Watching the
English

The Hidden Rules of English Behavior
Second Edition

KATE FOX

NICHOLAS BREALEY
PUBLISHING

BOSTON · LONDON

This edition first published by Nicholas Brealey Publishing in the United States of America in 2014.

53 State Street, 9th Floor
Boston, MA 02109, USA
Tel: + 617-523-3801
Fax: + 617-523-3708

3-5 Spafield Street, Clerkenwell
London, EC1R 4QB, UK
Tel: +44 (0)20 7239 0360
Fax: +44 (0)20 7239 0370

www.nicholasbrealey.com

Published in Great Britain in 2014 by Hodder & Stoughton
A division of Hodder Headlin

Printed in the United States of America

20 19 18 17 16 15   2 3 4 5 6 7 8 9 10

ISBN: 978-1-85788-616-0
E-ISBN: 978-1-85788-917-8

Library of Congress Cataloging-in-Publication Data

Fox, Kate.
Watching the English : the hidden rules of English behaviour / by Kate Fox. -- Revised and
updated.
pages cm
Published in Great Britain in 2014 by Hodder & Stoughton, a division of Hodder Headline.
Includes bibliographical references and index.
ISBN 978-1-85788-616-0 (pbk.) -- ISBN 978-1-85788-917-8 (ebook) 1. National characteris-
tics, English. 2. England--Social life and customs--21st century. I. Title.

DA566.4.F67 2014
390.0941--dc23

2014010674

To Henry, William, Sarah and Katharine

CONTENTS

PREFACE TO
THE AMERICAN EDITION

Since *Watching the English: The Hidden Rules of English Behaviour* was first published in the UK, I have had many letters and emails from Americans – both visitors and immigrants – about how the book has helped them understand and interact with the English.

Somewhat to my surprise, and slight anxiety, it seems that many Americans in the UK are using the book as a kind of 'how to be English' manual, never venturing out to a pub, an English home, or a business meeting without consulting the relevant chapters for 'instruction' on what to expect and how to behave. Some even go so far as to carry my book with them at all times – and one couple told me they now refer to it simply as 'The Book' ('you know, like the Bible') as in: 'What does The Book say we should do in this situation?' or 'No honey, don't you remember The Book says English people will cringe with embarrassment if you say that!'

I've also had quite a few letters from Americans married to English people, telling me that the book has proved invaluable in helping them understand the quirks and foibles of their English partners. Often, these poor souls had been under the impression for many years that their partners' bizarre behaviour and strange beliefs were personal peculiarities, or even symptoms of mental illness, until my book revealed that they were 'just being English.' Several correspondents claim that Watching the English has saved their marriages.

Perhaps the most unlikely and amusing example of this was the young American anthropology student who came up to me after a lecture I gave at Oxford University and said, without preamble, 'I am so grateful to you! Your book totally saved my relationship!' 'Gosh,' I said, a bit taken aback by such an intimate disclosure. 'Really? Er, how? I mean, which bit of the book did you find helpful?' 'The section on class differences in pea-eating,' she replied.

I thought she must be joking, but she was entirely serious. She had been terrified of meeting her English boyfriend's upper-middle-class parents, knowing that they were very snobbish and would look down on her as a crass, uncouth, low-class American. So when they invited her to dinner, she diligently studied and committed to memory the chapter on food rules, including the section on pea-eating, in which I explain that the upper-/upper-middle-class method of eating peas involves squashing the peas onto the convex back of your fork with your knife. This is of course a most perverse and impractical way of eating peas, but the obvious alternative – turning the fork prongs-up and scooping up the peas, as any sane person would do – is regarded as 'common' and frowned upon by the higher social echelons.

Fortunately for my new fan, peas were served at the dreaded dinner, and she duly ate them in the ludicrous upper-class English manner. The snobby mother could hardly contain her delight. 'Look, dear!' she nudged her husband and whispered, 'Look how she's eating her peas – she's one of us!' From that moment on, the parents' initial frosty wariness miraculously thawed, and their son's girlfriend was welcomed into the family.

England and America are, as George Bernard Shaw famously remarked, 'two countries divided by a common language'. This common language, and the so-called Special Relationship between our countries, lead many American visitors and immigrants to expect that we will share a common culture, attitudes, values, habits, and so on. They eventually discover that this is not the case, but the experience of 'acculturation' is often more frustrating for them than for other visitors and immigrants, because of these high expectations of compatibility.

Still, they mostly seem to cope and adjust rather better than I did as a child, when my family immigrated to the US. I was only about 5 or 6 at the time but already quite set in my English ways. For the entire 6 years that we lived in the US, I refused to adopt even a hint of an American accent. The New Jersey twang offended my aesthetic sensibilities ('sounds horrid,' was how I phrased it – ghastly little prig that I was). At my first school, I also refused point blank to pledge allegiance to the flag, as we were expected to do every morning. My objections to this were ostensibly on the grounds that I was English and therefore should not be asked to pledge allegiance to a foreign flag – but actually I just found the whole business excruciatingly embarrassing. What I was really saying was 'I am English, I should not be asked to put my hand on my heart and make a big sentimental patriotic fuss – we don't do that where I come from.'

As the daughter of an anthropologist, I really should have been rather better at adapting to native customs. My father was already training me to be an ethnographer, a 'participant observer,' but I was by nature much more of an observer than a participant. And an arrogant little observer at that. I am told that on one occasion, when I was about 7, an American friend of my parents' bent down, tweaked my cheek and asked, in what I clearly felt was a patronizing tone, 'So, what do you think of America, then?' I gave the matter due frowning consideration for a moment or two before replying, 'Well, I think it will probably be all right when it's finished.'

My father tells this little story with great pride, fondly imagining that this was some sort of profound cultural insight on my part. I suspect, however, that I was merely being obnoxious.

My father stayed in America, and after an interlude in France and then England, my mother and 2 sisters also returned to the States – all of them eventually becoming American citizens. My sisters have in fact spent so much of their lives there that they are in many ways more American than English. I made a much better fist of being French than I did of being American (I was an adolescent by then and, like all adolescents, desperate to fit in). When I finally returned to England, at the age of 16, I was obliged to re-learn the rules of Englishness – many of which, to be honest, I found rather silly.

But 'in spite of all temptations to belong to other nations,' I remain, like the Gilbert and Sullivan character, thoroughly English. And when my 'American' mother and youngest sister eventually came back to their native land, I found myself having to remind them of all the unwritten cultural rules they had forgotten. This experience was part of the inspiration for *Watching the English*, so I did quite often have an American reader in mind as I was writing the book.

Having said that, this is not and was never intended to be a guide book or an instruction manual. It is simply my attempt to understand and define my own native culture. It is somewhat unusual for an anthropologist's work to be critically scrutinized by the 'tribe' she is writing about, and to be honest I was somewhat apprehensive about this, especially as the book is a warts-and-all portrait, which pokes fun at our daft customs and irrational beliefs.

So I was surprised when the book became a big bestseller here in the UK, selling over a quarter of a million copies so far. I think this is because it has come at a time when the English are having a bit of an identity crisis. What with the 'loss,' through devolution, of Scotland and Wales, debates about our membership of the European Union and concerns about globalization, we have been rather thrown back on ourselves and forced to re-examine what it really means to be English. So any book that attempts to define Englishness is bound to be popular – especially one that allows us to indulge in one of our favourite national pastimes: laughing at ourselves.

An American friend pointed out to me that 'American readers will enjoy this book even more, as we get to laugh without wincing!'

I would like to dedicate this US edition to my 'transatlantic' sisters, Eleanor and Anne, with thanks for all their helpful insights and encouragement.

FOREWORD

I know this is going to sound like typical English false modesty, but I was truly surprised when *Watching the English* became a big bestseller – and I am still amazed by its continued popularity. The book has sold over half a million copies, been translated into many languages, received many rave reviews (as well as a few stinkers, of course) and all the usual hoohah.

Why? What can explain all this enthusiasm for a little pop-anthropology book about English behaviour?

Its success is almost entirely down to luck, no doubt, but in this case I think my good fortune may have something to do with what prompted me, ten years ago now, to write this book in the first place. I am often asked why I did it, and can only reply honestly, even though it makes me sound like a frightful geek, that it was because I didn't fully understand Englishness and this was keeping me awake at night. I know, I should have taken this as a cue to get a life. Instead, I read every book, article and research paper I could find on the subject, but still felt puzzled and frustrated – not to mention somewhat grumpy from lack of sleep. There was only one solution: if I really wanted to understand and define the English national character, I would have to do the research and figure it out for myself.

I can only assume that an awful lot of other people are equally perplexed by the English – including hundreds of thousands of English people. They may not be puzzled to the point of severe insomnia, but at least enough to splash out on a book that might help them to understand the inhabitants of this small, soggy, enigmatic island.

Perhaps I am also lucky to have published this book at a time when we English are having a bit of an identity wobble. Nothing as dramatic as a full-blown 'national identity crisis', as some have called it. Both the big fuss and the earnest navel-gazing implied by the term 'crisis' would be unseemly and un-English, so I'm sticking with 'wobble'. But I believe that various factors, including devolution (the 'loss' of Scotland and Wales), globalisation and immigration, have caused a degree of uncomfortable uncertainty about our national identity.

Oh – and it probably helped a bit that I obeyed one of the fundamental rules of Englishness, the one I call the Importance of Not Being Earnest. Earnest books about English national identity (some of them truly excellent) have not done so well, despite the wobble. Or perhaps because of it: in times of self-doubt and insecurity, the English take refuge in humour. And although this book has a fairly serious purpose, and is based on many years of solid research, I was writing to entertain the 'intelligent general reader', rather than to impress other anthropologists. This was no great hardship for me, as I am very English, find it hard to take things too seriously, and seem to be congenitally incapable of writing even a page without at least one or two little jokes.

Given that I had made no effort whatsoever to impress earnest academics, I was rather taken aback to find that *Watching the English* was being taught on the anthropology syllabus at a number of distinguished universities (and not, as I initially suspected, as a dire-warning example of how not to do anthropology). I found myself giving lectures and seminars at Oxford, Brown, University College London, Sussex, Pisa, etc. – and even the big scary Christmas Lecture at the Royal Geographical Society. At one of the universities where I lectured, the head of department told me that 50 per cent of new applicants cited my book as their inspiration for choosing to study anthropology. Fortunately, enough purist academic anthropologists still thoroughly disapprove of my light-hearted books for me to retain at least some vestiges of my maverick-outsider status.

I make no apology for my continued refusal, in this new edition, to pander to this stuffy minority by trying to show off my extensive reading, command of fancy jargon, mastery of abstruse concepts, ability to obfuscate simple ones, and all the other stuff that might make the book more palatable to them. Of course, there are many areas where I have no such impressive knowledge to show off, even if I wished to do so – where I am not so much 'dumbing down' as just plain dumb. But I firmly believe that any anthropological insight of genuine value or interest can, and should, be expressed in terms that a non-academic can understand – and ideally even enjoy. Whether I've achieved anything that might qualify as an interesting insight, or expressed things clearly or amusingly, is another question, but at least I try.

And, much as I enjoy trying, when my publishers asked for a revised edition, nearly a decade after *Watching the English* was first published, I was initially reluctant. 'I'm sorry,' I said, 'I know the world may have turned upside-down and inside-out quite a bit in the past ten years, and here in England we've had our share of terrorist bombings, economic crises, political upheavals, the Olympics and so on – but the English haven't changed. In this book, I was searching for the "defining characteristics of Englishness", and these should by definition be fairly timeless or, at least, not subject to any radical change in such a short period.'

I pointed out that neither my own continuing research nor any other studies or events had led me to revise my main conclusions. Quite the opposite: my own subsequent research on English behaviour, the findings of other relevant studies, and English reactions to events over the past decade have all actually confirmed and reinforced my original 'diagnosis'.

On the other hand, I thought, perhaps this new research evidence and these fresh observations might in themselves be of interest, both to readers of the original book and to new readers. On some aspects of Englishness, for example, I now have survey data to add weight to my original fieldwork findings. On others, I have more extensive field-research or experiments to back up early observations and hunches. A few intrepid readers have even taken it upon themselves to replicate some of my experiments, and I can report on their results. The 'defining characteristics' of Englishness remain essentially unchanged, but there are now some qualifications to add, some subtle nuances I hadn't noticed before, some emerging behaviour codes that need deciphering . . .

My publishers wisely left me to argue with myself over this, rather than putting me under any pressure, and eventually, much to their relief, I sort of talked myself into doing an updated edition.

Despite fairly extensive new research on many aspects of Englishness, I have undoubtedly missed many details that may have changed here or there in the past decade. I have continued to study the English, but other research interests and work commitments, and some frustrating health problems, have prevented me from revisiting some of the subcultures and some of the minutiae of English life that I covered in the original research. (Although the inconvenient illness has allowed me long periods as a 'participant observer' in English hospitals – field-research that would otherwise have required a lot of tiresome bureaucratic hassle over access.)

So, the updates are not as comprehensive as I would have wished, but there are over a hundred of them (about 150 new pages) scattered throughout this revised edition, so if you read the original book, you should not feel short-changed, at least in terms of the quantity of new material. The quality is for you to judge, of course.

Someone once said that the purpose of anthropology is to 'make the strange familiar and the familiar strange'. I have received many hundreds of letters and emails from immigrants and visitors to this country, and from foreigners married to English people, who tell me that the book has demystified this unfamiliar culture for them, helping them to understand the very strange behaviour of their English friends, colleagues, employers, neighbours, lovers and spouses. They write saying things like: 'Your book saved my marriage! I thought my English husband/wife must be mentally ill, but now I realise he/she is just being English!'

I also receive a constant flow of letters and emails from English people, telling me that reading this book has made them look afresh at familiar, 'normal' English behaviour, and realise just how strange we really are. Comments such as 'I kept cringing with embarrassment, thinking, Oh, God, I do that! and Oh no, that's me!' are a recurring theme from these readers, who take a typically English delight in laughing at themselves. Some of them (like the university applicants mentioned above) have even been inspired to go a bit beyond just laughing, and actually study anthropology.

So, for all its faults, it seems the book may have done at least some of its anthropological duty. I hope that this updated new edition will continue to make strange things familiar, and vice versa.

INTRODUCTION:
ANTHROPOLOGY AT HOME

I am sitting in a pub near Paddington station, clutching a small brandy. It's only about half past eleven in the morning – a bit early for drinking, but the alcohol is part reward, part Dutch courage. Reward because I have just spent an exhausting morning accidentally-on-purpose bumping into people and counting the number who said, 'Sorry'; Dutch courage because I am now about to return to the railway station and spend a few hours committing a deadly sin – queue-jumping.

I really, *really* do not want to do this. I want to adopt my usual method of getting an unsuspecting research assistant to break sacred social rules while I watch the result from a safe distance. But this time, I have bravely decided that I must be my own guinea pig. I don't feel brave. I feel scared. My arms are all bruised from the bumping experiments. I want to abandon the whole stupid Englishness project here and now, go home, have a cup of tea and lead a normal life. Above all, I do *not* want to go and jump queues all afternoon.

Why am I doing this? What exactly is the point of all this ludicrous bumping and jumping (not to mention all the equally daft things I'll be doing tomorrow)? Good question. Perhaps I'd better explain.

THE 'GRAMMAR' OF ENGLISHNESS

We are constantly being told that the English have lost their national identity – that there is no such thing as 'Englishness'. There has been a spate of books bemoaning this alleged identity crisis, with titles ranging from the plaintive *Anyone for England?* to the inconsolable *England: An Elegy*. Having spent much of the past twenty years doing research on various aspects of English culture and social behaviour – in pubs, at racecourses, in shops, in night-clubs, on trains, on street corners, in people's homes – I am convinced that there *is* such a thing as 'Englishness', and that reports of its demise have been greatly exaggerated. In the research for this book, I set out to discover the hidden, unspoken rules of English behaviour, and what these rules tell us about our national identity.

The object was to identify the *commonalities* in rules governing English behaviour – the unofficial codes of conduct that cut across class, age, sex, region, subcultures and other social boundaries. For example, Women's Institute members and leather-clad bikers may seem, on the surface, to have very little in common, but by looking beyond the 'ethnographic dazzle'[1] of superficial differences, I found that Women's Institute members and bikers, and other groups, all behave in accordance with the same unwritten rules – rules that define our national identity and character. I would also maintain, with George Orwell, that this identity 'is continuous, it stretches into the future and the past, there is something in it that persists, as in a living creature'.

My aim, if you like, was to provide a 'grammar' of English behaviour. Native speakers can rarely explain the grammatical rules of their own language. In the same way, those who are most 'fluent' in the rituals, customs and traditions of a particular culture generally lack the detachment necessary to explain the 'grammar' of these practices in an intelligible manner. That is why we have anthropologists.

Most people obey the unwritten rules of their society instinctively, without being conscious of doing so. For example, you automatically get dressed in the morning without consciously reminding yourself that there is an unspoken rule of etiquette that prohibits going to work in one's pyjamas. But if you had an anthropologist staying with you and studying you, she would be asking: 'Why are you changing

1. A term coined by my father, the anthropologist Robin Fox, meaning blindness to underlying similarities between human groups and cultures because one is dazzled by the more highly visible surface differences.

your clothes?' 'What would happen if you went to work in pyjamas?' 'What else can't you wear to work?' 'Why is it different on Fridays?' 'Does everyone in your company do that?' 'Why don't the senior managers follow the Casual Friday custom?' And on, and on, until you were heartily sick of her. Then she would go and watch and interrogate other people – from different groups within your society – and, hundreds of nosy questions and observations later, she would eventually decipher the 'grammar' of clothing and dress in your culture (see Dress Codes, page 385).

PARTICIPANT OBSERVATION AND ITS DISCONTENTS

Anthropologists are trained to use a research method known as 'participant observation', which essentially means participating in the life and culture of the people one is studying, to gain a true insider's perspective on their customs and behaviour, while simultaneously observing them as a detached, objective scientist. Well, that's the theory. In practice it often feels rather like that children's game where you try to pat your head and rub your tummy at the same time. It is perhaps not surprising that anthropologists are notorious for their frequent bouts of 'field-blindness' – becoming so involved and enmeshed in the native culture that they fail to maintain the necessary scientific detachment. The most famous example of such rose-tinted ethnography was, of course, Margaret Mead, but there was also Elizabeth Marshall Thomas, who wrote a book entitled *The Harmless People*, about a tribe who turned out to have a homicide rate higher than that of New York or Detroit.

There is a great deal of agonising and hair-splitting among anthropologists over the participant-observation method and the role of the participant observer. In a previous book, *The Racing Tribe*, I made a joke of this, borrowing the language of self-help psychobabble and expressing the problem as an ongoing battle between my Inner Participant and my Inner Observer. I described the bitchy squabbles in which these two Inner voices engaged every time a conflict arose between my roles as honorary member of the tribe and detached scientist. (Given the deadly serious tones in which this subject is normally debated, my irreverence bordered on heresy, so I was surprised and rather unreasonably annoyed to receive a letter from a university lecturer saying that he was using *The Racing Tribe* to *teach* the participant-observation method. You try your best to be a maverick iconoclast, and they turn you into a textbook.)

The more usual, or at least currently fashionable, practice is to devote at least a chapter of your book or Ph.D. thesis to a tortured, self-flagellating disquisition on the ethical and methodological difficulties of participant observation. Although the whole point of the participant element is to understand the culture from a 'native' perspective, you must spend a good three pages explaining that your unconscious ethnocentric prejudices, and various other cultural barriers, probably make this impossible. It is then customary to question the entire moral basis of the observation element, and, ideally, to express grave reservations about the validity of modern Western 'science' as a means of understanding anything at all.

At this point, the uninitiated reader might legitimately wonder why we continue to use a research method that is clearly either morally questionable or unreliable or both. I wondered this myself, until I realised that these doleful recitations of the dangers and evils of participant observation are a form of protective mantra, a ritual chant similar to the rather charming practice of some Native American tribes who, before setting out on a hunt or chopping down a tree, would sing apologetic laments to appease the spirits of the animals they were about to kill or the tree they were about to fell. A less charitable interpretation would see anthropologists' ritual self-abasements as a disingenuous attempt to deflect criticism by pre-emptive confession of their failings – like the selfish and neglectful lover who says, 'Oh, I'm such a bastard, I don't know why you put up with me,' relying on our belief that such awareness and candid acknowledgement of a fault is almost as virtuous as not having it. Or as Oscar Wilde put it: 'There is a luxury in self-reproach. When we blame ourselves, we feel that no one else has the right to blame us.'

But whatever the motives, conscious or otherwise, the ritual chapter agonising over the role of the participant observer tends to be mind-numbingly tedious, so I will forgo whatever pre-emptive absolution might be gained by this, and simply say that while participant observation has its limitations, this rather uneasy combination of involvement and detachment is still the best method we have for exploring the complexities of human cultures, so it will have to do.

The Good, the Bad and the Uncomfortable

In my case, the difficulties of the participant element are somewhat reduced, as I have chosen to study the complexities of my own native culture. This is not because I consider the English to be intrinsically more interesting than other cultures but because I have a rather wimpish aversion to the dirt, dysentery, killer insects, ghastly food and primitive sanitation that characterise the mud-hut 'tribal' societies studied by my more intrepid colleagues.

In the macho field of ethnography, my avoidance of discomfort and irrational preference for cultures with indoor plumbing are regarded as quite unacceptably feeble, so I have, until recently, tried to redeem myself a bit by studying the less salubrious aspects of English life: conducting research in violent pubs, seedy night-clubs, run-down betting shops and the like. Yet after years of research on aggression, disorder, violence, crime and other forms of deviance and dysfunction, all of which invariably take place in disagreeable locations and at inconvenient times, I still seemed to have risen no higher in the estimation of mud-hut ethnographers accustomed to much harsher conditions.

So, having failed my trial-by-fieldwork initiation test, I reasoned that I might as well turn my attention to the subject that really interests me, namely: the causes of *good* behaviour. This is a fascinating field of enquiry, which until fairly recently had been almost entirely neglected by social scientists. With a few notable exceptions, social scientists have tended to be obsessed with the dysfunctional, rather than the desirable, devoting all their energies to researching the causes of behaviours our society wishes to prevent, rather than those we might wish to encourage.

My co-director at the Social Issues Research Centre (SIRC), Peter Marsh, had become equally disillusioned and frustrated by the problem-oriented nature of social science, and we resolved to concentrate as much as possible on studying positive aspects of human interaction. With this new focus, we were now no longer obliged to seek out violent pubs, but could spend time in pleasant ones (the latter also had the advantage of being much easier to find, as the vast majority of pubs are congenial and trouble-free). We could observe ordinary, law-abiding people doing their shopping, instead of interviewing security guards and store detectives about the activities of shoplifters and vandals. We went to night-clubs to study flirting rather than fighting. When I noticed some unusually sociable and courteous interaction among the crowds at a racecourse, I immediately began what turned out to be three years of research on the factors influencing the good behaviour of racegoers. Other largely 'positive' research topics have included celebration, cyber-dating, summer holidays, beauty and body-image, social bonding, embarrassment, corporate hospitality, patriotism, cars and drivers, motherhood, menopause, risk-taking, crying, mobile phones, online social media, sex, gossip, the psychology of smell, the meaning of chips and the relationship between tea-drinking and DIY (this last dealing with burning social issues such as 'How many cups of tea does it take the average Englishman to put up a shelf?').

My professional life has thus been divided roughly equally between studying the problematic aspects of English society and its more appealing, positive elements (along with cross-cultural, comparative research in other parts of the world), so I suppose I can safely claim to have embarked on the specific research for this book with the advantage of a reasonably balanced overview.

My Family and other Lab Rats

My status as a 'native' gave me a bit of a head start on the participant element of the participant-observation task, but what about the observation side of things? Could I summon the detachment necessary to stand back and observe my own native culture as an objective scientist? Although in fact I was to spend much of my time studying relatively unfamiliar subcultures, these were still 'my people', so it seemed reasonable to question my ability to treat them as laboratory rats, albeit with only half of my ethnographer's split personality (the head-patting observer half, as opposed to the tummy-rubbing participant).

I did not worry about this for too long. After all, I had the advantage of having lived abroad for most of my 'formative years' (from the age of five to sixteen). And friends, colleagues, publishers, agents and others kept reminding me that I had more recently spent at least a decade minutely dissecting the behaviour of my fellow natives – with, they said, about as much sentimentality as a white-coated scientist tweezering cells around in a Petri dish. My family also pointed out that my father – Robin Fox, a much more eminent anthropologist – had been training me for this role since I was a baby. Unlike most infants, who spend their early days lying in a pram or cot, staring at the ceiling or at those dangly-animal mobile things, I was strapped to a Cochiti Indian cradle-board and propped upright, at strategic observation points around the house, to study the typical behaviour-patterns of an English academic family.

My father also provided me with the perfect role-model of scientific detachment. When my mother told him that she was pregnant with me, their first child, he immediately started trying to persuade her to let him acquire a baby chimp and bring us up together as an experiment – a case-study comparing primate and human development. My mother firmly vetoed the idea, and recounted the incident to me, many years later, as an example of my father's eccentric and unhelpful approach to parenthood. I failed to grasp the moral of the story, and said, 'Oh, what a great idea – it would have been *fascinating*!' My mother told me, not for the first time, that I was 'just like your bloody father'. Again missing the point, I took this as a compliment.

TRUST ME, I'M AN ANTHROPOLOGIST

By the time we left England, and I embarked on a rather erratic education at a random sample of schools in America, Ireland and France, my father had manfully shrugged off his disappointment over the chimp experiment, and begun training me as an ethnographer instead. I was only five, but he generously overlooked this slight handicap: I might be somewhat shorter than his other students, but that shouldn't prevent me grasping the basic principles of ethnographic research methodology. Among the most important of these, I learnt, was the search for rules. When we arrived in any unfamiliar culture, I was to look for regularities and consistent patterns in the natives' behaviour, and try to work out the hidden rules – the conventions or collective understandings – governing these behaviour patterns.

Eventually, this rule-hunting becomes almost an unconscious process – a reflex, or, according to some long-suffering companions, a pathological compulsion. Some years ago, for example, my fiancé (now husband) Henry took me to visit some friends in Poland. As we were driving in an English car, he relied on me, the passenger, to tell him when it was safe to overtake. Within twenty minutes of crossing the Polish border, I started to say, 'Yes, go now, it's safe,' even when there were vehicles coming towards us on a two-lane road.

After he had twice hastily applied the brakes and aborted a planned overtake at the last minute, he clearly began to have doubts about my judgement. 'What are you doing? That wasn't safe at all! Didn't you see that big lorry?'

'Oh, yes,' I replied, 'but the rules are different here in Poland. There's obviously a tacit understanding that a wide two-lane road is really three lanes, so if you overtake, the driver in front and the one coming towards you will move to the side to give you room.'

Henry asked politely how I could possibly be sure of this, given that I had never been to Poland before and had been in the country less than half an hour. My response, that I had been watching the Polish drivers and that they all clearly followed this rule, was greeted with perhaps understandable scepticism. Adding 'Trust me, I'm an anthropologist,' probably didn't help much either, and it was some time before he could be persuaded to test my theory. When he did, the vehicles duly parted like the Red Sea to create a 'third lane' for us, and our Polish host later confirmed that there was indeed a sort of unofficial code of etiquette that required this.[2]

2. I have since heard about a few Polish drivers being killed or injured in England because they did not realise that their 'third-lane' etiquette doesn't apply here.

My sense of triumph was somewhat diluted, though, by our host's sister, who pointed out that her countrymen were also noted for their reckless and dangerous driving. Had I been a bit more observant, it seemed, I might have noticed the crosses, with flowers around the base, dotted along the roadsides – tributes placed by bereaved relatives to mark the spots at which people had been killed in road accidents. Henry magnanimously refrained from making any comment about the trustworthiness of anthropologists, but he did ask why I could not be content with merely observing and analysing Polish customs: why did I feel compelled to risk my neck – and, incidentally, his – by *joining in*?

I explained that this compulsion was partly the result of promptings from my Inner Participant, but insisted that there was also some methodology in my apparent madness. Having observed some regularity or pattern in native behaviour, and tentatively identified the unspoken rule involved, an ethnographer can apply various 'tests' to confirm the existence of such a rule. You can tell a representative selection of natives about your observations of their behaviour patterns, and ask them if you have correctly identified the rule, convention or principle behind these patterns. You can break the (hypothetical) rule, and look for signs of disapproval, or indeed active 'sanctions'. In some cases, such as the Polish third-lane rule, you can 'test' the rule by obeying it, and note whether you are 'rewarded' for doing so.

BORING BUT IMPORTANT

This book is not written for other social scientists but, rather, for that elusive creature publishers used to call 'the intelligent layman'. My non-academic approach cannot, however, be used as a convenient excuse for woolly thinking, sloppy use of language, or failing to define my terms. This is a book about the 'rules' of Englishness, and I cannot simply assert that we all know what we mean by a 'rule', without attempting to explain the sense or senses in which I am using the term.

I am using a rather broad interpretation of the concept of a rule, based on four of the definitions allowed by the *Oxford English Dictionary*, namely:

- a principle, regulation or maxim governing individual conduct
- a standard of discrimination or estimation; a criterion, a test, a measure
- an exemplary person or thing; a guiding example
- a fact, or the statement of a fact, which holds generally good; the normal or usual state of things.

Thus, my quest to identify the rules of Englishness is not confined to a search for specific rules of conduct, but will include rules in the wider sense of standards, norms, ideals, guiding principles and 'facts' about 'normal or usual' English behaviour.

This last is the sense of 'rule' we are using when we say, 'As a rule, the English tend to be X (or prefer Y, or dislike Z).' When we use the term 'rule' in this way, we do not mean – and this is important – that all English people always or invariably exhibit the characteristic in question, only that it is a quality or behaviour pattern that is common enough, or marked enough, to be noticeable and significant. Indeed, it is a fundamental requirement of a social rule – by whatever definition – that it can be broken. Rules of conduct (or standards, or principles) of this kind are not, like scientific or mathematical laws, statements of a necessary state of affairs: they are by definition contingent. If it were, for example, utterly inconceivable and impossible that anyone would ever jump a queue, there would be no need for a rule prohibiting queue-jumping.[3]

When I speak of the unwritten rules of Englishness, therefore, I am clearly not suggesting that such rules are universally obeyed in

3. We do, in fact, have some rules prohibiting behaviours that, while not inconceivable, are unlikely or even 'unnatural' – see Robin Fox's work on the incest taboo, for example – cases where a factual 'it isn't done' becomes formalised as a proscriptive 'thou shalt not do it' (despite the claims of philosophers who hold that it is logically impossible to derive an 'ought' from an 'is'), but these tend to be universal rules, rather than the culture-specific rules that concern us here.

English society, or that no exceptions or deviations will be found. That would be ludicrous. My claim is only that these rules are 'normal and usual' enough to be helpful in understanding and defining our national character.

Often, exceptions and deviations may help to 'prove' (in the correct sense of 'test') a rule, in that the degree of surprise or outrage provoked by the deviation provides an indication of its importance and the 'normality' of the behaviour it prescribes. Many of the pundits conducting premature post-mortems on Englishness make the fundamental mistake of citing breaches of the traditional rules of Englishness (such as, say, the unsportsmanlike behaviour of a footballer or cricketer) as evidence for their diagnosis of death, while ignoring public reaction to such breaches, which clearly shows that they are regarded as abnormal, unacceptable and un-English.

THE NATURE OF CULTURE

My analysis of Englishness will focus on rules, as I believe this is the most direct route to the establishment of a 'grammar' of Englishness. But given the very broad sense in which I am using the term 'rule', my search for the rules of Englishness will effectively involve an attempt to understand and define English culture. This is another term that requires definition: by 'culture' I mean the sum of a society's or social group's patterns of behaviour, customs, way of life, ideas, beliefs and values. And this is essentially what we mean when we talk about 'national character'. Those who insist that there is no such thing often seem to fail to grasp that the term is a metaphor, a colloquial way of talking about 'culture'. Most would accept that there is such a thing as 'culture' and that there are differences between cultures.

I am not implying by this that I see English culture as a homogeneous or immutable entity – that I expect to find no variation in behaviour patterns, customs, beliefs, etc. – any more than I am suggesting that the 'rules of Englishness' are universally obeyed. As with the rules, I expect to find much variation and diversity within English culture, but hope to discover some sort of common core, a set of underlying basic patterns that might help us to define Englishness.

At the same time, I am conscious of the wider danger of cross-cultural 'ethnographic dazzle' – of blindness to the similarities between the English and other cultures. When absorbed in the task of defining a 'national character', it is easy to become obsessed with the distinctive features of a particular culture, and to forget that we are all members of the same species.[4] Fortunately, several rather more eminent anthropologists have provided us with lists of 'cross-cultural universals' – practices, customs and beliefs found in all human societies – which should help me to avoid this hazard. There is some lack of consensus on exactly what practices, etc., should be included in this category (but, then, when did academics ever manage to agree on anything?).[5] For example, Robin Fox gives us the following:

> Laws about property, rules about incest and marriage, customs of taboo and avoidance, methods of settling disputes with a minimum of blood-shed, beliefs about the supernatural and practices relating to it, a system of social status and methods of indicating it, initiation ceremonies for young men, courtship practices involving the adornment of females, systems of symbolic body ornament generally, certain activities set aside for men from which women are excluded, gambling of some kind, a tool- and weapons-making industry, myths and legends, dancing,

4. Although I was given a rather charming book, published in 1931, entitled *The English: Are They Human?* The question is rhetorical, as one might expect. The Dutch author (G. J. Renier) 'came to the conclusion that the world is inhabited by two species of human beings: mankind and the English'.
5. There is also considerable disagreement on whether or not such 'universals' should be regarded as hard-wired characteristics of human nature, but I'll wimp out of that debate as well, on the grounds that it is not directly relevant to our discussion of Englishness. My own view, for what it's worth, is that the whole nature/nurture debate is a rather pointless exercise, in which we engage because, as Lévi-Strauss has shown, the human mind likes to think in terms of binary oppositions (black/white, left/right, male/female, them/us, nature/culture, etc.). Why we do this is open to question, but this binary thinking pervades all human institutions and practices.

adultery and various doses of homicide, suicide, homosexuality, schizo-phrenia, psychoses and neuroses, and various practitioners to take advantage of or cure these, depending on how they are viewed.

George Peter Murdock provides a much longer and more detailed list of universals,[6] in convenient alphabetical order, but less amusingly phrased:

Age-grading, athletic sports, bodily adornment, calendar, cleanliness training, community organisation, cooking, cooperative labour, cosmology, courtship, dancing, decorative art, divination, division of labour, dream interpretation, education, eschatology, ethics, ethnobiology, etiquette, faith-healing, family, feasting, fire-making, folklore, food taboos, funeral rites, games, gestures, gift-giving, government, greetings, hairstyles, hospitality, housing, hygiene, incest taboos, inheritance rules, joking, kin-groups, kinship nomenclature, language, law, luck superstition, magic, marriage, mealtimes, medicine, modesty concerning natural functions, mourning, music, mythology, numerals, obstetrics, penal sanctions, personal names, population policy, postnatal care, pregnancy usages, property rights, propitiation of supernatural beings, puberty customs, religious rituals, residence rules, sexual restrictions, soul concepts, status differentiation, surgery, tool making, trade, visiting, weaning and weather control.

While I am not personally familiar with every existing human culture, lists such as these will help to ensure that I focus specifically, for example, on what is unique or distinctive about the English class system, rather than the fact that we have such a system, as all cultures have 'a system of social status and methods of indicating it'. This may seem a rather obvious point, but it is one that other writers have failed to recognise,[7] and many also regularly commit the related

6. To be fair, Fox was providing *examples* of human universals, while Murdock was attempting a comprehensive list.
7. Not Hegel, who captured the essence of the issue when he said that 'The spirit of the nation is . . . the universal spirit in a particular form.' (Assuming that I have correctly understood his meaning – Hegel is not always as clear as one might wish.)

error of assuming that certain characteristics of English culture (such as the association of alcohol with violence) are universal features of all human societies.

RULE-MAKING

There is one significant omission from the above lists,[8] although it is clearly implicit in both, and that is 'rule-making'. The human species is addicted to it. Every human activity, without exception, including natural biological functions such as eating and sex, is hedged about with complex sets of rules and regulations, dictating precisely when, where, with whom and in what manner the activity may be performed. Animals just *do* these things; humans make an almighty song and dance about it. This is known as 'civilisation'.

The rules may vary from culture to culture, but there are always rules. Different foods may be prohibited in different societies, but every society has food taboos. We have rules about everything. In the above lists, every practice that does not already contain an explicit or implicit reference to rules could be preceded by the words 'rules about' (e.g. rules about gift-giving, rules about hairstyles, rules about dancing, greetings, hospitality, joking, weaning, etc.). My focus on rules is therefore not some strange personal whim, but a recognition of the importance of rules and rule-making in the human psyche.

If you think about it, we all use differences in rules as a principal means of distinguishing one culture from another. The first thing we notice when we go on holiday or business abroad is that other cultures have 'different ways of doing things', by which we usually mean that they have rules about, say, food, mealtimes, dress, greetings, hygiene, trade, hospitality, joking, status-differentiation, etc., which are different from our own rules about these practices.

8. Actually, there are two: the second is 'use of mood- or consciousness-altering substances or processes', a practice found in all known human cultures, the peculiarly English version of which will be covered elsewhere in this book.

GLOBALISATION AND TRIBALISATION

Which brings us, inevitably, to the problem of globalisation. During the research for this book, I was often asked (by members of the academic/chattering classes) what was the point in my writing about Englishness, or indeed any other national identity, when the inexorable spread of American cultural imperialism would soon make this an issue of purely historical interest? Already, I was told, we are living in a dumbed-down, homogenised McWorld, in which the rich tapestry of diverse and distinctive cultures is being obliterated by the all-consuming consumerism of Nike, Coca-Cola, McDonald's, Disney and other multinational capitalist giants.

Really? As a fairly typical *Guardian*-reading, lefty-liberal product of the anti-Thatcher generation, I have no natural sympathy for corporate imperialists, but as a professional observer of sociocultural trends, I am obliged to report that their influence has been exaggerated – or, rather, misinterpreted. The principal effect of globalisation, as far as I can tell, has been an *increase* in nationalism and tribalism, a proliferation of struggles for independence, devolution and self-determination, and a resurgence of concern about ethnicity and cultural identity in almost all parts of the world, including the so-called United Kingdom.

OK, perhaps not an effect – correlation is not causation, as every scientist knows – but at the very least, one must acknowledge that the association of these movements with the rise of globalisation is a striking coincidence. Just because people everywhere want to wear Nike trainers and drink Coke does not necessarily mean that they are any less fiercely concerned about their cultural identity – indeed, many are prepared to fight and die for their nation, religion, territory, culture or whatever aspect of 'tribal' identity is perceived to be at stake.

The economic influence of American corporate giants may indeed be overwhelming, and even pernicious, but their cultural impact is perhaps less significant than either they or their enemies would like to believe. Given our deeply ingrained tribal instincts, and increasing evidence of fragmentation of nations into smaller and smaller cultural units, it does not make sense to talk of a world of seven billion people becoming a vast monoculture. The spread of globalisation is undoubtedly bringing changes to the cultures it reaches, but these cultures were not static in the first place, and change does not necessarily mean the abolition of traditional values. Indeed, new global media such as the internet have been an effective means of promoting traditional cultures – as well as the global subculture of anti-globalisation activists.

Within Britain, despite obvious American cultural influences, there is far more evidence of increasing tribalisation than of any reduction in cultural diversity. The fervour, and power, of Scottish and Welsh nationalists does not seem to be much affected by their taste for American soft drinks, junk food or films. Ethnic minorities in Britain are, if anything, increasingly keen to maintain their distinctive cultural identities, and even the English are becoming a bit more fretful (in our rather understated, moderate way) about our own cultural 'identity crisis'. In England, regionalism is endemic – and there is considerable resistance to the idea of being part of Europe, let alone part of any global monoculture.

So, I see no reason to be put off my attempt to understand Englishness by global warnings about the imminent extinction of this or any other culture.

CLASS AND RACE

When this book was in the planning stages, almost everyone I talked to about it asked whether I would have a chapter on class. My feeling all along was that a separate chapter would be inappropriate: class pervades all aspects of English life and culture, and will therefore permeate all the areas covered in this book.

Although England is a highly class-conscious culture, the real-life ways in which the English think about social class – and determine a person's position in the class structure – bear little relation either to simplistic three-tier (upper, middle, working) models, or to the rather abstract alphabetical systems (A, B, C1, C2, D, E), based entirely on occupation, favoured by opinion pollsters and market-research experts.[9] A schoolteacher and an estate agent would both technically be 'middle class'. They might even both live in a terraced house, drive the same make of car, drink in the same pub and earn roughly the same annual income. But we judge social class in much more subtle and complex ways: *precisely* how you arrange, furnish and decorate your terraced house; not just the make of car you drive, but whether you wash it yourself on Sundays, take it to a car wash or rely on the English weather to sluice off the worst of the dirt for you. Similar fine distinctions are applied to exactly what, where, when, how and with whom you eat and drink; where and how you shop; the clothes you wear; the pets you keep; how you spend your free time; and, especially, the words you use and how you pronounce them.

Every English person (whether we admit it or not) is aware of and highly sensitive to all of the delicate divisions and calibrations involved in such judgements. I will not therefore attempt to provide a crude 'taxonomy' of English classes and their characteristics, but will instead try to convey the subtleties of English thinking about class through the perspectives of the different themes mentioned above. It is impossible to talk about class without reference to homes, gardens, cars, clothes, pets, food, drink, sex, talk, hobbies, etc., and impossible to explore the rules of any of these aspects of English life without constantly bumping into big class dividers, or tripping over the smaller, less obvious ones. I will, therefore, deal with class demarcations as and when I lurch into them or stumble across them.

At the same time, I will try to avoid being 'dazzled' by class differences, remembering Orwell's point that such differences 'fade away the moment any two Britons are confronted by a European' and that 'even the distinction between rich and poor dwindles somewhat when one regards the nation from the outside'. As a self-appointed

9. The sociologist Pierre Bourdieu's concepts of economic, social and cultural capital are more helpful in understanding the English class system, but only if one is *very* specific about the *precise* nature of each type of capital associated with a particular social class.

'outsider' – a professional alien, if you like – my task in defining Englishness is to search for underlying commonalities, not to exclaim over surface differences.

Race is a rather more difficult issue, and again was raised by all the friends and colleagues with whom I discussed this book. Having noted that I was conveniently avoiding the issues of Scottish, Welsh and Irish national identities by confining my research to 'the English' rather than 'the British' or 'the UK', they invariably went on to ask whether or not Asians,[10] Afro-Caribbeans and other ethnic minorities would be included in my definition of Englishness.

There are several answers to this question. The first is that ethnic minorities are included, *by definition*, in any attempt to define Englishness. The extent to which immigrant populations adapt to, adopt and in turn influence the culture and customs of their host country, particularly over several generations, is a complex issue. Research tends to focus on the adaptation and adoption elements (usually lumped together as 'acculturation' or 'assimilation') at the expense of the equally interesting and important issue of influence. This is odd: we acknowledge that short-term tourists can have a profound influence on their host cultures – indeed, the study of the social processes involved has become a fashionable discipline in itself – but for some reason our academics seem less interested in the processes by which resident immigrant minority cultures can shape the behaviour patterns, customs, ideas, beliefs and values of the countries in which they settle. Although ethnic minorities constitute only about 10 per cent of the population of this country, their influence on many aspects of English culture has been, and is, considerable. Any 'snapshot' of English behaviour as it is now, such as I am attempting here, will inevitably be coloured by this influence. Although very few of the Asians, Africans and Caribbeans living in England would define themselves as English – most call themselves British, which has come to be regarded as a more

10. I am using the term 'Asian' – here and throughout the book – in the British sense, meaning (loosely) originating from the Indian subcontinent.

inclusive term[11] – they have clearly contributed to the 'grammar' of Englishness.

My second answer to the race question concerns the more well-trodden area of 'acculturation'. Here we come down to the level of the group and the individual, rather than the minority culture as a whole. To put it simply – perhaps too simply – some ethnic-minority groups and individuals are more 'English' than others. By this I mean that some, whether through choice or circumstance or both, have adopted more of the host culture's customs, values and behaviour patterns than others. (This becomes a somewhat more complex issue in the second, third and subsequent generations, as the host culture in question will have been influenced, at least to some degree, by their own forebears.)

Once you start to put it in these terms, the issue is really no longer one of race. When I say that some ethnic-minority groups and individuals are more 'English' than others, I am clearly not talking about the colour of their skin or their country of origin: I am talking about the degree of 'Englishness' they exhibit in their behaviour, manner and customs. I could, and do, make the same comment about white 'Anglo-Saxon' groups and individuals.

We all do, in fact. We describe a social group, a person, or even, say, just one of that person's reactions or characteristic mannerisms, as 'very English' or 'typically English'. We understand what someone means when they say, 'In some ways I'm very English, but in other ways I'm not,' or 'You're more English about that than I am.' We have a concept of 'degrees' of Englishness. I am not introducing anything new or startling here: our everyday use of these terms demonstrates that we all already have a clear grasp of the subtleties

11. Although I found that in real-life conversation, as opposed to ticking boxes on surveys, many people from ethnic-minority backgrounds tended, in casual discussions about Scotland or Wales, to refer to the English as 'we' and the Scots and Welsh as 'them'. This use of the first-person plural was common even among those who, when asked, would insist that they were British, not English. And that's not even counting the many ethnic-minority 'regionalists' who, like their Anglo-Saxon friends and neighbours, identified themselves more strongly as 'Geordies', 'Scousers', 'Brummies', 'Mancs', etc., than as British.

of 'partial' Englishness, or even 'piecemeal' or 'cherry-picking' Englishness. We recognise that we can all, at least to some extent, 'choose' our degree of Englishness. All I am saying is that these concepts can be applied equally to ethnic minorities.

In fact, I would go so far as to say that Englishness is rather *more* a matter of choice for the ethnic minorities in this country than it is for the rest of us. For those of us without the benefit of early first-hand influence of another culture, some aspects of Englishness can be so deeply ingrained that we find it almost impossible to shake them off, even when it is clearly in our interests to do so (such as, in my case, when trying to conduct field experiments involving queue-jumping). Immigrants have the advantage of being able to pick and choose more freely, often adopting the more desirable English quirks and habits while carefully steering clear of the more ludicrous ones.

I have some personal experience of such cultural cherry-picking. My family emigrated to America when I was five, and we lived there for six years, during which entire time I steadfastly refused to adopt any trace of an American accent, on the grounds that it was aesthetically unpleasing ('Sounds horrid' was how I put it at the time – dreadful little prig that I was), although I happily adapted to most other aspects of the culture. As an adolescent, I lived for four years in rural France. I attended the local state school and became indistinguishable in my speech, behaviour and manners from any other Briançonnaise teenager. Except that I knew this was a matter of choice, and could judiciously shed those elements of Frenchness that annoyed my mother when I got home from school in the evening – or, indeed, deliberately exaggerate them to provoke her (some teenage behaviours are universal) – and discard those that proved socially unfavourable on our return to England.

Immigrants can, of course, choose to 'go native', and some in this country become 'more English than the English'. Among my own friends, the two I would most readily describe as 'very English' are a first-generation Indian immigrant and a first-generation Polish refugee. In both cases, their degree of Englishness was initially a conscious choice, and although it has since become second nature, they can still stand back and analyse their behaviour – and explain the rules they have learnt to obey – in a way that most native English find difficult, as we tend to take these things for granted.

My sister had much the same experience when she married a Lebanese man and emigrated to Lebanon (from America), where she lived for about fifteen years. She became very quickly, to her Bek'aa Valley family and neighbours, a fully 'acculturated' Lebanese village housewife, but can switch back to Englishness (or Americanness, or indeed her teenage Frenchness) as easily as she changes languages – and often does both in mid-sentence. Her children are American-Arab, with a few hints of Englishness, and equally adept at switching language, manners and mores when it suits them.

Many of those who pontificate about acculturation are inclined to underestimate this element of choice. Such processes are often described in terms suggesting that the 'dominant' culture is simply *imposed* on unwitting, passive minorities, rather than focusing on the extent to which individuals quite consciously, deliberately, cleverly and even mockingly pick and choose among the behaviours and customs of their host culture. I accept that some degree of acculturation or conformity to English ways is often 'demanded' or effectively 'enforced' (although this would surely be true of any host culture, unless one enters it as a conquering invader or passing tourist), and the rights and wrongs of specific demands can and should be debated. But my point is that compliance with such demands is still a conscious process, and not, as some accounts of acculturation imply, a form of brainwashing.

My only way of understanding this process is to assume that every immigrant to this country is at least as bright and clever as I was when we immigrated to France, just as capable of exercising free will and maintaining a sense of their own cultural identity while complying with the demands, however irrational or unfair, of the local culture. I could crank up or tone down my Frenchness, by subtle degrees, in an entirely calculated manner. My sister can choose and calibrate her Arabness, and my immigrant friends can do the same with their Englishness, sometimes for practical social purposes, including the avoidance of exclusion, but also purely for amusement.

Perhaps the earnest researchers studying acculturation just don't want to see that their 'subjects' have got the whole thing sussed, understand our culture better than we do, and are, much of the time, privately laughing at us.

It should be obvious from all of this (but I'll say it anyway) that when I speak of Englishness I am not putting a value on it, not holding it up above any other '-ness'. When I say that some immigrants are more English than others, I am not (unlike Norman Tebbit with his infamous 'Cricket Test') implying that these individuals are in any way superior, or that their rights or status as citizens should be any different from those who are less English. And when I say that anyone *can* – given enough time and effort – 'learn' or 'adopt' Englishness, I am not suggesting that they *ought* to do so.

The degree to which immigrants and ethnic minorities should be expected to adapt to fit in with English culture is a matter for debate. Where immigrants from former British colonies are concerned, perhaps the degree of acculturation demanded should match that which we achieved as uninvited residents in their cultures. Of all peoples, the English are surely historically the least qualified to preach about the importance of adapting to host-culture manners and mores. Our own track-record on this is abysmal. Wherever we settle in any numbers, we not only create pockets of utterly insular Englishness, but also often attempt to impose our cultural norms and habits on the local population.

But this book is intended to be descriptive, not prescriptive. I am interested in understanding Englishness as it is, warts and all. It is not the anthropologist's job to moralise and pontificate about how the tribe she is studying ought to treat its neighbours or its members. I may have my opinions on such matters, but they are not relevant to my attempt to discover the rules of Englishness. I may sometimes state these opinions anyway (it's my book, so I can do what I like), but I will try to distinguish clearly between opinion and observation.

BRITISHNESS AND ENGLISHNESS

While I'm at it, this is a suitable place to apologise to any Scottish or Welsh (or even Northern Irish)[12] people who (a) still regard themselves as British and (b) are wondering why I am writing about Englishness rather than Britishness. (I am referring here to real, born-and-bred Scots, Welsh and Irish by the way, not English people – like me – who like to boast of their drop of Welsh, Scottish or Irish 'blood' when it suits them.)

The answer is that I am researching and writing about Englishness rather than Britishness:

- partly out of sheer laziness
- partly because England is a nation, and might reasonably be expected to have some sort of coherent and distinctive national culture or character, whereas Britain is a purely political construct, composed of several nations with their own distinctive cultures
- partly because although there may be a great deal of overlap between these cultures, they are clearly *not* identical and should not be treated as such by being lumped together under 'Britishness'
- and finally because 'Britishness' seems to me to be a rather meaningless term: when people use it, they nearly always really mean 'Englishness' – they do not mean that someone is being frightfully Welsh or Scottish.[13]

12. Yes, I know, technically Northern Ireland is not part of Britain, but part of the 'United Kingdom of Great Britain and Northern Ireland' – but I've had letters from Northern Irish people who see themselves as British and complained about not being included in this section.

13. For those who think I am being too glib and dismissive in this summary, the historian Krishan Kumar makes essentially the same points (apart from the confession of laziness, which I'm sure doesn't apply in his case) far more eloquently but at much greater length, in *The Making of English National Identity* – and so did the eminent political theorist and citizenship expert Sir Bernard Crick.

I only have the time and energy to try to understand one of these cultures, and I have chosen my own, the English.

I realise that one can, if one is being picky, pick all sorts of holes in these arguments – not least that a 'nation' is surely itself a pretty artificial construct – and Cornish nationalists and even fervent region- alists from other parts of England (Scousers, Geordies, Yorkshiremen, etc., etc.) will no doubt insist that they, too, have their own separate identity and should not be bundled together with the rest of the English.

The trouble is that virtually all nations have a number of regions, each of which invariably regards itself as different from, and superior to, all the others. This applies in France, Italy, the US, Russia, Mexico, Spain, Scotland, Australia – and more or less anywhere else you care to mention. People from St Petersburg talk about Muscovites as though they were members of a different species; east-coast and Midwestern Americans might as well be from different planets, ditto Tuscans and Neapolitans, Northern and Southern Mexicans, etc.; even cities such as Melbourne and Sydney see themselves as having radically different characters – and let's not start on Edinburgh and Glasgow. Regionalism is hardly a peculiarly English phenomenon. In all of these cases, however, the people of these admittedly highly individual regions and cities nevertheless have enough in common to make them recognisably Italian, American, Russian, Scottish, etc. I am interested in those commonalities.

STEREOTYPES AND CULTURAL GENOMICS

'Well, I hope you're going to get beyond the usual stereotypes' was another common response when I told people I was doing research for a book on Englishness. This comment seemed to reflect an assumption that a stereotype is almost by definition 'not true', that the truth lies somewhere else – wherever 'beyond' might be. I find this rather strange, as I would naturally assume that, although they are unlikely to be 'the truth, the whole truth and nothing but', stereotypes about English national character might possibly contain at least a grain or two of truth. They do not, after all, just come out of thin air, but must have germinated and grown from *something*. Most national-character stereotypes are widely accepted or even enthusiastically 'endorsed' among ordinary citizens of the nations in question, which does not make them 'true', but at the very least tells us something about a culture's self-image, and therefore about its beliefs and values.

So my standard reply was to say that I would try to get *inside* the stereotypes. I would not specifically seek them out, but would keep an open mind; and if my research showed that certain English behaviour patterns corresponded to a given stereotype, I would put that stereotype in my Petri dish, stick it under my microscope, dissect it, tease it apart, subject its component bits to various tests, unravel its DNA and, er, generally poke away and puzzle over it until I found those grains (or genes) of truth.

OK, there are probably some mixed metaphors in there, not to mention a somewhat hazy notion of what proper scientists actually do in their labs, but you get the idea. Most things look rather different when you put them under a microscope and, sure enough, I found that stereotypes such as English 'reserve', 'politeness', 'modesty', 'weather-talk', 'hooliganism', 'hypocrisy', 'privacy', 'anti-intellectualism', 'queuing', 'compromise', 'fair play', 'humour', 'class-consciousness', 'eccentricity', 'tolerance' and so on were not quite what they seemed. They all had complex layers of rules and codes that were not visible to the naked eye, and not one of them turned out to be a straightforward, unqualified 'truth'. Some of them nonetheless ended up on my list of 'defining characteristics', but redefined with many caveats and qualifications.

A few personality psychologists have wasted a lot of time 'proving' that national-character stereotypes are 'untrue' on the grounds that they do not correlate with aggregate scores on five personality factors. The supposedly 'reserved' English, for example, score high on 'extraversion' in personality questionnaires. While it is clear that so-called 'English reserve' is far more complex, contingent and contextual than the crude stereotype would suggest (as is its equally famous opposite, 'English hooliganism', a rowdy, 'extravert' stereotype that these researchers conveniently ignore), it is also part of a cultural 'grammar' of rules, norms, customs and behaviour codes that has nothing to do with individual personality traits. In real-life social situations, most people unconsciously obey the rules and norms of their culture, whatever their individual personalities. The term 'national character' is a metaphor, which should not be taken literally. A culture is not a person writ large, and cannot be understood or defined by adding up individual personality scores. But, then, 'When the only tool you have is a hammer, everything looks like a nail', and it is perhaps no accident that the main proponent of this aggregate-personality argument is a psychologist who designs personality questionnaires.

Without getting too carried away by my equally metaphorical DNA analogies, I suppose another way of describing my Englishness project would be as an attempt to sequence (or map, I'm never sure which is which) the English cultural genome – to identify the cultural 'codes' that make us who we are.

Hmm, yes, Sequencing the English Cultural Genome – that sounds like a big, serious, ambitious and impressively scientific project. The sort of thing that might well take three times longer than the period originally agreed in the publisher's contract, especially if you allow for all the tea-breaks.

Joking aside, I should probably explain the semi-scientific approach to understanding our national character that I actually used. It involved three stages:

- First, I used a variety of research methods (including observation studies, participant observation, interviews, discussion groups, national surveys, field experiments, etc., over the course of about two decades) to try to identify distinctive patterns or regularities in English behaviour.
- Then I tried to detect the unwritten social rules governing those behaviour patterns and, where possible, to 'test' or 'verify' these rules, mainly using field experiments, discussions and interviews.
- And, finally, I tried to figure out what these rules can tell us about Englishness.

The chapters in this book describe the behaviour patterns and unwritten rules relating to different aspects of English life (and in some cases how I discovered them). The brief sections at the end of each chapter are *not* summaries. This is not a textbook, and I would not insult your intelligence by summarising what you have only just read. These sections are where I examine each of the rules I have identified in that chapter, and try to tease out any 'defining characteristics of Englishness' these rules might reveal.

As I puzzled this out, methodically, rule by rule, chapter by chapter, many of the same characteristics – the same collective values, outlooks and unconscious reflexes – emerged again and again from the unwritten rules governing each aspect of English life and behaviour. So by the end I could see clearly which were the 'defining characteristics' I was seeking.

I have deliberately included this whole puzzling-out process in the book, as this seemed a more honest, transparent way of doing things – a bit like a maths exam at school, where the teacher says you have to show the 'workings out', rather than just putting down the final answer. So at the end of the book, if you think I've got the final answers to my 'What is Englishness?' question wrong, at least you can go back to the 'workings out' and see exactly where I made my mistakes.

PART ONE
CONVERSATION CODES

THE WEATHER

Any discussion of English conversation, like any English conversation, must begin with the weather. And in this spirit of observing traditional protocol, I shall, like every other writer on Englishness, quote Dr Johnson's famous comment that 'When two Englishmen meet, their first talk is of the weather', and point out that this observation is as accurate now as it was more than two hundred years ago.[14]

This, however, is the point at which most commentators either stop, or try, and fail, to come up with a convincing explanation for the English 'obsession' with the weather. They fail because their premise is mistaken: they assume that our conversations about the weather are conversations about the weather. In other words, they assume that we talk about the weather because we have a keen (indeed pathological) interest in the subject. Most of them then try to figure out what it is about the English weather that is so fascinating.

Bill Bryson, for example, concludes that the English weather is not at all fascinating, and presumably that our obsession with it is therefore inexplicable: 'To an outsider, the most striking thing about the English weather is that there is not very much of it. All those phenomena that elsewhere give nature an edge of excitement,

14. For stats-junkies: we (SIRC) recently did a national survey on this, in which, for example, 56 per cent said that they had talked about the weather within the previous six hours, 38 per cent within the previous hour. This suggests that, at any given moment, at least a third of us are probably talking about the weather. And that would be a conservative estimate: I suspect that the real weather-talk figures are even higher, as weather-speak is so automatic for the English that many people may not remember every instance when answering a survey question.

unpredictability and danger – tornadoes, monsoons, raging blizzards, run-for-your-life hailstorms – are almost wholly unknown in the British Isles.'

Jeremy Paxman, in an uncharacteristic and surely unconscious display of patriotism, takes umbrage at Bryson's dismissive comments, and argues that the English weather *is* intrinsically fascinating:

> Bryson misses the point. The English fixation with the weather is nothing to do with histrionics – like the English countryside, it is, for the most part, dramatically undramatic. The interest is less in the phenomena themselves, but in *uncertainty* . . . one of the few things you can say about England with absolute certainty is that it has a *lot* of weather. It may not include tropical cyclones but life at the edge of an ocean and the edge of a continent means you can never be entirely sure what you're going to get.

My research has convinced me that both Bryson and Paxman are missing the point, which is that our conversations about the weather are not really about the weather at all: English weather-speak is a form of code, evolved to help us overcome our social inhibitions and actually talk to each other. Everyone knows, for example, that 'Nice day, isn't it?', 'Ooh, isn't it cold?', 'Still raining, eh?' and other variations on the theme are not requests for meteorological data: they are ritual greetings, conversation-starters or default 'fillers'.

In other words, English weather-speak is a form of 'grooming talk' – the human equivalent of what is known as 'social grooming' among our primate cousins, where they spend hours grooming each other's fur, even when they are perfectly clean, as a means of social bonding.

These conclusions were based on my extensive participant-observation research, but even when confronted about their motives in a formal questionnaire survey (where people tend to try to appear rational and pragmatic) the majority of English people were prepared to admit that they used weather-talk for purely social purposes. And, perhaps even more striking, our survey findings show that this is by no means just an archaic custom practised mainly by older people.

In fact, young people proved to be the most acutely aware of the importance of polite conversation about the weather. The 18–24 age group, for example, was the most likely to say that weather-speak is so popular because it allows us to be nice/polite to people. These young people were also more than twice as likely as their elders to say that weather-talk helps us to gauge other people's moods.

THE RULES OF ENGLISH WEATHER-SPEAK

The Reciprocity Rule

Jeremy Paxman cannot understand why a 'middle-aged blonde' he encounters outside the Met Office in Bracknell says, 'Ooh, isn't it cold?', and he puts this irrational behaviour down to a distinctively English 'capacity for infinite surprise at the weather'. In fact, 'Ooh, isn't it cold?' – like 'Nice day, isn't it?' and all the others – is English code for 'I'd like to talk to you – will you talk to me?', or, if you like, simply another way of saying 'hello'. The hapless female was just trying to strike up a conversation with Mr Paxman. Not necessarily a long conversation – just a mutual acknowledgement, an exchange of greetings. Under the rules of weather-speak, all he was required to say was 'Mm, yes, isn't it?' or some other equally meaningless ritual response, which is code for 'Yes, I'll talk to you/greet you'. By failing to respond at all, Paxman committed a minor breach of etiquette, effectively conveying the rather discourteous message 'No, I will not exchange greetings with you'. (This was not a serious transgression, however, as the rules of privacy and reserve override those of sociability: talking to strangers is never compulsory.)

We used to have another option, at least for some social situations, but the 'How do you do?' greeting (to which the apparently ludicrous correct response is to repeat the question back 'How do you do?') is now regarded by many as somewhat archaic, and is no longer the universal standard greeting. The 'Nice day, isn't it?' exchange must, however, be understood in the same light, and not taken literally: 'How do you do?' is not a real question about health or well-being, and 'Nice day, isn't it?' is not a real question about the weather.

Comments about the weather are phrased as questions (or with an interrogative intonation) because they require a response – but the *reciprocity* is the point, not the content. Any interrogative remark on the weather will do to initiate the process, and any mumbled confirmation (or even near-repetition, as in 'Yes, isn't it?') will do as a response. English weather-speak rituals often sound rather like a kind of catechism, or the exchanges between priest and congregation in a church: 'Lord, have mercy upon us', 'Christ, have mercy upon us'; 'Cold, isn't it?', 'Yes, isn't it?', and so on.

It is not always quite that obvious, but all English weather conversations have a distinctive structure, an unmistakable rhythmic pattern, which to an anthropologist marks them out instantly as 'ritual'. There is a clear sense that these are 'choreographed' exchanges, conducted according to unwritten but tacitly accepted rules.

The Context Rule

A principal rule concerns the contexts in which weather-speak can be used. Other writers have claimed that the English talk about the weather all the time, that it is a national obsession or fixation, but this is sloppy observation: in fact, there are quite specific contexts in which weather-speak is prescribed. Weather-speak can be used:

- as a simple greeting
- as an ice-breaker leading to conversation on other matters
- as a 'default', 'filler' or 'displacement' subject, when conversation on other matters falters, and there is an awkward or uncomfortable lull
- as a signal that the speaker wishes to avoid more personal or intimate subjects
- as an excuse for a good moan
- as an opportunity for humour/wit
- as a way of gauging other people's moods
- as an opportunity to share 'Blitz Spirit' stoicism

Admittedly, this rule does allow for rather a lot of weather-speak – hence the impression that we talk of little else. A typical English conversation may well start with a weather-speak greeting, progress to a bit more weather-speak ice-breaking, and then 'default' to weather-speak joking, moaning, intimacy-avoidance, stoicism, etc., at regular intervals. It is easy to see why many foreigners, and even many English commentators, have assumed that we must be obsessed with the subject.

I am not claiming that we have no interest in the weather itself. The choice of weather as a code to perform these vital social functions is not entirely arbitrary, and in this sense, Jeremy Paxman is right: the changeable and unpredictable nature of the English weather makes it a particularly suitable facilitator of social interaction. If the weather were not so variable, we might have to find another medium for our social messages.

But in assuming that weather-speak indicates a burning interest in the weather, Paxman and others are making the same kind of mistake as early anthropologists, who assumed that certain animals or plants were chosen as tribal 'totems' because the people in question had a special interest in or reverence for that particular animal or plant. In fact, as the anthropologist Lévi-Strauss eventually explained, totems are symbols used to define social structures and relationships. The fact that one clan has as its totem the black cockatoo is not because of any deep significance attached to black cockatoos *per se*, but to define and delineate their relationship with another clan, whose totem is the white cockatoo. Now, the choice of cockatoos is not entirely random: totems tend to be local animals or plants with which the people are familiar, rather than abstract symbols. The selection of totems is thus not quite as arbitrary as, say, 'You be the red team and we'll be the blue team': it is almost always the familiar natural world that is used symbolically to describe and demarcate the social world.

The Agreement Rule

The English have clearly chosen a highly appropriate aspect of our own familiar natural world as a social facilitator: the capricious and erratic nature of our weather ensures that there is always something new to comment on, be surprised by, speculate about, moan about or, perhaps most importantly, *agree* about. Which brings us to another important rule of English weather-speak: always agree. This rule was noted by the Hungarian humorist George Mikes, who wrote that in England, 'You must never contradict anybody when discussing the weather.' We have already established that weather-speak greetings or openers such as 'Cold, isn't it?' must be reciprocated, but etiquette also requires that the response express agreement, as in 'Yes, isn't it?' or 'Mm, very cold.'

Failure to agree in this manner is a serious breach of etiquette. When the priest says 'Lord, have mercy upon us', you do not respond 'Well, actually, why should he?' You intone dutifully, 'Christ, have mercy upon us.' In the same way, it would be very rude to respond to 'Ooh, isn't it cold?' with 'No, actually, it's quite mild.' If you listen carefully, as I have, to hundreds of English weather-conversations, you will find that such responses are extremely rare, almost unheard of. Nobody will tell you that there is a rule about this – they are not even conscious of following a rule: it just simply isn't done.

If you deliberately break the rule (as I duly did, on several occasions, in the interests of science), you will find that the atmosphere becomes rather tense and awkward, and possibly somewhat huffy. No one will actually complain or make a big scene about it (we have rules about complaining and making a fuss), but they will be offended, and this will show in subtle ways. There may be an uncomfortable silence, then someone may say, in piqued tones, 'Well, it feels cold to *me*,' or '*Really*? Do you think so?' – or, most likely, they will either change the subject or continue talking about the weather among themselves, politely, if frostily, ignoring your *faux pas*. In very polite circles, they may attempt to 'cover' your mistake by helping you to redefine it as a matter of taste or personal idiosyncrasy, rather than of fact. Among highly courteous people, the response to your 'No, actually, it's quite mild' might be, after a slightly embarrassed pause, 'Oh, perhaps you don't feel the cold – you know, my husband is like that: he always thinks it's mild when I'm shivering and complaining. Maybe women feel the cold more than men, do you think?'

Exceptions to the Agreement Rule

This sort of gracious fudging is possible because the rules of English weather-speak are complex, and there are often exceptions and subtle variations. In the case of the agreement rule, the main variation concerns personal taste or differences in weather-sensitivity. You must always agree with 'factual' statements about the weather (these are almost invariably phrased as questions but, as we have already established, this is because they require a social *response*, not a rational answer), even when they are quite obviously wrong. You may, however, express personal likes and dislikes that differ from those of your companions, or express your disagreement in terms of personal quirks or sensibilities.

An appropriate response to 'Ooh, isn't it cold?', if you find you really cannot simply agree, would be 'Yes, but I really rather like this sort of weather – quite invigorating, don't you think?' or 'Yes, but you know I don't tend to notice the cold much – this feels quite warm to me.' Note that both of these responses start with an expression of agreement, even though in the second case this is followed by a blatant self-contradiction: 'Yes . . . this feels quite warm to me.' It is perfectly acceptable to contradict oneself in this manner, etiquette being far more important than logic, but if you truly cannot bring yourself to start with the customary 'Yes', this may be replaced by a positive-sounding 'Mm' accompanied by a nod – still an expression of agreement, but rather less emphatic.

Even better would be the traditional mustn't-grumble response: 'Yes [or Mm-with-nod], but at least it's not raining.' If you have a liking for cold weather, or do not find it cold, this response effectively guarantees that you and your shivering acquaintance will reach happy agreement. Everyone always agrees that a cold, bright day is preferable to a rainy one – or, at least, it is customary to express this opinion.

The personal taste/sensitivity variation is really more of a *modification* than an exception to the agreement rule: flat contradiction of a 'factual' statement is still taboo, the basic principle of agreement still applies; it is merely softened by allowing for differences in taste or sensitivity, providing these are explicitly identified as such.

There is, however, one context in which English weather-speakers are not required to observe the agreement rule at all and that is the male-bonding argument, particularly the pub-argument. This factor will come up again and again, and is explained in much more detail in Pub-talk (page 144), but for the moment, the critical point is that in English male-bonding arguments, particularly those conducted in the special environment of the pub, overt and constant disagreement – not just on the weather, but on everything else as well – is a means of expressing friendship and achieving intimacy.

The Weather Hierarchy Rule

I mentioned above that certain remarks about the weather, such as 'At least it's not raining' on a cold day, virtually guarantee agreement. This is because there is an unofficial English weather hierarchy to which almost everyone subscribes. In descending order, from best to worst, the hierarchy is as follows:

- sunny and warm/mild
- sunny and cool/cold
- cloudy and warm/mild
- cloudy and cool/cold
- rainy and warm/mild
- rainy and cool/cold

I am not saying that everyone in England prefers sun to cloud, or warmth to cold, just that other preferences are regarded as deviations from the norm.[15] Even our television weather forecasters clearly subscribe to this hierarchy: they adopt apologetic tones when forecasting rain, but often try to add a note of cheerfulness by pointing out that at least it will be a bit warmer, as they know that rainy/warm is preferable to rainy/cold. Similarly rueful tones are used to predict cold weather, brightened by the prospect of accompanying sunshine, because we all know that sunny/cold is better than cloudy/

15. In support of this (and as evidence of the importance of weather-speak) I would also cite the fact that of the seven synonyms for 'nice' in the Thesaurus, no less than five are exclusively weather-related, namely: fine, clear, mild, fair and sunny.

cold. So, unless the weather is both rainy and cold, you always have the option of a 'But at least it's not . . .' response.

If it is both wet and cold, or if you are just feeling grumpy, you can indulge what Jeremy Paxman calls our 'phenomenal capacity for quiet moaning'. This is a nice observation, and I would only add that these English 'moaning rituals' about the weather have an important social purpose, in that they provide further opportunities for friendly agreement, in this case with the added advantage of a 'them and us' factor – 'them' being either the weather itself or the forecasters. Moaning rituals involve displays of shared opinions (as well as wit and humour) and generate a sense of solidarity against a common enemy – both valuable aids to social bonding.

We now have yet another option for ritual humorous weather-moaning: in recent years, moans about global warming have become commonplace. The most popular form of this new moan is to say 'Huh, so much for global warming!' or 'So where's all this global warming they keep promising us?' on a cold, grey day.

An equally acceptable, and more positive, response to weather at the lower end of the hierarchy is to predict imminent improvement. In response to 'Awful weather, isn't it?', you can say, 'Yes, but they say it's going to clear up this afternoon.' If your companion is feeling Eeyorish,[16] however, the rejoinder may be 'Yes, well, they said that yesterday and it poured all day, didn't it?', at which point you may as well give up the Pollyanna approach and enjoy a spot of quiet moaning. It doesn't really matter: the point is to communicate, to agree, to have something in common; and shared moaning is just as effective in promoting sociable interaction and social bonding as shared optimism, shared speculation or shared stoicism.

For those whose personal tastes are at variance with the unofficial weather hierarchy, it is important to remember that the further down the hierarchy your preferences lie, the more you will have to qualify your remarks in accordance with the personal taste/sensitivity clause. A preference for cold over warmth, for example, is more acceptable

16. For those unfamiliar with English culture, Eeyore is the gloomy, pessimistic donkey in *Winnie the Pooh*.

than a dislike of sunshine, which in turn is more acceptable than an active enjoyment of rain. Even the most bizarre tastes, however, can be accepted as harmless eccentricities, providing one observes the rules of weather-speak.

Snow and the Moderation Rule

Snow is not mentioned in the hierarchy partly because it is relatively rare, compared to the other types of weather included, which occur all the time, often all in the same day. Snow is also socially and conversationally a special and awkward case, as it is aesthetically pleasing, but practically inconvenient. It is always simultaneously exciting and worrying. Snow is thus always excellent conversation-fodder, but it is only universally welcomed if it falls at Christmas, which it almost never does. We continue to hope that it will, however, and every year the high-street bookmakers relieve us of thousands of pounds in 'white Christmas' bets.

The only conversational rule that can be applied with confidence to snow is a generic, and distinctively English, 'moderation rule': too much snow, like too much of anything, is to be deplored. Even warmth and sunshine are only acceptable in moderation: too many consecutive hot, sunny days, and it is customary to start fretting about drought, muttering about hose-pipe bans and reminding each other, in doom-laden tones, of the summer of 1976. Or moaning about global warming.

The English may, as Paxman says, have a 'capacity for infinite surprise at the weather', and he is also right in observing that we like to be surprised by it. But we also *expect* to be surprised: we are accustomed to the variability of our weather, and we expect it to change quite frequently. If we get the same weather for more than a few days, we become uneasy: more than three days of rain, and we start worrying about floods; more than a day or two of snow, and disaster is declared, and the whole country slithers and skids to a halt.

The Weather-as-family Rule

While we may spend much of our time moaning about our weather, foreigners are not allowed to criticise it. In this respect, we treat the

English weather like a member of our family: one can complain about the behaviour of one's own children or parents, but any hint of censure from an outsider is unacceptable, and very bad manners.

Although we are aware of the relatively undramatic nature of the English weather – the lack of extreme temperatures, monsoons, tempests, tornadoes and blizzards – we become extremely touchy and defensive at any suggestion that our weather is therefore inferior or uninteresting. The worst possible weather-speak offence is one mainly committed by foreigners, particularly Americans, and that is to belittle the English weather. When the summer temperature reaches the high twenties, and we moan, 'Phew, isn't it *hot*?', we do not take kindly to visiting Americans or Australians laughing and scoffing and saying, 'Call *this* hot? This is *nothing*. You should come to Texas [Brisbane] if you wanna see *hot*!'

Not only is this kind of comment a serious breach of the agreement rule, and the weather-as-family rule, but it also represents a grossly *quantitative* approach to the weather, which we find coarse and distasteful. Size, we sniffily point out, isn't everything, and the English weather requires an appreciation of subtle changes and understated nuances, rather than a vulgar obsession with mere volume and magnitude.

Indeed, the weather may be one of the few things about which the English are still unselfconsciously and unashamedly patriotic. During my participant-observation research on Englishness, which naturally involved many conversations about the weather, I came across this prickly defensiveness about our weather again and again, among people of all classes and social backgrounds. Some of us may be too polite, or too inhibited, actually to *express* our irritation when faced with an unimpressed foreigner – although in the SIRC survey, nearly 50 per cent admitted to having 'got a bit defensive' when a foreigner belittled our weather.

In my more informal interviews, contempt for American size-fixation, in particular, was widespread – one outspoken informant (a publican) expressed the feelings of many when he told me: 'Oh, with Americans it's always "Mine's bigger than yours", with the weather or anything else. They're so crass. Bigger steaks, bigger buildings, bigger snowstorms, more heat, more hurricanes, whatever. No fucking subtlety, that's their problem.' Jeremy Paxman, rather more elegantly, but equally patriotically, dismisses all Bill Bryson's monsoons, raging blizzards, tornadoes and hailstorms as 'histrionics'. A very English put-down.

The Shipping Forecast Ritual

Our peculiar affection for our weather finds its most eloquent expression in our attitude towards a quintessentially English national institution: the Shipping Forecast. Browsing in a seaside bookshop, I came across an attractive large-format picture-book, with a seascape on the cover, entitled *Rain Later, Good*. It struck me that almost all English people would immediately recognise this odd, apparently meaningless or even contradictory phrase as part of the arcane, evocative and somehow deeply soothing meteorological mantra, broadcast immediately after the news on BBC Radio 4.

The Shipping Forecast is an off-shore weather forecast, with additional information about wind-strength and visibility, for the fishing vessels, pleasure craft and cargo ships in the seas around the British Isles. None of the information is of the slightest use or relevance to the millions of non-seafarers who listen to it, but listen we do, religiously, mesmerised by the calm, cadenced, familiar recitation of lists of names of sea areas, followed by wind information, then weather, then visibility – but with the qualifying words (wind, weather, visibility) left out, so it sounds like this: 'Viking, North Utsire, South Utsire, Fisher, German Bight. Westerly or south-westerly three or four, increasing five in north later. Rain later. Good becoming moderate, occasionally poor. Faroes, Fair Isle, Cromarty, Forties, Forth, Dogger. Northerly backing westerly three or four, increasing six later. Showers. Good.' And so on, and on, in measured, unemotional tones, until all of the thirty-one sea areas have been covered – and millions of English listeners,[17] most of whom have no idea where any of these places are, or what the words and numbers mean, finally switch off their radios, feeling strangely

---

17. Not all of them from the nostalgic older generations: the Shipping Forecast has many young devotees, and references to the Shipping Forecast have recently turned up in the lyrics of pop songs. I met a nineteen-year-old barman with a dog called Cromarty, after one of the sea areas.

comforted and even uplifted by what the poet Sean Street has called the Shipping Forecast's 'cold poetry of information'.

Some of my foreign informants – mostly immigrants and visitors who had been in England for some time – had come across this peculiar ritual, and many found it baffling. Why would we want to listen to these lists of obscure places and their irrelevant meteorological data in the first place – let alone insisting on hearing the entire pointless litany, and treating anyone who dared attempt to switch it off as though they had committed some sort of sacrilege? They were bemused by the national press, radio and television headlines, and fierce debates, when the name of one of the sea areas was changed (from Finisterre to FitzRoy), and would no doubt have been equally puzzled by the national outcry when the BBC had the temerity to change the time of the late-night broadcast, moving it back by a mere fifteen minutes ('People went ballistic,' according to a Met Office spokesman).

More recently, in 2011, the BBC seemed to have learnt their lesson: when the Shipping Forecast clashed with the broadcast of the final wicket in England's Ashes victory over Australia – a near-sacred moment in sporting history – the Shipping Forecast took priority. It was broadcast at its usual time, and cricket fans were advised to retune to digital, internet or medium-wave options to hear the end of this historic match. 'There's a Shipping Forecast heaving into view,' listeners were told, as though it were an approaching storm or some other immutable force of nature, 'Try to retune if you're listening on long wave.'[18]

'Anyone would think they'd tried to change the words of the Lord's Prayer!' said one of my American informants, of the hullabaloo over the Finisterre/FitzRoy issue. I tried to explain that the usefulness or

18. Yes, I know, the Shipping Forecast supposedly provides absolutely vital, potentially life-saving information for seafarers, and this is the ostensible reason for its immovable status. But the controller of Radio 4 himself has been quoted as saying that he would be 'slightly worried about anybody who is bobbing up and down in the Channel whose sole way of keeping from sinking is by listening to us on long wave. My advice would be to invest in a GPS system. But I still won't take it off because it has a glory of its own.'

relevance of the information is not the point, that listening to the Shipping Forecast, for the English, *is* like hearing a familiar prayer – somehow profoundly reassuring, even for non-believers – and that any alteration to such an important ritual is bound to be traumatic for us. We may not know where those sea areas are, I said, but the names are embedded in the national psyche: people even name their pets after them. We may joke about the Shipping Forecast (the author of *Rain Later, Good*[19] observes that some people 'talk back to it, "Thundery showers good? I don't think so"') but then we joke about everything, even, especially, the things that are most sacred to us. Like our weather, and our Shipping Forecast.

WEATHER-SPEAK RULES AND ENGLISHNESS

The rules of English weather-speak tell us quite a lot about Englishness. Already, before we even begin to examine the minutiae of other English conversation codes and rules of behaviour in other aspects of English life, these rules provide a number of hints and clues about the 'grammar' of Englishness.

In the reciprocity and context rules, we see some signs of social inhibition, but also the ingenious use of 'facilitators' to overcome this handicap. The agreement rule and its exceptions provide hints about the importance of politeness and avoidance of conflict (as well as the approval of conflict in specific social contexts) – and the precedence of etiquette over logic. In the variations to the agreement rule, and sub-clauses to the weather-hierarchy rule, we find indications of the acceptance of eccentricity and some hints of stoicism – the latter balanced by a predilection for Eeyorish moaning. The moderation rule reveals a dislike and disapproval of extremes, and the weather-as-family rule exposes a perhaps surprising patriotism, along with a quirky appreciation of understated charm. The Shipping Forecast ritual illustrates a deep-seated need for a sense of safety,

19. It is perhaps also worth noting that *Rain Later, Good*, first published in 1998, became an instant bestseller and has been reprinted many times (including a revised second edition in 2002, because of the controversial Finisterre name-change). More recent books about the Shipping Forecast have also been very popular.

security and continuity – and a tendency to become upset when these are threatened – as well as a love of words and a somewhat eccentric devotion to arcane and apparently irrational pastimes and practices. There seems also to be an undercurrent of humour in all this, a reluctance to take things too seriously.

Clearly, further evidence will be required to determine whether these are among the 'defining characteristics of Englishness' that we set out to identify, but at least we can start to see how an understanding of Englishness might emerge from detailed research on our unwritten rules.

GROOMING-TALK

I described weather-speak in the previous chapter as a form of 'grooming-talk'. Most of the much-vaunted human capacity for complex language is in fact devoted to such talk – the verbal equivalent of picking fleas off each other or mutual back-scratching.

THE RULES OF INTRODUCTION

Grooming-talk starts with greeting-talk. Weather-speak is needed in this context partly because greetings and introductions are such an awkward business for the English. The problem has become particularly acute since the decline of 'How do you do?' as the standard, all-purpose greeting. The 'How do you do?' greeting – where the correct response is not to answer the question, but to repeat it back, 'How do you do?', like an echo or a well-trained parrot[20] – is still in use in upper- and upper-middle-class circles, but the rest are left floundering, never knowing quite what to say. Instead of sneering at the old-fashioned stuffiness of the 'How do you do?' ritual, we would do better to mount a campaign for its revival: it would solve so many problems.

Awkwardness Rules

As it is, our introductions and greetings tend to be uncomfortable, clumsy and inelegant. Among established friends, there is less

20. To be fair, I should point out that although 'How do you do?' is technically a question, and written as such, it is spoken as a statement – with no rising, interrogative intonation at the end – so the custom of repeating it back is not quite as absurd as it might seem (almost, but not quite).

awkwardness, although we are often still not quite sure what to do with our hands, or whether to hug or kiss. The French custom of a kiss on each cheek initially became popular among the chattering classes and some other upper-middle-class groups, but was regarded as silly and pretentious by many other sections of society, particularly when it took the form of the 'air-kiss', and was in any case only acceptable between females, or males and females, never between males. Even in the social circles where cheek-kissing became customary, one could still never be entirely sure whether one kiss or two was required, resulting in much awkward hesitation and bumping as the parties tried to second-guess each other.

Over the past decade or so, the cheek-kissing custom has become much more widespread, and crept much further down the social scale. But most people are still just as uncertain about the 'correct' number of kisses (the higher social classes tend to do two kisses, the lower classes seem more inclined to stop at one, but one can never be sure) and the process is still just as self-conscious and uncomfortable. One often now sees bizarre attempts to combine a handshake, a cheek-kiss and a sort of brief, clumsy hug or back-pat. If anything, we seem to have become even more confused. Clearly, it is going to take the English a very long time indeed to arrive at a consensus on the simple matter of how to greet someone.

Handshakes are now the norm in business introductions – or, rather, they are the norm when people in business are introduced to each other for the first time. Ironically, the first introduction, where a degree of formality is expected, is the easiest. (Note, though, that the English handshake in these contexts is almost always somewhat awkward, very brief, performed 'at arm's length', and without any of the spare-hand involvement – clasping, forearm patting, etc. – found in less inhibited cultures.)

At subsequent meetings, particularly as business contacts get to know each other better, a handshake greeting often starts to seem *too* formal, but cheek-kisses would be too informal (or too pretentious, depending on the social circle), and in any case not allowed between males, so we revert to the usual embarrassed confusion, with no one being quite sure what to do. Hands are half extended and then withdrawn or turned into a sort of vague wave; there may be awkward, hesitant moves towards a cheek-kiss or some other form of physical contact such as an arm-touch – as no contact at all feels a bit unfriendly – but these are also often aborted halfway. This is excruciatingly English: over-formality is embarrassing, but so is an inappropriate degree of informality (that problem with extremes again).

The No-name Rule

In purely social situations, the difficulties are even more acute. There is no universal prescription of handshakes on initial introduction – indeed, they may be regarded as too 'businesslike' – and the normal business practice of giving one's name at this point is also regarded as inappropriate. You do not go up to someone at a party (or in any other social setting where conversation with strangers is permitted, such as a pub bar-counter) and say 'Hello, I'm John Smith,' or even 'Hello, I'm John.' In fact, the only correct way to introduce yourself in such settings is not to introduce yourself at all, but to find some other way of initiating a conversation – such as a remark about the weather.

The 'brash American' approach: 'Hi, I'm Bill, how are you?', particularly if accompanied by an outstretched hand and beaming smile, makes the English wince and cringe. The American tourists and visitors I spoke to during my research had been both baffled and hurt by this reaction. 'I just don't get it,' said one woman. 'You say your name and they sort of wrinkle their noses, like you've told them something a bit too personal and embarrassing.'

'That's right,' her husband added. 'And then they give you this tight little smile and say, "Hello" – kind of pointedly *not* giving their name, to let you know you've made this big social booboo. What the hell is so private about a person's *name*, for God's sake?'

I ended up explaining, as kindly as I could, that the English do not want to know your name, or tell you theirs, until a much greater degree of intimacy has been established – like maybe when you marry their daughter. Rather than giving your name, I suggested, you should strike up a conversation by making a vaguely interrogative comment about the weather (or the party or pub or wherever you happen to be). This must not be done too loudly, and the tone should be light and informal, not earnest or intense. The object is to 'drift' casually into conversation, as though by accident. Even if the other person seems happy enough to chat, it is still customary to curb any urges to introduce yourself.

Eventually, there may be an opportunity to exchange names, providing this can be achieved in a casual, unforced manner, although it is always best to wait for the other person to take the initiative. Should you reach the end of a long, friendly evening without having introduced yourself, you may say, on parting, 'Goodbye, nice to meet you, er – sorry, I didn't catch your name?' as though you have only just noticed the omission. Your new acquaintance should then divulge his or her name, and you may now, at last, introduce yourself – but in an offhand way, as though it is not a matter of any importance: 'I'm Bill, by the way.'

One perceptive Dutch tourist, after listening attentively to my explanation of this procedure, commented: 'Oh, I see. It is like *Alice Through the Looking Glass*: you do everything the wrong way round.' I had not thought of recommending *Alice* as a guide to English etiquette, but on reflection it seems like quite a good idea.

The 'Pleased to Meet You' Problem

In a small social gathering such as a dinner party, the host may solve the name problem by introducing guests to each other by name, but these are still awkward moments, as the decline of 'How do you do?' means that no one is quite sure what to say to each other when introduced in this manner. 'How are you?', despite having much the same meaning, and being equally recognised as a non-question (the correct response is 'Very well, thank you' or 'Fine, thanks' – or even the more American-sounding 'I'm good, thanks' – whatever your state of health or mind), will not do in initial introductions, as custom dictates that it may only be used as a greeting between people who already know each other. Even though it does not require an honest answer, 'How are you?' is far too personal and intimate a question for first-time introductions.

The most common solution, nowadays, is 'Pleased to meet you' or 'Nice to meet you', 'Good to meet you' or some other variation. But in some social circles – upper class and the higher ranks of upper-middle – the problem with this common response is that it is just that: 'common', meaning a lower-class thing to say. The people who hold this view may not put it quite like that – they are more likely to say that 'Pleased to meet you' is 'incorrect', and you will indeed still find etiquette books that confirm this. The explanation offered by some etiquette books is that one should not say, 'Pleased to meet you' as it is an obvious lie: one cannot possibly be sure at that point whether one is pleased to meet the person or not. Given the usual irrationalities, dishonesties and hypocrisies of English etiquette, this seems unnecessarily and quite uncharacteristically scrupulous.

Whatever its origins or dubious logic, the prejudice against 'Pleased to meet you' is still quite widespread in the higher social classes, often among people who do not know why it is that they feel uneasy about using the phrase. They just have a vague sense that there is something not quite right about it. 'Nice to meet you' is often preferred, presumably because 'nice' is a more neutral term than 'pleased' – and 'nice' is so overused as to be virtually meaningless – but there are still some who feel uncomfortable even with this restrained alternative.

Even among those with no class prejudice about 'Pleased/nice/good to meet you', who believe it is the correct and polite thing to say, this greeting is rarely delivered with ringing confidence: it is usually mumbled rather awkwardly, and as quickly as possible – 'Plstmtye' (or Nctmtye, Gdtmtye, etc.). This awkwardness may, perversely, occur precisely *because* people believe they are saying the 'correct' thing. Formality is embarrassing. But, then, informality is embarrassing. Everything is embarrassing.

The Embarrassment Rule

In fact, the only rule one can identify with any certainty in all this confusion over introductions and greetings is that, to be impeccably English, one must perform these rituals *badly*. One must appear self-conscious, ill-at-ease, stiff, awkward and, above all, embarrassed. Smoothness, glibness and confidence are inappropriate and un-English. Hesitation, dithering and ineptness are, surprising as it may seem, correct behaviour.[21] Introductions should be performed as hurriedly as possible, but also with maximum inefficiency. If disclosed at all, names must be mumbled; hands should be tentatively half proffered, then clumsily withdrawn; the approved greeting is something like 'Er, how, um, plstm– er, hello?'

If you are socially skilled, or come from a country where these matters are handled in a more reasonable, straightforward manner (such as anywhere else on the planet), you may need a bit of practice to achieve the required degree of embarrassed, stilted incompetence.

THE RULES OF ENGLISH GOSSIP

Following the customary awkward introductions and uncomfortable greetings, and a bit of ice-breaking weather-speak, we move on to other forms of grooming-talk. ('One must speak a little, you know,' as Elizabeth said to Darcy. 'It would look odd to be entirely silent.')

Strangers may stick to the weather and other relatively neutral topics almost indefinitely (although the weather is the only topic that is *entirely* safe – all other subjects are potentially 'dangerous', at least in some situations, and all carry at least some restrictions as to when, where and with whom they may be raised). But the most common form of grooming-talk among friends, in England as elsewhere, is gossip. The English are certainly a nation of gossips. Recent studies in this country have shown that about two-thirds of our conversation time is entirely devoted to social topics such as who is doing what with whom; who is 'in', who is 'out' and why; how to deal with difficult social situations; the behaviour and

21. I was rather chuffed, and at the same time slightly alarmed, to see that this observation has now been taken up (more or less verbatim) and enshrined in at least one English etiquette guide – alarmed because it was not my intention for the unwritten 'awkwardness is correct' rule to become an 'official' rule. I was also interested to see that *Debrett's* online guide to 'British behaviour' includes many observations from this book (more scrupulously paraphrased, of course).

relationships of friends, family and celebrities; our own problems with family, friends, lovers, colleagues and neighbours; the minutiae of everyday social life – in a word: gossip.[22]

If you want a more formal definition of gossip, the best I have come across is Noon & Delbridge (1993): 'The process of informally communicating value-laden information about members of a social setting.' This does not quite cover all aspects of gossip – it excludes gossip about celebrities, for example, unless the concept of 'members of a social setting' is intended to include film stars, sports stars, pop stars, television stars, royals and politicians, which seems unlikely. But, to be fair, there is a sense in which our gossip about celebrities does involve treating them as though they were members of our own social group – our conversations about the conflicts between characters in soap operas and 'reality' shows, the relationship problems of supermodels and the marriages, careers and babies of film stars are often indistinguishable from our gossip about family, friends and neighbours – so I'll give Noon & Delbridge the benefit of the doubt on this point.

In fact, one of the reasons I like this definition is that it gives some indication of the range of people about whom gossipy information may be communicated, including the gossipers themselves. Researchers have found that about half of 'gossip time' is taken up with discussion of the activities of the speaker or the immediate audience, rather than the doings of other people. This definition also helpfully conveys the *evaluative* nature of gossip. Although it has been shown that criticism and negative evaluations account for only about five per cent of gossip time, gossip does generally involve the expression of opinions or feelings. Among the English, you will find that these opinions or feelings may often be implied, rather than directly stated, or conveyed more subtly in the tone of voice, but we rarely share details about 'who is doing what with whom' without providing some indication of our views on the matter.

22. And this was research conducted in a manner of which I approve, not by questionnaire or lab experiments but by eavesdropping on real conversations in natural settings, so we can have some confidence in these findings.

Privacy Rules

In quoting the research findings on the pervasiveness of English gossip above, I am not suggesting that the English gossip any more than people in other cultures. I am sure that studies elsewhere would also find about two-thirds of conversation time dedicated to much the same social matters. The researcher responsible for the English findings (the evolutionary psychologist Robin Dunbar) is convinced that this is a universal human trait, and indeed maintains that language evolved to allow humans to gossip[23] – as a substitute for the physical 'social grooming' of our primate ancestors, which became impractical among the much wider human social networks.

What I am suggesting is that gossip may be particularly important to the English, because of our obsession with privacy. When I conducted interviews and focus-group discussions on gossip with English people of different ages and social backgrounds, it became clear that their enjoyment of gossip had much to do with the element of 'risk' involved. Although most of our gossip is fairly innocuous, it is still talk about people's 'private' lives, and as such involves a sense of doing something naughty or forbidden.

The 'invasion of privacy' involved in gossip is particularly relevant for the rather inhibited English, for whom privacy is an especially serious matter. It is impossible to overstate the importance of privacy in English culture. Jeremy Paxman points out that 'The importance of privacy informs the entire organisation of the country, from the assumptions on which laws are based, to the buildings in which the English live.' George Orwell observes that 'The most hateful of all names in an English ear is Nosy Parker.'

I would add that a disproportionate number of our most influential social rules and maxims are concerned with the maintenance of privacy: we are taught to mind our own business, not to pry, to keep ourselves to ourselves, not to make a scene or a fuss or draw

23. There are, of course, other theories of language evolution, the most appealing of which is Geoffrey Miller's proposition that language evolved as a courtship device – to enable us to flirt. Fortunately, the 'chat-up' theory of language evolution is not incompatible with the 'gossip' theory, providing one accepts that gossip has multiple functions, including status-display for courtship purposes.

attention to ourselves, and never to wash our dirty linen in public. It is worth noting again here that 'How are you?' is only treated as a 'real' question among very close personal friends or family;[24] everywhere else, the automatic, ritual response is 'Fine, thanks', 'OK, thanks', 'Oh, mustn't grumble', 'Not bad, thanks' or some equivalent, whatever your physical or mental state. If you are terminally ill, it is acceptable to say, 'Not bad, considering.'

As a result, thanks to the inevitable forbidden-fruit effect, we are a nation of curtain-twitchers, endlessly fascinated by the tabooed private lives of the 'members of our social setting'. The English may not gossip much more than any other culture, but our privacy rules significantly enhance the *value* of gossip. The laws of supply and demand ensure that gossip is a precious social commodity among the English. 'Private' information is not given away lightly or cheaply to all and sundry, but only to those we know and trust.[25]

This is one of the reasons why foreigners often complain that the English are cold, reserved, unfriendly and standoffish. In most other cultures, revealing basic personal data – your name, what you do for a living, whether you are married or have children, where you live – is no big deal: in England, extracting such apparently trivial information from a new acquaintance can be like pulling teeth; every question makes us wince and recoil.

The Guessing-game Rule

Unless you are the Queen, it is not considered entirely polite, for example, to ask someone directly, 'What do you do?', although if you think about it, this is the most obvious question to put to a new acquaintance, and the easiest way to start a conversation. But in addition to our privacy scruples, we English (especially the middle

24. This is even more evident in the USA, where 'Hi-how-are-you?' or 'Hey-how-are-you?' has become a standard throwaway greeting – similar to the English 'How do you do?' except that little or no response is required, whereas 'How do you do?' requires the polite repetition of the non-question.

25. There are some increasingly significant exceptions to these privacy rules – see 'The Print Exception' and 'The Internet Exception' (pages 62 and 64), for example.

classes) seem to have a perverse need to make social life difficult for ourselves, so etiquette requires us to find a more roundabout, indirect way of discovering what people do for a living. It can be most amusing to listen to the tortured and devious lengths to which English people will go to ascertain a new acquaintance's profession without actually asking the forbidden question. The guessing game, which is played at almost every middle-class social gathering where people are meeting each other for the first time, involves attempting to guess a person's occupation from 'clues' in remarks made about other matters.

A comment about traffic problems in the local area, for example, will elicit the response 'Oh, yes, it's a nightmare – and the rush hour is even worse: do you drive to work?' The other person knows exactly what question is really intended, and will usually obligingly answer the unspoken enquiry as well as the spoken one, saying something like 'Yes, but I work at the hospital, so at least I don't have to get into the town centre.' The questioner is now allowed to make a direct guess: 'Oh, the hospital – you're a doctor, then?' (When two or three possible occupations are indicated, it is polite to name the highest-status one as a first guess – doctor rather than nurse, porter or medical student; solicitor rather than secretary. Also, even though an explicit guess is permitted at this stage, it is best expressed as an interrogative statement, rather than as a direct question.)

Everyone knows the rules of this game, and most people tend to offer helpful 'clues' early in the conversation, to speed the process along. Even if you are shy, embarrassed about your job or trying to be enigmatic, it is considered very rude to prolong the clue-hunting stage of the game for too long, and once someone makes an explicit guess, you are obliged to reveal your occupation. It is almost equally impolite to ignore any obvious 'clue-dropping' by your new acquaintance. If (to continue the medical theme) he or she mentions in passing that 'My surgery is just round the corner from here', you are honour-bound to hazard a guess: 'Oh, so – you're a GP?'

When the person's occupation is finally revealed, it is customary, however boring or predictable this occupation might be, to express surprise. The standard response to 'Yes, I am a doctor [teacher, accountant, IT manager, secretary, etc.]' is 'Oh, *really*?!' as though the occupation were both unexpected and fascinating. This is almost invariably followed by an embarrassed pause, as you search desperately for an appropriate comment or question about the person's profession – and he or she tries to think of something modest, amusing, but somehow also impressive to say in response.

Similar guessing-game techniques are often used to find out where people live, whether they are married, what school or university they went to, and so on. Some direct questions are more impolite than others. It is less rude, for example, to ask, 'Where do you live?' than 'What do you do?', but even this relatively inoffensive question is much better phrased in a more indirect manner, such as 'Do you live nearby?', or even more obliquely, 'Have you come far?' It is more acceptable to ask whether someone has children than to ask whether he or she is married, so the former question is generally used as a roundabout way of prompting clues that will provide the answer to the latter. (Many married English males do not wear wedding rings, so the children question is often used by single females to encourage them to reveal their marital status. This can only be done in an appropriate conversational context, however, as asking the children question 'out of the blue' would be too obvious an attempt to ascertain a male's availability.)

The guessing-game rituals allow us, eventually, to elicit this kind of rudimentary census-form information, but the English privacy rules ensure that any more interesting details about our lives and relationships are reserved for close friends and family. This is 'privileged' information, not to be bandied about indiscriminately. The English take a certain pride in this trait, and sneer at the stereotyped Americans who 'tell you all about their divorce, their hysterectomy and their therapist within five minutes of meeting you'. This cliché, although not entirely without foundation, probably tells us more about the English and our privacy rules than it does about the Americans.

Incidentally, the English privacy rules, especially the taboo on prying, can make life quite difficult for the social researcher whose life-blood data can only be obtained by constant prying. I 'found' many of the findings in this book the hard way, by pulling metaphorical teeth or, more often, desperately trying to find sneaky tricks and stratagems that would help me to get round the privacy rules. Still, the process of devising and experimenting with such tricks led me to the identification of some unexpected and interesting rules, such as the distance rule.

The Distance Rule

Among the English, gossip about one's own private doings is generally reserved for intimates; gossip about the private lives of friends and family is shared with a slightly wider social circle; gossip about the personal affairs of acquaintances, colleagues and neighbours with a larger group; and gossip about the intimate details of public figures' or celebrities' lives with almost anyone. This is the distance rule. The more 'distant' from you the subject of gossip, the wider the circle of people with whom you may gossip about that person.

The distance rule allows gossip to perform its vital social functions – social bonding; clarification of position and status; assessment and management of reputations; transmission of social skills, norms and values – without undue invasion of privacy. More importantly, it also allows nosy-parker anthropologists to formulate their prying questions in such a roundabout manner as to bypass the privacy rules.

If, for example, you want to find out about an English person's attitudes and feelings on a sensitive subject, such as, say, marriage, you do not ask about his or her own marriage: you talk about someone else's marriage, preferably that of a remote public figure not personally known to either of you. When you are better acquainted with the person, you can discuss the domestic difficulties of a colleague or neighbour, or perhaps even a friend or relative. (If you do not happen to have colleagues or relatives with suitably dysfunctional marriages, you can always invent these people.)

The Reciprocal-disclosure Strategy

If you are determined to find out about your new English friend's own marital relations, or any other 'private' matter, you will probably have to resort to the reciprocal-disclosure strategy. There is a more or less universal rule whereby people almost unconsciously try to achieve some degree of symmetry or balance in their conversations, such that if you tell someone something about your own 'private' life, the other person will feel obliged, if only out of reflex politeness, to reciprocate with a comparably personal disclosure. You can then gradually escalate the level of intimacy by making your next disclosure somewhat more revealing, in the hope of eliciting an equivalent response, and so on.

Among the English, however, you would be advised to start with a very minor, trivial disclosure – something that barely counts as 'private' at all and can be dropped into the conversation casually – and work up, step by step, from this innocuous starting point. The reciprocal-disclosure strategy is a laborious, painstaking procedure, but it is often the only way of tricking the English into breaking their privacy taboos.

You might find it quite an amusing experiment, though, to pick the most reserved, buttoned-up English people you can find and see just how far you can get them to unbend using this technique. Being English myself, I often found it easier to make up my 'personal revelations' than to disclose anything about my real private life. I am sorry to bring my profession into disrepute by admitting to such deceptions, but this would not be an honest account of my research if I neglected to mention all the lies I told.

Exceptions to the Privacy Rules

The Print Exception

There is a curious exception to the privacy rules, which, although it applies mainly just to a certain rather privileged section of English society, is worth mentioning as it tells us something about Englishness. I call it the 'print exception': we may discuss in print (newspapers, magazines, books, etc.) private matters that we would be reluctant or embarrassed to talk about with, say, a new acquaintance at a party. It may seem strange or even perverse, but it is somehow more acceptable to divulge details of one's personal life in a book, newspaper column or magazine article than to do so in the much less public arena of a small social gathering.

Actually, this is one of those 'exceptions that proves the rule', in that what it really tells us is that the vogue for confessional journalism and other candid writing has not significantly affected the rules of behaviour in everyday English life. A newspaper or magazine columnist may tell millions of complete strangers about her messy divorce, her breast cancer, her eating disorder, her worries about cellulite, or whatever, but she will not take kindly to being asked personal questions about such matters by an individual stranger at a private social event. Her taboo-breaking is purely professional; in real life, she observes the English privacy and distance rules like everyone else, discussing private matters only with close friends, and regarding personal questions from anyone outside this inner circle as impertinent and intrusive. Just as you would not ask a professional topless model to take her top off at a family Sunday lunch, so you do not ask professional soul-barers to bare their souls over the canapés at a private party or pints at the pub.

The print exception is sometimes extended to cover other media such as television or radio documentaries and chat-shows. Generally, however, English professional soul-barers disclose rather less in these contexts than in the printed word. One sometimes sees the bizarre phenomenon of an English soul-barer, who has written a highly revealing book or column, coming over all coy and embarrassed and taking refuge in nervous jokes and euphemisms when interviewed about it on a chat-show. This is not to say that all soul-barers are more restrained in such contexts, but there does seem to be a subtle yet noticeable difference in degree of disinhibition between the written and the spoken word. And even those who do not observe this fine distinction, and talk freely about their private affairs in documentaries and chat-shows, will still subscribe to the privacy rules when they are not on air.

There are, of course, in England, as elsewhere, some people who will do or say or reveal almost anything, anywhere, to achieve their 'fifteen minutes of fame', or to score points off someone, or to make money. And in England as elsewhere, there are those who make a living providing outlets for them to do this; currently, *The Jeremy Kyle Show* (our rather tame imitation of *Jerry Springer*) seems to be the favoured television programme for this purpose, along with so-called 'reality' shows, such as *Big Brother*. But those who break the privacy rules – and these are clearly breaches, not exceptions – in this blatant manner are a very tiny minority, and their antics are generally reviled and ridiculed by the rest of the population, indicating that observance of these rules is still the norm.

The Internet Exception

Over the past decade or so, the 'print exception' has been extended to cover writing on the internet – blogs, online forums, chatrooms and social media sites such as Facebook and Twitter. Both public figures and ordinary people regularly – and sometimes regrettably – reveal intimate details in their Tweets, Facebook posts and other online chatter that they would be highly reluctant to divulge to a new acquaintance in a face-to-face encounter. The print exception has thus effectively been democratised: it now applies not only to privileged authors, journalists and celebrities, whose soul-baring words are published in traditional print media, such as books and newspapers, but to everyone with access to the internet.

The etiquette governing the print exception applies equally to the internet: just because your English Facebook, Twitter or forum 'friends' plaster intimate revelations about their private lives all over the internet does not mean that they will be happy to discuss these matters when you meet them face to face. In fact, they may take great offence if you so much as mention them. The English are by no means alone in finding cyberspace a disinhibiting place, and this disconnect between online and 'real life' communication applies in other cultures as well.[26] But the difference is perhaps more marked here: we may, if anything, be even more gleefully and giddily uninhibited in our online disclosures, but in face-to-face conversation, the normal English privacy rules apply.

26. I'll be coming back to the intriguing dissociation between cyberspace and 'realspace' and attempting some explanations, later on – see 'Cyberspace Rules' in Rules of Play (page 335).

Sex Differences in English Gossip Rules

Contrary to popular belief, researchers[27] have found that men gossip just as much as women. In one English study, both sexes devoted the same amount of conversation time (about 65 per cent) to social topics such as personal relationships; in another, the difference was found to be quite small, with gossip accounting for 55 per cent of male conversation time and 67 per cent of female time. As sport and leisure have been shown to occupy about 10 per cent of conversation time, discussion of football could well account for the difference.

Men were certainly found to be no more likely than women to discuss 'important' or 'highbrow' subjects, such as politics, work, art and cultural matters – except (and this was a striking difference) when women were present. On their own, men gossip, with no more than five per cent of conversation time devoted to non-social subjects, such as work or politics. It is only in mixed-sex groups, where there are women to impress, that the proportion of male conversation time devoted to these more 'highbrow' subjects increases dramatically, to between 15 and 20 per cent.

In fact, research has revealed only one significant difference, in terms of content, between male and female gossip: men spend much more time talking about themselves. Of the total time devoted to conversation about social relationships, men spend two-thirds talking about their own relationships, while women talk about themselves just one-third of the time.

Despite these findings, the myth is still widely believed, particularly among males, that men spend their conversations 'solving the world's problems', while the womenfolk gossip in the kitchen. In my discussion groups and interviews, most English males initially claimed that they did not gossip, while most of the females readily admitted that they did. On further questioning, however, the difference turned out to be more a matter of semantics than practice: what the women were happy to call 'gossip', the men defined as 'exchanging information'.

Clearly, there is a stigma attached to gossip among English males,

27. Including Professor Robin Dunbar's team, and my own SIRC project studying gossip on mobile phones.

an unwritten rule to the effect that, even if what one is doing is gossiping, it should be called something else. Perhaps even more important: it should *sound* like something else. In my gossip research, I found that the main difference between male and female gossip is that female gossip actually *sounds* like gossip. There seem to be three principal factors involved: the tone rule, the detail rule and the feedback rule.

The Tone Rule

The English women I interviewed all agreed that a particular tone of voice was considered appropriate for gossip. The gossip-tone should be high and quick, or sometimes a stage whisper, but always highly animated. 'Gossip's got to start with something like [quick, high-pitched, excited tone] "Ooh – guess what? Guess what?"' explained one woman, 'or "Hey, listen, listen [quick, urgent stage-whisper] – you know what I heard?"' Another told me: 'You have to make it sound surprising or scandalous, even when it isn't really. You'll go, "Well, don't tell anyone, but . . ." even when it's not really that big of a secret.'

Many of the women complained that men failed to adopt the correct tone of voice, recounting items of gossip in the same flat, unemotional manner as any other piece of information, such that, as one woman sniffed, 'You can't even tell it's gossip.' Which, of course, is exactly the impression the males wish to give.

The Detail Rule

Females also stressed the importance of detail in the telling of gossip, and again bemoaned the shortcomings of males in this matter, claiming that men 'never know the details'. 'Men just don't do the he-said-she-said thing,' one informant told me, 'and it's no good unless you actually know what people said.' Another said: 'Women tend to speculate more . . . They'll talk about *why* someone did something, give a history to the situation.' For women, this detailed speculation about possible motives and causes, requiring an exhaustive raking over 'history', is a crucial element of gossip, as is detailed speculation about possible outcomes. English males find all this detail boring, irrelevant and unmanly.

The Feedback Rule

Among English women, it is understood that to be a 'good gossip' requires more than a lively tone and attention to detail: you also need a good audience, by which they mean appreciative listeners who give plenty of appropriate feedback. The feedback rule of female gossip requires that listeners be at least as animated and enthusiastic as speakers. The reasoning seems to be that this is only polite: the speaker has gone to the trouble of making the information sound surprising and scandalous, so the least one can do is to reciprocate by sounding suitably shocked. English men, according to my female informants, just don't seem to have grasped this rule. They do not understand that 'You are supposed to say "NO! *Really?*" and "Oh, my GOD!"'

My female informants agreed, however, that a man who did respond in the approved female manner would sound inappropriately girly, or even disturbingly effeminate. Even the gay males I interviewed felt that the 'NO! *Really?*' kind of response would be regarded as decidedly 'camp'. The unwritten rules of English gossip etiquette do allow men to express shock or surprise when they hear a particularly juicy bit of gossip, but it is understood that a suitable expletive conveys such surprise in a more acceptably masculine fashion.

English Males, Animation and the Three-emotions Rule

It is possible that these sex differences in gossip rules may account for the persistence of the 'gossip is female' myth. If popular perceptions equate high-pitched, quick, animated speech, and frequent use of expressions such as 'Guess what? Guess what?' and 'NO! *Really?*' with gossip, then male conversations, at least in England, will very rarely sound like gossip, although their content may be identifiable as such. Gossiping English males sound as though they are talking about 'important issues' (or cars, or football) – which is, of course, precisely their intention.

Some of these rules and sex differences may not be peculiarly English. The detail rule, for example, may even be a universal female trait, it being well established that females tend to be more verbally skilled than males. I would also expect similar research in America and perhaps Australia to find significantly higher levels of animation in female gossip than male, both in the telling and in the response. But these are countries influenced at least to some extent by English culture, and my admittedly more limited research in other European cultures indicates that males in these societies are much less restrained, and considerably more animated, in their discussions of social matters. '*NON! C'est pas vrai? Ah, mon Dieu!*' is certainly a perfectly normal and acceptable male response to a scandalous bit of gossip in France, for example, and I have heard similarly animated male gossip in Italy, Spain, Belgium, Holland, Poland, Lebanon, Albania, Greece, Switzerland and Russia.

It is not that men in these cultures are any less concerned than English males about appearing effeminate. Fear of being seen as unmanly is undoubtedly a male cross-cultural universal. It is just that only the English (and some English-speaking former colonies) seem to regard animated tones and expressive responses as effeminate.

Nor am I saying that English conversation codes do not allow men to express emotion. English males are allowed to express emotion. Well, they are allowed to express some emotions. Three, to be precise: surprise, providing it is conveyed by expletives; anger, generally communicated in the same manner; and elation/triumph, which again often involves shouting and swearing. It can thus sometimes be rather hard to tell exactly which of the three permitted emotions an Englishman is attempting to express.

BONDING-TALK

English bonding-talk, another form of grooming-talk, is also largely sex-specific: male bonding-talk looks and sounds very different from female bonding-talk – although some of the underlying rules turn out to reflect the same basic values, which may qualify as 'defining characteristics' of Englishness.

Female Bonding: the Counter-compliment Rules

English female bonding-talk often starts with a ritual exchange of compliments. In fact, this ritual can be observed at almost every social gathering of two or more female friends. I have eavesdropped on female complimenting rituals in pubs, restaurants, coffee shops and night-clubs; at race-meetings and other sports events; at theatres, concerts, Women's Institute meetings and biker rallies; in shopping centres and on street corners; on buses and trains; in school play-grounds, university cafeterias and office canteens. I found that when women are accompanied by men, they tend to conduct a somewhat truncated version of the complimenting ritual, although they often retreat to the ladies' loos to complete the exchange (yes, I followed them); in all-female groups, the full version will be performed in public.

Observing the many variations of this ritual, and often participating as well, I noticed that the compliments are not exchanged at random, but often in a distinctive pattern, in accordance with what I came to call the 'counter-compliment rule'. The pattern is as follows. The opening line may be either a straight compliment, such as 'Oh, I like your new haircut!' or a combination of a compliment and a self-critical remark: 'Your hair looks great. I wish I had gorgeous hair like you – mine's so boring and mousy.' The counter-compliment rule requires that the response to either version contain a self-deprecating denial, and a 'counter-compliment', as in 'Oh, no! My hair's terrible. It gets so frizzy – I wish I could have it short like you, but I just don't have the bone structure. You've got such good cheekbones.' This must be countered with another self-critical denial, and a further compli-ment, which prompts yet another self-deprecating denial and yet another counter-compliment, and so the ritual continues. There are social 'points' to be gained by making amusing, witty, self-critical remarks – some English women have turned this kind of humorous self-deprecation into an art form, and there can almost be an element of competitiveness in their one-downmanship.

The conversation may jump from hair to shoes to thighs to profes-sional achievement, fitness, social skills, dating success, children, talents and accomplishments – but the formula remains the same. Few compli-ments are ever wholeheartedly accepted; no self-denigrating remark ever goes unchallenged. When a compliment is too obviously accurate to be received with the customary flat or humorous denial, it is deflected with a hasty, embarrassed 'Well, thank you, er . . .' and the inevitable counter-compliment, or at least an attempt to change the subject.

When I asked English counter-complimenters why they could not just accept a compliment, they usually responded by reiterating their denial of the specific compliment in question, and often attempting to throw in a counter-compliment to me while they were at it. This was not helpful, except in confirming that the rule was deeply ingrained, so I tried to phrase the question in more general terms, talking about the patterns I had observed in their conversation, and asking how they would feel about someone who just accepted a compliment, without qualification, and didn't offer one in return. The typical response was that this would be regarded as rather impolite and unfriendly, possibly even arrogant – one woman told me that it would be 'almost as bad as boasting', a slightly extreme view, but others felt that such a person would at least be seen as 'taking herself a bit too seriously'. One woman replied, and I swear this is true and was not prompted in any way, 'Well, you'd know she wasn't English!'

Women in other cultures frequently exchange compliments too, of course – this is a standard form of female bonding-talk almost everywhere – and English women, like women everywhere, often conduct much more 'simple' exchanges of compliments of the 'You look lovely', 'Thanks, you look great too' variety. But the counter-compliment ritual is common enough to be of interest to me as a 'pattern', and its one-downmanship is typically English.

Male Bonding: the Mine's Better Than Yours Game

The counter-compliment ritual may be distinctively English, but it is also distinctively female. One cannot imagine men, even English men, engaging in such an exchange. Think about it. 'I wish I could play pool as well as you do. I'm so hopeless at it'; 'Oh, no, I'm useless, really, that was just a lucky shot – and you're brilliant at darts!' If you find that remotely plausible, try: 'You're such a good driver – I'm always stalling and mixing up the gears!'; 'Me? No, I'm a terrible driver, honestly – and, anyway, your car is so much better than mine, faster and more powerful.' Not very likely, is it?

English men have different means of achieving social bonding, which at first glance would appear to involve principles diametrically opposed to those of the counter-compliment ritual. While English women are busy paying each other compliments, English men are usually putting each other down, in a competitive ritual that I call the Mine's Better Than Yours game.

'Mine', in this context, can be anything: a make of car, a football team, a political party, a holiday destination, a type of beer, a philosophical theory – the subject is of little importance. English men can turn almost any conversation, on any topic, into a Mine's Better Than Yours game. I once listened to a forty-eight-minute Mine's Better Than Yours conversation (yes, I timed it) on the merits of wet-shaving versus electric razors. And discussions of more 'highbrow' issues are no different: a lengthy debate on Foucault, conducted in the letters pages of the *Times Literary Supplement*, followed exactly the same pattern – and employed much the same kind of *ad hominem* arguments – as the shaving debate.

The rules of the game are as follows. You start either by making a statement in praise of your chosen 'Mine' (electric razors, Manchester United, Foucault, German cars, whatever) or by challenging someone else's assertion, or implication, or hint, that his 'Mine' is the best. Your statement will always be countered or challenged, even if the other male (or males) secretly agrees with you, or could not rationally disagree. One could hardly even imagine a male-bonding conversation in which a statement such as 'Don't know why you bought that piece of crap, when for the same price you could've had a BMW,' elicited the response 'Yes, I'm sure you're right.' It would be unthinkable, an unprecedented violation of macho etiquette.

Although these exchanges may become quite noisy, and much swearing and name-calling may be involved, the Mine's Better Than Yours game will still seem fairly good-natured and amicable, always with an undercurrent of humour – a mutual understanding that the differences of opinion are not to be taken too seriously. Swearing, sneering and insults are allowed, even expected, but storming off in a huff, or any other exhibition of *real* emotion, is not permitted.

The game is all about mock anger, pretend outrage, jokey one-upmanship. However strongly you may feel about the product, team, theory or shaving method you are defending, you must not allow these feelings to show. Earnestness is not allowed; zeal is unmanly; both are un-English and will invite ridicule. And although the name I have given the game might suggest boastfulness, boasting is not allowed either. The merits of your car, razor, politics or school of literary theory can be glowingly extolled and explained in minute detail, but your own good taste or judgement or intelligence in preferring these must be subtly implied, rather than directly stated. Any hint of self-aggrandisement or ostentation is severely frowned upon, unless it is done 'ironically', in such an exaggerated manner as to be clearly intended as a joke.

It is also universally understood that there is no way of actually winning the game. No one ever capitulates, or recognises the other's point of view. The participants simply get bored or tired and change the subject, perhaps shaking their heads in pity at their opponents' stupidity.

The Mine's Better Than Yours game is an exclusively male pastime. Accompanying females may occasionally spoil the fun by misunderstanding the rules and trying to inject an element of reason. They also tend to become bored with the predictability of the ritual, and may even do something unthinkable, such as asking the participants if they could not simply agree to disagree. These interjections are usually ignored. What some exasperated females fail to grasp is that there can be no rational resolution of such debates; neither is there even any desire to resolve the issue. These are no more genuine debates than the chanting of rival football supporters, and football fans do not expect their ritual chants to persuade their opponents to agree with them. (This is not to say that English female bonding is all 'sweetness and light'. It may be generally less competitive than the male variety, but I have recorded female-bonding sessions – mainly among younger women, but of all social classes – which consisted almost entirely of exchanges of heavily ironic mock-insults, and in which the participants all referred to each other, with great and obvious affection, as 'bitch' or 'slut'.)

The two examples of bonding-talk – counter-compliment and Mine's Better Than Yours – at first appear very different, and may indeed reflect some deep-seated universal differences between males and females. Much research in sociolinguistics has focused on this competitive/co-operative divide, and without subscribing to the more extreme of the 'genderlect' theories, it is clear that male bonding-talk often tends to be competitive, while female bonding-talk typically involves more 'matching' and co-operation.

But these bonding-talk rituals also have certain important features in common, in their underlying rules and values, which may tell us a bit more about Englishness. Both, for example, involve proscription of boasting and prescription of humour. Both also require a degree of polite hypocrisy – or, at least, concealment of one's real opinions or feelings (feigned admiration in the counter-compliment ritual, and fake light-heartedness in Mine's Better Than Yours) – and in both cases, etiquette triumphs over truth and reason.

AND FINALLY . . . THE LONG GOODBYE RULE

We started this grooming-talk chapter with greeting-talk, so it is appropriate to conclude with parting-talk. I wish I could end on a positive note and say that the English are rather better at partings than we are at greetings, but the truth is that our leave-takings tend to be every bit as awkward, embarrassed and incompetent as our introductions. Again, no one has a clear idea of what to do or say, resulting in the same aborted handshakes, clumsy cheek-bumping and half-finished sentences as the greeting process. The only difference is that while introductions tend to be hurried – scrambled through in an effort to get the awkwardness over with as quickly as possible – partings, as if to compensate, are often tediously prolonged.

The initial stage of the parting process is often, deceptively, an unseemly rush, as no one wants to be the last to leave, for fear of 'outstaying their welcome' (a serious breach of the privacy rules). Thus, as soon as one person, couple or family stands up and starts making apologetic noises about traffic, baby-sitters, or the lateness of the hour, everyone else immediately looks at their watch, with exclamations of surprise, jumps to their feet and starts hunting for coats and bags and saying preliminary goodbyes. (Although 'Pleased to meet you' can be problematic as a greeting, it is acceptable to say 'It was nice [lovely, great] to meet you' at this point, if you are parting from people to whom you have recently been introduced – even if you have exchanged no more than a few mumbled greetings.) If you are visiting an English home, be warned that you should allow a good ten minutes – and it could well be fifteen or even twenty – from these initial goodbyes to your final departure.

There is an old Dudley Moore piano-sketch – a spoof on the more flamboyant, self-indulgent, Romantic classical composers – in which he plays a piece that keeps sounding as though it has ended (da, da, DUM), but then continues with a trill leading to another dramatic 'ending' (diddly, diddly, dum, DUM, DA-DUM), followed by yet more 'final'-sounding chords (DA, DA-DUM) then more, and so on. This sketch has always reminded me of a typical group of English people attempting to say goodbye to each other. Just when you think that the last farewell has been accomplished, someone always revives the proceedings with yet another 'Well, see you soon, then . . .', which prompts a further chorus of 'Oh, yes, we must, er, goodbye . . .', 'Goodbye', 'Thanks again', 'Lovely time', 'Oh, nothing, thank you', 'Well, goodbye, then . . .', 'Yes, must be off – traffic, er . . .' 'Don't stand there getting cold, now!', 'No, fine, really . . .', 'Well, goodbye . . .' Then someone will say, 'You must come round to us next . . .' or 'So, I'll email you tomorrow, then . . .' and the final chords will begin again.

Those leaving are desperate to get away, and those hovering in the doorway are dying to shut the door on them, but it would be impolite to give any hint of such feelings, so everyone must make a great show of being reluctant to part. Even when the final, final, final goodbyes have been said, and everyone is loaded into the car, a window is often wound down to allow a few more parting words. As the leavers drive off, hands may be held to ears with thumbs and little fingers extended in a phone-shape, promising further communication. It is then customary for both parties to wave lingering, non-verbal goodbyes to each other until the car is out of sight. When the long-goodbye ordeal is over, we all heave an exhausted sigh of relief.

As often as not, we then immediately start grumbling about the very people from whom, a moment earlier, we could apparently hardly bear to tear ourselves. 'God, I thought they were never going to go!' 'The Joneses are very nice and all that, but she does go on a bit . . .' Even when we have thoroughly enjoyed the gathering, our appreciative comments following the long goodbye will be mixed with moans about how late it is, how tired we are, how much in need of a cup of tea/strong drink – and how nice it is to have the place to ourselves again (or to be going home to our own bed).

And yet if for any reason the long goodbye has been cut short, we feel uncomfortable, dissatisfied – and either guilty, if we have committed the breach of the rule, or somewhat resentful, if the other parties have been a bit hasty in their farewells. We may not be explicitly conscious of the fact that a rule has been broken, but we feel a vague sense of incompleteness; we know that somehow the goodbyes have not been said 'properly'. To prevent such malaise, English children are indoctrinated in the etiquette of the long-goodbye ritual from an early age: 'Say goodbye to Granny, now'; 'And what do we say? We say thank you, Granny!'; 'And say goodbye to Auntie Jane'; 'No, say goodbye NICELY!'; 'And say bye-bye to Pickles'; 'We're leaving now, so say goodbye again'; 'Come on now, wave, wave bye-bye!'[28]

The English often refer to this ritual not as 'saying goodbye' but as 'saying our goodbyes', as in 'I can't come to the station, so we'll say our goodbyes here.' I discussed this with an American visitor, who said, 'You know, the first time I heard that expression, I didn't really register the plural – or I guess I thought it meant you said one each or something. Now I know it means a LOT of goodbyes.'

---

28. Perhaps not surprisingly, some children rebel against this: teenagers in particular may go through a phase of refusing to participate in this ritual and, often, provoking their elders by going to the opposite extreme, where leave-takings consist of shouting, 'See ya,' and slamming the door. There does not seem to be a happy medium.

GROOMING-TALK RULES AND ENGLISHNESS

The weather-speak rules have already given us some clues about the 'grammar' of Englishness, and the grooming-talk rules can now help us to identify a few more of the defining characteristics we are seeking.

The rules of introduction confirm the weather-speaking findings on social inhibitions, and show that without 'facilitators' the English are quite unable to overcome these difficulties. A tendency to awkwardness, embarrassment and general social ineptitude must now be incorporated into our 'grammar' – an important factor, as this tendency must surely have a significant effect on all aspects of English social relations.

The no-name rule highlights an English preoccupation with privacy, and a somewhat suspicious standoffishness. This rule has also given us the first hint of the convoluted, irrational, *Looking-Glass* nature of English etiquette. The 'Pleased to meet you' problem provides our first evidence of the way in which class-consciousness pervades every aspect of English life and culture, but also exposes our reluctance to acknowledge the issue.

The gossip rules bring to light a number of important character-istics, the most striking of which is, again, the English obsession with privacy – also emphasised by the guessing-game rule, the distance rule, and the 'exceptions that prove the rule' of the print and internet media. The sex differences in gossip rules remind us that, in any culture, what is sauce for the goose is not always sauce for the gander. This sounds like a rather obvious point, but it is one that was often ignored by early anthropologists, and is sometimes glossed over by those who comment on Englishness today: both have a tendency to assume that 'male' rules are *the* rules. Anyone who believes, for example, that the English are not very excitable or animated in their everyday speech, has clearly never listened to two English females gossiping. The normal rules of restraint and reserve, in this case, apply only to gossiping males.

The rules of male and female bonding-talk reinforce the goose-and-gander point, but beneath striking (potentially dazzling) surface differences, they turn out to have critical features in common, including prohibition of boasting, prescription of humour and abhorrence of 'earnestness', polite hypocrisy and the triumph of etiquette over reason.

Finally, the long-goodbye rule highlights (again) the importance of embarrassment and ineptitude in English social interactions – our apparently congenital inability to handle simple matters such as greeting and parting with any consistency or elegance – but also provides a remarkable example of the irrational excesses of English politeness.

HUMOUR RULES

This heading can be read both in the straightforward sense of 'rules about humour' and in the (now rather dated) graffiti sense of 'Humour rules, OK!' The latter is in fact more appropriate, as the most noticeable and important 'rule' about humour in English conversation is its dominance and pervasiveness. Humour rules. Humour governs. Humour is omnipresent and omnipotent. I wasn't even going to do a separate chapter on humour because I knew that, like class, it permeates every aspect of English life and culture, and would therefore just naturally crop up in different contexts throughout the book. It did, but the trouble with English humour is that it is so pervasive that to convey its role in our lives I would have to mention it in every other paragraph, which would eventually become tedious – so it got its own chapter after all.

There is an awful lot of guff talked about the English Sense of Humour, including many patriotic attempts to prove that our sense of humour is somehow unique and superior to everyone else's. Many English people seem to believe that we have some sort of global monopoly, if not on humour itself, then at least on certain 'brands' of humour – the high-class ones such as wit and especially irony. My findings indicate that while there may indeed be something distinctive about English humour, the real 'defining characteristic' is the *value* we put on humour, the central importance of humour in English culture and social interactions.

In other cultures, there is 'a time and a place' for humour; it is a special, separate kind of talk. In English conversation, there is always an undercurrent of humour. We can barely manage to say 'hello' or comment on the weather without somehow contriving to make a bit of a joke of it, and most English conversations will involve at least some degree of banter, teasing, irony, understatement, humorous self-deprecation, mockery or just silliness. Humour is our 'default mode', if you like: we do not have to switch it on deliberately, and we cannot switch it off. For the English, the rules of humour are the cultural equivalent of natural laws – we obey them automatically, rather in the way that we obey the law of gravity.

THE IMPORTANCE OF NOT BEING EARNEST RULE

At the most basic level, an underlying rule in all English conversation is the proscription of 'earnestness'. Although we may not have a monopoly on humour, or even on irony, the English are probably more acutely sensitive than any other nation to the distinction between 'serious' and 'solemn', between 'sincerity' and 'earnestness'.

This distinction is crucial to any kind of understanding of Englishness. I cannot emphasise this strongly enough: if you are not able to grasp these subtle but vital differences, you will never understand the English – and even if you speak the language fluently, you will never feel or appear entirely at home in conversation with the English. Your English may be impeccable, but your behavioural 'grammar' will be full of glaring errors.

Once you have become sufficiently sensitised to these distinctions, the Importance of Not Being Earnest rule is really quite simple. Seriousness is acceptable; solemnity is prohibited. Sincerity is allowed; earnestness is strictly forbidden. Pomposity and self-importance are outlawed. Serious matters can be spoken of seriously, but one must never take *oneself* too seriously. The ability to laugh at ourselves, although it may be rooted in a form of arrogance, or at least complacency, is one of the more endearing characteristics of the English. (At least, I hope I am right about this: if I have overestimated our ability to laugh at ourselves, this book will be rather unpopular.[29])

To take a deliberately extreme example, the kind of hand-on-heart, gushing earnestness and pompous, Bible-thumping solemnity favoured

29. Update: the first edition became a big bestseller. I rest my case.

by almost all American politicians[30] would never win a single vote in this country. We watch these speeches on our news programmes with a kind of smugly detached amusement, wondering how the cheering crowds can possibly be so credulous as to fall for this sort of nonsense. When we are not feeling smugly amused, we are cringing with vicarious embarrassment: how can these politicians bring themselves to utter such shamefully earnest platitudes, in such ludicrously solemn tones? We expect politicians to speak largely in platitudes, of course – ours are no different in this respect; it is the earnestness that makes us wince.

The same goes for the gushy, tearful acceptance speeches of American actors at the Oscars and other awards ceremonies, to which English television viewers across the country respond with the same finger-down-throat 'I'm going to be sick' gesture. You will rarely see English Oscar-winners indulging in these heart-on-sleeve displays – their speeches tend to be either short and dignified or self-deprecatingly humorous, and even so they nearly always manage to look uncomfortable and embarrassed. Any English thespian who dares to break these unwritten rules, as Kate Winslet has done, is mercilessly ridiculed and condemned in our newspapers and other media. Winslet's emotional speech at the Golden Globes was described by one British newspaper as enough to 'make a corpse wince with embarrassment', for example, and others were even more scornful.

In fact, most expression of emotion constitutes a breach of the Importance of Not Being Earnest rule. We (SIRC) did a study on the 'emotional state of the nation', in which we found a curious mismatch between English attitudes and actual behaviour in this context. While the majority of us (72 per cent) will *say* that expressing emotion is 'healthy', only a minority – less than 20 per cent – had actually expressed any emotion in the previous 24 hours, and 19 per cent could not even *remember* the last time they had expressed any emotion. (Compare this with our survey on weather-talk, where 56 per cent had talked about the weather within the previous six hours, 38 per cent within the previous hour.) We English have become much

---

30. President Obama is an exception – still often rather too earnest for English tastes, but with flashes of dry wit that have endeared him to us.

better, in recent years, at talking *about* emotions – everyone has now mastered therapy-jargon, and can talk about 'emotional intelligence', the 'inner child' and the need to be 'in touch' with one's feelings. But most of us still don't actually express these feelings very much.

Americans, although among the easiest to scoff at, are by no means the only targets of our cynical censure. The sentimental patriotism of leaders and the portentous earnestness of writers, artists, actors, musicians, pundits and other public figures of all nations are treated with equal derision and disdain by the English, who can spot the slightest hint of self-importance at twenty paces, even on a grainy television picture and in a language we don't understand.

The 7/7 terrorist bombings in London in 2005 – our own mini-9/11, a series of suicide-bomb attacks during the morning rush-hour on the London Underground and on a bus, which killed 56 people and injured 700 – provided some striking illustrations of the Importance of Not Being Earnest rule. On the day of the bombings, some well-meaning Americans started a forum entitled 'London Hurts' on the international LiveJournal website, with a banner declaring 'Today I am A Londoner and Today I Hurt', and tearful sympathetic messages, poems and prayers began to pour in from around the world. But the swift response from actual Londoners was not quite what the effusive sympathisers expected: it consisted almost entirely of spoof and satire. The English poked fun at the sentimental banner with posts such as 'Today I am a Londoner and Today I Got a Day Off' and 'If you're all Londoners today, that's eight quid each for the congestion charge.[31] Come on, pony up!' The syrupy 'uplifting' poems sent in by foreigners prompted spoofs such as:

> Through blitz and bombs we did prevail
> We carried on by road and rail
> We soldiered on and in we mucked
> (Though if it snows, we're truly f**ked).

31. A fee we all have to pay for driving into central London, designed to reduce traffic congestion in the city.

The title 'London Hurts' inspired more gleeful lampooning: 'London Hurts . . . All the news concerns Norf London, but has anybody ever asked how Waterloo's feeling? Or checked to see if the Royal Festival Hall is OK? Some people are so self-centred.' To which another Londoner replied, 'I spoke to the Hayward Gallery earlier today – it is feeling slightly unsettled by events, but otherwise is in good health.' And later on another: 'Southwark Cathedral was a bit shaken, and went down the pub with the Imperial War Museum last night.'[32]

Most of the English responses were purely satirical, but some posters expressed the Importance of Not Being Earnest rule more explicitly: 'Please stop this drivel. We don't want it, it's not needed and it really is an embarrassment to everyone'; 'Calm down Americans . . . get a grip. London is over it – when's the chippy open?'; 'These sickly banners are actually sapping my morale more than any number of exploding buses. Please, for the love of God, stop.'

I can personally vouch for the fact that these responses were not just the reactions of armchair cynics unaffected by the bomb attacks. I was in London on the day of the bombings, on the Underground, waiting to catch the tube to Paddington – one of the many people who narrowly missed being on the wrong train at the wrong time. While quickly texting family and friends in London to make sure that they, too, were alive, I went into fieldwork mode and began observing, eavesdropping and talking with fellow passengers – breaking the English taboo on talking to strangers, but exceptions are allowed in such circumstances. The very first thing I overheard was a joke: 'I didn't realise the French were *such* sore losers!' (The day before the bombings, London had been chosen to host the 2012 Olympic Games, although Paris had been widely expected to win, and the French were clearly surprised and disappointed at the result – although not, as the joke implies, to the point of bombing London out of pique.) I am reliably informed, by friends who were on the

---

32. Admittedly none of these little parodies represents the height of erudite wit: I am quoting them here to illustrate a typically English reaction to earnestness, not as examples of brilliant comic writing.

spot, that similar jokes about the French were circulating even among actual survivors of the bombs as they emerged, filthy and coughing, from the Underground stations where the attacks had taken place. And for some the humour-reflex apparently kicked in even earlier: one of the survivors, who had been trapped in one of the bombed trains, reported that after the explosion, as the train filled with thick smoke, 'Silence descended on the carriage apart from people choking and coughing. Then someone near me quipped, "Well, at least we got the Olympics!"'

If, as someone once said, 'Comedy is tragedy plus time', it would seem that the time required for the English to turn tragedy into humour is about a nanosecond. Specifically, the Importance of Not Being Earnest rule applies before the dust has even settled, as the earnest would-be empathisers on 'London Hurts' were clearly shocked to learn. Monitoring the forum, I couldn't help feeling a bit sorry for them: their emotional outpourings were kindly meant, and would no doubt have been greatly appreciated by any other nation.

Seven years later, the opening ceremony for the London Olympics in 2012 seemed to me another particularly good example of English humour, self-mockery and aversion to earnestness. Although the spectacular parts of the ceremony were suitably grand and impressive, there was very little of the overblown self-important pomposity that normally characterises such ceremonies. Instead, almost every element included at least one ironic little twist, at least one humorous reminder that we don't take ourselves too seriously. A performance of the famously stirring and emotive *Chariots of Fire* music by the London Symphony Orchestra, for example, was subverted throughout by the antics of comedian Rowan Atkinson, acting the part of a bored and distracted musician. We couldn't even be serious about the arrival of our Queen to open the Games: this was done as a spoof of a James Bond film, with Her Majesty sportingly playing herself. If ever there were an excuse for patriotic pomp and grandeur, it must surely be hosting the Olympic Games – and yet we took this opportunity to poke fun at ourselves and our most cherished institutions.

Again, though, I suspect that English self-mockery is rooted in a rather smug complacency, if not outright arrogance. And this was evident in other aspects of the opening ceremony: there were some globally recognised, positive images of England and the English, but the chaotic display also featured dark, even deliberately ugly, unflattering moments, and was full of obscure parochial references and whimsical in-jokes that were incomprehensible to a global audience. Indeed, even the most delighted, admiring commentators from other nations found much of it 'baffling', 'odd', 'bizarre', 'impenetrable', 'weird', 'bewildering', 'insane' and 'What the f***?' Others were less polite. The majority of English people loved it, and didn't much care whether the rest of the world understood it or not. In fact, many were probably secretly pleased that they didn't. The degree of self-mockery, self-denigration, obscure self-reference and self-indulgent eccentricity exhibited in that ceremony required a breathtaking disregard for the opinion of others – in this case billions of others – which can only stem from a deep sense of superiority.

The Closet Patriot Rule

It is often said that the English suffer from a lack of patriotic feeling. And there is some evidence to support this claim: English people, on average, rate their degree of patriotism at just 5.8 out of 10, according to a European survey, far below the self-rated patriotism of the Scots, Welsh and Irish, and the lowest of all the European nations. Our 'national day', St George's Day, is on 23 April, but surveys regularly show that at least two-thirds of us are completely unaware of this. Can you imagine so many Americans not knowing 4 July, or Irish people unaware of St Patrick's Day?

I had a hunch, however, based on my participant-observation research, that our apparent lack of patriotism might have more to do with the ban on earnestness, and perhaps some other closely related aspects of Englishness, than an absence of national pride. So I did my own national survey, asking rather more detailed questions, which confirmed my impression that we are in fact a nation of 'closet patriots'. My survey findings showed that the vast majority (83 per cent) of English people do feel at least *some* sense of patriotic pride:

22 per cent 'always' feel proud to be English, 23 per cent 'often' and 38 per cent at least 'sometimes'. My survey and many others invariably show that the English quality we feel most proud of is our sense of humour.

Three-quarters of us think that more should be done to celebrate our national day, and of these, 63 per cent would like us to 'embrace' St George's Day as the Irish do St Patrick's Day. Nearly half would like to see more people flying the English flag on St George's Day. Only 11 per cent, however, would go so far as to fly the flag themselves, and 72 per cent said they would not be celebrating in any way or had no plans to celebrate, even though St George's Day was on a Saturday that year.

But why? If we are proud to be English, and feel that more should be done to celebrate our national day and national flag, why do we not celebrate or fly the flag ourselves?

If you look closely at the stats, the answers to this question are almost all clear.

First, there is a clue in the English quality of which we are most proud: our sense of humour. And a key element of this is the Importance of Not Being Earnest, the prohibition of excessive zeal. The boastful, sentimental, flag-waving patriotism of other nations is frowned upon and makes us cringe. We may feel proud to be English, but we are mostly too squeamish and too cynical – too conscious of the unwritten ban on earnestness – to make a big, gushy, patriotic fuss about it. Ironically, the English quality in which we take most pride, our sense of humour, prevents most of us from actually displaying this pride.

Second, you may well have noticed that the high percentage of English people who think that more should be done to celebrate St George's Day (75 per cent) is almost exactly the same as the high percentage who have no intention of celebrating our national day themselves (72 per cent). This pattern also strikes me as typically English, and related to two possible 'defining characteristics' already encountered: moderation and Eeyorishness. Our sense of moderation, as well as our horror of earnestness, means that we tend to be rather apathetic: we avoid extremes, excess and intensity. And we have an

Eeyorish tendency to indulge in a lot of therapeutic moaning about a problem rather than actually addressing it. We whinge and complain that 'more should be done' to celebrate our national day, but we don't organise a celebration or even so much as fly a flag.[33]

A few of us do emerge from our patriotic closet for big royal occasions, such as the Queen's Diamond Jubilee in 2012 and the Royal Wedding in 2011. You may have seen many images of flag-waving crowds in London and people holding street parties in their home towns to celebrate these events, but those images are unrepresentative: only a tiny minority of the population (six per cent at most) actually participate in such public celebrations.[34] Even this minority are not necessarily ardent monarchists. Royal events are brief episodes of what anthropologists call 'cultural remission' or 'festive inversion' – like carnivals or tribal festivals, where some of the usual social norms and unwritten rules are temporarily suspended and the English do things we would never normally do: waving national flags, cheering and dancing in the streets, and even talking to strangers. We welcome any opportunity to have a day off work, break the rules and indulge in disinhibited behaviour of this kind, and a royal wedding or jubilee is as good an excuse as any for a bit of 'legitimised deviance'.

Even with this powerful incentive, most of us cannot summon up much enthusiasm for royal events. Surveys showed, for example, that Americans were significantly more excited about the 2011 Royal Wedding than the English, the majority of whom remained underwhelmed, despite all the media hype. At least two-thirds of us either 'couldn't care less' or felt 'largely indifferent' about the wedding,

33. To be fair, our reasons for not flying the English flag are only partly rooted in these qualities. Although it has now been 'reclaimed', at least to some extent, the flag has in the fairly recent past been a symbol of the political far right and racism. (It is now gradually becoming more closely associated just with football fans, but this in itself is off-putting to many, for whom the flag is now tainted with a 'chavvy', lower-class image.) Still, the English flag was only 'available' for appropriation by extremists in the first place because the rest of the population already shunned it.
34. A significantly larger number of English people get excited (and even visibly patriotic) about big sporting events, for reasons that I'll explain later in Rules of Play (page 352).

and only about 10 per cent would admit to being 'very excited'. I say 'would admit' because I know that even with anonymous surveys we have to be aware of the Social Desirability Bias – defined as a standard error on self-report measures due to respondents attempting to present themselves in a socially desirable/acceptable light (otherwise known as 'lying'). But 'socially desirable responding' of this kind can itself be revealing: the fact that so many claimed to be unexcited, even if some simply could not bring themselves to admit to any excitement, tells us that the social norms prohibiting excitement about such things must be quite influential.

Our lack of excitement (normative or otherwise) does not mean that we are ardent anti-monarchists either. We just don't tend to get very ardent or fervent about anything. In fact, the majority of us support the monarchy, in a lukewarm sort of way. When asked, 'Would you favour Britain becoming a republic or remaining a monarchy?' most of us favour monarchy. Over the past twenty years or so, support for the monarchy – in this rather limited sense of not actively wanting to abolish it – has hovered around 75 per cent. About 17.5 per cent, on average, favour a republic, and about nine per cent 'don't know'.

Just one little caveat. When we are not being chronically underwhelmed, tepid or indifferent, we often engage in active criticism and moaning about the monarchy and the royals. But if you are not English, you would be wise to resist the temptation to join in. Remember: the English will happily moan about anything and everything, including things we are actually rather proud and fond of. We whinge endlessly about our weather, for example, but foreigners are not allowed to belittle it – just as one may criticise members of one's family but one is indignant if anyone else dares to do so. The same 'family' principle applies to our 'Auntie Beeb': there is a kind of tradition of grumpy affection and respect for the BBC, even among those who use the term 'BBC' as a metaphor for 'snooty middle class', and grumble about having to pay the annual licence fee. Our attitude towards the monarchy is essentially the same typically English contradictory cluster – much cynicism and moaning, but some grudging affection and pride, and twitchy indignation if outsiders dare to criticise.

In surveys, the BBC consistently gets roughly the same amount of support as the monarchy – around 75 per cent of us 'favour' the monarchy, and around 70 per cent feel largely 'positive' about the BBC. Respondents may be expressing a traditional, almost 'default' sense of affection and respect for the BBC and the monarchy, or revealing a need for the comfort of old, familiar institutions – or perhaps even expressing the patriotic pride that around 80 per cent of them acknowledged in my own survey.

Our humour, moderation and Eeyorishness may limit our public displays of affection for our country and its institutions, but in our jokey, moderate and grumpy way, we do manage to express this affection – if only when ticking boxes on anonymous surveys.

I generally favour participant observation and other qualitative research methods, and treat survey data with a degree of sceptical caution, but the ethnographic purists who disapprove of all quanti-tative methodologies should take note: there are embarrassing, private things that some people will only say in the safety of an anonymous survey. For the English, these things include 'Yes, all *right*, I'll admit that I feel proud to be English.'

The 'Oh, Come Off It!' Rule

I mentioned our derision at the sentimental pomposity of foreign politicians and public figures, but the English ban on earnestness, and specifically on taking oneself too seriously, means that our own poli-ticians and other public figures have a particularly tough time. The sharp-eyed English public is even less tolerant of any breaches of these rules on home ground, and even the smallest lapse – the tiniest sign that a speaker may be overdoing the intensity and crossing the fine line from sincerity to earnestness – will be spotted and picked up on immediately, with scornful, sneering cries of 'Oh, come off it!', or some equivalent remark, accompanied by a contemptuous snort.

And we are just as hard on each other, in ordinary everyday conversation, as we are on those in the public eye. In fact, if a country or culture could be said to have a catchphrase, I would propose 'Oh, come off it!' as a strong candidate for England's (although not as strong as 'Typical!', which I'll come to later). Jeremy Paxman's candidate is 'I know my rights' – well, he doesn't actually use the term 'catchphrase', but he refers to this one frequently, and it is the only such phrase that he includes in his personal list of defining characteristics of Englishness. I take his point, and 'I know my rights' does encapsulate a certain stubborn individualism and a strong sense of justice, but both the phrase and the attitude are equally common in the USA, so I am not sure it can be regarded as distinctively English. I would maintain that the armchair cynicism of 'Oh, come off it!' is more truly representative of the English psyche than the belligerent activism suggested by 'I know my rights'. This may be why, as someone once said, the English have satire instead of revolutions. It is worth noting, though, that this much-quoted line is deceptive. It makes us sound rather too nice – a cheeky but innocuous culture that prefers jokes to violent uprisings, that would rather sit around making up silly spoofs than take to the streets with guns and bombs. If you are familiar with the acid viciousness of English satire, you will know that the phrase means nothing of the sort: for the English, mockery is not a substitute for weapons but a lethal weapon in itself, and far more effective at bringing down unpopular political leaders than any amount of violent protest.

There have certainly been brave individuals who have campaigned and risked their lives for the rights and freedoms we now enjoy, but most ordinary English people now take these for granted, and prefer sniping, pin-pricking, grumbling and mocking from the sidelines to any sort of active involvement in defending or maintaining them. Many cannot even be bothered to vote in national elections, although the pollsters and pundits cannot seem to agree on whether our shamefully low turnout is due to cynicism or apathy – or, the most likely answer, a bit of both. Most of those who do vote do so in much the same highly sceptical spirit, choosing the 'best of a bad lot' or the 'lesser of two evils', rather than with any shining-eyed, fervent conviction that this or that political party is really going to make the world a better place. Such a suggestion would be greeted with the customary 'Oh, come off it!'

Among the young and others susceptible to linguistic fads and fashions, the current response might be the ironic 'Yeah, right', or other expressions of scornful scepticism such as 'Get over yourself', rather than 'Oh, come off it!' – but the principle is the same. Similarly, those who break the Importance of Not Being Earnest rule are described in current slang as being 'up themselves', rather than the more traditional 'full of themselves'. By the time you read this, these may in turn have been superseded by new expressions, but the underlying rules and values are deep-rooted, and will remain unchanged.

IRONY RULES

The English are not usually given to patriotic boasting – indeed, both patriotism and boasting are regarded as unseemly, so the combination of these two sins is doubly distasteful. But there is one significant exception to this rule, and that is the patriotic pride we take in our sense of humour,[35] particularly in our expert use of irony. The popular belief is that we have a better, more subtle, more highly developed sense of humour than any other nation, and specifically that other nations are all tediously literal in their thinking and incapable of understanding or appreciating irony. Almost all of the English people I interviewed subscribed to this belief, and many foreigners, rather surprisingly, humbly concurred.

Although we seem to have persuaded ourselves and a great many others of our superior sense of irony, I remain, as I have already indicated, not entirely convinced. Humour is universal. Irony is a universally important ingredient of humour: no single culture can possibly claim a monopoly on it. My research suggests that, yet again, the irony issue is a question of degree – a matter of quantity rather than quality. What is unique about English humour is the pervasiveness of irony and the importance we attach to it. Irony is the dominant ingredient in English humour, not just a piquant flavouring. Irony rules. The English, according to an acute observer

---

35. In my recent national survey on patriotism, our pride in the English sense of humour was significantly greater than our pride in qualities others might see as rather more admirable, such as our sense of fair play and our reputation for courtesy and tolerance. The English do value and take pride in these other qualities, but humour rules.

of the minutiae of Englishness,[36] are 'conceived in irony. We float in it from the womb. It's the amniotic fluid . . . Joking but not joking. Caring but not caring. Serious but not serious.'

It must be said that many of my foreign informants found this aspect of Englishness frustrating, rather than amusing: 'The problem with the English,' complained one American visitor, 'is that you never know when they are joking – you never know whether they are being serious or not.' This was a businessman, travelling with a female colleague from Holland. She considered the issue frowningly for a moment, then concluded, somewhat tentatively, 'I think they are mostly joking, yes?'

She had a point. And I felt rather sorry for both of them. I found in my interviews with foreign visitors that the English predilection for irony posed more of a problem for those here on business than for tourists and other pleasure-seekers. J. B. Priestley observed that 'The atmosphere in which we English live is favourable to humour. It is so often hazy, and very rarely is everything clear-cut.' And he puts 'a feeling for irony' at the top of his list of ingredients of English humour. Our humour-friendly atmosphere is all very well if you are here on holiday, but when you are negotiating deals worth hundreds of thousands of dollars, like my hapless informants quoted above, this hazy, irony-soaked cultural climate can clearly be something of a hindrance.[37]

For those attempting to acclimatise to this atmosphere, the most important 'rule' to remember is that irony is endemic: like humour in general, irony is a constant, a given, a normal element of ordinary, everyday conversation. The English may not always be joking, but they are always *in a state of readiness* for humour. We do not always say the opposite of what we mean, but we are always alert to the *possibility* of irony. When we ask someone a straightforward question (e.g. 'How are the children?'), we are equally prepared for either a straightforward response ('Fine, thanks') or an ironic one ('Oh,

36. The playwright Alan Bennett – or, to be precise, a character in one of his plays (*The Old Country*).

37. I will examine the role of irony in business culture-clashes in more detail in Work to Rule (page 274).

they're delightful – charming, helpful, tidy, studious . . .' To which the reply is 'Oh dear. Been one of those days, has it?').

The Understatement Rule

I'm putting this as a sub-heading under irony, because understatement is a form of irony, rather than a distinct and separate type of humour. It is also a very English kind of irony – the understatement rule is a close cousin of the Importance of Not Being Earnest rule, the 'Oh, come off it' rule and the various reserve and modesty rules that govern our everyday social interactions. Understatement is by no means an exclusively English form of humour, of course: again, we are talking about quantity rather than quality. George Mikes said that the understatement 'is not just a speciality of the English sense of humour; it is a way of life'. The English are rightly renowned for our use of understatement, not because we invented it or because we do it better than anyone else but because we do it so *much*. (Well, maybe we *do* do it a little bit better – if only because we get more practice at it.)

The reasons for our prolific understating are not hard to discover: our strict prohibitions on earnestness, gushing, emoting and boasting require almost constant use of understatement. Rather than risk exhibiting any hint of forbidden solemnity, unseemly emotion or excessive zeal, we go to the opposite extreme and feign dry, deadpan indifference. The understatement rule means that a debilitating and painful chronic illness must be described as 'a bit of a nuisance'; a truly horrific experience is 'well, not exactly what I would have chosen'; a sight of breathtaking beauty is 'quite pretty'; an outstanding performance or achievement is 'not bad'; an act of abominable cruelty is 'not very friendly', and an unforgivably stupid misjudgement is 'not very clever'; the Antarctic is 'rather chilly' and the Sahara 'a bit too warm for my taste'; and any exceptionally delightful object, person or event, which in other cultures would warrant streams of superlatives, is pretty much covered by 'nice', or, if we wish to express more ardent approval, 'very nice'.

Needless to say, the English understatement is another trait that many foreign visitors find utterly bewildering and infuriating (or, as we English would put it, 'a bit confusing'). 'I don't get it,' said one exasperated informant. 'Is it supposed to be funny? If it's supposed to be funny, why don't they laugh – or at least smile? Or *something*. How the hell are you supposed to know when "not bad" means "absolutely brilliant" and when it just means "OK"? Is there some secret sign or something that they use? Why can't they just say what they mean?'

This is the problem with English humour. Much of it, including and perhaps especially the understatement, isn't actually very funny – or at least not obviously funny, not laugh-out-loud funny, and definitely not cross-culturally funny. Even the English, who understand it, are not exactly riotously amused by the understatement. At best, a well-timed, well-turned understatement only raises a slight smirk. But, then, that is surely the whole point of the understatement: it is amusing, but only in an understated way. It is humour, but it is a restrained, refined, subtle form of humour.

Even those foreigners who appreciate the English understatement, and find it amusing, still experience considerable difficulties when it comes to using it themselves. My father tells me about some desperately Anglophile Italian friends of his, who were determined to be as English as possible – they spoke perfect English, wore English clothes, even developed a taste for English food. But they complained that they couldn't quite 'do' the English understatement, and pressed him for instructions. On one occasion, one of them was describing, heatedly and at some length, a ghastly meal he had had at a local restaurant – the food was inedible, the place was disgustingly filthy, the service rude beyond belief, etc., etc. 'Oh,' said my father, at the end of the tirade. 'So, you wouldn't recommend it, then?'

'YOU SEE?' cried his Italian friend. 'That's it! How do you *do* that? How do you *know* to do that? How do you know *when* to do it?'

'I don't know,' said my father, apologetically. 'I can't explain. We just do it. It just comes naturally.'

This is the other problem with the English understatement: it is a rule, but a rule in the fourth *Oxford English Dictionary* sense of 'the normal or usual state of things' – we are not conscious of obeying it; it is somehow wired into our brains. We are not taught the use of the understatement: we learn it by osmosis. The understatement 'comes naturally' because it is deeply ingrained in our culture, part of the English psyche.

The understatement is also difficult for foreigners to 'get' because it is, in effect, an in-joke about our own unwritten rules of humour. When we describe, say, a horrendous, traumatic and painful experience as 'not very pleasant', we are acknowledging the taboo on earnestness and the rules of irony, but at the same making fun of our ludicrously rigid obedience to these codes. We are exercising restraint, but in such an exaggerated manner that we are also (quietly) laughing at ourselves for doing so. We are parodying ourselves. Every understatement is a little private joke about Englishness.

The Self-deprecation Rule

Like the English understatement, English self-deprecation can be seen as a form of irony. It usually involves not genuine modesty but saying the opposite of what we really mean – or, at least, the opposite of what we intend people to understand.

The issue of English modesty will come up again and again in this book, so I should clear up any misunderstandings about it straight away. When I speak of 'modesty rules', I mean exactly that – not that the English are somehow naturally more modest and self-effacing than other nations but that we have strict rules about the *appearance* of modesty. These include both 'negative' rules, such as prohibitions on boasting and any form of self-importance, and 'positive' rules, actively prescribing self-deprecation and self-mockery. The very abundance of these unwritten rules suggests that the English are *not* naturally or instinctively modest: the best that can be said is that we place a high value on modesty, that we *aspire* to modesty. The modesty that we actually display is generally false – or, to put it more charitably, ironic.

And therein lies the humour. Again, we are not talking about obvious, thigh-slapping funniness: the humour of English self-deprecation, like that of the English understatement, is understated, often to the point of being almost imperceptible – and bordering on incomprehensible to those unfamiliar with English modesty rules.

To show how it works, however, I will take a relatively blatant example. My husband is a brain surgeon. When we first met, I asked what had led him to choose this profession. 'Well, um,' he replied, 'I read PPE [Philosophy, Politics and Economics] at Oxford, but I found it all rather beyond me, so, er, I thought I'd better do something a bit less difficult.' I laughed, but then, as he must have expected, protested that surely brain surgery could not really be described as an easy option. This gave him a further opportunity for self-deprecation. 'Oh, no, it's nowhere near as clever as it's cracked up to be. To be honest, it's actually a bit hit-or-miss.' It later emerged, as he must have known it would, that far from finding the intellectual demands of Oxford 'beyond him', he had entered with a scholarship and graduated with a First. 'I was a dreadful little swot,' he explained.

So was he being truly modest? No, but neither could his humorously self-deprecating responses really be described as deliberate, calculated 'false' modesty. He was simply playing by the rules, dealing with the embarrassment of success and prestige by making a self-denigrating joke of it all, as is our custom. And this is the point: there was nothing extraordinary or remarkable about his apparently humble self-mockery. He was just being English. We all do this, automatically, all the time. Even those of us with much less impressive achievements or credentials to disguise. I'm lucky – many people don't know what an anthropologist is, and those who do generally regard us as the lowest form of scientific life, so there is very little danger of being thought boastful when I am asked about my work. But just in case I might be suspected of being (or claiming to be) something vaguely brainy, I always quickly explain to those unfamiliar with the term that it is 'just a fancy word for nosy-parker', and to academics that what I do is in any case 'only pop-anthropology', and not even the proper, intrepid, mud-hut variety.

Among ourselves, this system works perfectly well: everyone understands that the customary self-deprecation probably means roughly the opposite of what is said, and is duly impressed, both by one's achievements and by one's reluctance to trumpet them. (Even in my case, when it barely counts as self-deprecation, being all too sadly true, people often wrongly assume that what I do must surely be somewhat more impressive than I make it sound.) The problems arise when we English attempt to play this game with people from outside our own culture, who do not understand the rules, fail to appreciate the irony, and therefore have an unfortunate tendency to take our self-deprecating statements at face value. We make our customary modest noises, the uninitiated foreigners accept our apparently low estimate of our achievements, and are duly unimpressed. We cannot very well then say, 'No, hey, wait a minute, you're supposed to give me a sort of knowingly sceptical smile, showing that you realise I'm being humorously self-deprecating, don't believe a word of it and think even more highly of my abilities *and* my modesty.' They don't know that this is the prescribed English response to prescribed English self-deprecation. They don't know that we are playing a convoluted bluffing game. They inadvertently call our bluff, and the whole thing backfires on us. And, frankly, it serves us right for being so silly.

If you think I may be inflating the importance of humorous self-deprecation in English everyday life – or if you are among those who believe that we English exaggerate the differences between English and American culture – try comparing the personal ads in the *New York Review of Books* and its exact English equivalent, the *London Review of Books*. This is a perfect 'natural experiment', as the readers of these two publications are demographically identical: same average age, socioeconomic class, level of education, professional achievements, etc. In the New York version, those seeking love and marriage invariably present themselves as flawless paragons, describing their physical, intellectual, professional, social and moral perfections at great length and with overwhelming earnestness. 'Slender, Sexy Professor and Poet' is a typical headline, plucked at random from my latest copies, along with 'Vital, Slender, Life-Affirming Woman', 'Exceptionally Beautiful', 'Smart and Beautiful', 'Million-Watt Smile, Remarkable' and the even more breathlessly braggy 'Sensual, Witty, Warm, Fit, Smart and Pretty'.

The men are all 'Handsome, Youthful, Intellectual', 'Extremely Handsome, Distinguished', 'Handsome, Gifted', 'Tall, Striking Gentleman' and so on.

The *NYRB* advertisers all boast of their wit and sense of humour – and even their modesty. In the typical ad I'm looking at, a woman describing herself as 'modest' is also, apparently, 'slender, athletic, fun, funny, very easy on the eyes, innovative, charitable, adventurous, curious, an accomplished photographer, former CEO, passionate hiker, laid-back and easy to talk to yet cosmopolitan and sophisticated . . .' She possesses 'casual elegance', a 'ready smile' and 'irreverent wit' – and is, above all, 'never full of herself'. Another woman, who headlines herself as 'Passionate, Smart, Always Interesting', also has a 'slim, sexy figure, blue, blue eyes, lots of depth, sophistication' as befits a 'non-profit executive director, writer, educator, also budding cabaret singer' who is, of course, 'good-looking, curious, athletic' and an 'independent non-traditional thinker' who 'values equality and fairness at all levels'. Most of all, she 'brings intelligence and humor to everything', has a 'definite mischievous and irreverent side' and, believe it or not, a 'touch of irony'.

The 'irreverent' wit, humour and irony professed by the *NYRB* advertisers might be sorely tested by the personal ads in its London counterpart, where their English demographic equivalents attract life-partners with ads describing themselves as 'fat, 47-year-old moody bitch', 'hostile and high-maintenance', 'clingy, over-emotional and socially draining', 'paranoid, jealous and often scary', 'serial divorcee', 'shallow', 'obsessive', 'menopausal', 'bulimic' and 'desperate'. The men typically describe themselves as 'bald, short, fat and ugly', 'run-of-the-mill beardy physicist', 'lonely, desperate and emotionally draining', 'lacklustre, melancholic and depressive', 'sinister-looking man with a face that only a mother would love' and 'man with low sperm count seeks woman in no hurry to see the zygotes divide'.

The London advertisers' impressive career achievements and *recherché* interests include 'care assistant and weekend league bowler', 'post-divorce comfort-eater and sex therapist' and 'my hobbies include crying and hating men'; and the delightful personal qualities they offer potential dates and mates are summed up in phrases such as 'tell me I'm pretty, then watch me cling'.

Incidentally, not one of the *LRB* advertisers ever claims to be modest. Neither do they ever describe themselves as sparkling with irreverent wit, mischievous humour or even a touch of irony.

HUMOUR AND COMEDY

Because the two are often conflated and confused, it is worth pointing out that I am talking here specifically about the rules of English humour, rather than English comedy. That is, I am concerned with our use of humour in everyday life, everyday conversation, rather than with the comic novel, play, film, poem, sketch, cartoon or stand-up routine. These would require another whole book to analyse – and a book written by someone much better qualified than I am.

Having said that, and without pretending to any expert knowledge of the subject, it seems clear to me that English comedy is influenced and informed by the nature of everyday English humour as I have described it here, and by some of the other 'rules of Englishness' identified in other chapters, such as the embarrassment rule (most English comedy is essentially about embarrassment). English comedy, as one might expect, obeys the rules of English humour, and also plays an important social role in transmitting and reinforcing them. Almost all of the best English comedy seems to involve laughing at ourselves.

While I would not claim that English comedy is superior to that of other nations, the fact that we have no concept of a separate 'time and place' for humour, that humour suffuses the English consciousness, does mean that English comic writers, artists and performers have to work quite hard to make us laugh. They have to produce something above and beyond the humour that permeates every aspect of our ordinary social interactions. Just because the English have 'a good sense of humour' does not mean that we are easily amused – quite the opposite: our keen, finely tuned sense of humour, and our irony-saturated culture probably make us harder to amuse than most other nations. Whether or not this results in better comedy is another matter, but my impression is that it certainly seems to result in an awful *lot* of comedy – good, bad or indifferent; if the English are not amused, it is clearly not for want of effort on the part of our prolific humorists.

I say this with genuine sympathy, as the kind of anthropology I do is not far removed from stand-up comedy – at least, the sort of 'observational' stand-up routines that involve a lot of jokes beginning 'Have you ever noticed how people always . . . ?' The best stand-up comics invariably follow this with some pithy, acute, clever observation on the minutiae of human behaviour and social relations. Social scientists like me try hard to do the same, but there is a difference: the stand-up comics have to get it right. If their observation does not 'ring true' or 'strike a chord', they don't get a laugh, and if this happens too often, they don't make a living. Social scientists can talk utter rubbish for years and still pay their mortgages. At its best, however, social science can sometimes be almost as insightful as good stand-up comedy.

HUMOUR AND CLASS

Although elsewhere in this book I scrupulously identify class differences and variations in the application and observance of certain rules, you may have noticed that there has been no mention of class in this chapter. This is because the 'guiding principles' of English humour are classless. The taboo on earnestness, and the rules of irony, understatement and self-deprecation transcend all class barriers. No social rule is ever universally obeyed, but among the English these humour rules are universally (albeit subconsciously) understood and accepted. Whatever the class context, breaches are noticed, frowned upon and ridiculed.

The rules of English humour may be classless, but it must be said that a great deal of everyday English humour is preoccupied with class issues. This is not surprising, given our national obsession with class, and our propensity to make everything a subject for humour. We are always laughing at class-related habits and foibles, mocking the aspirations and embarrassing mistakes of social-climbers, and poking gentle fun at the class system.

HUMOUR RULES AND ENGLISHNESS

What do these rules of humour tell us about Englishness? I said that the value we put on humour, its central role in English culture and conversation, was the main defining characteristic, rather than any specific feature of the humour itself. But we still need to ask whether there is something distinctive about English humour apart from its dominance and pervasiveness, whether we are talking about a matter of quality as well as quantity. I think the answer is a qualified 'yes'.

The Importance of Not Being Earnest rule is not just another way of saying 'humour rules': it is about the fine line between seriousness and solemnity, and it seems to me that our acute sensitivity to this distinction, and our intolerance of earnestness, are distinctively English.

There is also something quintessentially English about the nature of our response to earnestness. The 'Oh, come off it!' rule encapsulates a peculiarly English blend of armchair cynicism, ironic detachment, a squeamish distaste for sentimentality, a stubborn (empiricist?) refusal to be duped or taken in by fine rhetoric, and a mischievous delight in pin-pricking the balloons of pomposity and self-importance.

We also looked at the rules of irony, and its sub-rules of understatement and humorous self-deprecation, and I think we can conclude that, while none of these forms of humour is in itself unique to the English, the sheer extent of their use in English conversation gives a 'flavour' to our humour that is distinctively English. And if practice makes perfect, the English certainly *ought* to have achieved a somewhat greater mastery of irony and its close comic relations than other less compulsively humorous cultures. So, without wanting to blow our own trumpet or come over all patriotic, I think we can safely say that our skills in the arts of irony, understatement and self-mockery are, on the whole, not bad.

LINGUISTIC CLASS CODES

One cannot talk about English conversation codes without talking about class. And one cannot talk at all without immediately revealing one's own social class. This may, to some extent, apply internationally, but the most frequently quoted comments on the issue are English – from Ben Jonson's 'Language most shows a man. Speak that I may see thee' to George Bernard Shaw's rather more explicitly class-related 'It is impossible for an Englishman to open his mouth without making some other Englishman hate him or despise him.' We may like to think that we have become less class-obsessed in recent times, but Shaw's observation is as pertinent now as it ever was. All English people, whether they admit it or not, are fitted with a sort of social Global Positioning Satellite computer that tells us a person's position on the class map as soon as he or she begins to speak.

There are two main factors involved in the calculation of this position: terminology and pronunciation – the words you use and how you say them. Pronunciation is a more reliable indicator (it is relatively easy to learn the terminology of a different class), so I'll start with that.

THE VOWELS VS CONSONANTS RULE

Perhaps the most significant class indicator concerns which type of letter you favour in your pronunciation – or, rather, which type you fail to pronounce. Those at the top of the social scale like to think that their way of speaking is 'correct', as it is clear and intelligible and accurate, while lower-class speech is 'incorrect', a 'lazy' way of talking – unclear, often unintelligible, and just plain wrong. Exhibit A in this argument is the lower-class failure to pronounce consonants, in particular the glottal stop – the omission (swallowing, dropping) of *t* – and the dropping of *h*. But this is a case of the pot calling the kettle (or ke'le, if you prefer) black. The lower ranks may drop their consonants, but the upper class are often equally guilty of dropping their vowels. If you ask them the time, for example, the lower classes may tell you it is "'alf past ten' (which may even come out sounding like 'ah pass ten'), but the upper class will say 'hpstn'. A handkerchief in working-class speech is "'ankercheef', but in upper-class pronunciation becomes 'hnkrchf'.

Upper-class vowel-dropping may be frightfully smart, but it still sounds like a mobile-phone text message, and unless you are used to this clipped, abbreviated way of talking, it is no more intelligible than lower-class consonant-dropping. The only advantage of this SMS-speak is that it can be done without moving the mouth very much, allowing the speaker to maintain an aloof, deadpan expression and a stiff upper lip.

The upper classes at least pronounce their consonants correctly – well, you'd better, if you're going to leave out half of your vowels – whereas the lower classes often pronounce *th* as *f* ('teeth' becomes 'teef', 'thing' becomes 'fing') or sometimes as *v* ('that' becomes 'vat'; 'Worthing' is 'Worving'). A final *g* can become *k*, as in 'somefink' and 'nuffink'.

Pronunciation of vowels is also a helpful class indicator. The upper class only 'drop' some of their vowels: others are drawled, such that, for example, the upper-class *o* becomes *or*, as in 'naff orf', and the *a* in, say, 'plastic', becomes *aah* (plaahstic). The upper class *a* may also become a short *e*, so that 'actually' sounds like 'ectually' (or the even more vowel-economical 'eckshly'). The lower-class *a* is often pronounced as a long *i* – 'Dive' for Dave, 'Tricey' for Tracey. (Working-class northerners tend to elongate the *a*, and might also reveal their class by saying '*Our* Daaave' and '*Our* Traaacey'.) The very upper-class *i* may become a long *a*, such that 'I am' sounds like 'Ay am'.

But the upper class don't say 'I' at all if they can help it: one prefers to refer to oneself as 'one'. In fact, they are not too keen on pronouns in general, omitting them, along with articles and conjunctions, wherever possible – as though they were sending a frightfully expensive telegram. Despite all these peculiarities, the upper classes remain convinced that their way of speaking is the only proper way: their speech is the norm, everyone else's is 'an accent' – and when the upper classes say that someone speaks with 'an accent', what they mean is a working-class accent.

Although upper-class speech as a whole is not necessarily any more intelligible than lower-class speech, it must be said that mispronunciation of certain words is often a lower-class signal, indicating a less-educated speaker. For example: saying 'nucular' instead of 'nuclear', and 'prostrate' for 'prostate', are common mistakes, in both senses of the word 'common'. There is, however, a distinction between upper-class speech and 'educated' speech – they are not necessarily the same thing. What you may hear referred to as 'BBC English' or 'Oxford English' is a kind of 'educated' speech – but it is more upper-middle than upper: it lacks the haw-haw tones, vowel swallowing/drawling and pronoun-phobia of upper-class speech, and is certainly more intelligible to the uninitiated. The younger members of the Royal Family, including Princes William and Harry, and Princess Anne's daughter Zara, have deliberately toned down their speech to something much closer to BBC English, with the result that they now sound more upper-middle than upper class. Even the Queen's speech has gradually morphed into a more 'educated' than gratingly upper-class accent.

Most working-class people, however, and many lower middles, still regard 'BBC English' – and often the BBC itself and all its output – as 'posh'. As one of my (unemployed, working-class) interviewees put it, 'There's this posh girl in the flats where I live [she lived on a very run-down council estate] – single mum, struggling like the rest of us, but she's dead posh. Minute she opens her mouth, you know! Proper BBC accent – nobody round here talks like that!'

Another interviewee (working class, third-generation British Asian) told me, 'I worked in a call centre – shittiest job ever, but there were this couple of posh kids on the training day with me . . .'

'How did you know they were posh?' I asked.

'How do you think?' he replied. 'Only had to listen to them – sounded like the bloody Shipping Forecast!'

Incidentally, these comments illustrate the futility of using either income or occupation as a guide to a person's social class.

While mispronunciations are generally seen as lower-class indicators, and this includes mispronunciation of foreign words and names, attempts at overly *foreign* pronunciation of frequently used foreign expressions and place-names are a different matter. Trying to do a throaty French *r* in *'en route'*, for example, or saying 'Barthelona' with a lispy Spanish *c*, or telling everyone that you are going to Firenze rather than Florence – even if you pronounce them correctly – is affected and pretentious, which almost invariably betrays lower-middle or middle-middle origins. The upper-middle, upper and working classes usually do not feel the need to show off in this way. If you are a fluent speaker of the language in question, you might just, perhaps, be forgiven for lapsing into correct foreign pronunciation of these words – although it would be far more English and modest of you to avoid exhibiting your skill.

We are frequently told that regional accents have become much more acceptable nowadays – even desirable, if you want a career in broadcasting – and that a person with, say, a Yorkshire, Scouse, Geordie or West Country accent is no longer looked down upon as automatically lower class. Yes, well, maybe. I am not convinced. The fact that many presenters of popular television and radio programmes now have regional accents may well indicate that people find these accents attractive, but it does not prove that the class associations have somehow disappeared. We may like a regional accent, and even find it delightful, melodious and charming, while still recognising it as clearly working class. If what is really meant is that being working class has become more acceptable in many formerly snobby occupations, then that is what should be said, rather than a lot of mealy-mouthed polite euphemisms about regional accents.

Speaking of 'regional' accents, it is worth mentioning (particularly in the context of my remarks about the influence of immigrants in the Introduction) that many young working-class people in London and surrounding areas now speak a hybrid dialect known as

Multicultural London English (MLE), which incorporates elements of Caribbean, South Asian and African American speech patterns and vocabulary. Variants of MLE are also emerging in other 'multi-cultural' cities such as Birmingham and Manchester. In MLE, the *h* is no longer dropped, 'like' (a word used extensively) becomes 'lahke', 'that' can become 'dat' and virtually every sentence, interrogative or not, ends in 'innit?' or 'y'get me?'

TERMINOLOGY RULES – U AND NON-U REVISITED

Nancy Mitford coined the phrase 'U and Non-U' – referring to upper-class and non-upper-class words – in an article in *Encounter* in 1955, and although some of her class-indicator words are now outdated, the principle remains. Some of the shibboleths may have changed, but there are still plenty of them, and we still judge your class on whether, for example, you call the midday meal 'lunch' or 'dinner'.

Mitford's simple binary model is not, however, quite subtle enough for my purposes: some shibboleths may simply separate the upper class from the rest, but others more specifically separate the working class from the lower-middle, or the middle-middle from the upper-middle. In a few cases, working-class and upper-class usage is remarkably similar, and differs significantly from the classes in between.

The Seven Deadly Sins

There are, however, seven words that the English uppers and upper-middles regard as infallible shibboleths. Utter any one of these 'seven deadly sins' in the presence of these higher classes, and their on-board class-radar devices will start bleeping and flashing: you will immediately be demoted to middle-middle class, at best, probably lower – and in some cases automatically classified as working class.

Pardon

This word is the most notorious pet hate of the upper and upper-middle classes. Jilly Cooper recalls overhearing her son telling a friend 'Mummy says that "pardon" is a much worse word than "fuck".' He was quite right: to the uppers and upper-middles, using such an unmistakably lower-class term is worse than swearing. Some even refer to lower-middle-class suburbs as 'Pardonia'. Here is a good class-test you can try: when talking to an English person, deliberately say something too quietly for them to hear you properly. A lower-middle or middle-middle person will say, 'Pardon?'; an upper-middle will say 'Sorry?' (or perhaps 'Sorry – what?' or 'What – sorry?'); but an upper-class and a working-class person will both just say, 'What?' The working-class person may drop the *t* – 'Wha'?' – but this will be the only difference. Some upper-working-class people with middle-class aspirations might say 'pardon', in a misguided attempt to sound 'posh'.

Toilet

'Toilet' is another word that makes the higher classes flinch – or exchange knowing looks, if it is uttered by a would-be social-climber. The correct upper-middle/upper term is 'loo' or 'lavatory' (pronounced 'lavuhtry', with the accent on the first syllable). 'Bog' is occasionally acceptable, but only if it is said in an obviously ironic-jocular manner, as though in quotes. The working classes all say 'toilet', as do most lower-middles and middle-middles, the only difference being the working-class omission of the final *t*. (The working classes may also sometimes say 'bog', but without the ironic quotation marks.) Those lower- and middle-middles with pretensions or aspirations, however, may eschew 'toilet' in favour of suburban-genteel euphemisms such as 'Gents', 'Ladies', 'bathroom', 'powder room', 'facilities' and 'convenience', or jokey euphemisms such as 'latrines', 'heads' and 'privy' (females tend to use the former, males the latter).

Anyone who thinks that I'm exaggerating about the higher classes' extreme aversion to the terms 'pardon' and 'toilet' (or indeed about the general English obsession with class) should look back at the scathing press reports on Carole Middleton's use of these two words – described thus in a BBC News Online summary:

Negative stories about the Middleton family appeared in the press. These included allegations that Kate's mother . . . had used the words 'toilet' and 'pardon' in front of the Queen.

It is the BBC's use of the term 'allegations' that particularly amuses me here, as we normally only use this word in relation to the commission of a crime – or a sin.

Serviette

A 'serviette' is what the inhabitants of Pardonia call a napkin. This is another example of a 'genteelism', in this case a misguided attempt to enhance one's status by using a fancy French word rather than a plain old English one. It has been suggested that 'serviette' was taken up by squeamish lower-middles who found 'napkin' a bit too close to 'nappy', and wanted something that sounded a bit more refined. Whatever its origins, 'serviette' is now regarded as irredeemably lower class. Upper-middle and upper-class mothers get very upset when their children learn to say 'serviette' from well-meaning lower-class nannies, and have to be painstakingly retrained to say 'napkin'.

Dinner

There is nothing wrong with the word 'dinner' in itself: it is only a working-class hallmark if you use it to refer to the midday meal, which should be called 'lunch'. I've had fun at a few public lectures with a 'party trick' whereby I ascertain the social class of English audiences simply by asking those who call their midday meal 'dinner' to raise their hands, followed by those who call it 'lunch' (and then assess the degree of social mobility by asking the latter group to raise their hands if their *parents* called this meal 'dinner'). A *very* crude measure, obviously, but everyone immediately grasps the importance of linguistic 'cultural capital' in the English class system. And it never fails to get a laugh.

Calling your evening meal 'tea' is also a working-class indicator: the higher echelons call this meal 'dinner' or 'supper'. Technically, dinner is a somewhat grander meal than supper: if you are invited to 'supper', this is likely to be an informal family meal, often eaten in the kitchen – sometimes this is made explicit, as in 'family supper' or 'kitchen supper', although these are regarded as a bit twee. The uppers and upper-middles use the term 'supper' much more than the middles and lower-middles, rarely describing an evening meal as 'dinner' unless it is a particularly formal occasion – and never, ever using the term 'dinner party'.

The class connotations of 'supper' were the subject of much amusement – and many front-page headlines – in 2012, thanks to a text message revealed at the Leveson Inquiry into media ethics. The messsage was from a national newspaper editor, Rebekah Brooks, to the prime minister, David Cameron, and contained the sentence 'Let's discuss over country supper soon.' Although the message included far more embarrassing indicators of inappropriate collaboration and collusion (such as, 'professionally, we're definitely in this together'), it was the 'posh' term 'country supper' that sparked the most outrage, mockery, bafflement and mock-bafflement. Technically, 'country supper' is a pretty innocuous term, just meaning supper (i.e. an informal evening meal) at one's house in the country (where the prime minister and Rebekah Brooks are neighbours). But the media gleefully pounced on it as prime evidence of the elitism and upper-class chumminess of their relationship. The irony, which escaped almost all of the reporters, is that a truly upper-class person would not have used the term 'country supper' because it would be seen, like 'kitchen supper', as rather precious, simpering and cutesy (which are seen as lower-middle/middle-middle qualities).

'Tea', for the higher classes, is taken at around four o'clock, and consists of tea and cakes or scones (which they pronounce with a short o), and perhaps little sandwiches (pronounced 'sanwidges', not 'sandwitches'). The lower classes, for whom 'tea' means the evening meal, call this 'afternoon tea'. All this can pose a few problems for foreign visitors: if you are invited to 'dinner', should you turn up at midday or in the evening? Does 'come for tea' mean four o'clock or seven o'clock? To be safe, you will have to ask what time you are expected. The answer will help you to place your hosts on the social scale.

Settee

Or you could ask your hosts what they call their furniture. If an upholstered seat for two or more people is called a settee or a couch, they are no higher than middle-middle. If it is a sofa, they are upper-middle or above. There are occasional exceptions to this rule, which is not quite as accurate a class indicator as 'pardon', 'dinner' or 'toilet'. Some younger upper-middles, influenced by American films and television programmes, might say 'couch' – although they are unlikely to say 'settee', except as a joke or to annoy their class-anxious parents. If you like, you can amuse yourself by making predictions based on correlations with other class indicators such as those covered later in Home Rules (page 185). For example, if the item in question is part of a brand-new matching three-piece suite, which also matches the curtains, its owners are likely to call it a settee.

Lounge

And what do they call the room in which the settee/sofa is to be found? Settees are found in 'lounges' or 'living rooms', sofas in 'sitting rooms' or 'drawing rooms'. 'Drawing room' (short for 'withdrawing room') used to be the only 'correct' term, but many upper-middles and uppers feel it is bit silly and pretentious to call, say, a small room in an ordinary terraced house the 'drawing room', so 'sitting room' has become acceptable. You may occasionally hear an upper-middle-class person say 'living room', although this is frowned upon, but only middle-middles and below say 'lounge'. This is a particularly useful word for spotting middle-middle social-climbers trying to pass as upper-middle: they may have learnt not to say 'pardon' and 'toilet', but they are often not aware that 'lounge' is also a deadly sin.

Sweet

Like 'dinner', this word is not in itself a class indicator, but it becomes one when misapplied. The upper-middle and upper classes insist that the sweet course at the end of a meal is called the 'pudding' – never the 'sweet', or 'afters', or 'dessert', all of which are *déclassé*, unacceptable words. 'Sweet' can be used freely as an adjective, but as a noun it is piece of confectionary – what the Americans call 'candy' – and nothing else. The course at the end of the meal is always 'pudding', whatever it consists of: a slice of apple tart is 'pudding', so is a lemon sorbet. Asking 'Does anyone want a sweet?' at the end of a meal will get you immediately classified as middle-middle or below. 'Afters' will also activate the class-radar and get you demoted.

Some American-influenced young upper-middles are starting to say 'dessert', and this is therefore the least offensive of the three – and the least reliable as a class indicator. It can also cause confusion as, to the upper classes, 'dessert' traditionally means a selection of fresh fruit, served right at the end of a dinner, after the pudding, and eaten with a knife and fork.

'Smart' and 'Common' Rules

The 'seven deadly sins' are the most obvious and reliable class indicators, but a number of other terms will also register on our highly sensitive class-radar devices. If you want to 'talk posh', you will have to stop using the term 'posh', for a start: the correct upper-class word is 'smart'. In upper-middle and upper-class circles, 'posh' can only be used ironically, in a jokey tone to show that you know it is a low-class word.

The opposite of 'smart' is 'common' – a snobbish euphemism for 'working class'. But beware: using this term too often is a sure sign of class-anxiety. Calling things and people 'common' all the time is protesting too much, trying too hard to distance yourself from the lower classes. Only the insecure wear their snobbery on their sleeve in this way. 'Naff' is a better option, as it is a more ambiguous term, which can mean the same as 'common' but can also just mean 'tacky' or 'in bad taste'.

If you prefer, you can now use the term 'chav' (which started out as a noun, but can now also be used as an adjective, although 'chavvy' is the more widely used adjectival form). Officially, 'chav' refers only to a particular section of the working class – essentially the British version of what in the US would be called 'white trash', 'trailer trash' or just 'trash' ('bogan' is probably the closest equivalent in Australia and New Zealand). 'Respectable' working-class people are at pains to distinguish themselves from the brash, tacky, work-shy 'chavs'. For many members of the middle and upper classes, however, 'chav' has become yet another euphemism, yet another way of saying 'working class' without using the C-word, yet another way of sneering at working-class tastes without being branded a snob – although many articles and even whole books have been written about how offensive the term is.

'Chav' may eventually become unacceptable, at which point the middle and upper classes will simply find another snobby pejorative euphemism, as they always do. I would recommend reviving 'lumpen-proletariat'. Marx coined it (to describe the late-nineteenth-century equivalent of 'chavs'), which makes it a bit harder for class-warriors to object, and as a bonus its inevitable misuse would infuriate quite a few sociologists. It could be shortened to 'lumps' for catchiness. (Actually, I would recommend that the higher classes stop being such ghastly hypocritical snobs and learn some respect, but that won't happen.)

If they are 'common', young people will call their parents 'Mum' and 'Dad'; 'smart' children say 'Mummy' and 'Daddy' (some used to say 'Ma' and 'Pa', but these are now seen as very old-fashioned). When talking about their parents, common children refer to them as 'my mum' and 'my dad' (or 'me mam' and 'me dad'), while smart children say 'my mother' and 'my father'. These are not infallible indicators, as some higher-class children now say 'Mum' and 'Dad', and some very young working-class children might say 'Mummy' and 'Daddy'; but if the child is over the age of ten, maybe twelve to be safe, still calling his or her mother 'Mummy' is a fairly reliable higher-class indicator. Grown-ups who still say 'Mummy' and 'Daddy' are almost certainly upper-middle or above.

Prince Charles provided an example of this at the age of sixty-four, by addressing the Queen as 'Mummy' in his speech at her Diamond Jubilee celebrations. His use of this informal term was obviously intended to be humorous, but 'Mum' would have been equally informal and equally amusing.

Mothers who are called 'Mum' carry a 'handbag'; mothers called 'Mummy' just call it a 'bag'. Mums wear 'perfume'; mummies call it 'scent'. Parents called 'Mum' and 'Dad' go 'horseracing'; smart mummies and daddies call it 'racing'. Common people go to a 'do'; middle-middles might call it a 'function'; smart people just call it a party. 'Refreshments' are served at middle-class 'functions'; the higher echelons' parties just have food and drink. Lower- and middle-middles eat their food in 'portions'; upper-middles and above have 'helpings'. Common people have a 'starter'; smart people have a 'first course'

– although this one is rather less reliable. Referring to the main course (in, say, a three-course meal) as the 'main meal' is decidedly common.

Lower- and middle-middles talk about their 'home' or 'property'; upper-middles and above say 'house'. Common people's homes have 'patios'; smart people's houses have 'terraces'. Working-class people say 'indoors' when they mean 'at home' (as in 'Oh no, I've left it indoors' when they find they have forgotten something, and ''er indoors' meaning 'my wife'). This is by no means an exhaustive list: class pervades every aspect of English life, and you will find yet more verbal class indicators in almost every chapter of this book – as well as dozens of non-verbal class signals.

Class-denial Rules

We are clearly as acutely class-conscious as we have ever been, but in these 'politically correct' times, many of us are increasingly embarrassed about our class-consciousness, and do our best to deny or disguise it. The middle classes are particularly uncomfortable about class, and well-meaning upper-middles are the most squeamish of all. They will go to great lengths to avoid calling anyone or anything 'working class' – resorting to polite euphemisms such as 'low-income groups', 'less privileged', 'ordinary people', 'less educated', 'the man in the street', 'tabloid readers', 'blue collar', 'state school', 'council estate' and 'popular'.

These over-tactful upper-middles may even try to avoid using the word 'class' at all, carefully talking about someone's 'background' instead – which always makes me imagine the person emerging from either a Lowry street scene or a Gainsborough or Reynolds country-manor portrait, depending on the class to which 'background' is intended to refer. (This is always obvious from the context: 'Well, with that sort of *background*, you have to make allowances . . .' is Lowry; 'We prefer Saskia and Fiona to mix with girls from the same *background* . . .' is Gainsborough/Reynolds.)

All this diplomatic euphemising is quite unnecessary, though, as working-class English people generally do not have a problem with the C-word and, until very recently, were nearly all quite happy to call themselves working class. Upper-class English people are also often rather blunt and no-nonsense about class. It is not that these top and bottom classes are any less class-conscious than the middle ranks: they just tend to be less angst-ridden and embarrassed about it. Their class-consciousness is also, in many cases, rather less subtle and complex than that of the middle classes: they tend not to perceive as many layers or delicate distinctions. Their class-radar recognises at the most three classes: working, middle and upper; and sometimes only two, with the working class dividing the world into 'us and the posh' – with little or no distinction between levels of 'poshness', apart from actual aristocracy/royalty – and the upper class seeing only 'us and the plebs' (or 'ordinary people', if they are being polite).

Nancy Mitford is a good example, with her simple binary division of society into 'U and non-U', which takes no account of the fine gradations between lower-middle, middle-middle and upper-middle, let alone the even more microscopic nuances distinguishing, say, 'secure, established upper-middle' from 'anxious, borderline upper-middle' that are only of interest to the tortured middle classes – and to nosy anthropologists.

Having said that, it is worth noting that both the upper and working class do perceive finer distinctions and layers *within* their own classes – distinctions that may be unnoticed by the rest of the population. Only the upper classes notice or care about the distinctions between 'old family', 'landed gentry' and peerage, for example, or the arcane ranks (dukes, marquesses, earls and so on) within the peerage. And the working classes are far more sensitive to – and about – the important distinction between 'respectable working class' and the despised 'chavs' or 'pikeys'[38], and the factors distinguishing vulgar 'new money' from admirable 'working class made good' (the main difference being that the latter 'remember where they've come from' and don't become 'stuck up' or 'think they're better than us'). The English working class contains at least as many complex divisions and distinctions as the upper and middle classes.

The tendency of the middle and upper classes to ignore these

38. The term 'pikey' is technically only a pejorative word for gypsies or 'travellers', but some now use it more or less synonymously with 'chav'.

distinctions and lump all these working-class grades together and, even more shamefully, to tar them all with the same 'chav' brush is one of the causes of the recent 'identity shift' whereby more and more working-class people are defining themselves as middle class (in surveys, about half of those who used to call themselves 'working class' no longer do so – a very significant shift). 'Working class' has become a more pejorative term, associated with, ironically, people who do not work, so-called 'benefit scroungers', 'chavs', etc. There has always been a huge perceived gulf between the 'respectable', hard-working working class and the unemployed 'underclass' (well, perceived by the respectable working classes, at least). These are not entirely unlike the old sixteenth-century categories of 'deserving' and 'undeserving' poor. But now the demonisation of 'chavs', and the blurring of these categories, is adversely affecting the whole working class.

Other causes of the working-class 'identity shift' are the 'aspirational' ideologies promoted by Margaret Thatcher's Conservative government, and then by Tony Blair's New Labour, which have for many people eroded any sense of pride in being working class. The focus of governments for many years has been on promoting social mobility (which has remained stubbornly static at best), rather than improving conditions and life for the working class. Given the relentless message that being working class is a condition one should aim to escape from, it is hardly surprising that many working-class people now choose to call themselves 'middle class', a term that, for some, has been radically redefined. In response to my chatter about some research I was doing on class, for example, a working-class hairdresser told me, 'I'd like to say I'm middle class.'

'What does that mean to you,' I asked, 'that you're middle class, rather than working class?'

She answered: 'That I've got some class, I suppose – like, I dress nicely, I've got some ambition in life . . . I'm not just some lazy chav!'

With the decline of the manufacturing industry, many of the lowest-paid working-class jobs are now in service industries (call centres are the new coal mines) and can be seen as 'white collar', or 'pink collar', rather than traditional blue-collar manual labour. Those working in these occupations, however menial, undignified and poorly paid their jobs may be, can more easily define themselves as middle class – especially when they are being fobbed off with the illusion that they are middle class, as opposed to being paid a decent wage.

It is worth noting that, until very recently, things were the other way round: many people in what are classified as 'middle-class' occupations would identify themselves (correctly, and often proudly) as 'working class' when asked to state their social class in surveys. This discrepancy always caused much confusion and puzzled debate among those who believe that occupation is a reliable guide to social class – they would scratch their heads and wonder why all these ABC1s were insisting on calling themselves working class. Now they are wondering why all these C2DEs are calling themselves middle class.

LINGUISTIC CLASS CODES AND ENGLISHNESS

So, what do these linguistic class codes tell us about Englishness? All cultures have a social hierarchy and methods of signalling social status: what, apart from our perhaps disproportionate class-consciousness, is distinctive about the English class system and its signals?

For a start, the linguistic codes we have identified indicate that class in England has nothing to do with income or occupation. 'Cultural capital' is a more helpful concept, but the only form of cultural capital that functions as a near-infallible class indicator in real life (as opposed to surveys) is 'linguistic capital'. Speech is all-important. A person with an upper-class accent, using upper-class terminology, will be recognised as upper class even if he or she is earning poverty-line wages, doing grubby menial work and living on a grotty council estate. Or even unemployed, destitute and homeless. Equally, a person with working-class pronunciation, who calls his sofa a 'settee', and his midday meal 'dinner', will be identified as working class even if he is a multi-millionaire business tycoon living in a grand country house. There are other class indicators – such as one's taste in clothes, furniture, decoration, cars, pets, books, hobbies, food and drink – but speech is the most immediate and most obvious.

The importance of speech in this context may point to another English characteristic: our love of words. It has often been said that the English are very much a verbal rather than a visual culture, considerably more noted for our literature than for our art. We are also not particularly 'tactile' or physically expressive, not given to much touching or gesticulating. Words are our preferred medium, so it is perhaps significant that they should be our primary means of signalling and recognising social status.

This reliance on linguistic signals, and the irrelevance of wealth and occupation as class indicators, also reminds us that our culture is not a meritocracy. Your accent and terminology reveal the class you were born into and raised in, not anything you have achieved through your own talents or efforts. And whatever you do accomplish, your position on the class scale will always be identifiable by your speech, unless you painstakingly train yourself to use the pronunciation and vocabulary of a different class.

The sheer complexity of the linguistic rules reveals something of the intricate, convoluted nature of the English class system – all those layers, all those fine distinctions; the snakes-and-ladders game of social climbing. And the class-denial rules give us a hint of a peculiarly English squeamishness about class. This unease may be more pronounced among the middle classes, but most of us suffer from it to some degree – we would rather pretend that class differences do not exist, or are no longer important, or at least that we personally have no class-related prejudices.

Which brings me to another English characteristic: hypocrisy. Not that our pious denial of our class-obsession is specifically intended to mislead – it often seems to be more a matter of self-deception than any deliberate deception of others; a kind of collective self-deception, perhaps? I have a hunch that this distinctively English brand of hypocrisy will come up again, and might even turn out to be one of the 'defining characteristics' we are looking for.

EMERGING TALK-RULES: THE MOBILE PHONE

Almost everyone in England has a mobile phone, but because this is still relatively new, unfamiliar technology, there are no set rules of etiquette governing when, how and in what manner these phones should be used. We are having to 'make up' and negotiate these rules as we go along – a fascinating process to watch and, for a social scientist, very exciting, as one does not often get the opportunity to study the *formation* of a new set of unwritten social rules.

For example, I have found that most English people, if asked, agree that talking loudly about banal business or domestic matters on one's mobile while on a train is rude and inconsiderate. Yet a significant minority of people still do this, and while their fellow passengers may sigh and roll their eyes, they very rarely challenge the offenders directly – as this would involve breaking other well-established English rules and inhibitions about talking to strangers, making a scene or drawing attention to oneself. The offenders, despite much public discussion of this problem, seem oblivious to the effects of their behaviour, in the same way that people tend to pick their noses and scratch their armpits in their cars, apparently forgetting that they are not invisible.

How will this apparent impasse be resolved? There are some early signs of emerging rules regarding mobile-phone use in public places, and it looks as though very loud 'I'm on a train' conversations may eventually become as unacceptable as queue-jumping, but we cannot yet be certain, particularly given English inhibitions about confronting offenders. (I discuss the issue of loud mobile-phone talk on trains and buses in much more detail in Rules of the Road, page 225.) Inappropriate mobile-phone use on trains and in other public places is at least a social issue of which everyone is now aware. But there are other aspects of 'emerging' mobile-phone etiquette that are even more blurred and controversial.

There are, for example, as yet no agreed rules of etiquette on the use of mobile phones during business meetings. Do you switch your phone off, discreetly, before entering the meeting? Or do you take your phone out and make a big ostentatious *show* of switching it off, as a flattering gesture conveying the message 'See how important you are: I am switching off my phone for you'? Then do you place your switched-off phone on the table as a reminder of your courtesy and your client's or colleague's status? If you keep it switched on, do you do so overtly or leave it in your pocket or briefcase? Do you take calls during the meeting? My observations indicate that lower-ranking English executives tend to be less courteous, attempting to trumpet their own importance by keeping phones on and taking calls during meetings, while high-ranking people with nothing to prove tend to be more considerate.

Then what about lunch? Is it acceptable to switch your phone back on during the business lunch? Do you need to give a reason? Apologise? Again, my observations and interviews suggest a similar pattern. Low-status, insecure people tend to take and even sometimes make calls during a business lunch – often apologising and giving reasons, but in such a self-important 'I'm so busy and indispensable' manner that their apology is really a disguised boast. Their higher-ranking, more secure colleagues either leave their phones switched off or, if they absolutely must keep them on for some reason, apologise in a genuine and often embarrassed, self-deprecating manner.

There are many other, much more subtle social uses of mobile phones, some of which do not even involve talking on the phone at all – such as the competitive use of the mobile phone itself as a status-signal, particularly among young people, but also in some cases replacing the car as a medium for macho 'Mine's Better Than Yours' displays among older males as well, with discussions of the relative merits of different brands, networks, 'apps' and features taking the place of more traditional conversations about alloy wheels, nought-to-sixty, BHP, etc.

I have also noticed that many women use their mobiles as 'barrier signals' when on their own in coffee bars and other public places, as an alternative to the traditional use of a newspaper or magazine to signal unavailability – particularly to any potentially predatory males – and mark personal 'territory'. Even when not in use, the mobile acts as a kind of symbolic bodyguard, a protector against unwanted social contact: women will touch the phone or pick it up when a potential 'intruder' approaches. One woman explained, 'You just feel safer if it's there – just on the table, next to your hand . . . Actually it's better than a newspaper because it's real people – I mean, there are real people in there you could call or text if you wanted, you know? It's sort of reassuring.' The idea of one's social support network of friends and family being somehow 'inside' the mobile phone means that even just touching or holding it gives a sense of being protected.

This example provides an indication of the more important social functions of the mobile phone. I've written and lectured about this issue at great length elsewhere,[39] but it is worth explaining briefly here. The mobile phone has, I believe, become the modern equivalent of the garden fence or village green. The space-age technology of mobile phones has allowed us to recreate the more natural and humane communication patterns of pre-industrial society, when we lived in small, stable communities, and enjoyed frequent 'grooming-talk' with a tightly integrated social network of family and friends. In the fast-paced modern world, we had become severely restricted in both the quantity and quality of communication with our social network. Most of us no longer enjoy the cosiness of a gossip over the garden fence. We may not even know our neighbours' names, and communication is often limited to a brief, slightly embarrassed nod, if that. Families and friends are scattered, and even if our relatives or friends live nearby, we are often too busy or too tired to visit. We are constantly on the move, spending much of our time commuting

---

39. See K. Fox (2001), 'Evolution, Alienation and Gossip: the role of mobile telecommunications in the 21st century', www.sirc.org. (It's a lot less pompous than the title makes it sound, but also now *very* out of date. There will be much more about this in my next book.)

to and from work either among strangers on trains and buses, or alone and isolated in our cars. These factors are particularly problematic for the English, as we tend to be more socially inhibited than other cultures: we do not talk to strangers, or make friends quickly and easily.

Landline telephones allowed us to communicate, but not in the sort of frequent, easy, spontaneous, casual style that would have characterised the small communities for which we are adapted by evolution, and in which most of us lived in pre-industrial times. Mobile phones – particularly the ability to send short, frequent, cheap text messages – restore our sense of connection and community, and provide an antidote to the pressures and alienation of modern urban life. They are a kind of 'social lifeline' in a fragmented and isolating world.

Think about a typical, brief 'village-green' conversation: 'Hi, how're you doing?'/'Fine, just off to the shops – oh, how's your mum?'/'Much better, thanks.'/'Oh, good, give her my love – see you later.' If you take most of the vowels out of the village-green conversation, and scramble the rest of the letters into 'text-message dialect' (HOW R U? C U L8R), to me it sounds uncannily like a typical SMS or text exchange: not much is said – a friendly greeting, maybe a scrap of news – but a personal connection is made, people are reminded that they are not alone. Until the advent of mobile text messaging, many of us were forced to live without this kind of small but psychologically and socially very important form of communication.

But as a new medium for communication, texting requires a new set of unspoken rules, and the negotiations over the formation of these rules are currently causing a certain amount of tension and conflict – particularly the issue of whether mobile text is an appropriate medium for certain types of conversation. Flirting by text is accepted, even encouraged, but some women complain that men use texting as a way of avoiding talking. 'Dumping' someone by text message is widely regarded as cowardly and absolutely unacceptable, but this rule has not yet become firmly established enough to prevent some people from ending relationships in this manner.

I have been studying all these 'emerging' rules for well over a decade, but it seems that the negotiations on mobile-phone etiquette are still in progress, and although there have been some developments and advances, they have yet to result in unequivocal agreement on any well-defined rules.

Yes, *Debrett's* famous etiquette guides now include sections on mobile-phone etiquette, text messaging and related subjects – and, yes, some of their advice reflects what the majority of English people would consider to be 'good manners' in the use of this technology. If asked, most would agree, for example, that you should 'Ensure that your mobile phone conversation is not disturbing other people . . . don't shout' and that 'Intimate conversations are never appropriate in front of others.' In fact, the majority of English people were obeying these rules well before *Debrett's* rather belatedly acknowledged the existence of mobile phones, and are still obeying them now. But a minority persist in defying them, and get away with it because the rest of us tend to be too squeamishly English to make a scene or draw attention to ourselves by confronting them.

Even among the relatively courteous majority, some might have difficulty in obeying other *Debrett's* diktats, such as their assertion that 'People in the flesh deserve more attention than a gadget, so wherever possible turn off your phone in social situations.' Many would agree to this in principle, but in practice, the choice in social situations is not between 'people' and 'a gadget' – it is between the people you happen to be with and your friends, family or colleagues who keep in touch with you by phone. For the younger generation, there are few social situations in which it would be unacceptable to leave your mobile phone switched on, or even to take or make calls. Even among older people, a casual social gathering, say, in a pub, would not require the turning off of mobiles.

The *Debrett's* 'rules' are far too simplistic and rigid. The emerging unwritten rules of mobile-phone etiquette are much more complex and nuanced – a matter of degrees and types and timing of mobile-phone use, with variations for different social contexts, rather than blanket 'on or off' prescriptions.

The Three-degrees Rule

There are three basic degrees of mobile-phone 'use' in social situations, graded from the most passive to the most active:

- switched on
- taking calls/reading messages (texts, emails, PMs[40], etc.)
- making calls/typing messages (texts, emails, PMs, etc.)

In general terms, merely being passively 'switched on' is the least potentially offensive, more actively accepting calls or reading messages is more likely to cause offence, and actively making calls or typing messages is the most discourteous.

Some may consider that reading messages is a slightly lesser offence than taking calls, and that sending typed messages is less discourteous than making calls. Reading and typing messages are, indeed, less obviously disruptive than actual phone conversations, as they can be done in silence, but they still generally involve ignoring the people one is with – they are the electronic equivalents of reading or writing postcards in a social situation – so I'm putting them in the same broad categories as taking or making calls.

Some also argue that having your phone switched on but set to 'vibrate' rather than ring is, in courtesy terms, as good as having it switched off. But while a vibrating phone is certainly preferable to a ringing one in many situations, 'vibrate' is only the true social equivalent of 'switched off' if you *completely* ignore the phone when it vibrates – in which case it might as well be switched off.

Other types of 'silent' mobile-phone use – such as surfing the internet, updating your blog or Facebook status, tweeting or playing games – can actually be considerably *more* discourteous than the apparently more disruptive 'vocal' uses, such as taking calls. This is because when you are surfing, Googling, blogging, tweeting or gaming you really *are* giving a gadget – an inanimate object – priority over your human companions. Yes, you are 'talking' to other humans when you blog, tweet or update your Facebook status, but randomly

40. Private Messages or Personal Messages on internet social media sites.

addressing hundreds or even thousands of people in this manner, in the hope that some of them might be interested, is not a conversation – and certainly not a vital one that can't wait. It is bad enough to be neglected, even temporarily, while someone takes a call from a friend, colleague or family member – but to be neglected because they find Googling, tweeting or playing Angry Birds more interesting than your company is insulting. The rule of thumb is that if it would be rude to read a newspaper or magazine, write diaries or letters, or take out a deck of cards and play Patience[41] in a given social situation, then it is equally impolite to do the equivalent on your mobile. (This may all sound rather obvious, but even government ministers have had to be told off for tweeting during cabinet meetings.)

The only exception to this rule is when the internet is used to look something up as part of the conversation – using Google in the way that one might reach for a dictionary, encyclopaedia or other reference book in mid-conversation, for help in answering a question or resolving a debate. Even this legitimate reference-tool use, however, can become highly irritating if taken to excess, or employed when such help is not really needed. Gratuitous Googlers are regarded as rather childish – unable to sit still and listen to others without constant fiddling and fidgeting – or, even worse, as attention-seekers, trying to impress their companions with irrelevant factoids from Wikipedia.

Many breaches of mobile-phone etiquette can be softened by a pre-emptive apology. Taking a call will certainly cause less offence if you say, 'I'm so sorry, but I really have to take this,' and ideally leave the room or at least move away so that your conversation does not disturb your companions, apologising again upon your return. These must be genuine apologies, not disguised boasts about how important you are. The English are acutely sensitive to even the most subtle forms of bragging, and an apology that breaks our modesty rules will compound your offence rather than mitigating it.

In most situations, a (genuine) pre-emptive apology will also reduce the offence caused by ignoring your companions while you read or

41. The card-game known as Solitaire in the US.

reply to an incoming text message or email. There are, however, very few conceivable situations in which one simply 'must' update one's Facebook status, or tweet, or indulge in gratuitous Googling, so pre-emptive apologies for doing this will not minimise the offence.

The Formality Rule

As a general rule, the more formal the social gathering, the lower the degree of acceptable mobile-phone use. At very formal occasions, the phone should be switched off altogether. At, say, a less formal dinner with friends, it may be acceptable to leave it on 'for emergencies' (such as calls from one's children or babysitter). At very casual get-togethers, such as sharing a few drinks in the pub, or impromptu encounters, even the higher degrees of phone use may be acceptable.

The Numbers Rule

The smaller the number of people at a social gathering, however informal it may be, the more one should focus on them and avoid using one's phone. When just two friends get together, it would be rude and unfair for one to ignore the other and chat on a mobile with other people. With three people, it becomes *marginally* more acceptable for one person to have a *very brief* phone conversation or text exchange, providing the other two are happily chatting to each other and not feeling snubbed – although, in accordance with the three-degrees rule, taking a call/reading a message would be more acceptable than actively making a call/texting. With four people, one might feel free to have a *slightly* longer phone conversation/text exchange, again assuming that the other three were clearly happily engaged with each other. And so on. At a large, informal social gathering, even actively making calls is generally acceptable.

The Teenage Exception

There are exceptions to the above rules among teenagers, which may also be seen among some 'kidults' in their twenties and even thirties. I'm using the term 'teenage' here as an indicator of maturity, rather than necessarily just of chronological age.

Teenagers (and older kidults), who have grown up using mobile phones, tend to be highly skilled at a kind of 'split-screen' attention focus, which allows them, for example, to send text messages while simultaneously carrying on a conversation with the people around them. The texts may be of a poor literary standard, and the conversations may be somewhat disjointed and incoherent – but this is often the case even when the two activities are not performed in parallel.

Also, most teenagers are quite simply much less 'bothered' than adults about the niceties of mobile-phone etiquette. They may recognise, and even be irritated by, the more blatant offences described above – but they are generally more tolerant of such rule-breaking. If two teenage girls are out having coffee together, for example, and one is chatting away to someone else on her mobile, her companion may feel somewhat aggrieved, but rather than launching into the normal English repertoire of disapproving frowns, sighs, coughs, tuts and eye-rolls, she will probably just take out her own mobile and start sending texts or making calls herself. Getting all huffy about the offence would be 'uncool' and she would be told to 'chill' or 'get a life'.

Among teenagers and kidults, it is now the norm for any face-to-face social interaction to be constantly intermingled with electronic social interaction – and the face-to-face variety is not given much, if any, priority over the electronic. A mobile phone ringing in the middle of a face-to-face social gathering is not seen as an interruption, but as another person joining in the conversation. Indeed, a phone may often be passed around to allow the absent party to exchange greetings or brief chat with other members of the group.

Reactions to Rule-breaking: Body-language and Timed Frostiness Rules

Older people are generally much less tolerant of mobile misdemeanours, but even the most discourteous and socially unacceptable mobile-phone use is very rarely penalised in any direct or obvious way. The English have a remarkable capacity for accepting the unacceptable – or, at least, *appearing* to accept it, and certainly not making a big noisy fuss about it.

Unless you are close friends with your companions, the worst reaction you can expect for unacceptable use of your mobile is some disapproving body language. As you chat on your mobile, you may see raised eyebrows, frowns, eye-rolls, pursed lips and tapping feet or fingers, and hear sighs, tutting, pointed coughs, snorts and sniffs – and all the other barely noticeable signs of English outrage and indignation. (Our much-prized international reputation for 'tolerance' may well be partly thanks to this: we express any intolerance we may feel in such an understated manner that foreigners simply fail to notice it.)

When you eventually finish your ill-timed phone-chat, there will be more severe punishment, in the form of a certain frostiness in your companions' manner towards you. You have snubbed and ignored them while chatting on your mobile, so they will redress the balance and make things 'fair' by snubbing and ignoring you, often for an approximately equal amount of time. This remarkably accurate timing is not done consciously, but the English subconscious mind is quite precise in its calculation of fairness. And, yes, in accordance with the 'test a social rule by breaking it' principle, I deliberately committed breaches of mobile-phone etiquette, and timed both my offending phone calls and the duration of the resulting frostiness.

If you are not English, a few frowns and sighs and a bit of frostiness may not seem very worrying. But these are indications that you have caused quite considerable offence, and should be taken seriously – assuming that you wish to fit in and get on with the English (and if you don't, why on earth are you reading this book?). The only remedy is to apologise, immediately and profusely. A simple 'sorry' will not suffice. The English say 'sorry' all the time,[42] over anything or nothing, so a single 'sorry' does not count as an apology.

---

42. To be precise, the national average is at least eight 'sorries' a day, although some of us regularly say 'sorry' more than twenty times a day – see page 236 for more detail.

Mobile Phone Rules and Englishness

Of course, many of the emerging unwritten rules and exceptions I have described here are not peculiarly English. I'm sure that the three-degrees rule, the numbers rule and the formality rule – and the teenage exception – apply at least to some extent in most countries in which mobile phones are now widely used. It is our *reaction* to breaches of these rules that is distinctive: our squeamishness about confronting offenders, and the way we express our outrage in barely visible nano-gestures, tiny facial twitches and minimalist coughs, sniffs and sighs. There is a non-verbal dialect of disapproval that almost deserves to be called 'body English', rather than the generic 'body language'. More evidence of the social inhibitions and hand-icaps already flagged in previous chapters, which seem to be edging towards 'defining characteristic' status.

The exquisite timing of our 'frostiness' is also a quintessentially English response – our own very tame and moderate version of the Law of Talion: not so much 'an eye for an eye' as 'a five-minute snub for a five-minute snub'. Signs of social inhibition again, clearly – almost verging on passive-aggression here – combined with an acute sense of fairness.

These reactions to rule-breaking may be distinctively English, but the rules of mobile-phone etiquette are still being negotiated, and it is difficult to predict the future course of the negotiations. It would be a mistake, for example, simply to assume that what is customary and acceptable among English teenagers today will necessarily become the universal norm here in the future. Adolescents do grow up, and their social behaviour as mature adults differs in many ways from their teenage habits. I observed earlier in this chapter that in business and professional contexts, higher-ranking people – people with nothing to prove about their status – tend to be more consid-erate and courteous in their mobile-phone use. This applies in purely social contexts as well: those who feel more socially secure and confident are less likely to display their popularity and draw atten-tion to their busy social life by constantly taking and making calls. Teenagers and kidults tend to be highly socially insecure; as they mature, their need for such 'conspicuous consumption' of social connections should diminish.

Having said that, my hunch is that a toned-down version of the current teenage practice of amalgamating face-to-face and electronic social interaction, with the face-to-face participants given only marginally higher priority, will increasingly become more normal and acceptable, at least at larger and more casual social gatherings.

At the same time, as electronic communication becomes more and more commonplace, a mobile phone constantly pinging and bleeping with calls and messages is already becoming a far less effective indicator of one's 'social capital' – and those who continue to flaunt their social wealth in this manner are regarded as rather tiresome. Already, you will gain considerably more social cachet and respect by cultivating a degree of aloofness and traditional English reserve towards your mobile, rather than responding immediately to its every ring or bleep like an over-excited puppy. Excessive eagerness in social interaction is seen as embarrassing and frowned upon, and this applies to electronic hyper-sociability as well – particularly now that the novelty of mobile communication has worn off.

As I said, however, the rules of mobile-phone talk are still emerging. I hope that identifying more general, stable rules and 'defining characteristics' of Englishness will help us to predict, to some extent at least, the most likely future developments in this process.

To discover these defining characteristics, we first need to examine the rules of a much more stable, established form of English communication: pub-talk.

PUB-TALK

The pub is a central part of English life and culture. That may sound like a standard guidebooky thing to say, but I really mean it: the importance of the pub in English culture cannot be over-emphasised. More than three-quarters of the adult population go to pubs, and over a third are 'regulars', visiting the pub at least once a week. For many it is a second home. It also provides the perfect 'representative sample' of the English population for any social scientist, as pubs are frequented by people of all ages, all social classes, all education-levels and every conceivable occupation. It would be impossible even to *attempt* to understand Englishness without spending a lot of time in pubs, and it would almost be possible to achieve a good understanding of Englishness without ever leaving the pub.

I say 'almost' because the pub – like all drinking-places, in all cultures – is a special environment, with its own rules and social dynamics. My colleagues at SIRC and I have conducted quite extensive cross-cultural research on drinking-places[43] (well, someone had to do it), which showed that drinking is, in all societies, essentially a social activity, and that most cultures have specific, designated environments for communal drinking. Our research revealed three significant cross-cultural similarities or 'constants' regarding such drinking-places:

- In all cultures, the drinking-place is a special environment, a separate social world with its own customs and values.

43. See: Fox, K. (2000), *Social and Cultural Aspects of Drinking*, The Amsterdam Group, London.

- Drinking-places tend to be socially integrative, egalitarian environments, or at least environments in which status distinctions are based on different criteria from those operating in the outside world.
- The primary function of drinking-places is the facilitation of social bonding.

So, although the pub is very much part of English culture, it also has its own 'social microclimate'.[44] Like all drinking-places, it is in some respects a 'liminal' zone, an equivocal, marginal, borderline state, in which one finds a degree of 'cultural remission' – a structured, temporary relaxation or suspension of normal social controls (also known as 'legitimised deviance' or 'time-out behaviour'). It is partly because of this caveat that an examination of the rules of English pub-talk should tell us a lot about Englishness.

THE RULES OF ENGLISH PUB-TALK

The Sociability Rule

For a start, the first rule of English pub-talk tells us why pubs are such a vital part of our culture. This is the sociability rule: the bar counter of the pub is one of the very few places in England where it is socially acceptable to strike up a conversation with a complete stranger. At the bar counter, normal rules of privacy and reserve are suspended, we are granted temporary 'remission' from our conventional social inhibitions, and friendly conversation with strangers is considered entirely appropriate and normal behaviour.

Foreign visitors often find it hard to come to terms with the fact

---

44. The 'social microclimate' is a concept I introduced in *The Racing Tribe*, where I suggested that just as certain geographical locations (islands, valleys, oases, etc.) are said to 'create their own weather', so social environments (e.g. racecourses, pubs, universities, etc.) also have a distinctive 'microclimate', with behaviour patterns, norms and values that may be different from the cultural mainstream.

that there is no waiter service in English pubs.[45] Indeed, one of the most poignant sights of the English summer (or the funniest, depending on your sense of humour) is the group of thirsty tourists sitting patiently at a pub table, waiting for someone to come and take their order.

My first, callously scientific, response to this sight was to take out my stopwatch and start timing how long it would take tourists of different nationalities to realise that there was no waiter service. (For the record, the fastest time – two minutes, twenty-four seconds – was achieved by a sharp-eyed American couple; the slowest – forty-five minutes, thirteen seconds – was a group of young Italians although, to be fair, they were engrossed in an animated debate about football and did not appear much concerned about the apparent lack of service. A French couple marched out of the pub, complaining bitterly about the poor service and *les Anglais* in general, after a twenty-four-minute wait.) Once I had obtained sufficient data, however, I became more sympathetic, eventually to the point of writing a little paperback book on pub etiquette for tourists. The field research for that book – a sort of nine-month nationwide pub-crawl – also provided much useful material on Englishness.

In the pub-etiquette book, I explained that the sociability rule only applies at the bar counter, so having to go up to the bar to buy drinks gives the English valuable opportunities for social contact. Waiter service, I pointed out, would isolate people at separate tables. This may not be a problem in more naturally outgoing and sociable cultures, where people do not require any assistance to strike up a conversation with those seated near them, but, I argued rather defensively, the English are somewhat reserved and inhibited, and we need all the help we can get. It is much easier for us to drift casually into 'accidental' chat while waiting at the bar counter than deliberately to break into the conversation at a neighbouring table. The no-waiter-service system is designed to promote sociability.

45. There are now some exceptions to the no-waiter-service rule, which may not apply in pub-restaurants or 'gastro-pubs', or at least not in the 'restaurant' section of these pubs, if they are divided into 'bar' and 'restaurant' areas. These exceptions have only caused more confusion for foreign tourists.

But not rampant, uncontrolled sociability. 'Cultural remission' is not just a fancy academic way of saying 'letting your hair down'. It does not mean abandoning all inhibitions and doing exactly as you please. It means, quite specifically, a structured, ordered, convention-alised relaxation of normal social conventions. In English pubs, the suspension of normal privacy rules is limited to the bar counter, and in some cases, to a lesser degree, to tables situated very near the counter – those furthest from the bar being universally understood to be the most 'private'. I found a few other exceptions: the sociability rule also applies to a more limited extent (and subject to quite strict rules of introduction) around the dart-board and pool table, but only to those *standing* near the players: the tables in the vicinity of these games are still 'private'.

The English need the social facilitation of legitimised deviance at the bar counter, but we also still value our privacy. The division of the pub into 'public' and 'private' zones is a perfect, and very English, compromise: it allows us to break the rules, but ensures that we do so in a comfortingly ordered and rule-governed manner.

The Invisible-queue Rule

Before we can even begin to explore the complex etiquette involved in pub-talk, we stumble across another rule of pub behaviour that involves a brief digression from our focus on conversation rules, but will help us to prove (in the correct sense of 'test') a 'rule of Englishness'. The issue is queuing. The bar counter is the only place in England in which anything is sold without the formation of a queue. Many commentators have observed that queuing is almost a national pastime for the English, who automatically arrange them-selves into orderly lines at bus stops, shop counters, ice-cream vans, entrances, exits, lifts – and, according to some of the baffled tourists I interviewed, sometimes in the middle of nowhere for no apparent reason.

According to George Mikes: 'An Englishman, even if he is alone, forms an orderly queue of one.' When I first read this comment, I thought it was an amusing exaggeration, but then I started to observe people more closely, and found not only that it was often true, but also that I do it myself. When waiting alone for a bus or at a taxi stop, I do not just lounge about anywhere roughly within striking distance of the stop, as people do in other countries – I stand directly under the sign, facing in the correct direction, exactly as though I were at the head of a queue. I form an orderly queue of one. If you are English, you probably do this too.

In our drinking-places, however, we do not form an orderly queue at all: we gather haphazardly along the bar counter. At first, this struck me as contrary to all English instincts, rules and customs, until I realised that there is in fact a queue, an invisible queue, and that both the bar staff and the customers are aware of each person's position in it. Everyone knows who is next: the person who reached the bar counter before you will be served before you, and any obvious attempt to get served out of turn will be ignored by the bar staff and severely frowned upon by other customers. In other words, it will be treated as queue-jumping. The system is not infallible, but English bar staff are exceptionally skilled at identifying who is next in the invisible queue. The bar counter is 'the exception that proves the rule' about English queuing: it is only an apparent exception – and another example of the orderly nature of English disorder.

The Pantomime Rule

The rules of English pub-talk regulate non-verbal as well as verbal communication – in fact, some of them actively prohibit use of the verbal medium, such as the pantomime rule. Bar staff do their best to ensure that everyone is served in proper turn, but it is still necessary to attract their attention and make them aware that one is waiting to be served. There is, however, a strict etiquette involved in attracting the attention of bar staff: this must be done without speaking, without making any noise and without resorting to the vulgarity of obvious gesticulation. (Yes, we are back in *Looking-Glass* land again. The truth of English etiquette is indeed stranger than even the strangest of fiction.)

The prescribed approach is best described as a sort of subtle pantomime – not the kind of pantomime we see on stage at Christmas, but more like an Ingmar Bergman film in which the twitch of an eyebrow speaks volumes. The object is to make eye contact with the barman. But calling out to him is not permitted, and almost all other obvious means of attracting attention, such as tapping coins on the counter, snapping fingers or waving are equally frowned upon.

It is acceptable to let bar staff know one is waiting to be served by holding money or an empty glass in one's hand. The pantomime rule allows us to tilt the empty glass, or perhaps turn it slowly in a circular motion (some seasoned pub-goers told me that this indicates the passing of time). The etiquette here is frighteningly precise: it is permitted to perch one's elbow on the bar, for example, with either money or an empty glass in a raised hand, but not to raise one's whole arm and wave the notes or glass around.

The pantomime rule requires the adoption of an expectant, hopeful, even slightly anxious expression. If a customer looks too contented, bar staff may assume that he or she is already being served. Those waiting to be served must stay alert and keep their eye on the bar staff at all times. Once eye contact is made, a quick lift of the eyebrows, sometimes accompanied by an upward jerk of the chin, and a hopeful smile, lets the staff know you are waiting. They respond to these pantomime signals with a smile or a nod, a raised finger or hand, and perhaps a similar eyebrow-lift. This is code for 'I see that you are waiting and will serve you as soon as possible.'

The English perform this pantomime sequence instinctively, without being aware of following a rigid etiquette, and never question the extraordinary handicaps (no speaking, no waving, no noise, constant alertness to subtle non-verbal signals) imposed by the rule. Foreigners find the eyebrow-twitching pantomime ritual baffling – incredulous tourists often told me that they could not understand how the English ever managed to buy themselves a drink – but it is surprisingly effective. Everyone does get served, usually in the right order, and without undue fuss, noise or argument.

Researching the pantomime rule (and the other unwritten rules of pub behaviour) was something of a test of my own ability to stand back from my native culture and observe it as a detached scientist. As a native pub-goer, I had always performed the pantomime ritual automatically, like everyone else, without ever questioning or even noticing its strange and complex rules. But to write the little pub-etiquette book, I had to force myself to become a 'professional alien', even in my own local pub. It is quite an interesting (although somewhat disconcerting) mental exercise, to clear one's mind of everything one normally takes for granted – and to scrutinise, dissect and question every detail of a routine that is almost as familiar, mindless and mechanical as brushing one's teeth. When that book came out, some English readers told me that it was equally disconcerting to read the results of this exercise, and I have now received many similar comments from readers of *Watching the English*.

Exception to the Pantomime Rule

There is one important exception to the pantomime rule, and as usual it is a rule-governed exception. While waiting to be served at a pub bar-counter, you may hear people calling out to the bar staff, 'Oi, any chance of a bloody drink some time this millennium?' or 'Get a move on: I've been stood here since last Thursday!' or committing other blatant breaches of the pantomime rule. You would be advised not to follow their example: the only people permitted to speak in this manner are the established 'regulars' (regular customers of a particular pub), and the rude remarks are made in the context of the special etiquette governing relations between bar staff and regulars.

The Rules of Ps and Qs

The rules governing the ordering of drinks, however, apply to everyone. First, it is customary in England for just one or at the most two members of a group to go up to the bar to order drinks for the group, and for only one to make the actual payment. (This rule is not merely designed to make life easier for bar staff, or to avoid that English pet hate 'fuss'. It is related to another complex set of rules: the etiquette of round-buying, which will be covered later.) Second, the correct way to order a (draught) beer is 'Pint of bitter [or lager], please.' For a half-pint, this is always shortened to 'Half a bitter [or lager], please.' (When ordering a particular brand of draught bitter or lager, this would be 'Pint of [name], please,' or 'Half a [name], please.')

The 'please' is very important: foreigners or novices will be forgiven mistakes in other elements of the order, but omitting the 'please' is a serious offence. It is also vital to say 'thank you' (or 'thanks', or 'cheers', or at the very least the non-verbal equivalent – brief eye contact, nod and smile), when the drinks are handed over, and again when the change is given.

This rule applies not just in pubs, but when ordering or purchasing anything, anywhere in England: in shops, restaurants, trains, buses and hotels, staff expect to be treated politely, and this means saying 'please' and 'thank you'. The politeness is reciprocal: a bartender or shop assistant will say, 'That'll be four pounds fifty, then, please,' and will usually say, 'Thank you,' or a less formal equivalent, when you hand over the money. The generic rule is that every request (by either staff or customer) must end with 'please' and every fulfilment of a request (ditto) requires a thank-you.

During my research on Englishness, I diligently counted all the pleases and thank-yous involved in every purchase I made, and found that, for example, a typical transaction in a newsagent's or corner shop (such as, say, my usual purchase of a bar of chocolate and a newspaper) usually involves two pleases and three thank-yous (although there is no upper limit on thank-yous, and I have often counted five). The simple purchase of a drink and a packet of crisps in a pub also typically requires two pleases and three thank-yous.

England may be a highly class-conscious society, but these politeness rules suggest that the culture is also, in many ways, remarkably egalitarian – or at least that it is not done to *draw attention* to status differences. Service staff may often be of a lower social class than their customers (and linguistic class indicators ensure that where this is the case both parties will be aware of it), but there is a conspicuous lack of servility in their demeanour, and the unwritten rules require that they be treated with courtesy and respect. Like all rules, these are sometimes broken, but when this does occur, it is noticed and frowned upon.

The 'And One for Yourself?' Rule – and the Principles of Polite Egalitarianism

In the special social microclimate of the pub, I found that the rules of egalitarian courtesy are even more complex, and more strictly observed. For example, it is not customary in English pubs to tip the publican or bar staff who serve you. The usual practice is, instead, to buy them a drink. To give bar staff a tip would be an impolite reminder of their 'service' role, whereas to offer a drink is to treat them as equals. The rules governing the manner in which such drinks must be offered reflect both polite egalitarianism and a peculiarly English squeamishness about money. The prescribed etiquette for offering a drink to the publican or bar staff is to say, 'And one for yourself?' or 'And will you have one yourself?' at the end of your order. The offer must be clearly phrased as a question, not an instruction, and should be made discreetly, not bellowed out in an unseemly public display of generosity.

If you forget to add 'And one for yourself?' when ordering your drinks, it is acceptable to ask the bartender or publican, 'Will you have a drink?' at another time, but the 'And one for yourself?' approach is much preferred, as it implies that the customer and the bartender are having a drink together, that the bartender is being included in the 'round'. I observed that the English also tend to avoid using the word 'buy'. To ask, 'Can I buy you a drink?' would in theory be acceptable, but in practice is rarely heard, as it carries the suggestion that money is involved. The English are perfectly well aware that money is involved, but prefer not to call attention to the fact. We know that the publican and bar staff are providing us with a service in exchange for money – and indeed that the 'And one for yourself?' ritual is a somewhat convoluted way of giving them a tip – but it would be indecorous to highlight the pecuniary aspects of this relationship.

And the bar staff collude in this squeamishness. If the 'And one for yourself?' offer is accepted, it is customary for bar staff to say, 'Thanks, I'll have a half [or whatever],' and add the price of their chosen drink to the total cost of the order. They will then state the new total clearly, 'That'll be five pounds twenty, then, please' – thus indirectly letting you know the price of the drink you have just bought them, without actually mentioning the amount, which in any case will not be large, as the unwritten rules require them to choose a relatively inexpensive drink. By stating the revised total, they are also, in a subtle and oblique manner, making the customer aware of their abstemious choice of beverage.

The understanding that this is not a tip but an invitation to 'join' the customer in a drink is also reinforced by the behaviour of the bar staff when consuming the drink. They will always raise their glass in the customer's direction, and say, 'Cheers,' or 'Thanks', which is normal practice between friends on receiving a drink as part of a 'round'. When the bar is particularly busy, the staff may not have time to pour or consume the drink immediately. It is quite acceptable in these circumstances for them to accept the 'And one for yourself?' offer, add the price of their drink to the customer's order, and (if possible) enjoy the drink later when the bar is less crowded. On pouring the drink, however, even several hours later, bar staff will often go to some lengths to ensure that they catch the relevant customer's eye and raise the glass in acknowledgement, with a nod and a smile – and a 'Cheers' if the customer is within earshot.

It could be argued that, although more egalitarian than conventional tipping, this 'one-way commensality' – giving without receiving in return – is nonetheless a dominance signal. This argument would have some merit, were it not that the gesture is often reciprocated by publicans and bar staff, who will usually not allow a customer, particularly a regular, to buy them many drinks before attempting to return the favour. There will still, in the final reckoning, be some asymmetry, but such reckonings never occur, and even an occasional reciprocation on the part of the publican or bar staff serves to maintain the impression of a friendly exchange between equals.

To many foreign visitors, the 'And one for yourself?' ritual seems like an unnecessarily circuitous and complicated way of giving a tip – a gesture accomplished almost everywhere else in the world (and, indeed, everywhere in England apart from the pub) by the simple handing over of a few coins. A bemused American, to whom I explained the rule, expressed incredulity at the 'Byzantine' nature of English pub etiquette, and a French visitor bluntly dismissed the entire procedure as 'typical English hypocrisy'.

Although other foreigners told me that they found our convoluted courtesies charming, if somewhat bizarre, I have to admit that those two critics both had a point. English rules of politeness are undeniably rather complex, and, in their tortuous attempts to deny or disguise the realities of status differences, clearly hypocritical. But, then, surely all politeness is a form of hypocrisy: almost by definition, it involves pretence. The sociolinguists Penelope Brown and Stephen Levinson argue that politeness 'presupposes [the] potential for aggression as it seeks to disarm it, and makes possible communication between potentially aggressive parties'. Also in the context of a discussion of aggression, Jeremy Paxman observes that our strict codes of manners and etiquette seem 'to have been developed by the English to protect themselves from themselves'.

We are, perhaps more than many other cultures, intensely conscious of class and status differences. George Orwell correctly described England as 'the most class-ridden country under the sun'. Our labyrinthine rules and codes of polite egalitarianism are a disguise, an elaborate charade, a severe collective case of what psychotherapists would call 'denial'. Our polite egalitarianism is not an expression of our true social relations, any more than a polite smile is a manifestation of genuine pleasure or a polite nod a signal of real agreement. Our endless pleases disguise orders and instructions as requests; our constant thank-yous maintain an illusion of friendly equality; the 'And one for yourself?' ritual requires an extraordinary act of communal self-deception, whereby we all agree to pretend that nothing so vulgar as money or so degrading as 'service' is involved in the purchase of drinks in a bar.

Hypocrisy? At one level, clearly, yes: our politenesses are all sham, pretence, dissimulation – an artificial veneer of harmony and parity masking quite different social realities. But I have always understood the term 'hypocrisy' to imply conscious, deliberate deception of others, whereas English polite egalitarianism seems to involve a collective, even collaborative, *self*-delusion. Our politenesses are evidently not a reflection of sincere, heartfelt beliefs, but neither are they cynical, calculating attempts to deceive. And perhaps we need our polite egalitarianism to protect us from ourselves – to prevent our acute consciousness of class differences from expressing itself in less acceptable ways.

The Rules of Regular-speak

I mentioned above, in the context of the pantomime rule, that there is a special code of etiquette governing the behaviour and speech of a pub's 'regulars' (regular customers), which, among other privileges, allows them to break the pantomime rule. The special code does not, however, allow them to jump the invisible queue – as this would violate the overriding English rule about queuing, itself a subsidiary, it would seem, of a more general rule of Englishness about 'fairness'. It is worth examining the rules of regular-speak in more detail, as they represent a 'conventionalised deviation from convention', which should provide further clues that will help us in our search for the defining characteristics of Englishness.

Greeting Rules

When a regular enters the pub, there will often be a chorus of friendly greetings from the other regulars, the publican and the bar staff. Publicans and bar staff always address regulars by name, and regulars always address the publican, bar staff and each other by name. Indeed, I have noticed that in the pub, names are used rather more often than is strictly necessary, as though to emphasise the familiarity and personal connections between members of this small 'tribe'. This is particularly striking as a contrast to 'mainstream' English conversation codes, in which names are used significantly *less* than in other cultures, and where overuse of names is frowned upon as cloyingly American.

The bonding effect among pub regulars is further reinforced by the use of nicknames – pubs are always full of people called 'Shorty', 'Yorkshire', 'Doc', 'Lofty', etc. To call someone by a nickname universally indicates a high degree of familiarity. Normally, only family and close friends use nicknames. The frequent use of nicknames between regulars, publican and bar staff gives them a sense of belonging – and gives us a helpful insight into the nature of social relations in English pubs.[46] It is worth noting in this context that some regular pubgoers have a 'pub-nickname' that is not used by their friends and family outside the pub, and may not even be known to these groups. Pub-nicknames are often ironic: a very short regular may be known as Lofty, for example. In my own local pub, although I was normally known as 'Stick' (a reference to my rather scrawny figure), the landlord went through a phase of calling me 'Pillsbury'.

The greeting rules require the publican, bar staff and regulars to welcome a regular with a chorus of 'Evening, Bill', 'Wotcha, Bill', 'All right, Bill?', 'Usual, is it, Bill?', and so on. The regular must respond to each greeting, normally addressing the greeter by name or nickname: 'Evening, Doc', 'Wotcha, Joe', 'All right there, Lofty', 'Usual, thanks, Mandy.' The rules do not prescribe the exact words to be used in these exchanges, and one often hears inventive, idiosyncratic, humorous or even mock-insulting variations, such as 'Ah, just in time to buy your round, Bill!' or 'Back again, Doc? Haven't you got a home to go to?'

The Rules of Coded Pub-talk

If you spend hundreds of hours sitting eavesdropping in pubs, you will notice that many pub conversations could be described as 'choreographed', in the sense that they follow a prescribed pattern, and are conducted in accordance with strict rules – although participants are not conscious of this and obey the rules instinctively. While the rules of this choreographed pub-talk may not be immediately obvious to outsiders, the conversations can be followed and understood. One type of regular-speak, however, is utterly incomprehensible to outsiders, and can be understood only by the regular customers of a particular pub. This is because the regulars are effectively speaking in code, using a private language. Here is my favourite typical example of coded pub-talk, from the etiquette research:

46. Nicknames can also, of course, often be used for less friendly purposes, including expression of hostility, social division and social control, but that is not their function in the pub.

The scene is a busy Sunday lunchtime in a local pub. A few REGULARS *are standing at the bar, where the* PUBLICAN *is serving. A male* REGULAR *enters, and by the time he reaches the bar, the* PUBLICAN *has already started pouring his usual pint. The* PUBLICAN *places the pint on the counter in front of the* REGULAR, *who fishes in his pocket for money.*

REGULAR 1: 'Where's meat-and-two-veg, then?'
PUBLICAN: 'Dunno, mate – should be here by now.'
REGULAR 2: 'Must be doing a Harry!'
(*All laugh*.)
REGULAR 1: 'Put one in the wood for him, then – and yourself?'
PUBLICAN: 'I'll have one for Ron, thanks.'

To decode this conversation, you would need to know that the initial question about 'meat and two veg' was not a request for a meal, but an enquiry as to the whereabouts of another regular, nicknamed 'Meat-and-two-veg' because of his rather stolid, conservative nature (meat with two vegetables being the most traditional, unadventurous English meal). Such witty nicknames are common: in another pub, there is a regular known as TLA, which stands for Three Letter Acronym, because of his penchant for business-school jargon.

One would also have to know that 'doing a Harry', in this pub, is code for 'getting lost', Harry being another regular, a somewhat absent-minded man, who once, three years ago, managed to get lost on his way to the pub, and is still teased about the incident. 'Put one in the wood for him' is a local version of a more common pub-talk expression, meaning 'Reserve a pint of beer to give him when he arrives, which I will pay for now'. (The more usual phrase is 'Put one in for . . .' or 'Leave one in for . . .' – 'Put one in the wood for . . .' is a regional variation, found mainly in parts of Kent.) The phrase 'And yourself?' is shorthand for 'And one for yourself?', the approved formula for offering a drink. The 'Ron' referred to by the publican, however, is not a person, but a contraction of 'later on'.

So: Regular 1 is buying a drink now, to be served to the traditionalist Meat-and-two-veg when he arrives (assuming the latter has not repeated Harry's mistake and got lost) and offering the publican a drink, which he accepts, but will not consume until later on, when he is less busy. Simple, really – if you happen to be a member of this particular pub-tribe, and familiar with all its legends, nicknames, quirks, codes, abbreviations and in-jokes.

In our national scientific pub-crawls, we found that every pub has its own private code of in-jokes, nicknames, phrases and gestures. Like the 'private languages' of other social units, such as families, couples, school-friends and work-mates, this coded pub-talk emphasises and reinforces the social bonds between pub regulars. It also emphasises and reinforces the sense of *equality* among them. In the pub, your position in the 'mainstream' social hierarchy is irrelevant: acceptance and popularity in this liminal world are based on quite different criteria, to do with personal qualities, quirks and habits. 'Meat-and-two-veg' could be a bank manager or an unemployed bricklayer. His affectionately teasing nickname is a reference to his middle-of-the-road tastes, his rather conservative outlook on life. In the pub, he is liked, and mocked, for these idiosyncratic foibles; his social class and occupational status are immaterial. 'Harry' might be an absent-minded professor, or an absent-minded plumber. If he were a professor, he might be nicknamed 'Doc', and I heard of a plumber whose unfortunate pub-nickname was 'Leaky', but Harry's absent-mindedness, not his professional rank, is the quality for which he is known, liked and teased at the Rose and Crown.

So, coded pub-talk facilitates social bonding and reinforces egalitarian values. I mentioned earlier, however, that the primary function of *all* drinking-places, in *all* cultures, is the facilitation of social bonding, and that *all* drinking-places tend to be socially integrative, egalitarian environments – so what, if anything, is peculiarly English about the bonding and egalitarianism we find embedded in coded pub-talk?

There are aspects of this pub-talk that do seem to be identifiably English, such as the celebration of eccentricity, the constant under-current of humour, the wit and linguistic inventiveness. But the 'universal' features of facilitation of bonding and egalitarianism are distinctive here only in the *degree* to which they deviate from the mainstream culture – which is characterised by greater reserve and social inhibition, and more pervasive and acute class-consciousness, than many other societies. It is not that sociability and equality are peculiar to English drinking-places, but that the contrast with our conventional norms is more striking, and that, perhaps, we have a greater need for the drinking-place as a facilitator of sociable egalitarianism – as a liminal world in which the normal rules are suspended.

The Rules of the Pub-argument

I mentioned earlier that regulars are not only exempt from the pantomime rule but are allowed to make remarks such as 'Oi, Spadge, when you've quite finished your little chat, I wouldn't mind another pint, if it's not too much bloody trouble!' Banter, backchat and mock-insults of this kind (often involving the use of heavy irony) are a standard feature of conversations between regulars and bar staff, and among fellow regulars.

Pub-arguments, which are not like 'real' arguments in the 'real world', are an extension of this kind of banter. Arguing is probably the most popular form of conversation in pubs, particularly among males, and pub-arguments may often appear quite heated. The majority, however, are conducted in accordance with a strict code of etiquette, based on what must be regarded as the First Commandment of pub law: 'Thou shalt not take things too seriously.'

The rules of pub-arguments also reflect the principles enshrined in what might be called the 'unwritten constitution' governing all social interaction in this special environment. This pub constitution prescribes equality, reciprocity, the pursuit of intimacy and a tacit non-aggression pact. Students of human relations will recognise these principles as being among the foundations of all social bonding – and it seems that social bonding is indeed the underlying purpose of the pub-argument.

It is collectively understood, although never stated, that the pub-argument (like the Mine's Better Than Yours ritual described earlier) is essentially an enjoyable game. No strong views or deeply held convictions are necessary for pub regulars to engage in lively disputes

– in fact, they would be a hindrance. Regulars will frequently start an argument about anything, or nothing, just for the fun of it. A bored regular will deliberately spark off an argument by making an outrageous or extreme statement, then sit back and wait for the inevitable cries of 'Bollocks!' The instigator must then hotly defend his assertion, which he secretly knows to be indefensible. He will then counter-attack by accusing his adversaries of stupidity, ignorance or something less polite. The exchange often continues in this manner for some time, although the attacks and counter-attacks tend to drift away from the original issue, moving on to other contentious matters – and the need to argue among male[47] pub-goers is such that almost any subject, however innocuous, can become a controversial issue.

Pubgoers have a knack for generating disputes out of thin air. Like despairing auctioneers taking bids from 'phantom' buyers, they will vehemently refute a statement nobody has made, or tell a silent companion to shut up. They get away with this because other regulars are also looking for a good excuse to argue. The following example, recorded in my own local pub, is typical:

REGULAR 1: (*accusingly*): 'What?'

REGULAR 2: (*puzzled*): 'I didn't say anything.'

REGULAR 1: 'Yes, you did!'

REGULAR 2: (*still bemused*): 'No, I didn't!'

REGULAR 1: (*belligerent*): 'You did, you said it was my round – and it's not my round!'

REGULAR 2: (*entering into the spirit of things*): 'I didn't bloody say anything, but now you come to mention it, it *is* your round!'

REGULAR 1: (*mock-outraged*): 'Bollocks – it's Joey's round!'

REGULAR 2: (*taunting*): Then why are you hassling me about it, eh?'

REGULAR 1: (*now thoroughly enjoying himself*): 'I'm not – you started it!'

REGULAR 2: (*ditto*): 'Didn't!'

REGULAR 1: 'Did!'

47. Females do sometimes participate in these bantering pub-argument games, but much less frequently and usually with considerably less enthusiasm than males. When women argue, it tends to be 'for real'.

And so on. As I sat watching, sipping my beer, smiling the tolerant-but-slightly-superior smile characteristic of females listening patiently to male pub-arguments, the dispute meandered into other issues, but the opponents continued to buy each other drinks, and by the end everyone had, as usual, forgotten what the argument was supposed to be about. The rules state that no one ever wins a pub-argument, and no one ever surrenders. (The pub-argument is one context in which the traditional English gentlemanly edict that 'It is not the winning, but the taking part' that matters, still holds true.) The antagonists remain the best of mates, and a good time is had by all.

This sort of pointless, childish fight-picking might appear to be in contravention of the pub 'constitution', with its prescription of intimacy and non-aggression, but the fact is that arguing, for English males, is a crucial element of the pursuit of intimacy. The pub-argument allows them to show interest in one another, to express emotion, to reveal their personal beliefs, attitudes and aspirations – and to discover those of their companions. It allows them to become closer, more intimate, without acknowledging that this is their purpose. The pub-argument allows them to achieve intimacy under the macho camouflage of competition. The English male's tendency to aggression is channelled into harmless verbal fisticuffs, with the 'symbolic handshake' of round-buying serving to prevent any escalation into more serious, physical violence.[48]

Similar male-bonding arguments do, of course, take place outside the pub – among work-mates, for example, and among members of sports teams and clubs, or just among friends – and follow much the same rules. But the pub-argument is the best, most archetypal example of the English male-bonding argument. The English male-bonding argument also shares many features with similar practices in other cultures: all such 'ritual disputes' involve a tacit non-aggression pact, for example – in effect, an understanding that all

48. Of course, some arguments in pubs do escalate into physical violence, but pub-arguments of the type described take place *constantly*, and our research has shown that physical violence is very unusual, occurring only when the rules outlined here are broken. The issue of so-called 'alcohol-related' aggression and violence will be covered in more detail in Rules of Play (page 377).

the insults and attacks are not to be taken too seriously. What is distinctively English about the English version, it seems to me, is that our natural aversion to earnestness – and specifically our predilection for irony – makes this understanding much easier to achieve and to maintain.

The Free-association Rule

In the pub, even sticking to the same subject for more than a few minutes may sometimes be taken as a sign of excessive seriousness. Psychoanalysts use a technique called 'free-association', in which the therapist asks the patient to say whatever comes into his or her mind in association with a particular word or phrase. If you spend some time eavesdropping in pubs, you will notice that English pub-talk often exhibits the same qualities as free-association sessions, which may help to explain its socially therapeutic effects. In the pub, the normally reserved and cautious English shed some of their inhibitions, and give voice to whatever passing thought happens to occur to them.

The free-association rule states that pub conversations do not have to progress in any kind of logical or orderly manner; they need not stick to the point, neither must they reach a conclusion. When pubgoers are in free-association mode, which is much of the time, attempts to get them to focus on a particular subject for more than a few minutes are fruitless, and only serve to make one unpopular.

The free-association rule allows pub-talk to move in a mysterious way – mostly in apparently random sideways leaps. A comment about the weather somehow triggers a brief argument about football, which prompts a prediction about the fate of a television soap-opera character, which leads to a discussion of a current political scandal, which provokes some banter about the sex-life of the barman, which is interrupted by a regular demanding immediate assistance with a crossword clue, which in turn leads to a comment about the latest health-scare, which somehow turns into a debate about another regular's broken watch-strap, which sets off a friendly dispute about whose round it is, and so on. You can sometimes see a sort of vague logic in some of the connections, but most topic-shifts are accidental, prompted by participants free-associating with a random word or phrase.

The free-association rule is not just a matter of avoidance of seriousness. It is a licence to deviate from conventional social norms, to let one's guard down a bit. Among the English, this kind of loose, easy, disordered, haphazard conversation, in which people feel relaxed and comfortable enough to say more or less whatever occurs to them, is only normally found among close friends or family. In the pub, however, I found that free-association talk seems to occur naturally, even among people who do not know each other. It is most common among regulars, but at the bar counter, strangers can easily be drawn into the rambling chat. In any case, it must be understood here that people who regularly frequent the same pub are not necessarily, or even normally, close friends in the usual sense of the term. It is very rare for fellow regulars to invite each other to their homes, for example, even when they have been meeting and sharing their random thoughts every day for many years.

So: the free-association conversation patterns of English pub-goers, even among relative strangers, resemble those of a comfortable, close-knit family – which seems to contradict the usual perception of the English as reserved, standoffish and inhibited. But when I looked a bit closer, and listened a bit more carefully, the boundaries and restrictions emerged. I discovered that this was yet another example of strictly limited, and closely regulated, cultural remission. The free-association rule allows us to deviate from the normal codes of 'public' conversation, and to enjoy some of the looseness of 'private' or 'intimate' talk – but only up to a point. The clue is in the word 'patterns'. The *structure* of free-association pub-talk is like that of the private conversation among close friends or family, but the *content* is far more restricted. Even in free-association mode, fellow pub-goers (unless they also happen to be close friends) do not pour their hearts out to each other; they do not reveal – except inadvertently – their private fears or secret desires.

In fact, it is not done to talk about 'personal' matters at all, unless such matters can be aired in a non-serious manner, in accordance with the First Commandment. *Jokes* about one's divorce, depression, illness, work problems, delinquent children or other private difficulties and dysfunctions are fine – indeed, wry humour about life's tragedies is a standard feature of pub-talk. But earnest heart-to-heart outpourings are frowned upon. Such tearful exchanges do take place in pubs, of course, but these are private conversations, between friends or couples or family: it is not considered appropriate to conduct them at the bar counter and, most importantly, these private conversations are among the few that are *not* subject to the free-association rule.

PUB-TALK RULES AND ENGLISHNESS

So. What have we learnt? What do the rules of pub-talk tell us about Englishness?

The sociability rule confirms the characteristic revealed by the weather-speak rules of context and reciprocity – namely the ingenious use of 'facilitators' to overcome our social inhibitions. But this rule has added a couple of new twists to this theme. First, we find that in promoting sociability, the English are very careful to avoid sacrificing privacy. Second, the strict limits and caveats to the sociability rule indicate that even when we depart from convention we do so in a controlled, orderly manner.

In the invisible-queue rule, we find another example of 'orderly disorder', and evidence of the importance of queuing, which itself could be another indication of the importance of 'fairness' (this makes me wonder if perhaps the traditional English reverence for 'fair play' is still stronger than the doom-mongers would have us believe). In the pantomime rule, we see again the precedence of etiquette over logic – along with a marked dislike of fuss, noise and drawing attention to oneself, confirming earlier evidence indicating that social inhibition might be among the defining characteristics of Englishness.

The rules of Ps and Qs confirm the supreme importance of courtesy, and our squeamishness about calling attention to class and status differences. The 'And one for yourself?' rule exposes both the hypocrisies and the virtues of English 'polite egalitarianism'.

The deviations from convention involved in the rules of regular-speak provide a particularly rich source of indicators of Englishness. The excessive use of names (and nicknames) prescribed by the greeting rules contrasts sharply with mainstream English conversation-codes, in which overuse of names is frowned upon as too cloyingly familiar. It occurs to me that perhaps our official, snooty, well-bred contempt for such familiarity masks a secret need for it, expressed only in liminal zones.

As well as facilitating uncharacteristic sociability, the rules of coded pub-talk highlight another 'deviation': the escape from mainstream social hierarchies. We see that although sociability and egalitarianism are universal features of drinking-places, the contrast with conventional norms is particularly striking in the English case (only matched by the Japanese, also a culture noted for reserve, formality and acute sensitivity to status differences and also, perhaps significantly, a society inhabiting a small, overcrowded island[49]). In coded pub-talk and in the pub-argument rules, we also find that undercurrent of humour that characterises much English conversation, along with a sharp wit and linguistic inventiveness. Finally, the free-association rule provides yet another example of regulated deregulation, ordered disorder, method in (apparent) madness.

49. I know, Japan is actually a group of islands, not just one – but you get my point.

RACING-TALK

The world of horseracing, although much smaller than that of the pub, is almost equally representative. In fact, racing has more right, in demographic terms, to be called our national sport than football, as it attracts a far more balanced cross-section of the English population. Like the pub, race-meetings attract people of all ages and all social classes. The highest and lowest ends of the social spectrum are slightly over-represented at the racecourse, leaving a few minor gaps in the middle. The upper-middle-intelligentsia, for example, are rather under-represented, but as this vociferous minority receives more than enough attention elsewhere, its scarcity here need not concern us too much.

Like the pub, racing is a social microclimate – a special environment in which we find a degree of 'cultural remission', a temporary, conventionalised suspension of some of the normal social rules and constraints. In the case of racing, however, this microclimate is characterised by a highly unusual combination of relaxed inhibitions and exceptional good manners. I have never found this combination, or at least not to the same degree, in any other public setting in this country. The two elements usually seem to be mutually exclusive among the English (and indeed elsewhere): people will either shed their inhibitions and let rip *or* be frightfully polite and well behaved; you don't normally see both extremes at the same time.

This anomaly struck me the first time I went to the races, and I was so intrigued that I spent three years studying this subculture, and eventually wrote a book about it.[50] I am not, however, including

50. *The Racing Tribe: Watching the Horsewatchers* (published in the USA as *The Racing Tribe: Portrait of a British Subculture*).

racing as an example here merely because it is an English 'tribe' with which I am familiar, but because at the races we see the English in the behavioural equivalent of full national costume, in some respects almost a caricature of ourselves, but at our best and most likeable.

THE RULES OF ENGLISH RACING-TALK

Introduction Rules

To grasp the significance of microclimate codes, it is necessary to understand the prevailing 'mainstream' climatic conditions. I must therefore stress again that there are very few public places in England where it is socially acceptable to strike up a conversation with a stranger. We rarely speak to each other (and, indeed, rarely even make eye-contact or smile) in railway stations, on buses, in super-market queues, etc., without good reason. English commuters often travel on the same train together every morning for many years, without ever exchanging a word.[51] This is not a myth or even an exaggeration: I have observed it over many years and confirmed it in hundreds of interviews. We do not speak to strangers without good cause, and we certainly do not start chatting to random strangers in public places just to be friendly.

The pub bar counter is one exception to this normal rule of reserve; racecourses provide an even more remarkable example of deviation from this rule. In the pub, the bar counter is the only area in which mainstream rules on talking to strangers may be broken. At the races, you will see eye contact, smiles and amicable exchanges between complete strangers not only in the bars but also on the grandstands, around the parade ring, in the Tote queues – almost everywhere.

This is still England, though, so you will not be entirely surprised to learn that such conversations are conducted in accordance with strict and quite complex rules. They usually start with the question

51. The rules of behaviour on public transport will be covered in detail in Rules of the Road (page 217).

'What do you fancy in the next?' (or 'What are you on in the two-thirty?' or 'Got any tips for the next?' – or some variation on this theme: the exact words are not prescribed, but it should be an enquiry as to which horse the other person thinks might win a particular race).

'What do you fancy in the next?' is, of course, a grooming-talk conversation-starter with the same 'grammatical' function as 'Nice day, isn't it?' in weather-speak. In other words, it is not really a request for information or opinions on the likely winner of the next race, but a friendly greeting – code for: 'I'd like to talk to you: will you talk to me?' It is a basic, all-purpose initiator of social interaction, and understood as such by all racegoers. The rules require, however, that one respond as though one had been asked a real question.

To make the process easier, the use of 'props' is permitted. Well, one prop, to be exact: the race-card, but it is an extremely versatile prop. The race-card is a small booklet. It *looks* like a programme of the day's races, with details of the runners and riders in each race, form guides, a map of the racecourse and its facilities and other useful information. In fact, it is a vital social tool, used as a passport to conversation with strangers, as an ice-breaker in conversation with acquaintances, as an intimacy-escalator in courtship rituals and as a support in all debates and discussions. Perhaps its most important social function is as an indispensable 'displacement activity': whenever there is an awkward pause in a conversation, whenever English racegoers feel uneasy or self-conscious in a social situation, they consult their race-card.

The introduction rules state that the opening question – 'What do you fancy in the next?' or equivalent – should be accompanied by a suitable 'race-card gesture'. You may hold up your race-card and indicate the appropriate page, lean over to examine the race-card of the person you are addressing, place your race-card alongside theirs, or even, daringly, allow the two race-cards to touch or overlap – a symbolic indicator of the social contact you are attempting to initiate.

The Modesty Rule

Responses to the 'What do you fancy in the next?' opener vary, depending partly on the responder's level of knowledge about racing. But total lack of knowledge is no handicap – indeed, I soon discovered that it is, if anything, an advantage, as it enabled me to comply easily with the modesty rule. This is perhaps the most important rule of racing-talk. It goes well beyond 'Thou shalt not boast': there is an absolute prohibition on boasting, certainly, and indeed on any form of self-aggrandising or self-important behaviour. But the modesty rule goes further than this in actively prescribing humility and self-deprecation.

Even if you are a genius at picking winners, for example, you must not only refrain from trumpeting the fact, but also, whenever possible, make self-deprecating jokes about your ignominious failures. When the Tote screens or bookies' boards show a horse's odds lengthening – an indication that few punters are risking their money on the animal – the done thing is to say, with a rueful chuckle, 'Oh, I see word's got round that I backed it!'

Even professional racing journalists, who provide tips in their columns and compete with each other on who has the best track-record in picking winners, always obey the modesty rule in social situations. In fact, my favourite reply to the 'What do you fancy in the next?' opener came from one of these professionals, who laughed and said, 'Oh, you don't want to ask *me*: everyone knows I couldn't tip muck out of a barrow!'

I liked this response so much that I'm afraid I borrowed and used it shamelessly on many occasions during my research at racecourses; it never failed to get a laugh, and always prompted an immediate increase in warmth and friendliness. But silly puns are not necessary to achieve this effect: any self-effacing comment about your inability to pick winners is a correct response to the standard opener, and will instantly endear you to fellow racegoers. You may go on to name a horse that you fancy, but it is always best to preface this with the customary modest disclaimer.

Among jockeys and trainers, the taboo on boasting and the

prescription of humility are even stronger. There is almost a super-stitious belief that any hint of complacency, or even acceptance of praise, will bring bad luck. When they are interviewed by the media after winning a race, it is customary for both jockeys and trainers to disclaim all responsibility for their success, and attempt to give all the credit to the horse, each other, the favourable ground or weather conditions, the vet, the farrier or simple good luck.

Racehorse owners are also expected to be modest. If your horse is unsuccessful, this is relatively easy, but you must have a good repertoire of self-deprecating, affectionately humorous remarks about the beast's dismal form, your own folly in continuing to waste money on the poor creature, and your continued blind faith in its undiscovered talents. These comments must be accompanied by an apologetic shrug, a rueful, lopsided smile and a slightly bewildered frown. If your horse is successful (statistically the less likely scenario), you must avoid any hint of boastfulness about this. Even if you bred and raised the animal yourself, all credit for its wins must go to the horse, the trainer, the jockey, the stable staff, the horse's ancestors, the vet, the weather, etc. You must never appear complacent, but always somewhat puzzled and bemused by your good fortune.

The Courtesy Rules

While some of the conversation codes in this liminal microclimate represent a deviation from the 'mainstream' rules of English culture – a relaxation of normal constraints – others clearly involve an exaggeration of 'mainstream' restrictions and regulations. At the races, behaviours that are normally frowned upon (such as excessive drinking, exhibitionist dress, gambling and even talking to stran-gers) are not only permitted but actively encouraged. But at the same time racegoers are subject to codes and rules that impose greater controls and restraints – and, specifically, higher standards of courtesy – than those of everyday English culture. In the racing microclimate, we find a strange mixture of cultural remission and its exact opposite: cultural amplification, I suppose you could call it, or magnification.

The English have always been noted for their politeness, and despite our many lapses and deviations, this courtesy is still a 'rule' by any of the definitions outlined in my Introduction. It is still a guiding principle, a standard, and regarded as the normal or proper state of things. Like all rules, it often gets broken, but breaches are noticed and deplored, indicating that the principle still applies. At the races, however, we find an amplified, exaggerated version of the 'normal' politeness code – and breaches are rare.

At the races, it goes without saying that nothing can be accomplished without a full complement of pleases, thank-yous, excuse mes and endless apologies – but the courtesy code goes much further. Racegoers routinely open doors and hold coats and bags for each other; they automatically offer help or directions if someone looks a bit lost, as well as consolation on unsuccessful bets and congratulation on winners; and they always apologise if they inadvertently jostle or inconvenience you in any way. In my 'bumping' experiments, race-courses scored highest, with nearly 90 per cent of my victims being first to apologise when I accidentally-on-purpose bumped into them; in fact, at the races, even a 'near-miss' almost invariably elicited a 'sorry' (usually mumbled in the standard, barely audible English fashion, but sometimes even accompanied by brief eye-contact and a smile).

If you find you do not understand the complicated numbers and symbols printed in your race-card, you can go up to any fellow racegoer and ask for an explanation, which will almost always be patiently and politely given. If the person is as ill-informed as you, he or she may well apologise profusely – and, if possible, attempt to find someone who can help. I am not exaggerating: this was one of my favourite ways of getting into conversation with racegoers during my research, and it rarely failed.[52]

It even worked when my 'targets' were trainers, stewards, clerks and other busy officials, for whom my novicey questions were highly inconvenient interruptions to their work. Trainers would say, 'I'm

---

52. To make sure that these findings were not biased by my sex or appearance, I bribed and bullied 'guinea pigs' of the opposite sex to perform the same experiments, with much the same results. Being small and female is certainly an advantage when asking for 'help', in any social context, but even my tall male friends and colleagues had little difficulty initiating conversation in this way.

really sorry, but I must just go and saddle this horse. The owner is waiting for me and he's a dreadful fusser. I do hope you don't mind . . .' Stewards would apologise for having to hold enquiries, jockeys for having to go and ride in races, and so on.

Like the modesty rule, the courtesy rules pervade every aspect of racing-talk. In most cases, these rules are merely an exaggeration (though at times almost a caricature) of 'mainstream' English politeness principles. In one area, however, racing-talk courtesy is diametrically opposed to its 'mainstream' equivalent. Sports journalists are usually, in print, among the least polite people in English culture. Their style is generally highly confrontational, and they frequently attack and condemn players, coaches and managers who turn in sub-par performances or otherwise fail to meet their standards, accusing them of incompetence or corruption. Insulting headlines and cries of 'Shame!' and 'Disgrace!' are commonplace. Racing journalists, by contrast, are unfailingly polite in their reports and commentary, carefully avoiding any censure of the jockeys and trainers whose doings they record, and always very generous with praise.

When a much-hyped favourite trails in well beaten, its performance is almost always described as merely 'disappointing'. The explanations and excuses of jockeys and trainers are accepted and quoted with due respect. The courtesy rules dictate that blame should never be attributed directly, but only conveyed using the most diplomatic of euphemisms. Thus, racing journalists will not accuse a trainer of running a horse too often; instead, they will say that the animal's 'disappointing' performance 'was perhaps due to the effects of a long and tiring season'. Jockeys will not be directly accused of riding badly or adopting inappropriate tactics; rather, the journalists will say that a natural front-runner 'did not seem suited by being held up'. (Of course, everyone knows what these euphemisms really mean – in racing as elsewhere among the English, courtesy and hypocrisy tend to go hand in hand.)

And this strict observance of courtesy rules extends to other areas of racing celebrities' lives as well. Racing journalists have to report on horse-doping scandals or official enquiries into other forms of cheating or malpractice. But when the news and gossip pages of all the newspapers were full of salacious headlines about a 'sex scandal' in the racing world, the racing correspondents remained resolutely silent on the subject, continuing calmly to report on the week's runners, including those of the trainer in question, and politely ignoring all the unseemly fuss over his domestic difficulties. Although I found this restraint both extraordinary and admirable, it was not unexpected. In fact, I won some money by betting my friends that the racing-talk courtesy rules would prevail, and the racing correspondents would not be tempted to join in the fray. (My bets on social matters during the racing research were always much more successful than those on horses.) And when the mainstream newspapers started asking me, as racing's official anthropologist, to comment on the scandal, I obeyed the courtesy rules and politely declined. I still can't seem to bring myself to name those involved.

Finally, and perhaps most surprisingly, I found that observance of the courtesy rules is common where one would least expect it: among racegoers who, in their 'other lives', are aggressive football supporters and disruptive Saturday-night revellers of a type all too familiar to me from previous research on violence, disorder, 'lager-louts' and football hooligans. At the races, these very same young males are high-spirited and lively, but without the belligerence and anti-social tendencies that characterise their behaviour in other sporting and social contexts.

Their relatively decorous behaviour at the races defies all popular theories about the causes of violence and disorder, providing proof that it is entirely possible for hordes of young males to congregate, gamble and drink large amounts of alcohol at an exciting sports event without getting into fights or, indeed, causing any trouble at all. At the races, they may be extremely noisy and demonstrative, but they are not aggressive – in fact, they are remarkably well behaved. They open doors for women, they say 'please' and 'thank you', and if they drunkenly lurch into you, they apologise.

When I interviewed them, these young males freely admitted that their behaviour at football matches and on Saturday-night binges was quite different from their relatively good-mannered conduct at the races – although they could not provide a coherent explanation for this, beyond saying that 'Everyone knows you don't cause trouble at the races,' or 'It's just a fact, right?' In other words, there is an unspoken rule that everyone instinctively obeys. This seems to me to be largely a matter of expectation: where young males are treated as responsible, decorous adults, they will generally behave as such; where they are treated like children, criminals or wild beasts, they will also conduct themselves accordingly.

The Moaning Rules

Lest you start to think that the racing world is all sickly sweetness and light, I should point out that racegoers have their grumps and disgruntlements just like anyone else – and so do jockeys, trainers, journalists, officials and so on. The English predilection for quiet, Eeyorish moaning is as much in evidence at the races as anywhere else – and the rules and conventions governing talk about racing's irritations and discontents are much the same as those involved in the weather-speak 'moaning rituals' described earlier.

The subjects of complaint vary, although here, as elsewhere, the weather is a frequent source of dissatisfaction – and at the races it has the added power to affect the state of the 'going' (ground, turf) and thus ruin the chances of a horse that would otherwise have been a dead cert to win the three-thirty. Everyone moans about the weather, and the normal weather-hierarchy rules do not always apply, as sunshine can be as much of an evil as rain, for those whose horses prefer soft going.

Otherwise, different members of the racing tribe each have their own favourite whinges. Punters moan about lousy odds, greedy bookmakers, incompetent jockeys and inexplicably slow horses. Jockeys complain (quietly) to each other about 'pointless' stewards' enquiries, and about the unreasonable expectations of trainers and owners of slow horses (including my all-time favourite overheard moan: 'Guv'nor's complaining I didn't keep in touch with the leaders. Keep in touch! I told him I'd've needed an effing postcard!'). Owners whine about miserly prize money and the extortionate fees charged for this, that and the other. Everyone – even journalists – moans about the sport's governing bodies, the Jockey Club and the British Horseracing Authority (BHA). And then there are always temporary fads and fashions for ritual moaning on specific issues: during the period of my research on the racing tribe, a favourite whinge was 'The Derby Has Lost Its Atmosphere.' This kind of nostalgic moaning is typically English, and not confined to the elderly or conservative: one of my favourite examples is a homemade sign spotted at Glastonbury Festival, which read "Queue here to complain festival is not as good as it used to be'.

The rules of moaning ensure that, whatever the subject of the lament, all these conversations take much the same form. There must be some token disagreement on the causes of the evil in question, and on what the BHA (or 'someone') should do about it (or, rather, what they should have done about it ten years ago, if they'd had any sense). But the rules also require a great deal of fervent nodding and enthusiastic agreement on the key issues at stake. Minor differences of opinion on details are necessary to keep the conversation flowing, but the consensus on principles is the real point of the ritual. By ensuring expression and reaffirmation of shared values in this way, the rules of moaning help to reinforce solidarity and social bonding among racegoers.

Suggesting a practical solution to the problem under discussion (as I did on a few occasions, as an experiment) undermines this socially therapeutic function, by effectively bringing the subject to a close. This is therefore not allowed (my attempts were either frostily received or treated as a joke). The rules of moaning prohibit all attempts to introduce an element of reason or pragmatism into the debate, as this is likely to inhibit the bonding effect of the moaning ritual. As usual, social etiquette triumphs over logic. Or perhaps we should say that a different sort of logic applies. Participants in moaning rituals do not want to be given reasonable advice on how to solve their problems: they want to enjoy moaning about them. Reasonable advice is therefore, quite reasonably, forbidden.

Moaning is, of course, not an activity peculiar to the English. Woody Allen once said, in response to Noam Chomsky, 'Language may be innate, but whining is acquired.' Actually, whining is innate or, at least, certainly universal. But there does seem to be something distinctively English about the *kind* of whining involved in both weather-speak and racing-talk moaning rituals – a sort of grumpy and apathetic stoicism; complaining endlessly about unsatisfactory states of affairs, but in a resigned manner, without any real expectation that things could be improved, and certainly without any attempt to find means of improving them. I mentioned earlier that someone once said that the English have satire instead of revolutions (or something to that effect): we complain bitterly, and often wittily, but we do not actually do anything about it.

Post-mortem Rules

After each race, the trainers, owners and other 'connections' of the also-rans conduct a form of verbal 'post-mortem', in which the race is minutely dissected and the causes of failure diagnosed.

The unwritten rules governing such conversations express the tacit understanding that a horse very rarely loses a race because it is not fast enough. If you eavesdrop on a few post-mortem conversations (a most amusing pastime, I recommend it), you will soon find out that horses lose races because they get a bad draw, get upset in the stalls, miss the break, get boxed in, get bumped, can't act on the going, fail to settle, lose their action on a sharp bend, run wide, need the race, have got jaded from too much racing, should have gone for the gap, should have taken the outside, saw daylight too soon, didn't get a run until too late, might try him over a mile, might try him in blinkers and got bags of stamina and sure to improve next time out and ran a great race, really, considering.

You may have some difficulty keeping a straight face, but what you must not do, ever, is even to hint that an owner's horse might possibly have been beaten by twenty lengths and come fourteenth because it was up against thirteen better horses.

The post-mortem rules require jockeys riding also-rans to start mentally rehearsing their post-mortem speeches for the owners before they pass the post (or even earlier, in the case of obvious no-hopers: one jockey told me, 'I had a ride last week where the trainer told me exactly what to say the night before'). Jockeys may give their honest uncomplimentary opinion to the trainer, but this must be tactfully rephrased in more optimistic tones for the owner. The jockey's breathless comment to the trainer as he returns to the unsaddling enclosure, 'One-paced, and believe me it's a bloody slow one!' will, by the time they are joined by the owner, have become, 'Stayed on well, he's a real trier – a step up in distance might suit him.'

There is an element of self-interest in all this polite smoothing, in that brutal honesty about a horse's lack of talent could result in an empty box and loss of training fees – as the owner might decide to sell the 'dud' horse, or send it to a different trainer. But it is not really in a trainer's long-term interest to have a stable full of unsuccessful horses, and trainers are usually deluding themselves as much as the owners when they indulge in the customary post-mortem optimism. There is always a degree of courteous collusion in these conversations, whereby the owner and the trainer conspire to convince each other that the horse was unsettled in the stalls, or found the pace too fast or too slow, or the ground too soft or too hard, or was suffering from springtime hormonal mood-swings, or was unfairly handicapped, or hampered, or something.

The post-mortem prescription of polite optimism is also a subset of a more general rule to the effect that it is considered rude to bad-mouth a horse to its owner, or even to speak slightingly of a horse in public. Irate owners have been known to ring up racing journalists and broadcasters with heated complaints following a tactless comment about their horse in print or on air. The result is that journalists, and anyone speaking within earshot of an owner, tend to resort to gracious, diplomatic euphemisms. You do not tell an owner, or the world, that his horse is 'ungenuine' (a dire insult): you say that the animal is 'a bit of a character'. Everyone knows exactly what you mean. (I found that every racing enthusiast carries a mental glossary of these euphemisms, and, when pressed hard enough, could always tell me their real meanings.) But honour is preserved; face is saved. More of that delightful English hypocrisy.

The Money-talk Taboo

Although financial concerns pervade every aspect of racing, it is not done to talk about them – or, at least, not in any direct or straight-forward fashion.

There is an interesting contrast here with Irish racing. It starts with the signage. In Ireland, the betting ring is called the betting ring; in England, it is called 'Tattersalls' or some neutral made-up name such as 'The Gordon Enclosure'. In Ireland, the corporate hospitality boxes are boldly signposted 'Corporate Hospitality'; in England, this 'business' function is disguised with discreet signs to anonymous box numbers or the such-and-such suite or room. In Ireland, sponsors' logos are brazenly displayed around the inside fence of the parade ring; in England, the parade ring is sacred territory, where such a shameless exhibition of commercial interests would be considered crude and improper.

English squeamishness about money matters is equally evident in conversation codes. Where Irish racegoers enquire after your betting success with a brash 'Are you making money?', English racegoers say, 'Had any winners yet?' In both countries, the result of a race cannot be officially declared until the jockeys have 'weighed in', and the clerk of the scales has checked that they did not shed or add a few pounds since 'weighing out' before the race. At Irish racecourses, however, the announcements over the loudspeakers confirm the result of a race with the punter-friendly cry 'Winner all right!', meaning that if you backed the winner, your money is safe. The equivalent English announcement is another euphemism, repeated in a monotone: 'Weighed in, weighed in.'

Even in England, the money-talk taboo permits racegoers to exclaim loudly over their winnings – especially as it is universally understood that money won on the horses is not 'real money', and can therefore be spent on whims and luxuries (such as bottles of champagne, lavish ice-creams for the children, a new hat or dress), rather than saved to pay the mortgage or the gas bill.

But I found that other forms of money-talk, including conducting 'business' at the races, are strictly forbidden by the unwritten laws – particularly, and this is perhaps surprising, in exactly the places one would expect to hear business-talk: the corporate hospitality boxes. Almost all parties of 'suits' (as corporate racegoers are known) observe a complete ban on money-talk. It is understood, although rarely stated explicitly, that clients or potential clients have been invited to enjoy a pleasant day at the races, not to engage in discussion of business matters – or, worse, the ultimate heresy, to be subjected to any sort of a sales-pitch.

This is an unwritten, unofficial taboo, but it was observed by all of the corporate parties I studied over the course of a year's research on the racing 'suits' (a project referred to disparagingly by my SIRC colleagues as 'Kate's gatecrashing study', as it involved attending rather a lot of corporate-hospitality lunches and parties at race-meetings). When asked, the 'suits' told me that, yes, there was an unspoken understanding that one should not engage in 'shop-talk' (they couldn't even bring themselves to use the word 'money') at the races. A few corporate hosts operate a somewhat modified version of the taboo, whereby 'shop-talk' is occasionally allowed, if and only if the conversation on such topics is initiated and 'driven' by the client – in other words, where it would be rude to interrupt and change the subject. Even if the client insists on hearing about some new product or service, however, hosts must refrain from lengthy disquisitions, and remain alert to the slightest sign of fading atten-tion, whereupon they must immediately steer the conversation back to what will win the next race.

The 'suits' I interviewed maintained that the severe constraints imposed by the taboo do not hamper the function of corporate hospitality as a means of generating or retaining business. They insisted, on the contrary, that the taboo allows hosts and guests to get to know each other better, and to build closer, friendlier relation-ships, which in turn is good for business. Not one could provide any hard financial evidence to show a return on their hospitality 'invest-ment', and I read later about a survey showing that my sample was entirely typical in this respect: the overwhelming majority of English firms do not 'measure' the results of hospitality expenditure in any sort of systematic way, or indeed at all (and reading between the lines of the survey report, I got the impression that the respondents rather objected to being questioned too closely on the subject).

Whether the system works or not, 'You've invited them to enjoy the races and the company,' said one corporate host. 'And you don't spoil that by turning the thing into a vulgar sales-pitch. There is a time and a place for trade, and this is not it.' This successful busi-nessman's mouth made a little downturned *moue* of disgust as he said the words 'sales' and 'trade'. Which made me think of Mary Douglas, who famously defined 'dirt' as 'matter out of place' in her book about the concept of pollution. There is nothing intrinsically dirty, for example, about food or shoes – but food splattered on a tie or shoes on a dinner-table are dirty. Among the English, there are suitable times and places for money-talk: in the wrong place, such as the races, even euphemisms like 'sales' and 'trade' are so repugnant that they cannot be pronounced without a wince.

I was subsequently to find that the times and places considered appropriate for money-talk in English culture are few and far between, and that a degree of squeamishness and embarrassment about money is common even in those situations which *are* regarded as appropriate. The 'sordid subject of money', as it is commonly referred to among the English, will be covered in more detail in Work to Rule (page 288), but I should admit straight away that I am terribly English about money myself – and although I can laugh at our squeamishness, I found it very difficult to break the money-talk taboo, and my interviews on this subject were as embarrassing for me as they were for the unfortunate 'suits'.

RACING-TALK RULES AND ENGLISHNESS

The combination of cultural remission and cultural amplification in this subculture's social microclimate makes it a particularly rich source of insights on Englishness.

Remission first. The introduction rules underline the now familiar theme of English social inhibition, and the ingenious use of props and facilitators to overcome our awkwardness and difficulties in initiating social contact. It would seem that we are not by nature reserved or unsociable, as some observers have suggested, but merely socially incompetent, self-conscious and easily embarrassed. When we have a clear set of rules to follow, with prescribed, ready-made opening lines and helpful props, such as the race-card, we can actually talk to each other. (I start at this point to wonder whether the English obsessions with 'organised' hobbies, clubs and sports – much remarked upon but never really explained by other commentators – might be in some way connected with our need for social facilitators of this kind. I'll try to work this out when we get to Rules of

Play (page 313), but perhaps it's worth bearing in mind.)

While the unusual sociability of racegoers is an example of conventionalised deviation from English convention, the modesty rule and courtesy rules represent amplifications or exaggerations of 'mainstream' cultural constraints. Both self-deprecation and politeness have cropped up as persistent themes in previous chapters, but here, at the races, we see them taken to extremes – the 'behavioural equivalent of full national costume', or cartoon-Englishness factor, that I mentioned at the beginning of this chapter.

The degree of modesty and courtesy required by racecourse etiquette verges on the absurd, but this is balanced by very un-English disinhibition – a combination that I feel shows us the English at their best. At the races, we shed some of our more tiresome stuffiness and awkwardness, but without going to the usual opposite extreme of becoming boorish and aggressive. Normally, we seem to have a tendency to veer between these two almost equally unattractive modes; at the races, we somehow manage to combine relaxed inhibitions with good manners. I say 'somehow' because, despite having written a whole book on the racing subculture, I am still not sure that I completely understand the mechanisms behind this remarkable balancing act – or, at least, I have not yet explained them to my own satisfaction, although I am convinced, much to the annoyance of the neo-Puritan killjoys, that both alcohol and gambling are among the factors influencing good behaviour at the races.

On the modesty question, it strikes me that the racing-talk data might help to clarify an issue that has become somewhat muddled in discussions of Englishness. It seems obvious from the examples here that we are not talking about 'true' or 'genuine' modesty – the sort of humility that springs from a real conviction that one is nothing very special, undeserving of any praise or admiration. When people speak of 'English modesty', what they are really saying is not that we are naturally humble or self-effacing but that we have distinctive *rules* about modesty – rules that require us to affect an air of modesty, to deflect praise with an embarrassed shrug and a self-deprecating joke, even if we are actually feeling quite proud and pleased with ourselves. There does not seem to be too much difficulty in grasping this distinction when it comes to 'courtesy' – pretty much everyone[53] understands that politeness is a matter of obeying cultural rules about good manners, whatever one's natural inclinations may be.

The rules of moaning highlight (again) our predilection for incessant and apparently pointless whingeing. Pointless, that is, in a practical sense, because as pragmatic solutions are banned from such discussions, they never result in any effective action. The English have been described as stoical and uncomplaining: this is not true, we complain constantly – it is just that we rarely address our complaints to the sources of our dissatisfaction. But our bellyaching rituals are not at all pointless in a social or psychological sense, as we thoroughly enjoy our Eeyorish moans, and the rules involved (particularly the prescription of 'token dissent on detail but consensus on wider principles') ensure that these rituals promote a sense of solidarity and social bonding. The English are never so comfortably united and harmonious as when they are indulging in a collective grumble.

The post-mortem rules bring us back to the recurring theme of English polite hypocrisy – in this case involving a great deal of verbal ingenuity. To avoid causing offence or admitting failure, an impressive range of inventive euphemisms, tactful smoothings, imaginative excuses and skilful evasions are employed. As with the hypocrisies of 'polite egalitarianism', this is not a matter of deliberate deception, but of collusion in collective self-deception – a practice for which the English seem to have a peculiar talent.

Finally, the money-talk taboo provides a second example of the squeamishness about money first noted in Pub-talk (page 137). More evidence will be needed before we can include this characteristic in our definitive 'grammar' of Englishness, but it must surely be, as they say in racing, 'one to watch'.

Some of the other traits emerging from the racing-talk rules – the persistently recurring ones such as social inhibition/embarrassment,

53. Apart from a few psychologists, who confuse cultural rules with personality traits.

ingenious use of facilitators, modesty (affected), courtesy (ditto, by definition), humour, Eeyorish moaning and polite hypocrisy – begin to seem to me like strong contenders for inclusion in our 'grammar'. But I'm trying to be scientific about this, so I'll reserve judgement until we have some more data.

SQUADDIE-TALK AND
TWO TYPES OF RIDER-TALK

I will not attempt a complete conversational dissection of these three subcultures (soldiers, bikers and horse-riders) but just pick out some of their most distinctive features and their underlying rules, and see what these tell us about Englishness.

THE RULES OF SQUADDIE[54]-TALK[55]

The army. What does that make you think of? A highly controlled, hierarchical, literally 'regimented' society, the epitome of Erving Goffman's 'total institution'. And the soldiers at the bottom of the hierarchy – the squaddies? One thinks of obedience, discipline, forced marches, drilling, constant supervision, petty punishments, stiff upper lips, barked orders – and perhaps the occasional 'breakout' from all this repression in drunken rampages. So, what would you imagine is the single most important distinguishing feature of English squaddie-talk? Deference? Rank-consciousness? Army jargon/slang? Swearing?

54. I am using the term 'squaddie' for 'soldier', because it is the most common colloquial expression, but as some may regard it as derogatory, I should stress that no disrespect is intended.
55. I am greatly indebted to my sister, Dr Anne Fox, for much of the information in this section. She has been conducting research on soldiers (including extensive participant-observation fieldwork for her Ph.D. thesis) and working with the British Army for the past 15 years, and generously shares all her data with me.

Squaddie Humour Rules

No. All these are important, but the most striking, pervasive and distinctive feature is *humour*. When they are not 'speaking to order', saying, 'Yes, sir' and 'No, sir,' and 'Three bags full, Sergeant' (and sometimes even when they are), almost every aspect of squaddies' conversation is characterised by humour – jokes, ridicule, wit, puns, banter, irony, understatement, nicknames, satire, slapstick, mockery, teasing and, especially, black or 'gallows' humour. Rarely does an English soldier open his mouth to speak without showing at least a hint of humour – like a gold tooth, that little glint of humour is always there, even at serious moments, flashing and catching the light.

I have already discussed at some length the central importance of humour in English culture, but the squaddie example is significant because, in this particular respect, squaddies are 'like the rest of us only more so'. In squaddie humour, we see another 'amplification' of normal English conversation codes. Among squaddies, we see the English rules of humour taken to their logical extreme – and applied more strictly and obeyed more scrupulously than in any other group or subculture.

The Importance of Not Being Earnest Rule

Earnestness, for example, is severely frowned upon. The subtleties of the First Commandment of English humour – the Importance of Not Being Earnest rule – are clearly understood by all squaddies. Any who initially fail to grasp the fine distinctions involved, and cross the line between permitted seriousness and forbidden solemnity, are soon made painfully aware of their error – by relentless and merciless ridicule. You can take your duties and responsibilities as a soldier seriously, but if you take *yourself* too seriously, and become too humourlessly earnest, over-zealous, self-important or pompous about your soldiering, you will be branded a 'Green' (or 'Bleeds Green') – other terms have included 'Army Barmy' or 'Cabbage Head' – the military equivalents of a school 'swot' or teacher's pet. At Sandhurst, the excessively keen are those trying to win an accolade known as the Sword of Honour, and are therefore called 'Blade Runners'.

The Rules of Teasing and Mockery

Teasing and mockery, the most pervasive forms of squaddie humour, start from the moment of introduction – when raw trainee soldiers first meet each other on arrival at the barracks. Such introductions are, as we have seen, always a problem for the English: squaddies ingeniously overcome the usual painful awkwardness by the use of humour – in this case specifically teasing and mockery. The first question is usually 'Where do you come from?' often followed by 'Who do you support?' (meaning 'which football team' – it being automatically assumed among young working-class English males that everyone supports a football team). English regionalism and tribal football rivalries mean that the responses to these questions provide an instant basis for teasing, for the exchanges of mocking insults – 'Geordie wanker!', 'Swindon are pathetic!' and so on – that are the English male's favoured means of establishing rapport. In no time at all, this mutual mockery has the desired effect: the ice is broken, and the vital group-bonding process has begun.

Very quickly, the same humour rules become a means of reinforcing this in-group solidarity, by mocking and insulting other groups. The army is a highly tribal culture, with intricate systems of allegiances and loyalties at every level. A squaddie's first loyalty is to his own small section or 'squad' – these are his immediate peers, his mates. Next comes identification with and allegiance to his platoon, then company, then battalion, then regiment, then to his branch of the army (infantry, artillery, etc.), then to the army as a whole, and finally, last and very much least, the official loyalty to 'Queen and Country'. At each of these levels, there are endless opportunities to demonstrate one's loyalty to the group, and strengthen the bonds between its members, by poking fun at other, rival, groups.

The insults involved can be quite unpleasant, although often highly inventive – other types of infantrymen mock the Parachute Regiment, for example, by claiming that 'Only two things fall out of the sky: Paras and bird shit' – but they are, in the spirit of the Importance of Not Being Earnest rule, not to be taken seriously. John Hockey, in his excellent ethnography of squaddies, quotes a private explaining the nature of the rivalry between military units (in this case at 'company' level): 'They're all horrible, all the other companies are horrible . . . Well, they just are, they're not your company, so they're bound to be horrible. Not serious, like. I've got some good mates in them.'

Irony Rules

Squaddies are masters of irony, often remarkably skilled and witty satirists, and particularly good at laughing at themselves – poking fun at the army and its customs. In this context, rival military units often ridicule each other for breaches of the Importance of Not Being Earnest rule, and in particular for breaches of the sub-clause prescribing a strong sense of irony. Hockey cites a satirical article in the newsletter of an infantry battalion, the 3rd Battalion Royal Green Jackets, which mocks the over-zealous, excessively conformist and earnest approach to military appearance and discipline of a 'rival' battalion, the 1st Battalion Parachute Regiment, at the time serving alongside them:

> At Echelon they have a rather unorthodox regiment – 1 Para stationed with them. They look smart, have short hair, wear funny-coloured berets with badges above the left eye. The men without anything on their arms call the soldiers with stripes 'Corporal' or 'Sergeant' and hold their hand above their right eye when men with little marks on their shoulders pass. We are trying to find out when these quaint customs started.

In this passage, the Royal Green Jackets[56] combine mockery of a rival group with good-humoured ridicule of the orthodoxies of military dress and etiquette to which they are *all* required to conform. Their point is that they, the Royal Green Jackets, manage to do so while maintaining the proper degree of ironic detachment, while the Paras

56. The Royal Green Jackets have since been amalgamated with other regiments to form the Rifles.

allegedly take the whole ludicrous business of smartness, deferential forms of address and saluting much too seriously. You could hardly wish for a more perfect illustration of the English anti-earnestness and irony rules.

The Modesty Rule

After humour, perhaps the most striking feature of squaddie-talk is the taboo on boastfulness. At one level, this can be seen as an extension of the Importance of Not Being Earnest rule: it is accept-able to be a genuinely dedicated, serious soldier, as long as one does not talk about it in solemn, pompous, self-important tones – one must never take *oneself* too seriously. Collective pride is quite a different matter. Boasting about one's regiment is allowed, even prescribed: every soldier is expected to believe and loudly proclaim that his regiment is the best, and to disparage other rival regiments. (The humour rules, however, require that this be done with a degree of wit: the Paras are generally disliked by other regiments for being too arrogant and pompous about their alleged superiority. Their officers are aware of this, but believe that being disliked is good for them – that the constant need to 'fight back' makes them better soldiers.)

Any hint of *personal* boasting or immodesty is absolutely forbidden, and the penalties for breaking this unwritten rule can be very harsh indeed. During my sister's Ph.D. field-research with the army, a soldier who made 'Best Recruit' in Phase 1 training committed the cardinal sin of flaunting his new status, imagining that it gave him authority over his peers in Phase 2, and generally thinking rather too highly of himself. He was effectively 'shunned out' of the army – so utterly despised and rejected by his fellow trainees that it became impossible for him to stay.

This recruit might have got off more lightly had he responded appropriately to the initial scorn and ridicule provoked by his self-important manner. An important element of the squaddie modesty rule is the ability to 'take' mockery of this kind – the ability to swallow one's pride, laugh at oneself, learn a lesson and quietly mend one's ways without making a fuss. Humour of this sort can be a highly effective didactic tool: ridicule is often the quickest and most efficient way of teaching the unwritten rules – letting someone know exactly where the invisible lines are drawn, and conveying disapproval when they are overstepped. Our unfortunate 'Best Recruit', though clearly a promising soldier in other 'official' respects, failed to learn the unofficial modesty rule and persisted in his self-aggrandising behaviour.

The Fair-play Code

The fair-play code is, strictly speaking, a behaviour code rather than a conversation code, but it has significant implications for conversation, and some of its rules specifically prohibit certain ways of talking, so I'm including it here. The importance of this unwritten code among squaddies cannot be overstated: it governs their entire existence, affecting every aspect of their interactions with each other and with those in charge of them. The principal rules of the fair-play code are those prohibiting the following:

- shirking of responsibility
- failure to 'pull one's weight' or do one's 'fair share'
- excessive 'borrowing' and/or failure to return items or favours
- moaning and whining about one's lot or about perceived injustices ('personal' moaning, that is – collective moaning is not only permitted but part of the culture)
- and, worst of all, 'grassing'.

While breaches of other unwritten rules incur disapproval in the form of scorn, ridicule, ostracism or rejection, breaches of the fair-play code are even more serious, and persistent flouting can result in the offender receiving a severe beating. Physical violence is not exactly uncommon among soldiers, of course, but it mostly consists of heat-of-the-moment scuffles and brawls. By contrast, punishment-beatings for repeated breaches of the fair-play code tend to be carried out 'in cold blood'. The prohibition on 'grassing' then becomes even more important, as the battered victim's future will depend on whether or not he complains to the corporal or sergeant about the beating.

If he accepts his punishment, keeps his mouth shut and lies when asked how he got the bruises/broken nose/split lip (the correct response is 'Walked into a door, sir'), he gains respect and stands a strong chance of being fully reintegrated into the group, providing he does not repeat the fair-play breaches that got him into trouble in the first place. If he runs whining and squealing to the authorities and 'betrays' the 'mates' who beat him up, he is effectively 'finished', as he will lose the respect not only of his peers but also of the authorities to whom he complains. Contempt for 'grasses' is universal. Sergeants and officers *expect* the 'Walked into a door, sir' response when they question a soldier about such injuries. They will then say, as if reciting from a script, 'That's your story and you're sticking to it?' (This is invariably phrased more as a statement than as a question, and accompanied by a weary sigh.) The beaten-up squaddie, reading from the same unwritten script, simply replies, 'Yes, sir,' and that is the end of it.

THE RULES OF RIDER-TALK

In this section, I will focus exclusively on the 'greeting-talk' used by two English subcultures, rather than other aspects of their conversations, as it is their handling of initial encounters between strangers that might shed some light on Englishness.

In 'rider-talk', I am lumping together two English subcultures, bikers[57] and horse-riders, which most people, including the two groups themselves, would regard as having little or nothing in common. 'Don't be silly, Kate,' said one friend. 'Even you can't convince me that there's any of your precious "commonalities" between motorbike gangs and the Pony Club. I mean, Hell's Angels and the horsey set? Seriously? Apart from the trivial fact that they both ride things, these are opposite poles!'

So, I'd better explain what led me to make this unlikely connection. I was already very familiar, from personal involvement over

---

57. Some of whom prefer to call themselves 'motorcyclists', but I'm using 'bikers' here as it's less cumbersome – again, no offence intended.

many years, with the horsey subculture, when my sister suddenly developed an interest in motorbikes, and started hanging out with a group of bikers, going to rallies, biker pubs and so on. Intrigued, I pestered her for information and contacts, interviewed her biker friends, went to their meetings, and read their magazines, newsletters, blogs, online forums and anything else I could lay my hands on.[58] As soon as I had mastered a few words of biker-jargon, I also began seeking out and talking to bikers in the course of my rambling street-corner fieldwork in other parts of the country.

Despite my lack of familiarity with this subculture, there was something about it that felt remarkably, uncannily familiar. The terminology was new, but the patterns, structure and tone of the bikers' conversations, and the unspoken rules and tacit understandings I was starting to detect, kept reminding me of something; I had the strange sense of somehow having 'been here before'. It took me a while to realise what it was because I was suffering from 'ethnographic dazzle' – blinded by trivial surface differences – but eventually I twigged: bike-talk was exactly like horse-talk.

I also found that both bike-talk and horse-talk have much in common with the conversation patterns of other English 'hobby subcultures' or 'enthusiast subcultures', but I have deliberately chosen these two apparent opposites as representative examples.

The English, as we have already seen, have all sorts of difficulties with initiating social interaction: we tend to be awkward, inhibited and embarrassed. This social ineptitude can appear as shyness, reserve and dithering over-politeness, or as surliness, rowdiness and aggression – but the roots are the same.

The first thing you notice about bikers and horse-riders, however, is that they don't seem to have these problems. Bikers exchange friendly nods or raise a hand in acknowledgement and solidarity when they pass each other on the road, as do horse-riders. And when two English bikers or two English horse-people meet for the first time, they have an instant 'passport' to friendly conversation. They

58. Including one particularly good sociological study: *Bikers: Culture, Politics and Power* by Suzanne McDonald-Walker.

simply bypass the usual awkward greetings and preliminaries, sidestep the class, age or other social barriers that might otherwise separate them, and immediately start talking about motorcycles or horses.

In this context I should point out that, contrary to popular perceptions, both bikers and horse-riders come from all types of social background – and both groups insist that their passion, for bikes and horses respectively, is 'a great leveller'. This is not to say that either class divisions or class-consciousness miraculously vanish in these encounters (we are talking about the English here, after all): I specifically used the term 'sidestep', rather than 'ignore' or 'forget', to indicate that a mutual interest in bikes or horses allows *circumvention* of such barriers, without actually breaking them down.

The important point is that the bike and the horse serve as 'props', facilitators of social interaction – their function is a bit like that of the race-card, described in Racing-talk (page 152), but even more effective. If you watch an encounter between two bikers or two horse-riders – either at a bike rally/horse show or just at the roadside – you will notice that their bikes or horses are not only the focus of their conversation, but also of their gaze. Bikes and horses give the inhibited English something to talk about and, even better, an excuse to avoid making eye contact while we do so. We talk 'through' the bikes or horses, facing them, not each other: looking at them, standing back and admiring them, touching them, asking questions about them.

Meeting-talk customarily begins with a compliment of some sort, often immediately followed by a question: a first encounter between two horse people might start, for example, 'Lovely mover – how's he bred?' To which a typical response might be 'Thoroughbred with a dash of Welsh Cob, where he gets the knee action; bit green still, though – [to horse] Stop it! Stand still! No manners, as you can see . . .' Then, gesturing towards the other person's horse: 'Nice sort – very typey. Quite a decent size for an Arab, isn't he?' One must always find something complimentary to say about the other person's horse, even if the horse is unprepossessing or downright ugly. If one really can find nothing to admire, there are some stock lines one can trot out, such as 'lovely colour' or 'got a very kind eye'.

The equivalent greeting-conversation in biker-talk might be 'Nice bike, mate – what does it go like?' Which one of my motorcyclist informants admitted is a 'Daft question, really, as you'll have seen in countless mags opinions of how good a bike is, and by and large they go like the proverbial off a shovel.' Following which, 'It normally descends all too quickly into swapping technical specifications (for want of a better description) of your machines . . . more specific things like what tyres you use, do you like them, have you had the engine/suspension tuned, what do you think of the brakes? The list is endless.'

In both cases, the content of the endless questions and answers is not really important. Yes, there is often genuine interest, but these initial exchanges of technical information are more about conveying that one is a *bona fide* member of the biker or horsey 'tribe', by demonstrating knowledge and correct use of biker or horsey 'dialect'.

Suzanne McDonald-Walker, a social scientist who is also a biker, observes that there is an instant affinity or bond between bikers – which all the bikers I spoke to confirmed – and quotes a fellow biker who expresses the point rather well:

'The catalyst is that you're sitting there on two wheels, you're out in the open, you go past another biker and nine times out of ten they wave. And so there's that. And when you pull up, I mean, motorcyclists are interested in what they and other motorcyclists ride. Even if they would never ride it, they will still go across and look, and ask questions about it and that sort of thing. And, I mean *that* binds . . . We do not have much in common other than the machines we ride, but *that* is a significant bond.'

My horsey informants also repeatedly emphasised this instant-bonding factor, the usefulness of horses as facilitators of social interaction:

HORSEY INFORMANT *(young, female, trainee hairdresser)*: 'The thing about horses is it's like a magic word. I mean, you get that instant-friend thing even when you're not actually riding – even when the horses aren't there. Like, I was on a train and I mean you never talk to people on the train, but this girl was reading *Your Horse* [a magazine] and I just said, "Oh, is that the November one?" and she's, like, "Oh, yes, do you ride as well?" and I said yes and two seconds later we're chatting away like best friends . . . You know, you say the magic word "horse" and it's like a Masonic handshake or something.'

ME: 'Was she – did she look like the kind of person you might want to talk to, be friends with, apart from the magazine?'

HORSEY INFORMANT: 'To be honest, no. She looked quite posh, and quite a bit older than me, um, wearing a smart business suit – you know, like knee-length skirt, tights, smart shoes, and a posh briefcase and all. No, now I think about it, I'd have thought she was probably a bit snobby and, um, boring. But she wasn't, she was a good laugh, really nice – even though she's into poncy dressage and I like jumping. It's all horses, isn't it?'

It seems that being a member of the biker or horsey tribe allows circumvention not only of 'mainstream' class and other social barriers, but also of the many clannish sub-divisions within these subcultures. At an initial encounter, you are more likely to be judged and classified by the make of bike or the breed/type of horse you ride than by any indicators of your class or status in wider English society. Whether you are a doctor or a hairdresser is beside the point – the point being that you ride a Harley or a Honda, a hunter or a Hanoverian. Subculture conversation codes are not just about what is actually said, but also about the priorities implicit in what is said, and in what is not said. The clan or sub-group indicated by your choice of bike or horse is, at the moment of introduction, the second most important thing about you, the first being your membership of the bike or horse tribe. Another of McDonald-Walker's bikers and another of my horsey informants make this point in remarkably similar terms:

'And you've gone through that initial contact barrier so much more easily, you know, because you've already got something you can talk about. It's obvious . . . there's never a barrier in there by the different sort of criteria of bike you're riding. The fact that you ride one, and you're out there enjoying yourself on it, is enough to make you all right to sit down and talk to.'

'It's always a bit awkward when you meet new people, breaking the ice, but with horsey people it's so much easier to get over that initial hump – because you speak the same language, don't you? I mean obviously it's best if they're eventers, then it's practically like family, but anyone who rides or is into horses is all right, in my book. I'll talk with anyone about horses.'

As such conversations progress, both bikers and horse people may well move on to talk about matters unrelated to bikes or horses, and if they find they have enough other common views or interests, they may even end up exchanging more personal information, eventually becoming, as one of my informants put it, 'really proper friends, not just horse-friends'.

'We do have ordinary conversations as well, you know, just like everyone else,' said a horsey informant.

And a biker told me, 'I talk to my motorcycle friends about work, holidays, news, the weekend, families, friends and associates and bikes. Totally normal!'

In these 'normal' biker and horsey conversations on other subjects, the normal English conversation codes apply, and generally, apart from the effortless ease of their greeting-talk, the same goes for their bike-talk and horse-talk. In talk about bikes and horses, however, one is allowed to praise one's own bike or horse, often in glowing terms. This might appear to contravene the 'normal' prohibition on boasting, but if you listen carefully, you'll notice that most horse people and bikers avoid taking any credit themselves for the admirable qualities of their horses or bikes. As with the Mine's Better Than Yours game described earlier, the merits of one's chosen horse or bike can be extolled at great length, but one's own good taste or judgement in having chosen that horse or bike should be subtly implied (if possible through humorous self-deprecation) rather than directly stated – and one should also avoid boasting about one's skills as a rider, trainer or mechanic.

SQUADDIE-TALK, RIDER-TALK AND ENGLISHNESS

What do the conversation rules of these three subcultures tell us about Englishness? Do they help to confirm any of the candidates for 'defining characteristics' that we've tentatively identified so far – or reveal any additional nuances that might help us to define those characteristics more accurately?

I think it is safe to say that humour, modesty and fair play emerge as strong candidates, but the squaddie-talk rules, in which all of these characteristics are taken to extremes, add some new dimensions to our understanding of them.

In particular, the squaddie-talk rules highlight the English use of humour as a vital tool in social interaction and social bonding, both as an antidote to our awkwardness and discomfort in these contexts – our 'social dis-ease', one might call it – and as a didactic device, a way of teaching and reinforcing behaviour codes.

The squaddie-talk modesty rule provides the most dramatic illustration so far of the English taboo on boasting. I could be wrong, but I somehow doubt that an award-winning soldier in any other culture would actually be drummed out of the army just for being too boastful and cocky about his 'Best Recruit' status, or for taking this too seriously and failing to laugh at himself. Remember, he broke no official rules – quite the opposite, he was a model soldier – but this breach of the unwritten modesty and humour rules cost him his career.

The squaddies' fair-play rules provide more examples of severe penalties for breaches of unwritten codes – in this case, actual physical beatings for fair-play transgressions. An extreme subcultural example, of course, but still perhaps an indication of the importance of fair play in English culture.

The fair-play rules also add an interesting nuance to another candidate for 'defining characteristic' status. Our predilection for Eeyorish moaning seems to be cropping up regularly, but here we see that sub-clauses are involved: collective moaning is prescribed, personal moaning is forbidden – suggesting (as had already been hinted in the racing context) that English moaning is more of a social ritual than a genuine expression of grievance.

The rider-talk rules, indicate, I hope, that my search for 'common-alities' in English behaviour is perhaps not as quixotic as it might seem. Rider-talk was worth including for that reason alone, but the rules of these two subcultures also add to our understanding of English social interaction. Yet again, when we put that 'English reserve' stereotype under a sort of anthropological microscope, it is not quite as simple as it looks: we see significant evidence of social inhibition and discomfort, certainly, but very little of the misan-thropic or introverted tendencies that one might associate with the term 'reserve'. Almost every time we peer down this microscope and find those elements – molecules or whatever – of social dis-ease in English 'cultural DNA' (and, admittedly, we find a lot of them) they appear to be accompanied by antidotes: props and facilitators of sociability such as weather-talk, pubs, humour, games, alcohol, race-cards, horses, motorcycles, moaning rituals . . .

My hunch at the moment is that the English are *not* 'reserved' in the sense of unsociable. We may suffer from social dis-ease, but a truly unsociable, reclusive culture would not generate so many varied and ingenious antidotes to this dis-ease.

I'll tot all this up later, when I've examined enough different aspects of English culture to build up a representative sample of its unspoken rules, from which we can distil our 'quintessences of Englishness'. In this exploration of the minutiae of conversation codes, we are already starting to see some recurring themes, but I must be ruthless: will these themes appear again in other contexts, such as the way we decorate our homes, our behaviour on trains and buses, the customs and rituals of the workplace, the rules of eating and drinking, sex and shopping?

PART TWO
BEHAVIOUR CODES

HOME RULES

Some of the rules of Englishness do not require years of participant-observation research to discover. The privacy rules, for example, are so obvious that you could spot them from a helicopter, without even setting foot in the country. Hover above any English town for a few minutes, and you will see that the residential areas consist almost entirely of rows and rows of small boxes, each with its own tiny patch of green. In some parts of the country, the boxes will be a greyish colour, in others, a sort of reddish-brown. In more affluent areas, the boxes will be spaced further apart, and the patches of green attached to them will be larger. But the principle will be clear: the English all want to live in their own private little box with their own private little green bit.

THE MOAT-AND-DRAWBRIDGE RULE

What you cannot see from your helicopter, you will learn as soon as you try to visit an English home. You may have the address and a map, but you will have great difficulty in finding the house you are looking for. The Hungarian humorist George Mikes claimed that 'An English town is a vast conspiracy to mislead foreigners', citing the indisputable facts that our streets are never straight, that every time a street bends it is given a different name (except when the bend is so sharp that it really makes two different streets), that we have at least sixty confusing synonyms for 'street' (place, mews, crescent, terrace, rise, lane, gate, etc.), and that street names are in any case always carefully hidden. Even if you manage to find the correct street, the numbering of the houses will be hopelessly inconsistent and idiosyncratic, further complicated by many people choosing to give their houses names rather than numbers.

I would add that house numbers and names are usually at least as well camouflaged as the street names, indicating that an obsession with privacy, rather than a specific conspiracy to confuse Hungarians, is the real reason for all this muddle. We could not, even if we wanted to, demolish and redesign our muddled towns on a 'sensible' American grid system – but if we wanted to make it easier for others to find our house, we could at least paint the name or number reasonably clearly and in a position where it might be visible from the street.

But we do not. Our house numbers are at best highly discreet, and at worst completely obscured by creepers or porches, or even left off altogether, presumably on the assumption that our number may be deduced from those of our immediate neighbours. During the research for this book, I made a habit of asking taxi drivers why they thought this might be. They spend so much of their time crawling along, peering out of their side windows in search of a well-hidden or non-existent number, it struck me that they must at least have pondered the question, and perhaps come up with some interesting theories.

I was right about the pondering. Their initial response was almost always 'Bloody good question!' or words to that effect. The trouble was that it often seemed to be a cue for them to launch into a rant and moan about faded, camouflaged and absent house numbers – generally ending with something like 'Anyone would think they were doing it on purpose!' which, as far as I was concerned, was where we'd started. Trying a more devious tack, I would then ask the drivers if their own houses were clearly labelled. At this, most of them looked a bit sheepish and admitted that, no, come to think of it, their own house numbers and names were not particularly conspicuous. Why not? Why had they not painted their house number or name in big, bold lettering on the front door or gatepost? Well, it would look a bit odd, a bit flash; it would stand out, it would be drawing attention; and, anyway, they practically never took taxis, and their house was not hard to find, and all their friends and family knew where they were – and other lame excuses (much the same excuses, in fact, as those I received when I put this question to non-taxi-driving householders).

Apart from reminding me that there is an element of typically English reserve in our reluctance to display our house numbers, as well as a fixation with privacy, my initial taxi-driver interviews were not terribly helpful, but I persisted, and eventually one gave a succinct and astute response. He explained: 'An Englishman's home is his castle, right? He can't actually have the moat and drawbridge, but he can make it bloody difficult to get to.' From then on, I thought of the English practice of concealing our house numbers as 'the moat-and-drawbridge rule'.

But an Englishman's home is more than just his castle, the embodiment of his privacy rules, it is also his identity, his main status-indicator and his prime obsession. And the same goes for English women. This is why a house is not just something that you passively 'have', it is something that you 'do', something that you 'work on'.

NEST-BUILDING RULES

Which brings me to the English mania for 'home improvements', or 'DIY'. When Nikolaus Pevsner described 'the proverbial Englishman' as 'busy in house and garden and garage with his own hands', he hit the proverbial nail on the head. Never mind football, this is the real national obsession. We are a nation of nest-builders. Almost the entire population is involved in DIY, at least to some degree. In a survey conducted by some of my colleagues a while ago, only two per cent of English males and 12 per cent of females said that they never did any DIY.

We updated this research more recently, when SIRC was commissioned by the tea company who make PG Tips to do a study on home-improvers. (This was not quite as daft an idea as it sounds: we found that any DIY task requires the consumption of vast quantities of tea.) In terms of numbers, we found that nothing much had changed, except that the proportion of women involved in DIY is probably now even higher. And, if anything, the English were even more obsessed with their nest-building.[59]

I was not directly involved in the SIRC DIY study, but it was conducted in a manner of which I approve – not by ticking boxes on a telephone-questionnaire survey, but by actually going out and spending time in the temples of the DIY faith (Homebase, Wickes, B&Q, etc.), talking at length to DIYers about their motives, fears, stresses and joys. My colleague Peter Marsh, a devout DIYer himself, reasoned that some special temptation would be needed to persuade these fervent nest-builders to interrupt their Sunday-morning pilgrimage to talk to our researchers. His ingenious solution was tea and dough-nuts – a familiar, established part of the DIY ritual – offered free from the back of a van parked strategically in the DIY-store car parks.

It worked a treat. Stopping For Tea is such an integral element of the DIY routine that nest-builders who would never have allowed a conventional researcher with a clipboard to intrude on their twig-gathering were more than happy to hang around the SIRC van, gulping mugs of tea, munching doughnuts, and telling our researchers all about their home-improvement plans, hopes, worries and disasters.

The Territorial-marking Rule

The most common motive for DIYing among our car-park sample of typical nest-builders was that of 'putting a personal stamp on the place'. This is clearly understood as an unwritten rule of home ownership, and a central element of the moving-in ritual, often involving the destruction of any evidence of the previous owner's territorial marking. 'You've got to rip something out when you move in,' one young man explained. 'It's all part of the move, isn't it?'

He was right. Watch almost any residential street in England over a period of time, and you will notice that shortly after a For Sale sign comes down, a skip appears, to be filled with often perfectly serviceable bits of ripped-out kitchen or bathroom, along with

---

59. For stats-junkies: We now spend £8.5bn a year on DIY, considerably more per head than any other European country. Census data show that at least half of our adult males, and nearly a third of adult females, are regular, active DIYers.

ripped-out carpets, cupboards, fireplace-surrounds, shelves, tiles, banisters, doors and even walls and ceilings.

This is a 'rule' in a stronger sense than an observable regularity of behaviour: this kind of obsessive territorial marking is, for the majority of English people, an obligation, something we feel compelled, duty-bound to do: 'You've *got* to rip something out . . .'

This can be a problem for those who move into brand-new 'starter homes' or other new houses, where it would clearly be ludicrous to start ripping out virgin bathrooms and untouched kitchens. Yet we found the DIY temples full of such people, eager to add whatever 'personal touches' they could to mark their bland new territory. Even if you can't rip anything out, you've got to do *something*: a house that has not been tinkered with barely qualifies as a home.

CLASS RULES

The English obsession with home-improvements is not just about territorial marking, of course. It is also about self-expression in a wider sense: your home is not just your territory, it is your primary expression of your identity. Or, at least, that is how we like to think of it. Almost all of our DIY-temple sample saw themselves as exercising their creative talents, and other interviews with nest-builders in furniture shops, department stores and homes confirm that, although DIYing may be, for some, merely an economic necessity, we all see the arrangement, furnishing and decorating of our homes as an expression of our unique personal taste and artistic flair.

And it is, but only up to a point. The more closely I researched this question, the more it became clear that the way in which we arrange, furnish and decorate our homes is largely determined by social class. This has little or nothing to do with wealth. Upper-class and upper-middle-class homes tend to be shabby, frayed and unkempt in a way no middle-middle or lower-middle would tolerate, and the homes of the wealthiest working-class *nouveaux-riches* are full of extremely expensive items that the uppers and upper-middles regard as the height of vulgarity. The brand-new leather sofas and repro-duction-antique dining chairs favoured by the middle-middles may cost ten times as much as the equivalent items in the houses of upper-middles, who despise new leather and 'repro'.

In the homes of the middle-middles and below, the 'lounge' (as they call it) is more likely to have a fitted carpet (among the older working classes, this may be a patterned carpet). The higher castes prefer bare floorboards, often part-covered with old Persian carpets or rugs. The contents of lower-middle and some upper-working 'front rooms' will often be obscured by net curtains (useful as a class-indicator, but otherwise something of an annoying obstacle to peeping-Tom researchers) but they are likely to be dominated by huge flat-screen television sets and, among the older generations, may also boast carefully displayed 'collections' of small objects (spoons, glass animals, Spanish dolls, figurines or other 'collectables') from package holidays or mail-order catalogues.

Younger lower-middles and upper-workings may have less fussy tastes – their 'lounges' are often uncluttered to the point of dentist's-waiting-room bleakness (perhaps aspiring to, but never approaching, stylish minimalism). They will compensate for this lack of visual interest with an even bigger wide-screen television, which they call the TV or telly and which is always the focal point of the room (and, incidentally, currently shows at least six programmes every week about homes and home-improvement). Many upper-middle homes also have big televisions, but they are usually hidden in another sitting room, sometimes called the 'back room' or 'family room'.

Among the more well-off upper-middles, many of their rooms are likely to be painted with Farrow & Ball, Little Greene or Sanderson paint, in 'heritage' colours. The more insecure upper-middles will somehow find an opportunity to tell you this – and explain at tedious length exactly why these high-class paints are so much better than ordinary cheap Dulux. They will try to avoid mentioning the considerable difference in price, as it is unseemly to mention money or to appear to boast about one's wealth – although such boasts can be subtly disguised as moans about the 'silly' prices charged by the posh-paint manufacturers.

Coasters or drink mats (little mats for putting drinks on to stop them damaging the tables) are another fairly useful class-indicator:

you are less likely to find these in upper-middle or upper-class houses, nor will you often see them in lower-working-class homes. Coasters/ drink mats are mainly the preserve of the middle-middle and lower-middle classes, and those among the upper-working class who aspire to middle-class status.

Matching and Newness Rules

Lower-middle and working-class lavatories, which they call toilets, used to have matching coloured loos and basins (which they still call bathroom suites) and even matching coloured loo paper. Those of the upper-middles and above have always been plain white, although you will sometimes see a wooden loo seat.

At the highest and lowest ends of the scale (upper-middle and above, lower-working and below) you will find old, threadbare and mismatched furniture, while the classes in between favour brand-new 'suites' of matching 'settees' and armchairs, 'sets' of matching dining tables and chairs, and yet more 'suites' of bedroom furniture with matching bedspreads, cushions and curtains. (These carefully co-ordinated furnishings may involve cottagey-chintzy flowers, Ikea 'simplicity', or television-inspired 'themes' but the principle is the same.) The upper echelons, proud of their eclectic antiques, look down their noses at matching 'suites'; the lower echelons, ashamed of their ill-assorted cast-offs, aspire to them.

In fact, an English person's social class can be gauged immediately from his or her attitude to expensive brand-new furniture: if you think it is 'posh', you are no higher than middle-middle at best; if you think it is 'naff', you are upper-middle or above. An upper-class Tory MP once sneered at fellow Tory Michael Heseltine by remarking that Heseltine had 'had to buy all his own furniture' – the put-down implication being that only *nouveaux* have to buy their furniture: genuinely upper-class furniture is inherited.

Thanks to the influence of the upper-middle-class interior designers who dominate the many home-improvement programmes on television, some formerly clear class-indicators are no longer so reliable. Middle-middle, lower-middle and even working-class homes may now have wooden floors rather than fitted carpets (and even the

naffest of *nouveaux riches* now avoid the deep-pile variety).
Coloured bathroom suites have been so comprehensively mocked
and vilified on every home-improvement show that people of all
classes now regard them as dated and in poor taste. To the untrained
eye, many middle-middle, lower-middle and upper-working-class
homes may now be hard to distinguish from those of the upper-
middle classes.

Look more closely, however, and you will see that the 'matching and
newness' rules still apply. Only the upper-middles and above seem
consistently free of the irresistible urge to match. Some television-
designer-inspired, upwardly mobile middle-middles may strive for a
more 'eclectic' look – eschewing the three-piece suite, for example,
in favour of less obviously matched sofas and chairs, but they tend
to betray their origins by adding carefully matched (and brand new)
cushions, often with a perfectly 'toning' rug and precisely 'co-ordi-
nating' curtains to complete the effect. They may have avoided the
most glaring signs of petit-bourgeois matching, but it all still looks
new, neat, pristine, effortful and 'designed'. If a room looks like a
photograph from a catalogue, even if the floors are wood and the
principal items of furniture are not matching sets, its owners' origins
are no higher than middle-middle.

When it comes to bathrooms, however, even some upper-middles
have been seduced by the fashion for 'wet rooms', and you may see
brand-new wet rooms, or bathrooms with trendy ultra-modern wash-
basins and other fashionably avant-garde fittings, in some otherwise
poshly shabby homes. The true upper classes, and most of the upper-
middle intelligentsia, have so far resisted these trends – and tend to
look down upon them as flashy and pretentious.

The Brag-wall Rule

Another helpful class-indicator is the siting of what Americans would
call your 'brag wall'. In which room of your house do you display
prestigious awards you have won, or photographs of yourself shaking
hands with famous people? If you are middle-middle or below, these
items might be proudly on show in your sitting room or entrance
hall or some other very prominent place. For the upper-middles and

above, however, the *only* acceptable place to exhibit such things is the downstairs loo.

This trick is 'smart' in both senses of the word (posh and clever): visitors are highly likely to use the downstairs loo at some point, and to be impressed by your achievements, but by displaying them in the loo you are making a joke out of them (taking the piss, even) and thus cannot be accused of either boasting or taking yourself too seriously.

The Satellite-dish Rule

From the outside of an English house, even if you are not familiar with the class-semiotics of plants and flowers, which I will come to later, you can sometimes make a quick broad-brush class assessment based on the presence (lower class) or absence (higher class) of a satellite dish. This is not an infallible indicator, and has become much less reliable with the advent of cable – although many people classify entire neighbourhoods by counting satellite dishes – but a house with a satellite dish can still be classified at the lower end of the social scale until proven otherwise by the presence of unequivocal upper-middle or upper-class features.

A satellite dish on a very grand old house in an upper-class area could, however, be a sign of *nouveau* colonisation. But to be sure, you would have to go inside and look for brand-new leather sofas, fancy Jacuzzi baths and multiple giant televisions. If instead you found faded colours, priceless but threadbare Oriental rugs, shabby damask sofas covered with dog hair and cracked wooden loo seats, you would revise the occupants' social class upwards, and assume that they had some suitable reason for watching satellite television – work in broadcasting or journalism, perhaps (check for BAFTAs in the downstairs loo), a liking for obscure foreign-language programmes or an eccentric passion for basketball or old sit-coms or some other aspect of popular culture.

Having said that, a lot of the lowbrow television channels that previously required satellite are now available on cable, so the higher classes can now indulge without defacing their houses with a 'chavvy' satellite dish. And continue to pretend that they only watch highbrow programmes.

The Eccentricity Clause

Which brings me to a further complicating factor: taste is often judged, in social terms, not by the deed but by the doer. If someone is securely established as a member of a particular class, his or her house may feature a number of exceptions to the rules I have mentioned without any danger of reclassification downwards or upwards. I read somewhere that Princess Anne's house, Gatcombe Park, is cluttered with displays of every gift she has ever received, including the sort of tacky national dolls and cheap African carvings normally only found in working-class 'front rooms'. Such signs of plebeian tastes among the upper classes or even long-established upper-middles are generally regarded as harmless eccentricities.

And it works the other way round as well. I had a friend of impeccable working-class credentials – a school cleaner, living on a run-down council estate – who had a passion for the upper-class equestrian sport of eventing (also known as horse trials, and also, incidentally, favoured by Princess Anne). She kept a horse (free in return for mucking-out) at a nearby riding school, and her council-house kitchen was festooned with rosettes and photographs of herself competing in local hunter trials and one-day events. Her working-class friends and neighbours accepted her 'posh' horsey doings and decorations as an innocuous quirk, a somewhat eccentric hobby that in no way affected her status as their social equal.

This 'eccentricity clause' seems to be most reliably effective at the top and bottom ends of the social scale. The middle-middle, lower-middle, upper-working and even upper-middle zones are more vulnerable to reclassification on the grounds of perceived deviation from the class norm. Here, a single lapse in home-decorating taste may be forgiven or disregarded, but two or more could be damaging. Even among the less vulnerable, it is safest to choose your eccentricity from a class at the opposite end of the scale, rather than from the one immediately adjacent to your own. An upper-middle showing evidence of middle-middle tastes, for example, is much more likely to be suspected and downgraded than an upper-middle with a penchant for an unmistakably proletarian item of furniture or decoration.

In borderline cases, well-intentioned gifts can pose a problem for the class-conscious English. I was once given some very pretty wooden coasters, and not having any tables worth protecting from drink-stains – nor, I must admit, wishing to be suspected of the bourgeois instinct to do so – I use them to prop open my dodgy windows. I could get the broken sashes mended instead, of course, but then what would I do with the coasters? Being English can be quite tricky sometimes.

HOUSE-TALK RULES

Whatever your social class, there are rules governing not only what you must *do* when you move into a house, but also how you should talk about it – or, rather, to be more precise, how you should moan about it.

The 'Nightmare' Rule

When talking about your house-move, it must always be described as traumatic, fraught with difficulty and disruption, even if the process was completed smoothly and without noticeable stress. This rule applies to the initial house-hunting, the purchase of the house, the move itself, any DIY undertaken upon moving in, and 'having the builders in': it is universally understood that all of these are 'a nightmare'. To describe them in any more favourable or even neutral terms would be regarded as odd, possibly even as arrogant – as somehow implying that you are immune to the stresses and upsets afflicting all normal house-buyers.

There is a modesty rule implied here as well. The more grand or desirable your new residence, the more you must emphasise the troubles, inconveniences and 'nightmares' involved in its acquisition and improvement. One does not boast about one's purchase of a beautiful Cotswold cottage or even a château in France: one moans about the awfulness of the estate agents, the carelessness of the removal men, the obtuseness of the local builders or the dire state of the plumbing, roof, floors or garden.

Done well, with just the right air of long-suffering humour, this kind of English moaning can be remarkably convincing, and highly effective in deflecting envy. I have found myself sympathising – *genuinely sympathising* – with the beleaguered new owners of just such bijou cottages and grand châteaux. Even if you are not convinced, and indeed even if you are boiling with envy, resentment or righteous indignation, the correct response is to express sympathy: 'How infuriating!' 'You must be exhausted!' 'What a nightmare!'

At one level, this ritual moaning is, of course, an indirect boast – an excuse to talk about one's new property and convey its attractions without appearing to crow. At the same time, however, it can also be seen as another manifestation of English 'polite egalitarianism', a less invidious form of hypocrisy. The moaners, by emphasising the mundane practical details and difficulties of home-buying or moving, are focusing on problems they and their listeners have in common, matters with which we can all identify, and politely deflecting attention from any potentially embarrassing disparity in wealth or status. I could sympathise with my château-buying friends because their laments centred on the only element of their situation that could be compared with my own humble removals from one cheap flat to another. But this practice is observed by all classes, and in circumstances of much less dramatic income-disparity. Only the most vulgar *nouveaux-riches* break the rule and tell house-move stories that blatantly advertise their superior wealth.

Money-talk Rules

Similar modesty rules apply to the discussion of house prices, compounded by the usual English squeamishness about money-talk. Although conversations about house prices have become a staple at middle-class dinner parties, they are conducted in accordance with a delicate etiquette. It is absolutely forbidden to ask directly what someone paid for their house (or indeed any item in it): this is almost as unforgivably rude as asking them what they earn.

In the interests of science, I deliberately broke this rule a few times. Well, to be honest, I only really did it twice. My first attempt doesn't count, as I hedged my price-enquiry about with so many anxious apologies and qualifiers and excuses (such as a fictitious friend thinking of buying a house in the area) that it could not possibly be considered a direct question. Even so, the experience was not wasted, as the reactions of my unwitting lab-rats indicated that my apologies and excuses were not seen as at all excessive or out of place.

On the two occasions when I managed to steel myself, take a deep breath and ask the house-price question properly (or, rather, improperly), the lab-rats responded with predictable embarrassment. They answered my question, but in an awkward, uncomfortable manner: one forced himself to mutter an approximate price, then hastily changed the subject; the other, a female, laughed nervously and replied with her hand half covering her mouth, while her other guests looked sideways at me, coughed uneasily and exchanged raised-eyebrow glances across the table. Yes, all right: raised eyebrows and a bit of embarrassed throat-clearing are probably the worst that can happen to you when you commit breaches of English dinner-party etiquette, so my experiments might not sound particularly heroic. Maybe you have to be English to know just how wounding those eyebrows and coughs can be.

The house-talk rules also state that it is not done to introduce the price paid for your own house into the conversation without good cause and suitable preamble. The price of your house can only be mentioned 'in context', and even then only if this can somehow be done in a self-deprecating manner, or at least in such a way as to make it clear that you are not engaging in an ostentatious display of wealth. You can mention the price of your house, for example, if you bought it many years ago, for what now seems a ludicrously low sum.

The current *value* of your house, for some unfathomable reason, is a different matter, and may be the subject of endless discussion and speculation – although high property prices, including the estimated value of your own property, must always be described as 'silly', 'crazy', 'absurd' or 'outrageous'. This perhaps gives us a clue as to why value can be discussed while price cannot: it seems that the current value of a house is regarded as a matter entirely outside our control, rather like the weather, while the price actually paid for a house is a clear indicator of a person's financial status.

In times of economic recession, when house prices are falling, these conversations are actually rather more comfortable for the

English, as moaning about the considerably *reduced* value of one's home is so much easier than trying to disguise one's pride in its absurdly inflated value. In general, however, excessive talk about house prices is a class-indicator: if you indulge in too much moaning or speculation about house prices, you may be categorised as a petit-bourgeois reader of the *Daily Mail* (a tabloid newspaper that is much ridiculed for its burning obsession with house prices).

Improvement-talk Rules

Whatever your class or financial status, and whatever the value of the house you are moving into, it is customary to disparage the taste of the previous occupant. If you do not have the time, skill or funds necessary to rip out all evidence of the former owner's bad taste, you must, when showing friends around your new house, sigh deeply, roll your eyes or grimace and say, 'Well, it's not what we would have chosen, obviously, but we'll just have to live with it for the moment,' or, more succinctly, 'We haven't done this room yet.' This will also save your guests from the dire embarrassment of complimenting you on a room that has not been 'done', then having to backtrack with awkward face-savers such as 'Oh, of course, when I say "lovely" I mean the proportions, er, the view, um, er, I mean, it's got such *potential . . .*'

When showing visitors the results of your DIY efforts, or talking about your home-improvements at a party or in the pub, a strict modesty rule applies. Even if you are highly skilled, you must always play down your achievements and, if possible, play up your most embarrassing mistakes and blunders. The SIRC DIY-temple sample of nest-builders, and my own department-store and pub-eavesdropping samples, invariably followed this rule – sometimes even engaging in almost competitive self-deprecation, trying to cap each other's amusing stories of disastrous incompetence. 'I managed to burst three pipes just laying the carpet!'; 'We bought an expensive carpet, but I ruined it by cutting it four inches short, so I had to build some bookcases to cover the gap'; 'I somehow managed to put the sink in the wrong way round – and I'd done all the tiles before I noticed'; 'You think that's bad: it took me an hour and three cups of tea to put up a coat-hook board, and then I found I'd hung it upside-down!'; 'So I painted over the dodgy bit and tried to pretend it was meant to look like that, but my girlfriend was, like, "You complete muppet!"'

If your home has been 'improved' by professional builders, rather than your own DIY efforts, it is customary (as under the moving-nightmare rules above) to indulge in humorous moaning about their incompetence, laziness, etc. Unless the builders in question were Polish, in which case the current convention is to rhapsodise about how skilled, efficient, punctual and courteous they were – although this generally turns, by way of unpatriotic comparisons, into another moan about the ineptitude and indolence of home-grown builders. Revealing the price of your new kitchen or loft-conversion is *only* permitted in the context of nightmare-builders moaning – but even then, do be very careful: the English are well aware that money-related moans can often be disguised boasts. Asking about the cost of someone else's improvements might just, but only just, be permissible if you first apologise for the nosiness and explain that you are considering having similar work done on your house and wondering what the going rate is.

But there is no excuse, ever, for talking about the price of your furniture, curtains, rugs or any other possessions. Or for asking anyone else what they paid for theirs. This would cause considerably more embarrassment than talking about the price of your house or asking someone what their house cost them. As I mentioned above, the taboo on house-price talk is relaxed a bit when prices are falling, as such talk tends to be more anxious than boastful. But talk about the price of furnishings is only ever permitted among immediate family and very close friends, and even then can easily cause offence. The only exception would be if you had picked up the item in question for an astoundingly low bargain price – but it would have to be something like getting a beautiful antique table for two pounds at a car-boot sale to make the disclosure acceptable. An ordinary 50-per-cent-off type of bargain would certainly not justify breaking the money-talk taboo. Even if you did snag an incredible bargain, a brief, casual mention, sounding surprised at your good fortune, is more than enough. Best to throw in a 'Couldn't possibly afford something like this in a real antique shop, of course', even if you could, but don't bang on about the low price you paid and the real value of the item: this will be seen as either boasting about your bargain-hunting skills, or showing an unseemly obsession with money, both equally distasteful.

Class Variations in House-talk Rules

House-talk, like everything else in England, is also subject to class rules. Unless you have recently moved in and are 'housewarming', or happen to live in a particularly odd or unusual house (such as a converted lighthouse or church), it is considered rather lower-class to give visitors guided tours, or to invite them to inspect your new bathroom, kitchen extension, loft conversion or recently redecorated 'front room'. Middle-middles and below are inclined to engage in such ritual displays – and may even invite friends round specifically to show off their new conservatory or kitchen – but among upper-middles and above, this is frowned upon. Among the highest echelons of English society, this affected lack of interest is required of visitors as well as hosts: it is considered incorrect to notice one's surroundings when visiting someone at home, and paying compliments is regarded as decidedly 'naff', if not downright rude. A duke was said to have huffed in outrage, 'Fellow praised my chairs, damned cheek!' after a visit from a new neighbour.

Some traces of this upper-class squeamishness about house-display have trickled down, at least to the middle classes: they may indulge in a bit of showing-off of conservatories and so on, but there are often hints of awkwardness or embarrassment. They will lead you to their new pride-and-joy kitchen, but will then attempt to appear dismissive, indifferent or jokey about it, making modest, self-effacing remarks ('Well, we had to do *something* – it had got into such a state'), damning themselves with faint praise ('At least it's a bit brighter with the skylight') or focusing on the inevitable difficulties ('nightmares') involved in the refurbishment ('It was supposed to take a week, but we've had plaster and dust and total chaos in here for over a month').

Unlike the higher castes, however, these modest middles will not be offended by praise, although it is generally advisable to be vague rather than specific in your compliments. The English tend to be terribly touchy about their homes, and if you are too precise, there is always the danger of praising the wrong aspect of their latest improvement, or praising it in the wrong terms – calling a room 'cosy' or 'cheerful', say, when your hosts were aiming for an impression of stylish elegance. It is best to stick to generic expressions of approbation such as 'lovely' or 'very nice' unless you know the people well enough to be more explicit.

The Awful Estate-agent Rule

This extreme touchiness, evidence of the extent to which our identity is bound up with our homes, helps to explain the universal and apparently quite irrational English dislike of estate agents. You will rarely hear a good word spoken about estate agents in this country: even people who have never had any dealings with them invariably speak of them with contempt. There is a clear unwritten rule to the effect that estate agents must be constantly mocked, sneered at, censured and abused. They are on a par with traffic wardens and double-glazing salesmen – but while the offences of traffic wardens and salesmen are obvious, I found that no one could quite put a finger on exactly what estate agents do to deserve their vilification.

When I asked people to account for their aversion to estate agents, the responses were vague, inconsistent and often contradictory: estate agents were ridiculed as stupid and incompetent 'twits', but also reviled as sly, grasping, cunning and deceitful. Finding it hard to see how estate agents could manage to be simultaneously dim-witted and deviously clever, I eventually gave up pressing for a rational explanation of their unpopularity, and tried instead to look for clues in the detailed mechanics of our interactions with them. What *exactly* do estate agents do? They come to inspect your house, look around it with an objective eye, put a value on it, advertise it, show people round it and try to sell it. What is so terribly offensive about that? Well, everything, if you replace the word 'house' with 'identity', 'personality', 'social status' or 'taste'. Everything that estate agents do involves passing judgement not on some neutral piece of property but on *us*, on our lifestyle, our social position, our character, our private self. And sticking a price tag on it. No wonder we can't stand them. By making them the butt of our jokes and scorn, we minimise their power to hurt our feelings: if estate agents are universally agreed to be stupid, ineffectual and insincere, their opinions and judgements become less meaningful, their intrusions into our private sphere less traumatic.

GARDEN RULES

From our helicopter at the beginning of this chapter we saw that the English all want to live in their own private box with their own private green bit. Indeed, it is our insistence on the private green bit that is, ironically, largely responsible for the desecration of the English countryside, with the construction of 'invincible green suburbs'[60] and all the environmental damage and pollution that they entail. The English simply will not live in flats or share courtyards like urban dwellers in other countries: we must have our private boxes and green bits.[61]

However small, the green bit is at least as important as the box. Tiny scraps of land, which almost anywhere else in the world would be regarded as too insignificant to bother with, are treated as though they were grand country estates. Our moats and drawbridges may be imaginary, but every Englishman's castle has its miniature 'grounds'. Take a typical, undistinguished street in a typical suburban or 'residential' area, with the usual two rows of smallish, nondescript semi-detached or terraced houses – the kind of street in which the vast majority of English people live. Each house will usually have a minuscule patch of garden at the front, and a larger green bit at the back. In slightly more affluent areas, the patch at the front will be a little bigger, and the house set a few feet further back from the road. In less well-off areas, the front patch will shrink to a token

60. As former prime minister John Major called them, in a rather sickly, sentimental speech, for which he was of course much mocked.
61. Of course, we may soon be forced to accept that this insistence on private boxes with private gardens is economically as well as environmentally unsustainable.

tiny strip, although there may still be a front gate, a path to take you the one or two steps to the front door, and a plant or smidgen of greenery of some sort on either side of the path to prove that it still qualifies as a 'front garden'. (The front garden with its path can also be seen as a kind of symbolic moat and drawbridge.)

'Your Own Front Garden, You May Not Enjoy'

In all typical streets of this kind, all of the little patches of garden, front and back, will have walls or fences around them. The wall around the front garden will be low, so that everyone can see into the garden, while the one enclosing the back garden will be high, so they can't. The front garden is likely to be more carefully arranged, designed and tended than the back garden. This is not because the English spend more time enjoying their front gardens. Quite the opposite: the English spend no time at all in their front gardens, except the time necessary to weed, water, tend and keep them looking 'nice'.

This is one of the most important garden-rules: we never, ever *sit* in our front gardens. Even when there is plenty of room in a front garden for a garden seat of some sort, you will never see one. Not only would it be unthinkable to sit in your front garden, you will be considered odd if you even stand there for very long without squatting to pull up a weed or stooping to trim the hedge. If you are not squatting, stooping, bending or otherwise looking busy and industrious, you will be suspected of a peculiar and forbidden form of loitering.

Front gardens, however pretty and pleasant they might be to relax in, are for display only; they are for others to enjoy and admire, not their owners. This rule always reminds me of the laws of tribal societies with complicated gift-exchange systems, in which people are not allowed to consume the fruits of their own labour: 'Your own pigs, you may not eat.' is the most famous and frequently quoted tribal example; the English equivalent would be 'Your own front garden, you may not enjoy.'

The Front-garden Social-availability Rule
(and 'Sponge' Methodology)

If you do spend time squatting, bending and pruning in your front garden, you may find that this is one of the very few occasions on which your neighbours will speak to you. A person busy in his or her front garden is regarded as socially 'available', and neighbours who would never dream of knocking on your front door may stop for a chat (almost invariably beginning with a comment on the weather or a polite remark about your garden). In fact, I know of many streets in which people who have an important matter to discuss with a neighbour (such as an application for planning permission), or a message to convey, will wait patiently – sometimes for days or weeks – until they spot the neighbour in question working in his front garden, rather than committing the 'intrusion' of actually ringing his doorbell.

This social availability of front-gardeners proved very helpful during my research, as I could approach them with an innocuous request for directions, follow this with a weather-speak ice-breaker and a comment on their garden, and gradually get them talking about their gardening habits, their home improvements, their pets, their children and so on. Sometimes, I would pretend that I (or my mother or sister or cousin) was thinking of moving to the area, which gave me an excuse to ask more nosy questions about the neighbours, the local pubs, schools, shops, clubs, societies and events – and find out a lot about their unwritten social rules. In front-garden interviews, although I might sometimes focus on a specific current obsession, such as, say, the estate-agent question, I would often just soak up a whole lot of random data on a variety of subjects, and hope to make sense of it all at some later stage. This is not such a daft research method as it might sound – in fact, I think there may even be an official scientific name for it, but I can never remember the correct term, so I call it the 'sponge' method.

The Counter-culture Garden-sofa Exception

There is just one minority exception to the 'Your own front garden, you may not enjoy' principle, and as usual, it is one that proves the rule. The front gardens of left-over hippies, New Agers and various other 'counter-culture' types may sometimes boast an old, sagging sofa, on which the inhabitants will sit, self-consciously defying convention and actually enjoying their front garden (which, also in defiance of convention, will be unkempt and overgrown).

This 'exception' to the no-sitting-in-front-gardens rule is clearly an act of deliberate disobedience: the seat is always a sofa, never a wooden bench or plastic chair or any other piece of furniture that might possibly be regarded as suitable for outdoor use. This flaccid, often damp and eventually rotting sofa is a statement, and one that tends to be found in conjunction with other statements, such as eating organic vegan food, smoking ganja, wearing the latest eco-warrior fashions, decorating the windows with anti-fracking posters . . . the themes and fashions vary, but you know what I mean: the usual counter-culture cluster.

The garden-sofa sitters may be the subject of much tutting and puffing among their more conservative neighbours, but in accordance with the traditional English rules of moaning, the curtain-twitchers will usually just air their grievances to each other, rather than actually confronting the offenders. In fact, as long as the sofa-sitters abide by their own clearly defined set of counter-culture rules and conventions, and do not do anything original or startling – such as joining the local Women's Institute or taking up golf – they will generally be tolerated, with that sort of grudging, apathetic forbearance for which the English seem to have a peculiar talent.

The Back-garden Formula

The back garden, the one we are all allowed to enjoy, is often relatively scruffy, or at least utterly bland, and only very rarely the pretty, colourful, cottagey profusion of roses, hollyhocks, pansies, trellises, little gates and whatnot that everyone thinks of as a typical English garden. It is verging on blasphemous to say this, but I have to point out that the truly typical English back garden is actually a fairly dull rectangle of grass, with some sort of paved 'patio' at one end and a shed of no particular aesthetic or architectural merit at the other, a path down one side and perhaps a bed of rather unimaginatively arranged shrubs and flowers along the other side.

There are variations on this theme, of course. The path may run alongside the flower-bed, or down the middle of the grass rectangle, with flower-beds along both walls. There may be a tree or two. Or some bushes or pots, or maybe climbing-plants on the walls. The edges of the flower-beds may be curved rather than straight. But the basic pattern of the conventional English garden – the 'high walls, paved bit, grass bit, path, flower bed, shed' formula – is reassuringly unmistakable, instantly identifiable, comfortingly familiar. This pattern must be somehow imprinted on the English soul, as it is reproduced faithfully, with only minor twists and variations, behind almost every house in every street in the country.[62]

Tourists are unlikely ever to see an ordinary, typical English back garden. These very private places are hidden from the street behind our houses, and even hidden from our neighbours by high walls, hedges or fences. They never feature in glossy picture-books about The English Garden, and are never mentioned in tourist brochures or indeed in any other publications about England, all of which invariably parrot the received wisdom that the English are a nation of green-fingered creative geniuses. That is because the authors of these books do not do their research by spending time in ordinary people's homes, or climbing onto roofs and walls at the back of standard suburban semis and peering through binoculars at the rows and rows of normal, undistinguished English gardens. (Now you know: that person you thought was a burglar or a peeping Tom was me.) Aesthetically, it must be said, the duped tourists, Anglophiles and garden enthusiasts who read this English Garden stuff are perhaps not missing much.

But I am being unfair. The average English garden, however unoriginal and humdrum, is actually, on a mild sunny day, a rather pleasant place to sit and drink a cup of tea and chuck bits of bread about

62. If you don't believe me, try looking out of the window of a train next time you are travelling anywhere in England: I can guarantee that almost all of the back gardens you see will be variations on this 'formula'. An Anglophile American friend was reluctantly converted to my theory when she tried this experiment.

for the birds and grumble quietly about slugs, the weather forecast, the government and the neighbours' cat. (The rules of garden-talk require that such moans be balanced by more cheerful noticing of how well the irises or columbines are doing this year.)

And it must also be said that even the average, bog-standard English garden represents considerably more effort than most other nations typically invest in their green bits. The average American garden, for example, does not even deserve the name, and is rightly called a 'yard', and most ordinary European gardens are also just patches of turf.[63] Only the Japanese – our fellow crowded-small-island-dwellers – can be said to make a comparable effort, and it is perhaps no coincidence that trendy, design-conscious English gardeners are often influenced by Japanese styles (witness the fashions for pebbles, raked sand and water-features). But these avant-gardeners are a tiny minority, and it seems to me that our reputation as a 'nation of gardeners' must derive from our *obsession* with our small patches of turf, our *love* of gardens, rather than any remarkable artistic flair in garden design.

The NSPCG Rule

Our ordinary back gardens may not be particularly beautiful, but almost all show evidence of interest, attention and effort. Gardening is probably the most popular hobby in the country – at the last count, at least two-thirds of the population were described as 'active gardeners'. (Reading this, I couldn't help wondering what 'passive gardening' might consist of – would being irritated by the noise of other people's lawnmowers count, like passive smoking? – but the point is clear enough.)

Almost all English houses have a garden of some sort, and almost all gardens are tended and cared for. Some are tended more carefully and expertly than others, but you rarely see a completely neglected garden. If you do, there is a reason for it: the house may be

---

63. Although the English passion for gardening has been catching on in some other European countries – particularly in Germany, where I am told that translations of English gardening books are very popular.

unoccupied, or rented by a group of students (who feel it is the landlord's responsibility to do the garden); or occupied by someone for whom neglecting the garden constitutes some sort of ideological or lifestyle statement; or by someone who is poor, deprived, disabled or depressed and has more serious problems than weeds or untidy lawns to worry about.

This last category may be grudgingly forgiven, but you can be sure that the others will be the subject of much muttering and tut-tutting among the neighbours. There is a sort of unofficial National Society for the Prevention of Cruelty to Gardens, for whose members the neglect of a garden is on a par with the mistreatment of animals or children.

The NSPCG rule, perhaps as much as our genuine interest in gardening, may explain why we feel obliged to devote so much time and effort to our gardens.[64]

Class Rules

The garden historian Charles Quest-Ritson boldly rejects the rather pretentious current vogue for studying gardening as an art form and garden history as a branch of the history of art. Gardening, he says, 'has little to do with the history of art or the development of aesthetic theories . . . It is all about social aspirations, lifestyles, money and class.' I am inclined to agree with him, as my own research on the English and their gardens suggests that the design and content of an English person's garden is largely determined – or at least very strongly influenced – by the fashions of the class to which he or she belongs, or to which he or she aspires.

'Why,' asks Quest-Ritson, 'do hundreds of middle-class English women have a white garden and a potager and a collection of old-fashioned roses? Because these features are smart, or may have been smart about ten years ago – not because their owners think they are beautiful or useful, but because they make them feel good, better

---

64. For stats-junkies: in the latest national census survey, 52 per cent of men and 45 per cent of women reported that they had spent time gardening in the four weeks prior to the census date.

than the neighbours. Gardens are symbols of social and economic status.' I would soften this slightly, and suggest that we may not be quite as *conscious* of the socio-economic determinants of our flower-beds as Quest-Ritson implies. We may genuinely think that our class-bound choices of plants and designs are beautiful – although this does not make them any less socially determined.

Class Indicators and the Eccentricity Clause

Our taste is influenced by what we see in the gardens of our friends, family and neighbours. In England, you grow up learning to find some flowers and arrangements of flowers 'pretty' or 'tasteful' and others 'ugly' or 'vulgar'. By the time you have your own garden, you will, if you are from the higher social ranks, instinctively turn up your nose at gaudy bedding plants (such as zinnias, salvia, marigolds and petunias), ornate rockeries, pampas grass, hanging baskets, busy lizzies, chrysanthemums, gladioli, gnomes and goldfish ponds. You will, on the other hand, be likely to find other horticultural (haugh-tycultural?) features such as box hedges, old-fashioned shrub roses, herbaceous borders, clematis, laburnum, Tudor-revival/Arts-and-Crafts patterns and York stone paths aesthetically pleasing.

Garden fashions change, and in any case it would be a mistake to be too precise and attempt to classify a garden socially on the basis of one or two flowers or features. The 'eccentricity clause' applies here as well, as Quest-Ritson observes: 'Once a garden-owner has acquired a reputation as a general plantsman, it is quite permissible for him to express a tenderness for the unfashionable, the plebeian and the naff.' I would say that being firmly and unequivocally established as a member of the upper- or upper-middle classes would be enough, with or without plantsmanship, but the point is much the same. The odd garden gnome or zinnia does not necessarily result in automatic demotion, but may be tolerated as a personal idiosyncrasy.

To gauge the social class of a garden owner, it is therefore better to look at the general style of the garden, rather than becoming too obsessed with the class-semiotics of individual plants – particularly if you can't tell an old-fashioned rose from a hybrid tea. As a rule-of-thumb, gardens lower down the social scale tend to be both more garish (their owners would say 'colourful' or 'cheerful') and more regimented in appearance (their owners would call them 'neat' or 'tidy') than those at the higher end.

Higher-class gardens tend to look more casual, more natural, less effortful, with more faded or subtle colours. Like the 'natural look' in make-up, this effect may require a great deal of time and effort to achieve – perhaps more than the pastry-cut flowerbeds and disciplined rows of flowers of the lower-class garden – but the effort does not show; the impression is of a charming, uncontrived confusion, usually with little or no earth visible between the plants. Excessive fretting and fussing about the odd weed or two and over-zealous manicuring of lawns are regarded, by the upper classes and upper-middles, as rather lower class.

The wealthier uppers, of course, have lower-class gardeners to do their fretting and manicuring for them, so their gardens may sometimes look rather too neat – but if you talk to them, you will find that they often complain about the perfectionism of their gardeners ('Fred's a dreadful fusser – has a fit if a daisy dares to rear its ugly head on "his" lawn!') in the same patronising way that some businessmen and professionals mock the tidiness of their super-efficient secretaries ('Oh, I'm not allowed *near* the filing cabinet – I might mess up her precious colour-coding system!').

The Ironic-gnome Rule

Leaving aside the proletarian neatness of paid gardeners, if you do spot an unexpectedly and unmistakably plebeian feature in a higher-class garden, it is worth asking the owner about it. The response will tell you much more about the owner's class than the feature itself. I once expressed mild surprise at the presence of a garden gnome in a very grand and tasteful garden (I said something intelligent like 'Oh, a gnome'). The owner of the garden explained that the gnome was 'ironic'. I asked him, with apologies for my ignorance, how one could tell that his garden gnome was supposed to be an ironic statement, as opposed to, you know, just a gnome. He rather sniffily replied that I had only to look at the rest of the garden for it to be obvious that the gnome was a tongue-in-cheek joke.

But surely, I persisted, garden gnomes are always something of a joke, in any garden – I mean, no one actually takes them seriously or regards them as works of art. His response was rather rambling and confused (not to mention somewhat huffy), but the gist seemed to be that while the lower classes saw gnomes as *intrinsically* amusing, his gnome was amusing only because of its incongruous appearance in a 'smart' garden. In other words, council-house gnomes were a joke, but his gnome was a joke about council-house tastes, effectively a joke about class. A subtle but clearly very important distinction. Needless to say, I was not invited back.

This man's reaction to my questions clearly defined him as inse-cure-upper-middle, rather than upper class. In fact, his pointing out that the gnome I had noticed was 'ironic' had already demoted him by half a class from my original assessment. A genuine member of the upper classes would either have boldly admitted to a passion for garden gnomes (and eagerly pointed out other examples of the genre dotted about his otherwise effortlessly elegant garden) or said some-thing like 'Ah, yes, my gnome. I'm very fond of my gnome,' and left me to draw my own conclusions. The upper classes do not care what a nosy anthropologist (or indeed anyone else) thinks of them, and in any case do not need ironic gnomes to emphasise their status.

HOME RULES AND ENGLISHNESS

Can the unwritten rules of English homes and gardens help to clarify, refine or expand our 'grammar' of Englishness? Have we found or confirmed any more candidates for 'defining characteristic' status? Given that our homes and gardens are two of our principal obses-sions, it would be surprising if an analysis of their underlying rules did not yield some helpful insights into our national character.

All humans have a territorial instinct, but the English obsession with our homes and mania for nest-building goes much further than this. Almost all commentators have remarked on this English home-fixation, but none has yet offered a satisfactory explanation. Jeremy

Paxman comes closest to an understanding of this characteristic when he says that '"Home" is what the English have instead of a Fatherland,' echoing (although he does not mention it) the sentiment of the Edwardian rhyme 'The Germans live in Germany/ The Romans live in Rome/The Turkeys live in Turkey/ But the English live at home.' But this does not entirely explain why we should be so neurotically obsessive about our homes. Attempts to attribute our home-fixation to the English climate are unconvincing – other countries have weather conditions much more likely to drive their inhabitants indoors, but do not share our fanatical nesting tendencies.

Historical explanations can be equally misleading. Harry Mount, in *How England Made the English,* claims that 'a lack of invasions since 1066 – and of civil wars for over 350 years – has led to a confidence that property rights will last forever, and so to the high percentage of home ownership in England.' This sounds plausible, until one looks at international statistics on home ownership, in which we score a measly one per cent or so above the international average, with a much lower rate of home ownership than many countries, Europe and elsewhere, who have suffered far more recent invasions, civil wars etc. If anything the figures demonstrate the opposite of Mount's theory: the most recently troubled, unstable, precarious countries tend to have the *highest* rates of home ownership.

Within Europe, for example, Romania tops the list with 97.5 per cent, closely followed by Lithuania, Croatia and Slovakia (all with over 90 per cent); we are well below this on 64 per cent, and neutral, peaceful Switzerland has the lowest home-ownership rate of all, 44.3 per cent. Although we are indeed *currently* obsessed with property ownership, our home-obsession long pre-dates this. As Mount points out, the notion that 'an Englishman's home is his castle' was first invoked in English law in 1623, but this had nothing to do with what he calls 'an affection for property ownership'. At the time, only a very tiny fraction of the English owned their homes. The popular precept enshrined into law by Sir Edward Coke was about *privacy,* not property, about refuge and *freedom from intrusion*, not ownership. The full quote from Coke's *Institutes of the Laws of England* makes this clear: 'A man's house is his castle – *et domus sua cuique est tutissimum refugium.*' The Latin bit means: 'and each man's home is his safest refuge.' Or, as William Pitt (then Prime Minister) explained in 1763, what is meant by 'castle' is that 'the poorest man may in his cottage [which would have been a 'tied' or rented cottage] bid defiance to all the forces of the crown. It may be frail – its roof may shake . . . the rain may enter – but the King of England cannot enter.' Even in 1918, nearly 300 years after the establishment of the 'castle' law, 77 per cent of the English did not own their homes, and as recently as 1970 there were still more renters than owners. Our current mania for ownership is of very recent origin, shared with many other countries, and should not be confused with our deep-seated, centuries-old passion for privacy.

I think that some more helpful insights into our home-obsession can be found in the 'rules of Englishness' that we have identified in this and previous chapters. The moat-and-drawbridge rule represents the fifth 'sighting' so far of the English fixation with privacy (a preoccupation also evident in the awful-estate-agent rule, the front-garden rules and the back-garden formula) and at least the tenth or eleventh occurrence of the social-inhibition theme. My hunch at this stage is that these are likely to qualify as 'defining characteristics' of Englishness, and that they are closely connected. It seems to me that our home-obsession is directly related to our almost pathological need for privacy, and that this in turn is inextricably bound up with our problems of social inhibition and embarrassment – our lack of ease and skill in social interaction.

The English seem to have three main ways of dealing with this 'social dis-ease': one is the ingenious use of props and facilitators to overcome our inhibitions and mask our incompetence; another is to become aggressive; the one that concerns us here is the tendency to retreat into the privacy and sanctuary of our castle-like homes, shut the door, pull up the imaginary drawbridge and avoid the issue. Home may indeed be our substitute for a Fatherland, but at another level, I would suggest that *home is what the English have instead of social skills*.

The class rules reveal a new aspect of our acute class-consciousness – which I call the 'adjacent classes problem'. We noted that it is always safest to choose one's eccentricity from a class at the opposite end of the social scale, rather than from an immediately adjacent class. Each English class particularly despises the one immediately below it, and the prospect of being mistaken for a member of this adjacent class is therefore especially abhorrent.

The brag-wall rule reflects another kind of typically English hypocrisy, and brings us back to the recurring theme of humour. In this case, we see the use of wit and humour as a sort of cover for breaking the modesty and anti-earnestness rules. The house-talk 'nightmare' rule reminds us, again, of the English penchant for moaning, but is also yet another manifestation of the modesty rule, which must surely be a strong contender for 'defining characteristic' status. The nightmare rule is also a hypocritical 'cover': a way of boasting without appearing to boast. (Hypocrisy seems to be yet another recurring theme.)

The improvement-talk rules highlight an extreme version of the generic modesty rule, involving an exercise in competitive modesty that can only be described as 'one-downmanship'. Other nations have rituals of polite modesty and self-deprecation (the Japanese immediately spring to mind here), but the English improvement-talk one-downmanship is distinctive for the importance of *humour*: it is not enough merely to speak disparagingly of one's incompetent DIY efforts (in the way that, say, Japanese etiquette requires denigration of a gift one is offering), one must do so in a witty and amusing manner.

The 'non-specific praise' requirement raises a misunderstanding about English 'reserve' and politeness that needs to be addressed. There is a distinctively English form of bland, insipid politeness, which is primarily concerned, even when paying compliments, with the avoidance of offence or embarrassment rather than with actually giving pleasure or expressing positive feelings. This reserve, which foreigners often interpret as coldness or standoffishness, must be understood in the light of the crucial distinction the English make between friends and acquaintances, and between friends and close friends. It is not that the English are cold or incapable of being open and expressive, it is just that we find it more difficult than many other cultures to be uninhibited among people we do not know well – and this reticence in turn means that it takes us longer to get to know people well enough to shed our inhibitions. A vicious circle resulting in, among many other problems, misuse of alcohol and chronic overuse of the word 'nice'.

The awful-estate-agent rule highlights not only the extent to which our identity is bound up with our homes, but also, again, the importance of humour in English culture. Estate agents are an intrusive threat to our sense of identity, so we 'neutralise' their power by making fun of them. This is to some extent a universal human coping mechanism: in all cultures, people who are perceived to be threatening tend to be the subject of such defensive jokes, but the use of this strategy does seem to be more marked, and more frequently employed, among the English than elsewhere. We use humour to deal not only with the threatening or unfamiliar but with any and every social or practical difficulty, from the most trivial problems to issues of national importance.

Both the front- and back-garden rules confirm the English pre-occupation with privacy. The front-garden rules also highlight the related themes of social inhibition and politeness: if home equals self, the front garden is our 'public face' – formal and carefully arranged in the horticultural equivalent of a blank social smile.

The counter-culture garden-sofa exception underlines the now familiar themes of 'orderly disorder' and ineffectual but socially therapeutic moaning – but it also brings to light a rather more amiable quality: a distinctive English capacity for *tolerance*. Admittedly, our tolerance of counter-culture sofas and other odd behaviour tends to be grudging and stoical rather than warm and open-hearted – but even this passive, grumbling forbearance is worth noting, and perhaps worthy of commendation. It may be the quality responsible for the relatively good race relations in this country (the key word here is 'relatively', of course: race relations in England are, as Jeremy Paxman puts it, 'by and large, not bad' only in comparison with other much less tolerant nations).

The back-garden formula, as well as dispelling a few rose-tinted myths about The English Garden, highlights the quiet, restrained aspects of Englishness, our dislike of flashy extremes, our predilection for moderation, for domesticity, for the comfortably tame and familiar. The NSPCG rule also indicates a strong tendency to comply with unwritten social rules and expectations, a sense of duty and obligation. Finally, the class rules, the eccentricity clause and the ironic-gnome rule remind us of the convoluted nature of English class distinctions, and also the complexities of the rules governing English eccentricity. We find that contrived eccentricities, such as ironic gnomes, can backfire: idiosyncrasies and unconventional tastes are applauded only if they are seen to be genuine, unaffected – products of authentic nuttiness, not manufactured foibles.

I am now starting to see some patterns, which may lead to the development of a diagram that will encapsulate not only the defining characteristics of Englishness, but also the relationships and interactions among these core qualities. I am not good at diagrams – I tried to do one once of a particular kind of social network I was studying, and it looked like the webs produced by spiders on LSD – but, if the next few chapters help to clarify the 'grammatical' relationships between rules of Englishness, it should be possible even for me to represent these on a chart of some sort.

RULES OF THE ROAD

If home is what the insular, inhibited English have instead of social skills, how do we cope when we venture outside our castles? The quick answer, as you might expect, is 'not very well'. But after more than twenty years of participant observation in railway stations, on buses and on the streets, I should be a bit more specific than that, and try to decipher the unwritten codes of conduct involved. I'm calling these 'rules of the road' for shorthand, but I'm really talking about every kind of transport – cars, trains, aeroplanes, taxis, buses, bicycles, motorbikes, feet, etc. – and every aspect of the process of getting from A to B.

Speaking of cars, I should mention that I can't drive. I did try to learn, once, but after a few lessons the driving instructor and I agreed that it was not a good idea, and that I could save a lot of innocent lives by sticking to public transport. From a research point of view, this apparent handicap has proved a blessing in disguise, as it means that I get to spend a lot of time observing English behaviour and conducting devious little field-experiments on trains and buses, and interviewing captive taxi drivers about the quirks and habits of their passengers. And whenever I do travel by car, some long-suffering friend or relative is always doing the driving, which leaves me free to scrutinise their behaviour and that of other road users.

PUBLIC TRANSPORT RULES

But I'll start with the rules of behaviour on public transport, as these more graphically illustrate the problems faced by the English when we step outside the security and privacy of our homes.

The Denial Rule

Our main coping mechanism on public transport is a form of what psychologists call 'denial': we try to avoid acknowledging that we are among a scary crowd of strangers, and to maintain as much privacy as possible, by pretending that they do not exist – and, much of the time, pretending that we do not exist either. The denial rule requires us to avoid talking to strangers, or even making eye contact with them, or indeed acknowledging their presence in any way unless absolutely necessary. At the same time, the rule imposes an obligation to avoid drawing attention to oneself and to mind one's own business.

It is common, and considered entirely normal, for English commuters to make their morning and evening train journeys with the same group of people for many years without ever exchanging a word. The more you think about this, the more utterly incredible it seems, yet everyone I spoke to confirmed the story.

'After a while,' one commuter told me, 'if you see the same person every morning on the platform, and maybe quite often sit opposite them on the train, you might start to just nod to each other when you arrive, but that's about as far as it goes.'

'How long is "a while"?' I asked.

'Oh, maybe a year or so – it depends. Some people are more outgoing than others, you know?'

'Right,' I said (wondering what definition of 'outgoing' she could possibly have in mind). 'So, a particularly "outgoing" person might start to greet you with a nod after seeing you every morning for say, what, a couple of months?'

'Mm, well, maybe,' my informant sounded doubtful, 'but actually that would be a bit, um, forward – a bit pushy. That would make me a bit uncomfortable.'

This informant – a young woman working as a secretary for a PR agency in London – was not an especially shy or retiring person. In fact, I would have described her as quite the opposite: a friendly, lively, gregarious extravert. I am quoting her here because her responses are typical – almost all of the commuters I interviewed said that even a brief nod constituted a fairly drastic escalation of intimacy, and most were highly cautious about progressing to this stage because, as another typical commuter (a man in his late thirties, commuting daily from Skipton into Leeds) explained, 'Once you start greeting people like that – nodding, I mean – unless you're very careful, you might end up starting to say "good morning" or something, and then you could end up actually having to *talk* to them.' I recorded other commuters using expressions such as 'tip of the iceberg' and 'slippery slope' to explain their avoidance of premature nodding, or even making eye contact with other commuters (eye contact in public places in England is never more than a fraction of a second: if you do accidentally meet a stranger's eye, you must look away immediately – to maintain eye contact for even a full second may be interpreted as either flirtation or aggression).

But what would be so awful, I asked each of my informants, about a brief friendly chat with a fellow commuter? This was clearly regarded as an exceptionally stupid question. Obviously, the problem with actually speaking to a fellow commuter was that if you did it once, you might be expected to do it again – and again, and again: having acknowledged the person's existence, you could not go back to pretending that they did not exist, and you might end up having to exchange polite words with them *every day*. You would almost certainly have nothing in common, so these conversations would be highly awkward and embarrassing. Or else you would have to find ways of avoiding the person – standing at the other end of the platform, for example, or hiding behind the coffee kiosk, and deliberately choosing a different compartment on the train, which would be rude and equally embarrassing. The whole thing would become a nightmare; it didn't bear thinking about.

I laughed at all this at first, of course, but after a little soul-searching realised that I have often practised much the same kind of contact-avoidance myself, and actually with rather less justification. How can I laugh at the fears and elaborate avoidance strategies of English commuters when I employ much the same tactics to save myself from a mere half-hour or so of potentially uncomfortable interaction on a one-off journey? They could be 'stuck with' someone *every day* for *years*. They're right: it doesn't bear thinking about. Best not even to nod for at least a year, definitely.

The one exception to my utterly typical English behaviour on public transport is when I am in 'fieldwork mode' – that is, when I have burning questions to ask or hypotheses to test, and I am actively looking for 'subjects' to interview or upon whom to conduct experiments. Other forms of fieldwork, such as simple observation, are entirely compatible with squeamishly English contact-avoidance – in fact, the researcher's notebook serves as a useful barrier-signal. But to interview people or conduct field-experiments, I have to take a deep breath and try to overcome my fears and inhibitions. When interviewing the English on public transport, I have to overcome their inhibitions as well. In a sense, all my field-interviews with commuters and other bus, train and tube passengers were also experiments in rule-breaking, as by speaking to them at all I was automatically in breach of the denial rule. Whenever possible, therefore, I tried to minimise the distress (for both of us) by taking advantage of one of the exceptions to the denial rule.

Exceptions to the Denial Rule

There are three situations in which one is allowed to break the denial rule, acknowledge the existence of other passengers, and actually speak directly to them.

The Politeness Exception

The first situation is one I call the 'politeness exception': when not speaking would constitute a greater rudeness than the invasion of privacy by speaking – such as when one accidentally bumps into people and must apologise, or when one must say, 'Excuse me,' to get past them, or ask if the seat next to them is free, or if they mind having the window open. It is important to note, however, that these politenesses are *not* regarded as ice-breakers or legitimate preludes to any further conversation: having made your necessary apology or request, you must immediately revert to the denial state, both parties pretending that the other does not exist. The politeness exception is therefore not of much use for research purposes, except as a means of gauging the degree of distress or irritation likely to be caused by any attempt at further interaction: if the response to my polite apology or request was grudgingly monosyllabic, or a mere non-verbal signal such as a curt nod, I would be less inclined to regard the person as a potential informant.

The Information Exception

Somewhat more helpful was the 'information exception', whereby one may break the denial rule to ask another passenger for vital information, such as 'Sorry, is this the right train for Paddington?' or 'Sorry, do you know if this one stops at Reading?' or ''Scuse me, sorry, but do you know if this is the right platform for Clapham Junction?'[65] The responses to such questions are often mildly humorous: I've lost count of the number of times my panicky 'Is this the right train for Paddington?' has prompted replies such as 'Well, I certainly hope so!' or 'If it's not, I'm in trouble!' When I ask: 'Is this the fast train to London?' (meaning the direct train, as opposed to the 'stopping' train that calls at lots of small stations), some Eeyorish wit is sure to respond with 'Well, depends what you mean by "fast" . . .' (I have even had this jokey reply from conductors and railway-station staff.) Although technically the same principle applies as with the politeness exception, in that one is supposed to revert to the denial state once the necessary information has been imparted, the more humorous responses can sometimes indicate a greater willingness to exchange at least a few more words – particularly if one can subtly engineer the conversation towards the 'moan exception' category.

The Moan Exception

The 'moan exception' to the denial rule normally only occurs when something goes wrong – such as an announcement over the loudspeakers that the train or plane will be delayed or cancelled, or the train or tube stopping in the middle of nowhere or in a tunnel for no apparent reason, or an inordinately long wait for the bus to change drivers, or some other unforeseen problem or disruption.

65. The 'sorries' are a standard prefix to any question in this context – I explain this later in Bumping Experiments and the Reflex-apology Rule, page 234.

On these occasions, English passengers appear suddenly to become aware of each other's existence. Our reactions are always the same and minutely predictable, almost as though they had been choreographed. A loudspeaker platform announcement of a delayed train, or an abrupt jerking stop in the middle of the countryside, prompts an immediate outbreak of sociable body language: people make eye contact; sigh noisily; exchange long-suffering smiles, shrugs, raised eyebrows and eye-rolling grimaces – invariably followed or accompanied by snide or weary comments on the dire state of the railway system. Someone will always say, 'Huh, *typical*!' Another will say, 'Oh, *now* what?' or 'For Christ's sake, what is it *this* time?' or the more succinct ''Kinell!'

Nowadays, you will also often hear at least one comment containing the phrase 'the wrong sort of . . .', a reference to the now legendary excuses offered by the railway operators when 'leaves on the line' (and, on a later occasion, snow) caused extensive disruptions to large parts of the railway system. When it was pointed out to them that fallen leaves were a perfectly normal feature of autumn (and snow not exactly unprecedented in winter) and had never previously brought the railways to a halt, they responded plaintively that these were 'the wrong sort of leaves' (and 'the wrong sort of snow'). These admittedly daft remarks made headlines in all the newspapers and news broadcasts at the time, and have been a standing joke ever since. The joke is often adapted to suit the circumstances of the delay or disruption in question: if the loudspeaker announcement blames rain for the delay, someone will invariably say, 'The wrong sort of rain, I suppose!' I was once waiting for a train at my local station in Oxford when the loudspeaker announced a delay due to 'a cow on the line outside Banbury'.[66] Three people on the platform simultaneously piped up: 'The wrong sort of cow!'

Such problems seem to have an instant bonding effect on English

---

66. This is not as improbable as it might sound: cows on the line are quite a frequent problem in this country. According to one Network Rail report, cows are the fifth most common reason for train delays and cancellations, causing 15 cancellations in just one month in 2011, for example, so many regular rail passengers will have heard a similar announcement at least once.

passengers, clearly based on the 'them and us' principle. The opportunity to moan or, even better, the opportunity to indulge in *witty* moaning, is irresistible. The moan-fests prompted by delayed trains or other public-transport disruptions are very much like weather-moaning: utterly pointless, in that we all know and stoically accept that nothing can or will be done to remedy the situation, but enjoyable and highly effective as facilitators of social interaction.

The moan exception turns out, however, to be yet another of those 'exceptions that prove the rule'. Although we appear to break the denial rule to indulge in this favourite pastime, and may even engage in quite prolonged discussion of the flaws and failings of the relevant public-transport system (and by extension the incompetence of the authorities, companies or government departments deemed responsible for its inadequacies), it is universally understood that such conversations are a 'one-off'. What is involved is not a true breach of the denial rule, but a temporary suspension. Commuters know that they can share an enjoyable moan about a delayed train without incurring any obligation to talk to their fellow moaners again the next morning, or even to acknowledge their existence. The denial rule is suspended only for the duration of the collective whinge. Once we have completed our moan, silence is resumed, and we can go back to ignoring each other for another year or so – or until the next plague of delinquent leaves or suicidal cows. The moan exception proves the rule precisely because it is specifically recognised as an exception.

The temporary suspension of the denial rule during moaning opportunities does, however, offer the intrepid researcher a little chink in the privacy armour of the English commuter – a brief chance to ask a few pertinent questions without seeming to pry or intrude. I had to be quick, though, to avoid giving the impression that I had misunderstood the strictly temporary nature of the moan exception and was settling in for a long chat.

Waiting for moan-worthy mishaps and disruptions may sound like a rather unsatisfactory and unreliable way to conduct field-research interviews – if you are unfamiliar with the vagaries of English public transport, that is. Anyone who lives in England will know that few journeys are completed without at least one delay or interruption, and if you are English (and generous-spirited), you will no doubt be pleased to hear that there is one person in the country who actively benefits from all those leaves, cows, floods, engine troubles, bottle-necks, AWOL drivers, signal faults, points failures and other obscure malfunctions and obstructions.

Apart from moan-exception interview opportunities, public transport was one of the field locations in which I was often obliged to conduct 'formal' interviews, by which I mean interviews where the subjects knew that they were being interviewed. My preferred method of disguising interviews as casual, ordinary conversations – a highly effective technique at pub bar counters, at the races, at parties and other locations where conversation between strangers is permitted (although regulated by strict protocols) – was not suitable in environments subject to the denial rule. Under these conditions, it was less threatening to come clean and tell people that I was doing research for a book, asking politely if they would mind answering 'just a couple of questions', rather than attempting to break the denial rule and engage them in spontaneous chat. A researcher with a notebook is a nuisance, of course, but much less scary than a random stranger trying to start a conversation for no apparent reason. If you simply start chatting to English people on trains or buses, they tend to assume that you are either drunk, drugged or deranged.[67] Social scientists are not universally liked or appreciated, but we are still marginally more acceptable than alcoholics and escaped lunatics.

This formal approach was not necessary with foreigners, however, as they do not suffer from English fears, inhibitions and privacy obsessions, and seemed generally quite happy to engage in casual chat. In fact, many tourists were positively delighted to encounter,

67. If you are female, lone males may instead assume that you are chatting them up. They are therefore more than willing to break the denial rule and talk to you, but it can then be difficult to extricate yourself from the conversation. Even the 'formal interview' approach can be misinterpreted, so I tended to avoid speaking to unaccompanied males unless I was (a) surrounded by other passengers and (b) getting out at the next stop.

at last, a 'sociable', 'friendly' native, especially one who expressed genuine interest in their impressions of England and the English. Quite apart from my preference for informal, incognito interviews, I could not bring myself to dispel their illusions and spoil their holiday by revealing my ulterior motives – although I must admit to an occasional twinge of conscience when effusive visitors confided that I had caused them to revise their view of the English as a cold and standoffish race. Whenever possible, I did my best to explain that most English people observe the denial rule on public transport, and tried to direct them towards more sociable environments such as pub bar counters – but if you are one of the hapless tourists who were misled by my 'interviews', I can only apologise, thank you for your contribution to my research, and hope that this book will clear up any confusions I may have caused.

The Mobile-phone Ostrich Exception

I mentioned earlier that there are two aspects to the denial rule: pretending that other people do not exist, and also, much of the time, pretending that we do not exist either. On public transport, it is considered unseemly to draw attention to oneself. There are people who violate this rule, talking and laughing loudly with each other instead of hiding quietly behind their newspapers in the approved manner, but they have always been a much-frowned-upon minority.

Until the advent of the mobile phone, which brings out the ostrich in us: just as the dimwit ostrich with its head in the sand believes that it is invisible, the dimwit English passenger on a mobile phone imagines that he or she is inaudible. People on mobiles often seem to go about in a little personal bubble, oblivious to the crowds around them, connected only to the person at the other end of the phone. They will happily discuss the details of their domestic or business affairs, matters that would normally be considered private or confidential, in tones loud enough for half a train carriage to hear. Tremendously useful for eavesdropping nosy researchers – I get a lot of data from mobile-phone ostriches – but irritating for all the other passengers. Not that they would actually *do* anything about it, of course, except tut and sigh and roll their eyes and shake their heads.

We are not all ostriches. Many English passengers – the majority, even – are smart enough to realise that other people can hear what you are saying on your mobile, and we do our best to keep our voices down. The oblivious loudmouths are still a minority, but they are a highly noticeable and annoying minority. Part of the problem is that the English will not complain, not directly, to the person making the noise, only quietly to each other, or to colleagues when they get to work, or to their spouse when they get home, or in letters to the newspapers, or on internet social media. Our television and radio comedy programmes are full of amusing sketches about the infuri- ating stupidity of noisy mobile-phone ostriches, and the banality or utter pointlessness of their 'I'm on a train!' conversations. Newspaper columnists are equally witty on the subject.

In typically English fashion, we channel our anger into endless clever jokes and ritual moans, reams of print and hours of airtime, but fail to address the real source of the problem. Not one of us is brave or blunt enough to go up to a mobile-phone ostrich and simply ask him or her to keep it down. At least, this is *extremely* rare: I travel by train a lot, and have only witnessed a direct verbal rebuke once (the man confronting the ostrich was clearly drunk, swore loudly at the ostrich to 'shut the f*** up', and ended up getting more disap- proving looks from other passengers than the startled ostrich). The train companies are aware of the issue, and some have designated certain sections of their trains as 'quiet' carriages, where the use of mobile phones is prohibited. Most people observe this rule, but when an occasional rogue ostrich ignores the signs, nobody dares to confront the offender. Even in a designated 'quiet' carriage, the worst an ostrich can expect is a lot of glares and pointed sighs. It's not that the English are naturally shy, timid introverts: this is about unconscious obedience to cultural norms, in this case the taboos on 'causing a scene', 'making a fuss' or 'drawing attention to oneself' in public. Yes, the ostriches are breaking the rules (and in designated 'quiet' carriages, they are breaking official rules as well as the unwritten ones) but addressing them directly would be a breach of the denial rules.

Passive Disapproval Rules

I gave up smoking a few years ago – replacing real cigarettes with 'electronic cigarettes'. These clever devices are a sort of glorified version of nicotine inhalators, which look and feel rather more like a real cigarette, and emit a totally harmless, odourless steam or vapour that looks a bit like smoke. Many people are now accustomed to seeing these electronic cigarettes, and know that they are harmless. Even for those to whom they are unfamiliar, it is usually immediately obvious that they are not actual cigarettes.

Some people, however, do not instantly grasp this (especially if the e-cig is one of the more realistic-looking brands, with a tan-coloured band at one end and a red light at the other) and I have been conducting informal cross-cultural research on their reactions. In England, there are the usual raised eyebrows, frowns, pursed lips, tuts and mutters – and slightly more than the usual number of disapproving coughs, which I suppose is appropriate. But in all the years that I have been using these e-cigarettes on public transport and in restaurants, pubs and other public places where smoking is banned, only one English person has ever actually 'confronted' me about it. (This was an elderly lady on a train, who approached me very hesitantly, and said, 'I'm sorry, dear, but, um, you know smoking really isn't allowed here?' I explained, very politely, about electronic cigarettes; she apologised for the intrusion; I apologised for confusing her with my strange gadget; we laughed and she went back to her seat.)

In other countries, by contrast, people regularly come up to me and tell me that smoking is forbidden, that I must put out my ciga-rette, etc. Some do so politely, others more forcefully, but they have no qualms or inhibitions about confronting me and verbalising their disapproval. They do not rely entirely, like the English, on barely perceptible non-verbal signals. Yes, they use raised eyebrows and frowns, but these signals are delivered with full eye-contact (often a sustained glaring scowl) and frequently accompanied by more overt gestures such as pointing, finger-wagging and vigorous head-shaking.

In almost all countries, this disapproval quickly turns to friendly laughter, or curiosity, once I have explained that my 'cigarette' is an innocuous electronic device. The only exception I have found so far is the US, where some people seem to object almost as much to completely risk-free e-cigs as they do to the real thing – an irrational reaction that brings to mind my favourite definition of Puritanism: 'The haunting fear that someone, somewhere, may be having fun.' At least, I get the impression that some Americans feel that e-cigs make giving up smoking a bit too easy, that not enough suffering and self-denial is involved . . . that I might even, God forbid, be deriving some modicum of pleasure from my smoke-free electronic substitute.

The most charming reactions, by contrast, were in Albania. Smoking is officially banned in restaurants there, and when I visited e-cigs were still a very rare sight, often mistaken for the real thing. And yet every time I took out my electronic cigarette in a restaurant, a waiter would immediately bring me an ashtray.

Emerging Contact-avoidance Rules

Some years ago, an excited young American visitor remarked to me, 'English people are all so brainy!' I knew from our own (SIRC's) studies that this is a fairly common perception among young Americans: in our most recent US survey, 40 per cent of 18- to 24-year-old Americans chose 'academic' as a typically English characteristic (it was an even more popular stereotype with this age-group than 'polite' and 'stiff upper lip') Still I suspected a severe case of deluded Anglophilia, so I asked her what she meant. 'Well,' she replied, 'it's like even on the trains *everyone* is always *reading* – seriously, they've all got their noses in books and newspapers the *whole* time! I was on the subway and even people standing up were reading; they looked really uncomfortable, like this [she mimed someone struggling to hang on to a pole with one upstretched hand and hold a book up to his face with the other], but *nothing* was gonna stop them reading!' I had to explain that although her observation was perfectly accurate – I saw the same thing myself on every train journey, and many other visitors had commented on it – she had drawn the wrong conclusion: all this dedicated reading is about contact avoidance, not studious braininess. In our desperate need to avoid any interaction with strangers on public transport, the English have elevated the use of 'barrier signals' to a fine art.

This in itself is nothing new: we have always been experts in the use of newspapers, books and magazines to signal to others that we are occupied, unavailable and have no desire for any human interaction. On trains and on the Underground, the majority of English passengers have always hidden behind these 'do not disturb' props, carefully avoiding even the possibility of accidentally making eye contact with fellow passengers. And my American informant was right: even standing passengers on very crowded trains and tubes will often somehow manage to extract a paperback or newspaper from their pocket and focus intently on it, resolutely denying the existence of the other passengers squashed up against them. A journey without reading matter has always been torture for many English passengers, particularly on the Underground, where there is nothing to see out of the windows and passengers sit in long rows facing each other, which makes accidental eye contact with those opposite you very hard to avoid. In desperation, we resort to reading every word of the advertisements and Underground maps above their heads,[68] studying the safety instructions, scrutinising the small print on our tickets, digging out crumpled old chocolate-bar wrappers from our bags and reading the lists of ingredients . . . anything to avoid the embarrassment of even a fleeting millisecond of eye contact.

In more recent times, however, the range of potential 'barrier signals' has expanded beyond our wildest dreams. Mobile phones, tablet computers, laptops, e-books and other electronic gadgets have given us countless new denial-enablers, new ways to ignore each other, signal our frosty unavailability and cocoon ourselves in a private little world of words and pictures. And iPods give us the

---

68. Unless we are very lucky and happen to be in a tube-carriage where the London Underground's 'Poems on the Underground' project displays poems on the advertising boards – a hugely popular initiative, prompting heartfelt thanks from commuters, who, although perhaps not as intellectually voracious as my American informant imagined, would much rather avoid eye contact by reading bits of Shakespeare, Byron and Donne than ads for insurance companies and internet providers.

perfect excuse to plug our ears and ensure that even the usually minimal sounds made by fellow passengers cannot impinge on our consciousness and remind us of their existence. Now that almost all of us carry at least a mobile phone, we no longer have that heart-sinking moment when we board a tube-train and realise we've forgotten to bring any reading material: we can dig out our mobiles and scroll through our text messages, emails, contacts lists, notes and diaries. Yes, this is rather boring, but our primary objective is contact avoidance, not entertainment – and it beats staring at ads, maps and safety notices. Only trouble is, reading mobiles and tablets and so on doesn't make us look brainy. But as this was a false impression anyway, it's a very small price to pay.

The Smoker Solidarity Exception

In England, as in many other countries, smoking is now banned on public transport and in any 'enclosed public places' such as train stations, bus stations, workplaces, pubs, cafes, etc., and has also become increasingly stigmatised as a socially unacceptable act in any context. Smokers are not only vilified for health reasons but also looked down upon for class reasons: smoking is increasingly seen as a lower-class habit, allowing non-smokers to regard themselves as both morally and socially superior. The result is an increasing sense of solidarity among the dwindling numbers of despised and ostracised smokers. All this is true in other countries as well, but for English smokers there is at least one positive outcome: a new exception to the 'denial' and contact-avoidance rules. Smokers lighting up outside the entrances to railway stations, or shivering outside office buildings, cafés, etc., often make eye contact with each other (still only briefly – it's a matter of not studiously avoiding eye contact rather than actively seeking it) and this can prompt a small nod of mutual acknowledgement, maybe even an exchange of tentative little smiles. These are often accompanied by a humorous grimace – an eye-roll with a lopsided lip-shrug that somehow, in a nanosecond, simultaneously conveys mock-ruefulness about one's 'filthy' habit, stoicism in the face of disapproval and discomfort, and defiant solidarity with one's fellow rebels and outcasts. The correct response, as with 'how do you do?', is to repeat the same humorous grimace back.

These non-verbal exchanges are not necessarily a prelude to actual conversation – for many English smokers, the brief eye contact, nod, tiny smile and nano-grimace cover all that needs to be said – but there is at least the possibility of a humorous-moaning opportunity, which as you know is an established exception to the 'no talking to strangers' rule. Before I gave up smoking, I was an avid collector of suitable smoker-moan opening lines, and I have pretended to smoke quite a few times recently to check that they are still current.[69] Huddled outside a station entrance on a bitterly cold, wet day, for example, a fellow smoker opened with the standard eye-roll/shrug combo and 'Nice weather for non-smokers, eh?' – a jokey variation on the traditional English weather-moan 'Nice weather for ducks' or 'Nice day, if you're a duck.' I laughed, and we ended up having a brief amicable moan about the weather and the smoking ban. My contribution, 'Only about ten per cent of smokers get lung cancer. I wonder how many die of hypothermia?' got a laugh and the cynical reply, 'That's their plan: freeze us to death, save the NHS a few quid' (note how we had progressed to 'them and us' solidarity within a few seconds of meeting).

Bad weather helps, of course, but is not essential. On an earlier, sunnier occasion, sneaking outside for a cigarette during a long day of radio interviews, I noticed a group of three smokers[70] in the doorway of an office building across the street. As I lit up, we did the customary eye-contact/nod/smile/grimace exchange, then one of them beckoned me over with a typical opening line: 'Come join the leper colony?' In accordance with the ritual, I mimed ringing a bell – 'ding-ding' – as I crossed the street, and we enjoyed a little comradely moan. Later the same day, I snuck out again, and saw a

69. Yeah, I know, inhaling a bit of smoke and risking a renewal of my smoking addiction, even on freezing-cold rainy days, is hardly comparable with the risks and hardships endured by proper intrepid ethnographers.

70. What should be the collective noun for smokers? I've heard 'a billow of smokers', and also a 'cloud', 'wheeze', 'gasp', etc.; 'confraternity' comes closest of those proposed, but I would suggest that 'a defiance of smokers' now seems most appropriate.

different group of smokers standing outside the same office building. Spotting the perfect opportunity for a 'control' experiment, I refrained from lighting up and just stood there, leaning against the wall, drinking my coffee, as though simply out for a bit of fresh air and sunshine. As I expected from many previous such experiments, the smokers glanced at me briefly, noted that I lacked the essential little white 'prop' that would allow them to break the contact-avoidance rules, and returned to their chat.

Of course, smoker solidarity and friendly encounters between smokers are common in other cultures as well – the point here is the dramatic contrast with normal English behaviour. In most other cultures, smokers chatting with strangers are only indulging in one 'prohibited' pleasure: here, their sociable chat is 'illicit' as well. They are gorging on double portions of forbidden fruit.

There seems to be an unconscious understanding of a 'causal' connection between these two forbidden fruits. I observed that English smokers are significantly more inclined to initiate the non-verbal ritual, and strike up conversations with strangers, in contexts where their marginalised 'leper' status is most obvious, such as the entrances to public buildings or workplaces where smoking is prohibited. I noted the very highest degree of sociability among smokers outside the entrances to hospitals, especially among those standing directly under the 'No Smoking on Hospital Grounds' sign. In open parks and on random street corners, smokers are considerably more reticent and inhibited. The rule of thumb seems to be that the further you are from a no-smoking area, the less effective your cigarette will be as a facilitator of social interaction. English smokers seem to need that immediate reminder of their 'outlaw' status to give themselves permission to break unwritten social rules.

COURTESY RULES

Although many of the foreign visitors I interviewed complained about English reserve, they all tended to be impressed by our courtesy. Appreciation of our courtesy/politeness and complaints about our reserve/coldness were also among the most common responses in SIRC's international discussion-groups and surveys. This apparent contradiction is accurately expressed by Bill Bryson, who is amazed and somewhat spooked by the 'orderly quiet' of the London Underground: 'All these thousands of people passing on stairs and escalators, stepping on and off crowded trains, sliding off into the darkness with wobbling heads, and never speaking, like characters from *Night of the Living Dead*.' A few pages later, at another station, he is full of praise for the courteous behaviour of a large crowd of rugby fans: 'They boarded with patience and without pushing, and said sorry when they bumped or inadvertently impinged on someone's space. I admired this instinctive consideration for others, and was struck by what a regular thing that is in Britain and how little it is noticed.'

'Negative Politeness' Rules

But our much-maligned reserve and our much-admired courtesy are, it seems to me, two sides of the same coin. In fact, at one level, our reserve is a *form* of courtesy – the kind of courtesy that the sociolinguists Penelope Brown and Stephen Levinson call 'negative politeness', meaning that it is concerned with other people's need not to be intruded or imposed upon, as opposed to 'positive politeness', which is concerned with their need for inclusion and social approval. The restraint, cautiousness and contact-avoidance of English public-transport passengers – the standoffishness that foreigners complain about – are all characteristic features of negative politeness. What looks like unfriendliness is really a kind of consideration: we judge others by ourselves, and assume that everyone shares our obsessive need for privacy – so we mind our own business and politely ignore them.

All cultures practise both forms of politeness, but most incline somewhat more towards one than the other. The English are a predominantly negative-politeness culture, while the Americans, for example, tend to favour the warmer, more inclusive positive-politeness mode. Although these are crude distinctions, and there are class, regional and other subcultural variations in both types of culture, it seems probable that visitors from positive-politeness cultures are more likely to misunderstand and be offended by the 'polite' aloofness of the English than those from cultures that are similar to our own in this respect (according to Brown and Levinson, these negative-politeness cultures also include Japan, certain sections of Indian society and Madagascar).

Bumping Experiments and the Reflex-apology Rule

Which brings me to the bumping experiments. I spent many amusing afternoons in busy, crowded public places (railway stations, tube stations, bus stations, shopping centres, street corners, etc.) accidentally-on-purpose bumping into people to see if they would say 'sorry'. A number of my informants, both natives and visitors, had cited this habit of apologising when bumped as a particularly striking example of English courtesy, and I was fairly sure I had experienced it (and done it) myself – but I felt obliged to do the proper scientific thing and actually test the theory in a field-experiment or two.

If you would like to try this yourself, it is important to make your bumps appear genuinely accidental, as even the English will not apologise to someone who seems to be crashing into them deliberately. I found that the best method was to pretend to be searching for something in my shoulder-bag: with my head down and hair over my eyes, I could still actually see my 'target' and calculate my trajectory to achieve a relatively gentle bump, while giving the impression that I was genuinely distracted by my bag-fumblings.

My bumping got off to a rather poor start. The first few bumps were technically successful, in that I managed to make them seem convincingly accidental, but I kept messing up the experiment by blurting out an apology before the other person had a chance to speak. As usual, this turned out to be a test of my own Englishness: I found that I could not bump into someone, however gently, without automatically saying 'sorry'. After several of these false starts, I finally managed to control my knee-jerk apologies by biting my lip – firmly and rather painfully – as I did the bumps. Having perfected the technique, I tried to make my experiments as scientific as possible by bumping into a representative cross-section of the English population, in a representative sample of locations. Somewhat to my surprise, the English lived up to their reputation: about 80 per cent of my victims said 'sorry' when I lurched into them, even though the collisions were quite clearly my fault.

There were some minor variations in the response: I found that older people were very slightly more likely to apologise than younger people (late-teenage males were the least apologetic, particularly when in groups), and British Asians seemed to have a somewhat stronger sorry-reflex than British Afro-Caribbeans (possibly a reflection of the negative-politeness tendency in Indian culture – such apologies being a clear example of politeness that is primarily concerned with the avoidance of imposition or intrusion). But these differences were marginal: the vast majority of the bumped, of all ages, classes and ethnic origin, apologised when I 'accidentally' jostled them.

These experiments would tell us little or nothing about Englishness if exactly the same results were obtained in other countries, so by way of 'controls' I diligently bumped into as many people as I could in France, Belgium, Italy, Russia, Poland, Lebanon, Switzerland, Greece, the USA and Albania. Recognising that this would not constitute a representative international sample, I also bumped into tourists of different nationalities (American, German, Japanese, Spanish, Australian, Scandinavian) at tourist-trap locations in London and Oxford. And just for good measure I got friends and contacts in some of these countries, and in Canada and China, to conduct the same experiments in their own countries.

Only the Japanese (surprise, surprise) seemed to have anything even approaching the English sorry-reflex, and they were frustratingly difficult to experiment on, as they appeared to be remarkably adept at sidestepping my attempted collisions.[71] (Canadians were slightly more likely to say 'sorry' than other nationalities, but still nowhere near the English percentage.)

This is not to say that my bumpees of other nationalities were discourteous or unpleasant – most just said, 'Careful!' or 'Watch out!' (or the equivalent in their own language), and many reacted in a positively friendly manner, putting out a helpful arm to steady me,

71. I have since been told about a cross-cultural study of pedestrians, which showed that the Japanese are indeed much more skilled than other nations at avoiding bumping into each other in crowded public places – so this was not just my imagination.

sometimes even solicitously checking that I was unhurt before moving on – but the automatic 'sorry' did seem to be a peculiarly English response. It must be said, however, that the English 'sorries' were usually muttered, often barely audible (if you try this experiment yourself, you will have to listen *extremely* carefully to catch the rapidly mumbled or even whispered 'sorry', which may well sound more like 'sry' or 'so-y') and with no eye contact, smile or other friendly signal.

George Orwell said that the English are 'inveterate gamblers, drink as much beer as their wages will permit, are devoted to bawdy jokes and use probably the foulest language in the world', but he nevertheless concluded, without contradiction, that 'The gentleness of the English civilisation is perhaps its most marked characteristic.' As evidence of this, along with the good-temperedness of bus-conductors and unarmed policemen, he cited the fact that 'In no country inhabited by white men is it easier to shove people off the pavement.' Quite so, and if your shove appears to be genuinely accidental, they might even apologise as they stumble into the gutter.

Since this book was first published (in 2004), I have been surprised by the number of letters and emails I have received from intrepid readers who took it upon themselves to replicate my bumping experiments. Pleasantly surprised, as the results reported by those who managed to bump into a decent-sized sample seem to be much the same as mine – between 65 and 88 per cent of their English 'targets' said 'sorry' when bumped. So my figure of 'about 80 per cent' was clearly not too far off (to my shame, I didn't always keep count quite as precisely as these diligent readers, although in my defence I have clocked up many hundreds of bumps over the years, whereas their bumping samples were much more limited).

Female experimenters seemed to receive a higher percentage of 'sorries' than males, which may be partly down to a degree of chivalry in the response, but also perhaps because male experimenters reported having greater difficulty in making their bumps appear accidental.

Also, while one should always be a bit sceptical of survey findings, I was pleased when one recent survey showed 60 per cent of us admitting to saying sorry when we are bumped into or someone treads on our feet, and in another survey 75 per cent of us admitted to saying sorry when bumped. These figures are very slightly lower than mine, but I suspect that quite a few of us (probably at least 5 or 10 per cent) don't even realise that we do this – I wasn't even entirely aware that I did myself until I started this research.

You may be wondering why the English seem to assume that any accidental collision is our fault, and immediately accept the blame for it by apologising. If so, you are making a mistake. The apology is reflex – an automatic, knee-jerk response, *not* a considered admission of guilt. This is a deeply ingrained rule: when any inadvertent, undesired contact occurs (and to the English, almost any contact is by definition undesired), we say 'sorry'.

In fact, any intrusion, impingement or imposition of any kind, however minimal or innocuous, generally requires an apology. We mumble 'sorry' if our arm accidentally brushes against someone else's when passing through a crowded doorway; even a 'near miss', where no actual physical contact takes place, can often prompt an automatic 'sorry' from both parties. The apology is so habitual and mechanical that we sometimes even say 'sorry' when we bump into an inanimate object, such as a door or a lamp-post. I caught myself saying 'sorry' when I bumped into an unattended shopping trolley in a supermarket recently, which prompted me to do a quick informal poll, in which the majority of English people admitted that they too had often apologised to trolleys, chairs, trees, street-signs . . .

As noted earlier, we use the word 'sorry' as a prefix to almost any request or question: 'Sorry, but do you know if this train stops at Banbury?'; 'Sorry, but is this seat free?'; 'Sorry – do you have the time?'; 'Sorry, but you seem to be sitting on my coat.' We also often say 'sorry' when we mean 'excuse me' (or 'get out of my way'), such as when asking someone to move so we can get past them. An interrogative 'sorry?' means 'I didn't quite hear what you said – could you repeat it?' (or 'what?'). According to the recent survey mentioned above, we say 'sorry' on average eight times a day, with a significant minority who say 'sorry' at least twenty times a day – and of course these are just the 'sorries' that people actually *remember* saying when they are asked a survey question. I suspect that the real total, including all the unconscious, reflex 'sorries', is even higher.

Clearly, all these sorries are not heartfelt, sincere apologies. Like 'nice', 'sorry' is a useful, versatile, all-purpose word, suitable for all occasions and circumstances. When in doubt, say 'sorry'. Being English means *always* having to say you're sorry.

Rules of Ps and Qs

The English may not speak much on public transport, but when they do open their mouths, the words you are most likely to hear, apart from 'sorry', are 'please' and, especially, 'thank you'. The latter may often be shortened to 'thanks', ''anks' or ''kyou',[72] or replaced with an informal equivalent such as 'cheers' or 'ta' – or even, among younger people and kidults, 'cool', 'nice one', 'wicked' or 'fab'.

According to yet another survey, we say 'thank you' thirteen times a day, on average – and again these are just the 'thank-yous' that people actually remember saying when they are asked a survey question, so the real figure is probably even higher. And this figure doesn't include the more casual equivalents (ta, cheers, etc.), which at least a third of us are more likely to use.

It's worth noting that this last survey finding, about the 'casual equivalents', was reported by the press in typically Eeyorish fashion, with headlines about 'The Death of Thank-you', in line with the popular myth that as a society we are becoming less courteous, standards are declining, young people especially are all ill-mannered and obnoxious, etc., etc. In almost every survey I've seen, about 75 per cent of people in this country bemoan the 'fact' that we are becoming less polite. But think about that figure for a moment. This 75 per cent invariably feel that they themselves are still polite, that their own personal standards of courtesy have not declined in the slightest. So, either they are all considerably less courteous than they think they are, or they are mistaken: a society in which at least 75 per cent of us are still perfectly polite is hardly one that has lost its manners. I say 'at least' because there is no reason to suppose that the other 25 per cent – those who are *not* convinced that we are becoming less polite – are all a bunch of badly behaved thugs and

72. ''kyou' is a particularly common abbreviation, hence the 'Q' in 'Ps and Qs'.

louts either. They may simply be more observant, and perhaps less susceptible to doom-mongering headlines.[73]

During the research for this book, I made a point of counting Ps and Qs. Whenever I took a bus, I would sit or stand as near as possible to the driver (outside central London, buses nowadays do not have conductors – if passengers don't have a travel card or pre-purchased ticket, they buy their tickets directly from the driver) to find out how many of the people boarding the bus said 'please' and 'thank you' when purchasing their ticket. I found that the majority of English passengers mind their Ps and Qs, and most of the drivers also say 'thank you' when accepting money for tickets. If you want statistics, I came across a cross-cultural study showing that 70 per cent of public-transport passengers in London say 'please' and 'thank you' when buying tickets, compared with 50 per cent in Tokyo, 30 per cent in Hamburg and 10 per cent in New York. (It is interesting to note that, as with the 'sorries' in my bumping experiments, the Japanese come closest to English etiquette regarding Ps and Qs, although again this is perhaps not quite as much of an automatic 'reflex' for them.)

Not only that, but many English passengers also thank the bus driver again when they get off at their stop. This practice is less common in very big cities, but in smaller cities and towns it is the norm. On a typical short bus journey from a council estate on the outskirts of Oxford to the city centre, for example, I noted that all of the passengers said ''kyou' or ''anks' or 'cheers' as they alighted from the bus – with the noticeable exception of a group of foreign students, who had also omitted the 'please' when buying their tickets. Many tourists and other visitors have commented to me on the politeness of English passengers, and from my own cross-cultural research, I know that this degree of courtesy is unusual. In other countries, the only circumstances in which I have

73. Or perhaps they read reports of an excellent study on civility in Britain by the Young Foundation, which confirmed that 'Although subjectively civility is perceived to be deteriorating there is no objective evidence for this.' The study even concluded that in some respects our behaviour is actually now *better* than a generation or two ago.

found people consistently thanking bus drivers in this way were in small communities where the passengers all knew the regular drivers.

Having said that, I should point out that there is nothing particularly warm or friendly about English Ps and Qs – they are generally muttered, usually without any eye contact or smiles. If you listen *very* closely, you may even sometimes hear English passengers absent-mindedly murmuring 'thanks,' while alighting through the doors halfway down the bus, from where the driver cannot possibly hear them – clearly just an automatic habit rather than an actual attempt to thank the driver. I caught myself doing this, and realised that my 'thanks' was simply a reflex, a word I just instinctively mumble as I step off a bus, even when I've failed to notice that I am nowhere near the driver. This prompted me to listen more carefully to fellow passengers at the central doors on subsequent bus journeys, and I heard quite a few muttering 'thanks'– more than enough to convince me that this is not just some odd personal habit of mine, but yet another habitual oddity of Englishness. Just because we are distinctively polite and courteous in our public conduct does not mean that we are good-natured, generous, kind-hearted people. We just have rules about Ps and Qs, which most of us observe, most of the time, often without being conscious of doing so.

Our scrupulous pleasing and thanking of bus drivers, conductors, taxi drivers and the like can also be another manifestation of the 'polite egalitarianism' discussed earlier – reflecting our squeamishness about drawing attention to status differences, and our embarrassment about anything to do with money. We like to pretend that these people are somehow doing us a favour, rather than performing a service for financial reward. And they collude with us in this pretence. Taxi drivers, in particular, expect to be thanked as well as paid at the end of their journey, and feel offended if the passenger simply hands over the money – although they are usually tolerant towards foreigners who 'don't know any better', as one London cabbie put it when I questioned him on the subject. 'With most English people, it's just automatic,' he explained. 'They say "thanks" or "cheers" or something when they get out – and you say "thanks" back. You get the occasional rude bastard who doesn't, but most people just automatically say "thanks."'

Taxi Exceptions to the Denial Rule

In return, English taxi drivers are generally courteous towards their customers – and often positively friendly, to the extent of breaking the normal 'denial' rules of privacy and reserve. There is a sort of standing joke among the English about the excessive chattiness of taxi drivers and, indeed, many live up to their garrulous reputation. The main popular stereotype is of the would-be-tabloid-columnist cabbie, who bores or infuriates his passengers with endless heated monologues on everything from the inadequacies of the current government or the England football coach to the latest celebrity-gossip scandal. I have come across drivers of this type and, like most English passengers, I tend to be too embarrassed either to ask them to shut up or to argue with their more objectionable opinions. We grumble about taxi drivers' breach of the denial rule, but in typically English fashion we make a national joke out of it rather than actually tackling them directly.

There is also, however, another type of chatty cabbie, who does not deliver tabloid monologues but rather attempts to engage his passengers in friendly conversation – usually beginning, in accordance with English protocol, with a comment on the weather, but then breaking with tradition by expressing interest in the passengers' destination and the purpose of their journey (a railway station, for example, often prompts the question 'Are you off somewhere nice, then?'). The questions can become more personal (or at least what the English regard as personal – such as perfectly innocuous enquiries about one's job or family), but most such drivers are remarkably sensitive to nuances of tone and body language, and will not persist if the passenger comes over all English and gives monosyllabic answers or looks squirmy and uncomfortable. Many English people do find these enquiries intrusive, but we are nearly all too polite, or too embarrassed, to tell the cabbie to mind his own business – so these signals are all he has to go on.

There is also an element of 'cultural remission' in conversations with taxi drivers – and with certain other professionals such as hairdressers – whereby the normal rules of reticence and discretion are temporarily suspended, and one can, if one wishes, indulge in much more personal and intimate chat than is usually permitted between strangers.

The English Patient Rules

A slight digression from the transport/public-places theme of this chapter, but it occurs to me that doctors might well wish that the same suspension of cultural privacy rules applied in their consulting rooms and surgeries, where the English tend to be their usual inhibited, embarrassed selves. In the 2004 edition of this book, I half-jokingly suggested that they try speaking to their patients 'through a mirror', either by standing behind them like a hairdresser, or by rigging up a rear-view mirror like a taxi driver, as it seems to be at least partly the lack of direct face-to-face eye contact that allows the English to shed their inhibitions in these contexts.

This may to some extent be one of those 'human universals' – Catholic priests of all nationalities have long been aware of the effectiveness of the screen in promoting greater openness in confessions, and psychoanalysts' use of the couch to avoid eye contact with their patients cannot be a coincidence, but as usual we are probably talking about a question of degree here, and it seems that the English find it particularly difficult to 'open up' in the absence of such tricks, and are particularly susceptible to the illusion of anonymity that they provide. In fact, if you think about it, my advice to English doctors goes against all the touchy-feely 'communication skills' training they now receive, in which they are told to sit close to the patient, not use their desk as a shield, lean forward, make eye contact, etc.: all measures that seem to me calculated to make the average English person clam up entirely. Which, according to doctors I asked about this, is precisely their effect on most English patients, who do not confess to the doctor what is *really* bothering them until they are on their way out of the consulting room, usually with their back half turned and their hand on the door-knob.

Since this book was first published in 2004, I have been invited to speak at a few medical conferences on this subject, and at one of these a doctor told me that the best trick is to find an excuse to stand *behind* English patients, such as listening to their breathing or heartbeat with a stethoscope, when one has difficult or personal questions to ask. Anything to avoid the dreaded eye contact! As the stethoscope trick could be a bit implausible when a patient 'presents with', say, a sprained ankle or some other clearly non-respiratory/cardiac complaint, I suggested at another medical gathering that doctors could perhaps achieve the same effect by turning away to look stuff up on their computer screens – then maybe just very casually saying, without looking at the patient, 'So, while you're here, anything else you want to ask me about?' or something like that. The doctors laughed, and told me that their 'communications' training specifically forbids focusing on their computer screens while talking with patients. Apparently this makes them look aloof and uncaring. One doctor said, 'But you're absolutely right, Kate. You only get that "Oh, while I'm here, it's probably nothing, but . . ." (you know, the line where you always sit up and think, OK, here comes the real problem) when you turn away and start fiddling with the computer trying to find their notes or do their prescriptions.'

The other doctors all nodded agreement with him, and one added, 'Yep, spot on, often the best time to ask the really awkward questions, too, while you're on the computer . . . exact opposite of what they tell us on the comms training, of course! Perhaps you could explain this to them, Kate? Tell them they've got it all wrong.'

'Yeah, but break it to them gently,' joked another doctor, 'y'know, with lots of eye contact . . .'

Clearly, not enough doctors are adopting this highly effective 'taxi driver' approach, as English patients' inhibitions about visiting or talking to doctors have recently been blamed for the fact that we have far lower cancer survival rates than other developed nations, despite free access to skilled doctors and cutting-edge treatments. A survey by the British Heart Foundation found that we also wait on average ninety minutes (often much longer) before calling the emergency services when we experience heart-attack symptoms. Even seriously ill English patients in hospital are often reluctant to complain or 'make a fuss' about their ailments. I have spent quite a lot of time in hospital over the past decade or so (as a patient, but the silver lining was the chance to do 'undercover' participant-observation research), and have lost count of the number of times I witnessed variations on the following exchange during the doctors' ward-rounds:

DOCTOR: So, how are you today?

ENGLISH PATIENT (clearly very ill): Not too bad, thanks.

DOCTOR (frowning, concerned): Are you sure? It says here in your notes 'Patient complains of severe abdominal pain'.

ENGLISH PATIENT (highly offended): I wasn't *complaining*! Why did they put that? I mean, I might have said my guts hurt but I didn't *complain*! And I only said it because they *asked* – I wasn't making a fuss or anything!

DOCTOR (reassuring, slight sigh, has heard this before): No don't worry, sorry, 'complains' is kind of a technical term here – it doesn't mean you were making a fuss, I promise.

After the doctor had moved on, these English patients would often engage in moaning-rituals with fellow patients, complaining about their pain, the lousy hospital food and many other discomforts – and, indignantly and repeatedly, about the medical jargon in which their dignified response to a question had been classified as 'complaining'. As with our moans about trains and buses, we seem perversely disinclined to address our complaints to anyone who might actually be able to help.

These participant-observation findings were confirmed in many informal interviews with both English doctors and foreign doctors working in English hospitals. When I asked foreign doctors (especially Americans) 'Have you noticed any differences between English patients and patients in your country?' almost all of them commented on our squeamishness about complaining.

Some commentators attribute our reluctance to visit doctors or complain about illness to tough English stoicism and the 'stiff upper lip', but I would suggest that embarrassment and inhibition, and unwritten rules about 'making a fuss', are the more likely explanations. Now I come to think of it, these factors, rather than any exemplary fortitude or ability to suffer in silence, are also perhaps the most likely explanations for our 'stiff upper lip' reputation. Much of what looks like stoicism could just be social dis-ease.

QUEUING RULES

'And the Lord said unto Moses, "Come forth!" And he came third, and got sent to the back for pushing.'[74]

In 1946, the Hungarian humorist George Mikes described queuing as our 'national passion'. 'On the Continent,' he said, 'if people are waiting at a bus-stop they loiter around in a seemingly vague fashion. When the bus arrives they make a dash for it . . . An Englishman, even if he is alone, forms an orderly queue of one.' In an update over thirty years later, in 1977, he confirmed that this was still the case. After more than another thirty years, nothing much seems to have changed – and foreigners are still bemused by our queuing habits. An Italian participant in one of SIRC's discussion-groups echoed Mike's description: 'The queue for the bus, for example . . . everybody stands in a line and gets on one by one in order. It drives me crazy – it is so slow! Here in Italy we stand near the sign and when the bus comes we all get on – quickly!' But English queuing is not quite as simple as Mikes makes it sound.

I saw a headline in a Sunday newspaper, bemoaning the fact that the English had 'lost the art of queuing'. Puzzled, as this was not what my own observation fieldwork had shown, I read on. It turned out that the author had been in a queue, someone had tried to jump it and both she and the other queuers had been outraged and disgusted – but no one had had the courage to tackle the queue-jumper in a sufficiently forceful manner (they just humphed and tutted), so he had got away with it. Far from constituting any sort of evidence for its loss, this struck me as a perfectly accurate description of the English art of queuing.

The Indirectness Rule

The English expect each other to observe the rules of queuing, feel highly offended when these rules are violated, but seem unable to

74. A joke I remember from childhood.

express their annoyance in a straightforward manner. In other countries, this is not a problem: in America, where a queue-jumper has committed a misdemeanour rather than a cardinal sin, the response is loud and prescriptive: the offender is simply told, 'Hey, you, get back in line!' or words to that effect. On the Continent, the reaction tends to be loud and argumentative; in some other parts of the world, queue-jumpers may simply be unceremoniously pushed and shoved back into line – but the end result is much the same. Paradoxically, it is only in England, where queue-jumping is regarded as deeply immoral, that the queue-jumper is likely to get away with the offence. We huff and puff and scowl and mutter and seethe with righteous indignation, but only rarely do we actually speak up and tell the jumper to go to the back of the queue.

Try it yourself if you don't believe me. I had to, so I don't see why you shouldn't suffer as well. Sorry to sound so grumpy, but my queue-jumping experiments were the most difficult and distasteful and upsetting of all the rule-breaking field experiments I conducted during the research for this book. Far worse than bumping, much worse even than asking people the price of their house – just the *thought* of queue-jumping was so horribly embarrassing that I very nearly abandoned the whole project rather than subject myself to such an ordeal. I just couldn't bring myself to do it. I hesitated and agonised and procrastinated, and then even when I thought I had managed to steel myself, I would lose my nerve at the last minute, and slink humbly to the back of the queue, hoping no one had noticed that I had even been *considering* jumping it.

The Paranoid Pantomime Rule

That last bit might sound silly, or at least pathetically feeble, but I actually learnt something from all my wimpish hovering in the vicinity of likely queues, which is that the English *do* notice when someone is even just 'considering' jumping a queue. They start glancing at you sideways, through narrowed, suspicious eyes. Then they shuffle a bit closer to the person in front of them, just in case you might try to insert yourself in the gap. They adopt a more belligerent, territorial posture – putting a hand on a hip, 'squaring up' to the potential threat, or ostentatiously turning a shoulder away from you. The body language is quite subtle – perhaps not even visible to a foreigner unaccustomed to our ways – but to an English would-be queue-jumper the non-verbal message is clear. It says, 'We know what you're thinking, you cheating little fiend, but don't imagine you're going to get away with it because we're on to you.'

The Ambiguity Rule

It is important to note that this kind of paranoid pantomime – and indeed queue-jumping itself – only occurs when there is some ambiguity in the structure of the queue. No one would even think of simply barging to the front of a single, straightforward, obvious queue. This is so unthinkable that if it does happen, we will often assume that it is a genuine dire emergency, or perhaps an ignorant foreigner making a mistake – in which case, one of the more intrepid among us might actually speak up and inform the jumper of his or her grave error. The speaker may then look around with an expression of defiant pride, as though expecting the other queuers to award him a medal for bravery. I have often heard such people say things like 'Well, someone had to do it!' to nods of grateful approval from the queue. Normally, however, the potential for queue-jumping only arises when there is some doubt about exactly where the queue starts and ends – when there is a break or gap in a queue due to some obstruction or to allow people to pass through, for example, or when two people are serving behind the same counter and it is not entirely clear whether there is one queue or two separate queues, or some other element of confusion or uncertainty.

The English have an acute sense of fairness, and what in other cultures would be seen as entirely legitimate opportunistic behaviour – such as heading directly for the 'free' cashier when there are two people already waiting to be served in front of the cashier alongside, who have simply not been quick enough to move across – is here regarded as queue-jumping, or tantamount to queue-jumping. I am not saying that English people do not perform this manoeuvre, they do, but it is obvious from their self-consciously disingenuous manner, particularly the way they carefully avoid looking at the queuers, that they know they are cheating, and the reactions of the queuers indicate that such behaviour is severely frowned upon. You can tell by the severe frowns.

Body-language and Muttering Rules

But frowns, glares, raised eyebrows and contemptuous looks – accompanied by heavy sighs, pointed coughs, scornful snorts, tutting and barely audible muttering ('A*hem*'; 'Well, *really*!'; 'Bloody hell!'; 'Huh, *typ*ical'; 'What the . . .') – are usually the worst that you will be subjected to if you jump such a queue. The queuers are hoping to shame you into retreating to the back of the queue, without actually having to break the denial rule and 'cause a scene' or 'make a fuss' or 'draw attention to themselves' by addressing you directly.

Ironically, they will often in these circumstances break the denial rule by addressing *each other*. A queue-jumper can prompt complete strangers to exchange raised eyebrows, eye-rolls, pursed-lipped head-shakes, tuts, sighs and even (quiet) verbal comments. These verbal exchanges between queuers include the standard mutters mentioned above, and some that clearly ought to be addressed to the jumper, such as '*Hello*, there's a queue here!'; 'Oh, don't mind us!'; 'Oi, are we invisible or what?' Occasionally, some brave souls will make these remarks in tones loud enough for the jumper to overhear, but they will avoid looking at the jumper, and glance away immediately if they should happen inadvertently to make eye contact.

Feeble and utterly irrational as they may sound, these indirect measures can often be remarkably effective. Yes, it is probably easier to get away with queue-jumping in England than anywhere else, but *only* if you can bear the humiliation of all those eyebrows, coughs, tuts and mutters – in other words, only if you are not English. In my endless queue-watching, I noticed that many foreigners are simply oblivious to all of these signals, much to the mute fury of English queuers, but that most English queue-jumpers find it hard to ignore the barrage of sighs and scowls. Having jumped the queue, they may brazen it out, but one gets the impression that they will think twice about doing it again. In many cases, queue-jumping is effectively 'nipped in the bud' by non-verbal signals alone: 'body English' is a rich and eloquent language. I have often seen would-be jumpers start to approach, and then, faced with a scornful eyebrow or two, a warning cough and a bit of territorial posturing, rapidly think better of it and retreat meekly to the back of the queue.

Sometimes, a muttered remark, loud enough to overhear but not actually addressed to the queue-jumper, can also have the desired effect, even at a much later stage in the attempted queue-jump. In these cases, I found the behaviour and reactions of both parties fascinating to watch. The queuer mutters (to his or her neighbour, or to no one in particular) 'Oh, don't mind me!' – or some other sarcastic gibe. The jumper, feigning wide-eyed innocence, says something like 'Oh, sorry! Were you in front of me?' and immediately moves aside to give his or her place to the mutterer. Now the tables are turned, and it is the mutterer who is blushing, squirming and avoiding eye contact – the degree of discomfort usually being in proportion to the unpleasantness of the original muttered gibe, which has now been recast as an unwarranted or at least excessively rude response to an honest mistake. The mutterer will usually resume his or her rightful place in the queue, but with bowed head and mumbled thanks or apology – clearly deriving no pleasure or sense of triumph from the victory. In some cases, I have even seen such humbled mutterers backtrack completely, saying, 'Oh, er, no, that's all right, you go ahead.'

The Unseen Choreographer Rule

All of this embarrassment and hostility would be avoided, of course, if the English could just manage to be straightforwardly assertive, and simply say to queue-jumpers, 'Excuse me, but there is a queue here.' But no. Our typical responses are closer to what psychotherapists would call 'passive-aggressive'. The same psychotherapists, reading this, would probably recommend that the entire nation be sent on one of those assertiveness-training courses. And they might well be right: assertiveness is clearly not our strong point. We can do aggression, including both outright violence and devious, ineffectual passive-aggression – and we can do the opposite, over-polite self-effacement and stoical, passive resignation. But we veer between these two extremes: we can never seem to achieve that happy medium of grown-up, socially skilled, rational assertion. But then, the world would really be awfully dull if everyone behaved in the correct, sensible, assertive manner, as taught on communication-skills courses – and much less amusing for me to watch.

And, anyway, there is a positive side to the English approach to queuing. Where there is an ambiguity, such as the 'two cashiers at one counter' problem described above, we often simply resolve it of our own accord, silently and without fuss – in this case by forming a single orderly queue, a few feet back from the counter, so that the customer at the front can step forward whenever one of the cashiers becomes free. We also often form these scrupulously fair single queues when buying tickets from a row of machines.

If you are English, you may be reading this and thinking, Yes? Well? So what? Of course. Obvious thing to do. We tend to take this kind of thing for granted – in fact, we do it automatically, as though some unseen fair-minded choreographer were controlling our movements, arranging us into a tidy, democratic line. But many of the foreign visitors I interviewed regard these processes with open-mouthed amazement. Bill Bryson comments glowingly on exactly the same typical queuing scenario in his book about England; I met some American tourists who had read his book and didn't believe him, or at least assumed that he was exaggerating for comic effect, until they came here and saw the procedure for themselves. They were even less inclined to believe my account of the 'invisible queue' mechanism in pubs – in the end I had to drag them to the nearest pub to prove that I was not making it up.

The Fair-play Rule

And there are smaller, more subtle, everyday queuing courtesies that even sharp-eyed foreigners may not notice. One of my many scribbled fieldwork notes on this subject concerns a queue in a railway-station coffee shop.

Man in queue ahead of me moves out of queue briefly to take a sandwich from nearby cooler cabinet. Then seems a bit hesitant, unsure as to whether he has thereby forfeited his place in the queue. I make it clear (by taking a step back) that he has not, so he resumes his position in front of me, with a little nod of thanks. No speech or eye contact involved.

Another railway-station note reads:

Two males ahead of me at information-desk counter, not entirely clear which of them is first (there were two people serving, now only one). They're doing the pantomime, sideways glances, edging forward, hints of territorial posture, etc. Clever cashier notices this and says, 'Who's next?' They both look embarrassed. Man on left makes open-palm, go-ahead gesture to the other man. Man on right mumbles, 'No, s'all right, you go.' Man on left hesitates. 'Well, um . . .' Person behind me gives oh-do-get-on-with-it cough. Man on left says hurriedly 'Oh, all right – 'anks, mate' and proceeds with his enquiry, looking a bit uncomfortable. Man on right waits patiently, looking rather smug and pleased with himself.

These incidents were by no means isolated or unusual: I have transcribed these accounts from the dozens in my queuing-observation notes precisely because they are the most typical, mundane, everyday examples. Now, I see that the common denominator, the unwritten rule governing these incidents, is immediately obvious: if you 'play fair' and explicitly acknowledge the rights and prior claims of those in front of you in a queue – or generously give them the benefit of the doubt where there is some ambiguity – they will instantly drop all their paranoid suspicions and passive-aggressive tactics, and treat you fairly, or even generously, in return.

Queuing is all about fairness. As George Mikes points out, 'A man in a queue is a fair man; he is minding his own business; he lives and lets live; he gives the other fellow a chance; he practises a duty while waiting to practise his own rights; he does almost everything an Englishman believes in doing.' And these unwritten principles apply even when the Englishman in question is breaking the law. During the London riots in August 2011, I witnessed looters *forming an orderly queue* to squeeze, one at a time, through the smashed window of a shop they were looting. They even did the 'paranoid pantomime', deterring potential queue-jumpers with disapproving frowns, pointed coughs and raised eyebrows. And it worked. Nobody jumped the queue. Even amid rioting and mayhem – and while committing a blatant crime – the unwritten laws of queuing can be 'enforced' by a raised eyebrow.

The Silent Fury Rule

Mikes, however, does tend to make it sound as though the English actively enjoy queuing. We don't. We hate it, like everyone else. It makes us cross and resentful and irritable, perhaps even more so than other nations, because we take the rules and principles of queuing more seriously – and all that constant vigilance and deterring of potential queue-jumpers with eyebrows and coughs and the rest of the non-verbal 'body English' repertoire is jolly hard work. We may not actually complain out loud about being kept waiting in a queue – at least, we are unlikely to address our complaints to the cashier or whoever is keeping us waiting – but do not mistake our silence for contentment or even patience. Look closer, and you will see that we convey our intense displeasure and frustration with queuing through yet more non-verbal micro-signals: heavy sighs, exasperated eye-rolls, pursed lips, fidgeting, tutting, finger tapping and pointedly looking at our watches every few seconds. We curse under our breath to ourselves, and we may even break the denial rule to exchange raised eyebrows and grimaces with fellow sufferers, and perhaps even mutter '*Typical!*' to each other.

Festive Queuing Rules

Although most of our queuing time is spent in a state of mute fury or righteous indignation, there are some special queues that could be described as 'national pastimes', queues that the English actively enjoy. Perhaps ironically, they are the longest, most uncomfortable, most exhausting queues of all. But queuing all day, and even overnight, for tickets at Wimbledon, the Proms, the Globe Theatre and other big events is somehow not really queuing: these special queues have been elevated to the status of festive rituals in their own right, and as such are periods of 'cultural remission' or 'festive inversion', where the normal social rules are temporarily suspended or even inverted. The ritual, liminal status of these queues is often emphasised with special names: queuing for cheap day-tickets at the Proms is called 'Promming', and the queuers are 'Prommers', while those queuing for cheap tickets to performances at Shakespeare's Globe Theatre are known as 'Groundlings'. These queues may even *look* like festivals: we bring picnics, folding chairs, sleeping bags and little tents. At Wimbledon, the queue – or rather, The Queue, always capitalised, as befits an important national institution – becomes an overnight tent-village campsite.

In these special queues (I'll call them 'festive queues' for shorthand) we eat, drink and make merry. We play games. We sing songs. In a total inversion of normal English etiquette, talking to strangers is actively prescribed: you will be regarded as rather snooty and frowned upon if you 'keep yourself to yourself' in the usual English manner. There is an atmosphere of camaraderie, a sense of solidarity. Many of the same people come back year after year – returning 'Prommers' often greet each other with 'Happy New Year!', although the Proms take place in the summer. Lifelong friendships and even marriages have been initiated in these queues.

There are special 'festive queues' for big concerts and sporting events in other countries too, of course – the phenomenon itself is not peculiarly English – but it is the contrast with our normal queues and the contact avoidance that characterises our normal public behaviour that is so striking here, and that may perhaps explain why we love and treasure these queues.

It is worth reminding ourselves, however, that 'cultural remission' is not just fancy academic jargon for 'letting rip' or 'anything goes': English festive queues are a *conventionalised* deviation from convention, a rule-governed form of rule-breaking. They have their own etiquette, in which, although some of our normal rules are suspended or inverted, others may be even more strictly enforced. Queue-jumping is regarded with even more abhorrence than usual: attempting to barge or sneak in ahead of people who have been patiently queuing all day or overnight is an even more heinous breach of the fair-play principle. And the inversion of the normal prohibition on talking to strangers means that here people will, for once, feel free to address offenders directly, giving full verbal vent to all the pent-up righteous outrage we usually try to express with eyebrows and coughs.

In these festive queues, the normal unwritten rules about 'place saving' are also still in force. In normal queues, leaving the queue for whatever reason means forfeiting your place in it, although a quick dash to grab a suddenly remembered item in a shop or supermarket may be permitted by the person behind you, if you ask nicely – and someone may take pity and 'keep your place' for you in a very long queue if you are desperate to use the loo, again if your request is suitably polite and apologetic. In festive queues, the same principle essentially applies, but during these marathon queuing rituals you are allowed to leave the queue for somewhat longer periods, after politely asking those around you if they 'could possibly' or 'would mind very much' keeping your place (and perhaps leaving a few objects such as your blankets or newspapers as markers) while you go off to buy a snack or an ice-cream, find a loo, etc. The length of absence permitted by the unwritten rules varies, but among Prommers, for example, half an hour is the unofficial maximum: longer than this, and, although you may not forfeit your place, you will be punished with frowns, pursed lips and other frosty expressions on your return. Sincere apologies and thanks will be required to restore goodwill.

The Drama of Queuing

Foreigners may find the complexities of our unwritten queuing rules somewhat baffling, but to the English they are second nature. We obey all of these laws instinctively, without even thinking about it. And despite all the apparent contradictions, irrationalities and downright absurdities I have just described, the result is, as the rest of the world recognises, that we are really very good at queuing. Admittedly, most of the rest of the world does not say this as a compliment: when people talk about the English talent for queuing, they generally do so with a slight sneer, implying that only rather dull, plodding, sheep-like creatures would actually take pride in their ability to stand patiently in orderly lines. ('The English would have done well under Communist rule,' they laugh, 'you are so good at queuing.') Our

critics – or those damning us with faint praise – will readily acknowledge that a man in a queue is a fair man, but point out that he is
not exactly what you'd call dashing or exciting.

But that is because they have not looked closely enough at English
queues. It's a bit like watching ants or bees. To the naked eye, an
English queue does indeed look rather dull and uninteresting – just
a tidy line of people, patiently waiting their turn. But when you
examine English queues under a social-science microscope, you find
that each one is a little mini-drama – not just an entertaining 'comedy
of manners', but a real human-interest story, full of intrigue and
scheming, intense moral dilemmas, honour and altruism, shifting
alliances, shame and face-saving, anger and reconciliation. I now
look at the ticket-counter queues at Clapham Junction and see, well,
perhaps not quite *War and Peace*, but . . . something a bit more
understated and English. Let's say *Pride and Prejudice*.

A Very English Tribute

One of the things that amused me about media coverage of the death
of Diana, Princess of Wales was the reporters' constant breathless
amazement at the 'un-Englishness' of the public response. This was
(and still is) invariably described as 'an unprecedented public
outpouring of grief' or 'an unprecedented public display of emotion',
amid extravagant claims that this extraordinary disinhibition marked
a 'sea-change' in the English character, that the stiff upper lip was
trembling, that we were all now wearing our hearts on our sleeves,
that we would never be the same again, and so on and so forth.

And what, exactly, did this 'unprecedented display of emotion'
consist of? Look at the pictures and videos of the crowds. What are
all those people doing? Queuing, that's what. Queuing to buy flowers,
queuing to lay flowers, queuing for miles to sign books of condolence,
queuing for hours to catch trains and buses home after a long day
of queuing. Then, a week or so later, queuing to catch buses and
trains to get to the funeral; queuing overnight to secure a good position to watch the procession; queuing to buy more flowers, drinks,
flags, newspapers; standing patiently in lines for hours waiting for
the cortège to file past; then queuing again for buses, coaches, tubes

and trains. Quiet, orderly, disciplined, dignified queuing.

Certainly, there were tears, but we did not scream or wail or rend our clothing or cover ourselves in ashes. Watch the videos. You will hear one or two rather feeble 'wails' as the coffin first emerges from the Palace gates, but these are clearly deemed inappropriate, quickly shushed, and not taken up by the rest of the crowd, who watch the procession in silence. The first people to turn up on the day after Diana died laid flowers; this was taken as the correct thing to do, so all subsequent visitors dutifully laid flowers. After the funeral, a few people started throwing flowers as the hearse drove past, and again the rest obediently followed their example. (No one threw flowers at the horse-drawn coffin earlier, of course: however overcome by unprecedented, un-English emotion, we know better than to frighten the horses.)

So, there were tears and flowers – neither of which strikes me as a particularly abnormal response to the death of a very popular young princess. Nor are the tears even 'unprecedented'. There were, according to commentators, 'few dry eyes' among the crowds watching Winston Churchill's funeral more than thirty years earlier. And going back even further, the death of twenty-one-year-old Princess Charlotte in 1817 prompted what would now be described as a frenzy of public mourning. Churches were full day and night, many shops in London closed for two weeks (not just a day as some did for Diana), and there was mayhem verging on a riot among the crowds trying to get tickets to see her lying in state. By comparison, the response to Diana's death seems remarkably restrained. The English paid tribute to Diana in the most English possible manner, by doing what we do best: queuing.

CAR RULES

Before we can even start to look at English unwritten social rules about cars and driving, there are a few 'universals' about cars that need clarifying. Across all cultures, humans have a strange and complex relationship with the car. The first thing we need to be clear about in this context is that the car is not primarily a means of transport – or, rather, if that sounds a bit too extreme, that our relationship with the car has very little to do with the fact that it gets us from A to B. Trains and buses get us from A to B: cars are part of our personal territory, and part of our personal and social identity. A bus can take you to the shops and back, but you do not feel at home in it or possessive about it. A train can get you to work, but it does not make socially and psychologically significant statements about you.

These are cross-cultural universals – basic, rather obvious facts about humans and cars. But we can now move straight back into discussions of Englishness, because the English, of all nations, are the most likely to resist or even vehemently deny at least one of these basic facts.

The Status-indifference Rule

Specifically, the English like to believe, and will often doggedly insist, that social-status considerations play no part in their choice of car. Even at the height of the BMW's yuppie-image heyday, for example, upwardly mobile English executives claimed that they bought their BMWs for their excellent German engineering and design, comfort, reliability, speed, handling, BHP, torque, low drag-coefficients and other rational, no-nonsense qualities. Nothing to do with social image. Nothing to do with status. Nothing to do with vanity. Nothing to do with impressing colleagues or neighbours or girlfriends. Oh, no. It's just a bloody good car.

English women, and some English men, will admit to aesthetic and even emotional reasons for choosing a particular car. Men will say that their flashy Porsche or big Mercedes is 'a beautiful car'; women will tell you that they want the trendy new Mini or Fiat because it is 'so cute'; both will even confess that they 'fell in love with' a 'gorgeous' car in the showroom, or that they have always had 'a passion' for MGs, or that they are 'sentimentally attached' to their rusty old banger.

We might even go so far as to acknowledge that we choose cars that we feel express our individual 'personality' or some aspect of our self-image (cool, sophisticated, stylish, fun, quirky, eccentric, sporty, sassy, sexy, honest, understated, down-to-earth, manly, professional, serious, etc.). But not our social status. We will not admit to buying or wanting a particular make of car because it is associated with a social class or category to which we wish to be seen to belong.

Class Rules

The 'Mondeo Test'

But the truth is that car choice, like almost everything else in England, is mostly about class. If you are conducting research – or just have a mischievous nature – you can trick English people into revealing, albeit indirectly, the real social-class reasons for their car choice. You do this not by talking about the make of car they actually own or would like to own, but by asking about the brands they do not like and would not buy. If you don't mind causing offence in the name of science, try saying 'I'd guess you probably drive a Ford Mondeo?' to some older members of the middle-middle or upper-middle classes. 'Mondeo Man' was for many years the generic euphemism for a lower-middle-class, suburban-salesman type, so class-anxious middles and upper-middles will be highly miffed at being 'demoted' to this social category. Many upper-middles may be too polite, or too squeamish about appearing snobbish, to show their annoyance in any obvious way, so you will have to watch their faces carefully for the indignant micro-signals – the raised eyebrows, brief wince, nose-wrinkle, or little *moue* of distaste. Among the higher or more secure reaches of upper-middle, the reaction is more likely to be mild, benign, somewhat condescending amusement,[75] and the genuinely upper class may simply have no idea what you are talking about. I found that the Mondeo-test can be a pretty good indicator of class-anxiety: the more huffy English people are about the suggestion that they drive a Mondeo, the more insecure they are about their own position in the social hierarchy.

75. Or even, among the very class-secure, approval: I know one unquestionably upper-middle woman who actually drives a Mondeo, and says that she bought it precisely because of its Mondeo-Man association with salesmen. 'If the big companies buy it for their travelling salesmen, it must be a reliable car that can take a lot of abuse,' she argues. Such confidence and admirable disdain for the opinion of others is, however, quite rare.

This is *not* a question of price. The cars driven by Mondeo-despising upper-middles may well be considerably cheaper than the reviled Mondeo, and the almost equally ridiculed Vauxhalls and other British-made 'fleet'[76] cars. But however inexpensive and lacking in comfort or luxury features, the Mondeo-despiser's car will be a foreign, preferably Continental make (or possibly, among the environmentally concerned, a 'green' Toyota Prius). The only exceptions to this anti-British rule are Minis, Jaguars and big, four-wheel-drive 'country' vehicles such as Land Rovers and Range Rovers. Those who regard themselves as being a class or two above Mondeo Man may well drive a small, cheap, second-hand Peugeot, Renault, VW or Fiat hatchback – but they will still feel smugly superior as Mondeo Man glides past them in his bigger, faster, more comfortable car.

I noted in a footnote in the 2004 edition of this book that the Mondeo example 'might be out of date by the time you read this'. As it turns out, although sales reps, aspiring middle-managers and other lumpen-lower-middle types are now just as likely to be driving bottom-of-the-range BMWs, the Mondeo is still remarkably popular, and the term 'Mondeo Man' is still quite a common euphemism for this social category. As the Mondeo is now regarded as slightly more downmarket, the Mondeo Test might now be slightly more insulting.

The 'Mercedes Test'

Upper-middles who pass the Mondeo Test – those who are merely mildly amused by your suggestion that they might drive a Mondeo – may still reveal hidden class anxieties over the Mercedes. When you've had your complacent little chuckle about Mondeos, try saying 'Now, let me guess . . . I'd say you probably drive a big Mercedes.'

If your subject looks hurt or annoyed (watch for the same micro-expressions as in the Mondeo Test) or responds with a forced laugh and perhaps a bit of barbed humour about 'flashy rich trash' or 'wealthy businessmen', you have hit the adjacent-class insecurity button. Your subject has made it into the upper-middle 'intelligentsia',

---

76. Cars purchased in large quantities ('fleets') by companies, generally for the use of travelling sales staff, area managers and other relatively low-grade employees.

'professional' or 'country' set, and is anxious to distinguish himself from the despised middle-middle 'business' class (or *nouveaux riches*) with which he almost certainly has some family connections. You may well find that his father (or even grandfather – these prejudices are passed down the generations) was a petit-bourgeois middle-class businessman of some sort – perhaps a successful shopkeeper or sales manager or even a well-off car dealer – who sent his children to smart private schools where they learnt to look down on petit-bourgeois middle-class businessmen.

Many English people will tell you that there is no longer any Jane-Austenish stigma attached to being 'in trade'. They are mistaken. And it is not just the tiny minority of aristocrats and landed gentry who turn up their noses at the commercial world. Upper-middle-class people in 'respectable' professions, such as barristers, doctors, civil servants and senior army officers, can often be equally snooty – and the upper-middle chattering classes (with their 'nice work' careers in the media, the arts, academia, publishing, charities, think-tanks and so on) are the most disparaging of all. Very few of this last group will drive a Mercedes, and most will regard the Mercedes-driving classes with at least some degree of disfavour, but only the insecure will get all huffy and heated and scornful at the thought of being associated with such a vulgar, business-class vehicle.

Again, the price of the car is not really the issue here. Mercedes-despisers may drive either equally expensive, more expensive or much cheaper cars than the Mercedes they find so abhorrent. Nor is wealth *per se* the problem. Upper-middle Mercedes-despisers come in all income brackets: they may make as much money as the 'vulgar rich businessman' driving the 'Merc' (as he would call it), or even more, or much less. The class issue concerns the means by which one acquires one's wealth, and how one chooses to display it. A Mercedes-despising barrister or publisher might well drive a top-of-the-range Audi, which costs about the same as a big Mercedes, but is regarded as more elegantly understated. This is presumably why the Royal Family all drive Audis, and have done for many years. Cynics claim that this is only because Audi gives the royals very favourable 'VIP' discounts, supports their charities and sponsors their polo matches, but it seems naïve to assume that other luxury-car manufacturers have never offered them similar terms. I suspect that their choice of respectable, discreet Audis, rather than flashy, wealth-displaying Mercedes or BMWs, was a judicious one.

At the moment, BMWs are tainted, to some extent, with the same business-class image as the Mercedes, although generally associated with a younger, City-dealer, 'yuppie' stereotype (and now, at the lower end of the BMW range, with the same lower-level managers and salesmen who drive Mondeos). Jaguars have also suffered a bit from a vulgar 'trade' connection, being associated with wealthy used-car dealers, slum-landlords, bookmakers and shady underworld characters. But Jaguars have also been for many years the official cars of our prime ministers and important cabinet ministers, which to some lends them an air of respectability – although others feel that this only confirms their inherent sleaziness. In both cases, however, these associations may be fading, and I did not find either Jaguars or BMWs reliable as a class-anxiety indicator. Should you wish to replicate my highly scientific class-anxiety experiments – or if you just fancy tormenting some socially insecure upper-middles – use the Mercedes test.

These rules and tests apply to normal saloon cars – SUVs are a different category. The upper classes and many upper-middles tend to look down upon SUVs, particularly the huge, brash, ostentatious ones, which they regard as the height of vulgarity, although they still buy the more traditional 'country' four-wheel-drive cars, such as Land Rovers and Range Rovers. For the snooty higher classes, driving a Mercedes SUV would put you even lower down the social scale than a normal Mercedes saloon car – you would be seen as a 'chav with money' rather than a rich bourgeois businessman. Even the new Bentley SUV is viewed as a vulgar monstrosity and a disgrace to a grand old name.

Car-care and Decoration Rules

But class distinctions, and class anxieties, don't stop with the make of car you choose to drive. The English will also gauge your social rank by the appearance and condition of your car – the way in which you care for it, or do not care for it.

The unwritten class rules involved in car care are even more revealing than those governing our choice of car, as we are less consciously aware of following them. The English all know, although we won't admit it, that our car choice is a class indicator; and we all know, although we pretend not to, exactly which cars are associated with which classes. But many people are unaware that the state and condition of their car may be broadcasting even more powerful class signals than its make.

How clean and shiny – or dirty and scruffy – is your car? As a crude rule of thumb: spotless, shiny cars are the hallmark of the middle-middle, lower-middle and upper-working classes while dirty, neglected cars are characteristic of the uppers, upper-middles and lower-workings (or in many cases 'not-workings' – the deprived, unemployed underclasses). In other words, dirty cars are associated with both the highest and very lowest ends of the social scale, clean cars with the middle ranks.

But it's not quite as simple as that. More specific class distinctions depend not only on the cleanliness of your car, but also on precisely how it got that way. Do you wash and polish the car yourself, lovingly and religiously every weekend, in the driveway or street outside your house? Then you are almost certainly lower-middle or upper-working. Do you take it frequently to a car-wash? Then you are probably either middle-middle or lower-middle with middle-middle aspirations (if you are upper-middle, your car-care habits betray middle-middle origins). Do you simply rely on the English weather to sluice off the worst of the grime for you, only resorting to a car-wash or bucket when you can no longer see out of the windows, or when people start finger-writing graffiti in the dirt on the boot? Then you are either upper class,[77] upper-middle or lower-working/underclass.

---

77. The exception being very wealthy members of the upper class, whose servants are responsible for their car care, and whose cars are therefore cleaned to impeccable upper-working-class standards.

This last rule might seem to suggest that one cannot distinguish between an upper-class car and an underclass one. In terms of degree of neglect, it is indeed impossible to tell the difference, but this is where one has to take the make of car into consideration as well. At the higher end of the social scale, the filthy car is more likely to be a Continental make (or, if British, either a 'country' four-wheel drive, a Mini or something grand such as an old Jaguar, Bentley or Daimler); at the lower end, the grubby vehicle is more likely to be British, American or Japanese.

More or less the same principle applies to the state of the interior of the car. A scrupulously tidy car indicates an upper-working to middle-middle owner, while a lot of rubbish, apple cores, biscuit crumbs, crumpled bits of paper and general disorder suggests an owner from either the top or the bottom of the social hierarchy. And there are still smaller clues and finer distinctions. If you not only have a tidy car, but also hang your suit-jacket carefully on the little hook thoughtfully provided for this purpose by the car manu-facturers, you are lower-middle or possibly at the lower end of middle-middle class. (All other classes simply sling their jacket on the back seat.) If you hang your jacket on a coat-hanger attached to the little hook, you are definitely lower-middle. If you also hang a neatly ironed shirt on a coat-hanger from the little hook, to change into before arriving at your 'important meeting', you are lower-middle of working-class origins, and anxious to proclaim your white-collar status.

There are minor variations to the interior car-care class rules, relating mainly to sex-differences. Women of all classes generally tend to have somewhat less tidy cars than men – they are rather more prone to scattering sweet-wrappers and tissues, and leaving stray gloves, scarves, maps, notes and other paraphernalia strewn over the seats. Men are usually a bit more 'car-proud', a bit more anal about keeping such things in the glove-compartment or side-pockets, rather less tolerant of clutter and muddle. Having said that, the upper and upper-middle classes of both sexes have a high tolerance of *dog-related* dirt and disorder (an immunity they share, again, with the lower-working/underclass). The interiors of their cars are often

covered in dog hair, and the upholstery scratched to bits by scrab-
bling paws. The middle-middles and lower-middles confine their dogs
to a caged-off section behind the back seats.

The lower-middles might even hang a flat, often tree-shaped,
scented dangly-thing from their rear-view mirror to counteract any
doggy smells, or indeed any smells. Their houses also tend to be full
of air-fresheners, loo-fresheners, carpet-fresheners and other deodor-
isers – as are those of the middle-middle class, but the middle-middles
know that hanging scented tree-things or any other dangly objects
from your rear-view mirror is lower class. In fact, you will not see
any decorative objects anywhere in cars belonging to the middle-
middle and higher social ranks. Nodding dogs on the back shelf,
Garfields clinging to windows and other cutesy animal motifs are
lower-middle and working-class indicators, as are bumper-stickers
and windscreen-stickers informing you of the car's occupants' taste
in holiday destinations and leisure activities. There are only two
exceptions to the no-sticker rule, and these are virtuous animal-
charity stickers and smugly safety-conscious 'Baby on Board' notices,
which you will see on the rear windscreens of both lower-middle and
middle-middle cars – although the middle-middle notices are less
likely to sport the logo of a nappy-manufacturer. (A few borderline
upper-middles may also display 'Baby on Board' signs, but they are
sneered at by the majority of upper-middles, particularly the intelligentsia.)

Electronics Rules

Your social class may also be judged on the amount of electronic
gadgetry in your car – the rule of thumb being that the more you
festoon the interior with all the latest 'In Vehicle Infotainment', or
IVI, as it is now called, the lower your position on the social scale.
Most cars now have at least a radio and a CD player, so these don't
count, and satnav and hands-free mobile-phone systems are also
becoming too ubiquitous to function as class indicators. But cars
tricked out with too many high-tech luxuries – such as video screens
built into seat-backs, games consoles, back-massagers and chilled
drinks cabinets – are regarded as vulgar and ostentatious, and only

driven by flashy *nouveaux-riches*. This applies especially if the car in question is one of those mammoth tank-like SUVs.

The Mobile Castle Rule

I mentioned at the beginning of this section that the 'personal-territory' factor is an important element of our relationship with the car. When Ford described their 1949 model as 'a living-room on wheels', they were cleverly appealing to a deep-seated human need for a sense of territory and security. This aspect of car psychology is a cross-cultural universal, but it is of particular significance to the English because of our obsession with our homes, which is in turn related to our pathological preoccupation with privacy.

An Englishman's home is his castle, and when an Englishman takes to the road in his car, a part of his castle goes with him. We have seen that on public transport, the English go to great lengths to maintain an illusion of privacy: we try to pretend that the strangers surrounding us simply do not exist, and assiduously avoid any contact or interaction with them. In our mobile castles, this self-delusion becomes much easier: rather than an invisible 'bubble' of standoffishness, we are enclosed in a real, solid shield of metal and glass. We can pretend not only that we are alone, but also that we are at home.

The Ostrich Rule

This illusion of privacy results in some rather strange and decidedly un-English behaviour. Like ostriches with their heads in the sand, English people in their cars seem to believe that they are invisible. You will see drivers picking their noses, scratching themselves in intimate places, singing and 'bopping' along to music on their radios, having screaming rows with their partners, kissing and fondling – things that most of us would normally only do in the privacy of our own homes, all performed in full view of dozens of other drivers and pedestrians, who may often be only a few feet away.

The sense of home-like security and invulnerability provided by our mobile castles also encourages some more offensive forms of disinhibition. Even normally fairly polite English people find them-selves making rude gestures and mouthing insults and threats at other road users from the safety of their cars – in many cases saying things we would never dare to say outside this protective shield.

Road-rage and the 'Nostalgia Isn't What It Used To Be' Rule

Despite these lapses, most foreign visitors acknowledge that the English are, generally speaking, remarkably courteous drivers. In fact, many visitors are surprised, and often rather amused, to read the now regular diatribes in British newspapers about how we are suffering from an 'epidemic' of 'road rage'. 'Have these people never been abroad?' asked one incredulous, well-travelled tourist. 'Don't they realise how polite and well-behaved English drivers are, compared to just about anywhere else in the world?'

'You call this "road rage"?' said another. 'You want to see road rage, go to America, go to France, go to Greece – hell, go anywhere but England! What you people call "road rage" is just normal driving.'

'This is so typically English,' an Anglophile but perceptive immigrant friend told me. 'You have a few incidents where a couple of drivers lose their temper and start hitting each other, and immediately it is a big national issue, it is a new dangerous disease sweeping the country, it is not safe to go out, the roads are full of violent maniacs . . . It makes me laugh. The English are the most fair and courteous drivers in the world, but you are always so determined to believe that the country is going to rack and ruin.'

He has a point. The English do suffer from a sort of 'nostalgia isn't what it used to be' syndrome. The belief that the country is going to the dogs, that things are not what they were, that some cherished bastion or emblem of Englishness (such as the pub, queuing, sportsmanship, the monarchy, courtesy, or even nostalgia itself) is dead or dying, seems to be endemic.

The truth about 'road rage' is that humans are territorial animals, and the car, as a 'home on wheels', is a special kind of territory, so our defensive reactions are aroused when we perceive that this territory is being threatened. So-called 'road rage' is therefore, not surprisingly, a universal phenomenon, and for all the sensationalist headlines, English manifestations of this universal human trait tend to be rather less common, and rather less violent, than in most other countries.

I am always somewhat wary of making such positive statements about the English, and tend to overload them with endless hesitant qualifiers, as I know from experience that praising the English – whether in published work or in ordinary conversation – invariably provokes much more argument and controversy than criticising them. When I make critical or even damning remarks about some aspect of English culture or behaviour, English people invariably nod gloomily in agreement, sometimes even providing supporting examples from their own experience. But praise, however mild and anxiously qualified, is always challenged: I am accused of wearing rose-tinted spectacles, and bombarded with counter-examples – everyone has some anecdote or statistic that contradicts my observations and proves that the English are really quite an awful and unpleasant lot.[78]

This is partly because social scientists are supposed to study problems (deviance, dysfunction, disorder, delinquency and other bad things beginning with D), and I am breaking the unwritten rules of my own profession by insisting on studying nice things instead. But that does not explain why it is only the determinedly unpatriotic English who object to my more positive findings about them. When I am interviewed by foreign journalists, or just chatting to tourists, visitors and immigrants, they are always quite happy to acknowledge that the English have some pleasant and even admirable qualities. The English themselves just cannot seem to accept this – at the merest hint of a compliment, they become sceptical, stroppy and argumentative. Well, I'm sorry, but I'm afraid I cannot alter my findings just to appease all these Eeyorish grouches and doom-mongers, so they will just have to swallow the odd bit of well-deserved praise.

---

78. I have noticed that those on the political left tend to believe that we have always been awful and unpleasant (citing colonialism, Victorian hypocrisy, etc., etc.), while those on the right favour the 'going to rack and ruin' line, harking back to an earlier age when we still had manners, respect, dignity and hard-backed blue passports.

Courtesy Rules

I will now stick my neck out and say that, apart from occasional territorial lapses, English drivers are quite rightly renowned for their orderly, sensible, courteous conduct. My foreign informants noticed well-mannered customs and practices that most of us take for granted: that you never have to wait too long before someone lets you out of a side-road or driveway, and that you are always thanked when you let someone else out; that almost all drivers keep a respectful distance from the car in front of them and do not 'tailgate', flash their head-lights or lean on their horns when they wish to overtake; that on single-track roads, or streets lined with cars on both sides making them effectively single-track, people are remarkably considerate about pulling in to let each other pass, and almost always raise a hand in thanks; that drivers stop for pedestrians at zebra crossings, even when the pedestrians are still standing waiting on the pavement and have not set foot on the crossing (I met one tourist who found this so astonishing that he kept repeating the experiment, marvelling at the fact that he could single-handedly bring streams of traffic to a defer-ential halt, without the aid of red lights or stop-signs); that horn-honking is regarded as rude, and only used in emergencies or special circumstances, as a warning, not as an all-purpose means of commu-nication or emotional outlet, as it is elsewhere in Europe and most other parts of the world. Even if you fail to notice that the traffic lights have changed to green, the English drivers behind you will often hesitate for a few moments, hoping you will move off of your own accord, before giving a small, almost apologetic 'beep' to draw your attention to the green light.

The standard driver's 'thank you' signal – a raised hand, or sometimes just a minimal raised index-finger, with the hand still on the steering wheel – is an infinitely more common sight among English drivers than any rude gestures. We use headlight-flashes primarily to say, 'I'm letting you pull out ahead of me,' or 'You go first', or to warn another driver of some danger or problem, or to say 'Thank you', not as a 'Get out of my way' signal. Some of us also use an alternating-indicator 'wave' to say 'Thank you' to a driver behind us for letting us pass.

Drivers in many countries no doubt feel as hampered as the English by the limited range of messages that can be conveyed with hand-signals and headlight- or indicator-flashes, but a study by my SIRC colleagues showed that there is one word that English drivers experience the most intense frustration at not being able to communicate to other drivers. That word is 'sorry'. 'Sorry' (or, more specifically, 'Oops, sorry!') is the message English drivers would most like to express, but for which there is no standard signal or gesture, as we've rather foolishly used up all the possible ones with our umpteen different ways of saying 'thank you'. When we inadvertently commit some error and impinge upon, confuse or inconvenience another driver, we often use the raised-hand 'thank you' gesture as a makeshift 'sorry', but this is ambiguous and unsatisfactory. We almost invariably *say* or silently mouth 'sorry' in such circumstances, and adopt a cringing posture and pained expression, even when we know the other driver can't possibly hear or see us.

I am not saying that English drivers are paragons of automotive virtue, or somehow magically endowed with any more saintly forbearance than other nations, just that we have rules and customs that prescribe a certain degree of restraint and courtesy. When frustrated or angry, English drivers are inclined to shout insults at each other just like anyone else, and the language used is no less colourful, but we mostly tend to do this from behind closed windows, rather than winding them down or getting out and 'making a scene'. If someone does lose their temper to the point of stand-up ranting and raving, or physically threatening behaviour, this is a noteworthy incident, deplored and tutted over in indignant tones for days, cited as evidence of a 'road-rage epidemic', a decline in moral standards, etc. – not, as it would be almost anywhere else, an annoying but relatively unremarkable event.

Fair-play Rules

English driving behaviour can be seen as an extension of our queuing behaviour, in that the same principles of fairness and good manners apply. As with queuing, people do 'cheat', but breaches of automotive fair-play rules provoke the same righteous indignation as pedestrian queue-jumping. Like pedestrian queuers, drivers are acutely aware of 'potential' cheats, and will, for example, inch forward in a pointed manner, with suspicious sideways glances, closing gaps to thwart another driver who appears to be considering an opportunistic manoeuvre, while carefully avoiding eye contact.

When the turn-off lane on a motorway or other main road is moving very slowly, some unscrupulous drivers will 'cheat' by zipping down the outside, faster-moving lanes and then trying to edge back into the turn-off lane at a later point. This is tantamount to queue-jumping, but the only punishment such sinners receive is much the same barrage of scowls, filthy looks and muttered insults that faces pedestrian queue-jumpers – perhaps with the addition of a few irate or obscene gestures, almost always performed from behind the safety of closed windows. The horn is rarely used in such cases, there being an unwritten rule to the effect that honking and beeping 'in anger' should be reserved for admonishing driving behaviour that is potentially dangerous, rather than just deeply immoral.

These tactics seem to be somewhat less effective at maintaining fair play among drivers than among pedestrians, because there is less potential for embarrassment. In the security of their mobile castles, with the ability to escape quickly from disapproving looks or angry gestures, the English are less vulnerable to these rather subtle deterrents and sanctions, and thus more inclined to break the fair-play rules. It is worth noting, however, that although queue-jumping and other opportunistic behaviours are more common among drivers than among pedestrians, only a small minority of drivers break the rules: the majority of English drivers, most of the time, 'play fair'.

ROAD RULES AND ENGLISHNESS

What do these rules tell us about Englishness? The denial rule provides yet another striking example of English social inhibition and embarrassment, and further evidence of our insularity and obsession with privacy. In the last chapter, I suggested that these two tendencies were related: that our excessive need for privacy is at least partly due to our social awkwardness, that 'home is what the English have instead of social skills'. A rather bold claim, perhaps, but none of the data in this road-rules chapter, which has been concerned with what happens when we venture outside the privacy and security of our homes, has caused me to revise this opinion. Both the denial rule and the mobile-castle rule confirm our inability to deal with the realities of social interaction: we can only cope by practising various forms of self-delusion, pretending either that other people do not exist, or that we are still at home.

The courtesy rules, both in the public-transport and driving contexts, also remind us of the importance of politeness in English culture, but I think we are now getting closer to a more precise understanding of the subtleties and nuances of English politeness. The identification of England as a predominantly 'negative-politeness' culture – concerned mainly with the avoidance of imposition and intrusion – seems to me quite helpful. The important point here is that politeness and courtesy, as practised by the English, have very little to do with friendliness or good nature.

A pattern seems to be emerging as we examine different aspects of English life and culture, a recurring theme that I think may be crucial to our understanding of the English character. What I am noticing is that there is rarely anything straightforward or direct or transparent about English social interaction. We seem to be congenitally incapable of being frank, clear or assertive. We are always oblique, always playing some complex, convoluted game. When we are not doing things backwards (saying the opposite of what we mean, not introducing ourselves until the end of an encounter, saying sorry when someone bumps into us and other *Looking-Glass* practices), we are doing them sideways (addressing our indignant mutterings about queue-jumpers to other queuers, and our complaints about delayed trains to other passengers, rather than actually tackling the offenders). Every social situation is fraught with ambiguity, knee-deep in complication, hidden meanings, veiled power-struggles, passive aggression and paranoid confusion. We seem perversely determined to make everything as difficult as possible for ourselves. Why, as one American visitor plaintively asked me, can't the English just be 'a bit more direct, you know, a bit more upfront?' We would, as she pointed out, save ourselves and everybody else a great deal of trouble.

The problem is, I think, that when we are 'direct and upfront', we tend to overdo it, becoming noisy, aggressive, rude and generally insufferable. Whenever I talk to English people about my research on Englishness, and mention that we tend to be inhibited and have lots of rules about politeness, they say, 'But we're not inhibited and polite – look at our football hooligans and drunken louts all over the place – we're loud and obnoxious and a disgrace.' Leaving aside what this response reveals about our penchant for national self-denigration, I would argue that our inhibited politeness and our loud obnoxiousness are two sides of the same coin. Both tendencies reflect a fundamental and distinctively English form of social dis-ease, a chronic and seemingly incurable inability to engage normally and directly with other human beings. We have developed many ingenious ways of disguising and overcoming this unfortunate disability ('facilitators' such as the weather, the pub and taxi-drivers' rear-view mirrors), but it can never be entirely eradicated.

Despite our idiopathic social handicaps, we do have some redeeming qualities. Many of the rules examined in this chapter, for example, highlight the immense importance of the concept of 'fairness' in English culture. This is not to say that other nations lack such a concept – what is distinctively English is our overwhelming national obsession with 'fair play'. (In my survey on patriotism, remember, our reputation for fair play came second only to our sense of humour as the quality in which the English take the most pride.)

Most of the remaining rules in this chapter seem to be concerned with that other great English obsession: class. The car-care rules relating to dirt, tidiness and dogginess indicate a curious but apparently consistent pattern in which we find that the top and bottom ends of the social scale have more in common with each other than either has with the middle ranks. The common factor usually turns out to be some form of disregard for social niceties or a lack of concern about 'what the neighbours will think'. It occurs to me that this may be why the majority of the more notable and flamboyant English eccentrics tend to come from either the highest or the lowest social classes. There seem to be fewer examples of brazen, colourful eccentricity among the middle-middle or lower-middle classes.

Finally, the 'road-rage' issue sheds some new light on the question of English patriotism or, rather, our apparent lack of it. Can there be any other nation so resolutely unpatriotic, so prone to self-flagellation, so squeamishly reluctant to accept praise? This dearth of national *amour-propre*, this seemingly unshakeable conviction that our country has nothing much to recommend it and is in any case rapidly going to the dogs, must surely be one of the defining characteristics of the English. Although, having said that, I suspect that this trait is in fact a sub-category, a symptom or side effect of our modesty, moaning and humour rules (particularly the self-deprecation rule and the Importance of Not Being Earnest rule)[79] rather than a defining characteristic in itself.

In the 2004 edition of this book, I confidently predicted that, despite all my many critical comments on the English, I would be taken to task when the book came out for being too positive, for painting too flattering a portrait, for ignoring or glossing over our darker side – and so on and so gloomily forth. As predicted, I received no complaints over any of my critical observations on English behaviour (or at least not from English people; some foreigners thought I was too harsh) but there were a couple of reviews and some letters and emails from grouchy English readers, complaining that I had failed to do full justice to our many flaws and failings. To be fair, though, many English readers and reviewers offered unstinting praise for the way this book had made them 'cringe with embarrassment'. Only in masochistic England would this be such a flattering compliment.

---

79. As noted in Humour Rules (page 78), my recent national survey on patriotism confirmed this suspicion.

WORK TO RULE

To identify and analyse the behaviour codes of the English at work is a huge, complex and difficult task – so daunting that most other recent books on the English either simply ignore the subject of work altogether or gloss over it with a few brief mentions. At least, I'm assuming that this aspect of English life and culture is neglected because it is too difficult, as it seems to me that it cannot be regarded as either irrelevant or uninteresting. Perhaps I am being supremely arrogant in even attempting to tackle this subject. My direct personal experience of the English world of work and business is somewhat unorthodox, as almost all of my own working life has been spent in a tiny, struggling, independent research organisation, the Social Issues Research Centre (SIRC), run by two very unbusinesslike social scientists (myself and my co-director Dr Peter Marsh, a social psychologist). But while SIRC itself may not be a typical workplace, the work we do has taken us into a varied and reasonably representative sample of working environments across the country (and in other countries as well, providing at least some basis for cross-cultural comparison).

During the research for this book, almost all of the foreigners I spoke to were somewhat perplexed and confused by English attitudes to work and behaviour at work; they all seemed to feel there was a 'problem', but they found it hard to pin down or express exactly what the problem was. To some extent, the differing opinions I encountered reflected my informants' own cultural backgrounds – those from Mediterranean, Latin American, Caribbean and some African cultures tended to see the English as rather rigid adherents of the Protestant work ethic, while many Indians, Pakistanis, Japanese and northern Europeans saw us as lazy, feckless and irresponsible (the Asians and Japanese usually tried to put this politely, although their meaning was clear enough; the Germans, Swedes and Swiss were more blunt).

But some of the contradictions seemed inherently English: the same people often expressed admiration for our inventiveness and innovation while deploring our stuffy, pig-headed traditionalism. Americans, supposedly our closest cultural relations, seemed if anything to be the most mystified and disoriented (not to mention irritated) by the anomalies and oddities of English work-culture. This may be partly because they have higher expectations of compatibility and mutual understanding ('two nations divided by a common language' and all that) and are therefore more surprised and unsettled when they find themselves dealing with an 'alien' culture, but even English observers find English attitudes to work confusing. In a textbook entitled *British Cultural Identities*, the authors claim on one page that 'The dominant British view is that work is a treadmill from which people dream of escaping' and on the next that 'The work ethic is very strong in the UK.' Quite apart from their apparent uncertainty as to which country or countries they are talking about,[80] this contradiction indicates that there are a number of elusive and entangled inconsistencies in English work-culture, which are 'indigenous' and quite independent of the cultural perspective from which they are viewed. I will now try to identify and untangle them.

THE MUDDLE RULES

The French writer Philippe Daudy remarked that 'Continentals are always disconcerted by the English attitude to work. They appear neither to view it as a heavy burden imposed by Fate, nor to embrace it as a sacred obligation.' In other words, our attitude to work does not conform to either the Catholic-fatalist or the Protestant-work-ethic

---

80. If the work ethic is very strong in the UK but negligible or absent in Britain, as they appear to be saying, then the nation's entire 'supply' of work ethic must be concentrated in Northern Ireland. With no disrespect to the Irish, this seems rather unlikely.

model, one or the other of which characterises the work-cultures of most other European countries. Our position is sort of somewhere in between these two extremes – a typically English exercise in compromise and moderation. Or a typically English muddle, depending on your point of view. But it is not an incomprehensible muddle; it is a rule-governed muddle, the guiding principles of which are as follows:

- We are serious about work, but not *too* serious.
- We believe that work is a duty, but we wouldn't go so far as to call it a 'sacred' duty, and we also believe it is a bit of a fag and a nuisance, imposed by practical necessity, though, rather than by some mystical 'Fate'.
- We constantly moan and complain about work, but we also take a kind of stoical pride in 'getting on with it' and 'doing our best'.
- We indignantly disapprove of those who avoid work – from rich aristocrats at the top of the social scale to the alleged 'benefits scroungers' at the bottom – but this reflects our strict, almost religious belief in fair play, rather than a belief in the sanctity of work itself (such people are seen as 'getting away with' idleness, while the rest of us, who would equally like to be idle, have to work, which is just not fair).
- We often maintain that we would rather not work, but our personal and social identity is in fact very much bound up with work (either the mere fact of being 'in work', bringing home a wage, or, for those with more intrinsically interesting or prestigious jobs, the rewards and status attached to the work).
- We find the whole subject of money distasteful, and there are still vestiges of a deep-seated prejudice against 'trade' or 'business', which can make 'doing business' a rather awkward business.
- We also have vestigial traces of a 'culture of amateurism', involving an instinctive mistrust of 'professionalism' and businesslike efficiency, which again can be a handicap when trying to run professional, efficient businesses.

- Finally, we carry into the workplace all the familiar English rules of humour, embarrassment, inhibition, privacy, modesty, moaning, courtesy, fairness, etc. – most of which are also incompatible with productive and effective work.
- But despite all this, we seem to muddle through somehow, and some of our work is not bad, considering.

It is from these principles that many of the specific rules governing behaviour at work are formed or derived.

The Parable of the Biscuit Chief

One of my encounters with an English businessman provides a real-life illustration of some of these principles, and a starting point for talking about the more specific rules. My colleague Peter Marsh and I once went with our begging bowl to try to persuade the chief executive of a large British company – a biscuit manufacturer – to provide funding for some of our research. We went through the usual polite preliminaries: slightly awkward handshakes and mumbled introductions; some wryly humorous comments about the weather; enquiries about our journey and apologies for the place being a bit difficult to find; comments on the compensating pleasantness of the view; offers of tea or coffee, fussing over milk and sugar; a few jokes about the proffered biscuits, and so on – the whole ritual taking the customary full fifteen minutes.

When we were finally settled, and had run out of excuses for avoiding discussion of business, the distinguished CEO said, 'So, well, where should we start?' One of us tentatively suggested that as he knew a bit about us and the Social Issues Research Centre from our letter, perhaps he could tell us a bit about himself and his company. 'Right,' said the CEO. 'Um, well, I've been running this company for the past eight years . . .' he paused for a fraction of a second before adding '. . . badly.' We laughed, but he protested, with a rueful expression, 'No, it's true, really – you only have to look at the figures.' Another pause, then he smiled broadly and added, 'But you can tell by looking at me [patting his ample stomach cheerfully] that I'm very fond of biscuits.' Having reassured us that his mismanagement of the company was not due to any personal antipathy towards its products, he seemed to feel that he had said more than enough about himself, and steered the conversation back to SIRC and our proposed research projects, for which he later generously agreed to provide some of the necessary funds.

Later, out of curiosity, we did 'look at the figures', and found that the company had indeed experienced something of a slump, to put it mildly, under his leadership. He later moved on to be chairman of an even bigger, multinational firm, which also promptly started going downhill. His appointment to this post provoked some grumbles in the City about his poor track-record, and the fact that he had no experience or knowledge whatsoever of the industry sector he was going to, but we could see why he had been chosen: he was such a nice, affable, amusing, unpretentious chap – and so disarmingly candid about his failings that one had the feeling he must be concealing great talents.

His is perhaps not an entirely typical English business story – but neither is it in any way atypical. In the course of our many encounters with people at all levels in English companies large and small, from shop-floor and front-line workers to managing directors and chairmen, we found that the most successful people – those most likely to be promoted or given plum jobs, that is – were not the most competent, or the most hard-working, or the most 'businesslike' or 'professional', but tended to have other, less tangible, qualities, particularly the self-deprecating humour exhibited by our biscuit chief. Of course, incompetent-but-charming people get promoted in other countries, too, but generally because they use their charm to distract attention *away* from their poor performance – not because they cheerfully tell everyone what a terrible job they are doing, and show them the results to prove it.

HUMOUR RULES

Spend a day in any English workplace, from a street-market to a merchant bank, and you will notice that one of the most striking features of English working life is the undercurrent of humour. I do not mean that all English workers and businessmen spend their time telling raucous, thigh-slapping jokes, or that we are 'good-humoured' in the sense of happy or cheerful: I am talking about the more subtle forms of humour – wit, irony, understatement, banter, teasing, pomposity-pricking – which are an integral part of almost all English social interaction.

Actually, I lied in that first sentence: if you are English, you could easily spend a day among English workers and business people without noticing the omnipresent humour – in fact, you probably do this every day. Even now that I've prompted you to be conscious of it, the humour in your workplace interactions will be so familiar, so normal, so ingrained that you may find it hard to 'stand back' far enough to see it. Foreigners, on the other hand, tend to notice it straight away – or, rather, to notice *something*, not always immediately identifiable as humour, which they find baffling. In my discussions with immigrants and other foreign informants, I found that the English sense of humour, in various guises, was one of the most common causes of misunderstanding and confusion in their dealings with the English at work. All of the unwritten rules of English humour contributed in some measure to this confusion, but the biggest stumbling blocks appeared to be the Importance of Not Being Earnest rule and the rules of irony.

The Importance of Not Being Earnest Rule

Our acute sensitivity to the distinction between seriousness and solemnity, between sincerity and earnestness, is not always fully understood or appreciated by foreign visitors, whose cultures tend to allow rather more blurring of these boundaries than is permitted among the English. In most other cultures, taking oneself too seriously may be a fault, but it is not a sin: a bit of self-important pomposity or over-zealous earnestness is tolerated, perhaps even expected, in discussion of important work or business matters. In the English workplace, however, the hand-on-heart gusher and the pompous pontificator are mercilessly ridiculed – if not to their faces, then certainly behind their backs. There are such people, of course, and the higher their status, the less likely they are to be made aware of their errors, but the English in general tend to be subconsciously sensitive to these taboos, and usually avoid overstepping the invisible lines.

The Importance of Not Being Earnest rule is implicit in our whole attitude to work. The first 'guiding principle' I mentioned was that we take work seriously, but not *too* seriously. If your work is interesting, you are allowed to be interested in it – even to the point of being 'a bit of a workaholic'; but if you are too much of a workaholic, or over-zealous about an intrinsically uninteresting job, you will be regarded as 'sad' and pathetic and it will be suggested that you should 'get a life'. It is not done to be too keen.

Training in Not Being Earnest starts early: among English schoolchildren, there is an unwritten rule forbidding excessive enthusiasm for academic work. In some schools, working hard for exams is permitted, but one must moan about it a lot, and certainly never admit to enjoying it. Even at the most academically-minded establishments, the over-earnest 'swot' or teacher's pet – currently known as a 'geek', 'nerd', 'suck' or 'boffin' – will be unpopular and subject to ridicule. Pupils who actively enjoy studying, or find a particular subject fascinating, or take pride in their academic prowess, will carefully conceal their eagerness under a mask of feigned boredom and cynical detachment.

The English are often accused of being anti-intellectual, and while there may be a grain of truth in this, I am inclined to think that it is a slight misinterpretation: what looks like anti-intellectualism is often in fact a combination of anti-earnestness and anti-boastfulness. We don't mind people being 'brainy' or clever, as long as they don't make a big song-and-dance about it, don't preach or pontificate at us, don't show off and don't take themselves too seriously. If someone shows signs of any of these tendencies – all unfortunately rather common among intellectuals – the English respond with our cynical national catchphrase 'Oh, come off it!' We may use whatever slang equivalent is currently favoured, such as 'Get over yourself', 'Oooh – get you!' or 'Could he be more up himself?' (often muttered under our breath, as is our custom, rather than addressed directly to the speaker), but the meaning is the same.

Our instinctive avoidance of earnestness results in a way of conducting business or work-related discussions that the uninitiated foreigner finds quite disturbing: a sort of offhand, dispassionate, detached manner – always giving the impression, as one of my most perceptive foreign informants put it, 'of being rather underwhelmed by the whole thing, including themselves and the product they were supposed to be trying to sell me'. This impassive, undemonstrative demeanour seems to be normal practice across all trades and professions, from jobbing builders to high-price barristers. It is not done to get too excited about one's products or services – one must not be seen to care too much, however desperate one may in fact be to close a deal: this would be undignified. The dispassionate approach works perfectly well with English customers and clients, as there is nothing the English detest more than an over-enthusiastic salesman, and excessive keenness will only make us cringe and back off. But our unexcitable manner can be a problem when dealing with foreigners, who expect us to show at least a modicum of enthusiasm for our work, particularly when we are trying to persuade others of its value or benefits.

Irony and Understatement Rules

The English predilection for irony, particularly our use of the understatement, only makes matters worse. Not only do we fail to exhibit the required degree of enthusiasm for our work or products, but we then compound the error by making remarks such as 'Well, it's not bad, considering' or 'You could do a lot worse,' when trying to convince someone that our loft conversions or legal acumen or whatever are really the best that money can buy. Then we have a tendency to say, 'Well, I expect we'll manage somehow,' when we mean 'Yes, certainly, no trouble', and 'That would be quite helpful,' when we mean 'For Christ's sake, that should have been done yesterday!', and 'We seem to have a bit of a problem,' when there has been a complete and utter disaster.

It takes foreign colleagues and clients a while to realise that when the English say, 'Oh, *really*? How interesting!' they might well mean 'I don't believe a word of it, you lying toad.' Or they might not.

They might just mean 'I'm bored and not really listening but trying to be polite.' Or they might be genuinely surprised and truly interested. You'll never know. There is no way of telling: even the English themselves, who have a pretty good 'sixth sense' for detecting irony, cannot always be entirely sure. And this is the problem with the English irony-habit: we do sometimes say what we mean, but our constant use of irony is a bit like crying wolf – when there really is a wolf, when we *do* mean what we say, our audience is not surprisingly somewhat sceptical, or, if foreign, completely bewildered. The English are accustomed to this perpetual state of uncertainty, and as J. B. Priestley says, this hazy atmosphere in which 'very rarely is everything clear-cut' is certainly favourable to humour. In the world of work and business, however, even one of my most staunchly English informants admitted that 'A bit more clarity might be helpful,' although, he added, 'We seem to muddle through well enough.'

A kind reader sent me a wonderful article about English irony and indirectness from, of all unlikely sources, the medical journal *Pediatric Pulmonology*, in which researchers report on a study of how Dutch professionals (but it could equally apply to most other nationalities) frequently misunderstand their English colleagues and employers. The study, based on interviews and tests in which Dutch and English subjects were asked to explain the meanings of common English phrases and expressions, confirms my view that when the English say, for example, 'With the greatest respect', foreigners not unreasonably assume that the speaker respects them or their views, when in fact the message is 'You must be a fool.' I would add that 'With all due respect' is often an even greater insult, as there is a convenient ambiguity, in the expression itself, regarding how much respect might actually be 'due'.

The researchers note that when the English say, 'I'm sure it's my fault . . .' foreigners naturally assume that we mean exactly this, when in fact we are just as likely to mean 'It's your fault!' I would add that the 'I'm sure' is nearly always a dead giveaway. When the English preface a statement with 'I'm sure', we generally mean the exact opposite of what we say. Similarly, a statement prefaced with a casual 'Oh, by the way . . .' is taken by foreigners to indicate an unimportant afterthought, when to the English it may well mean 'Pay attention, this is the primary purpose of our whole conversation.'

It is worth noting here that while the two Dutch co-authors of this paper charitably put this 'indirectness' down to the 'gentleman-like, polite nature' of the English, their English co-author attributes it to our 'utter dishonesty'. A typical example of unpatriotic English self-deprecation, perhaps, but he has a point. English politeness almost always goes hand-in-hand with English hypocrisy.

An Indian immigrant, who has been valiantly trying to do business with the English for many years, told me that it took him a while to get to grips with English irony because although irony is universal, 'the English do not do irony the way Indians do it. We do it in a very heavy-handed way, with lots of winks and raised eyebrows and exaggerated tones to let you know we are being ironic. We might say, "Oh yes, do you think so?" when we don't believe someone, but we will do it with all the signals blazing. In fact, most other nations do this – give lots of clues, I mean – in my experience. Only the English do irony with a completely straight face. I do realise that is how it should be done, Kate, and, yes, it is much more amusing – Indian irony is not funny at all, really, with all those big neon signs saying, "Irony" – but, you know, the English can be a bit too bloody subtle for their own good sometimes.'

Most English workers, however, far from being concerned about the difficulties it poses for foreigners, are immensely proud of our sense of humour. In a survey conducted by a social psychologist friend of mine, Peter Collett, experienced Euro-hopping British businessmen perceived the business climate in this country to be more light-hearted and humorous than in any other country in Europe, except Ireland (it was not entirely clear whether we felt the Irish had a better sense of humour, or just that we found them funnier). Only the Spanish even came close to matching us, and the poor Germans got the lowest humour-score of all, reflecting the popular stereotype in this country that Germans have absolutely no sense of humour – or perhaps that we find them difficult to laugh at, which is not quite the same thing.

THE MODESTY RULE –
AND THE 'BUMPEX' SCHOOL OF ADVERTISING

A further potential impediment to the successful conduct of business is the English modesty rule. While the English are no more *naturally* modest or self-effacing than other cultures – if anything, we are inclined to be rather arrogant – we do put a high value on these qualities, and have a number of unwritten rules prescribing at least the *appearance* of modesty. Perhaps the modesty rules act as a counter-balance to our natural arrogance, just as our courtesy rules protect us from our aggressive tendencies? Whatever their source, the English rules forbidding boastfulness, and prescribing a modest, unassuming manner can often be at odds with modern business practices.

I was once asked, as the official anthropologist of the horseracing 'tribe', to talk to a group of English racecourse owners and managers about how they might generate more business. I suggested that they could perhaps do more to publicise the unique social attractions of racing – the sunny 'social microclimate' of racecourses. With a look of horror, one of the racecourse managers protested, 'But that would be *boasting*!' Trying to keep a straight face, I said, 'No, I think nowadays it's called "marketing",' but the modesty rule proved stronger than any of my arguments, and he and a number of his colleagues remained unpersuadable.

That is an extreme example, and most English business people would now laugh at this old-fashioned attitude, but there are still some traces of this mindset in the majority of English businesses. While most of us would not go to the extreme of rejecting any kind of marketing effort as 'boasting', there is a near-universal distaste for the 'hard sell', for 'pushiness', for the sort of brash, in-your-face approach to advertising and marketing that the English invariably describe, in contemptuous tones, as 'American'. As usual, this stereotype reveals more about the English than it does about the maligned Americans: we like to think that our approach to selling things is more subtle, more understated, more ironic – and certainly less overtly boastful.

And, on the whole, it is. As I have said before, we do not have a monopoly on these qualities, but they tend to be more pervasive here than in other cultures, and we take them to greater extremes, particularly in our approach to advertising. The most striking example of this was a series of television advertisements for Marmite[81] in which people were shown reacting with utter revulsion – to the point of gagging – to even the faintest trace of a Marmitey taste or smell. The campaign was so successful that Marmite have been running variations on the same theme ever since. In 2012, for example, Marmite was repackaged as 'Ma'amite' to celebrate the Queen's Diamond Jubilee, but in the accompanying ads, even a dog (a royal corgi, of course) turns up his nose at a piece of toast spread with Marmite – and then emphasises his disgust by cocking a leg and urinating on it. It is well known that Marmite is something one either loves or hates, but an advertising campaign focusing exclusively on the disgust some people feel for your product strikes many foreigners as somewhat perverse. 'You couldn't get away with that anywhere else,' said an American informant. 'I mean, yes, I get it. People either love Marmite or find it disgusting, and as you're never going to convert the ones who find it disgusting, you might as well make a joke out of it. But an ad with the message "some people eat this stuff but a lot of people can't even bear the smell of it"? Only in England!'

The humorist George Mikes claimed in 1960 that 'All advertisements – particularly television advertisements – are utterly and hopelessly un-English. They are too outspoken, too definite, too boastful.' He suggested that instead of 'slavishly imitating the American style of breathless superlatives' the English should evolve their own style of advertising, recommending, 'Try your luck on Bumpex fruit juice. Most people detest it. You may be an exception,' as a suitably un-boastful English way of trying to sell a product.

This was clearly intended as a bit of comic exaggeration, a caricature of a stereotype, and yet, over fifty years on, the avoidance of breathless superlatives is now the norm in English advertising, and Marmite's

81. A salty, dark brown spread made from the yeast by-products of the beer-brewing process.

highly successful advertising campaign has precisely the same message as Mikes's fictitious Bumpex brand. The resemblance is uncanny: the ad agency might have taken their brief directly from Mikes's book. This suggests to me that his main point, that advertising itself is essentially un-English, and would have to be radically reinvented to comply with English modesty rules, is also much more than just an amusing exaggeration. He was quite right, and spookily prophetic. Advertising, and by extension all forms of marketing and selling, is almost by definition boastful – and therefore fundamentally at odds with one of the guiding principles of English culture.

For once, however, our self-imposed constraints have had a positive effect: advertising does not fit our system of values, so, rather than abandon our unwritten rules, we have twisted and changed the rules of advertising, and developed a form of advertising that allows us to comply with the modesty rule. The witty, innovative advertising for which the English are, I am told by people in the trade, internationally renowned and much admired, is really just our way of trying to preserve our modesty.

We English can blow our own trumpet if we have to; we can put on displays of heartfelt, gushing enthusiasm for our products or services, but the anti-boasting and anti-earnestness rules mean that many of us find this unseemly and acutely embarrassing, and we tend therefore to be somewhat unconvincing. And this problem is not just a feature of the higher echelons of English work: I found that workers at the bottom of the social scale are no less squeamish or cynical about trumpet-blowing than the educated middle- and upper-middle classes.

THE POLITE PROCRASTINATION RULE

Although the rules governing initial workplace encounters allow us to sidestep the problems normally posed by the no-name rule and the handshake dilemma, that's pretty much where the reassuring formality ends and the potential for embarrassment begins.

For a start, as soon as the initial introductions are completed, there is always an awkward period – usually lasting around five to ten minutes, but it can often take up to twenty – in which all or some of the parties feel that it would be rude to start 'talking business' straight away, and everyone tries to pretend that this is really just a friendly social gathering. We procrastinate politely with the usual weather-speak, enquiries about journeys, the obligatory wryly humorous traffic-moan, courteous comments on the host's excellent directions and rueful jokes about one's own poor navigation skills, interminable fussing over tea and coffee – including the usual full complement of pleases and thank-yous, appreciative murmurs from the visitors and humorously self-deprecating apologies from the host, and so on, and on.

I always find it hard to keep a straight face during this 'polite procrastination' ritual, because I am reminded of images from wild-life documentaries in which we see birds and other creatures engaging in 'displacement activity' – turning aside and nervously pecking at the ground or grooming themselves when they are in the middle of a confrontation over territory or mating rights or something. In tense, hostile situations, animals often perform these meaningless 'displacement' routines, as a kind of coping mechanism. It is much the same with the English in business meetings: the whole process of doing business makes us uncomfortable and embarrassed, so we distract ourselves and attempt to delay things by performing a lot of irrelevant little rituals.

And woe betide anyone who dares to cut short our therapeutic pecking and fussing. A visiting Canadian businessman complained, 'I wish someone had warned me about this earlier. I had a meeting the other day and they'd all been dithering and talking about the weather and making jokes about the M25 for what seemed like half an hour, so I suggested maybe we could get started on the contract and they all looked at me like I'd farted or something! Like, how could I be so crass?' Another told me he had worked in Japan and been invited to participate in tea ceremonies 'but there you are *either* having a tea ceremony *or* you are doing business. They don't try to pretend the business meeting is really a tea party, like you do here.'

THE MONEY-TALK TABOO

'But *why*?' asked another mystified foreigner – an Iranian immigrant with whom I was discussing the 'polite procrastination' rituals. 'You are right, this is exactly how they behave. It takes forever. It drives me crazy. But *why* do they do this? What is the *matter* with them? Why are they so reluctant to get down to business?'

Good question – to which I'm afraid there is no rational answer. The English find 'doing business' awkward and embarrassing at least partly because of a deep-seated but utterly irrational distaste for money-talk of any kind. At some stage, business-talk inevitably involves money-talk. We are comfortable enough, allowing for our usual social inhibitions, with most of the other aspects of business discussions. As long as boasting or earnestness are not required, we'll talk reasonably happily about the details of the product or project, and pragmatic issues such as objectives, what needs to be done, how, where, by whom and so on. But when it comes to what we call 'the sordid subject of money', we tend to become tongue-tied and uncomfortable. Some of us cover our embarrassment by joking, some by adopting a blustering, forthright, even aggressive manner; some become flustered and hurried, others may be over-polite and apologetic, or prickly and defensive. You will not often see an English person entirely at ease when obliged to engage in money-talk. Some may appear brash and bullish, but this is often as much a symptom of dis-ease as the nervous joking or apologetic manner.

A frustrated American immigrant told me that she had 'finally figured out that it is best to do all the financial negotiating in letters or emails. The English just can't talk about money face to face, you have to do it in writing. In writing they're fine – they don't have to look you in the eye and they don't have to say all those dirty words out loud.' As soon as she said this, I realised that this is exactly how I have always managed to get round the problem myself. I am typically, squeamishly English about money, and when negotiating fees for consultancy work or speaking engagements, or trying to get research funding, I will always try to put all those dirty words – money, cost, price, fees, payment, etc. – in writing rather than say them face to face or even on the telephone. (To be honest, I don't even like writing them, and usually try to cajole my long-suffering co-director into doing all the negotiating for me – with the feeble excuse that I am useless at maths.)

Being English, I had always rather taken it for granted that this avoidance of money-talk was normal, that everyone found it easier to discuss the taboo subject in writing, but my well-travelled inform-ants were adamant that this is a peculiarly English problem. 'I never get this anywhere else in Europe,' said one. 'Everywhere else you can be up-front about money. They're not ashamed or embarrassed about it; you just talk normally, they don't try to skirt round it or feel they have to apologise or make a joke out of it – that's it, with the English you always get that sort of nervous laughter, someone always tries to make a joke out of it.'

The joking is, of course, another coping mechanism, our favourite way of dealing with anything we find frightening or uncomfortable or embarrassing. Even high-powered City bankers and brokers – people who have to talk about money all day long – are affected by the money-talk taboo. One merchant banker told me that some types of dealing and negotiating are OK because 'it's not real money', but that when negotiating over his own fees he suffers from the same squeamish discomfort as everyone else. Other City financiers echoed this, and explained that, like everyone else, money-men cope with embarrassment about money-talk by joking. When things go wrong, one of them told me, 'You'll say, "So, are we still on your Christmas-card list?"'

'What about the image we all have of bankers bragging about their huge bonuses?' I asked. 'Sorry, touchy subject, I know, but would that be an exception to the taboo?'

My informants grimaced and embarked on long-winded explana-tions, the gist of which was that boasts about bonuses, like all 'personal' money-talk, must be heavily disguised as either humorous banter or mock-moaning.

To be honest, I am somewhat puzzled by the money-talk taboo, despite my own instinctive adherence to it. Introspection does not really help me to figure out the origins of the English squeamishness about money-talk at work. Our distaste for money-talk in everyday social life is well established: you never ask what someone earns, or disclose your own income; you never ask what price someone paid for anything, or announce the cost of any of your own possessions. In social contexts, there is a sort of 'internal logic' to the money-talk taboo in that it can be explained, to some extent, with reference to other basic 'rules of Englishness' to do with modesty, privacy, polite egalitarianism and other forms of hypocrisy. But to extend the money-talk taboo to the world of work and business seems, to put it mildly, perverse. Surely this should be an exception to the rule – the one arena in which, for obvious practical reasons, we set aside or suspend our prissy distaste and 'talk turkey', like everyone else. But, then, that would be expecting the English to behave rationally.

While I'm being ruthlessly honest, I have to admit that saying there is an 'internal logic' to the money-talk taboo is a bit of a cop-out. Yes, the taboo is clearly related, in a 'grammatical' sort of way, to the rules of privacy, modesty and polite egalitarianism, but this is how anthropologists always try to explain the more outlandishly irrational beliefs or grotesque practices of the tribes and societies they study. A belief or practice may seem irrational (or in some cases downright stupid or cruel), but, we argue, it makes sense in relation to other elements of the cultural system of beliefs and practices and values of the tribe or community in question. Using this clever little trick, we can find an 'internal logic' for all sorts of daft and apparently unintelligible notions and customs, from witchcraft and rain-dances to female circumcision. And, yes, it does help to make them more intelligible, and it is important to understand why people do these things. But it doesn't make them any less daft.

Not that I'm putting the English money-talk taboo on a par with female circumcision: I'm just saying that sometimes anthropologists should come clean and acknowledge that a particular native belief or practice is pretty bloody weird, and perhaps not entirely in the natives' own best interest. At least in this case I can't be accused of being ethnocentric or colonial or patronising (anthropological equivalents of blasphemy, for which one can be excommunicated) as the daft taboo I am denigrating is an unwritten rule of my own native culture, and one that I blindly and slavishly obey.

The Income-talk Taboo

The taboo on asking what someone earns, or disclosing one's own income, is possibly the strictest of all English money-talk taboos. I recently observed a perfect example of this, while chatting with a couple of new English acquaintances – two young male students (let's call them George and Mark) – over a cup of tea at a neighbour's flat. One of the young men, George, mentioned that he had lived for a while in America as a child, so naturally I asked him about any cultural differences he might have noticed. He talked about being shocked by how willing Americans are to ask people what they earn, and to reveal their own incomes.

Two minutes later, the conversation moved on a bit, and George mentioned that on their return from America, his father had changed careers and become a schoolteacher. Here is the dialogue that ensued:

MARK (*speaking very clearly, with a straight face*): Oh, so what did he earn?

GEORGE (*sounding slightly confused*): What did I learn?

MARK (*enunciating even more clearly*): No. I asked, What Did He *Earn*?

GEORGE (*even more puzzled*): Oh, sorry – what did *he* learn?

At this point, Mark, my neighbour and I burst out laughing. 'Oh, that is *so* English!' I giggled. 'The question is so utterly unthinkable here that you can't even hear it – you assume Mark must be asking something else. Even I thought I must have misheard him the first time. It was only when he repeated the question that I realised he was playing a joke on you!'

George finally twigged, joined in the laughter and said, 'But I *still* didn't get it! Even though we'd only just been discussing how Americans do this. That was so strange. It never even occurred to me that he could possibly be asking *that* question. My brain must have translated it into something more acceptable.'

We chatted a bit more about the money-talk taboo, then moved on to other topics. George never did answer the question about his father's salary, of course. No one expected him to: it was a question that could only ever have been asked as a joke.

It is worth noting that this ultra-embarrassing question was not even about the current income of anyone in the room: it was a question about a father's schoolteacher salary, many years ago. And yet still so unimaginable that our English ears couldn't even hear it.

Variations and the Yorkshire Inversion

The money-talk taboo is a distinctively English behaviour code, but it is not universally observed. There are significant variations: southerners are generally more uncomfortable with money-talk than northerners, and the middle and upper classes tend to be more squeamish about it than the working classes. Indeed, middle- and upper-class children are often brought up to regard talking about money as 'vulgar' or 'common'.

In the world of business, observance of the taboo increases with seniority: whatever their individual class or regional origins, higher-ranking people in English companies are more likely to be squeamish about money-talk. Those from working-class and/or northern backgrounds may start out with little or no 'natural' embarrassment about money-talk, but as they rise through the ranks they learn to be awkward and uncomfortable, to make apologetic jokes, to procrastinate and avoid the issue.

There are, however, pockets of stronger resistance to the money-talk taboo, particularly in Yorkshire, a county that prides itself on being forthright, blunt and plain-spoken, especially on matters that mincing, hesitant southerners find embarrassing, such as money. To illustrate this no-nonsense, no-frills attitude, Yorkshiremen jokingly describe a standard conversation between a Yorkshire travelling salesman and a Yorkshire shopkeeper as follows:

SALESMAN (*entering shop*): 'Owt?'
SHOPKEEPER: 'Nowt.'[82]
SALESMAN *leaves.*

This is a caricature, of course – most Yorkshire people are probably no more blunt than any other northerners – but it is a caricature with which a great many people from this area identify, and some actively do their best to live up to it. Far from beating about the bush, dithering and euphemising about money in the usual English manner, the proud-to-be-Yorkshire businessman will take a perverse pleasure in blatantly flouting the money-talk taboo – saying, directly and without jokes or preamble, 'Right, and what's all that going to cost me, then?'

But this is not an exception that invalidates or even questions the rule. It is a deliberate, dramatic *inversion* of the rule – something that can only occur where a rule is well established and understood. It is the flip side of the same coin, not a different and separate coin. Blunt Yorkshiremen *know* that they are turning the rules upside-down: they do it on purpose; they make jokes about it; they take pride in their maverick, iconoclastic status within English culture. In most other cultures, their directness about money would pass without notice: it would simply be normal behaviour. In England, it is remarked upon, joked about, recognised as an aberration.

It is also worth noting that despite the un-English bluntness of the salesman/shopkeeper scenario described above, the travelling salesman still politely refrains from any pushy insistence on actually *selling* anything to the shopkeeper. That would be unseemly – far too brash and un-English, even for an extreme caricature of a brash and un-English Yorkshireman.

Class and the Vestigial Trade-prejudice Rule

Without attempting to defend or justify the money-talk taboo, I can see that there might be historical explanations for this peculiar

82. For those who do not speak Yorkshire: 'owt' means 'anything' and 'nowt' means 'nothing'.

practice, as well as the rather circular 'grammatical' ones. I mentioned earlier that we still suffer from vestigial traces of a prejudice against 'trade', left over from the days when the aristocracy and landed gentry – and, indeed, anyone wishing to call himself a gentleman – lived off the rents from their land and estates, and did not engage in anything so vulgar as the making and selling of goods. Trade was low-class, and those who made their fortune by commerce were always quick to purchase a country estate and attempt to conceal all evidence of their former undesirable 'connections'. In other words, the upper-class prejudice against trade was in fact shared by the lower social ranks, including those who were themselves engaged in trade.

Every English school pupil's essay on Jane Austen notes that while she pokes fun at the snobbish prejudices against trade of her time, she does not seriously question them – but schoolchildren are not told that residual, subconscious traces of the same snobberies are still implicit in English attitudes towards work and behaviour in the workplace. These prejudices are strongest among the upper classes, the upper-middle professional classes (that's 'professional' in the old sense, meaning those belonging to one of the traditionally respectable professions, such as the law, medicine, the Church or the military) and the intelligentsia or chattering classes.

These classes have a particularly ingrained distaste for the 'bourgeois businessman', but the stigmatisation of anyone involved in 'sales' is widespread. Even the makes of car associated with either wealthy businessmen (Mercedes) or sales representatives (Mondeo) are sneered at by the socially insecure of all classes – and remember the near-universal contempt for another breed of salesman, the estate agent.

These examples indicate that the English prejudice against trade, as well as being eroded (though not eradicated), has shifted slightly since Austen's time, in that the making of goods has become significantly more acceptable than the selling of them. Although, of course, the two are often inextricably connected, it seems to be the pushy, undignified, money-focused selling of things that we find most distasteful, and most untrustworthy. There is an unwritten rule – a truth universally acknowledged, even – to the effect that anyone selling anything is not to be trusted. Distrust of salesmen is clearly not a uniquely English trait, but our suspicion and scepticism, and above all our contemptuous distaste, seem to be more acute and more deep-seated than other cultures'. The English are less litigious than the Americans when we feel cheated or dissatisfied with what we are sold (despite some shifts towards greater litigiousness, our tendency is still to complain indignantly to each other, rather than tackling the source of our discontent) but our more marked mistrust and dislike of salesmen means that we tend to be less gullible in the first place.

In other cultures, salesmen may not be trusted, but they are somehow socially accepted in a way that they are not among the English. In other parts of the world, selling things is regarded as a legitimate way of earning a living, and successful businessmen who have made their fortune by doing so are accorded a degree of respect. In England, money will buy you a lot of things, including access to power and influence, but it will not buy you any respect – quite the opposite, in fact: there seems to be almost as much of a taboo on making money as there is on talking about it. When the English describe someone as 'rich' or 'wealthy', we almost always do so with a slight sneer, and those who can be so described will rarely use these terms of themselves: they will admit, reluctantly, to being 'quite well off, I suppose'. We may well be, as Orwell said, the most class-ridden country under the sun, but I think it is safe to say that in no other country is social class so completely independent of material wealth. And social acceptability in the wider sense is, if anything, inversely related to financial prosperity – there may be some surface syco-phancy, but 'fat cats' are objects of contempt and derision, if not to their faces, then certainly behind their backs. If you do have the misfortune to be financially successful, it is bad manners to draw attention to the fact. You must play down your success, and appear ashamed of your wealth.

It has been said that the main difference between the English system of social status based on class (that is, birth) and the American 'meritocracy' is that under the latter, because the rich and powerful believe that they deserve their wealth and power, they are more complacent, while under the former they tend to have a greater sense of social responsibility, more compassion towards those less privileged than themselves. I'm grossly oversimplifying the arguments – whole books have been written on this[83] – but it may be that the English embarrassment about money and lack of respect for business success have something to do with this tradition.

Having said that, it is clear that much of all this English squeamishness about money is sheer hypocrisy. The English are no less naturally ambitious, greedy, selfish or avaricious than any other nation – we just have more and stricter rules requiring us to hide, deny and repress these tendencies. Our modesty rules and rules of polite egalitarianism – which I believe are the 'grammatical laws' or 'cultural DNA' behind the money-talk taboo and the prejudice against business success – are a veneer, an exercise in collective self-delusion. The modesty we display is generally false, and our apparent reluctance to emphasise status differences conceals an acute consciousness of these differences. But, hey, at least we value these virtuous qualities, and obey the rules despite their often deleterious effect on our business dealings.

THE MODERATION RULE

The phrase 'work hard, play hard' became popular in England in the 1980s, and you will still quite often hear people use it to describe their exciting lifestyle and their dynamic approach to work and leisure. They are almost always lying. The English, on the whole, do not 'work hard and play hard': we do both, and most other things,

---

83. Not least by the Englishman Michael Young, who coined the term 'meritocracy' in 1958 – and never intended the positive connotations it has acquired. In 2001, he wrote: 'If meritocrats believe, as more and more of them are encouraged to, that their advancement comes from their own merits, they can feel they deserve whatever they can get. They can be insufferably smug, much more so than the people who knew they had achieved advancement not on their own merit but because they were, as somebody's son or daughter, the beneficiaries of nepotism. The newcomers can actually believe they have morality on their side.'

in moderation. Of course, 'work moderately, play moderately' does not have quite the same ring to it, but I'm afraid it is a far more accurate description of typical English work and leisure habits. We work fairly diligently, and have a modest amount of fun in our free time.

I will not be thanked for this rather dull portrait, so I should make it clear that it is not just an impression or subjective judgement: these are the findings not only of SIRC's own quite extensive research on work habits and attitudes, but also of every other study I could find on this subject. Neither are these rather staid, conventional, conservative habits confined to the middle-aged or middle-class. Contrary to popular opinion, the 'youth of today' are not feckless, irresponsible, thrill-seeking hedonists. If anything, both our own research and other surveys and studies have found that the young of all classes are *more* sensible, industrious, moderate and cautious than their parents' generation. I find this rather worrying, as it suggests that unless our younger generation grows out of these middle-aged attitudes as they get older (which seems somewhat unlikely) the English will as a nation become even more ploddingly moderate than we are now.

If you think I'm exaggerating either the extent or the dangers of English youthful moderation, a few examples from the SIRC research might help to convince you:

Safe, Sensible, Bourgeois Aspirations

In our survey, when asked where they would like to be in ten years' time, nearly three quarters (72 per cent) of young people chose the safe, sensible options of being 'settled down' or 'successful at work', compared with just 38 per cent of the older generation. Only 20 per cent of 16–24-year-olds chose the more adventurous option of 'travelling the world/living abroad', compared with 28 per cent of 45–54-year-olds. The older age group was also *twice* as likely as the youngsters to want to be 'footloose and fancy-free'. In discussion groups and informal interviews, when we asked about their aspirations in life, almost all young working people wanted to be 'financially secure and stable'. Home ownership was a long-term goal.

Future Stability More Important Than Fun

Gosh, what a dull lot, I thought, when those results first came in. In the hope of finding some more imaginative and rebellious attitudes, I turned to the questions on 'fun'. I was disappointed to find that on the issue of 'having fun now vs thinking about the future', where one might expect the younger generation to be at least a bit less mature and responsible, the views of young people and their elders were more or less identical. Only 14 per cent of 16–24-year-olds felt that 'At my age it's more important to have fun than to think too much about the future' – and about the same minority of 45–54s were also carefree fun-lovers.

Our discussion-group and interview findings indicated that young working people's only major 'fun' indulgence is going out to pubs and clubs on Friday and Saturday nights, or perhaps a clothes-shopping spree. Many of our discussion-group participants tried to make all this sound as 'wild' as possible, one proudly announcing that 'I spend most of my money abusing my body, really – going out to pubs and clubs, smoking' but essentially it boiled down to a rather tame routine of weekend drinking, dancing and shopping.

I was not much cheered by the next lot of findings, which showed that young people also seem to be more industrious than their parents' generation: 70 per cent of 16–24s believe that 'getting ahead in life is down to hard work and dedication'. Only 53 per cent of the older generation share this diligent attitude, with 41 per cent adopting the more laid-back view that success is a matter of luck, contacts or 'the right breaks'.

The Dangers of Excessive Moderation

I felt like saying, 'Oh, for heaven's sake, lighten up! Live a little! Rebel a bit! Whatever happened to "Turn on, tune in, drop out"?' All right, I did, and still do, realise that many people will find these results reassuring. Even some of my colleagues felt that I was making rather an unnecessary fuss. 'Surely it is a good thing that most young people are being diligent, prudent and responsible,' they said. 'Why do you find this so depressing?'

My concern is that these largely commendable tendencies are also symptoms of a wider and more worrying trend: our findings indicated that young people are increasingly affected by the culture of fear, and the risk-aversion and obsession with safety that have become defining features of contemporary society. This trend, described by one sociologist as a 'cultural climate of pervasive anxiety' – which has no doubt been further exacerbated by economic recession – is associated with the stunted aspirations, cautiousness, conformism and lack of adventurous spirit that were evident among many of the young people in our survey and discussion groups.

There has always, of course, been a significant degree of exaggeration and even invention in the standard laments and outcries about 'the youth of today', their fecklessness and irresponsibility. So perhaps our findings merely showed what has always been the case: that young people are rather more conventional and responsible than they are cracked up to be. Well, yes. And in their adherence to the moderation rule, the young people we studied were to some extent just 'being English'. Whether I like it or not, we are a deeply conservative, moderate people. But what worried me was that these young people were *more* conservative, moderate and conformist than their parents' generation, that there seemed to be a trend towards even *greater* excesses of moderation (if one can say such a thing). And although I am in many ways very English, I can only take so much moderation. Moderation is all very well, but only in moderation.

THE FAIR-PLAY RULE

But, to be fair, there were plenty of more positive findings in our research on English workers as well, not least to do with fairness. Although I often use the terms interchangeably, I have chosen the term 'fair-play rule' rather than 'fairness rule' for the title of this section, as I feel that 'fair play' conveys a wider and somewhat less rigidly egalitarian concept that more accurately reflects the English values I am trying to describe. 'Fair play', with its sporting overtones, suggests that everyone should be given an equal chance, that no one should have an unfair advantage or handicap, and that people should conduct themselves honourably, observe the rules and not cheat or shirk their responsibilities. At the same time, 'fair play' allows for differences in ability and accepts that there will be winners and losers – while maintaining that playing well and fairly is more important than winning. Some would claim that this last element is archaic and no longer observed, but my research has convinced me that it is still a rule in the sense of an ideal standard to which the English aspire, even if it is not often achieved.

In some respects, the fair-play rule serves us well in the world of work and business. While we undoubtedly have our share of rogues and cheats, and the rest of us are by no means saints, the English are generally still regarded, with some justification, as *relatively* fair and straight in their conduct of business – and there is certainly less blatant *tolerance* of bribery, corruption and cheating here than in many other countries. When we hear of such incidents, most of us do not shrug in a knowing, worldly manner, as if to say, 'Well, yes, what do you expect?' We are shocked, outraged, righteously indignant. This may be partly because the English take great pleasure in being shocked and outraged, and righteous indignation is one of our favourite national pastimes, but the feelings expressed are nonetheless genuine. And they are expressed, vehemently, even when the 'cheating' in question is perfectly legal – as in the recent outrage over tax avoidance by some big multinational corporations. These companies had broken no official laws: our indignation was over their serious breach of the unwritten 'fair play' principle.

When asked to compare English working and business practices with those of other cultures, all of my foreign and immigrant informants commented on the English sense of fair play, and specifically on our relative freedom from the corruption they felt was endemic and tacitly accepted (albeit in varying degrees) in other parts of the world. Many felt that we were not sufficiently aware or appreciative of this fact. 'You just take it for granted,' a Polish immigrant complained. 'You assume that people will play fair, and you are shocked and upset when they do not. In other countries there is not that assumption.'

So, we may be a bit dull and excessively moderate, but perhaps, without wishing to come over all patriotic, we can still take a little bit of pride in this fair-play ideal. (And we do in my survey, 'fair play' came second only to 'humour' as the English quality of which we are most proud.)

MOANING RULES

The rather less admirable English habit of constant moaning is another distinguishing feature of our workplace behaviour, and of our attitude to work. The principal rule in this context is that work is, almost by definition, something to be moaned about. There is a connection here with the Importance of Not Being Earnest rule, in that if you do not indulge in the customary convivial moaning about work, there is a danger that you will be seen as too keen and earnest, and labelled a 'sad geek', a sycophantic 'suck' or 'brown nose', or a self-important 'pompous git'.

The Monday-morning Moan

English work-moaning is a highly predictable, regular, choreo-graphed ritual. On Monday mornings, for example, in every work-place in England, from factories and shops to offices and boardrooms, someone will be conducting a Monday-morning moan. I can guarantee it. It is universally understood that everyone hates Mondays; that we all had trouble dragging ourselves out of bed; that we really could have done with an extra day to get over the weekend; that the traffic/tube/trains/buses just seem to be getting worse and worse; that we have far too much to do this week, as per bloody usual; that we are already tired and our back/head/feet are hurting, and the week's only just started, for God's sake; and, look, now this effing printer's on the blink again, just for a change, huh, typical!

There are endless variations on this Monday-morning moan, and no two such moans are ever exactly alike – but, like the infinitely variable snowflake,[84] they are all nonetheless remarkably similar. Most of them start and sometimes end with a bit of weather-speak:

84. Although I've always wondered: how do we *know* that no two snowflakes are identical? I mean, has someone actually *checked* them all?

'Bloody cold,' or 'Raining again,' we grumble, as we shed our coats and scarves on arrival, which sets the tone and triggers another complaint, either about the weather or the traffic, trains, etc. At the end of the first morning-moan ritual, someone may close the proceedings with '*And* it's still raining,' or 'Well,' stoical sigh, 'at least it's stopped raining.' This is the cue for everyone to shift from their habitual moan-position and start reluctantly getting on with the day's work, muttering, 'Right, well, s'pose we'd better make a start,' or 'Back to the grind, then,' or, if in a position of authority, 'All right, c'mon, you lot, let's get some work done.'

Then we all work, moderately diligently, until the next moaning opportunity, usually the first tea- or coffee-break, when the Monday litany of complaint is revived with a new set of moans: 'God, is it only eleven o'clock? I'm so tired.' 'Well, it's been a long week.' 'Eleven already? I've got so much to do and I've barely made a dent in it.' 'That bloody coffee machine's eaten my 50p again! Typical!' And so on. Followed by yet more congenial moaning over lunch, at subsequent breaks, and at the end of the day, either on leaving work or over after-work drinks in a local pub or bar.

The Time-moan and the Meeting-moan

There are variations in our workplace moans, but even these are largely predictable. Everyone moans about time, for example, but junior and low-grade employees are more likely to complain that it passes too slowly, that they have another seven sodding hours of this shift to get through, that they are bored and fed up and can't wait to get home, while more senior people usually whine that time just seems to fly past, that they never have enough of it to get through their ridiculous workload, and now there's another bloody meeting they have to go to.

All white-collar executives and managers – right up to top boardroom level – *always* moan about meetings. To admit to enjoying meetings, or finding them useful, would be the secular equivalent of blasphemy. Meetings are by definition pointless, boring, tedious and awful. A bestselling training video on how to conduct meetings (or at least make them marginally less awful) was called *Meetings, Bloody*

Meetings – because that is how we always refer to these ordeals. English workers struggle to get to the rung on the corporate ladder where they are senior enough to be asked to attend meetings, then spend the rest of their career moaning about all the meetings they have to attend.

We all hate meetings, or at least loudly proclaim that we hate them. But we have to have a lot of them, because of the fair-play, moderation, compromise and polite-egalitarianism rules, which combine to ensure that few individuals can make decisions on their own: a host of others must always be consulted, and a consensus must be reached. So we hold endless meetings, everyone is consulted, we discuss everything, and eventually we reach a consensus. Sometimes we even make a decision.

Then we go and have a good moan about it all.

The Mock-moaning Rule and the 'Typical!' Rule

All this talk of moaning may be making the English sound rather sad and depressing, but that is not the case. The curious thing about all of these moan sessions is that the tone is actually quite cheerful, good-natured and, above all, humorous. In fact, this is probably one of the most important 'rules of moaning': you must moan in a relatively good-humoured, light-hearted manner. However genuinely grumpy you may be feeling, this must be disguised as *mock*-grumpiness. The difference is subtle, and may not be immediately obvious to the naked ear of an outsider, but the English all have a sixth sense for it, and can distinguish acceptable mock-moaning from real, serious complaining at twenty paces.

Serious moaning may take place in other contexts, such as heart-to-heart conversations with one's closest friends, but it is regarded as unseemly and inappropriate in collective workplace moaning rituals. Here, if you become too obviously bitter or upset about your griev-ances, you will be labelled a 'moaner', and nobody likes a 'moaner' – 'moaners' have no place in ritual moaning sessions. Ritual moaning in the workplace is a form of social bonding, an opportunity to estab-lish and reinforce common values by sharing a few gripes and groans about mutual annoyances and irritations. It is worth a reminder here that in all English moaning rituals, there is a tacit understanding that nothing can or will be done about the problems we are moaning about. We complain to each other, rather than tackling the real source of our discontent, and we neither expect nor want to find a solution to our problems – we just want to enjoy moaning about them. Our ritual moaning is purely therapeutic, not strategic or purposeful: the moan is an end in itself.

Genuine grievances may be raised in these sessions, about pay, working conditions, tyrannical bosses or other problems, but even these moans must be delivered with humorous grimaces, shrugs, eye-rolling, mock-exasperated eyebrow-lifts and exaggerated stoical sighs – not with tear-filled eyes, trembling lips or serious scowls. This is sociable light entertainment, not heavy drama. The appropriate tone is encapsulated in the English moan-ritual catchphrase 'Typical!' which you will hear many times a day, every day, in every workplace in the country. 'Typical!' is also used in moaning rituals in many other contexts, such as on delayed trains or buses, in traffic jams, or indeed whenever anything goes wrong. Along with 'nice', 'typical' is one of the most useful and versatile words in the English vocabulary – a generic, all-purpose term of disapproval, it can be applied to any problem, annoyance, mishap or disaster, from the most insignificant irritation to adverse events of national or even international importance. On the morning of the 7/7 bombings in London, when news of the horrifying terrorist attacks on the Underground reached the tube station where I was waiting for a train, the passengers around me incorporated this inconvenience into their standard ritual moans, with grumbles such as, 'Of course bloody Al Qaeda had to pick the one day I really needed to get to work on time! Typical!'

There is something quintessentially English about 'Typical!' It manages simultaneously to convey huffy indignation and a sense of passive, resigned acceptance, an acknowledgement that things will invariably go wrong, that life is full of little frustrations and difficulties (and highly inconsiderate terrorists), and that one must simply put up with it. In a way, 'Typical!' is a manifestation of what used to be called the English 'stiff upper lip': it is a complaint, but a complaint that also expresses a very English kind of grudging forbearance and restraint – a sort of grumpy, cynical stoicism.

THE AFTER-WORK DRINKS RULES

I was talking with my sister (Anne Fox, also an anthropologist) about after-work drinks, and she started to tell me about a study she had just seen on stress in English workplaces. 'Don't tell me,' I interrupted. 'It showed that employees who go to the pub for after-work drinks with their colleagues suffer less stress than those who don't, right?'

'Yes, of course it did,' she replied. 'I mean, duh, we knew that!' And pretty much any English worker familiar with the after-work drinks ritual could have told you the same thing – and would no doubt add that social scientists have a habit of stating the bloody obvious. But it is nonetheless nice, I think, to have our instinctive 'knowledge' of such matters properly measured and confirmed by objective research. Being a social scientist is a pretty thankless job, though, particularly among the ever-cynical English, who generally dismiss all of our findings as either obvious (when they accord with 'common knowledge') or rubbish (when they challenge some tenet of popular wisdom) or mumbo-jumbo (when it is not clear which sin has been committed, as the findings are couched in incomprehensible academic jargon). At the risk of falling into one or all of these categories, I will try to explain how the hidden rules of the after-work drinks ritual make it such an effective antidote to the stresses of the workplace.

First, there are some universal rules about alcohol and about drinking-places. In all cultures, alcohol is used as a symbolic punctuation mark – to define, facilitate and enhance the transition from one social state or context to another. The transitional rituals in which alcohol plays a vital role range from major life-cycle 'rites of passage' such as birth, coming-of-age, marriage and death to far less momentous passages, such as the daily transition from work-time to play-time or home-time. In our culture, and a number of others, alcohol is a suitable symbolic vehicle for the work-to-play transition because it is associated exclusively with play – with recreation, fun, festivity, spontaneity and relaxation – and regarded as antithetical to work.[85]

There are also universal 'laws' about the social and symbolic functions of drinking-places. I mentioned these at the beginning of the chapter on pub-talk, but it is worth reminding ourselves here that all drinking-places, in all cultures, have their own 'social microclimate'. They are 'liminal zones' in which there is a degree of 'cultural remission' – a temporary relaxation or suspension of normal social controls and restraints. They are also egalitarian environments, or at least places in which status distinctions are based on different criteria from those operating in the outside world. And, perhaps most important, both drinking and drinking-places are universally associated with social bonding.

So, the English after-work drinks ritual functions as an effective de-stressor partly because, by these universal 'laws', the hierarchies and pressures of the workplace are soluble in alcohol, particularly alcohol consumed in the sociable, egalitarian environment of the pub. The funny thing is that the after-work drinks ritual in the local pub has much the same stress-reduction effect even if one is drinking only Coke or fruit juice. The symbolic power of the pub itself is often enough to induce an immediate sense of relaxation and conviviality, even without the social lubricant of alcohol.

The specific, self-imposed rules of the English after-work drinks ritual are mainly designed to reinforce this effect. For example, discussion of work-related matters is permitted – indeed, after-work drinks sessions are often where the most important decisions get made – but both the anti-earnestness rules and the rules of polite egalitarianism are much more rigorously applied than they are in the workplace.

The anti-earnestness rules state that you can talk with colleagues

85. This is not universally the case: in many cultures, specifically those with a healthier, more 'integrated' attitude to drinking, alcohol is equally used to mark the transition from home/play to work. In parts of France and Spain, for example, men may stop at a bar or café on their walk to work for a 'fortifying' glass of wine, calvados or brandy – although recently this practice has been dying out, a worrying sign of a shift towards a more 'ambivalent', 'episodic' drinking culture. I discuss these differences in more detail in Rules of Play (page 377).

or work-mates about an important project or problem in the pub, but pompous, self-important or boring speeches are not allowed. You may, if you are senior enough, get away with these in workplace meetings (although you will not be popular), but in the pub, if you become too long-winded, too serious or too 'up yourself', you will be summarily told to 'come off it' or 'put a sock in it'.

The polite-egalitarianism rules prescribe not exactly a dissolution of workplace hierarchies, but a much more jocular, irreverent attitude to distinctions of rank. After-work drinks sessions are often conducted by small groups of colleagues of roughly the same status, but where a mixing of ranks does occur, any deference that might be shown in the workplace is replaced in the pub by ironic *mock*-deference. Managers who go for after-work drinks with their 'team' may be addressed as 'Boss', but in a jokey, slightly insolent way, as in 'Oi, Boss, it's your round!' We do not suddenly all become equals in the pub, but we have a licence to poke fun at workplace hierarchies, to show that we do not take them too seriously.

The rules of after-work drinks, and of pub-talk generally, are deeply ingrained in the English psyche. If you ever find that a business discussion or interview you are conducting with an English person is somewhat stilted, over-formal or heavy going, ask the person to 'just talk as though we were in the pub,' or 'tell me about it as you would if we were in the pub'. Everyone will know exactly what you mean: pub-talk is relaxed, informal, friendly talk, not trying to impress, not being too serious. Of course, if you can actually take the person to the nearest pub, so much the better, but I have found that even just 'invoking' the social microclimate of the pub in this way can reduce tensions and inhibitions.

OFFICE-PARTY RULES

The same principles apply, in intensified form, to office parties (I'm using this, as most people do, as a generic term, covering all parties given by a firm or company for its employees, whether white- or blue-collar) – particularly the annual Christmas party, an established ritual, now invariably associated with 'drunken debauchery' and various other forms of misbehaviour. I have done a couple of studies on this, as part of SIRC's wider research on social and cultural aspects of drinking, and I always know when the run-up to Christmas has officially started, as this is when I start getting phone calls from journalists asking, 'Why do people always misbehave at the office Christmas party?' The answer is that we misbehave because misbehaviour is what office Christmas parties are all about: misbehaviour is written into the unwritten rules governing these events; misbehaviour is expected, it is customary.

By 'misbehaviour', however, I do not mean anything particularly depraved or wicked – just a higher degree of disinhibition than is normally permitted among the English. In my SIRC surveys, 90 per cent of respondents admitted to some form of 'misbehaviour' at office Christmas parties, but simple over-indulgence was the most common 'sin', with nearly 70 per cent confessing to eating and drinking too much. We also found that flirting, 'snogging', telling rude jokes and 'making a fool of yourself' are standard features of the office Christmas party.

Among the under-thirties, 50 per cent see the office Christmas party as a prime flirting and 'snogging' opportunity, and nearly 60 per cent confessed to making fools of themselves. Thirty- and forty-somethings were only slightly more restrained, with 40 per cent making fools of themselves at Christmas parties, often by 'saying things they would never normally say'. Although this festive 'blabbing' can sometimes cause embarrassment, it can also have positive effects: 37 per cent had made friends with a former enemy or rival, or 'made up' after a quarrel, at a Christmas party, and 13 per cent had plucked up the courage to tell someone they fancied them.

But even the most outlandish office-party misbehaviours tend to be more silly than sinful. In my more casual interviews with English workers, when I asked general questions about 'what people get up to at the office Christmas party', my informants often mentioned the custom of photocopying one's bottom (or sometimes breasts) on the office photocopier. I'm not sure how often this actually occurs, but the fact that it has become one of the national standing jokes about office parties gives you an idea of how these events are regarded, the expectations and unwritten rules involved – and how the English behave under conditions of 'cultural remission'.

I will have much more to say about different kinds of 'cultural remission', 'legitimised deviance' and 'time-out behaviour' in later chapters, but we should remind ourselves here that these are not just fancy academic ways of saying 'letting your hair down'. They do not mean letting rip and doing exactly as you please, but refer quite specifically to temporary, *conventionalised* deviations from convention, in which only certain rules may be broken, and then only in certain, rule-governed ways.

English workers like to talk about their annual office parties as though they were wild Roman orgies, but this is largely titillation or wishful thinking. The reality, for most of us, is that our debauchery consists mainly of eating and drinking rather too much; singing and dancing in a more flamboyant manner than we are accustomed to; wearing skirts cut a bit too high and tops cut a bit too low; indulging in a little flirtation and maybe an illicit kiss or fumble; speaking to our colleagues with rather less restraint than usual, and to our bosses with rather less deference – and perhaps, if we are feeling really wanton and dissolute, photocopying our bottoms.

There are exceptions and minor variations, but these are the permitted limits in most English companies. Some young English workers learn these rules 'the hard way', by overstepping the invisible boundaries, going that little bit too far, and finding that their antics are frowned upon and their careers suffer as a result (particularly if they are stupid enough to post photos or descriptions of their indiscretions on internet social media sites). But most of us instinctively obey the rules, including the one that allows a significant degree of exaggeration in our accounts of what happened at the office Christmas party.

WORK RULES AND ENGLISHNESS

Looking at the guiding principles identified at the beginning of this chapter, and trying to figure out what they tell us about Englishness, I am immediately struck by all the ambivalence and contradictions in English attitudes to work. The 'muddle rules' seem to be full of 'buts'. We are serious but not serious, dutiful but grudging, moaning but stoical, inventive but also stuffily set in our ways. I would not go so far as to say that we have a 'love/hate' relationship with work. That would be too passionate and extreme and un-English. It is more a sort of 'quite like/rather dislike' relationship – a somewhat uneasy compromise, rather than an angst-ridden conflict.

There is something quintessentially English, it seems to me, about all this middling, muddling and fence-sitting. English work-culture is a mess of contradictions, but our contradictions lack the sense of dramatic tension and struggle that the word normally implies: they are generally half resolved, by means of a peculiarly English sort of grumpy, vague, unsatisfactory compromise. We can neither embrace work with wholehearted Protestant zeal, nor treat it with Latin-Mediterranean insouciant fatalism. So we sit awkwardly on the fence, somewhere in the middle ground, and grumble about it all – quietly.

The concept of compromise seems to be deeply embedded in the English psyche. Even on the rare occasions when we are roused to passionate dispute, we usually end up with a compromise. The English Civil War was fought between supporters of the monarchy and supporters of Parliament – and what did we end up with? Well, er, both. A compromise. We are not keen on dramatic change, revolutions, sudden uprisings and upheavals. A truly English protest march would see us all chanting: 'What do we want? GRADUAL CHANGE! When do we want it? IN DUE COURSE!'

When in doubt, which would seem to be much of the time, we turn to our favourite, all-purpose coping mechanism: humour. I think that the workplace humour rules have added a new dimension to our understanding of English humour and its role in our cultural codes. We already knew that the English put a high value on humour, but we had only seen this 'in operation' in purely social contexts, where there is perhaps less need for clarity, certainty and efficiency than in the workplace. We can only calculate the value of humour now that we have seen what the English are prepared to sacrifice in its honour – things like clarity, certainty and efficiency.

The workplace humour and modesty rules have also helped us to get 'inside' another stereotype, that of English anti-intellectualism, which we stuck under our microscope and broke down into its component parts – namely prohibitions on earnestness and boastfulness. Having got anti-intellectualism in my Petri dish, I've now poked away at it a bit more and tweezered out another component, which looks awfully like 'empiricism', particularly the anti-theory, anti-dogma, anti-abstraction elements of the English empiricist tradition, our stolid preference for the factual, concrete and common-sense, and deep mistrust of obscurantist, 'Continental' theorising and rhetoric. There is something fundamentally empiricist about the English 'Oh, come off it!' response. In fact, there is something essentially empiricist about most aspects of the English sense of humour.[86] I've got a feeling we'll be coming back to this.

The modesty rule seems to be yet another consistently recurring theme – and, as with humour, the workplace provides a useful and revealing 'test' of the strength of this rule. We found that when the requirements of advertising and marketing are at odds with the English modesty rule, the rule wins, and advertising must be reinvented to comply with the prohibition on boasting.

The polite-procrastination rule highlights another familiar trait, the one I have taken to calling the English 'social dis-ease', as a shorthand way of referring to our chronic inhibitions, our perverse obliqueness, our congenital inability to engage in a direct and straightforward fashion with other human beings. The money-talk taboo, a symptom of this dis-ease, brings us back to the usual-suspect themes of class-consciousness, modesty and hypocrisy – all increasingly strong candidates for defining-characteristic status, along with our penchant for excessive moderation.

I have a hunch that fair play will also turn out to be a fundamental law of Englishness. Like humour and 'social dis-ease', the fair-play ideal seems to pervade and influence much of our behaviour, although it is often manifested as polite egalitarianism, suggesting that hypocrisy is an equally powerful element.

---

86. When I wrote this somewhat throwaway little observation about the essentially empiricist nature of English humour, I had not come across Anthony Easthope's fascinating book, *Englishness and National Culture*, in which I now discover that he makes much the same point, albeit at much greater length and in a far more scholarly manner.

More familiar themes recur in the workplace moaning rules, but with some new twists. We find that even our constant Eeyorish moaning is subject to the ubiquitous humour rules, particularly the injunction against earnestness. And the 'Typical!' rule reveals what may be a modern variant of the 'stiff upper lip' – a distinctively English quality, which for the moment I am calling 'grumpy stoicism'.

Finally, the after-work-drinks and office-party rules bring us back again to the theme of English social dis-ease, in particular to our need for 'props' and facilitators – such as alcohol and special settings with special rules – to help us overcome our many social inhibitions. More of these in the next chapter.

RULES OF PLAY

I am using the term 'play' here in a very broad sense, to mean any leisure activity: pastimes, hobbies, holidays, sport – anything that is not work, anything that we do in our spare time (with the exception of the specific things covered in later chapters on food, sex and rites of passage).

The English have three different approaches to leisure, relating to our three main methods of dealing with our social dis-ease, our incompetence in the field – minefield might be a better term – of social interaction:

- First, there are private and domestic pursuits, such as DIY, television, the internet, gardening and hobbies (the 'go home, shut the door, pull up the drawbridge' method).
- Second, we have public, social activities such as pubs, clubs, sports and games (the 'ingenious use of props and facilitators' method).
- Third, we have anti-social pursuits and pastimes, such as getting very drunk and fighting (our least attractive way of dealing with social dis-ease, the 'become loud, aggressive and obnoxious' method).

PRIVACY RULES – PRIVATE AND DOMESTIC PURSUITS

Like 'humour rules', this heading can be read to mean 'rules of privacy' but also in the (now somewhat dated) graffiti sense of 'Privacy rules, OK!' – conveying the way in which the English obsession with privacy dominates our thinking and governs our behaviour. The easiest way for the English to cope with our social dis-ease is to avoid social interaction altogether, by choosing either leisure activities that can be performed in the privacy of one's own home, or outdoor pursuits that require no significant contact with anyone other than one's immediate family, such as going for a walk, or to the cinema, or shopping – anything that takes place in environments governed by the 'denial rule', which covers almost all public places.

In surveys, over half of all the leisure activities mentioned by respondents are of this private/domestic type, and of the top ten pastimes, only two (having friends round for a meal or drinks, going to the pub and chatting on the internet) could be unequivocally described as 'sociable'. The most domestic pursuits are the most popular: watching television, 'sofalising' on the internet, listening to the radio, reading, DIY and gardening. Even when the English are being sociable, the survey findings show that most of us would much rather entertain a few close friends or relatives in the safety of our own homes (or chat online from inside this sanctuary) than venture out among strangers.

Homes and Gardens

I have already discussed at some length (in Home Rules, page 185) the English home-fixation and privacy-obsession, but it is worth repeating here my theory that 'home is what the English have instead of social skills'. Our love-affair with our homes and gardens is, I believe, directly related to our obsession with privacy, which in turn is due to our social dis-ease.

Watching television is a universal pastime – nothing uniquely English about this. Nor is there anything peculiarly English about the other main domestic leisure pursuits mentioned here, such as reading, gardening and DIY, or at least not *per se*. There is, however, something distinctive about the phenomenal *extent* of their popularity, particularly in the case of DIY and gardening. On any given evening or weekend, in at least half of all English households, someone will be 'improving' the home, with bits of wood or tins of paint, or the garden, by digging or just 'pottering'. In my SIRC colleagues' studies on English DIY habits, only 12 per cent of women and two per cent of men said that they never did any DIY. In the latest national census survey, at least half of the entire adult male population had been DIYing in the four weeks before the census date. Nearly a third of the female population had also been busily improving their homes, and our obsession with our gardens was equally evident: 52 per cent of all English males and 45 per cent of females had been out there pruning and weeding.

Compare these figures with those for church attendance, and you will find the real national religion. Even among people claiming to belong to a particular religion, only eight per cent attend religious services every week. The rest of us are more likely to be found on Sundays at our local garden centre or DIY superstore. And when we want a break from obsessing about our own homes and gardens, we go on mini-pilgrimages to gawp at bigger and better houses and gardens, such as the stately homes and gardens opened to the public by the National Trust and the Royal Horticultural Society. Visiting grand country houses consistently ranks as one of the most popular national pastimes. This is not at all surprising, as these places have everything an English person could wish for in a Sunday outing: not just inspiration for home and garden improvements ('Oooh, look, that's just the sort of pinky-beige colour I was thinking of for our lounge!') and indulgence in class-obsession and general nosiness, but also reassuring queues, refreshing cups of tea, and a sense that the whole thing must be virtuously educational – or at least a lot more so than going to the DIY store or garden centre – because it is, after all, 'historic'.[87] This little puritanical streak, this need to show that one's leisure activities are more than just mindless consumerist pleasure-seeking, is most evident among the middle classes; the working classes and upper classes are generally more open and honest

87. But perhaps I am being too harsh. Jeremy Paxman thinks that the millions who visit historic houses and gardens are expressing, among other things, a 'deeply felt' sense of history. I'm not convinced; we are chronically nostalgic, yes, but that is not the same thing. Still, it is somewhat disturbing to find myself sounding more cynical than Paxman.

in their consumption of pleasure, being less fussily concerned about
what others might think of them.

Television Rules

Those who do worry about such things can take comfort from the
research findings showing that we are not, in fact, a nation of telly-
addicted couch potatoes. At first glance, survey figures tend to give
a rather misleading impression: television-watching appears to be by
far the most popular domestic leisure pursuit, with 99 per cent of
the population recorded as regular viewers. But when we note how
the survey questions are phrased – 'Which of these things have you
done in the past month?' – the picture changes. After all, it would
be hard, in the space of an entire month, not to switch on the news
occasionally. Ticking the 'yes' box for television does not necessarily
mean that one has been glued to the set every night.

We do watch quite a lot of television – the national average is
about four hours a day (including online viewing) – but television
cannot be said to be killing the art of conversation. In the same
survey, 97 per cent of respondents had also entertained or visited
friends or relations in the past month. I have been somewhat sceptical
about television viewing figures since I was involved in a research
project some years ago in which a team of psychologists installed
video-cameras in ordinary people's sitting rooms to monitor how
much television they watched and how they behaved while doing so.
I was only a lowly assistant researcher on this study; my job was to
monitor the videotapes with a stopwatch and time exactly how long
our subjects actually looked at the television screen, as well as making
notes on anything else they might be doing. The subjects filled in
forms every day, saying what programmes they had seen and estimating how much of each programme they had actually watched.

The differences between their estimates and the reality, as clocked
by my stopwatch, showed that when people tell a survey researcher
that they spent an evening, or an hour, 'watching television', it is
highly likely that they were doing no such thing. What they often
mean is that they had the television on while they chatted with family
or friends, played with the dog, read the newspaper, squabbled over

the remote, gossiped on the telephone, cut their toenails, nagged their spouse, cooked and ate supper, fell asleep, did the ironing and hoovering, had sex, shouted at their children and so on, perhaps occasionally glancing at the television screen.

If we were to repeat this experiment now, we would also see many people chatting with friends, family and strangers on the internet, on sites such as Facebook or Twitter, while ostensibly watching television. Often, they are posting and tweeting about the programmes they are 'watching', conducting a sort of running commentary consisting mainly of humorously derogatory remarks. But many find the internet chatter far more engrossing than the programme itself, so we are probably now actually *watching* less television than ever. This is certainly true of younger people, who spend considerably more time on the internet than watching television.

There are also, of course, people who grossly underestimate the amount of television they watch, but they are usually lying, unlike our study participants who were at least trying to be accurate. The sort of people who claim that they 'never watch television' are usually trying to convince you that they are somehow morally and/or intellectually superior to the lumpen masses, who have nothing better to do than 'goggle at hours of mindless rubbish' every night. You are most likely to find this attitude among middle-aged, middle-class males, suffering from the same class-insecurities as those who sneer at Mercedes drivers. This anti-telly posturing always strikes me as a particularly irrational affectation in England, where we have what is generally acknowledged to be the best television in the world, and there really is something worth watching almost every day, even for those with haughtily highbrow tastes.

For the rest of us ordinary mortals, television seems to *promote* the art of conversation, providing the socially challenged English with yet another much-needed 'prop'. In a recent survey, television programmes came out as the most common topic of conversation among friends and family, even more popular than moans about the cost of living. Television is second only to the weather as a facilitator of sociable interaction among the English. It is something we all have in common. When in doubt, or when we have run out of weather-speak starters and fillers, we can always ask: 'Did you see . . . ?' The likelihood is that many of us will have watched at least some of the same recent programmes, and despite the relatively high quality of English television, we can nearly always find something to share a good moan about.

Soap Rules

Our social inhibitions and obsession with privacy are also reflected in the kind of television programmes we make and watch, particularly our soap operas. The most popular English television soap operas are highly unusual, utterly different from those of any other country. The plots, themes and storylines may be very similar – the usual mix of adultery, violence, death, unwanted pregnancies, paternity disputes and other improbable incidents and accidents – but only in England does all this take place entirely among ordinary, plain-looking, working-class people, often middle-aged or old, doing menial or boring jobs, wearing cheap clothes, eating beans and chips, drinking in scruffy pubs and living in realistically small, poky, unglamorous houses.

American soaps are aimed at the same lower-class audience as our *EastEnders* and *Coronation Street* (you can tell the market from the kind of products advertised in the breaks), but the characters, their settings and lifestyles are all middle class, glamorous, attractive, affluent and youthful. They are all lawyers and doctors and successful entrepreneurs, beautifully groomed and coiffed, leading their dysfunctional family lives in immaculate, expensive houses, and having secret meetings with their lovers in smart restaurants and luxurious hotels. Virtually all soaps throughout the rest of the world are based on this 'aspirational' American model. Only the English go in for gritty, kitchen-sink, working-class realism. Even the Australian soaps, which come closest, are glamorous by comparison with the grim and grubby English ones. Why is this? Why do millions of ordinary English people want to watch soaps about ordinary English people just like themselves, people who might easily be their next-door neighbours?

The answer, I think, lies partly in the empiricism and realism[88] that are so deeply rooted in the English psyche, and our related qualities of down-to-earthness and matter-of-factness, our stubborn obsession with the real, concrete and factual, our distaste for artifice and pretension. If Pevsner were to write today on 'The Englishness of English Soap Opera', I think he would find the same eminently English 'preference for the observed fact and personal experience', 'close observation of what is around us' and 'truth and its everyday paraphernalia' in *EastEnders* and *Coronation Street* that he found in Hogarth, Constable and Reynolds.

But this is not sufficient explanation. The Swiss painter Henry Fuseli may have been correct in his observation that our 'taste and feelings all go to realities' but the English are quite capable of appreciating much less realistic forms of art and drama; it is only in soap opera that we differ so markedly from the rest of the world, demanding a mirror held up to reflect our own ordinariness. My hunch is that this peculiar taste is somehow closely connected to our obsession with privacy, our tendency to keep ourselves to ourselves, to go home, shut the door and pull up the drawbridge. I have discussed the privacy-fixation in some detail in earlier chapters, and suggested that a corollary of it is our extreme nosiness, which is only partially satisfied by our incessant gossiping. A forbidden-fruit effect is operating here: the English privacy rules mean that we tend to know very little about the personal lives and doings of people outside our immediate circle of friends and family. It is not done to 'wash one's dirty linen in public', or acceptable to ask the kind of personal questions that would elicit any such washing.

So we do not know what our neighbours get up to behind their closed doors (unless they are so noisy that we have already complained to the police and the local council about them). When

88. I do realise that there is a distinction between empiricism and realism as philosophical doctrines (holding that all knowledge is derived from sense experience, and that matter exists independently of our perception of it) and the broader, more colloquial senses that are implied here, but I would maintain that there is a strong connection between our formal philosophical traditions and our informal, everyday attitudes and mindsets, including those governing our taste in soap operas.

a murder is committed in an average English street, the response from neighbours questioned by the police or journalists is always the same: 'Well, we didn't really know them . . .', 'They kept themselves to themselves . . .', 'They seemed pleasant enough . . .', 'We mind our own business, round here . . .', 'A bit odd, but one doesn't like to pry, you know . . .' Actually, we would dearly love to pry: we are a nation of insatiably curious curtain-twitchers, constantly frustrated by the draconian nature of our unwritten privacy rules. The clue to the popularity of kitchen-sink soap operas is in the observation that soap-opera characters are 'people who might easily be our next-door neighbours'. Watching soaps such as *EastEnders* and *Coronation Street* is like being allowed to peer through a spyhole into the hidden, forbidden, private lives of our neighbours, our social peers – people like us, but about whom we can normally only guess and speculate. The addictive appeal of these soaps lies in their vicarious satisfaction of this prurient curiosity: soaps are a form of voyeurism. And, of course, they confirm all of our worst suspicions about what goes on behind our neighbours' firmly closed doors and impenetrable net curtains: adultery, alcoholism, wife-beating, shoplifting, drug-dealing, AIDS, teenage pregnancy, murder . . . The soap-opera families are 'people like us', but they are making an even more spectacularly dysfunctional mess of their lives than we are.

So far, I have mentioned only the most popular English soaps – which are the unequivocally working-class ones: *EastEnders* and *Coronation Street*. But our television producers are a shrewd and kindly lot, and do their best to provide soaps catering to each layer of the English class system, and even to different demographic groups within these layers. *EastEnders* and *Coronation Street* represent, respectively, the southern and northern urban working classes. *Emmerdale* is one or two social notches up from these, with a number of significant lower-middle and middle-class characters, and also rural rather than urban. *Hollyoaks* is essentially a more youthful, teenage, suburban version of *EastEnders*, deviating somewhat from the warts-and-all norm in actually featuring attractive-looking characters, although they are still dressed in realistically cheap high-street fashions. Even the middle- to upper-middles occasionally get their own soaps: for a while there was *This Life*, featuring a group of well-spoken but neurotic thirty-something lawyers. They were fairly attractive and smartly dressed, but they did not, like American soap characters, wake up in the morning with their faces immaculately made-up and hair perfectly blow-dried; their (frequent) drunkenness was convincingly vomitous; their rows and squabbles involved a believable amount of swearing; and they had dirty dishes in the sink.

Sit-com Rules

Much the same warty-realism rules apply to English situation-comedy programmes. Almost all English sit-coms are about 'losers' – unsuccessful people, doing unglamorous jobs, having unsatisfactory relationships, living in, at best, dreary suburban houses. They are mostly working class or lower-middle class, but even the more well-off characters are never successful high-flyers. The heroes – or rather, anti-heroes, the characters we laugh at – are all failures.

This has caused a few problems in the export market: when popular English sit-coms, such as *Men Behaving Badly* and *The Office*, are 'translated' for the American market, the original English characters are often found to be too low-class, too unsuccessful, too unattractive, too crude – and generally just a bit too uncomfortably real. In the American versions, they tend to be given job promotions, more regular features, better hair, smarter clothes, more glamorous girlfriends, more up-market houses and lifestyles. Their disgusting habits are toned down, and their language is sanitised along with their bathrooms and kitchens.[89] (This process has itself more recently been the subject of a satirical comedy, *Episodes*.)

This is not to say that there are no losers in American sit-coms: there are losers, but they tend to be a rather better class of loser; less irredeemably hopeless, squalid, grubby and unappealing than the English variety. One or two of the characters in *Friends*, for

---

89. I am indebted to Simon Nye, who wrote *Men Behaving Badly*, and Paul Dornan, who was involved in its translation for the American market, for this information, and other helpful insights into the nature of English comedy.

example, did not have successful careers, but neither did they ever have a hair out of place. The girls in 2 *Broke Girls* may be broke, and working as waitresses, but perfect features and permanently flawless make-up must be some consolation. There has only been one long-running, popular American sit-com, *Roseanne*,[90] that comes close to the degree of realistic kitchen-sink seediness that is the norm in English television, and that is demanded by the empiricist, down-to-earth, cynical, prurient, curtain-twitching English audience, who want to see Pevsner's 'truth and its everyday paraphernalia' in their sit-coms as well as their soap operas.

I am not trying to claim here that English comedies are necessarily better or more subtle or more sophisticated than American ones or anyone else's. If anything, the humour in most English sit-coms is rather *less* subtle and sophisticated than the Americans', and usually considerably more childish, crude and silly. In everyday life and conversation, I would maintain that the English do have a keener and more subtle sense of humour than most other nations, and this mastery of wit, irony and understatement is also evident in a few of our television comedy productions – but there are still a vast number in which farting and saying 'arse' a lot, or indeed virtually anything to do with bottoms, is regarded as the pinnacle of hilarious repartee.

We may legitimately pride ourselves on the sparkling wit of programmes such as *Yes, Minister/Yes, Prime Minister* and the offbeat genius of *The Thick of It*, *The Office* and *The Royle Family*. The English are also undeniably brilliant at spoof and satire (we should be, it's what we do instead of getting angry and having revolutions) but let's not forget that we are also responsible for Benny Hill and the *Carry On* films, which differ from bog-standard sexual Euro-slapstick (and its American, Australian and Japanese equivalents) only in their excessive reliance on bad puns, *double-entendres* and innuendo – a measure of the English love of words, I suppose, but

90. I mean home-grown sit-coms here, so I'm not counting US adaptations of gritty British comedies such as *Shameless*. Having said that, the US version of *Shameless* is somewhat less sanitised and prettied-up than other attempts.

otherwise not much to our credit. *Monty Python* is in a different class from these, both socially and verbally, but it is still rather a childish, schoolboy form of humour.

The important question, it seems to me, is not whether our comedies are better or worse than other nations', or cleverer, or cruder, but whether they have some distinctive common theme or characteristic (apart from the empiricism already mentioned) that might tell us something about Englishness. I've worked on this question long and hard, consulted quite a few comedy writers and other experts, dutifully watched dozens of television sit-coms, satires, spoofs and stand-ups – and thoroughly annoyed all my family and friends by insisting on calling this 'research'. But I did eventually arrive at an answer: as far as I can tell, almost all of the cruder type of English television comedy, as well as much of the more sophisticated, is essentially about that perennial English preoccupation: embarrassment.

Embarrassment is a significant element in other nations' television comedy as well – and perhaps in all comedy – but the English seem to have a greater potential for embarrassment than other cultures, to experience it more often, and to be more constantly anxious and worried about it. We tend to make jokes about the things that frighten us (we humans, that is, not just we English), and the English have an unusually acute fear of embarrassment, so it is not terribly surprising that so much of our comedy should deal with this theme. To the socially challenged English, almost any social situation is potentially highly embarrassing, so we have a particularly rich source of comic material to play with. In the field of situation-comedy, we do not even have to invent odd or unlikely 'situations' to produce the necessary embarrassment: many of our sit-coms have no 'sit' to speak of, unless you count 'an average suburban family going about its utterly normal and uneventful life' (*My Family*, *2.4 Children*, *Butterflies*, *Outnumbered*, etc.) or 'ordinary boring days in the life of an ordinary boring office' (*The Office*), or even 'an average working-class family sitting around watching television' (*The Royle Family*), and yet they seem to generate quite enough amusingly embarrassing moments. I could be wrong, but I suspect that it would be very hard to 'pitch' these as great sit-com ideas in any other country.[91]

'Reality TV' Rules

So-called 'reality TV' provides yet more evidence, if any were needed, of English social inhibitions, and what a psychotherapist would probably call our 'privacy issues'. Reality TV bears little resemblance to what any sane person would regard as 'reality', as it often involves putting people in bizarre, highly improbable situations and getting them to compete with each other in the performance of utterly ludicrous tasks. The people, however, are 'real', in the sense that they are not trained actors but ordinary unsuccessful mortals, distinguished only by their desperate desire to appear on television. Reality TV is by no means a uniquely English or British phenomenon. The most famous and popular of these programmes, *Big Brother*, originated in Holland, and many other countries now have their own versions, making it an ideal example for cross-cultural comparison. The format is quite simple. A dozen or so participants are selected from the many thousands who apply, and put together in a specially constructed house, where they live for nine weeks, with hidden cameras filming their every move, twenty-four hours a day, the 'highlights' of which are shown every night on television. Their lives are entirely controlled by the show's producers (collectively known as 'Big Brother'), who set them tasks and dish out rewards and punishments. Every week, the housemates each have to nominate two of their fellow participants for eviction, the viewing public then votes for the one it wants to evict, and one housemate is chucked out. At the end, the winner – the last surviving competitor – is awarded a fairly substantial cash prize. All participants get their fifteen minutes of fame, and a few go on to become D-list 'celebrities'.

Britain and America are the only countries in which none of the *Big Brother* housemates has been seen having sex (I think the reasons

91. Other nations may watch and enjoy (and remake) some of our sit-coms, and we certainly watch and enjoy many of theirs, but I am interested in what English television comedy, the comedy we produce, tells us about Englishness.

are slightly different: we are inhibited, while the Americans are prudish). In Holland, they apparently had to be told to stop having sex all the time, as viewers were starting to find the non-stop humping rather tedious. In Britain, the newspapers went into paroxysms of excitement if two housemates so much as kissed. When, in the third series, a pair of housemates finally took things a little bit further, they made sure that they were carefully concealed under a duvet (another pair later used a bubbling Jacuzzi) and it was impossible to tell what was going on. Even when our *Big Brother* producers, in a desperate attempt to spice up the show a bit, provided a special little lovers' den, allowing couples to cavort away from the prying eyes of their fellow housemates (although still filmed by the hidden cameras), none of the inhibited housemates could be tempted. They used the den for 'private' gossip sessions instead. In 2003, a tabloid newspaper offered a reward of £50,000 (almost as much as the prize-money for winning *Big Brother*) to tempt the housemates to have sex, but still nothing happened.

In other countries, *Big Brother* housemates regularly have screaming rows, and even stand-up fights and brawls, with broken chairs and flying crockery. For some years on the British *Big Brother* even a raised voice or a mildly sarcastic comment was a major incident, discussed and speculated over for days, both within the house and among the show's many fans. Our housemates' language is often foul, but this reflects their limited vocabulary, rather than powerful emotions. For the first few series, their behaviour was quite remarkably restrained, and even polite. They rarely expressed anger at a fellow housemate directly, but rather, in true English fashion, bitched and complained constantly about the person behind their back.

Although the show is a competition, any sign of actual competitiveness was severely frowned upon by our *Big Brother* contestants. 'Cheating' was the worst sin – a violation of the all-important fair-play ethos – but even admitting to having a game-plan, 'playing to win', was taboo, as one competitor discovered to his cost, when his boastful remarks about his clever strategy resulted in him being ostracised by the rest of the group and swiftly evicted. Had he kept quiet about his motives, pretended to be 'in it for fun' like all the others, he would have had as good a chance as any. Hypocrisy rules.

Inhibition, embarrassment, indirectness, hypocrisy, gritted-teeth politeness – all very English, and, you might say, not particularly surprising. But think for a minute about who these *Big Brother* participants were. The people who applied and auditioned to take part in this programme *actively wanted* to be exposed to the public gaze, twenty-four hours a day, for nine weeks, with absolutely no privacy, not even on the loo or in the shower – not to mention being obliged to perform idiotic and embarrassing tasks. These were not normal, ordinary people: these were the most shameless, most brazen, most attention-seeking, least inhibited people you could hope to encounter, anywhere in England. And yet their behaviour in the *Big Brother* house was largely characterised by typically English inhibition, squeamishness and awkwardness. They only broke the rules when they were very drunk – or, rather, they got drunk to legitimise their deviance from the rules[92] – and even then there were boundaries that were never crossed.

For the first few series, I saw *Big Brother* as an interesting experiment, testing the strength of the 'rules of Englishness': if even the shameless attention-seekers on *Big Brother* conform to these rules, they must be very deeply ingrained in the English psyche.

But then the producers became desperate to find some way of livening up the show – of manufacturing some drama and conflict and shedding of English inhibitions. They resorted to more and more extreme tactics, both in the increasingly degrading 'tasks' and gimmicks they inflicted upon the unfortunate housemates, and in the selection of these housemates. They began choosing people who were not merely loud, lewd and obnoxious, but clearly suffering from mental health problems – and even neuropsychiatric disorders such as Tourette's (well, that's one way to guarantee a lot of swearing, I suppose).

---

92. I will have more to say on English beliefs about alcohol and the etiquette of drunken comportment later in this chapter.

The criminologist Professor David Wilson resigned as an adviser to the show, in disgust, after less than a week. He said that the producers filled the house with 'bullies, egomaniacs, predators and exhibitionists . . . A personality disorder became the prime qualification for entry into the house.' Having selected mentally unstable people, they then got them drunk as often as possible, engineered situations guaranteed to cause conflict and aggression – in some cases actually instructing housemates to insult and provoke each other – and encouraged lewd behaviour, accusing housemates of being 'boring' when they failed to indulge in enough mayhem and debauchery.[93]

All of these increasingly desperate tactics eventually resulted in one actual physical fight (still mainly just shouting and swearing, but with some pushing and shoving, and a few bits of food and crockery were thrown). No one was even slightly injured, but security personnel were sent in to break up what has 'gone down in history' as 'Fight Night'. Another shouting-and-swearing incident, in which the only physical violence consisted of one housemate spitting at another, was promptly labelled 'Fight Night Two' by the media. There were also a few incidents of sexual exhibitionism (falling short of any actual visible intercourse). By international *Big Brother* standards this was all pretty tame, but many English viewers rightly felt that the programme had become little more than an embarrassing freak-show: viewing figures duly declined and Channel 4 eventually decided that enough was enough and cancelled it. The show has now migrated to the less discerning Channel 5, where the freakery continues and audience numbers decline even further.

So, although the typical English inhibition exhibited in the early seasons was not maintained, I stand by my conclusions. The fact

93. I could find no responses to Professor Wilson's comments from the production company responsible for *Big Brother*, although the broadcaster, Channel 4, did issue a statement saying that the programme-makers were confident in the 'rigorous vetting procedures, full-time monitoring and security and on-site psychological support' provided. Wilson's concerns and criticisms have been echoed by other psychologists, the mental health charity SANE and the British Association for Counselling and Psychotherapy.

that disinhibition could only be achieved by selecting emotionally unstable contestants, and even then required deliberate and constant extreme provocation from the producers, shows that this 'reality' programme was clearly no longer in any way representative of 'real' English behaviour.

Reading Rules

The English love of words features, in some form, on a large proportion of the lists of our 'national characteristics' that I came across during the research for this book. And the fact that there are so many such lists only reinforces the point: our response to insecurities about our national identity is to make lists about it – to throw words at the problem. Orwell may have started the list-making trend, but now everyone seems to be at it.

Jeremy Paxman, whose own Orwellian list of quintessential Englishnesses includes 'quizzes and crosswords', calls the English 'a people obsessed by words', and cites the phenomenal output of our publishing industry (150,000 new books a year, more per head than any other country), more newspapers per head than almost any other country, our 'unstoppable flow of Letters to the Editor', our 'insatiable appetite' for all forms of verbal games and puzzles, our thriving theatres and bookshops.

I would add that reading is consistently a top-ranked pastime in national surveys of leisure activity, even more popular than gardening and DIY. About 80 per cent of us read newspapers (either in print or online), and we spend considerably more time reading our newspapers than any other European nation. Our passion for word games and verbal puzzles is well known, but it is also worth noting that every one of the *non*-verbal hobbies and pastimes that occupy our leisure time – such as fishing, DIY, gardening, collecting, bird-watching, walking, sports, pets and knitting – has many specialist magazines devoted to it. The more popular hobbies each have at least half a dozen dedicated weekly or monthly publications, as well as hundreds of internet sites, and we often spend much more time reading about our favourite pastime than we do practising it.

The Rules of Bogside Reading

We read compulsively, anytime, anywhere. In many English homes, you will find what I call 'bogside reading': piles of books and magazines placed next to the loo, or even neatly arranged in a special rack or bookcase for reading while sitting on the loo. I have occasionally come across the odd book or magazine in loos in other countries, but bogside reading does not seem to be a firmly established custom or tradition elsewhere in the way that it is in England. There are many English people – particularly males – who find it very hard to defecate at all unless they have something to read. If there is no proper bogside reading, they will read the instructions on the soap-dispenser or the list of ingredients on the can of air-freshener.

A cynical friend pointed out that this might have more to do with the English propensity to constipation than our love of words, but I am not convinced. It is often said that the English are obsessed with their bowels, and judging by the contents of people's bathroom cabinets (yes, I always snoop – don't you?) and of chemists' shelves, we do indeed seem to use more than our fair share of constipation and diarrhoea remedies, suggesting a constant struggle to maintain some elusive ideal state of regularity and solidity. But are we more obsessed than the Germans? We do not, as they do, construct our lavatory-bowls with a little shelf for the anxious inspection or smug contemplation of our faeces (at least, I assume that's what those shelves are for: they seem to have no other discernible purpose). In fact, our bogside-reading customs indicate a degree of embarrassment about the whole process: we would rather distract ourselves with words than focus too intently (Germanically? anally?) on the products of our bowels. But maybe this is just more English hypocrisy.

The unwritten rules of bogside reading state that the books and magazines in question should be of a relatively unserious nature – humour, books of quotations, collections of letters or diaries, odd or obscure reference books, old magazines; anything that can be dipped into casually, rather than heavy tomes requiring sustained concentration.

Bogside reading, like pretty much everything else in an English home, is a useful class-indicator:

- Working-class bogside reading tends to be mostly humorous, light entertainment or sports-related – books of jokes, cartoons, maybe the occasional puzzle- or quiz-book, and perhaps a few glossy gossip or sports magazines. You will also sometimes find magazines about hobbies and interests, such as motorcycles, music or skateboarding.

- Lower-middles and middle-middles are not so keen on bogside reading: they may well take a book or newspaper into the loo with them, but do not like to advertise this habit by having a permanent bogside collection, which they think might look vulgar. Females of these classes may be reluctant to admit to reading on the loo at all.

- Upper-middles are generally much less prudish about such things, and often have mini-libraries in their loos. Some upper-middle bogside collections are a bit pretentious, with books and magazines that appear to have been selected to impress, rather than to entertain,[94] but many are genuinely eclectic, and so amusing that guests often get engrossed in them and have to be shouted at to come to the dinner table.

- Upper-class bogside reading is usually closer to working-class tastes, consisting mainly of sport and humour, although the sporting magazines are more likely to be of the hunting/shooting/fishing sort than, say, football. Some upper-class bogside libraries include fascinating old children's books, and ancient, crumbling copies of *Horse and Hound* or *Country Life*.

---

94. A little spasm of ruthless honesty just propelled me to our own loo to check the current bogside reading matter. I found a paperback edition of Jane Austen's letters and a mangled copy of the *Times Literary Supplement*. Oh dear. Could possibly be seen as a bit pretentious. I suppose it's no use saying that both are gloriously bitchy and extremely funny. Perhaps I should be less quick to cast aspersions on other people's bogside libraries. Maybe some people really do enjoy reading Habermas and Derrida on the loo. I take it all back.

Newspaper Rules

When I say, in support of my claims about the English love of words, that around 80 per cent of us read newspapers,[95] some of those unfamiliar with English culture may mistakenly imagine a nation of super-literate highbrows, engrossed in the solemn analyses of politics and current affairs in the pages of *The Times*, the *Guardian* or another big, serious-looking paper. In fact, although we have four of them to choose from, only about 16 per cent of us read the so-called 'quality' national daily papers.

These quality papers are also still known as 'broadsheets', because all of them used to be twice as wide (and twice as tall) as the tabloids. I could never understand why they were such an awkward, unwieldy size, until I started watching English commuters reading them on trains, and realised that readability and manoeuvrability were not the point: the point is clearly to have a newspaper large enough to hide behind. The English broadsheet is a formidable example of what psychologists call a 'barrier signal' – in this case more like a 'fortress signal'. Not only can one conceal oneself completely behind its outsize, outstretched pages – effectively prohibiting any form of interaction with other humans, and successfully maintaining the comforting illusion that they do not exist – but one is enclosed, cocooned, in a solid wall of *words*. How very English.

Tabloids, otherwise known as the 'popular' press, are smaller (although still large enough to conceal one's head and shoulders) and somewhat less challenging, both intellectually and physically.

Since the last edition of this book was published (in 2004), three of the four broadsheet papers have adopted a smaller, more manageable, tabloid format – amid much vociferous protest from traditionalists. The *Daily Telegraph* resisted the change, and was rewarded with increased circulation. But people still use the terms 'tabloid' and 'broadsheet' to distinguish the 'popular' from the 'quality' papers.

95. Apparently we read more newspapers than any other nation, except – surprise, surprise – the Japanese. What *is* it about small, overcrowded islands?

There is also a further distinction between 'red-top' and 'compact' tabloids – the latter regarding themselves as both more serious and 'classier' than the former, although it could be argued that the compacts are merely more coy, hypocritical and self-righteous. The red tops unashamedly feature photos of topless models, for example, while the compacts' paparazzi photos of almost equally scantily clad 'celebrities' are presented as 'showbiz gossip' stories, which may even include disapproving comments on the amount of flesh revealed. The *Daily Mail*, the archetypal compact, panders to the fears of the less-educated middle classes, and is endlessly mocked for its obsession with house prices, while the *Sun*, the bestselling red top, is more squarely aimed at a working-class readership, and is more likely to get irate about the price of beer. The philosopher Julian Baggini summarises the difference between these two papers as 'the *Sun* + money + fear = the *Daily Mail*'. A nice point, but I would quibble slightly with the 'money' element, as social class in England is not determined by material wealth: the *Daily Mail* appeals to those with higher social aspirations – those who self-identify as 'middle class' and are anxious to proclaim and maintain this status – rather than simply those with higher incomes.[96]

Broadsheets are favoured by the higher social classes – upper-middle, upper and the more educated middle-middles. Within these groups they also serve, to some extent, as signals of political affiliation (unlike the tabloids, which are all essentially conservative). Both *The Times* and the *Daily Telegraph* are somewhat to the right of centre – although the *Telegraph*, also known as the *Torygraph*, is traditionally regarded as more right-wing than *The Times*. The *Independent* and the *Guardian* balance things out neatly by being somewhat to the left of centre – again with one, the *Guardian*, being seen as slightly more left-wing than the other. The term

96. To be fair to Baggini, he does acknowledge these nuances, and the complexities of English social class are difficult to convey in a catchy little formula like this. I'm not sure why I'm being so scrupulously fair, as Baggini reduces all of my careful analyses of our dysfunctional relationship with alcohol to an equally simplistic (and misleading) equation that I have never used.

'*Guardian*-reader' is often used as shorthand for a woolly, lefty, politically correct, knit-your-own-tofu sort of person. This is England, though, so none of these political positions is in any way extreme; indeed, the differences may be hard to discern unless you are English and familiar with all the subtle nuances. The English do not like extremism, in politics or any other sphere: apart from anything else, political extremists and fanatics, whether on the right or the left, invariably break the all-important English humour rules, particularly the Importance of Not Being Earnest rule. Among their many other sins, Hitler, Stalin, Mussolini and Franco were not noted for their use of the understatement. No such totalitarian leaders would ever stand a chance in England: even leaving aside their ethical shortcomings, they would be rejected immediately for taking themselves too seriously. George Orwell, for once, was wrong: 1984 would be unlikely to happen in England; our response to Big Brother (the original, not the television programme) would be 'Oh, come off it!' and a lot of mockery. This is effectively what happened to our own would-be fascist leader Oswald Mosley – the vast majority simply found him ridiculous and treated him as a pathetic joke.

The people who read the broadsheets occasionally lower their printed barrier signals to look down their noses at those who read the tabloids. When broadsheet readers complain about the awfulness of 'the press', which they do constantly, they usually mean the tabloids.

A MORI survey found that more people are 'dissatisfied' than 'satisfied' with our national press, but the margin was quite small, and, the researchers pointed out, 'filled with an irony'. The balance against the press was tipped by broadsheet readers (the minority), who are much more likely to say they are 'dissatisfied' with our national press than tabloid readers (the majority). Broadsheet readers are unlikely to be dissatisfied with the papers they actually buy, say the MORI researchers, so they are presumably expressing dissatisfaction with newspapers they do not read. The press as a whole is condemned by 'people who don't actually read what they take exception to!' Fair point. The English love to complain, and the English educated classes do have a tendency to complain noisily about matters of which they have little or no knowledge. But I would hazard a guess that the broadsheet readers are in fact quite likely to be expressing dissatisfaction with the papers they do read, as well as the ones they don't. Just because the English buy something, it doesn't follow that we actually *like* it, or are even 'satisfied' with it, and it certainly doesn't mean we won't moan and complain about it. Given an opportunity for a pointless whinge – such as a MORI researcher showing interest in our opinions – we will complain about pretty much anything.

Now that most newspapers have free online editions, many of the snooty broadsheet readers, who sneer at the low-class tabloids, secretly read these tabloids online. In public, they may still signal their class and education by only ever reading the 'quality' papers, but a history-search on their computers would reveal sneaky visits to the tabloids' websites. Even without performing such searches, I know that many upper-middle-class people lie about the newspapers they read. They may get away with this in survey responses, but in conversation it is easy to trip them up: I have smoked out quite a few closet online tabloid readers just by dropping in a casual reference to a story covered *only* in that day's tabloids. My victims' familiarity with the details of the *Daily Mail* and *Daily Express* exclusives in question proved to be quite remarkable for people who 'would never read that rubbish'.

As a paid-up member of the broadsheet-reading classes, I will probably be regarded as a traitor for saying anything nice about the tabloids, but I think that in some respects they are unfairly maligned. Yes, I get fed up with their sensationalism and scaremongering, but the so-called 'quality' press is often just as guilty of these sins. We have no less than eight main national daily papers – four tabloids, four broadsheets – in cut-throat competition with each other, and all of them sometimes feel obliged to mislead or exaggerate in their efforts to attract our attention. But leaving the moral issues to one side, the quality of the writing on both broadsheets and tabloids is generally excellent. There is a difference in style between the 'popular' and the 'quality' press, but the skill of the writers is equally outstanding. This is not surprising as they are often the same writers:

journalists move back and forth between tabloids and broadsheets, or even write regularly for both.

It seems to me that the English love of words – and particularly the universal nature of this passion, which transcends all class barriers – is most perfectly demonstrated not by the erudite wit of the broadsheet columnists, brilliant though they are, but by the journalists and sub-editors who write the headlines in the tabloids. Take a random selection of English tabloids and flip through them: you will soon notice that almost every other headline involves some kind of play on words – a pun, a double meaning, a deliberate jokey misspelling, a literary or historical reference, a clever neologism, an ironic put-down, a cunning rhyme or amusing alliteration, and so on.

Yes, many of the puns are dreadful; much of the humour is laboured, vulgar or childish; the sexual innuendo is overdone; and the relentlessness of the wordplay can become tiresome after a while. You may find yourself longing for a headline that simply gives you the gist of the story, without trying to be funny or clever. But the sheer ingenuity and linguistic playfulness must be admired, and all this compulsive punning, rhyming and joking is uniquely and gloriously English. Other countries may have 'quality' newspapers at least as learned and well written as ours, but no other national press can rival the manic wordplay of English tabloid headlines. So there we are: something to be proud of.

Cyberspace Rules

In recent times, the English have found a new and perfect excuse to stay at home, pull up the imaginary drawbridge and avoid the traumas of face-to-face social interaction: the internet. Email, chatrooms, forums, social networking sites, surfing, blogging, messaging – the whole thing could have been invented for the insular, socially handicapped, word-loving English.

In cyberspace, we are in our element: a world of disembodied words. No need to worry about what to wear, whether to make eye contact, whether to shake hands or kiss cheeks or just smile. No awkward pauses or embarrassing false starts; no need to fill uncomfortable silences with weather-speak; no polite procrastinating or tea-making or other displacement activity; no need for the usual prolonged goodbyes. Nothing physical, no actual corporeal human beings to deal with at all. Just written words. Our favourite thing.

And, best of all, cyberspace is a disinhibitor. The disinhibiting effect of cyberspace is a universal phenomenon, not peculiar to the English. People from many cultures find that online they are more open and chatty, less reticent than they are face to face or even on the telephone. But this disinhibiting effect is particularly important to the English, who have a greater need for such social facilitators than other cultures.

In my discussion groups and interviews with English internet users, the disinhibiting effect of online communication is a constantly recurring theme. Without exception, participants say that they express themselves more freely, with less reserve, in cyberspace than in what they invariably call 'real life' encounters: 'I say things on Facebook that I would never dare to say in real life'; 'That's right, you lose your inhibitions when you're online – it's almost like being a bit drunk.'

It seems particularly significant to me that so many of my informants contrast their online communication style with what they would (or would not) say in 'real life'. This curious slip provides a clue to the nature of the disinhibiting effects of online communication. It seems that William Gibson, who coined the term 'cyberspace', was right when he said that 'It's not really a place, it's not really space.' We regard cyberspace as somehow separate from the real world: our behaviour there is different from our conduct 'in real life' (or 'IRL', as it is now called in webspeak).

In this sense, cyberspace can be seen as what anthropologists would call a 'liminal' place – a marginal, borderline state, segregated from everyday existence, in which normal rules and social constructions are suspended, allowing brief exploration of alternative ways of being. Just as we abandon the conventional rules of spelling and grammar in our emails and other cyber-talk, so we ignore many of the social inhibitions and restrictions that normally govern our behaviour. The English behave in remarkably un-English ways. In cyberspace social media sites, chatrooms and forums, for example, unlike most 'real-space' public environments in England, striking up conversations with complete strangers is normal behaviour, indeed actively encouraged. We then go on to reveal personal details that we would never disclose in 'real life'. This may explain why studies regularly find that cyberspace friendships form more easily and develop more rapidly than traditional 'real-space' relationships.

Much of this sociable disinhibition is based on an illusion. Because of the liminality effect, chatting online *feels* more ephemeral and less binding than 'putting something in writing' on paper, or talking face to face, but it is in fact, if anything, more permanent and considerably less discreet. So although many English people find the alternative reality of online communication a liberating experience, it can have adverse consequences. Just as we may sometimes regret things we have said or done while under the influence of alcohol, we may also sometimes regret our unrestrained behaviour in cyberspace. The problem is that cyberspace is not separate from the 'real' world, any more than the office Christmas party takes place in a parallel universe. Excessively uninhibited emails, posts or tweets, like office-party misdemeanours, may come back to haunt us. But I would still argue that the benefits of the cyberspace liminality effect in overcoming English social dis-ease far outweigh these disadvantages.

As I pointed out in the Introduction, the term 'national character' is a metaphor and should not be taken literally: English inhibitions are *cultural*, a matter of obedience to unwritten cultural rules and norms. These rules may be deeply ingrained, and our obedience to them largely unconscious, but they are not personality traits. In contexts where the unspoken rules permit a degree of 'cultural remisswion' (such as pubs, racecourses, festive queues, etc., etc.), we shed some of our inhibitions. 'Cyberspaces' such as social media sites, forums, etc. have their own sets of social rules (both official and unwritten), and we English adapt our behaviour, and relax our inhibitions, in accordance with the rules of the sites and forums we frequent. Many of these social sites and forums are international, and in in these contexts, apart from a few obvious linguistic indicators, it can be hard to distinguish English participants from other nationalities. We do not suddenly or entirely 'shed' all of our cultural quirks along with our inhibitions, but when our social dis-ease symptoms are 'in remission' to the extent permitted in cyberspace, we become far less distinctively English.

I am not the slightest bit surprised to learn that chatting online and surfing the internet are now considerably more popular pastimes among children and teenagers in this country than watching television. Neither am I inclined to share the hand-wringing concern that many parents and pundits seem to feel about this trend. Instead of staring passively at a television screen, our children and teenagers are spending their time actively interacting with what used to be called pen-pals, including pen-pals in foreign countries, or Googling and internet-surfing to read about subjects that interest them. They are, much of the time at least, reading and writing. What is so terrible about that? The subjects they choose to read and write about may not be to our taste, but surely 'twas ever thus.

And, incidentally, it is perhaps no accident that our young people's increasing obsession with online social media has coincided with a substantial decline in public vandalism. Who needs to smash up bus shelters, spray graffiti on buildings or scribble angry messages on the walls of public lavatories when you can express your teenage angst, get attention, win friends and influence people on Facebook, Twitter, forums, chatrooms and blogs?[97]

The Rules of Shopping

It may seem strange to include shopping in this section on 'private and domestic' pursuits, as, despite the rise of online shopping, this activity mostly does not take place in the home but in shops, which are public places. We are talking about the English, however, which means that 'public' activities can be almost as 'private' as domestic ones. Shopping is not, for most English people, a particularly social pastime. Indeed, for most people, most of the time, it is not a 'pastime' at all, but a domestic chore – and should really have been covered in the chapter on work, not here.

But you would probably have found it odd to see a section on

---

97. The internet is changing human social interaction in many other profound (and I believe largely beneficial) ways. As with mobile phones, we are using the internet to recreate more collectivist, 'tribal' social dynamics. But a book about Englishness is not the place to discuss these much wider sociocultural shifts, so I am trying to write another book about them.

shopping under the heading of 'work'. Shopping is not generally regarded as 'work'. There is a curious mismatch between shopping as a concept, and shopping as a real-life activity, between the way we talk in the abstract about shopping, and the realities of our actual experience of it.[98] Discussions about shopping – in the media, among researchers and social commentators, and often in ordinary conversation – tend to focus on the hedonistic, materialistic, individualistic view of shopping: we talk about shopaholics, about 'retail therapy', about the power of advertising, about people spending lots of money they don't have on lots of things they don't need, about the 'sex and shopping' novel, about shopping as self-indulgence, shopping as pleasure, shopping as leisure.

Shopping may indeed sometimes be all of these things. But apart from the very rich and the very young, most people's day-to-day experience of shopping bears little resemblance to this image of mindless hedonism. Most of the shopping we do is 'provisioning' – buying the mundane necessities of life such as food, drink, washing powder, loo paper, light-bulbs, toothpaste and so on, and my survey on shopping showed that 87 per cent of us do this kind of routine provisioning at least once a week. This is no more an act of materialistic self-indulgence than the gathering and foraging of our hunter-gatherer ancestors. Shopping is not work in the sense of 'production', it is a form of 'consumption', and the people who do it are 'consumers', but for many shoppers it is work in the sense of 'providing a service', albeit an unpaid service.

On the other hand, shopping *can* be a pleasurable leisure activity, even for those who mainly experience it as a tedious chore. In my survey, 81 per cent said that they go shopping for pleasure or leisure items at least once a month. In my informal fieldwork interviews with shoppers, most of the people I spoke to made a distinction between 'routine' shopping and 'fun' shopping, provisioning and pleasure, work and play. In fact, if I introduced the topic without qualification, I would often be asked to specify which type of shopping I meant (one woman asked, 'Do you mean the baked-beans-and-nappies sort

98. Daniel Miller makes this observation in his excellent ethnographic study of shoppers in North London – I was intrigued by it and subsequently 'tested' it in various semi-scientific ways in my own fieldwork.

of shopping or the girly-day-out sort?'). On other occasions, it would be clear from people's answers that they assumed I was talking specifically about either one type or the other. This often depended on the location in which the interview took place: people in supermarkets were more likely to assume that I was talking about 'routine' shopping, while the same sort of people interviewed in clothes shops, antiques shops and garden centres tended to think I meant 'fun' shopping. Age was also a factor: teenagers, students and some twentysomethings mainly tended to assume that 'shopping' referred to the play/leisure/fun variety, while older people were much more likely to focus on the chore/provisioning/routine aspects.

Sex and Shopping Rules

There were also significant sex differences: men were less likely than women to distinguish between different types of shopping, and less inclined to admit to enjoying any sort of shopping, even the 'fun' type. Among older English males, in particular, there seems to be an unwritten rule prohibiting any enjoyment of shopping, or at least prohibiting the disclosure or acknowledgement of such enjoyment. Taking pleasure in shopping is regarded as effeminate. The correct masculine line is to define any shopping one does, including the purchase of luxuries and inessentials, as something that has to be done, a means to an end, never a pleasure in itself. The majority of women, by contrast, will readily admit to enjoying 'fun' shopping, and some even say that they quite like the 'provisioning' sort of shopping, or at least take some pride and pleasure in doing it well. There are males and females who do not conform to these rules, but they are seen as deviating from the norm, and they recognise that they are unusual.

The rules regarding attitudes towards shopping are also reflected in the manner in which males and females are expected to shop. I call them the 'hunter/gatherer rules': men, if they can be persuaded to shop at all, tend to shop like hunters; women tend to shop like gatherers. Male shopping (or, more accurately, masculine shopping) is teleological: you select your prey, then single-mindedly and purposefully hunt it down. Female (feminine) shopping is more flexible, more opportunistic: you browse, you see what's available; you know roughly what you're looking for, but you might spot something better, or a bargain, and change your mind.[99]

A significant number of English males, however, choose to prove their masculinity by emphasising how hopelessly bad they are at shopping. Shopping is seen as a female skill; being too good at it, even in the approved hunter-like manner, might cast doubt upon your macho credentials, or even raise questions about your sexual orientation. Among anxious heterosexuals, it is tacitly understood that only gay men – and a few ultra-politically-correct, New Man, feminist types – take pride in their shopping skills. The done thing for 'real men' is to avoid shopping, to profess to hate it, and to be completely useless at it.

This can be partly just a matter of laziness, the employment of a practice the Americans call 'klutzing out' – deliberately making such a poor job of a domestic chore that one is unlikely to be asked to do it again. But among English men, uselessness at shopping is also a significant source of pride. Their female partners often play along with this, helping them to display their manliness by performing elaborate pantomimes of mock-exasperation at their inability to find their way around the supermarket, teasing them constantly and telling stories about their latest doofus mistakes. 'Oh, he's hopeless, hasn't got a clue, have you, love?' said a woman I interviewed in a supermarket coffee shop, smiling fondly at her husband, who pulled a mock-sheepish face. 'I sent him out to get tomatoes and he comes back with a bottle of ketchup and he says, "Well, it's made of tomatoes, isn't it?" So I go, "Yes, but it's not much bloody use in a salad!" Men! Typical!' The man positively glowed with pride, laughing delightedly at this confirmation of his virility.

The 'Shopping as Saving' Rule

For many English females, who still do most (93 per cent at the last count) of the 'routine' 'provisioning' type of shopping, shopping is a

99. My research on shopping indicates a slight but significant recent shift, among younger males, towards a more female/feminine approach to shopping, and a similar shift among older females towards a more male/masculine approach – but, in general, the hunter/gatherer rules still apply.

skill, and it is customary, even among the relatively well-off, to take some pride in doing it well, which is understood to mean with a concern for thrift. Not necessarily getting everything as cheaply as possible, but getting value for money, not being extravagant or wasteful. There is a tacit understanding among English shoppers to the effect that shopping is not an act of spending, but an act of saving.[100] You do not speak of having 'spent' X amount on an item of food or clothing, but of having 'saved' X amount on the item. You would certainly never boast about having spent an excessive sum of money on something, but you are allowed to take pride in finding a bargain.

This rule applies across all social classes: the upper echelons would regard boasting about extravagant expenditure as vulgar, while the lower classes would regard it as 'stuck up' or showing off. The English will tell you that only brash, crass Americans display their wealth by boasting about how much something cost them. Congratulating yourself on a bargain or saving, however – boasting about how *little* something cost you – is universally acceptable among English shoppers of all classes. It is one of the very few exceptions to the money-talk taboo. What constitutes a bargain, what counts as cheap or good value, may well differ according to class and income level, but the principle is the same: whatever price you paid, you should if possible claim that it somehow constituted a saving.

The Apology and Moan Options

When it is not possible to make saving claims – when you have indisputably paid full price for something undeniably expensive – you should ideally just keep quiet about it. Failing that, you have two options, both very English: either apologise or moan. You can apologise for your embarrassing extravagance ('Oh dear, I know I shouldn't have, it was terribly expensive, just couldn't resist it, very naughty of me . . .') or you can moan and grumble about the extortionate cost of things ('Ridiculously expensive, don't know how they get away with charging that much, stupid prices, total rip-off . . .').

100. Another Danny Miller observation, again 'tested' and successfully 'replicated' in my fieldwork.

Both of these options are sometimes used as indirect boasts, ways of subtly indicating one's spending power without indulging in anything so vulgar as an overt display of wealth. And both can also be a form of 'polite egalitarianism': even very rich people will often pretend to be either apologetically embarrassed or grumpy and indignant about the cost of expensive things they have bought, when in fact they can easily afford them, in order to avoid drawing attention to any disparity in income. Shopping, like every other aspect of English life, is full of courteous little hypocrisies.

The 'Bling' Exception

There is one significant exception to the 'shopping as saving' principle, and its associated apologising and moaning. Young people influenced by the black American hip-hop/gangsta/rap culture – a significant youth subculture in England – have adopted a style that requires deliberate ostentatious displays of wealth. This involves wearing expensive designer clothes and flashy gold jewellery (a look originally known as 'bling-bling', now shortened to just 'bling'), drinking expensive champagne (Cristal) and cognac, driving expensive cars – and certainly not being the slightest bit embarrassed about all this extravagance; in fact, taking great pride in it.

Even those who cannot afford the champagne and cars (the majority: this style is particularly popular among low-income teenagers) will do their best to acquire at least a few items of the correct designer clothing, and will boast to anyone who will listen about how much they cost. The 'bling' culture is not so much an exception as a deliberate challenge to mainstream rules of Englishness; it is sticking up two heavily be-ringed fingers at all our unwritten codes of modesty, restraint, diffidence, polite egalitarianism and general hypocrisy. In its own way, it provides confirmation of the enduring importance of these codes – assertion by negation, if you like.

As a form of rebellion, however, 'bling' has not been particularly effective. The style, like the word, has gradually become more 'mainstream'. 'Bling' now simply means pretty much anything shiny, sparkly or glittery. As with many youth subculture fashions, a very diluted version is now to be found in the wardrobes of all age groups and classes. Most important, *mainstream* bling is no longer about displaying wealth. In typical English fashion, mainstream bling-wearers of all ages now often boast about how *little* they paid for their new 'blingy' sandals or necklace.

Class and Shopping Rules

The shopping-as-saving rule applies across class barriers, and even the bling exception is not class-bound: this style appeals to young people from all social backgrounds, including some upper-class schoolboys, who seem quite unaware of how silly they look, trying to dress like pimps and walk and talk like tough black gangstas from American inner-city ghettos. (Other young upper-class males have adopted the slang but not the clothing, and somehow look even sillier, addressing each other as 'bro' and 'homie' while dressed in country tweeds, Barbour jackets and green wellies.)

Most other aspects of shopping, however, are deeply entangled in the complexities of the English class system. As might be expected, where you shop is a key class indicator. But it is not a simple matter of the higher social ranks shopping in the more expensive shops, while the lower echelons use the cheaper ones. The upper-middle classes, for example, will hunt for bargains in second-hand and charity shops, which the lower-middle and working classes 'would not be seen dead in'. Until recently, many upper-middles and middle-middles were reluctant to buy their groceries in the cheap supermarkets, some with names that emphasise their price-consciousness such as Poundland and Costcutter, favoured by the working classes. Instead, they shopped in middle-class supermarkets such as Sainsbury's and Tesco (buying the cheaper 'value' ranges offered by these stores if necessary), or the more upper-middle Waitrose.

Not that anyone would admit to choosing a supermarket for its class status, of course. No, we shop in middle-class supermarkets because of the superior quality of the food and the wider range of organic and exotic vegetables, even when we are just buying exactly the same ubiquitous brand-name basics as the working-class shoppers in cheaper supermarkets such as Asda and Morrisons, or the now ubiquitous German discount supermarkets such as Lidl and

Aldi. We may have no idea what to do with *pak choi* or how to eat organic celeriac, but we like to know they are there, as we walk past with our Kellogg's cornflakes and Andrex loo paper.

The economic recession has resulted in a slight shift in these attitudes, in that at least some upper-middles are now much less reluctant to shop in the cheaper, working-class supermarkets. The more secure, less class-anxious upper-middles will even boast about this, in much the same way as they display their charity-shop purchases with an air of virtuous pride. In fact, the flaunting of an Aldi or Lidl shopping bag, and enthusing over all the 'bargains' they have 'discovered' in these supermarkets can be, in itself, a means of drawing attention to their secure higher-class status. They are effectively saying, 'I am so obviously, unquestionably higher class that I have nothing to fear from these lower-class symbols.' Except that they still tend to favour Lidl and Aldi, the slightly more 'exotic' Continental discount-stores, rather than the more humdrum Asda and Morrisons, which have been around too long to count as 'discoveries'.

The M&S Test

If you want to get an idea of the convoluted intricacy of shopping class-indicators, spend some time observing and interviewing the shoppers in Marks & Spencer. In this very English high-street chain, you trip over invisible class barriers in every aisle. M&S is a sort of department store, selling clothes, shoes, furniture, linen, soap, make-up, etc. – as well as food and drink – all under its own brand name.

- The upper-middle classes buy food in the very expensive but high-quality M&S food halls, and will also happily buy M&S underwear and perhaps the occasional plain, basic item, such as a T-shirt, but will not often buy any other clothes there, except perhaps for children – and certainly not anything with a pattern, as this would identify it as being from M&S. They would never buy a party dress from M&S, and are squeamish about wearing M&S shoes, however comfortable or well made they may be. They will buy M&S towels and bed-linen, but not M&S sofas, curtains or cushions.

- The middle-middles also buy M&S food, although those on a lower budget would not do their entire weekly shop there. They complain a bit (to each other, not to M&S) about the high prices of M&S food, but tell themselves it is worth it for the quality, and buy their cornflakes and loo paper at Sainsbury's or Tesco. Most will buy a much wider range of clothes from M&S than the upper-middles, including some things with prints and patterns, although the class semiotics of M&S have shifted a bit in recent years, and more educated, upwardly mobile middle-middles have now joined the upper-middles in rejecting M&S's patterned clothing – and reserve particular scorn for the heavily patterned and embellished Per Una range (a supposedly 'youthful' collection that in fact caters almost entirely to middle-aged and older women). They will still condescend to buy the occasional plain item from the Limited Edition or Autograph ranges, and they are generally happy to buy M&S sofas, cushions and curtains. Their teenage children, however, may turn up their noses at M&S clothes, not for class reasons but because they prefer the more fashionable high-street chains.

- Lower-middles and some upwardly mobile upper-workings buy M&S food, but usually only as a special treat: for some, particularly those with young children, an M&S 'ready-meal' is an alternative to eating out at a restaurant, something they might have as an indulgence, maybe once a week. They cannot afford to food-shop here regularly, and regard anyone who does as extravagant and quite possibly 'stuck up'. 'My sister-in-law buys all her veg and washing-up liquid and everything from Marks, stupid cow,' a middle-aged woman told me, with a disdainful, disapproving sniff. 'It's just showing off – thinks she's better than us.' M&S clothes, on the other hand, are generally regarded as 'good value' by the thrifty, respectable, genteel sort of lower-middles: 'Not cheap, mind you, but good quality.' Some lower-middles feel the same about the cushions and duvets and towels, while others regard them as 'very nice, but a bit too pricey'.

If you need to make a quick assessment of an English shopper's social class, don't ask about her family background, income, occupation or the value of her house (all of which would in any case be rude): ask her what she does and does not buy at Marks & Spencer. I say 'she' because this test only works reliably on women: men are often blissfully unaware of the yawning social gulf between M&S knickers and an M&S patterned dress.

Pet Rules and 'Petiquette'

Keeping pets, for the English, is not so much a leisure activity as an entire way of life. In fact, 'keeping pets' is an inaccurate and inadequate expression – it does not begin to convey the exalted status of our animals. An Englishman's home may be his castle, but his dog is the real king. People in other countries may buy luxurious five-star kennels and silk-lined baskets for their pets, but the English let them take over the whole house. The unwritten rules allow our dogs and cats to sprawl all over our sofas and chairs, always hogging the best places in front of the fire or television. They get far more attention, affection, appreciation, encouragement and 'quality time' than our children, and often better food. Imagine the most over-indulged, fêted, adored *bambino* in Italy, and you will get a rough idea of the status of the average English pet. The Royal Society for the Prevention of Cruelty to Animals was established more than half a century before the National Society for the Prevention of Cruelty to Children, which appears to have been founded as a somewhat derivative afterthought.

Why is this? What is it about the English and animals? Yes, many other cultures have pets, and some are in their own ways as soppy about them as we are, but the English inordinate love of animals is still one of the characteristics for which we are renowned, and which many foreigners find baffling. The Americans may outdo us in gushy sentimentality and extravagant expenditure on pets – all those cheesy tear-jerker films, elaborate pet cemeteries, luxury toys and dogs got up in ludicrous designer costumes. But then they always outdo us in gushiness and conspicuous consumption.

The English relationship with animals is different: our pets are more than status indicators (although they do serve this purpose) and our affinity with them goes well beyond sentimentality. It is often said that we treat them like people, but this is not true. Have you *seen* how we treat people? It would be unthinkable to be so cold and unfriendly to an animal. OK, I'm exaggerating – a bit. But the fact is that we tend to be far more open, easy, communicative and demonstrative in our relationships with our animals than with each other.

The average Englishman will assiduously avoid social interaction with his fellow humans, and will generally become either awkward or aggressive when obliged to communicate with them, unless certain props and facilitators are available to help the process along. He will have no difficulty at all, however, in engaging in lively, amicable conversation with a dog. Even a strange dog, to whom he has not been introduced. Bypassing all the usual stilted embarrassments, his greeting will be effusive: 'Hello there!' he will exclaim. 'What's your name? And where have you come from, then? D'you want some of my sandwich, mate? Mm, yes, it's not bad, is it? Here, come up and share my seat! Plenty of room!'

You see, the English really are quite capable of Latin-Mediterranean warmth, enthusiasm and hospitality; we can be just as direct and approachable and emotive and tactile as any of the so-called 'contact cultures'. It is just that these qualities are only consistently expressed in our interactions with animals. And, unlike our fellow Englishmen, animals are not embarrassed or put off by our un-English displays of emotion. No wonder animals are so important to the English: for many of us, they represent our only significant experience of open, unguarded, emotional involvement with another sentient being.

An American visitor I met had suffered for a week as a guest in a fairly typical English household ruled by two large, boisterous and chronically disobedient dogs, whose ineffectual owners engaged them in non-stop, stream-of-consciousness chatter, indulged their every whim and laughed affectionately at their misdemeanours. She complained to me that the owners' relationship with their dogs was 'abnormal' and 'unhealthy' and 'dysfunctional'. 'No, you don't understand,' I explained. 'This is probably the only normal, healthy, functional relationship these people have.' She was, however, sensitive enough to have picked up on an important rule of English 'petiquette' – the one that absolutely forbids criticism of a person's pets. However badly your hosts' ghastly, leg-humping, shoe-eating dog behaves, you must not speak ill of the beast. That would be a worse social solecism than criticising their children.

We are allowed to criticise our own pets, but this must be done in affectionate, indulgent tones: 'He's so naughty – that's the third pair of shoes he's wrecked this month, ah, bless!' There is almost a hint of pride in such 'isn't he awful?' complaints, as though we are secretly, perversely, rather charmed by our pets' flaws and failings. In fact, we often engage in one-upmanship over our pets' misdemeanours. At a party, I listened to two Labrador-owners capping each other's stories of the items their dogs had eaten or destroyed.

'It wasn't just shoes and ordinary things, mine used to eat mobile phones.'

'Well, mine chewed a whole hi-fi system to bits!'

'Mine ate a Volvo!' (How do you top that? I wondered. Mine ate a helicopter? Mine ate the QE2?)

I am convinced that the English get great vicarious pleasure from our pets' uninhibited behaviour. We grant them all the freedoms that we deny ourselves: the most repressed and inhibited people on Earth have the most blatantly unreserved, spontaneous and badly behaved pets. Our pets are our alter egos, or perhaps even the symbolic embodiment of what a psychotherapist would call our 'inner child' (but not the sort of inner child they mean, the one with big soulful eyes who needs a hug – I mean our snub-nosed, mucky, obnoxious 'inner brat'). Our animals represent our wild side; through them, we can express our most un-English tendencies: we can break all the rules, if only by proxy.

The unspoken law states that our animal alter egos/inner brats can do no wrong. If an English person's dog bites you, you must have provoked it; and even if the attack was clearly unprovoked – if the animal just took a sudden irrational dislike to you – the owners will assume that there must be something suspect or objectionable about you. The English firmly believe that our dogs (and cats, guinea pigs, ponies, parrots, etc.) are shrewd judges of character. If our pet takes against someone, even if we have no reason at all to dislike the person, we trust the animal's superior insight and become wary and suspicious. People who object to being jumped on, climbed over, kicked, scratched and generally mauled by English animals who are 'just being friendly' also clearly have something wrong with them.

Although our pets usually provide a vital therapeutic substitute for emotional relationships with human beings, the superior quality of our communication and bonding with animals can sometimes also have beneficial side effects on our relations with other humans. We can even manage to strike up a conversation with a stranger if one of us is accompanied by a dog, although it must be said that both parties are sometimes inclined to talk to the canine chaperone rather than address each other directly. Non-verbal as well as verbal signals are exchanged through the blissfully oblivious dog, who happily absorbs all the eye contact and friendly touching that would be regarded as excessively forward and pushy between newly acquainted humans. And pets can act as mediators or facilitators even in more established relationships: English couples who have trouble expressing their feelings to each other often tend to communicate through their pets. 'Mummy's looking really pissed off, isn't she, Patch? Yes, she is. Yes, she is. Do you think she's annoyed with us?'

'Well, Patchy-poo, Mummy's vewy, vewy tired and she would appreciate it if lazy old Daddy gave her a bit of help round here instead of sitting on his arse reading the paper all day.'

Most of the above rules apply across class barriers, but there are a few variations. The middle-middles and lower-middles, although just as dotty about their pets as the other classes, tend to be somewhat less tolerant of mess, and rather more squeamish about the lewder kinds of misbehaviour than those at the top and bottom of the social scale. Middle-middle and lower-middle pets are not necessarily any better behaved, but their owners are more zealous about cleaning up after them, and more embarrassed when they sniff people's crotches or try to have sex with their legs.

The type and breed of pet you keep, however, is a more reliable class indicator than your attitude towards animals. Dogs, for example, are universally popular, but the upper echelons prefer Labradors, golden retrievers, King Charles spaniels and springer spaniels, while the lower classes are more likely to have Rottweilers, Alsatians, poodles, Afghans, chihuahuas, bull terriers and cocker spaniels.

Cats are less popular than dogs with the upper class, although those who live in grand country houses find them useful for keeping mice and rats at bay. The lower social ranks, by contrast, may keep mice and rats as pets – as well as guinea pigs, hamsters and gold-fish. Some middle-middles, and lower-middles with aspirations, take great pride in keeping expensive exotic fish such as Koi carp in their garden pond. The upper-middles and upper classes think this is 'naff'. Horses are widely regarded as 'posh' animals, and social-climbers often take up riding or buy ponies for their children in order to ingratiate themselves with the 'horsey' set to which they aspire. Unless they also manage to perfect the appropriate accent, arcane vocabulary, mannerisms and dress, they don't fool the genuinely 'posh' horse-owners – who may well in any case be a minority, as horses are owned by people of all social ranks.

What you do with your pet can also be a class indicator. Generally, only the middle-middles and below go in for dog shows, cat shows and obedience tests, and only these classes would put a sticker in the back window of their car proclaiming their passion for a partic-ular breed of dog or warning other motorists that their vehicle may contain 'Show Cats in Transit'. The upper classes regard showing dogs and cats as rather vulgar, but showing horses and ponies is fine. There is no logic to any of this.

Middle-middles and below are also more likely to dress up their dogs and cats in coloured collars, bows and other tweenesses – and if you see a dog with its name in inverted commas on its collar, the animal's owners are almost certainly no higher than middle-middle. Upper-middle and upper-class dogs usually just wear plain brown leather collars. Only a certain type of rather insecure working-class male goes in for big, scary, aggressive-looking guard dogs (or bull terriers) with big, scary, studded, black collars.

English pet-owners are highly unlikely to admit that their pet is a status signal, or that their choice of pet is in any way class-related. They will insist that they like Labradors (or springer spaniels, or whatever) because of the breed's kind temperament. If you want to get them to reveal their hidden class anxieties, or if you just like causing trouble, you can try the canine equivalent of the Mondeo and Mercedes tests: put on your most innocent face, and tell a Labrador-owner, 'Oh, I'd have seen you more as an Alsatian [or poodle, or chihuahua] sort of person.'

If you are of a more kind and affable disposition, note that the quickest way to an English person's heart, no matter what their class, is through their pet. Always praise people's pets, and when you speak to our animals directly (which you should do as much as possible) remember that you are addressing our inner child. If you are a visitor eager to make friends with the natives, try to acquire or borrow a dog to act as a passport to conversation and as a chaperone.

PROPS AND FACILITATORS – PUBLIC/SOCIAL ACTIVITIES

If you do not have a dog, you will need to find another kind of passport to social contact. Which brings me neatly to the second type of English approach to leisure mentioned at the beginning of this chapter: the public/social pursuits and pastimes – sports, games, pubs, clubs and so on. All of these relate directly to our second main method of dealing with our social dis-ease: the 'ingenious use of props and facilitators' method.

Rules of the Game

It is no accident that almost all of the most popular sports and games played around the world today originated in England. Football, base-ball, rugby and tennis were all invented here, and even when we did not actually invent a sport or game, the English were usually the first to lay down a proper, official set of rules for it (hockey, horseracing, polo, swimming, rowing, boxing – and even skiing, for heaven's sake). And that's not counting all the rather less athletic games and pastimes such as darts, pool, billiards, cards, cribbage and skittles. And let's not forget hunting, shooting and fishing. We didn't create or codify all of these, of course, but sports and games are widely recognised as an essential part of our culture, our heritage and our legacy – one cannot talk about Englishness without talking about sports and games.

Testosterone Rules

A number of students of Englishness have tried to explain the English obsession with games. Most of these commentators attempt to find historical explanations. Jeremy Paxman wonders whether the development of this obsession might have had something to do with 'safety and prosperity and the availability of leisure time' or perhaps 'the fact that duelling was frowned upon earlier than in the rest of Europe meant there was a need to find alternative challenges'. Hmm, well, maybe. He comes closer with the observation that our great boys' boarding schools had to 'find ways of exercising the hormonally challenged'. But this is what I would call a 'cross-cultural universal', a valid reason for *any* human society to develop sports and games, and indeed one of the reasons every human society has done so. We all have testosterone-fuelled adolescent and post-adolescent males to deal with, and we all deal with them by trying to channel their potentially destructive aggression and other disruptive tendencies into relatively harmless sports and games.

The universal testosterone problem cannot in itself explain why the English in particular should have developed so many of these pastimes, although I would argue that the young English male, being socially uneasy as well as hormonally challenged, has perhaps a more pressing need for such channelling. And the rest of us also need some means of overcoming our social inhibitions and dis-ease. The real reasons for the English love of games are perhaps best explained through an example from my research.

The 'Props and Facilitators' Method

It was during my study on pub etiquette that I began to understand the importance of games. In conversations with tourists, I found that, to foreign visitors, many English pubs seem more like children's playgrounds than adult drinking-places. One American tourist I interviewed expressed his bewilderment at the number and variety of games in a local pub: 'Look at this place! You've got a dartboard, a bar-billiards table, four different board games, and card games and dominoes and some weird thing with a box and a bunch of little sticks – and then you tell me this pub has a football team and a cricket team and quiz nights . . . You call this a bar? At home we'd call it a kindergarten!' Fortunately for me, this scornful tourist had only noticed about a dozen or so typical pub games, and had not heard of all the more obscure regional eccentricities such as Aunt Sally, wellie-throwing, shove ha'penny, marrow-dangling, conger-cuddling and Wetton Toe Wrestling. Another equally puzzled but marginally more polite visitor asked, 'What is it with you English? Why do you have to play all these silly games? Why can't you just go to a bar and drink and talk like the rest of the world?'

Somewhat defensively, I explained that the rest of the world is not as socially inhibited and inept as the English. We do not find it easy to initiate friendly conversation with strangers, or to develop closer relationships with fellow pubgoers. We need help. We need *props*. We need excuses to make contact. We need toys and sports and games that get us involved with each other.

What works in the microcosm of the pub also works in English society as a whole. More so, in fact. If we need games and sports even in the special social microclimate of the pub, where the usual restraints are relaxed somewhat, and it is acceptable to strike up a conversation with a stranger, we clearly have an even greater need for such props and facilitators outside this sociable environment.

The Self-delusion Rule

But sports and games do not only provide the props we need to initiate and sustain social contact, they also prescribe the nature of that contact. This is not 'random' sociability, but sociability hedged about with a lot of rules and regulations, ritual and etiquette, both official and unofficial. The English are capable of engaging socially with each other, but we need clear and precise guidelines on what to do, what to say, and exactly when and how to do and say it. Games ritualise our social interactions, giving them a reassuring structure and sense of order. By focusing on the detail of the game's rules and rituals, *we can pretend that the game itself is really the point, and the social contact a mere incidental side-effect.*

In fact, it is the other way round: games are a means to an end, the end being the kind of sociable interaction and social bonding that other cultures seem to achieve without all this fuss, subterfuge and self-delusion. The English *are* human; we are social animals just like all other humans, but we have to trick ourselves into social interaction and bonding by disguising it as something else, such as a game of football, cricket, tennis, rugby, darts, pool, dominoes, cards, Scrabble, charades, wellie-throwing or toe-wrestling.

Closet Patriotism and Effervescent Exceptions

I have already mentioned that the English are mostly a nation of 'closet patriots' – we may feel proud of our country but, apart from a tiny minority, we are normally too inhibited and squeamishly embarrassed, perhaps too cynical, to make a big gushy flag-waving fuss about it. Except over sport: big sporting events such as the London 2012 Olympic Games provide an antidote to our social dis-ease, a temporary remission from our usual Eeyorishness – an excuse to shed some of our inhibitions and be a bit more emotive and demonstrative.

The 2012 Olympics were like a carnival or tribal festival, a period of 'cultural remission', 'legitimised deviance' and 'festive inversion', where some of the usual social norms and unwritten rules are temporarily suspended and we behave in ways we wouldn't normally – dancing in the streets, waving national flags, shouting, cheering and indulging in other wildly disinhibited acts such as maybe even talking to strangers.

Sport can also have a unifying effect, to which even the socially inhibited English are not immune. At big sporting events, spectators experience a special sort of communal energy. Anthropologists have a bunch of jargon words for this – Durkheim called it 'collective effervescence', Victor Turner called it 'communitas' – a sort of special crowd-energy that has a bonding and unifying effect. Some psychologists use the terms 'limbic resonance', 'emotional contagion' or 'mood contagion' to describe this effect. To put it very simply, when others around us are clapping, dancing, laughing and cheering, the mirror neurons in our brains are activated and mimic these actions, and there is a link between these neurons and the limbic system, so our emotions are activated as well: we feel happy and connected. (This even works to some extent for those only watching on television: 'laugh tracks' on comedy programmes provide people alone at home with the sense that others around them are laughing, and this is probably all about limbic resonance. The same applies to television viewers watching the cheering crowds at the Olympics.) These effects are common to all nations, of course, but only the English need the huge drug-like collective 'high' of a sporting event as big as the Olympics to get strangers on trains to exchange a few friendly words with each other.

And, of course, it didn't last. As I predicted in some radio interviews just before the London Olympics, there was a brief outbreak of un-English sociability on public transport during the Games, but we very quickly reverted to our usual contact-avoidance, hiding behind our newspapers, tablets and laptops, and only breaking the taboo on talking to strangers when there is a delay or disruption to grumble about. It has been said that if moaning were an Olympic sport, the English would win all the gold medals. But looking on the bright side, we should remember that moaning – or, rather, our special kind of humorous mock-moaning – is probably the primary form of social bonding in this country, way ahead of sport and much more reliably effective. Olympic effervescence is ephemeral, but we can always rely on the delayed and cancelled trains that allow us to indulge in a more traditional, comfortable form of social bonding: exchanging the same old familiar grumpy jokes about 'the wrong sort of leaves' and saying, 'Typical!' a lot.

Games Etiquette

Each of our many games and sports has its rules – not just the official rules of the game itself, which the English like to be as complex as possible, but an equally complex set of unofficial, unwritten rules governing the comportment and social interactions of the players and spectators. Again, pub games are a good example. Even in this sociable microclimate, our diffidence and reluctance to intrude on other people means that we are more comfortable when there are established 'rules of introduction' to follow. Knowing the etiquette, the correct form of address, gives us the courage to take the initiative. Even if we are feeling in need of company, we are unlikely to approach a stranger who is sitting at a table with his pint, or with his mates, but if they are playing pool or darts or bar-billiards, there is not only a valid excuse to make an approach, but also a set formula to follow, which makes the whole process much less daunting.

For pool and bar-billiards players, the formula is straightforward. You simply approach a player and ask, 'Is it winner stays on?' This traditional opening is both an enquiry about the local rules on turn-taking, which may vary from region to region and even from pub to pub, and an invitation to play the winner of the current game. The reply may be 'Yeah, coins down,' or 'That's right – name on the board.' This is both an acceptance of your invitation, and an instruc-tion on the pub's system for securing the table, which may be by placing your coins on the corner of the table, or writing your name on a nearby chalkboard. Either way, it is understood that you will pay for the game, so there is no need for any embarrassing breach of the money-talk taboo. If the reply to your original question is simply 'Yes,' you may ask, 'Is it coins down?' or 'Is it names on the board?'

Having completed the correct introductions, you may now stand around and watch the current game, gradually joining in the banter as you wait your turn. Further enquiries about local rules are the most acceptable way of initiating conversation. These usually begin with the same somewhat impersonal 'Is it . . .' as in 'Is it two shots on the black?' or 'Is it stick pocket or any pocket?' rather than using anything so intimate as a personal pronoun. Once you are accepted as a player, the unwritten etiquette also allows you to make appropriate comments on the game. Well, actually there is only one entirely safe and appropriate comment you can make, particularly among male players, and this is to say, 'Shot,' when a player makes a particularly good shot. Perhaps to compensate, this one word is pronounced in a drawn-out fashion, as though it had at least two syllables: 'Sho-ot.' Other players may also tease and taunt each other over bad shots (the same drawn-out 'sho-ot' can be used ironically in this context), but newcomers wisely tend to avoid making any derogatory remarks until they are better acquainted.

Sex Differences and the 'Three-emotions Rule'

There are some sex differences in the codes of conduct governing pub games, and indeed many sports and games played in other contexts. As a rule of thumb, males are supposed to adopt a strong, stiff-upper-lip, manly approach to the game, both as players and as spectators. It is not done to jump about and exclaim over one's own or another player's luck or skill. In darts, for example, swearing at one's mistakes, and making sarcastic comments on those of one's opponents is allowed, but clapping one's hands in glee upon scoring a double-twenty, and excessive laughter on failing to hit the board at all, are regarded as 'girly' and inappropriate.

The usual 'three-emotions rule' applies. English males are allowed to express three emotions: surprise, providing it is conveyed by shouting or swearing; anger, also communicated in expletives; and elation/triumph, displayed in the same manner. For the untrained eye and ear, it can be difficult to distinguish between the three permitted emotions, but English males have no trouble grasping the nuances. Female players and spectators are allowed a much wider range of acceptable emotions, and a much more extensive vocabulary with which to express them. This often seems to happen – that one sex is required to be 'more English' than the other, in a certain context. Here, males are subject to more restrictions than females, but in other contexts – such as, say, the giving and receiving of compliments – the unwritten rules place more complex constraints on female behaviour. It may all balance out, but my suspicion is that, overall, the rules of Englishness are probably a bit harder on males than on females.

The Fair-play Rule

The English concern with fair play is, as we have seen, an underlying theme in almost all aspects of our life and culture, and in the context of sports and games, fair play is still – despite the rantings of the doom-mongers – an ideal to which we cling, even if we do not always manage to live up to it.

At the top national and international level, sport has become, for the English as for all other nations, a rather more cut-throat business, and there seems to be more focus on winning and on the exploits of individual superstar 'personalities' (a misnomer if ever there was one) than on high-minded notions of team spirit and sportsmanship.

Until, that is, there is some accusation of cheating, unfairness, loutishness or unsporting behaviour, whereupon we all seethe with righteous indignation – or cringe with shame and embarrassment, and
tell each other that the country is going to the dogs. Both reactions
suggest that the sporting ethic, which the English are often credited
with inventing, is still very important to us.

In *Anyone for England?*, one of the many premature obituaries
for English national identity, Clive Aslet bemoans the loss of all these
gentlemanly ideals, claiming that even cricket, 'the game synonymous
with the sporting ideal, has changed beyond recognition in terms of
the spirit in which it is played'. But, apart from the rather unseemly
row between Ian Botham and Imran Khan in 1996, the worst sin of
which he accuses the England team is that the players 'make little
effort to cultivate an image of gentlemanliness through their dress'.
He objects to the baseball caps, stubble, T-shirts and shorts worn
by off-duty cricketers. He refers to the 'ungentlemanly tactics' of
national players, without giving any examples, and then is 'shocked
to learn from cricketing friends' that these are even being adopted
at village-cricket level. Intimidating 'war-paint' and helmets, as seen
in televised international matches, are sometimes worn; opposing
batsmen, it seems, are no longer *always* clapped to the crease; and
the Woodmancote team, from Hampshire, was expelled from the
National Village Cricket Knock-out Tournament for being 'too
professional'. The first two of these examples do not strike me as
particularly shocking, and the third seems to indicate that, if
anything, the old values of amateurism and fair play are very much
alive and well in village cricket.

Even Aslet admits that people have been mourning the demise of
this sporting ethic for at least a century – indeed, the obituaries
started almost as soon as the Victorians invented the gentlemanly
'sporting ideal' in the first place. The English have a habit of inventing
'traditions' out of thin air, to suit the spirit of the times, and then
almost immediately waxing mournfully nostalgic about them, as
though they were a vital and now tragically dying part of our cultural
heritage.

Which brings me to football. And the modern evil of football hooliganism, of course. The subject of football hooliganism was raised by participants in all of SIRC's discussion-groups on national identity, and chosen as a core feature of our national character by nearly 30 per cent of survey respondents. And football violence is always wheeled out as Exhibit A by those who complain that the country is going to the dogs, that we have become a nation of louts, that sport isn't what it used to be, and so on. These complainers admittedly constitute quite a large proportion of the population, but that is an indication of our Eeyorish love of moaning and national self-flagellation, rather than evidence for the truth of our moans.

What all the mourners and moaners fail to understand is that football violence is nothing new. You know the well-worn joke about 'I went to a fight and a football match broke out'? Well, that's pretty much how football started. The game of football has been associated with violence since its origins in thirteenth-century England. Medieval football matches were essentially pitched battles between the young men of rival villages and towns. They involved hundreds of 'players', and were often used as opportunities to settle old feuds, personal arguments and land disputes. Some forms of 'folk-football' existed in other countries (such as the German *Knappen* and the Florentine *calcio in costume*), but the roots of modern football are in these violent English rituals.

The much more restrained, disciplined form of the game with which we are now familiar was the reformed pastime of the Victorians, but the violent traditions and rivalries have persisted, mainly among spectators, on the terraces and in the towns. Only two quite brief periods in English history – the inter-war years and about a decade or so following the Second World War – have been relatively free of football-related violence. Historically, these periods are the exception rather than the rule. So I'm sorry, but I cannot accept modern football hooliganism as evidence of a recent decline in sporting manners or values.

In any case, the rule or ideal I am concerned with here is not the entire Victorian gentlemanly package, but just the basic notion of fair play, which is not necessarily incompatible with a desire to win, or with inelegant dress, or with financial gain and commercial sponsorship – or, for that matter, with violence. My colleague Peter Marsh (among others) has shown that human violence – including specifically English football-hooligan violence – is not a random free-for-all but a rule-governed affair, in which considerations of fairness may often play a part. Football violence is not as widespread, or indeed as violent, as it is cracked up to be. There is a lot of aggressive chanting and taunting, some intimidating displays and threats, and a few scuffles, but serious physical violence is actually relatively uncommon. The hooligans' aim is to scare rival fans into running away, and then jeer at their cowardice, not to beat them to a pulp. A typical football chant (this one sung to the tune of 'Seasons in the Sun') encapsulates the hooligans' mission:

> We had joy, we had fun, we had Swindon on the run
> But the joy didn't last, cos the bastards ran too fast!

I am not trying to whitewash or defend football hooligans here. They are loud, ill-mannered and often racist. All I am saying is that they do have their own codes of conduct, and that 'fair play' is very much part of the etiquette governing their aggressive and violent encounters.

The Underdog Rule

In 1990, the Tory MP Norman Tebbit caused much outrage and uproar when he complained that too many Asian immigrants in Britain failed what he called the 'cricket test' – by cheering for India or Pakistan when these countries played England at cricket, rather than cheering for England. His remarks were aimed primarily at second-generation Asian and Caribbean immigrants, whom he accused of having 'split loyalties', when they should be demonstrating their Britishness by supporting the England cricket team. 'When people come to a new country, they should be prepared to immerse themselves totally and utterly in that country,' he declared.

The racism, ignorance and arrogance of the 'Tebbit Test', as it came to be known, are quite breathtaking. Was Tebbit suggesting that Asian immigrants in Britain should follow the shining example we provided as uninvited residents in their countries? And for whom would he suggest that English settlers in Australia should cheer, when England plays Australia in their adopted home? And what about

Scottish and Welsh people living in England – whom should they support? Did he realise that the Scots *always*, on principle, cheer for whatever country is playing *against* England? As do many members of the cynical English intelligentsia, among whom any display of patriotism, particularly over sport, is regarded as deeply unsophisticated. Not to mention all the other English people who just find patriotic fervour somewhat embarrassing, and would feel silly and self-conscious if obliged to cheer for England. Should we all be denied full citizenship?

But even leaving all of this aside, the 'Tebbit Test' would still not work as a test of Englishness. Those who are truly, culturally 'English' – whatever their race or country of origin – can be distinguished by their automatic, instinctive inclination to cheer for the underdog. I am by no means the first to notice this trait: the English tendency to support the underdog is one of those national stereotypes that I was determined to 'get inside' during my field research. I saw plenty of examples, but the one that sticks in my mind, the one that really helped me to understand the depth and complexities of the underdog rule, was the men's final at Wimbledon in 2002.

Tennis buffs apparently found this match rather dull, for a Wimbledon final, but I was there to watch the spectators, not the players, and I found it fascinating. The match was between the world-famous, top-seed Australian player Lleyton Hewitt, and a virtually unknown Argentine called David Nalbandian, who had never even played at Wimbledon before. The result was a predictably easy victory for the Australian champion, who beat Nalbandian 6–1, 6–3, 6–2.

At the start of the match, all the English spectators were cheering for Nalbandian, clapping and whooping and shouting, 'Come on, David!' every time he scored a point or even made a good shot (or whatever it's called in tennis), while Hewitt only got a few token, polite claps. When I asked the English spectators around me why they were supporting the Argentine – particularly given that there was no great love between England and Argentina; indeed, we had been at war not so long ago – they explained that nationality was irrelevant, that Nalbandian was the underdog, highly unlikely to win, and therefore obviously deserved their support. They seemed surprised that I should have to ask such a question, and several people even spelt out the rule for me – 'You always support the underdog'; 'You have to support the underdog.' Their tone suggested that I really should already know this, that it was a fundamental law of nature.

Fine, I thought, good, another 'rule of Englishness' in the bag. Feeling rather smug, I watched complacently for a bit, and was just beginning to get bored, and thinking about maybe sloping off in search of an ice-cream, when something strange happened. Hewitt did something particularly good (don't ask me what, I don't understand tennis) and the people around me started whooping and cheering and clapping him. 'Eh?' I said. 'Hang on. I thought you were supporting Nalbandian, the underdog? Why are you now cheering for Hewitt?' The explanations offered by the English spectators were a bit less clear-cut, but the gist was that Hewitt was, after all, playing exceptionally well, and that everyone had been cheering for Nalbandian, because he was the underdog, which meant that poor Hewitt, despite playing brilliantly, was getting little or no support and encouragement from the crowd, which seemed rather unfair, so they felt sorry for him, out there all alone with everyone cheering his opponent, so they were cheering for him to redress the balance a bit. In other words, Hewitt, the overdog (is that a word? never mind – you know what I mean), had somehow become the underdog, the one who deserved their support.

For a while, that is. I was now alert, shaken out of my complacency, and paying close attention to the behaviour of the spectators, so when the cheering for Hewitt dwindled, and the spectators began giving all their support to Nalbandian again, I was ready with my questions: '*Now* what? Why aren't you cheering for Hewitt any more? Is he not playing so well?' No, apparently he was playing even better. And that was the point. Hewitt was now clearly heading for an easy win. Nalbandian was struggling, was going to be 'slaughtered', had absolutely no chance – so obviously it was only fair to give him all the noisy vocal encouragement and praise, and only clap politely for the all-conquering overdog Hewitt.

So, in the logic of English fair play, you must always support the underdog, but too much support for the underdog can be unfair on the overdog, who then becomes a sort of honorary underdog, whom you must support until balance is restored, or until the real underdog is clearly going to lose, at which point you must support the real underdog again. Simple, really. Once you know the rules. Or at least at Wimbledon it was relatively simple, as there could be no doubt as to who was the real underdog. When this is not immediately obvious, there can be difficulties, as the English dither over who is most deserving of their cheers; and further problems can arise when an English player (or team) happens to be the overdog, as fairness demands that we give at least some token support to the underdog opposition.

A top-level English athlete (multiple Olympic gold medallist) told me that this English habit of supporting the underdog is most irritating – 'Drives me nuts' were his exact words – for competitors like him, who are, of course, almost always in the 'overdog' category. It must indeed be rather galling, when one has worked so hard to get to the top of one's sport, to hear English supporters dutifully cheering on one's less talented rivals.

Football fans, the most patriotic of sports spectators, do not suffer from these fair-play anxieties at the international level, or when the local team they support is playing, but even they may be inclined to cheer for the underdog when they have no prior loyalties to either team involved in a match, particularly if the overdog-team has been too boastful about its successes, or too insultingly confident about the result of the match. Many English football fans will also doggedly support a hopeless, talentless, third-division team throughout their entire lives, never wavering in their loyalty, however badly their team performs. There is an unwritten rule that says you choose which football team to support at a very young age, and that's it, for ever: you never switch your allegiance to another team. You can appreciate or even admire the skills and talent of, say, a top team such as Manchester United, but the team you *support* is still Swindon, or Stockport, or whoever – the team you have supported since you were a child. You are not obliged to support your local team: many young people from all parts of the country support Manchester United, or Chelsea, or Arsenal. The point is that once you have chosen, you stay loyal; you don't switch from Chelsea to Arsenal just because the latter happen to be playing better, or indeed for any other reason.

At the races, however, you will see even more extreme examples of English observance of the fair-play and underdog rules – and indeed of Englishness in general or, rather, the more pleasant aspects of Englishness. I mentioned in Racing Talk (page 151) that the unique 'social microclimate' of the racecourse, characterised by a rare combination of (relatively) relaxed inhibitions and exceptionally good manners, seems to bring out the best in us. At the Cheltenham Festival, which is traditionally regarded as an 'England versus Ireland' contest, with national pride at stake in every race, I have witnessed English racegoers fretting because it was nearly the end of the first day and the Irish still had not had a winner. 'It would be awful if the Irish didn't get a winner,' these young men told me. 'The buzz will really start as soon as we have an Irish winner – they need to celebrate, and they've a good chance in the next, so cross your fingers for them!' When an Irish horse finally won, these English racegoers whooped and cheered and celebrated. All of them had just lost money, as they had backed the English favourite in the race in question. But the 'underdog' had won, everyone could celebrate: somehow the balance of the universe had been restored.

Club Rules

There is an apparent contradiction, which has puzzled a number of commentators, between the strong individualism of the English and our penchant for forming and joining clubs, between our obsession with privacy and our 'clubbability'. Jeremy Paxman notes that the supposedly insular, individualistic, privacy-fixated English have clubs for almost everything: 'There are clubs to go fishing, support football teams, play cards, arrange flowers, race pigeons, make jam, ride bicycles, watch birds, even for going on holiday.' I won't attempt a more comprehensive list – it would take up half of the book: just as every conceivable English leisure pursuit has a magazine or six, each one also has clubs, if not a National Society, with a whole network of Regional Groups and subdivisions. Usually there are two rival National Societies, with marginally different views on the activity in question, who spend most of their time happily bickering and squabbling with each other.

Citing de Tocqueville, Paxman wonders how 'the English manage to be simultaneously so highly singular, yet to be forever forming clubs and societies: how could the spirit of association and the spirit of exclusion be so highly developed in the same people?' He seems to accept de Tocqueville's pragmatic, economic explanation, that the English historically have always formed associations in order to pool resources, when they could not get what they wanted by individual effort – and he also emphasises that joining clubs is very much a matter of individual choice.

I would argue that clubs are more about social needs than practical or economic ones, but I agree that the issue of choice is important. The English are not keen on random, unstructured, spontaneous, street-corner sociability; we are no good at this, and it makes us uneasy. We prefer to socialise in an organised, ordered manner, at specific times and places of our choosing, with rules that we can argue about, an agenda, minutes and a monthly newsletter. Above all, as with sports and games, we need to pretend that the activity of the club or society (flower-arranging, amateur dramatics, charity, breeding rabbits, whatever) is the real point of the gathering, and that social bonding is just a secondary side-effect.

It's that self-delusion thing again. The English constantly form clubs and societies for exactly the same reason that we have so many sports and games: we need props and facilitators to help us engage socially with our fellow humans, to overcome our social dis-ease, and we also need the illusion that we are doing something else, that we have come together for some practical purpose, to pursue a specific shared interest, to pool resources in order to achieve something we could not manage alone. The pragmatic de Tocqueville/Paxman explanation of English clubbiness is a very English one: it perfectly describes this illusion, but fails to recognise that it is an illusion – that the real purpose of all these clubs is the social contact and social bonding that we desperately need, but cannot admit to needing, not even to ourselves.

If you are very English, you may well choose to reject my explanation. I don't like it much myself. I would much rather believe that I joined, say, the Arab Horse Society, and attended meetings of its Chiltern Regional Group, because I had an Arab stallion and was interested in breeding and riding Arab horses and participating in shows, events and discussions with other aficionados. I would like to think that at university I joined umpteen left-wing political groups, and went on countless demonstrations and marches and CND rallies, because of my firmly held convictions and principles.[101] And, indeed, these were the conscious reasons. I am not saying that the English *deliberately* set out to trick ourselves into sociability. But if I'm ruthlessly honest with myself, I have to admit that I also liked the sense of belonging, the ease of socialising with people with whom I shared an interest or a cause – compared to the awkwardness of trying to make conversation with strangers in public places or at gatherings where the sole purpose is to gather, to be sociable, without any shared hobbies or horses or political hobby-horses to help things along.

If you are a member of an English club or society, you may also resent my lumping them all together like this, as though there were no significant difference between the Arab Horse Society and the Campaign for Nuclear Disarmament, or between, say, a Women's Institute meeting and that of a bikers' club. Well, sorry, but I have to report that there is indeed very little difference. In the case of the Women's Institute and motorbike-club meetings that I attended, the only significant difference was that the bikers spent considerably more time discussing their charity work and planning their next charity events.

I've been a member of many English clubs and societies, and gate-crashed a few others in the course of my research, and they are all much of a muchness. Meetings of regional or local branches of the AHS, CND, WI, MAG (Motorcycle Action Group) and Neighbourhood Watch groups or residents' associations all follow more or less the same pattern. They start with the usual English awkward greetings and jokes and some preliminary weather-speak. There is tea or alcohol, and sandwiches or biscuits (both if you're lucky), a lot of

---

101. Lest I be suspected of rather un-English humourless earnestness, I should add that I also joined a jokey organisation called SAVE, which stood for Students Against Virtually Everything.

gossip, a lot of ritual moaning and a lot of in-jokes. These are followed by a bit of throat-clearing and attempts to get the meeting started without seeming pompous or officious. The unwritten rules prescribe slightly self-mocking tones when using official meeting-speak terms such as 'agenda', 'minutes', 'procedures' and 'chairman', to show one is not taking the thing too seriously, and eye-rolling at the long-winded speeches of the inevitable club bore who does take it all too seriously.

This self-important bore quite often ends up being 'the chair', and uses this title at every possible opportunity, in endless bossy round-robin emails explaining at great length exactly why it really is vital for 'all communications to be sent to myself as Chair, in accordance with Article 13 of the Association Rules . . .' This might seem very odd – why would the English, with their horror of earnestness, elect such tediously earnest people to run so many of their clubs, societies, committees and associations? The answer is simple: these people are often the only ones who are eager to take on all the tiresome admin (which they insist on calling 'management') involved in organising meetings, agendas, rotas, minutes, guest speakers and so on – although they adopt a martyrish air about this, and regularly complain that no one appreciates all their hard work. The other members understand that regularly thanking and placating the chair is the price they pay for not having to do all the boring stuff them-selves. Although there is always one member, usually a newcomer or desultory and infrequent attendee, who fails to grasp this unwritten rule, laughs too openly at some pomposity or other, and causes huge huffy offence ('*You* may think that my responsibilities as chair are a big joke, but *if* you could ever be bothered to show up for meet-ings, you *might* realise that this association doesn't just run itself.'). But as these self-aggrandising chairs tend to be socially unpopular, this role is their chance to get attention and be at the centre of things, so at the next AGM, with much huffing and puffing about expecting 'maybe just a *bit* of help from other members this time', they agree to shoulder the onerous burden for yet another year.

Despite the efforts of some officious chairs, Englishness prevails during the actual 'agenda' part of club meetings as well as the preliminary socialising. There is some discussion of important matters, punctuated by jokes, bitching about enemies (or rival clubs with the same interests – MAG members bitch about the British Motorcycle Federation, for example), and polite territorial squabbling among members over largely irrelevant details. Occasionally, a decision or resolution is reached, or at least a consensus of opinion, with the actual decision deferred until the next meeting. Then more tea or alcohol, with more joking, gossiping and moaning – especially moaning: I defy you to find an English club or society whose members do not feel misunderstood or put-upon in some way. To go back to my surprisingly similar examples, the WI ladies moaned about being stereotyped as stuffy and old-fashioned ('People *still* think it's all jam and Jerusalem!'), while the bikers complained about public and media misperceptions of them as wild, irresponsible and scary ('We're hardly Hell's Angels – got two lawyers and a GP here tonight: practically the bloody Rotary!'). Then the meeting winds up with the usual prolonged English goodbyes. Sometimes there is a guest speaker, who must be fêted and fussed over and politely applauded, however dull and unenlightening their speech. But the basic pattern is always the same. If you've seen one meeting of an English club or society, you've seen them all. Even an Anarchist meeting I attended followed the same sequence, although it was much better organised than most, and at the demonstration the next day the members were all dressed in uniform black, carrying professional-looking banners, chanting in unison and marching in step.

Pub Rules

You've probably got the message by now that I think pubs are quite an important part of English culture. Of all the 'social facilitators' that help the inhibited English to engage and bond with each other, the pub is the most popular. There are around fifty thousand or so pubs in England, frequented by three-quarters of the adult population. Nearly a third of the adult population are 'regulars', visiting the pub at least once a week, in some cases treating their 'local' almost as a second home.

I talk about 'the pub' as though they were all the same, but nowadays there is a bewildering variety of different types: student pubs, youth pubs, theme pubs, family pubs, gastro-pubs, sports pubs – as well as a number of other kinds of drinking-places such as café-bars and wine bars. Much fuss has been made about these novelties, of course, much huffing and puffing, dire warnings and doom and gloom. Pubs aren't what they used to be. It's all trendy bars now, you can't find a proper traditional pub. The country's going to the dogs. The end of the world is nigh, or at least a lot nigher than it was.

The usual nostalgic moaning. The usual premature obituaries (I mean this quite literally: there was a book published about twenty years ago entitled *The Death of the English Pub*: I can't help wondering how the author feels now every time he passes a Rose and Crown or a Red Lion and sees people still happily drinking and playing darts). But a lot of this precipitate mourning is just typical English Eeyorishness, and the rest is the result of a syndrome similar to 'ethnographic dazzle': the doom-mongers are so dazzled by superficial differences between the new types of pub and the traditional sort that they cannot see the underlying, enduring similarities – the customs and codes of behaviour that make a pub a pub. Even if the Eeyores were right, the new pubs and bars they object to are still only a small minority, concentrated largely in city centres, and there are still tens of thousands of more traditional 'local' pubs.

It is true that a number of village pubs are struggling, and increasing numbers in smaller villages have had to close, which is very sad, as a village is not really a proper village without a pub. When this happens, there are often howls of protest in the local papers, and a morose group of villagers is photographed with a handmade 'Save Our Pub' placard. What *would* save their pub, of course, would be lots of them spending lots of money drinking and eating in it, but they never seem to make this connection. We have the same problem with the Death of the Village Shop: everyone wants to save their village shop; they just don't particularly want to shop there. The usual English hypocrisies.

But the English pub, as an institution, as a micro-society, is still alive and well. And still governed by a stable, enduring set of unspoken rules. I have already described most of these in Pub-talk (page 129) – the pub is an institution devoted to sociability, which even among the English involves communication, so it is not surprising that most of its rules are concerned with language and body language. Some more pub rules were covered in the section on Games Etiquette (page 356) but that still leaves a few quite significant ones, such as the rules governing the consumption of alcohol. I don't mean the official licensing laws, but the much more important unwritten codes of social drinking.

Drinking Rules

You can learn a lot about a culture by studying its drinking rules. And every culture has rules about alcohol: there is no such thing as random drinking. In every culture where alcohol is used, drinking is a rule-governed activity, hedged about with prescriptions and norms concerning who may drink how much of what, when, where, with whom, in what manner and with what effects. This is only to be expected. I have already pointed out that one of the distinguishing characteristics of *Homo sapiens* is our passion for regulation – our tendency to surround even the most basic, essential activities such as eating and mating with a lot of elaborate rules and rituals. But even more than with sex and food, the specific unwritten rules and norms governing the use of alcohol in different cultures invariably reflect the characteristic values, beliefs and attitudes of those cultures. The anthropologist Dwight Heath put it much more eloquently when he wrote that 'just as drinking and its effects are imbedded in other aspects of culture, so are many other aspects of culture imbedded in the act of drinking'. So, if we want to understand Englishness, we need to look more closely at the Englishness of English drinking.

The Rules of Round-buying

Round-buying is the English form of a universal practice: the sharing or reciprocal exchange of drinks. The consumption of alcohol, in all cultures, is a quintessentially social activity, whose ritual practices and etiquettes are designed to promote friendly social interaction.

There is certainly nothing uniquely English about reciprocal drink-giving, or even the buying of rounds. What is distinctively English, and often baffling or even frightening for foreigners, is the immense, almost religious significance attached to this practice among English pubgoers. Obeying the rules of round-buying is not just good manners, it is a sacred obligation. Failing to buy your round is not just a breach of drinking etiquette: it is heresy.

When I talk to foreign visitors about this they find it all a bit extreme. Why, they ask, is round-buying so desperately important to English pubgoers? I tell them that round-buying is important to us because it prevents bloodshed. This often sounds even more extreme, at least to non-anthropologists, so I try to explain a bit further. Reciprocal gift-giving has always been the most effective means of preventing aggression between groups (families, clans, tribes, nations) and between individuals. Among English drinkers, more specifically English male drinkers, this peacekeeping system is essential. This is because the socially challenged English male has a tendency to become aggressive. Male pub-talk, as we have seen, is often highly argumentative, and there is a need for an antidote to these verbal fisticuffs, a means of ensuring that the argument is not taken seriously, and does not escalate into physical aggression. Buying your 'opponent' a drink is a kind of 'liquid handshake': it proves that you are still mates. A particularly shrewd (female) publican told me, 'If the men didn't buy each other drinks, they'd be at each other's throats. They can be shouting and swearing, but as long as they are still buying each other drinks, I know I won't have a fight on my hands.' I have personally witnessed many apparently heated slanging matches which were amicably concluded with 'And, anyway, it's your round!' or 'And I suppose it's my bloody round again an' all, right?' or 'Oh, put a sock in it and get the beers in, will you?'

As well as preventing carnage and mayhem, round-buying is also vitally important because it is an Englishman's substitute for the expression of emotion. The average English male is terrified of intimacy, but he is also human, and therefore has a need to bond with other humans, particularly with other males. This means finding some way of saying, 'I like you' to other males, without, of course, actually having to utter anything quite so soppy. Fortunately, such positive feelings can be expressed, without any loss of masculine dignity, by the reciprocal buying of rounds of drinks.

The importance we attach to round-buying is also yet another indicator of our obsession with fair play: round-buying, like queuing, is all about taking turns. But, like every aspect of English etiquette, the unwritten rules of round-buying are complicated, with all the usual sub-clauses and exceptions, and 'fairness' is a somewhat slippery concept – it is not just a simple matter of ensuring roughly equal expenditure on drinks. The rules of round-buying are as follows:

- In any group of two or more people, one person must buy a 'round' of drinks for the whole group. This is not an altruistic gesture: the expectation is that the other member or members of the group will each, in turn, buy a round of drinks. When each person has bought a round, the process begins again with the first person.

- Unless the group is drinking at the bar counter, the person who buys the round must also act as waiter. 'Buying your round' means not only paying for the drinks, but going to the bar, ordering the drinks and carrying them all back to the table. If there are a lot of drinks, another member of the group will usually offer to help, but this is not compulsory, and the round-buyer may have to make two or three trips. The effort involved is as important as the expenditure: it is part of the 'gift'. (Exceptions to this rule are often made for frail or elderly people, however, and chivalrous males will often perform this service for female round-buyers, or at least offer some assistance.)

- 'Fairness' in round-buying is not a matter of strict justice. One person may well end up buying two rounds during a 'session', while the other members of the group have only bought one round each. Over several 'sessions', rough equality is usually achieved, but it is extremely bad manners to appear overly concerned about this.

- In fact, any sign of miserliness, calculation or reluctance to participate wholeheartedly in the ritual is severely frowned upon. For an English male, saying that someone 'doesn't buy his round' is a dire insult. It is thus important to try always to be among the earliest to say 'It's my round' rather than waiting until the other members of the group have bought 'their' rounds and it is quite obviously your turn.

- Perhaps surprisingly, I found that on average 'initiating' round-buyers (those who regularly buy the first round) actually spend no more money in the long term than 'waiting' round-buyers (those who do not offer a round until later in the session). In fact, far from being out-of-pocket, 'initiators' often end up rather better off than those who wait, because their popularity and reputation for generosity means that others are inclined to be generous towards them.

- One should never wait until all one's companions' glasses are empty before offering to buy the next round. The correct time to say, 'It's my round' is when the majority of the glasses are about three-quarters empty. This rule is only partly about proving one's generosity, more a matter of ensuring that the flow of alcohol is continuous – that no one is ever left without a drink for even a few minutes.

- It is acceptable occasionally to refuse a drink during the round-buying process, as long as you do not attempt to make an issue or a moral virtue out of your moderate intake, but this does not exempt you from the round-buying obligation. Even if you are drinking less than the others, you should still 'buy your round'. It would be very rude, however, to refuse a drink that is offered as a 'peace-making' gesture, or that is clearly a significant, personal friendship-signal.

There is usually no excuse for failing to perform the sacred round-buying ritual, but there are a few exceptions to the round-buying rules, relating to the size of the drinking group and the demographics of its members.

THE NUMBERS EXCEPTION—In a very large group, traditional round-buying can sometimes be prohibitively expensive. This is not, however, usually seen as a valid reason to abandon the ritual altogether. Instead, the large group divides into smaller sub-groups (nobody suggests or organises this, it just happens), each of which follows the normal round-buying procedure. Alternatively, the principle of gift-giving is maintained by having a 'whip-round' – collecting a relatively small sum of money from each person to put into a 'kitty', which is then used to buy rounds of drinks for the whole group, with the members of the group taking turns to perform the 'waiter' service. Only as a last resort, perhaps among students or others on very low incomes, will members of a large group agree to purchase drinks individually.

THE COUPLE EXCEPTION—In some social groups, couples are treated as one person for the purposes of round-buying, in that only the male half of the couple is expected to 'buy his round'. In a slightly different variation, where the group consists of both couples and singles, a couple will be treated as two people, but the male partner will buy the female's rounds for her. These 'couple exceptions' are somewhat less common among younger people, so you are more likely to see these practices when the males in the group are over forty. Some older English males cannot cope with the idea of women buying them drinks at all, and extend the couple exception to cover all females in a group, whether or not they are accompanied by an attached male. When out alone with a female, these older, old-fashioned males will also insist on buying all the drinks, whereas younger males are more likely to expect a female companion to take turns buying rounds in the usual manner, or at least to offer to buy a round.

THE FEMALE EXCEPTION—Women generally have considerably less reverence for the round-buying rules than men. In mixed-sex groups, they play along, humouring their male companions by following the prescribed etiquette, but in all-female gatherings you see all sorts of odd variations and even outright flouting of the rules. They do buy each other drinks, but round-buying is just not such a big issue for them – they don't keep track of whose round it is, or have endless friendly disputes about who has or hasn't bought their round, and they tend to find the male obsession with round-buying somewhat tedious and irritating.

This is mainly because English females have much less need for the 'liquid handshake' of reciprocal drink-buying than English males: the argument is not their primary form of communication, so there is no need for peacekeeping gestures, and they are quite capable of conveying that they like each other and achieving intimacy by other means, such as compliments, gossip and reciprocal disclosure. English women may not be as free-and-easy with their disclosures as women from other, less inhibited, cultures: they do not tend to tell you all about their messy divorce and what their therapist said within five minutes of meeting you. But once English females become friends, such discussions are commonplace, whereas many English males never get to this stage, even with their best and closest friends.

   Even the word 'friend' is a bit difficult, a bit too touchy-feely, for some English males: they prefer to use the term 'mate'. You can be 'mates' with someone without necessarily knowing anything at all about his personal life, let alone his feelings, hopes or fears – except where these concern the performance of his football team or his car. The terms 'mate', 'good mate' and 'best mate' are ostensibly used to convey varying degrees of intimacy, but even your 'best mate' may know little or nothing about your marital problems – or only as much as can be conveyed in a jokey-blokey, mock-moaning manner, to which he can respond, 'Women! Huh! Typical!' You would, of course, risk your life for him, and he for you. Your 'best mate' may have a better idea of your golf handicap than the names of your children, but you actually care deeply about each other. Still, that goes without saying, right, so there's no need to cause unnecessary embarrassment by saying it. And anyway, it's your round, mate.

You Are What You Drink

Another 'human universal' is important here: in all cultures where more than one type of alcoholic drink is available, drinks are classified in terms of their social meaning, and these classifications help to define the social world. No alcoholic drink is ever 'socially neutral'. In England, as elsewhere, 'What's yours?' is a socially loaded question, and we judge and classify people on their answer. Choice of beverage is rarely just a matter of personal taste.

Among other symbolic functions, drinks can be used as indicators of social status, and as gender differentiators. These are the two most important symbolic functions of alcoholic beverages among the English: your choice of drink (in public at least) is determined mainly by your sex and social class, with some age-related variations. The rules are as follows:

- Working-class and lower-middle-class females have the widest choice of drinks. Almost anything is socially acceptable – cocktails, sweet or creamy liqueurs, all soft drinks, beers, spirits and alcopops (pre-mixed alcoholic drinks in bottles, usually vodka- or rum-based, such as WKD, Smirnoff Ice and Bacardi Breezer, which are very popular with young drinkers). There is really only one restriction: the size of glass from which some lower-class women may drink beer. Drinking 'pints', in some working-class and lower-middle circles, is regarded as unfeminine and unladylike, so some women in these social groups, if they drink beer at all, will drink 'halves' (half-pints) of beer. Drinking pint glasses of beer would classify you as a 'ladette' – a female 'lad', a woman who imitates the loutish, raucous behaviour of hard-drinking males. Some women are happy with this image, but they are still a minority.
- Next on the freedom-of-choice scale are middle-middle to upper-class females. Their choice is more restricted: the more sickly-sweet alcopops, cream-based liqueurs and cocktails are regarded as a bit vulgar – ordering a Bailey's would certainly cause a few raised eyebrows and sideways looks – but they

can drink more or less any wines, spirits, sherries, soft drinks, ciders or beers. Female pint-drinking is also more acceptable in this social category, at least among the younger women, particularly students. Among upper-middle-class female students, I found that some felt they had to give an explanation if they ordered a 'girly' half rather than a pint of beer.

- The choices of middle- and upper-class males are far more restricted than those of their female counterparts. They may drink only beer, spirits (mixers are acceptable), wine (must be dry, not sweet) and soft drinks. Alcopops are permitted for the young, but anything too sweet or creamy is regarded as suspiciously 'feminine', and cocktails are only acceptable at cocktail parties or in a cocktail bar – you would never order them in an ordinary pub.

- Working-class males have virtually no choice at all. They can drink only beer or spirits – everything else is effeminate. At least, this is the unwritten rule among older working-class males, for whom even some mixers may be forbidden: gin-and-tonic may be just about acceptable in some circles, but more obscure combinations are frowned upon. Younger working-class males have quite a bit more freedom: spirits with mixers are acceptable, for example, as are alcopops, providing they have a high enough alcohol content and a suitably macho name and image.

RULES OF DRUNKENNESS – ANTI-SOCIAL PASTIMES

Another 'universal': the effects of alcohol on behaviour are determined by social and cultural rules and norms, not by the chemical actions of ethanol. There is enormous cross-cultural variation in the way people behave when they drink alcohol. In some societies (such as the UK, the US, Australia and parts of Scandinavia – about one-fifth of all cultures worldwide), drinking is associated with aggression, violence and anti-social behaviour, while in others (such as Latin/Mediterranean cultures in particular, but in fact the vast majority of all cultures) drinking is not associated with these undesireable behaviours. This variation cannot be attributed to different levels of consumption or genetic differences, but is clearly related to different cultural beliefs about alcohol, different expectations regarding the effects of alcohol and different social norms regarding drunken comportment.

This basic fact has been proved time and again, not just in qualitative cross-cultural research but also in carefully controlled proper scientific experiments – double-blind, placebos and all. To put it simply, the experiments show that when people think they are drinking alcohol, they behave according to their cultural beliefs about the behavioural effects of alcohol. The English believe that alcohol is a disinhibitor, and specifically that it makes people amorous or aggressive, so when they are given what they think are alcoholic drinks – but are in fact non-alcoholic 'placebos' – they shed their inhibitions: they become more flirtatious, and some (young males in particular) may become aggressive.

Which brings me to the third method the English use to deal with their chronic, incurable social dis-ease: the 'become loud and aggressive and obnoxious' method. I am certainly not the first to have noticed this dark and unpleasant side to the English character. Both English observers and foreign visitors have been commenting on it for centuries, and our habit of national self-flagellation ensures that not a week goes by without some mention of it in our own newspapers. Binge drinkers, football hooligans, rowdy ladettes, neighbours-from-hell, drunken brawling, delinquency, disorder and downright impudence. These infelicities are invariably attributed either to a vague, idiopathic 'decline in moral standards' or to the effects of alcohol, or both. Neither of these explanations will do. Even the most cursory scan of English social history confirms that our current bouts of obnoxious drunken disorder are nothing new.[102]

102. There are plenty of well-worn examples, but a reader sent me a more obscure book, *The Little Londoner*, published in 1901, in which the German author R. Kron observes that 'London pubs are crowded with drunken men and women' and 'In no city in the world is drunkenness amongst the lower classes so obtrusive as in the British Metropolis'.

And even leaving aside the placebo experiments, it is clear that many other nations manage to consume much larger quantities of alcohol than us without becoming rude, violent and generally disgusting.

Our *beliefs* about the behavioural effects of alcohol are certainly at least partly to blame, as they act as self-fulfilling prophecies. If you firmly believe and expect that alcohol will make you aggressive, then it will do exactly that. But this still leaves the question of why we should hold such strange beliefs. The notion that alcohol is a dangerous disinhibitor is not peculiar to the English: it is shared by a number of other cultures, known to the anthropologists and other social scientists who take an interest in such matters as 'ambivalent', 'dry', 'Nordic' or 'temperance' cultures – cultures with an ambivalent, morally charged, love/hate, forbidden-fruit relationship with alcohol, usually associated with a history of temperance movements. These are contrasted with 'integrated', 'wet', 'Mediterranean' or 'non-temperance' cultures – those for whom alcohol is simply a normal, integral, taken-for-granted, morally neutral part of everyday life; generally cultures that have been fortunate enough to escape the attentions of temperance campaigners. 'Integrated' drinking-cultures, despite usually having much higher levels of *per-capita* alcohol consumption, experience few of the 'alcohol-related' social problems that afflict 'ambivalent' cultures.

These basic facts are, among my fellow cross-cultural researchers and other dispassionate 'alcohologists', so obvious and commonplace as to be tedious. We are certainly all very weary of repeating them, endlessly, to English audiences who either cannot or will not accept their validity. Much of my professional life has been spent on alcohol-related research of one sort or another, and my colleagues and I have been trotting out the same irrefutable cross-cultural and experimental evidence for over twenty years, every time our expertise is called upon by government departments, police conferences, worried brewers and other concerned agencies.

Everyone is always highly surprised – 'Really? You mean there are cultures where people don't believe that alcohol causes violence? How extraordinary!' – and politely determined to let nothing shake their faith in the evil powers of the demon drink. It's like trying to explain the causes of rain to some remote mud-hut tribe in thrall to the magic of witch-doctors and rain-makers. Yes, yes, they say, but of course the *real* reason it hasn't rained is because the ancestors are angry that the shaman did not perform the rain-dance or goat-sacrifice at the correct time and someone allowed uncircumcised boys or menstruating women to touch the sacred skulls. Everyone knows that. Just like everyone knows that drinking alcohol makes people lose their inhibitions and start bashing each other's heads in.

Or, rather, according to the concerned believers at the conferences on 'Alcohol and Public Disorder', alcohol makes *other people* do this. They themselves are somehow immune: they can get quite squiffy at the office Christmas party, or over a few bottles of good cabernet sauvignon with their friends, or gin-and-tonic in the pub or whatever, without ever throwing a single punch, or even using bad language. Alcohol, it seems, has the specific power to make *working-class* people violent and abusive. Which, if you think about it, is truly miraculous – a much more impressive magical feat than rain-making. We hold these strange beliefs about the powers of alcohol because, like other irrational religious tenets, they help us to explain the inexplicable – and, in this case, to avoid the issue. By blaming the booze, we sidestep the uncomfortable question of why the English, so widely admired for our courtesy, reserve and restraint, should also be renowned for our oafishness, crudeness and violence.

My view is that our courteous reserve and our obnoxious aggression are two sides of the same coin. More precisely, they are both symptoms of the same social dis-ease. We suffer from a chronic sociability-disorder, a set of deeply ingrained inhibitions that make it difficult for us to express emotion and engage in the kind of casual, friendly social interaction that seems to come naturally to most other nations. How we have come to be like this, why we are afflicted with this dis-ease, is a bit of mystery, which I may or may not be able to solve by the end of this book, but it is possible to diagnose an illness or disorder without necessarily knowing its cause. With psychological disorders such as this one, whether at the individual or national level, the cause is often difficult or even impossible to determine, but that does not prevent us pronouncing the patient to be autistic, or agora-phobic, or whatever. Those were supposed to be random examples, but now that I come to think of it, the English social dis-ease has some symptoms in common with both autism and agoraphobia. But let's be charitable and politically correct and just say that we are 'socially challenged'.

Whatever we choose to call it, the symptoms of the English social dis-ease involve opposite extremes: when we feel uncomfortable or embarrassed in social situations (that is, most of the time), we become either over-polite, buttoned-up and awkwardly restrained, or loud, loutish, aggressive, violent and generally insufferable. There seem to be no in-between states, and certainly no happy medium. Both extremes are regularly exhibited by English people of all social classes, with or without the assistance of the demon drink.

The worst of the 'loud and obnoxious' extreme tends, however, to be largely confined to specific, well-defined periods of 'cultural remission', such as town centres on Friday and Saturday nights, and holidays at home and abroad, when it is customary for hordes of young people to congregate in pubs, bars and night-clubs and get drunk. Getting drunk is not an accidental by-product of the evening's entertainment: it is the primary objective – young English revellers and holidaymakers (male and female) set out quite deliberately to achieve this goal, and they are almost invariably successful (we're English, remember, we can get roaring drunk on non-alcoholic placebos). To prove to their companions that they have attained the socially desirable degree of drunkenness, they generally feel obliged to do something 'mad' – to put on some sort of display of outra-geously disinhibited behaviour. The repertoire of approved displays is actually quite limited, and not terribly outrageous, ranging from relatively tame shouting and swearing to rather more ambitiously offensive antics such as 'mooning' (pulling down one's trousers to show one's naked bottom – bottoms being regarded as intrinsically funny among young English males) and, much more rarely, fighting.

For a *very small minority*, a Saturday night's revelry is just not complete without a bit of a punch-up. These are generally rule-governed, predictable, almost choreographed affairs, consisting mainly of a lot of macho posturing and bravado, very occasionally escalating to a drunken, clumsy exchange of blows. Such incidents are often sparked off by nothing more than a fraction of a second too much eye contact. It can be remarkably easy to start a fight with the average young, inebriated English male: all you have to do is make eye contact, hold it a little too long (anything over about a second will do – the English are not keen on eye contact), then say, 'What you lookin' at?' The response may well be a repetition of the question, 'What *you* lookin' at?' – very like the traditional English 'How do you do?' exchange: our obnoxiousnesses are about as awkward, irrational and inelegant as our politenesses. But just as the polite 'How do you do?' ritual very rarely leads to more intimate conversation, the belligerent 'What you lookin' at?' exchange is merely a ritual display of manliness, only occasionally resulting in an actual physical fight.

This aggressive behaviour is much less evident, it must be said, among those young people who use illegal 'recreational drugs' such as cannabis and ecstasy as their social facilitators, rather than alcohol. We believe that cannabis makes you mellow and pleasantly relaxed ('chilled out', 'chilled' or 'chillaxed', in current parlance) and that ecstasy makes you lively, euphoric, full of goodwill towards fellow revellers, and a brilliant dancer. Apart from the quality of the dancing, these beliefs are largely self-fulfilling prophecies, and a good time is had by all.

PLAY RULES AND ENGLISHNESS

The rules of play have provided further confirmation of all the main 'quintessences of Englishness' identified so far – all the usual suspects: humour, hypocrisy, class-anxiety, fair play, modesty and so on. Empiricism now also seems to be emerging as a strong candidate for inclusion in the English cultural genome. But most of the rules in this chapter have been about one particular defining characteristic of Englishness – the one I have taken to calling our 'social dis-ease', our inhibited insularity, our chronic social awkwardness, bordering on a sort of sub-clinical combination of autism and agoraphobia.

Almost all of our leisure activities are, one way or another, a response to this unfortunate condition. And almost all of our responses are forms of denial and self-delusion. In fact, our phenomenal capacity for collective self-deception is beginning to look like a defining characteristic in its own right.

The collective self-deception involved in the English use of sports, games and clubs as social facilitators is particularly interesting – the fact that we have to trick ourselves into social interaction and bonding by pretending that we are doing something else. Our belief in the magical disinhibiting powers of alcohol is part of the same delusional syndrome. We have a desperate need for social contact and emotional bonding, but we cannot simply acknowledge this need, and get on with the pursuit of human warmth and intimacy in a natural, straightforward fashion. We have to create elaborate structures and myths and rituals to disguise our craving for social contact as a burning desire to throw balls at each other, or to perfect our flower-arranging or motorcycle-maintenance skills, or to save the whales, or the world, or something – and then go to the pub, where we can pretend that we are only there for the beer, and attribute any embarrassing evidence of normal human emotion to its miraculous properties.

Really, I don't see why anthropologists feel they have to travel to remote corners of the world and get dysentery and malaria in order to study strange tribal cultures with bizarre beliefs and mysterious customs when the weirdest, most puzzling tribe of all is right here on our doorstep.

DRESS CODES

Before we can even begin to examine the rules of English dress, we need to be clear about a few cross-cultural universals. Apart from the obvious need for warmth in cold climates, and for protection from the elements, dress, in all cultures, is essentially about three things: sex differentiation, status signals and affiliation signals. Sex differentiation is usually the most obvious: even if a society shows very little variation in dress or personal adornment, there will always be at least some minor differences between male and female attire – differences that are often emphasised to make each sex more attractive to the other. By 'status' I mean social status or position in the broadest sense, and I am including age-differentiation in this category. Affiliation, to a tribe, clan, subculture, social or 'lifestyle' group, covers pretty much everything else.

I'm sorry if this offends some fashion editors of glossy magazines, or their readers, who believe that dress is all about individual 'self-expression' or some such guff. What modern, Western, post-industrial cultures like to see as 'style' or 'self-expression' – or fashion itself, for that matter – is really just a glorified combination of sex-differentiation, status signals and affiliation signals. I have probably also offended those in these societies who insist that they have no interest in fashion, that their clothes do not make any social statements and that they dress purely for comfort, economy and practicality. Some people may indeed have no conscious interest in fashion, but even they cannot help choosing one cheap, comfortable and practical garment over another, so they are making sartorial social statements whether they like it or not. (And, besides, claiming to be above such trivialities as dress is in itself a socially significant proclamation, usually a rather loud one.)

The English have no 'national costume' – an omission noted and lamented by all those wringing their hands over our national identity crisis. Some such commentators then go about trying to understand English dress in what seems to me a most peculiar and irrational manner, in that they attempt to discover what English dress says about the English by scrutinising specific, stereotyped, 'stage-English' items of clothing, as though the secret of Englishness might somehow be hidden in the colour, the cut, the seams or the hems. Clive Aslet, for example, tells us that 'The quintessential English garment must be the slurry-coloured waxed Barbour jacket.' It is perhaps not surprising that the former editor of *Country Life* should choose this particular stereotype, but the fixation with clichés of English dress seems to be universal. Aslet then bemoans the decline in popularity of Harris tweed, which he claims reflects a decline in traditional 'country' values. When in doubt, he blames the weather: 'The British generally have lacked style in summer clothes, largely because traditionally we have never had much of a summer.' Harry Mount, in *How England Made the English*, also attributes our lamentable lack of taste in summer clothing to the English climate. At the first ray of unaccustomed summer sunshine, he observes, 'the English think "God it's hot. Let's wear something special/ludicrous to celebrate, something that exposes as much skin as possible."' This typically English weather-moaning is amusing, but not terribly helpful as an explanation, as there are plenty of other countries with unimpressive summers where people still manage to dress much more stylishly than we do. And we do not exactly become paragons of stylish elegance during the autumn and winter either, despite long familiarity with cold, damp and grey skies. Finally, Aslet complains that we have become too informal, that 'outside the military, the county set, the royal family and certain ceremonial occasions' we no longer have any codes telling us how to dress.

Others seem to give up the attempt to understand English dress before they've even started. Jeremy Paxman includes punk and street-fashion in his initial list of 'Englishnesses', but then avoids the dress issue, apart from the brief assertion that 'There is no longer even any consensus on questions like dress, let alone any prescriptive rules.' This notion that 'there are no longer any rules' is a typically English nostalgic complaint, and, on the part of those trying to explain Englishness, a bit of a typically English cop-out. But these plaintive comments are at least based on a very sound principle: that national identity is about rules, and lack of rules is symptomatic of loss of identity. The diagnostic criteria are correct, but both Aslet and Paxman have misidentified the symptom. There *are* still rules and codes of English dress, although they are not as formal or as clear-cut as they were fifty years ago. Some of the current unofficial, unwritten rules are even highly prescriptive. The most important rule, however, is a descriptive one – it could even be called a 'meta-rule', a rule about rules.

THE RULES RULE

The English have an uneasy, difficult and largely dysfunctional relationship with clothes, characterised primarily by a desperate need for rules, and a woeful inability to cope without them. This meta-rule helps to explain why the English have an international reputation for dressing in general very badly, but with specific areas (pockets, you might say) of excellence, such as high-class gentlemen's tailoring, sporting and 'country' clothes, ceremonial costume and innovative street-fashion. In other words, we English are at our sartorial best when we have strict, formal rules and traditions to follow – when we are either literally or effectively 'in uniform'. Left to our own devices, we flounder and fail, having little or no natural sense of style or elegance – suffering from, as George Orwell put it, an 'almost general deadness to aesthetic issues'.

Our need for rules has been highlighted in recent years by the 'Dress-down Friday' or 'Casual Friday' custom imported from America, whereby companies allow their employees to wear their own choice of casual clothes to the office on Fridays, rather than the usual formal business suits. A number of English companies adopted this custom, but quite a few have been obliged to abandon it, as many of their more junior staff started turning up in ludicrously inappropriate clothes – tasteless outfits more suited to the beach or a night-club than to any normal office. Others just looked unacceptably scruffy. Clients were put off, colleagues were embarrassed, and in any case most of the senior management simply ignored the Casual Friday rule, choosing, perhaps wisely, to maintain their dignity by sticking to the normal business-suit uniform. This served only to emphasise hierarchical divisions within the business – quite the opposite of the chummy, democratising effect intended by the Casual Friday policy. In short, the experiment was not a great success.

Other nations may have their flaws and foibles in matters of dress, but only among our colonial 'descendants', the Americans and Australians, is this deplorable absence of taste as marked or as widespread as it is in England. Ironically, given our supposed obsession with our weather and our pride in its changeable nature, even these sartorially undistinguished nations are rather better than us at dressing appropriately for different climatic conditions. We may spend inordinate amounts of time discussing weather forecasts, but we somehow never seem to be wearing the right clothes: for example, I have spent many rainy afternoons on the streets counting umbrellas, and calculated that only about 25 per cent of the population (mainly middle-aged or older) actually manage to arm themselves with this supposedly quintessentially English item, even when heavy rain has been forecast for days. These perverse habits give us a good excuse to moan and grumble about being too hot, cold or wet – and, incidentally, would seem to bear out my contention that our constant weather-speak is a social facilitator rather than evidence of a genuine obsession.

THE ECCENTRIC-SHEEP RULE

Sharp-eyed readers will have noticed that I seem to be including 'innovative street-fashion' in the category of 'uniform' – and you might perhaps be questioning my judgement. Surely this is a contradiction? Surely the quirky, outlandish, subculture street-fashions – cockatoo-haired punks, Victorian-vampire Goths, scary-booted skinheads – for which the English are renowned are evidence of our eccentricity and originality, not conformist, conservative rule-following? The idea that English street-fashion is characterised by eccentricity and imaginative creativity has become a universally accepted 'fact' among fashion writers – not only in popular magazines but also in academic, scholarly works on English dress.[103] Even the normally cynical Jeremy Paxman fails to question this stereotype, reiterating the widely accepted view that English street-fashions 'all express a basic belief in the liberty of the individual'. But what most people think of as English eccentricity in dress is really the opposite: it is tribalism, a form of conformity, a uniform. Punks, Goths and so on may look outlandish, but this is everyone – or, rather, a well-defined group – all being outlandish *in exactly the same way*. There is nothing idiosyncratic or eccentric about English street-fashions: they are just subcultural affiliation signals.

Design houses such as Vivienne Westwood and Alexander McQueen pick up on these street-fashion trends and interpret and glamorise them on the international catwalks, and everyone says, 'Ooh, how eccentric, how English,' but really there is nothing terribly eccentric about a diluted copy of a uniform. Street-fashions do not even function for very long as effective subcultural affiliation signals, as these styles invariably and rapidly become 'mainstream': no sooner do youth subcultures invent some daft new tribal costume than the avant-garde designers pick it up, then a somewhat more muted interpretation appears in the high-street shops and everyone is wearing a version of it, including one's mother. This is infuriating for the young originators of these street-styles. English youth tribes spend a lot of time and energy trying to avoid being 'mainstream' – a dirty word, used as an insult – but this does not make them eccentric, anarchic individualists: they are still conformist sheep, all disguised in the same wolf's clothing.

The most truly eccentric dresser in this country is the Queen, who pays no attention whatsoever to fashion, mainstream or otherwise, continuing to wear the same highly idiosyncratic style of clothing (a kind of modified 1950s-retro look, if you had to define it in

103. Such as, for example, Alison Goodrum's *The National Fabric* and Christopher Breward's edited volume, *The Englishness of English Dress*.

fashion-speak, but very much her own personal taste) with no regard for anyone else's opinion. Because she is the Queen, people call her style 'classic' and 'timeless' rather than eccentric or weird, politely overlooking the fact that absolutely no one else dresses in this peculiar way. Never mind the herds of street-sheep and their *haute-couture* imitators: the Queen is the best example of English sartorial eccentricity.

Having said that, young English subcultural sheep do invent clothing styles that are significantly more wacky and outrageous than any other nations' street-fashions – indeed, the rebellious youth of many other nations tend to imitate English street-fashions rather than going to the trouble of inventing their own. We may not be individually eccentric, apart from the Queen, but our youth subculture groups do have a sort of collective eccentricity, if that is not a contradiction in terms. At any rate, we *appreciate* originality, and we take pride in our reputation for eccentricity, however undeserved it may be.

THE AFFECTED-INDIFFERENCE RULE

This is partly because of another set of unwritten rules about dress, which derive in part from the humour rules that are so deeply ingrained in the English psyche. In particular, our attitude to dress is governed by the omnipresent Importance of Not Being Earnest rule. Dress, like pretty much everything else, is not to be taken too seriously. It is not done to be too intensely interested in one's clothes – or, rather, one should not be *seen* to be overly concerned about being fashionable or well dressed. We admire eccentricity, because genuine eccentricity means not caring a hoot about the opinion of others. This state of perfect indifference may never in fact be achieved, except perhaps among the clinically insane and some elderly aristocrats, but it is an ideal to which we all aspire. We make do with the next best thing: affected indifference – we *pretend* that we do not care very much about what we wear or how we look.

The affected-indifference rule applies most strictly to English males, among whom any expression of interest in fashion or appearance is regarded as effeminate. And it doesn't even have to be verbally expressed – any slight *evidence* of interest in dress, of taking a bit of care over one's appearance, can cast doubt on one's masculinity. Many English males almost feel obliged to dress badly, just to prove they are not homosexual.

Younger males are, in fact, secretly highly concerned about conforming to the current street-fashions, sporting the required tribal affiliation-signals, but only their mothers, from whom they beg the money to purchase these items, know how deeply important this is to them. Females are generally less restricted by the affected indifference rule, although outside 'fashionista' circles, obsessive interest in fashion is frowned upon. Teenage girls are the only real exception to the rule: they are allowed to express their passionate interest in clothes and concerns about their appearance – at least among themselves: in the company of males, all English females tend to play down these anxieties, and avoid mentioning the hours they spend poring over fashion magazines and eagerly debating the merits of the latest trends.

EMBARRASSMENT RULES

I had a hunch that the rest of the English, even the males, share these concerns, and that observing the affected-indifference rule helps us to hide a deep-seated insecurity about dress, a desperate need to 'fit in' and an acute fear of embarrassment. My most perceptive informant on matters of dress was the fashion 'agony-aunt' Annalisa Barbieri, whose 'Dear Annie' column in the *Independent on Sunday* attracted hundreds of anxious letters every week from the sartorially challenged English. She had interviewed me a few times for features she was writing on a variety of subjects, and when I found out that she was 'Dear Annie', I jumped at the chance to interrogate an expert on the real, usually hidden, dress concerns and problems of the English – particularly as her international background meant that she could compare these with other cultures' preoccupations.

She confirmed that the English are much more worried about our clothes and appearance than the affected-indifference rule allows us to admit. And her postbag indicates that our main concern is indeed about 'fitting in', being acceptably dressed and, above all, that perennial English preoccupation, avoiding embarrassment. Yes, we want to look attractive, to make the most of our physical assets and disguise our flaws, but we do not, like other nations, want to stand out or show off – quite the opposite: most of us are scared of any form of ostentation, or even of seeming to make too much effort, to care too obviously. We just want to fit in. The overwhelming majority of the questions addressed to Dear Annie are not about whether a certain garment or outfit is beautiful or glamorous, but whether it is socially acceptable, suitable, appropriate. 'It's all "Is it OK to wear X with Y?"; "Can I wear such-and-such to a wedding?"; "Is this suitable for the office?"; "Is that too tarty?"' Annalisa told me. 'Up to the 1950s, there were lots of official rules about dress – there were uniforms, really – and the English dressed well. Since the 1960s, there have been fewer formal rules, and lots of confusion and embarrassment, and the English dress very badly, but there is still an obsession with etiquette. What they really want is more rules.'

It is worth noting in this context that the outlandish youth subculture styles for which we are renowned are worn only by a very small minority. The vast majority of English youth are not even collectively eccentric. After school each day, when they change out of their 'oppressive' school uniforms and are free to 'express themselves' in clothing of their own choice, they still all look virtually identical. At one girls' boarding school I visited, for example, all the girls came to the cafeteria in the evening wearing exactly the same loose shirts or sweatshirts in the same muted colours, the same skinny jeans or matte leggings, and the same flat pumps. They all carried the exact same type of flower-patterned shoulder-bag, and all wore their hair roughly the same length, and either loose or tied back in the same casual, messy ponytail. The homogeneity was so striking that I asked the teachers if there were any rules about what the girls could wear when not in school uniform. No, they replied, there are no rules at all – they can wear whatever they choose. 'So they choose another strict uniform,' I laughed. The teachers seemed slightly surprised at my comment, but then looked around at all their identically clad pupils and laughed along with me. Of course, this 'unofficial uniform' varies from school to school – but every school has its unwritten dress code, which almost all pupils slavishly obey.

Ironically, this desperate desire to fit in and conform can often, particularly among the most fashion-conscious, lead to the most dramatic and ludicrous of our sartorial mistakes. Edina, the ridiculously overdressed character in the television sit-com *Absolutely Fabulous*, is a caricature of a certain type of English fashion-victim. She combines a burning need to be fashionable with a typically English lack of any natural taste or sense of style – decking herself out indiscriminately in all of the most outrageous of the latest designer catwalk creations, and invariably ending up looking like an over-decorated Christmas tree. Edina is a caricature, a deliberate comic exaggeration, but the caricature is based on features and behaviours that are all too familiar and recognisable among English females. There are plenty of Edinas among our pop-stars and other celebrities, and you can see down-market, chain-store versions of Edina-like bad taste walking around on every high street.

Women of most other nations can watch *Absolutely Fabulous* and just laugh at Edina's absurd outfits. English women may laugh at Edina, but we also wince with vicarious embarrassment, and our amusement is tinged with a little frisson of fear, a little anxiety about our own fashion-victim errors of judgement. Edina's mistakes may be more extreme than most, but English women do seem to be particularly susceptible to the more preposterous products of designers' fevered imaginations: almost every English female had a ludicrous puffball skirt in her wardrobe in the 1980s; we wear microminis every time they come into fashion, whether we have the legs for them or not; ditto thigh-boots, leg-warmers, hot pants, bra-tops and other inventions that are unflattering on all but the skinniest, and often look remarkably silly even on them.

At night, English town-centre bars and night-clubs are full of herds of young women wearing very little clothing at all, and certainly leaving little or nothing to the imagination. You could be forgiven for thinking that the women displaying their legs, bellies and bosoms in these tight, shiny micro-garments are trying very hard to 'stand out' and be noticeable – until you notice that they are *all* 'standing out' in exactly the same hooker-like manner, that they are all trying very hard to conform and blend in, that this is in fact yet another uniform. To wear a less embarrassingly revealing outfit would be drawing attention to oneself, and therefore deeply embarrassing.

Of course, we are not alone in conforming to the fashion norms of our social group – I stated at the beginning of this chapter that affiliation signals are one of the primary functions of dress in all cultures. It's just that most other cultures manage to signal their tribal affiliations in a more aesthetically pleasing manner. We are not entirely alone in our aesthetic inadequacies – our American and Australian cousins can be equally tasteless – but my female friends, acquaintances and informants from around the world tend to be particularly scornful about English women's sartorial awkwardness and incompetence. On one occasion, when I protested that singling us out in this way was a bit unfair, a rather grand French lady replied, 'It is perfectly fair. One does not expect much from the colonies, but you English are supposed to be civilised Europeans. You really should know better. Paris is, what, an hour away?' She lifted an immaculate eyebrow, shrugged her elegant shoulders and sniffed delicately, meaning, presumably, that if we could not be bothered to learn from our neighbours and betters, we were beneath her notice. I wouldn't have minded so much, but this impromptu interview took place at Royal Ascot, in the Royal bloody Enclosure, no less, with all of us Englishwomen (even undercover social scientists) in our very smartest frocks and hats. And I'd been especially proud of my pink mini-dress and pink shoes with amusing snaffle-shaped buckles on them – a little horsey reference (footnote, even) that had struck me as charmingly witty for a day at the races, but now, under the withering gaze of Madame Style-Police, seemed rather silly and childish, a typically English attempt to make a joke out of everything.

Dress is essentially a form of communication – one could even call it a social skill – so perhaps it should not be surprising to find that the socially challenged English are not terribly good at it. We have difficulties with most other aspects of communication, particularly when there are no clear, formal rules to follow. Perhaps the loss of our old 1950s rigid dress codes has had the same effect as the decline of 'How do you do?' as the standard greeting. In the absence of the formal 'How do you do?' exchange, we never know quite what to say, and our attempts at informal greetings are awkward, clumsy, inelegant and embarrassing. In the same way, the decline of formal dress codes – now regarded by many, like the 'How do you do?' ritual, as stuffy and old-fashioned – means that we never know quite what to wear, and our informal dress has become as embarrassingly awkward as our greetings.

We do not like formality; we object to being dictated to by prissy little rules and regulations – but we lack the natural grace and social ease to cope with informality. We are like rebellious teenagers whose parents complain, with some justification, that they want to be treated like adults and given the freedom to make their own choices and decisions, but do not have the sense or maturity to handle such freedom, and when granted it just make a big mess of things and get into trouble.

MAINSTREAM RULES AND TRIBAL UNIFORMS

Our solution is to invent more rules. The rigid dress codes of the past have *not* given way to complete sartorial anarchy. Although fashion magazines regularly proclaim that 'Nowadays, anything goes', this is clearly not the case. What is now known as 'mainstream' dress certainly does not conform to the same kind of official, universal dress codes as in the pre-1960 eras – when, for example, all women were supposed to wear hats, gloves, skirts of a particular length and so on, with only relatively minor, and well-defined, class and subcultural variations. But there are broad-brush rules and fashion trends that most of us still obey: show a crowd-scene photograph from the 1960s, 1970s, 1980s, 1990s, 2000s, etc., and anyone can immediately identify, just from the clothing and hairstyles, the period in which it was taken. The same will no doubt be true of the current period, although as usual we imagine that this one is more bewilderingly anarchic and fast-changing than any previous time. Even a photograph featuring 'retro' fashions, recycling the style of, say, the 1970s in the 1990s, or the 1960s and 1980s in the year 2003, or the 1950s and 1970s again in 2011, the 1960s again in 2013, and so on, would not fool us, as these styles are never simply repeated 'verbatim', but always piecemeal, with many subtle changes, and different hairstyles and make-up. Look at a few crowd-pictures, or just flip through some family photo albums, and you realise not only that dress is far more rule-governed than you might have thought but also that you are probably far more aware of the detail and nuances of current dress codes than you imagined – even if you think you have no interest in fashion. You are obeying these rules unconsciously, whether you like it or not, and will, when future people see you in a photograph, be identifiable as an example of your time.

Even if I showed you a photograph of a specific subcultural youth group, rather than a mainstream crowd, you would still, probably quite easily, identify the period in which that subculture was prominent. Which brings me to 'tribal' dress codes. English subcultures with different styles of dress from the mainstream majority are nothing new. In the mid-nineteenth century, the counter-culture Pre-Raphaelites influenced a style of 'artistic' dress – a sort of medieval-retro look, but with modern naturalistic touches – which in turn led to the droopy, 'aesthetic' subculture look of the late nineteenth century, and then the loose but more vivid 'Bohemian' styles of the early twentieth century. Teddy boys, students and arty types had their own distinctive styles in the 1950s; then there were the sharp mods and hard-looking rockers; then the softer, artistic-Bohemian look was reinvented by the hippies (not realising the whole thing had been done before) in the late 1960s and early 1970s; followed by the harsher punks, skinheads and Goths (this last still a fairly popular subculture genre) in the late 1970s and 1980s. Then in the 1990s we were back to the recurring droopy-Bohemian-natural theme again with grunge, indies, crusties and eco-warriors, succeeded in the 2000s by the usual pendulum swing to a harder-edged style with new-metallers, gangsta-bling, 'hoodies' – and Goths reincarnated as slightly more punk-like emos. Although these harsher styles are still with us, the subculture fashion pendulum at least partly swung back to yet another reinvention of the softer Boho-ish look in the latter part of the decade – this time in the form of surfer/skater/festival styles, and the latest incarnations of indie (short for 'independent', although it is of course nothing of the sort).

This potted summary is over-simplified, by no means exhaustive, and may well already be out of date by the time you read it, but my point is that we've always had subcultures, and they have always distinguished themselves from the mainstream, and from each other, by their dress codes – until their distinctive style of dress becomes mainstream and they are forced to think of a new one.

The only significant change that I can see in recent times is an increase in the sheer number of different subcultural styles – an increase in tribalism, perhaps a reaction to the 'globalisation' affecting our mainstream culture. In the past, young English people looking for a sense of identity and a means of annoying their parents had a choice of just one or two, at the most three, counter-culture youth tribes; now there are at least half a dozen, each with its own sub-groups and splinter groups. Since the 1950s, all youth subculture styles have been closely identified with different types of music, almost all originally derived from American black music, usurped and modified by young whites. The current batch conforms largely to this pattern, with aficionados of garage (must be pronounced to rhyme with 'marriage', not 'barrage'), R&B, hip-hop, drum&bass, techno, trance and house (and, more recently, dubstep, grime and grindie) each sporting marginally different clothing – the techno/house/trance groups being more smart-casual, the others more 'gangsta' and show-off glamorous, with designer labels and varying degrees of 'bling'. I have already mentioned indie, a more middle-class (and increasingly mainstream) youth subculture, again with many sub-divisions (indie-pop, grunge, sadcore, shoegaze, math rock, indietronica, etc.), which favours angst-ridden lyrics, guitar-based music and a softer, more arty, Bohemian style of dress.

The minor style distinctions differentiating many of these groups are subtle, and some may not be visible to the naked eye of an uninitiated observer, just as much of the music may sound alike to the untrained ear. As a member of one of these youth-tribes, however, you can not only see and hear important differences between, say, house, techno and trance, but also, within these categories, between sub-genres such as acid house, deep house, tech house, progressive house, hi-NRG, nu-NRG, old skool, Goa trance, psy trance, hardcore, happy hardcore, electro house, fidget house, psycho house, reg house, etc. You know, for example, that hard house and hi-NRG are particularly popular among gay men, and associated with a more flamboyant, body-conscious style of dress, but you can easily distinguish this type of glamour from the ostentatious, blingy variety associated with hip-hop. You can discuss the various sub-genres in a dialect utterly incomprehensible to outsiders, and read specialist magazines with reviews written in this private coded language, such as:

> Slam drop a looping tech-house mix and Unkle provide a more twisted beatz version.

> A rich mix of textures that will satisfy floors and purist swots alike.

> For some acid mayhem, Massive Power reveals its Mr Spring influence in a spiralling 290bpm breakdown.[104]

I noted in the 2004 edition of this book that many of these sub-genres of 'house', 'trance' etc. would probably be out of date by the time it was published, and indeed that some were already being described as '*so* last week' (the expression itself an indication of how fast the music fashions change). Sure enough, some have either been superseded or 'gone mainstream', but as 'house' and some

---

104. Review quotes from the magazines *Muzik* and *MixMag*. These particular music-based subcultures have a penchant for cutely misspelled words, wherever possible involving the letter 'k', as in 'kamaflage', Nukleuz, old skool, Muzik, etc. 'Old skool' means pre-1993–4, usually house. 'Floors' are people on the dance-floor, people who are into dancing. 'Purist swots' are anoraks, trainspotters, who instead of dancing to the music develop an encyclopaedic knowledge of every aspect of it, with which they bore you at every opportunity; 'bpm' is beats per minute. The rest is a bit of a mystery.

related genres are still very popular among clubbers, and this is still a good example of the variety of sub-divisions within youth music-based subcultural styles, I'll let it stand.

The Collective Distinctiveness Rule

So you get to rebel against the mainstream culture, and proclaim your non-conformist individual identity, but with the comforting security of belonging to a structured, rule-governed social group, with shared tastes, values and jargon, and well-defined boundaries and behaviour codes. And no risk of mistakes or embarrassment because, unlike the mainstream culture where you only have rather vague guidelines, there are clear and precise instructions on what to wear. No wonder so many English teenagers choose this form of rebellion.

The dress codes of youth subcultures are 'codes' in both senses of the word: rules, but also ciphers. The tribes' sartorial statements, like the verbal ones in the reviews quoted above, are delivered in dialect, a private code that is difficult for outsiders to decipher. These coded dress codes are highly prescriptive – strict to a degree that would feel oppressive if these were rules imposed by parents or schools. Deviation from the uniform is not tolerated, as anyone who has tried to get into a popular subculture night-club wearing the wrong thing will know. And it's not just what you wear but precisely how you wear it. If woolly hats are being worn pulled right down to the eyebrows and completely covering the ears, then that is how you wear your woolly hat. The fact that it makes you look like a six-year-old dressed by an over-anxious mother is neither here nor there. If hooded sweatshirts are worn zipped to the neck with the hoods up – again somehow looking curiously vulnerable and childlike – then that is how you wear your sweatshirt. If you are a Goth, you wear a lot of black clothes and dyed-black hair, with white make-up, heavy black eyeliner and dark lipstick. And long hair. Even with all the correct funereal fancy-dress and make-up, short hair will mark you out (at least in some goth circles) as a novice or 'baby' Goth. Either grow it quickly, buy a wig or get extensions.

This is not to say that there is no variety or diversity or scope for individual self-expression within subcultural styles, just that such variation must remain within clearly defined boundaries: you can pick and choose, but you do so from a limited range of core themes. A Goth must be recognisably a Goth, and an emo identifiable as an emo, otherwise there is no point. Some members of youth subcultures have more insight into their own conformity than others. In his excellent study of the Goth subculture, Paul Hodkinson quotes an informant who responded to the question 'What is the Goth scene all about?' by declaring that it is about 'having the absolute freedom to dress as you want and to express yourself as you want'. Hodkinson comments that 'The ways in which subcultural participants choose to respond to direct questioning can sometimes result in debatable conclusions' – which is a polite academic way of saying, 'Yeah, right.'

Another of his informants was more perceptive. Responding to a question about the importance of being 'different', she said, 'Yeah, although you always say that, like, you're all individuals, but everyone's got the same boots on! Do you know what I mean? "Oh, aren't we all individual with all our ripped fishnets and our New Rocks [a make of boot]?"' And a third respondent gave a beautifully concise and endearingly honest explanation of the apparent contradiction: 'It's not like you're a Goth because you want to stand out, but you do like sort of being different from everyone else, although when you're with a load of Goths you blend in, but you're all different, if you know what I mean, from everyone else.'

This comment would seem to support my point about alleged English sartorial 'eccentricity' being something of a team effort, more often a matter of collective distinctiveness than individual originality. We want to be creative and different, but we're squeamish about 'standing out', and we also want to fit in and belong – so let's join a subculture and all be eccentric in the same way, together. That way, we get the best of both worlds: the excitement of rebellion and the comfort of conformity. A delightfully English compromise. And only a tiny bit hypocritical, really.

HUMOUR RULES

The coded language of subcultural dress statements is, like all English communication, infused with humour. I have already mentioned the role of the Importance of Not Being Earnest rule (the First Commandment of English humour) in mainstream English attitudes to dress, but I was surprised to find that this rule was equally powerful and as strictly observed among youth subcultures.

It is well known, after all, that young people, especially self-obsessed teenagers, are inclined to take themselves a bit too seriously. And given the immense social importance of dress in these youth tribes – clothing style being the primary means by which they distinguish themselves from the dreaded mainstream and from each other, the principal way in which they express their tribal affiliation and identity – they could be forgiven for taking their clothes and appearance very seriously indeed. I had fully expected these subcultures to be an exception to the Importance of Not Being Earnest rule and the irony rules. I assumed that members of youth tribes would be, understandably, unable or at least very reluctant to stand back and laugh at their cherished sartorial affiliation signals.

But I was wrong. I had underestimated the sheer strength and pervasiveness of the English humour rules. Even among those whose subcultural identity is most closely bound up with their tribal uniform, such as Goths, I found an astonishing degree of ironic detachment. Goths, in their macabre black costumes, might *look* as though they are taking themselves very seriously, but when you get into conversation with them, they are full of typically English self-mockery. In many cases, even their clothes are deliberately ironic. I was chatting at a bus stop to a Goth in full vampire regalia – with chalk-white face, deep-purple lipstick, long black hair and all – when I noticed that he was also wearing a T-shirt with 'GOTH' printed in large letters on the front. 'So, what's that about?' I asked, indicating the T-shirt.

'It's just in case you missed the point,' he replied, mock-seriously. 'I mean, I couldn't have people thinking I was just a boring, mainstream, normal person, right?' We both looked at his highly conspicuous, unmistakable, fancy-dress costume and burst out laughing. He then confided that he had another T-shirt with 'SAD OLD GOTH' on it, and that these were very popular among his Goth friends, who wore them 'to stop people taking it all too seriously – well, to stop us from taking ourselves too seriously as well, which to be honest we're a little bit inclined to do if we're not careful. You've got to be able to take the piss out of yourself.'

Once you learn to decode a subculture's sartorial dialect, you find that many of the dress-statements are self-mocking in-jokes, often ridiculing the tribe's own rigid dress codes. Some Goths, for example, poke fun at the whole sombre, morbid, black-only colour rule by wearing bright, girly pink – a colour that is traditionally despised by this subculture. 'The pink thing is a joke,' explained a young female Goth with pink hair and pink gloves, 'because pink is, like, totally against the whole Goth ideology.' So, Goths with pink hair or sporting items of pink clothing (even ultra-cutesy My Little Pony or Hello Kitty T-shirts) are laughing at themselves, deliberately mocking not just their dress codes but all the tastes and values that define their tribal identity. That seems to me about as ironically detached as you can get.

I've been rather critical of the English so far in this discussion of dress, but this ability to laugh at ourselves is surely a redeeming quality. Where else would you find dedicated members of dress-obsessed youth tribes who can look at themselves in the mirror and say, 'Oh, come off it!' or 'Get over yourself!'? I have certainly never come across this degree of self-mockery among comparable groups in any other culture.

So. Vampires in ironic pink. Another thing to be proud of. I think my last little burst of patriotic pride was over bad puns in tabloid headlines. Hmm. You may be starting to worry about my taste and judgement, but at least there's a consistent pattern: my rare moments of unqualified admiration for the English all seem to relate to our sense of humour, clearly something I prize above many other perhaps more worthy qualities. How very English of me.

This sense of humour may perhaps help to explain the otherwise puzzling English mania for fancy-dress parties. Other nations may have masked balls and national or regional festivals involving fancy-dress costumes, but they don't have fancy-dress parties every weekend, for no apparent reason or on the flimsiest of excuses, the way the English do. English males seem to have a particular penchant for cross-dressing, seizing every opportunity to deck themselves out in corsets, fishnet stockings and high heels. And it is always the most macho, the most blatantly heterosexual of English men (soldiers, rugby players, etc.) who find it most amusing to dress up as tarty women. This strikes me as yet another form of 'collective eccentricity': we love to break the rules, providing we can all do it together, in a context of rule-governed cultural remission such as a fancy-dress party or a stag night, so there's no individual embarrassment.

CLASS RULES

It is much harder nowadays to tell a person's class by his or her dress, but there are still a few fairly reliable indicators. Nothing as obvious as the old distinctions between cloth-caps and pinstripes, but if you look closely, you can identify the unwritten rules and subtle status-signals.

Youth Rules and Yoof Rules

Class indicators are most difficult to detect among the young, as young people of all classes tend to follow either tribal street-fashions or mainstream trends (which are in any case often diluted versions of street-fashions). This is annoying for class-conscious parents as well as class-spotting anthropologists. One upper-middle-class mother complained, 'Jamie and Saskia look just like those yobbos from the council estate. Honestly, what *is* the point?' Meaning, presumably, what is the point of taking the trouble to give your children 'smart' upper-middle-class names and send them to expensive upper-middle-class schools, when they insist on dressing exactly like Darren and Chantelle from the local comprehensive.

But a more observant mother might have noticed that Jamie and Saskia do not, in fact, look *exactly* like Darren and Chantelle. Jamie may have his hair cut very short and even gelled into spikes (or whatever the latest street-fashion shape may be), but Darren will go one step further and have his shaved off almost entirely, leaving just a few millimetres of fuzz. Saskia's multiple ear-piercings may horrify her parents, and the more audacious Saskias may even have their belly-buttons pierced, or get a small, discreet tattoo, but most Saskias will not, like the Chantelles, sport multiple large tattoos, or rings and studs in their eyebrows, noses and tongues. Princess Anne's daughter, Zara, had a tongue-stud, but this was shocking enough to make front-page headline news in all the tabloids. The upper class and aristocracy, like those at the bottom end of the social scale, can ignore the unwritten dress codes because they don't care what the neighbours think. They do not suffer from middle-class class anxiety. If middle-class Saskia gets her tongue pierced, she is in danger of being thought 'common': if aristocratic Zara does it, it is daring and eccentric.

Leaving aside the occasional upper-class exceptions, sartorial differences between middle-class youth and working-class 'yoof' are generally a matter of degree. Both Jamie and Darren might wear low-slung baggy jeans (a gangsta-influenced style, of black American origin), but Darren's will be lower and baggier – four sizes too big for him, rather than just two. And working-class Darrens will start wearing this style at a younger age than middle-class Jamies. The same goes for their sisters: Chantelles tend to wear more extreme versions of the latest tribal costume than Saskias,[105] and to start younger. They are also generally allowed to 'grow up' earlier and faster than Saskias. If you see a pre-pubescent girl dolled up in sexy teenage fashions and make-up, she is almost certainly not middle class.

As a rule, middle-class children's and teenagers' dress tends to be both more restrained and somewhat more natural-looking than working-class yoof attire. Chantelle and Saskia may both wear the same fashionable style and shape of T-shirt and trousers, but Saskia's will be matte rather than shiny, with a higher proportion of natural fibres, at least in the daytime. The class indicators are quite subtle. Saskia and Chantelle may shop at the same teenage high-street chains, and often buy the same items, but they combine them and wear them in slightly different ways. They may both have, say, the latest skinny jeans from Topshop, but Chantelle is more likely to wear hers with

105. At least, this rule applied to punk and now to the current 'blingy' gangsta/hip-hop fashions, but a relatively high proportion of Goths are middle class, as are most indies, so there are exceptions.

a 'blingy' designer-logo top and teetering high heels, while Saskia's identical jeans might be worn with a woolly jumper, boots and a big, soft scarf wrapped several times round her neck. For some reason, middle- and upper-class young people are much more inclined to wear scarves than the lower ranks – that big, soft scarf is one of the most reliable class indicators – and generally more willing to wrap up warmly in cold weather. Darren and Chantelle often seem perversely determined to be cold, going out on freezing January nights wearing just a T-shirt and jeans (Darren) or a strappy top and a mini-skirt with bare legs (Chantelle).

This is not a question of money, and the cost of clothes is not a reliable guide to the class of the wearer. Saskia's and Jamie's clothes are no more expensive than Chantelle's and Darren's (they may even be cheaper, as the former are more likely to hunt for 'indie'/Boho items in charity shops), and Chantelle and Darren are just as likely to have a number of expensive items of 'designer' clothing in their wardrobes. But, again, there are tell-tale differences. When working-class yoof, male or female, wear 'designer' clothes, they tend to go for the ones with the big, obvious logos. The reasoning seems to be: what is the point in having a Juicy Couture or Tommy Hilfiger sweatshirt if no one can tell? The upper-middles and above regard big designer logos as rather vulgar.

If in doubt, look at the hair. Hair is a fairly reliable class-indicator. Chantelle's haircut is likely to look more 'done', more contrived, more artificial than Saskia's – and her style will involve more obvious use of gel, dye and spray. Almost all upper-middle to upper-class schoolgirls have shiny-clean, floppy hair, falling loose so that they can be constantly pushing it back, running their fingers through it, flipping and tossing it, tucking it behind their ears, pulling it into a rough twist or ponytail then letting it fall back again, in a sequence of apparently casual, unconscious gestures. This floppy-hair display is a highly distinctive ritual, rarely seen among working-class females. Many lower-working-class females currently wear their hair pulled up into an extremely tight, high pony-tail, sneeringly known as a 'Croydon facelift', 'council-house facelift' or 'chav facelift'. A popular variation on this style involves leaving two very thin sections of hair hanging down over the face.

The more restrained/natural appearance of middle-class youth is only partly due to the diktats of class-anxious parents. English children and teenagers are no less class-conscious than their elders, and although some middle-class Jamies and Saskias may use 'common' items of clothing or jewellery as a form of rebellion, they have their own sartorial snobberies, and their own class anxieties. Their parents may not realise it, but they do not, in fact, wish to be indistinguishable from the 'council-estate yobbos'. They may even use derogatory names for those whose dress and manner put them in this low-class category, such as 'townies', 'scallies', 'oiks', 'yobs', 'pikeys' or 'plebs' – or, of course, the now ubiquitous 'chavs'. The working-class children and teenagers, in turn, have absolutely no wish to emulate the 'posh gits', 'yahs', 'Sloanes', 'hoorays', etc.

The more sensitive English middle-class youths are slightly embarrassed about their snobbery, and were somewhat hesitant, in interviews, about admitting to using these terms. Discussions touching on class issues were always punctuated by nervous laughter. An upper-middle-class teenage girl confessed that she had been hankering after a particular rather expensive item of jewellery, until she noticed that it seemed to have become very popular among hairdressers, which, she said, 'put me off it a bit,' adding, 'I know it shouldn't, that it's really snobbish of me, but I can't help it: if they're all wearing it, I don't like it so much.' Her class-anxious mother, with her concerns about appearing 'common', would no doubt be pleased at this evidence of her influence.

Although young English people are more class-conscious than they like to admit, many of them are more worried about being seen as 'mainstream' than about the class-labels attached to their clothing. To call someone's taste in dress, music or anything else 'mainstream' is always derogatory, and in some circles a dire insult. Definitions of 'mainstream' vary. Taking me through the lists of clubs and other dance-venues in *Time Out* magazine, young music-lovers offered different opinions as to which clubs were 'cool' (a term that is now becoming less cool) and which were 'mainstream'. In extreme cases, 'mainstream' encompassed anything that was not unquestionably 'underground': for some young clubbers, *any* club or venue listed in

Time Out was automatically 'mainstream' – 'cool' events were those advertised only by word of mouth.

These are serious issues for young English people, but I was pleased to find that there was still an undercurrent of humour, even an element of self-mockery, in discussions of coolth and mainstream-ness. Some teenagers even make sartorial jokes about their own mainstream-phobia. In the mid-1990s, for example, when the Spice Girls were the epitome of mainstream, despised by all those with cool, underground pretensions, some counter-culture 'grungers' took to wearing Spice Girls T-shirts – a little ironic in-joke, poking fun at themselves, refusing to take the mainstream-avoidance rules too seriously. Such jokes can be successfully carried off only by those already established as 'cool', of course: you are effectively saying 'I'm so cool that I can wear a blatantly mainstream Spice Girls T-shirt without anyone thinking that I might actually like the Spice Girls.'

Adult Class Rules

Grown-up sartorial semiotics are marginally less complex than the teenage rules and signals, and the class indicators are somewhat clearer.

Debrett's Guide to Etiquette and Modern Manners advises us to 'forget the old British adage that it is ill-bred to be overdressed'. The author claims that this rule dates from a time when 'it was the accepted norm to dress up for any activity more than gardening'. At this time, he says, 'overdressing meant being got up in a flashy, overly elaborate or embarrassing way and took no account of the modern invasion of sports-inspired clothes that has enslaved whole swathes of the nation into sweats and trainers'. He has a point, and higher-class people tend not to wear sweats for going out. But flashy, over-elabo-rate dress is also still a lower-class indicator, while the higher echelons still manage to 'dress up' without looking fussy and overdone.

Female Class Rules

Too much jewellery (especially gold jewellery, necklaces spelling out one's name or initials and large hoop earrings), too much make-up, over-coiffed hair, fussy-dressy clothes, shiny tights and uncomfortably tight shoes are all lower-class hallmarks, particularly when worn for relatively casual occasions. Deep, over-baked suntans – whether real or fake – are also regarded as vulgar by the higher social ranks. A ruddy complexion, however, is perfectly acceptable, providing it is the obvious result of much walking, riding, hunting, gardening and other hearty outdoor activity. This rugged, weather-beaten type of tan, confined to the face, neck and forearms, and always clearly an accidental by-product of country life, is often seen among upper-class women. Deliberate tans – those achieved by spit-roasting oneself on a beach or sunbed, or applied with a spray-can – are 'effortful' and contrived, and therefore seen as lower class.

As with furniture and home-decoration, too much twee, laboured matching of clothes or accessories is also a lower-class signal, particularly if the scheme involves a bright colour – say, a navy dress with a red belt, red shoes, a red bag and a red hat (take off two more class points if any of these items are shiny as well as red). This kind of overdressing is often seen at working-class weddings or other special occasions. The same over-careful matching but with a more muted 'accent' colour, such as cream, would be lower-middle class; reducing the number of matched accessories to just two or three might raise the whole outfit to middle-middle status – but it would still be an 'outfit', still too fussy and Sunday-best, still too obviously dressed-up for the upper-middles.

For the crucial distinction between lower/middle-middle and upper-middle dress, think Margaret Thatcher (careful, stiff, smart, bright-blue suits; shiny blouses; matching shoes and bags; coiffed helmet of hair) versus Shirley Williams (worn, rumpled, thrown-together – but good quality – tweedy skirts and cardigans; dull, sludgy colours; nothing matching; messy, unstyled hair).[106] This is most emphatically *not* to say that any sort of scruffiness is 'posh',

---

106. Apologies to those too young to remember Shirley Williams in her heyday, but I could not find a good contemporary example, as all female politicians now seem to dress in a rather lower/middle-middle manner – or at least I have seen none with Williams's unmistakably high-class brand of unkemptness.

or that any attempt at dressing up is automatically lower-class. An upper-middle or upper class woman will not wear Waynetta Slob leggings and a grubby velour sweatshirt to go out to lunch at a smart restaurant – but she will turn up in something fairly simple and understated, without lots of heavy-handed matching and effortful accessorising. Her hair may be casually 'unstyled', but it will not be greasy, or display several inches of dark roots straggling into a brassy-blonde dye.

Among adult English females, the amount of flesh on display can also be a class indicator. As a rule, the amount of visible cleavage is inversely correlated with position on the social scale – the more cleavage revealed by a garment, the lower the social class of its wearer (a daytime garment, that is: party dresses and ball gowns can be more revealing). For the middle-aged and over, the same rule applies to upper arms. And skimpy, skin-tight clothes clinging to bulges of fat are also lower class. The higher ranks have bulges too, but they hide them under looser or more substantial clothing.

The class rules on legs are rather less clear-cut, as there are two more factors to complicate the issue: fashion and the quality of the legs in question. Lower-working-class females (and *nouveaux-riches* of working-class origin) tend to wear short skirts, when they are in fashion and often when they are not, regardless of whether they have good enough legs, while 'respectable' upper-working, lower-middle and middle-middle women do not display very much leg, even when both fashion and leg-quality would allow it. Among the higher social ranks, the more youthful and fashionable women may wear shorter hemlines, but only if they have very good legs. The upper-middle and upper classes regard thick legs – and in particular thick ankles – as not only unattractive, but also, worse, working class. The myth that all upper-class females have elegant legs and slim ankles is perpetuated by the fact that those with thick ones usually take care to hide them.

So, if you see an English woman with thick legs in a short skirt, she is probably working class; but a woman with elegant legs in a short skirt could be from either the bottom or the top of the social scale. You will have to look for other clues, in the details described above such as cleavage-display, visible bulginess, make-up, tanning, matching, shininess, fussiness, jewellery, hairstyle and shoes. All of these indicators can be used in judging work-clothes – suits and so on – as well as casual dress. English dress codes and sartorial class-indicators may have become somewhat less formal and obvious since the 1950s, but to say that it is no longer possible to judge class from dress is just nonsense. It is more difficult, certainly, but there are still plenty of clues – particularly once one has grasped the difference between higher-class and lower-class notions of smartness and, perhaps even more importantly, between higher-class and lower-class types of scruffiness.

In genuinely tricky or borderline cases, where you cannot simply 'sight-read' the sartorial class-statements, you may have to focus on other aspects of dress, such as shopping habits and dress-talk, to determine an Englishwoman's social position. Over a certain age, only the upper-middles and above, for example, will readily and cheerfully admit to buying clothes in charity shops. This rule is not so strictly observed among teenagers and twenty-/thirty-somethings, as hunting for charity-shop 'vintage' bargains has become a fashionable pastime, endorsed by glossy magazines and working-class supermodels, and some lower-class young females have followed their example. But among older females, only those at either the higher end or the very bottom of the scale buy clothes from Oxfam, Cancer Research or Sue Ryder shops – and only those at the higher end want to tell you about it. An upper-middle female will proudly twirl and flounce a skirt at you, and announce gleefully that it was 'Only four pounds fifty from Oxfam!', expecting you to admire her for being so clever, so thrifty, so charmingly eccentric, Bohemian and un-snobbish.

In some cases, she may be genuinely hard-up and, knowing that class in England is not judged on income, she won't be ashamed to admit it. But upper-middle females will often buy cheap clothes in charity shops and second-hand shops on principle (exactly what principle is not entirely clear), even when they can perfectly well afford new clothes. And boast about their purchases. But have a bit of compassion: this is the only chance these women get to break both the modesty rule and the money-talk taboo in the same breath – surely they can be forgiven for getting a bit over-excited? Their delight would, however, be incomprehensible to the women at the bottom of the social *and* income scales, who shop in charity shops out of dire necessity and get no social kudos or sense of pride from doing so – quite the opposite: many of them find it deeply shaming.

Two factors, the economic recession and the rise of eBay, have given women in the higher social ranks more reason to boast about their thrifty purchases, and more opportunities to do so. Extravagant spending on clothes has always been frowned upon as rather vulgar by the upper-middles and upper class, but the recession allows them to 'frame' their disapproval as moral rather than social. And their own second-hand purchases can be displayed with even greater self-righteousness. In these hard times, it has become customary among higher-class women to claim that any designer-label or expensive-looking item they are wearing was picked up for a fraction of its value on eBay. I know for a fact that some will say, 'Well, yes, it is Marc Jacobs [or Chanel, Marni, Chloé, etc.] but I got it for half-nothing on eBay' even when they have in fact paid full price for the item in a fancy shop.

Although they are proud to shop in charity shops and on eBay, the more class-anxious of the upper-middles are often reluctant to admit to buying clothes at certain high-street chains, such as Marks & Spencer (except for underwear and the odd plain T-shirt or man's jumper), or the supermarket clothing ranges, such as George at Asda or Tu at Sainsbury's (both no-go zones, even for knickers). If they do buy something more important, such as a jacket, from Marks & Spencer, they do not normally twirl and flaunt it and exclaim over how cheap it was, but if a friend admires the garment and asks where it is from, they say, 'Would you believe *M&S*?' in a high-pitched, surprised tone, as though they don't quite believe it themselves. The friend replies, '*No!* Really?' in the same tone.[107] (Their teenage daughters might have much the same conversation about

107. See page 345 for a more detailed discussion of the class-semiotics of shopping at M&S.

some of the cheaper high-street chains aimed at their age-group, such as New Look or Claire's Accessories.)

The more secure upper-middle shoppers, those with little or no anxiety about their social position, will cheerfully admit to buying supermarket or ultra-cheap high-street clothes. These confident upper-middles will often even flaunt their virtuously thrifty 'discoveries' with pride.

Male Class Rules

One way or another, it is usually possible to gauge English women's social class from their dress. Men, however, pose rather more of a problem for the class-spotter. There is far less variety in adult male clothing, particularly work-clothes, which means less choice, which means fewer opportunities to make either deliberate or inadvertent sartorial class-statements. The old blue-collar/white-collar distinction is no longer reliable. The decline of the manufacturing industry and the casual dress codes of many of the newer companies and industries mean that a suit *per se* no longer distinguishes the lower-middle from the working-class male. The young man going to work in jeans and a T-shirt could be a construction-site labourer, but he could equally be the managing director of an independent software or internet company. Uniforms are more helpful, but not infallible. Yes, a shop assistant's or bus driver's uniform is probably a working-class indicator, but a barman's or waiter's is not, as middle-class students (and struggling graduates) often take jobs in bars and restaurants. Generally, occupation is not a very reliable guide to social class, particularly in the 'white-collar' occupations: accountants, doctors, lawyers, businessmen, teachers and estate agents can come from any social background. So, even if you could tell a man's occupation from his dress, you would not necessarily be any the wiser regarding his class.

Although dress codes are now more relaxed in some occupations, the majority of 'white-collar' men still go to work in a suit – and at first glance, be-suited male commuters catching their trains in the morning all look pretty much alike. Well, to be honest, they all look pretty much alike at second and third glance as well. If I were a menswear expert, and could distinguish between an Armani suit and a Marks & Spencer's one without grabbing the commuter by his collar and peering at the label, I would still only have information on the man's income, not his social class. Class in England is no more determined by wealth than it is by occupation. I know that an upper-class English man, with sufficient money, is more likely to choose a tailor-made Jermyn Street suit than an Armani one, and that if he is broke he might prefer a charity-shop tailored suit to a new high-street-chain one, but this is not really a great deal of help to me as they all still just look like suits.

Jewellery and accessories are a better guide. Size is important. Large, bulky, ostentatious metal watches, especially gold ones, are a lower-class signal – even if they are frightfully expensive Rolexes (or those James-Bond-wannabe gadgety ones that tell you what time it is in six countries and will work at the bottom of the sea and withstand a small nuclear attack). Upper-middles and above tend to wear more discreet watches, usually with a simple leather strap. A similar principle applies to cufflinks: big, flashy, show-off cufflinks are lower class; small, simple, unobtrusive ones are higher. Again, the cost of the items is irrelevant.

Any rings other than a plain wedding band indicate that the wearer is probably no higher than middle-middle. Some upper-middle and upper-class males might wear a signet ring, engraved with their family crest, on the little finger of their left hand, but these are also often sported by pretentious middle-middles, so they are not a reliable guide. A signet ring with initials on it rather than a crest, and worn on any other finger, is lower middle. Ties are marginally more helpful. Very brash, garish colours and loud patterns (especially cartoony/jokey ones) are lower class; ties in a single, solid colour (particularly if pale, bright and/or shiny) are no higher than middle-middle; the upper-middles and above wear ties in relatively subdued, usually dark colours, with small, discreet patterns.

But I'll come clean and admit that I rarely, if ever, manage to identify be-suited males' class by dress alone: I have to cheat and look at their body language or their newspaper. (Whatever they are wearing, only working-class males sit on trains or buses with their legs wide apart; and most upper-middle-class males do not read the tabloids – or at least not in public.)

Casual clothes are a bit more revealing than suits, in both the physical and class-indicator sense, as there is more variety and men have to exercise more choice. The trouble is that when allowed free rein to choose what to wear – without the rules and constraints of the suit – adult English men of all classes tend to dress rather badly. The vast majority have no natural sense of style, and indeed no wish to be stylishly dressed – quite the opposite: to describe a man as stylish, or even just well dressed, is to cast doubt upon his masculinity. A man who is too well dressed is automatically suspected of being gay. English men are concerned about being *correctly* or *appropriately* dressed, but this is because they do not want to stand out or draw attention to themselves. They just want to fit in, to blend, to look pretty much like any other unquestionably heterosexual male. The result is that they all look very much alike. When they are not wearing the work uniform of suit and tie, they all wear more or less the same undistinguishing and undistinguished dress-down uniform of jeans and T-shirt/sweatshirt or casual trousers and shirt/jumper.

Yes, I do realise that all T-shirts are not created equal, and that there are casual trousers and casual trousers. So it should be possible to spot class distinctions between different styles and fabrics and brands and so on. And it is possible. But it is not easy. (I'm not whining here – well, actually I am: I just want you to know that this has taken a lot of effort, not to mention a lot of funny looks from men who misinterpreted my attempts to scrutinise the label on the back of their trousers.)

The class rules of male casual dress are based on more or less the same basic principles as the female class rules, except that fussy over-dressing is regarded as camp, rather than lower class. The shiny nylon versus natural-fibre principle applies to adult males as well as females, but it is much less useful as a class indicator because men of all classes tend to avoid obviously shiny man-made fibres as they are both effeminate and uncomfortable. And although the working-class male's shirt might not be pure cotton, it is quite difficult to tell just by looking, and you can't go around pinching men's sleeves to check the quality of the fabric.

There is also the same inverse correlation between amounts of visible flesh and position on the social scale. Shirts unbuttoned to display an expanse of chest are lower class – the more buttons undone, the lower the class of the wearer (and if a chain or medallion round the neck is also revealed, take off another ten class points). Even amounts of arm on display can be significant. Among older males, the higher classes tend to prefer shirts to T-shirts, and would certainly *never* go out in just a vest or singlet, however hot the weather – these are strictly working-class garments. Bare chests, anywhere other than a beach or swimming pool, are lower-working-class.

If you are wearing a shirt, the class divide seems to be at the elbow: on a warm day, lower-class men will roll their shirt-sleeves up to above the elbow, while the higher ranks will roll them to just below the elbow – unless they are engaged in some significant physical activity, such as gardening. The visible-flesh rule also applies to legs. Upper-middle and upper-class adult males are rarely seen in shorts unless they are playing sports, running/jogging, hill-walking or perhaps gardening at home. Middle-middles, lower-middles and some younger upper-middle and upper-class males might wear shorts on holiday abroad, but only working-class males exhibit their legs in public in their home town.

There is an upper-middle-class male summer uniform, also worn by some members of the upper class, and favoured especially by upper/upper-middle-class television presenters, consisting of a plain pale-blue shirt and pale-beige or string-coloured loose-fitting trousers. On a recent episode of the television show *Antiques Road Trip*, both of the male presenters, and one upper-class interviewee, were wearing this uniform. But the presenter of lower-class origins (judging by his accent) had got it just slightly wrong in that his shirt was boldly striped and slightly shiny, and he was wearing a black belt and shoes, instead of the 'correct' brown.

As a general principle, winter or summer, higher-class males just seem to wear *more clothes*. More layers, more coats, more scarves, hats and gloves. They are somewhat more likely to carry umbrellas as well, but only in cities: there is an old unwritten taboo against gentlemen carrying an umbrella in the country, except at the races or other occasions where chivalry might require them to protect dressed-up ladies from the rain. So, an umbrella in the city can sometimes be a higher-class signal – particularly if it is a very large, old-fashioned, sturdy-looking umbrella, with a proper solid wood handle – but an umbrella on a country walk is lower class. Unless you are a vicar, that is: for some reason country clergymen are exempt from the no-umbrella rule.

Upper-class English males generally take the 'don't stand out' rule to extremes, dressing to blend in not only with each other but also with their surroundings: tweedy greens and browns in the country; sombre greys and dark blue pinstripes in town – a sort of high-class camouflage. Wearing inappropriate 'city' clothes in the country, for both males and females, is a serious social solecism. In some very old and grand upper-class country circles, this taboo extends to the wearing of anything even remotely fashionable: the more frumpy and out-of-date you look, the higher your social status.

There are, however, a few striking exceptions to this upper-class camouflage rule. These are mainly special-occasion exceptions, such as the dandyish striped blazers worn at regattas and garden parties, and the flashy waistcoats worn by members of exclusive university dining clubs, but some upper-class males also seem to have a penchant for wearing brightly coloured trousers in more everyday settings. Red in particular, to the extent that 'toffs in red trousers' have become a bit of a national joke, although a violent shade of mustardy-yellow is also quite popular. But if you wish to infiltrate this class by emulating the red-trouser look, do be very careful, as any old red trousers won't do: the unwritten rules are complex and precise. Your red trousers must be matte, not shiny (stick to corduroy or heavy cotton) and always loose-fitting (tight red trousers are camp, not posh). Raspberry-pink shades of red are favoured, orangey-reds less so; bright is fine, but neon is forbidden. Red trousers must never be worn with black shoes or belts, only brown, and always with a shirt, not a T-shirt. The shirt must be in a pale, muted colour (pale blue is again the most popular), never dark or bright; fine stripes are permitted, but not big bold ones. Jumpers (knitted wool jumpers, not sweatshirts) may be any colour, but your jacket must be blue, beige, string-coloured, tweed or Barbour. To be safe, you should also add a soft woollen scarf – almost always a higher-class signal. But, frankly, upper-class red-trouser etiquette is a minefield, best avoided altogether by the uninitiated, as the loud trousers only draw attention to one's *faux pas*.

Vivid exceptions to the posh camouflage rule – flamboyant stripy blazers, brightly coloured trousers, peacocky waistcoats and so on – may seem highly eccentric, but as with Goth, punk and other apparently outlandish street-fashions, these upper-class dandies are eccentric sheep, all prancing about in the same strict tribal uniform.

DRESS CODES AND ENGLISHNESS

Oh dear. Dress seems to be yet another thing that the English are not very good at, yet another important 'life skill' we have somehow failed to master. Unless we have strict rules to follow – either official uniforms or tribal-subculture uniforms – our sartorial statements tend to be at best inarticulate and at worst downright ungrammatical.

Of course, there are a few exceptions, a few English people who speak the language of dress with effortless fluency. But on average, as a nation, our grasp of this idiom is poor. More evidence, if any were needed, of the social dis-ease that seems to be the most distinctive of our national characteristics.

My attempt to dissect English dress codes has also helped me to 'get inside' another stereotype: that of English eccentricity. Under the microscope, our much-vaunted eccentricity is not quite as admirably individual, original and creative as we might wish. Most of what passes for English eccentricity turns out, on closer inspection, to be a rather sheep-like conformity. But still – we do at least appreciate and value originality, and we can take some pride in the collective eccentricity of our street-fashions.

We are at our best when we are 'in uniform' but rebelling just slightly against it, refusing to take ourselves too seriously, indulging that peculiarly English talent for self-deprecating humour. We may lack the sartorial fluency of other nations, and our dress sense may be laughable, but at least we can always laugh at ourselves.

FOOD RULES

In 1949, the Hungarian George Mikes famously declared that 'On the Continent people have good food; in England they have good table manners.' Later, in 1977, he observed that our food had improved somewhat, while our table manners had deteriorated. He still did not, however, seem impressed by English food, and he acknowledged that our table manners were still 'fairly decent'.

Nearly forty years on, Mikes's comments still reflect the general international opinion of English cooking, as the travel writer Paul Richardson discovered when he told foreign friends that he was going to spend eighteen months researching a book on British gastronomy. His Spanish, French and Italian friends, he says, informed him that there was no such thing as British gastronomy, as this would require a passionate love of food, which we clearly did not have. They implied 'that our relationship with the food we ate was more or less a loveless marriage'.

Among the litany of complaints, which I have also heard from my own foreign friends and informants, was the fact that we regard good food as a privilege, not a right. We also have no proper regional cookery; families no longer eat together but instead consume junk food in front of the television; our diet consists mainly of salty or sweet snack foods – chips, crisps, chocolate bars, ready-meals, microwave pizzas and other rubbish. Even those with an interest in good food, and able to afford it, tend to have neither the time nor the energy to shop for and cook fresh ingredients in what other nations would regard as a normal or proper manner.

These criticisms are largely justified, and confirmed by statistics: for example, we consume more microwave ready-meals than all the rest of Europe put together. But they are not the whole truth. The same goes for the opposite extreme – the current fashion for proclaiming that English cooking has in recent years improved out of all recognition, that London is now the gastronomic capital of the world, that food is the new rock 'n' roll, that we have become a nation of gourmets and 'foodies', and so on.

I am not going to spend too much time here arguing about the quality of English cooking. My impression is that it is neither as awful as its detractors would have us believe, nor as stupendous as its recent champions have claimed. It is somewhere in between. Some of it is very good, some is quite inedible. On average, it's probably about fair to middling. I am only interested in the quality of English food in so far as it reflects our relationship with food, the unwritten social rules governing our food-related behaviour, and what these tell us about our national identity. Every culture has its own distinctive food rules – both general rules about attitudes towards food and cooking, and specific rules about who may eat what, how much, when, where, with whom and in what manner – and one can learn a lot about a culture by studying its food rules. So, I am not interested in English food *per se*, but in the Englishness of English food rules.

THE AMBIVALENCE RULE

'Loveless marriage' is not an entirely unfair description of the English relationship with food, although marriage is perhaps too strong a word: our relationship with food and cooking is more like a sort of uneasy, uncommitted cohabitation. It is ambivalent, often discordant, and highly fickle. There are moments of affection, and even of passion, but on the whole it is fair to say that we do not have the deep-seated, enduring, inborn love of food that is to be found among our European neighbours, and indeed in most other cultures. Food is just not given the same high priority in English life as it is elsewhere. Even the Americans, whose 'generic' (as opposed to ethnic) food is arguably no better than ours, still seem to care about it more, demanding hundreds of different flavours and combinations in each category of junk food on their supermarket shelves, for example, whereas we will put up with just twenty or so.

In most other cultures, people who care about food, and enjoy cooking and talking about it, are not singled out, either sneeringly or admiringly, as 'foodies'. Keen interest in food is the norm, not the exception: what the English call a 'foodie' would just be a normal person, exhibiting a standard, healthy, appropriate degree of focus on food. What we see as foodie obsession is in other cultures the default mode, not something unusual or even noticeable.

Among the English, such an intense interest in food is regarded by the majority as at best rather odd, and at worst somehow morally suspect – not quite proper, not quite right. In a man, foodie tendencies may be seen as unmanly, effeminate, possibly even casting doubt upon his sexual orientation. In this context, foodieness is roughly on a par with, say, an enthusiastic interest in fashion or soft furnishings. English male 'celebrity' chefs who appear on television tend to go out of their way to demonstrate their masculinity and heterosexuality: they use blokeish language and adopt a tough, macho demeanour; they parade their passion for football, mention their wives, girlfriends or children ('the wife' and 'the kids' in bloke-speak), and dress as scruffily as possible. Jamie Oliver, the TV chef who has done so much to make cooking a more attractive career choice for English boys, is a prime example of this 'please note how heterosexual I am' style, with his Cockney brashness and laddish 'Chuck in a bi' o' this an' a bi' o' that an' you'll be awright, mate' approach to cookery. Other English celebrity chefs prove their manliness by shouting and swearing all the time.

Foodieness is somewhat more acceptable among females, but it is still noticeable, still remarked upon – and in some circles regarded as pretentious. No one wishes to be seen as too deeply fascinated by or passionate about food. Most of us are proud to claim that we 'eat to live, rather than living to eat' – unlike some of our neighbours, the French in particular, whose excellent cooking we enjoy and admire, but whose shameless devotion to food we rather despise, not realising that the two might perhaps be connected.

ANTI-EARNESTNESS AND OBSCENITY RULES

Our ambivalence about food may be due in part to the influence of the Importance of Not Being Earnest rule. Excessive zeal on any subject is embarrassing, and getting all earnest and emotional about something as trivial as food is, well, frankly rather silly.

But it seems to me that our uneasiness about food and foodieness involves something more than this. There is a hint here of a more general discomfort about sensual pleasures. Flaunting one's passion for good food, and talking openly about the pleasure of eating it, is not embarrassing just because it is over-earnest but also because it is somehow a bit obscene.

It has been said that the English have a puritanical streak, but I'm not sure this is quite accurate. Sex, for example, is not regarded as sinful, but as private and personal and therefore a bit embarrassing. Jokes about sex, even quite explicit ones, are acceptable; earnest or fervent talk about the same intimate physical details is obscene. The sensual pleasures of eating, it seems to me, are in the same category – not exactly a taboo subject, but one that should only be talked about in a light-hearted, unserious, jokey manner.

Foodies (or foreigners) who dwell too lyrically, too erotically, on the delights of a perfectly executed, voluptuously creamy *sauce Béarnaise* will make us squirm, blush and look away. To avoid offending, all they need do is lighten up a bit, laugh at themselves, not take the whole thing quite so seriously. Without such ironic detachment, foodie-talk becomes a form of 'gastro-porn' (the term normally refers to lavishly illustrated foodie magazines and cookbooks, with detailed, mouth-watering descriptions of each luscious dish – but can equally be applied to over-enthusiastic foodie conversation).

TV-DINNER RULES

Although the idea that we are becoming a nation of discerning gastronomes is, I'm afraid, over-optimistic foodie propaganda – well, a gross exaggeration, anyway – interest in food and cooking has certainly increased in recent years. There is usually at least one food-related programme on every television channel every day. Admittedly, some of the game-show-style programmes, in which amateur chefs compete to cook a three-course meal in twenty minutes from five ingredients, are more entertainment than cookery – and most of my foreign informants found this approach to food either amusingly daft or shockingly irreverent. But there are plenty of genuinely informative cookery shows as well.

Whether this actually translates into much real cooking in English homes is a matter for debate. It is probably true that many English people avidly watch the celebrity TV chefs preparing elaborate dishes from fresh ingredients, while their own plastic-packaged supermarket ready-meals circle sweatily for three minutes in the microwave. (I've often done exactly this myself.) It has been estimated that of the 171 million cookbooks we own, 61 million are never even opened, and even from those that are, only a few recipes are ever used.

But there are exceptions – people who are genuinely inspired by these programmes, and rush out to buy the TV chefs' cookbooks and try their recipes. And I'm not just talking about a middle-class, trendy-foodie elite. A small but significant number of my working-class friends and informants have become much more enthusiastic and adventurous cooks as a result of watching television cookery programmes. A bus driver told me he was a 'big fan' of Gary Rhodes. 'I love his recipes,' he said. 'I'd never even tried to cook fish before – not real fish, proper fresh fish. Now I can go to the fishmonger and get, oh, red snapper or whatever and make a really beautiful meal. I did roasted sea bass last weekend. It's very pricey, is sea bass, but it's worth it. Beautiful, it was.'

Like most other English born-again food lovers, however, he only does this sort of 'proper cooking' once a week, on Saturday nights. There are still very few households in England where fresh ingredients, pricey or otherwise, are painstakingly prepared and carefully cooked on a daily basis. The shelves of the more up-market supermarkets may be full of exotic vegetables, herbs and spices, but the majority of shoppers still have no idea what these ingredients are or how to cook them. I spent some time hanging around the fruit and veg sections in supermarkets, staring at things like *pak choi*, wild mushrooms and lemongrass, and randomly asking fellow shoppers if they knew what one was supposed to do with them. Most did not, and neither, for that matter, did the supermarket staff.

THE NOVELTY RULE

I am, however, falling into a very English trendy-foodie trap here – equating 'good' food and 'genuine' interest in cooking with novel, foreign ingredients and new ways of preparing them. My foreign friends and informants find the frantic novelty-seeking of English foodies somewhat bizarre, and laugh at our constantly changing fads and fashions – from *nouvelle* to Cajun to Fusion to Tuscan to Pacific Rim to Modern British. One minute it's sun-dried tomatoes with everything, the next these are *passé* and it's raspberry vinegar, or garlic mash, or polenta, or, oh, I don't know, *confit* of black pudding and potato *rösti* layered into a precarious tower in the middle of a huge white plate, with goat-cheese filo parcels and a balsamic reduction or rosemary *jus* or horseradish *sabayon* or something.

Now the teetering towers are out and the latest fashion is for, say, scallops and chorizo with thin slices of purple and yellow beetroot and some obscure 'foraged' wild herbs, arranged in arty patterns on a piece of slate, with an elongated-teardrop smear of shallot purée and a watercress foam, decorated with pea shoots and edible flowers. Oh, and a fiendishly complicated dried and powdered ingredient, or tiny cubes of some equally high-tech jelly, or something theatrical involving liquid nitrogen. 'Molecular gastronomy' is one of the latest fads, and seems to be more about playing with big sciencey machines than making nice food – and yet another way for chefs to look manly on television.

This novelty-obsession is not peculiarly English: the same trend can be observed in America and Australia, but they are much younger nations, composed of immigrants from a variety of cultures, with no traditional indigenous cuisine to speak of, so they have some excuse. We are supposed to be an old, established European culture, with centuries of tradition and a sense of history. Yet when it comes to food, we behave like teenage fashion-victims. Presumably because, when it comes to food, despite our seniority, we are actually in much the same position as these teenage former colonies, having no great culinary tradition of our own. Some historically minded food lovers claim that English food has not always been so undistinguished, citing the great banquets of former times, with rich game pies and exotic spices and so on. But these things were largely the preserve of a very small, wealthy minority – and foreigners have been complaining about the poor quality of most English cooking for centuries. Now they marvel at our indiscriminate mixing and matching of foreign influences.

'I thought the English were supposed to be resistant to change,' said one of my confused foreign informants. 'This is not what I see in your restaurants. In Italy, we are much more traditional, much less open-minded about food. And the French are even more . . .' He curved his hands like blinkers alongside his eyes, in a gesture indicating tunnel vision or narrow-mindedness. He had a good point, I thought. The English have a reputation as sticks-in-the-mud, but our attitude to food suggests that we can be remarkably flexible, willing to try new things and absorb different culinary practices. The wilder extremes of the most recent novelty-seeking trends are mainly confined to the young and fashion-conscious, but Greek, Italian, Indian and Chinese food have been part of the English diet for decades – as familiar and established as meat-and-two-veg. Indian food in particular is an integral part of English culture. Our customs revolve around it. No Saturday night pub-crawl would be complete without a visit to the local tandoori or balti restaurant. And when the English go on holiday abroad, the food they most miss, according to surveys, is not fish and chips or steak-and-kidney pie but 'a proper English curry'.

MOANING AND COMPLAINING RULES

In restaurants, as elsewhere, the English may moan and grumble to each other about poor service or bad food, but our inhibitions, our social dis-ease, make it difficult for us to complain directly to the staff. We have three very different ways of dealing with such situations, all more or less equally ineffective and unsatisfying.

The Silent Complaint

Most English people, faced with unappetising or even inedible food, are too embarrassed to complain at all. Complaining would be 'making a scene', 'making a fuss' or 'drawing attention to oneself' in public – all forbidden by the unwritten rules. It would involve a confrontation, an emotional engagement with another human being, which is unpleasant and uncomfortable and to be avoided if at all possible. English customers may moan indignantly to their companions, push the offending food to the side of their plate and pull disgusted faces at each other, but when the waiter asks if everything is all right they smile politely, avoiding eye contact, and mutter, 'Yes, fine, thanks.' Standing in a slow queue at a pub or café food counter, they sigh heavily, fold their arms, tap their feet and look pointedly at their watches, but never actually complain. They will not go back to that establishment, and will tell all their friends how awful it is, but the poor publican or restaurateur will never even know that anything was amiss. Despite claims that we have become more assertive and litigious, this pattern is still standard consumer behaviour in England: recent surveys show that nearly three-quarters of us *never* complain about poor customer service, and of those who do, many now just vent their frustrations on online social media or anonymous review-sites such as Tripadvisor, which is simply another version of 'telling all your friends' – a wider circle of 'friends', perhaps, but still not a direct complaint to the actual restaurant.

The Apologetic Complaint

Some slightly braver souls will use method number two: the apologetic complaint, an English speciality. 'Excuse me, I'm terribly sorry, um, but, er, this soup seems to be rather, well, not very hot – a bit cold, really . . .' 'Sorry to be a nuisance, but, um, I ordered the steak and this looks like, er, well, fish . . .' 'Sorry, but do you think we could order soon? [This after a twenty-minute wait with no sign of any service.] It's just that we're in a bit of a hurry, sorry.' Sometimes these complaints are so hesitant and timid, so oblique, and so carefully disguised as apologies, that the staff could be forgiven for failing to grasp that the customer is dissatisfied. 'They look at the floor and mumble, as though *they* have done something wrong!' an experienced waiter told me.

As well as apologising for complaining, we also tend to apologise for making perfectly reasonable requests: 'Oh, excuse me, sorry, but could we possibly have some salt?'; 'Sorry, but could we have the bill now, please?' and even for spending money: 'Sorry, could we have another bottle of this, please?' I am guilty of all of these, and I always feel obliged to apologise when I haven't eaten much of my meal: 'Sorry, it was lovely, really, I'm just not very hungry.'

The Loud, Aggressive, Obnoxious Complaint

Finally, there is, as usual, the other side of the social dis-ease coin – English complaint-technique number three: the loud, aggressive, obnoxious complaint. The red-faced, blustering, rude, self-important customer who has worked himself into a state of indignation over some minor mistake – or, occasionally, the patient customer who eventually explodes in genuine frustration at being kept waiting hours for disgusting food.

It is often said that English waiters and other service staff are surly, lazy and incompetent. While there may be some truth in these accusations – we lack the professionalism and servility of some cultures, and cannot bring ourselves to adopt the gushing over-friendliness of others – one should look at the nonsense English servers have to put up with before casting stones. Our inept complaints alone would try the patience of a saint, and our silent ones require an understanding of non-verbal behaviour that would tax many psychologists, particularly if they had to fry chips or carry plates at the same time.

They may seem very different, but the silent or apologetic complaint and the aggressive-obnoxious one are closely related. The symptoms of the English social dis-ease involve opposite extremes: when we feel uncomfortable or embarrassed in social situations, we become either over-polite and awkwardly restrained or loud, loutish, aggressive and insufferable.

The 'Typical!' Rule Revisited

Our reluctance to complain in restaurants is, however, only partly due to social dis-ease. There is also a wider issue of low expectations. I mentioned at the beginning of this chapter Paul Richardson's observation that the English regard good food as a privilege, not as a right. Unlike other cultures with a tradition of caring about food and culinary expertise, the English on the whole do not have very high expectations when we go to a restaurant, or indeed of the food we prepare at home. With the exception of a handful of foodies, we don't really expect the meals we are served to be particularly good: we are pleased when the food is good, but we do not feel as deeply offended or indignant as other nations when it is mediocre. We may feel a bit annoyed about an overcooked steak or flabby chips, but it is not as though some fundamental human right has been infringed. Mediocre food is the norm.

And it's not just food. Many of my foreign informants, Americans in particular, commented on our inability to complain effectively about incompetence or failings in most other products and services. 'I get the impression,' said one frustrated American, 'that at some deep-down, fundamental level the English just don't really *expect* things to work properly – do you know what I mean?'

'Yes,' I said, 'especially compared with America. Americans expect good service, value for money, products that do what they're supposed to do – and if their expectations are not met they get pissed off and sue somebody. English people mostly don't expect particularly good service or products, and when their pessimistic assumptions are confirmed they say, "Huh! Typical!"'

'That's it exactly!' said my informant. 'My wife's English and she's *always* saying that. We go to a hotel and the food's crap and I want to complain and she says, "But hotel food's always crap – what did you expect?" We buy a new dishwasher and they don't deliver it when they said they would and she goes, "Typical!" The train's two hours late and she says, "Oh, isn't that just typical!" I'm like, "Well, yes, it is typical and it always will be because you people never *do* anything about it except sit around saying, "Typical!" to each other.'

He is right. We do tend to treat such failings as though they were acts of God, rather than instances of human incompetence. A delayed train or an undelivered dishwasher is 'typical' in the same way that rain on a bank-holiday picnic is 'typical'. These inconveniences may be frustrating, but they are normal, familiar, 'only to be expected, I suppose'. And acts of God do not require us to engage in embarrassing confrontations with other humans.

But there is more to it than that. I observed earlier that the quintessentially English 'Typical!' combines huffy indignation with a sense of passive, resigned acceptance, an acknowledgement that things are bound to go wrong, that life is full of little irritations and difficulties and that one must simply put up with it. There is a sort of grudging forbearance, a very English kind of grumpy stoicism, in 'Typical!'. But now I see that there is also almost a perverse sense of *satisfaction*. When we say, 'Typical!' we are expressing annoyance and resentment, but we are also, in some strange way, *pleased* that our gloomy predictions and cynical assumptions about the ways of the world have been proved accurate. We may have been thwarted and inconvenienced, but we have not been taken unawares. We knew this would happen, we 'could have told you' that the hotel food would be dire, the dishwasher would not be delivered, the train would be delayed, for we in our infinite wisdom know that such is the nature of hotels, deliveries and trains. We may be useless at complaining, incapable of even the most basic assertiveness, at the mercy of incompetent providers of sub-standard goods but, hey, at least we are omniscient.

That's the way things are. Cars are 'temperamental'; boilers are 'a bit unpredictable'; washing machines 'have off days'; toasters, kettles and doorknobs 'have a bit of a tendency to play up'; flush mechanisms 'only work if you pump it twice and hold it down the second time – there's a bit of a knack to it'; computers can be guaranteed to 'go on the blink' at the wrong moment and wipe out your files; you always choose the slowest queue; deliveries are always late; builders never finish a job properly; you always wait ages for a bus and then three come along at once; nothing ever works properly; something always goes wrong, and on top of that it's bound to rain.

To the English, these are established, incontrovertible facts; they are on a par with two-plus-two-is-four and the laws of physics. We start learning these mantras in our cradles, and by the time we are adults this Eeyorish view of the world is part of our nature.

Unless you fully appreciate this peculiar mindset and its implications you will never truly understand the English. Try repeating the above mantras to yourself every day for about twenty years, and you'll get the idea. Recite them in a resignedly humorous tone, adding the odd 'mustn't grumble' or 'never mind' or 'better make the best of it', and you will be well on your way to becoming English. Learn to greet every problem, from a piece of burnt toast to World War Three, with 'Typical!', somehow managing to sound simultaneously peeved, stoical and smugly omniscient, and you will qualify as a fully acculturated English person.

CULINARY CLASS CODES

Along with the lists of ingredients and calorie-counts, almost every item of English food comes with an invisible class label. (Warning: this product may contain traces of lower-middle-class substances. Warning: this product has *petit-bourgeois* associations and may not be suitable for upper-middle-class dinner parties.) Socially, you are what you eat – and when, where and in what manner you eat it, and what you call it, and how you talk about it.

The popular novelist Jilly Cooper, who has a better instinctive understanding of the English class system than most sociologists, quotes a shopkeeper who told her, 'When a woman asks for back I call her "madam"; when she asks for streaky I call her "dear".' Nowadays, in addition to these two different cuts of bacon, one would have to take into account the class semiotics of extra-lean, organic and 'locally sourced' bacon, *lardons*, *prosciutto*, *pancetta*, *speck* and Serrano ham (all favoured by the 'madam' class rather than the 'dear', but more specifically by the educated-upper-middle branch of the 'madam' class), as well as 'bacon bits', pork scratchings and bacon-flavoured crisps (all decidedly 'dear'-class foods, rarely eaten by 'madams').

English people of all classes love bacon sandwiches (the northern working classes call them 'bacon butties'), although some more pretentious members of the lower- and middle-middle classes pretend to have daintier, more refined tastes, and some affectedly health-conscious upper-middles make disapproving noises about fat, salt, cholesterol and heart disease.

Other foods that come with invisible labels warning of lower-class associations include:

- prawn cocktail (the prawns are fine, but the pink 'cocktail' sauce is lower-middle class – and, incidentally, it does not suddenly become any 'posher' if you call it 'Marie-Rose' sauce)
- egg and chips (both ingredients are relatively classless on their own, but working class if eaten together)
- pasta salad (nothing wrong with pasta *per se*, but it's 'common' if you serve it cold and mixed with mayonnaise)
- rice salad (lower class in any shape or form, but particularly with sweetcorn in it)
- tinned fruit (in syrup it's working class, in fruit juice it's still only about lower-middle)
- sliced hard-boiled eggs and/or sliced tomato in a green salad (whole cherry tomatoes are just about OK, but the class-anxious would be advised generally to keep tomatoes, sliced eggs and lettuce away from each other)
- tinned fish (all right as an ingredient in something else, such as fishcakes or a tuna-mayonnaise sandwich, but very working class if served on its own)
- chip butties (a mainly northern tradition; even if you call it a chip sandwich rather than a butty, it is about as working class as food can get).

Very secure uppers and upper-middles, with the right accents and other accoutrements, can admit to loving any or all of these foods with impunity – they will merely be regarded as charmingly eccentric. The more class-anxious should take care to pick their charming eccentricity from the very bottom of the scale (chip butties) rather than the class nearest to them (tinned fruit in juice), to avoid any possibility of a misunderstanding.

The Health-correctness Indicator

Since about the mid-1980s, health-correctness has become the main gastronomic class-divider. As a general rule, the middle social ranks are highly susceptible to the latest healthy-eating fads and fashions, while the highest and lowest classes are more robust in their views and secure in their food preferences, and apparently largely immune to the blandishments and exhortations of the middle-class health police.

Food, we are told, is the new sex. It is certainly true that food has taken over from sex as the principal concern of the 'interfering classes' – the nannyish, middle-class busybodies who have appointed themselves guardians of the nation's culinary morals, and who are currently obsessed with making the working class eat up its vegetables. We no longer have the prudish Mary Whitehouse complaining about sex and 'bad language' on television; instead, we have armies of middle-class amateur nutritionists and dieticians complaining about all the seductive advertisements for junk food, which are supposedly corrupting the nation's youth. By which they mean *working-class* youth: everyone knows that it's mainly the Darrens and Chantelles who are stuffing their faces with fatty and sugary snack foods, not the Jamies and Saskias.

Particularly not the upper-middle Saskias, many of whom may be borderline anorexic or bulimic, or restricting their diets because of imaginary food 'intolerances'. None of this seems to worry the health-correctness evangelists, who are only interested in force-feeding Darren and Chantelle their five daily portions of fruit and vegetables, and confiscating their crisps.

The upper-middle chattering classes are the most receptive and suggestible adherents of the health-correctness cults. Among the females of this class in particular, food taboos have become the primary means of defining one's social identity. You are what you *do not* eat. No chattering-class dinner party can take place without a careful advance survey of all the guests' fashionable food allergies, intolerances and ideological positions. 'I've stopped giving dinner parties,' one upper-middle-class journalist told me. 'It's become simply impossible. Catering for the odd vegetarian was OK, but now everyone's got a wheat allergy or a dairy intolerance or they're vegan or macrobiotic or Atkins or they can't eat eggs or they've got "issues" about salt or they're paranoid about E-numbers or they'll only eat organic or they're detoxing . . .'

While I have every sympathy for anyone with a genuine food allergy, the fact is that only a very small percentage of the population actually have such identifiable medical conditions – far fewer than the number who believe they are afflicted. These English chattering-class females seem to hope that, like the Princess and the Pea, their extreme sensitivities about food will somehow demonstrate that they are exquisitely delicate, highly tuned, finely bred people, not like the vulgar *hoi-polloi* who can eat anything. In these rarefied circles, you are looked down upon if you have no difficulty digesting proletarian substances such as bread and milk.

If you really cannot manage to have any modish food problems yourself, then make sure that your children have some, or at least fret noisily about the possibility that they *might* be allergic to something: 'Ooh, no! Don't give Tamara an apricot! She hasn't been tested for apricots yet. She had a bit of a reaction to strawberries, so we can't be too careful'; 'Milly can't have bottled baby food – too much sodium – so I buy organic vegetables and purée them myself . . .' Even if your children are unfashionably robust, you must take the trouble to keep up with the latest food-fear trends: fat was the big bogey in the eighties, then carbohydrates were the new fat, so high-fibre diets were out, high-protein and low-GI diets were in, and so on. On the genetic-modification debate, the official chattering-class party line is still 'two genes good, four genes bad'. As a rule of thumb, assume that there is no such thing as a 'safe' food, except possibly an organic carrot personally hand-reared by Prince Charles.

The lower- and middle-middles, taking their cue from the upper-middles (and from the *Daily Mail*, with its regulation five health-scares per day), are rapidly succumbing to the full range of 'posh' food-fears. There tends to be a bit of a satellite-delay effect, a pause in transmission of a beat or two, before the latest upper-middle food fads and taboos are taken up by the inhabitants of mock-Tudor and neo-Georgian detached houses, and then another delay before they reach the 1930s semi-detacheds. Some semi-detached suburbanites have only just realised that fat-phobia and fibre-worship are *passé*, long since superseded by carbo-phobia and protein-mania. I said in the 2004 edition of this book that once all the current carcinogens-*du-jour* and other food-fear fashions were adopted by the lower-middles, the upper-middles would have to think of some new ones, as there is no point in having a wheat intolerance if all those common people who say 'pardon' and 'serviette' have one too.

Exactly as predicted, Atkins eventually reached lower-middle suburbia and is therefore now *passé*, so although carbo-phobia is still the norm, fat-phobia has been resurrected and protein is no longer revered. Wheat intolerance has become much less popular among the upper-middles since the lower classes cottoned on and started using it as an excuse for being overweight. Also as predicted, the upper-middles are casting about for other food-fears to replace this. The latest fashionable upper-middle 'intolerance' seems to be preservatives – allowing sufferers to claim that they cannot digest, or 'have a reaction to', yet another proletarian food group: cheap, processed, packaged food, or indeed anything that isn't fresh, organic and locally sourced from a named farmer.

The working classes generally have no truck with this sort of nonsense. They have real problems, and most do not need to invent fancy food allergies to make their lives more interesting. At the opposite end of the social scale, the upper classes tend to be equally down-to-earth and sceptical about such matters. Although they may have the time and money to devote to whimsical food taboos, they do not suffer from the same insecurities about their identity as the fretful middle classes, so do not need to define themselves through conspicuous non-consumption of bread and butter. There are a few exceptions, such as the late Princess of Wales, but they tend to prove the rule by being noticeably more insecure and self-conscious than the average aristocrat.

Timing and Linguistic Indicators

Dinner/Tea/Supper Rules

What do you call your evening meal? And at what time do you eat it?

- If you call it 'tea', and eat it at around half past six, you are almost certainly working class or of working-class origin. (If you have a tendency to personalise the meal, calling it 'my tea', 'our/us tea' and 'your tea' – as in 'I must be going home for my tea', 'What's for us tea, love?' or 'Come back to mine for your tea' – you are probably northern working class.)
- If you call the evening meal 'dinner', and eat it at around seven o'clock, you are probably lower-middle or middle-middle.
- If you normally only use the term 'dinner' for much more formal evening meals, and call your informal, family evening meal 'supper' (pronounced 'suppah'), you are probably upper-middle or upper class. The timing of these meals tends to be more flexible, but a family 'supper' is generally eaten at around half past seven, while a 'dinner' would usually be later, from half past eight onwards.

To everyone but the working classes, 'tea' is a light meal taken at around four o'clock in the afternoon, and consists of tea (the drink) with cakes, scones, jam, biscuits and perhaps little sandwiches – traditionally including cucumber sandwiches – with the crusts cut off. The working classes call this 'afternoon tea', to distinguish it from the evening 'tea' that the rest call supper or dinner.

Lunch/Dinner Rules

The timing of lunch is not a class indicator, as almost everyone has lunch at around one o'clock. The only class indicator is what you call this meal: if you call it 'dinner', you are working class; everyone else, from the lower-middles upwards, calls it 'lunch'. People who say 'd-lunch' – which Jilly Cooper notes has a slightly West Indian sound to it – are trying to conceal their working-class origins, remembering at the last second not to call it 'dinner'. (I've noticed that they may also say 't-dinner' – which confusingly sounds a bit Yorkshire – for the evening meal, just stopping themselves from calling it 'tea'.) Whatever their class, and whatever they may call it, the English do not take the middle-of-the-day meal at all seriously: most make do with a sandwich or some other quick, easy, hand-held meal.

The long, lavish, boozy 'business lunch' is nowadays somewhat frowned upon (more of that American-inspired puritanical health-correctness), which is a great shame, as it was based on very sound anthropological and psychological principles. The giving and sharing of food is universally known to be one of the most effective forms of human social bonding. Anthropologists even have a special jargon-word for it: 'commensality'. In all cultures, the offering and acceptance of such hospitality constitutes at the very least a non-aggression pact between the parties – you do not 'break bread' with your enemies – and at best a significant move towards cementing friendships and alliances. And it is even more effective if the social lubricant of alcohol is involved.

You would think that the English, with our desperate need for social 'props and facilitators', not to mention ways of detracting from the inevitable awkwardness of money-talk, would seize upon and embrace this tried-and-tested tradition. And, indeed, I am convinced that the current misguided disdain for the business lunch is, to borrow a term from the environmentalists, 'unsustainable', and will prove to be a temporary aberration. It does, however, provide further evidence to support my argument that the English generally do not take food seriously, and in particular that we grossly underestimate the social importance of sharing food, of eating together – something most other cultures seem to grasp instinctively.

In this respect, the middle-class 'foodies' are often no more enlightened than the rest of us. Their obsessive focus on the food itself – the fruity virginity of the cold-pressed olive oil, the gooey ripeness of the unpasteurised Brie de Meaux – is often curiously devoid of the human warmth and intimacy that should be associated with its consumption. They claim to understand this social dimension, waxing lyrical and misty-eyed about the conviviality of mealtimes in Provence and

Tuscany, but they have an unfortunate tendency to judge their English friends' dinner parties, and restaurant lunches with business contacts, on the quality of the cooking rather than the friendliness of the atmosphere. 'Well, the Joneses are very nice people and all that but, *really*, they have no *idea* – overcooked pasta, boiled-to-death vegetables, and God knows *what* that chicken thing was supposed to be . . .' Their patronising and sneering sometimes makes one long for the old, pre-foodie-revolution days, when the higher classes considered it vulgar to make any comment at all on the food they were served, and the lower classes defined a good meal as a filling one.

Breakfast Rules – and Tea Beliefs

The traditional English breakfast – tea, toast, marmalade, eggs, bacon, sausages, tomatoes, mushrooms, etc. – is both good and filling, and breakfast is the only aspect of English cooking that is frequently and enthusiastically praised by foreigners. Few of us eat this 'full English breakfast' regularly, however: foreign tourists staying in hotels get far more traditional breakfasts than we natives ever enjoy at home.

The tradition is maintained more at the top and bottom of the social scale than among the middle ranks. Some members of the upper class and aristocracy still have proper English breakfasts in their country houses, and some working-class people (mostly males) still believe in starting the day with a 'cooked breakfast' of bacon, eggs, sausages, baked beans, fried bread, toast and so on.

This feast may often be eaten in a 'caff' rather than at home, and is washed down with industrial quantities of strong, brick-coloured, sweet, milky tea. Lower-middles and middle-middles drink a paler, 'posher' version, Twining's English Breakfast, say, rather than PG Tips. The upper-middle and upper classes drink weak, dishwater-coloured, unsweetened Earl Grey. Taking sugar in your tea is regarded by many as an infallible lower-class indicator: even one spoonful is a bit suspect (unless you were born before about 1955); more than one and you are lower-middle at best; more than two and you are definitely working class. Putting the milk into the cup first is also a lower-class habit, as is over-vigorous, noisy stirring. Some pretentious middles and upper-middles make an ostentatious point of drinking Lapsang Souchong, without milk or sugar, as this is about as far removed from working-class tea as they can get. More honest (or less class-anxious) upper-middles and uppers often admit to a secret liking for the strong, rust-coloured 'builders' tea'. How snooty you are about 'builders' tea', and how careful you are to avoid it, is quite a good class-anxiety test.

Tea is still believed, by English people of all classes, to have miraculous properties. A cup of tea can cure, or at least significantly alleviate, almost all minor physical ailments and indispositions, from a headache to a scraped knee. Tea is also an essential remedy for all social and psychological ills, from a bruised ego to the trauma of a divorce or bereavement. This magical drink can be used equally effectively as a sedative or stimulant, to calm and soothe or to revive and invigorate. Whatever your mental or physical state, what you need is 'a nice cup of tea'.

Perhaps most importantly, tea-making is the perfect displacement activity: whenever the English feel awkward or uncomfortable in a social situation (that is, almost all of the time), they make tea. It's a universal rule: when in doubt, put the kettle on. Visitors arrive; we have our usual difficulties over greeting protocol. We say, 'I'll just put the kettle on.' There is one of those uneasy lulls in the conversation, and we've run out of weather-speak. We say, 'Now, who'd like more tea? I'll just go and put the kettle on.' A business meeting might involve having to talk about money. We postpone the uncomfortable bit by making sure everyone has tea. A bad accident – people are injured and in shock: tea is needed. 'I'll put the kettle on.' War breaks out – a nuclear attack is imminent. 'I'll put the kettle on.'[108]

You get the idea. We are rather fond of tea.

We are also very partial to toast. Toast is a breakfast staple, and an all-purpose, anytime comfort food. What tea alone does not cure,

108. I wasn't joking with those last two scenarios – at the sites of the 7/7 bombings in 2005 (when terrorist suicide-bombers attacked the London transport system, blowing up a bus and Underground trains) concerned local shopkeepers rushed out to provide aid and comfort to the injured, shocked and walking wounded. What did they bring? Cups of tea, of course.

tea and toast surely will. The 'toast rack' is a peculiarly English object. My father, who lives in America and has become somewhat American in his tastes and habits, calls it a 'toast cooler' and claims that its sole function is to ensure that one's toast gets stone cold as quickly as possible. English supporters of the toast rack would argue that it keeps toast dry and crisp, that separating the slices and standing them upright stops them becoming soggy, which is what happens to American toast, served piled up hugger-mugger in a humid, perspiring stack on the plate, sometimes even wrapped in a napkin to retain yet more moisture. The English would rather have their toast cool and dry than warm and damp. American toast lacks reserve and dignity: it is too sweaty and indiscreet and emotional.

But toast is not much use as a class indicator: everybody likes toast. Some of the higher social ranks do have a bit of a prejudice against packaged sliced bread, but only the very class-anxious will go to great lengths to avoid it. What you choose to spread on your toast, however, can provide clues to your social position. Margarine and most other butter-substitute 'spreads' are regarded as decidedly 'common' by the middle and upper classes, who use butter (unless they are on a diet or have a dairy intolerance, that is). Marmalade is universally popular, but the dark, thick-cut Oxford or Dundee marmalade is favoured by the higher echelons, while the lower ranks generally prefer the lighter-coloured, thin-cut brands such as Golden Shred.

The unwritten class rules about jam are much the same: the darker the colour and the bigger the lumps of fruit, the more socially elevated the jam. Some class-anxious middles and upper-middles secretly prefer the paler, smoother, low-class marmalades and jams, but feel obliged to buy the socially superior chunky ones. Home-made jam or marmalade is favoured by the higher social ranks, who often labour the point by making it even more lumpy than the shop-bought varieties, and sometimes also watery (not enough pectin) and sharp (not enough sugar). Only the lower classes – older-generation lower-middles in particular – try to sound posh by calling jam 'preserves'.

Table Manners and 'Material Culture' Indicators

Table Manners

English table manners, across all classes, have deteriorated somewhat but are still, as the humorist George Mikes acknowledges, fairly decent. The genuinely important aspects of eating etiquette – showing consideration for others; not being selfish or greedy; general fairness, politeness and sociability – are known to, if not always strictly observed by, most English people of all social classes. No class has a monopoly on either good or bad eating behaviour.

Although proper 'family meals' may nowadays occur on average only once a week, rather than every day, most English children of all classes are still brought up to say 'please' and 'thank you' when asking for and being given food, and most adults are also reasonably polite. We all know that we should ask for things rather than just grabbing them; not serve ourselves huge helpings leaving insufficient food for the others; wait until everyone has been served before starting to eat, unless urged, 'Please start, or it will go cold'; not take the last piece of anything without asking if anyone else wants it; not talk with our mouths full; not cram vast, unsightly amounts of food into our mouths or masticate noisily; take part in the conversation without monopolising or dominating it; and so on.

When eating at a restaurant, we know that in addition to the above we should be polite to the waiters and, in particular, never, ever try to summon a waiter by snapping our fingers or bellowing across the room. The correct procedure is to lean back in your chair with an expectant look, endeavour to make eye contact, then perform a quick eyebrow-lift/chin-lift. Raising a hand is permissible, as is a quiet 'Excuse me?' (or preferably, if irrationally, 'Er, sorry?') if the waiter is nearby and has not noticed you, but this should not be done in an imperious manner. We know that orders should be phrased as requests, with the usual full complement of pleases and thank-yous. We know that it is unseemly to make a fuss or a scene or in any way draw attention to oneself when eating in public. Making any sort of fuss about money is especially distasteful, and ostentatious displays of wealth are as bad as conspicuous meanness. People who insist on calculating in detail exactly who had what when it comes to dividing up the bill are despised, not just because they are miserly, but also because such discussions involve a prolonged breach of the money-talk taboo, which is hugely embarrassing for everyone.

We may not abide by all of these codes, but we know the rules. If you ask English people about 'table manners', they may assume that you mean prissy, pointless etiquette about which fork to use, but if you start a conversation about what is and isn't acceptable when eating with other people, what they were taught and what they teach their children, these rather more basic, universal, classless courtesies will emerge. Many of them, if you look closely, are essentially about that perennial English preoccupation: fairness.

Some lower-class parents – particularly 'respectable upper-working' and lower-middle mothers – tend to be, if anything, more strict on these basic points than some middle-middle and upper-middle parents, who are influenced by 'child-centred' parenting books that frown upon rules and regulations, and encourage unfettered self-expression.

Those at the top of the social scale, as so often seems to be the case, have more in common with the working classes than with the middle ranks: upper-class mothers tend to be quite strict on basic good eating manners, although upper-class men do not necessarily practise what their wives and nannies preach to their children. Some aristocratic males are notorious for their appalling table manners, in this trait resembling some lower-working/underclass males, who also do not care about other people's opinion of them.

But these are just minor and patchy variations: on the whole, the basic courtesy rules are fairly classless. It is only when you look beyond these essential courtesies that the significant class divisions start to appear. The more arcane, esoteric rules of table etiquette – the peas-on-the-back-of-the-fork minutiae for which the English are famous and widely ridiculed – tend to be the preserve of the higher social classes. Indeed, one could be forgiven for suspecting that the only function of such rules is to distinguish these classes from the lower ones, as in most cases it is hard to see what other purpose they might serve.

'Material Culture' Indicators

Many of these class-indicator rules concern the use of objects and implements – knives, forks, spoons, glasses, bowls, plates and so on. Which is where 'material culture' comes in. I remember a conversation I had during my first week at Cambridge with a rather earnest and self-important graduate student in the coffee room of the archaeology and anthropology library. He told me he was writing his thesis on 'material culture' in something or other. 'What do you mean by "material culture"?' I asked.

'Well, now,' he replied, 'let me explain.' He took a deep breath, and launched into a long, involved, jargon-ridden disquisition. I listened attentively, for about twenty minutes.

When he had finished his lecture, I said, 'Oh, I see. You mean "things". Pots and knives and clothes and so on. Things.' He was most put out, although he agreed huffily that, yes, I could put it that way if I wanted to be simplistic. I've been longing for an excuse to use the gloriously pompous term 'material culture' ever since, but actually what I mean is just 'things'.[109]

The Knife-holding Rule

The bossy *Debrett's* etiquette guide tries hard to pretend that there is some rational point to all the minutiae of English material-culture table etiquette, that it is all about consideration for others, but I find it difficult to see how the precise positioning of your fingers on your knife – whether the handle goes under your palm (correct) or, like a pencil, rests between the base of your thumb and your index finger

---

109. Although I didn't know it at the time, I was not alone in preferring this 'simplistic' term: one of the classic texts in material culture is Arjun Appadurai's edited volume *The Social Life of Things*, and more recently the gloriously *un*-pompous Danny Miller, professor of material culture at University College London, has written a splendid book about this subject, even more unpretentiously entitled *Stuff*.

(incorrect) – could in any way affect your dinner companions' enjoyment of their meal. And yet *Debrett's* insists that 'on no account' should you ever hold your knife like a pencil. The only possible effect your pencil-method could have on your fellow diners would be to activate their class-radar bleepers and alert them to your inferior social status. So one must assume that, for the class-conscious English, this is in itself a good enough reason not to do it.

Forks and the Pea-eating Rules

The same goes for the prongs of your fork. When the fork is being held in your left hand and used in conjunction with a knife or spoon, the prongs of the fork should always point downwards, not upwards. 'Well-brought-up' English people must therefore eat peas by spearing two or three peas with the downturned prongs of their fork, using their knife to hold the peas still while spearing, then pushing a few more peas on to the convex back of the fork with their knife, using the speared peas on the prongs as a sort of little ledge to help stop the slightly squashed, pushed peas on the back of the fork from sliding straight off. It is actually much easier than it sounds, and, when one describes the procedure in proper detail, marginally less idiotic than all the jokes about English pea-eating would suggest. Although it must be said that the lower-class pea-eating methods – turning the fork over and using the knife to push a larger quantity of peas onto the concave side of the fork, or even abandoning the knife, transferring the fork to your right hand, and shovelling up peas with it as though it were a spoon – are clearly rather more sensible, or at least more ergonomic, in that more peas per forkful are transported from plate to mouth. The socially superior spear-and-squash system carries no more than about eight peas at a time, at best, while the prongs-up, scoop-and-shovel technique can hold up to about thirteen, by my calculations – depending on the size of the fork, and the size of the peas, of course. (I really should get a life.)

There is obviously, then, no practical reason for *Debrett's* and other etiquette guides to insist on the prongs-down method of pea-eating. And again, it is hard to see how adopting the lower-class prongs-up practice could possibly have any adverse effects on one's eating companions, so the consideration-for-others argument doesn't wash either. We are forced to conclude that, like the knife-holding rule, the pea-eating rule is a class indicator and nothing more.

In recent years, the 'uncouth', prongs-up style of pea-eating has spread somewhat further up the social scale, perhaps because of increasing American influences, to the extent that the majority of lower-middle and middle-middle English people now eat their peas in this fashion (it used to be just those of working-class origin, inadvertently revealing their roots). Most upper-middles and uppers, however, resolutely continue to spear and squash.

The 'Small/Slow Is Beautiful' Principle

And it's not just peas. I chose peas as an example because people poke fun at English pea-eating – and because peas are somehow intrinsically more amusing than other foods – but our codes of class-indicator table etiquette prescribe the prongs-down, spear-and-squash method for *all* eating that is done with a knife and fork. And as almost all eating is supposed to be done with both implements, almost all foods must be speared and/or squashed onto the backs of forks. Only a limited number of specified foods – first courses and salads, for example, or spaghetti or shepherd's pie – may be eaten with the fork alone, in the right hand, with the prongs pointing upwards.

When using both knife and fork, only the lower classes adopt the American system of first cutting up all or most of the food, then putting down the knife and shovelling up the food with the fork alone. The 'correct' – or, rather, socially superior – approach is to cut up and eat your meat and other foods one small piece at a time, each time spearing and squashing a little selection of food on to the prongs and the back of your fork.

The same 'small is beautiful' and 'slow is beautiful' principles seem to be at the root of many of the class-indicator rules, or at any rate a large proportion of these rules appear to be designed to ensure that only small amounts of food are transferred from plate to mouth at a time, with clear pauses between mouthfuls for cutting, spearing and so on. The cut-spear-squash system for peas, meat and pretty much everything else on your plate is the main example, but these principles extend to other foods as well.

Take bread, for example. The correct ('posh') way to eat anything involving bread – rolls and butter, pâté and toast, breakfast toast and marmalade – is to break off (not cut off) a bite-sized piece of the bread or toast, spread butter/pâté/marmalade onto just that small piece, eat it in one small bite, then repeat the procedure with another small piece. It is considered vulgar to spread butter or whatever across the whole slice of toast or half-roll, as though you were making a batch of sandwiches for a picnic, and then bite into it. Biscuits or crackers served with cheese must be eaten in the same way as bread or toast, breaking off and spreading one small, bite-sized piece at a time.

With fish on the bone, the 'small/slow is beautiful' principle requires that we fillet the fish one small bit at a time, lifting each mouthful away from the bone, eating it, then filleting off the next mouthful. Grapes must be broken off in a small bunch, and eaten one at a time, not in handfuls. At the table, apples and other fruit are peeled, quartered and eaten one segment at a time, not bitten into whole. Bananas must not be eaten 'monkey style' but should be peeled and cut into discs, which are then eaten one at a time. And so on.

Do you see the recurring small-and-slow pattern here? Class-indicator rules are not about eating with any degree of ease, speed, efficiency or practicality. Quite the opposite: they are designed to slow us down, to make things deliberately difficult, to ensure that we eat the smallest possible mouthfuls in the most time-consuming, laborious manner. Now that we've identified the pattern and the principle behind it, the purpose becomes clear. What it all boils down to is not appearing to be greedy and, more specifically, not appearing to give food too high a priority. Greed of any sort is a breach of the all-important fair-play rule. Letting one's desire for food take priority over making conversation with one's companions involves giving physical pleasure or gratification a higher value than words. In polite society, this is frowned upon as un-English and highly embarrassing. Over-eagerness about anything is undignified;

over-eagerness about food is disgusting and even somehow faintly obscene. Eating small mouthfuls, with plenty of pauses in between them, shows a more restrained, unemotional, English approach to food.

Napkin Rings and Other Horrors

Napkins are useful and versatile objects – as class indicators, that is. We have already seen that to call them 'serviettes' is a grave social solecism – one of the 'seven deadly sins' unmistakably signalling lower-class origins. But there are many other ways in which napkins can set off English class-radar bleepers, including, in chronological order from the beginning to the end of a meal:

- setting the table with napkins folded into over-elaborate, origami-like shapes (higher-class people just fold them simply)
- standing folded napkins upright in glasses (they should be placed either on or next to the plates)
- tucking one's napkin into waistband or collar (it should be left loose on the lap)
- using one's napkin to scrub or wipe vigorously at one's mouth (gentle dabbing is correct)
- folding one's napkin carefully at the end of the meal (it should be left carelessly crumpled on the table)
- or, even worse, putting rolled-up napkins into napkin rings (only people who say 'serviette' use napkin rings).

The first two of these napkin-sins are based on the principle that over-fussy, 'genteel' daintiness is a lower-middle-class trait. Inelegant use of the napkin – tucking and scrubbing – is working class. The last two napkin-sins are abhorrent because they indicate that the napkins will be used again without being washed. Higher-class people would rather be given a paper napkin than a used cotton or linen one. The upper-middle classes joke about 'the sort of people who use napkin rings' – meaning lower/middle-middles who think they are being elegant and dainty, but are in fact being rather grubby.

While there is some point to these napkin rules (at least, the objection to reusing napkins strikes me as perfectly reasonable), the prejudice against fish knives is harder to justify. At one time, quite a number of middle-class and even upper-class English people used special knives (and forks) for eating fish. Some may have regarded this practice as a bit over-dainty and pretentious, but the outright taboo seems to date from the publication of John Betjeman's 'How to Get On in Society', in which he lampoons the affectations and pretensions of a lower-middle-class housewife preparing for a dinner party. The poem begins:

> Phone for the fish knives, Norman
> As cook is a little unnerved;
> You kiddies have crumpled the serviettes
> And I must have things daintily served.

Fish knives, possibly always a bit suspect, were from that moment irrevocably associated with people who say 'pardon' and 'serviette' and 'toilet' – and use napkin rings. Now, fish knives are also seen as hopelessly old-fashioned, and are probably only used by lower/middle-middle people of older generations. Steak knives are regarded as equally suburban, as are doilies, pastry-forks, salt-and-pepper 'cruets', drink mats/coasters and anything gold.

You would have thought that finger bowls – little bowls of tepid water for washing your fingers when eating food by hand – would come into the same category of precious, twee, affected, suburban daintiness, but for some reason they are acceptable, and are still seen at upper-middle and upper-class dinners. There is very little logic to any of this. Tales are often told of ignorant lower-class guests drinking from finger bowls – and of ultra-polite hosts then drinking from the bowls themselves, so as not to embarrass the guests by drawing attention to their error. You are supposed to dip your fingers briefly in the finger bowl, then pat them gently dry with your napkin – not wash and scrub and rub as though it were a bathroom sink, unless you want to activate your hosts' class-radar systems.

Port-passing Rules

Another way you can set off English class-radar bleepers is to pass the port the wrong way. Port is served at the end of a dinner – sometimes, among the upper classes, to men only, as the women follow the old-fashioned practice of 'withdrawing' to another room to drink coffee and talk girl-talk, leaving the men to their male bonding. Port must always travel round the table clockwise (if it were to go anticlockwise, the world would end), so you must always pass the bottle or decanter to your left.

Even if you somehow miss your turn, you must *never* ask for the port to be passed back to you, as this would mean port travelling in the wrong direction, which would be a disaster. Either wait for it to come all the way round again, or pass your glass along to the left to catch up with the port and be filled for you. Your glass can then be passed back to you without danger, as port can travel anti-clockwise if it is in a glass: the taboo on passing to the right only applies to port in bottles and decanters.

No one has the slightest idea why clockwise port-passing is so important. The rule serves no discernible purpose, other than to cause embarrassment to those who are not aware of it, and, presumably, a peculiarly English sense of smug self-satisfaction among those who are.

A number of kind readers of the 2004 edition of this book wrote to me helpfully explaining that clockwise port-passing is in fact an application of the 'fairness' principle: passing the port round the table in only one direction ensures that everyone gets to pour themselves a glass of port – whereas if it were just passed around randomly, some people might end up missing out. Good point. I can see the logic of passing the port in one direction, in an orderly fashion, to ensure fairness. This makes sense and sounds typically English. It also makes sense to continue passing the port in the same direction on its second or third 'circuits' of the table, so that those whose glasses are most likely to be empty get their refills first.

The fairness principle does not explain, however, why that direction must absolutely, always, as a sacred rule, be clockwise. At any given dinner, consistently passing the port anti-clockwise would have exactly the same scrupulously fair result.

So, the 'one direction' rule may well be all about fairness, but the 'clockwise' rule, the strict taboo on ever passing port to the right, is still useful only as a class-indicator. Our port-passing customs thus somehow manage to combine courteous fairness with snobby class-obsession. How very English.

THE MEANING OF CHIPS

The SIRC research report on *The Meaning of Chips* dealt with a food issue of great national importance. Ninety per cent of us are chip eaters, the majority indulging at least once a week, and the chip is a vital part of English heritage, but little was known, until our ground-breaking study, about our relationship with the chip, its role in our social interactions, and its place in the cultural *Zeitgeist*.

Chips, Patriotism and English Empiricism

Although chips were invented in Belgium, and are popular – as French fries (or just fries) in America, and as *frites*, *patate fritte*, *patatas fritas*, etc., in many other parts of the world – we found that English people tend to think of them as British or, rather more specifically, English. 'Fish and chips' is still regarded as the English national dish. The English are not normally inclined to be either patriotic or passionate about food but we found that they could be surprisingly patriotic and enthusiastic about the humble chip.

'The chip is down to earth,' explained one of our discussion-group participants. 'It's basic, it's simple in a good way, which is why we like the chip. We have that quality and it's a good quality . . . This is what we are – no faffing about.' It hadn't occurred to me that a chunk of fried potato could so eloquently express the earthy empiricism and no-nonsense realism that I had tentatively identified as defining characteristics of Englishness, so I was grateful to him for this insight.

Chip-sharing Rules and Sociability

Chips are also an important social facilitator. This is the only English food that actually lends itself to sharing (or at least the only hot, cooked, mealtime food – I'm not counting snack-foods such as crisps and nuts) and that the unwritten rules allow us to share. When we are eating chips, you will often see the English behaving in a very sociable, intimate, un-English manner: all pitching in messily to eat with our fingers off the same plate or out of the same bag, pinching chips off each other's plates – and even feeding chips to each other. Even with foods that are clearly supposed to be shared, such as Indian food, you may still see English groups sticking to the practice of each person ordering and eating his or her own dish. But chips seem to promote sociability, which for many English people is part of their attraction – perhaps because we have a greater need than other nations for props and facilitators that encourage 'commensality'.

FOOD RULES AND ENGLISHNESS

The food rules have revealed yet more symptoms of the English social dis-ease. It seems that an awful lot of irrational and apparently inexplicable aspects of English behaviour – such as our silent, apologetic and obnoxious approaches to complaining – are traceable to this unfortunate affliction.

Looking closely at food-related behaviour has also helped us to refine our analysis of the 'Typical!' rule and what it tells us about Englishness. More than just 'grumpy stoicism', this rule is a reflection of our cynically low expectations of the world, our chronic pessimism, our assumption that it is in the nature of things to go wrong and thwart us and generally be disappointing. Perhaps even more important is the discovery of our perverse sense of satisfaction, even pleasure, at seeing our gloomy predictions fulfilled. Understanding this peculiar, Eeyorish mindset will, I think, prove critical to our understanding of Englishness. It is worth noting that the theme of English empiricism also came up again, in the somewhat unlikely context of our relationship with the chip.

The class rules in this chapter expose, perhaps even more than previous ones, the truly mind-boggling silliness of the English class system. I mean, really. How many peas can dance on the back of a fork? I'm ashamed to write this stuff. I'm ashamed to *know* this stuff, even though it is my job to observe and describe and try to understand it. Yes, I know that every human society has 'a system of social status and methods of indicating it', but the English do seem to take this to the most utterly ludicrous extremes.

The 'small/slow is beautiful' principle is rather less silly than the other class-related rules. Although it does serve as a class indicator, it also reflects important English ideals such as courtesy and fair play, and highlights our appreciation of restraint and distaste for greedy selfishness. There is something to be said for giving pleasant conversation priority over stuffing one's face.

The Meaning of Chips rules indicate that our apparent lack of passion about food, and perhaps our apathy in other areas as well, such as patriotism, may be more a matter of observing anti-earnestness rules than the natural indifference to which they are often attributed. We *can* be emotional and even sometimes quite passionate about things. Well, about chips, anyway. It is just that we normally suppress these impulses, in our efforts to comply with the earnestness taboo. Is our much-ridiculed lack of passion about sex part of the same syndrome? Are English humour rules stronger than our sex-drive? I'll try to find out in the next chapter.

RULES OF SEX

'How's the Englishness book going? What chapter are you working on?'

'The one about sex.'

'So, that'll be twenty blank pages, then?'

THE KNEE-JERK HUMOUR RULE

I've lost count of the number of times I heard this response – or others like it, such as: 'That'll be a short chapter!'; 'Oh, that won't take long, then!'; 'Oh, that's easy: "No Sex Please, We're British!"'; 'But we don't have sex, we have hot water-bottles!'; 'Lie back and think of England, you mean?'; 'Will you explain the mystery of how the English manage to reproduce?' And these were all from *English* friends and informants. Foreigners occasionally made similar jokes, but the English almost invariably did so. Clearly, the notion that the English do not have much sex, or have a laughably low sex-drive, is widely accepted as fact – even, indeed especially, among the English themselves.

Or is it? Do we really believe in the popular international stereotype of the passionless, reserved, sexually naïve, amorously challenged English? The bloke who would really rather be watching football, and his wife who would prefer a nice cup of tea? And, moving up the social scale, the awkward, tongue-tied, timid, public-schoolboy character, and his equally clueless horsey female counterpart who cannot stop giggling? Is this really how we see ourselves? Is this really how we are?

In purely factual, quantitative terms, our sexless image is

inaccurate. The English are human, and sex is naturally as important to us as to any other members of the species. Our sexually incompetent reputation is not borne out by the facts and figures, which suggest that we manage to copulate and reproduce just like the rest of the world. If anything, we start younger: the English have the highest rates of teenage sexual activity in the industrialised world, with 86 per cent of unmarried girls sexually active by the age of nineteen (the US comes a poor second, with 75 per cent). There are also plenty of other nations that are far more prudish and repressive about sex than the English, and where the English are regarded as dangerously permissive. Our censorship laws may be stricter than many other European countries', and our politicians more likely to be forced to resign over what some other Europeans would consider minor sexual peccadilloes, but in most respects, by international standards, we are fairly liberal.

Stereotypes do not come out of thin air, however, and one as widely recognised and acknowledged as the unsexy English must surely have at least some basis in reality. Sex may be a natural, instinctive, universal human activity, which the English must perform like everyone else – but it is also a social activity, involving emotional engagement with other humans, contact, intimacy, and so on, which we have already established are not exactly our strong points. Still, our apparent readiness to accept this decidedly unflattering stereotype (we are much more patriotically defensive about our weather than about our sexual prowess) could be seen as somewhat bizarre, and requires explanation.

Looking back at my research notes, I find that I was continually struck by the difficulty of having any sort of sensible conversation about sex with English informants. 'The English simply cannot talk about sex without making a joke of it,' I complained in my notebook, 'usually the same joke: if one more person offers to "help me with my research" for the sex chapter, I'm going to scream.' The mere mention of the word 'sex' seems automatically to trigger a quip or witticism or, among the less articulate, a crude nudge-nudge remark, a bit of *Carry-On*-style oohing and face-pulling, or at the very least a snigger. This is more than a rule: it is an involuntary, unthinking reflex – a knee-jerk response. Mention sex, and the English humour reflex kicks in. And we all know that self-deprecating jokes are the most effective, the most widely appreciated form of humour. The 'blank pages' quips about my sex chapter were thus not necessarily a sign that we fully accept the sexually-challenged-English stereotype, but just a typically English reaction to the word 'sex'.

Why do we find sex so funny? We don't, not really: it's just that humour is our standard way of dealing with anything that makes us feel uncomfortable or embarrassed. This is surely one of the Ten Commandments of Englishness: when in doubt, joke. Yes, other nations joke about sex, but none, in my experience or to my knowledge, does so with the same tedious knee-jerk predictability as the English. In other parts of the world, sex may be regarded as a sin, an art form, a healthy leisure activity, a commodity, a political issue and/ or a problem requiring years of therapy and umpteen self-help 'relationship' books. In England, it is a joke.

FLIRTING RULES

There is nearly always a tiny grain of truth in stereotypes of national character, and the notion that the English are sexually inhibited is, I'm afraid, quite accurate. We may be as competent and, indeed, as passionate as anyone else, once we actually get into bed, but the process of getting there is often awkward and inept.

The idea that our inhibitions stem from lack of interest in sex, however, is mistaken. We may find the subject embarrassing, but the English have a keen interest in sex. In particular, thanks to the forbidden-fruit effect of our privacy rules, we have a prurient, insatiable fascination with other people's sex lives, only partially assuaged by a constant stream of sex scandals and kiss-and-tell stories in our tabloid newspapers and on the internet.

Our interest in our own sex lives ensures that we do our best to overcome our inhibitions, and if we are somewhat inept at flirtation, it is certainly not for want of practice. I have conducted two big studies on flirting among the English and, in the most recent, only one per cent of survey respondents – aged eighteen to forty – said that they 'never flirted', and over a third had flirted with someone 'today' or 'within the past week'. You would, of course, get much the same result in any other country, as flirting is a 'human universal', a basic instinct, without which our species would have become extinct a long time ago. If some evolutionary psychologists are to be believed, flirting may even be the foundation of civilisation as we know it. They argue that the large human brain – our complex language, superior intelligence, culture, everything that distinguishes us from animals – is our equivalent of the peacock's tail: a courtship device evolved to attract and retain sexual partners. If this theory – which I jokingly call the 'chat-up theory of human evolution' – is correct, human achievements in everything from art to literature to rocket science may be merely a side effect of the essential ability to charm.

The idea of NASA, *Hamlet* and the *Mona Lisa* as accidental by-products of primeval chat-ups might seem somewhat far-fetched, but it is clear that evolution favours flirts. The most skilful charmers among our distant ancestors were the most likely to attract mates and pass on their charming genes. We are descended from a long line of successful flirts, and the flirting instinct is hard-wired into our brains. Even when modern humans are not engaged in mate-selection, we still flirt: all of us practise two types of flirting, which for shorthand I call 'flirting with intent' (flirting designed to lead to mating, and possibly pair-bonding) and 'recreational flirting' (flirting for fun, for other social reasons, or perhaps just for practice). *Homo sapiens* is, by nature, a compulsive flirt.

So, the English are genetically programmed to flirt, just like everyone else, and we probably do about as much of it as everyone else. It's just that we do not do it with the same degree of skill, ease or assurance. Or, rather, about 50 per cent of us are noticeably deficient in these qualities. If you look more closely at the stereotype of the sexually challenged English, it is the English *male* who is most often singled out for criticism and ridicule in this department. A few of the standard jokes and quips allude to the supposed frigidity or ignorance of the English female, but the vast majority are about the alleged impotence, indifference or incompetence of English males. These failings of English men are often assumed to account for any sexual inadequacies or shortcomings among their frustrated women-folk. In the early eighteenth century, a Swiss commentator[110] described English women as 'little spoilt by the attentions of men who give but a small part of their time to them. Indeed most men prefer wine and gaming to women, in this they are more to blame as women are much better than the wine in England.' Many of my own foreign informants made much the same kind of remarks, although they substituted beer for wine, and did not complain about the quality of English beer.

The first two of these charges against English males – impotence and indifference – are unfounded and unfair; they are not based on fact or direct observation, but mainly on an impression created by the third defect of which English men stand accused: incompetence in the art of seduction. 'Englishmen seem little made for gallantry,' observed our Swiss critic, 'they know no mean between complete familiarity and respectful silence.' The average English male may be highly sexed, but he is not, it must be said, an accomplished flirt. He is not at his best when confronted with what one of my male informants called 'a female person of the opposite species'.[111] He is usually either reticent, tongue-tied and awkward, or, at worst, boorish, crass and clumsy.[112] In the belief that it will help him to shed his inhibitions, he tends to consume large quantities of alcohol: this merely results in a shift from awkward, tongue-tied reticence to crass, clumsy boorishness. From the perspective of the unfortunate

110. B. L. de Muralt in *Lettres sur les Anglais*.

111. Harry Mount puts this down to 'schools that were largely segregated until the twentieth century' and the long-standing English male tradition of spending their evenings drinking in pubs with other men instead of going home to their wives and families. Trouble is, the gender-segregated schools argument would apply equally to almost all other European countries, and the Englishman's preference for male-bonding sessions in the pub over wife and family is a *choice*, which makes this argument somewhat circular.

112. Some observers have puzzled over the fact that English males have nonetheless managed to produce some of the finest love poetry in the world. I see no contradiction: fine love poetry tends to be written when the object of one's affections is at a safe distance; also it often reflects a love of words more than a love of women, and the Englishman's love of words has never been in question.

English female, this is not much of an improvement – unless her own judgement is severely impaired, as it often is, by a similar quantity of alcohol, in which case chat-up lines such as 'Er, fancy a shag?' may seem like the height of wit and eloquence.

And there, in a nutshell, or rather a bottle, is the answer to the mystery of how the English manage to reproduce. All right, I'm exaggerating – but only a little. The role of alcohol in the passing on of English DNA should not be underestimated.

The SAS Test

There are other factors, of course. As part of a public-spirited effort to help the English improve their seduction skills, I once devised a test, based on extensive field research, to locate the best 'flirting zones' – the social settings most conducive to enjoyable and successful flirtation in this culture; I called it the 'SAS test'. SAS stands for Sociability (by which I mean specifically the acceptability and ease of initiating conversation with strangers), Alcohol (an essential flirting aid among the inhibited English) and Shared-interest (environments in which people have interests in common, or a shared focus – settings likely to have the kind of props and facilitators that help the English to overcome their social dis-ease). The results of my application of this test provide some insights into English flirting habits and the unwritten rules of mate-seeking in English culture.

Pubs

Pubs and bars, which seem at first glance like prime candidates, actually only pass two elements of the test – Sociability and Alcohol – failing on 'Shared interest'. In English pubs and bars, striking up a conversation with an attractive stranger is permitted by the unwritten rules (although subject to certain restrictions and caveats), but the lack of an obvious common interest means that one still has to struggle to think of something to talk *about*. Generic English etiquette provides a universally acceptable subject in the weather, but without a shared focus of interest, the introductory process still requires considerable effort.

Having said that, one survey showed that 27 per cent of us first met our current partner in a pub, so it is clearly an effort we are prepared to make. My own observation studies and interviews with English pubgoers, however, indicate that the majority of these pairings were probably not the result of someone approaching a complete stranger, cold, at the bar counter, but rather of people being introduced, albeit informally, by friends or acquaintances, the encounter happening to take place in the pub because that is where the English spend a great deal of their time and do much of their socialising.

Clubbers and the 'No Sex Please, We're Too Cool' Rule

Night-clubs score somewhat higher on the Shared-interest factor than pubs and bars, as clubbers usually share a common interest in music. In any case, the problem of initiating conversation is reduced by the volume at which the music is played, which restricts verbal communication to a few monosyllabic shouted exchanges, allowing clubbers to flirt mainly through non-verbal channels. With very high scores on Sociability and Alcohol, night-clubs should in theory be near the top of my English flirt-zone league table. And most of them are, but there is a curious and apparently perverse unwritten rule among a significant minority of young English clubbers whereby dancing – and by extension clubbing in general – is regarded as an asexual activity. At least, this is true of the many clubbers who favour EDM (electronic dance music – the various forms of house, trance, etc., mentioned in Dress Codes, page 398). Their focus is on group bonding, and the euphoric, almost transcendental experience of becoming one with the music and the crowd (which sounds like a version of what anthropologists call 'communitas' or 'collective effervescence' – an intense, intimate, liberating kind of group bonding, experienced only in 'liminal' states). They take great exception to any suggestion that they might be there for the vulgar, crass purpose of 'pulling'.

In a national survey, for example, only six per cent of these clubbers admitted that 'meeting prospective sexual partners' was an important part of 'dance events' for them. This finding strikes me as an instance of what we researchers call the Social Desirability Bias. You will remember that the SDB is 'a standard error on self-report measures due to respondents attempting to present themselves in a socially desirable light' – in other words: lying. In the clubber survey, we can tell that the respondents were being a bit economical with the truth, as responses to other questions revealed that over half of them had had sex with 'someone they met at a dance event', which suggests that meeting prospective sexual partners was perhaps a more important element of clubbing than they were prepared to acknowledge.

The SDB can be quite useful, though, as a consistent pattern of such 'socially desirable' responses can indicate an unwritten social rule or norm within a group or subculture. In this case, it seems pretty clear to me that among some young English clubbers, particularly those who regard themselves and their musical tastes as 'non-mainstream', there is an unspoken 'no sex please, we're too cool' rule. It is considered deeply 'uncool' to go clubbing to meet prospective partners, so clubbers will naturally be reluctant to admit to this motive. If they should happen to end up in bed with someone they met while out clubbing, this is a fortuitous by-product of the evening's entertainment, not something they set out to achieve. The 'no sex please' rule seems to be honoured more in speech than in observance. We pretend not to be too interested in sex, but we still manage accidentally-on-purpose to have quite a lot of sex. More of that lovely English hypocrisy.

I found that gay clubbers tend to be rather more open and honest than straight clubbers about their interest in sex: although some subscribe to the 'no sex please, we're too cool' rule, the majority candidly admit that flirtation, mate-selection and sex are important elements of clubbing for them. Aficionados of other currently popular music genres (such as hip-hop, R&B and rock) are also much less likely to subscribe to these asexual, euphoric-group-bonding norms than the EDM clubbers. They are far more overtly sexual in their behaviour and dance styles, and, like the gay clubbers, more likely to admit that flirting and mate-seeking are important motivations.

Parties

Private parties and celebrations generally score high on Alcohol, but vary on Sociability: although it is officially acceptable to strike up a conversation with a stranger at a private party, this is still, for most of us, awkward and uncomfortable, so we tend to stay in little huddles with people we already know. Parties are redeemed, however, by scoring a bit higher than pubs, bars and night-clubs on Shared interest, as the guests generally have at least one helpful thing in common: their relationship with the hosts. This can provide enough conversation-fodder (of the 'So, how do you know Sarah, then?' variety) to get us through the inevitable English difficulties with introductions.

Workplaces

Both 'flirting with intent' and 'recreational flirting' are common in most English offices and other workplaces. Surveys have found that about 20 per cent of us meet our spouses or current sexual partners at work, and some research findings show that flirting is good for relieving workplace anxiety and stress: the playful atmosphere created by flirtatious banter helps to reduce friction, and exchanges of compliments boost self-esteem.

We knew that, of course, but it needs saying, as workplace flirting may be under threat from puritanical influences imported from America, where flirting has been officially banned in many offices and other workplaces (an 'unsustainable' move on the part of the political-correctness lobby, as attempts to forbid behaviours that are as deeply ingrained in the human psyche as flirting are doomed to failure). At the moment, workplaces are still among the better flirting zones in England. Technically, they only pass two elements of the SAS test, as alcohol is not commonly available in offices or factories, but in practice work colleagues tend to find opportunities to drink together – and workplaces score very highly on the Sociability and Shared-interest factors. Training courses, sales conferences, academic conferences and other such work-related excursions and gatherings were highlighted by my English informants as particularly conducive to flirting, combining all the benefits of common interests and ease of sociable communication with the added lubricant of celebratory drinking.

In the English workplace itself, however, flirting is usually acceptable only in certain areas, with certain people and at specific times or occasions. Each workplace has its own unwritten etiquette governing flirtatious behaviour. In some companies, I found that the coffee machine, photocopier or cafeteria was the unofficial 'designated flirting zone'. In one it was a balcony mainly used by smokers, who often tend to be more sociable than non-smokers, or at least have a sense of defiant solidarity. One woman told me that she was a non-smoker, but pretended to smoke, because the smokers were 'more fun to hang out with'. I have already mentioned the 'smoking exception' to the contact-avoidance rules in public places, where cigarettes have increasingly become, for this marginalised minority, a highly effective prop, facilitating social interaction between strangers. They can be equally effective as facilitators of flirtation between co-workers – again with that 'causal' connection whereby one illicit activity prompts or enables another.

Learning-places

Almost all educational establishments are hot-beds of flirting. This is mainly because they are full of young single people making their first attempts at mate selection, but they also pass all three elements of the SAS test – schools, colleges and universities score very high on the Sociability and Shared-interest factors, and while alcohol is not usually served in classrooms, students have plenty of opportunities for drinking together.

The Shared-interest factor is particularly important to English adolescents. Adolescents everywhere tend to be self-conscious, but English ones are often especially awkward, lacking the social ease necessary to strike up conversations without an obvious point of contact. The shared lifestyle and concerns of students, and the informal atmosphere, make it easier for them to initiate conversation with each other. Simply by being students, prospective partners automatically have a great deal in common, and do not need to struggle to find topics of mutual interest.

Participant Sports, Clubs and Hobbies – and the Incompetence Rule

Almost all participant sports and hobbies score highly on the Sociability and Shared-interest factors in my SAS test – with the

Alcohol element usually requiring some deliberate effort rather than being built into the activity itself.

I found that the level of flirtatious behaviour among members of amateur English sports teams or hobby-clubs tends to be *inversely* related to the standards achieved by participants and their enthusiasm for the activity. With some exceptions, one tends to find a lot of flirting among incompetent tennis players, unfit hill-walkers, cack-handed painters and tangle-footed dancers, but somewhat less among more proficient, serious, competitive participants in the same activities. Even the most blatantly incompetent will usually *pretend* that they are really there for the sport or activity to which the club is ostensibly dedicated. They may even genuinely believe this – the English are masters of self-delusion – but the truth is that their tennis racquets, Ordnance Survey maps and paintbrushes are all primarily props, facilitators of sociability, and often come in very handy as flirting tools.

Spectator Events

While they have the advantage of providing conversation topics of mutual interest, and some achieve a reasonable score on the Sociability factor, most sporting events and other spectator pastimes such as theatre or cinema are not particularly conducive to flirting or mate-seeking, as social interaction of any kind is usually limited to a short interval or requires 'missing the action'.

The most striking exception to this rule is horseracing, where all of the 'action' takes place in just a few minutes, the half-hour interval between races is dedicated to sociability, and friendly interaction between strangers is actively encouraged by racecourse etiquette. Race-meetings pass all three elements of the SAS test, with the added advantage of a ready-made conversation-starter that includes the word 'fancy': 'What do you fancy in the three-thirty?'

Singles' Events, Dating Agencies and the No-date Rule

Singles' parties, singles' clubs and agency-arranged dates pass the SAS test, but only just. They don't score very highly on Shared interest. This may sound daft, as participants have an obvious shared interest in finding a mate, but this interest is rather embarrassing to acknowledge, and therefore not much use as a conversation-starter. Even in non-sexual contexts, the English need to pretend that they are gathering for some reason other than just gathering, and the need for another ostensible motive is even greater when something as personal and intimate as mate-seeking is the real purpose of the event. Even when we are on a 'date', the English do not like to use this term; English males are particularly squeamish about the idea of 'dating' – it makes the whole thing too embarrassingly open and official. And too earnest. We don't like being forced to take the whole courtship process too seriously: the very word 'date' seems to contravene the spirit of English humour rules.

There is also still an element of stigma attached to 'organised matchmaking'. Singles' events and dating agencies are regarded as somehow unnatural, too contrived, too artificial, lacking in the serendipity and spontaneity that ought to characterise romantic encounters. Many people are still ashamed to admit to 'resorting' to dating agencies or organised singles' parties: they feel it is undignified, an admission of failure. The truth is, of course, that there is nothing at all unnatural or undignified about organised matchmaking. It is a practice that has been the norm throughout human history, and is still customary in most cultures around the world. But the English obsession with privacy makes us even more reluctant than other modern Western nations to accept the need for such practices.

Cyberspace – and the Liminality Effect

Online flirtation is a different matter. Cyberspace technically 'fails' the Alcohol element of the SAS Test, in that booze is not actually supplied, but cyber-flirts can easily provide their own. The internet scores increasingly highly on the Shared-interest factor – and, above all, very highly indeed on Sociability. In cyberspace, unlike most 'real-space' public environments in England, striking up conversations with complete strangers is normal behaviour, indeed actively encouraged. Shared interest can be ensured by joining a suitable community or forum on social media sites, or an online dating agency catering to a specific social or cultural group[113] – or just choosing a prospective partner with similar interests from a more generic online dating-agency portfolio. The 'liminality effect' of cyberspace – the perception of the internet as somehow separate from the real world, as a place where normal social constraints and restrictions don't apply – gives it disinhibiting powers equal to those of alcohol, making it an ideal environment for socially challenged English flirts. So, the internet passes the SAS test with flying colours, which is probably why three in five of us are now happy to flirt and meet our prospective partners online, and about 17 per cent of marriages now start this way (a figure that is bound to increase, and may well be out of date by the time you read this).

THE COURTESY-FLIRTING RULE

One of my English informants observed that: 'You can have a sort of platonic flirting with people who are married or attached. In some situations it is almost expected – almost like you have to flirt to be polite.'

This comment refers to an unwritten rule prescribing a special form of 'safe', 'recreational' flirting that I call 'courtesy flirting'. This is mainly practised by men, who engage in mild flirtation with women as a form of politeness. (Women do it to some extent as well, but tend to be more cautious, knowing that men are a bit inclined to misread the signals.) Courtesy flirting is common throughout Continental Europe as well as in England, but there are some subtle differences: English men tend more towards playful teasing, Continental Europeans towards gallant compliments. Both forms can be confusing for Americans, who often mistake courtesy flirting for the real thing.

---

113. It took them a while, but the online matchmakers finally grasped that human mate-seekers are by nature socially 'endogamous', tending to marry people from the same sociocultural background, and created these specialist sites. I predicted/ recommended this in a privately commissioned and therefore unpublished research report many years ago, but as I have no business acumen whatsoever, it didn't even occur to me to set up any such sites myself. Typical.

THE UNCERTAINTY PRINCIPLE

Even when English males *are* genuinely interested in a female, they may often be reluctant to convey their interest in any obvious or straightforward fashion. We have already established that the English male is: (a) not an accomplished flirt, tending to be either awkward and tongue-tied or crass and boorish, and (b) somewhat uncomfortable with the whole concept of 'dating'. Defining an encounter with a female as a 'date' is a bit too explicit, too official, too clear-cut and unambiguous – the sort of embarrassing 'cards on the table' declaration of intent that the naturally cautious, indirect English male prefers to avoid.

Even when full of Dutch courage, he is unlikely to use the word 'date' in his drunken amorous advances, generally opting for 'shag' (or some equivalent expression) instead. This may seem strange, as 'shag' (or 'bonk', 'hook up', 'pull', etc.) might be regarded as rather more explicit than 'date', but it makes sense in the context of beer-sodden English male logic, where asking a female to have sex with you (or just clumsily trying to kiss or grope her) is somehow less personal, intimate and embarrassing than inviting her out for coffee or dinner.

Ideally, the English male would rather not issue any definite invitation at all, sexual or social, preferring to achieve his goal through a series of subtle hints and oblique manoeuvres, often non-verbal and either so understated as to be almost undetectable or so sexually (but not romantically) explicit that they can easily be dismissed as a meaningless drunken mistake or joke if they backfire. This 'uncertainty principle' has a number of advantages: the English male is not required to exhibit any emotions; he avoids entangling himself too soon in anything that could possibly be described as a 'relationship' (a term he detests even more than 'date'); he does not have to do or say anything 'soppy', so he maintains his masculine dignity; and, above all, by never making any direct, unequivocal, verbal request, he avoids the humiliation of a direct, unequivocal, verbal rejection. Somehow, being shoved away or even slapped during a vague beery lunge at a female is regarded as less humiliating than having one's invitation to coffee politely turned down. (It's all about the post-mortem with one's mates the next day, where 'I tried to get off with her but she wasn't having any' at least sounds cocky and laddish, whereas 'I asked her out for coffee but she said no' just sounds pathetic.)

English females are accustomed to this rather hazy, ambivalent form of courtship – although even we sometimes find it hard to read the signals accurately, and may spend inordinate amounts of time discussing the possible 'meaning' of some obscure hint or ambiguous gesture with our female friends. The uncertainty principle has its advantages for English females as well: although less emotionally guarded than our menfolk, we are easily embarrassed, and prefer to avoid precipitate declarations of amorous attraction. The uncertainty principle allows us time to gauge the suitability of a prospective mate before expressing any interest in him, and we can 'reject' unwanted suitors without having to tell them out loud that we are not interested.

Foreign females, however, tend to be confused or even seriously irritated by the elusive, uncertain nature of English courtship practices. My non-English female friends and informants constantly complain about English men, whose protean behaviour they attribute to shyness, arrogance or repressed homosexuality, depending on their degree of exasperation. What they fail to understand is that English courtship is essentially an elaborate face-saving game, in which the primary object is not so much to find a sexual partner as to avoid offence and embarrassment.

The offence-avoidance element of this game is yet another example of English 'negative politeness' – politeness that addresses other people's need not to be intruded or imposed upon, as opposed to 'positive politeness', which is concerned with their need for inclusion and approval. Many of the seemingly bizarre courtship practices of English males – the wariness, ambiguity and inhibitions that foreign females complain about – are characteristic features of 'negative politeness'. The embarrassment-avoidance aspect of our courtship game may seem rather more selfish, but it is also to some extent a matter of courtesy. The uncertainty principle, whereby neither attraction nor rejection is ever made verbally explicit, and advances and retreats are a matter of vague hints rather than direct invitations and refusals, allows *both* parties to save face. The courtship game, like other sports, is governed by the fair-play principle.

THE RULES OF BANTER

In most other cultures, flirtation and courtship involve exchanges of compliments: among the English, you are more likely to hear exchanges of insults. Well, mock-insults, to be precise. 'Banter', we call it, and it is one of our most popular forms of verbal interaction generally (on a par with moaning), as well as our main flirting method. The key ingredients of flirtatious banter are all very English: humour, particularly irony; wordplay; argument; cynicism; mock-aggression; teasing; indirectness – all our favourite things. And banter specifically excludes all the things we don't like and that make us uncomfortable: emotion, soppiness, earnestness and clarity.

The rules of flirtatious banter allow courting couples to communicate their feelings for each other without ever saying what they really mean, which would be embarrassing. In fact, the banter rules require them to say the opposite of what they mean – something at which the English excel. Here is a verbatim extract from a typical flirtatious encounter, recorded on a bus, between two teenagers. The exchange was conducted in full view and hearing of a group of their friends.

'You gotta licence for that shirt? Or are you wearing it for a bet?'

'Huh! Look who's talking – I can see your knickers, you slag!'

'It's a thong, you nerd – not that you'd know the difference. And that's the closest you'll ever get to it.'

'Who says I'd want to? What makes you think I fancy you? You're such a slag!'

'Better than being a sad geek!'

'Bitch!'

'Geek!'

'Sla— Oh, that's my stop – you coming out later?'

'Yeah – come round about eight.'

'Right.'

"Bye.'

From the conversation among their friends afterwards, it was clear that this pair had been attracted to each other for some time, had just started 'sort of going out' together (in that rather vague, non-dating way the English do these things), and were expected to become 'an item' in the near future. Even if I had not heard this subsequent discussion, I would have recognised the exchange of insults as a typical flirtation – perhaps not the wittiest or most articulate flirtatious banter I've come across, but a normal, unremarkable, everyday English courtship sequence. I only recorded it in my notebook because I happened to be doing a study on flirting at the time, and was collecting examples of real-life chat-up routines.

I also noted that English teenagers sometimes conduct a special form of 'group courtship', in which a small group of males will exchange banter – consisting mainly of sexually charged insults – with a small group of females. This group-courtship banter is most common among working-class youth, among whom I have even seen male and female groups hurling flirtatious abuse at each other from opposite sides of a street. English teens and twentysomethings can also be seen indulging in this peculiar form of collective courtship at holiday resorts abroad, where bemused local inhabitants must wonder how such raucous taunting and heckling can possibly be a prelude to love and marriage. (Although I can confirm that it is, I have some sneaking admiration for shrewd local males in Spanish and Greek holiday resorts, who rightly suspect that young English females might be susceptible to more conventionally flattering approaches, and often succeed in poaching them from their loutish English suitors.)

Among older adults, I found that flirtatious banter is less overtly abusive than in these teenage examples, but that the same basic rules of irony, teasing, mock-insults and so on still apply. English females of all ages might very well prefer a more chivalrous, less perversely oblique form of courtship – but the banter rules, like the uncertainty principle, are tuned more to the sensibilities of the emotionally constipated and socially challenged English male than to those of his somewhat less inhibited and more socially skilled female counterpart. We females are, however, accustomed to complying with these rules, and generally do so unconsciously. We know that arguing is the English male's primary means of bonding with other males, and that banter is thus a form of intimacy with which he is familiar and comfortable. We know that when a man persistently taunts and teases us, it usually means he likes us, and that if the sentiment is reciprocated, taunting and teasing back is the best way to express this.

As with the uncertainty principle, foreign females do not have this instinctive, in-built understanding of English male peculiarities, and so tend to be baffled and sometimes offended by the banter rules. I find myself having to explain to them that 'silly cow' really can be a term of endearment, and 'You're just not my type', uttered in the right tone and in the context of banter, can be tantamount to a proposal of marriage. I'm not saying that English men never pay straightforward compliments or formally ask women out on dates. They often do both of these things, albeit rather awkwardly, and they even propose marriage; it's just that if they can possibly find a more vague or circuitous way of achieving the same end, they will.

MALE-BONDING RULES – AND THE GIRL-WATCHING RITUAL

The English male may not be an accomplished flirt, or adept at the finer points of pair bonding, but when it comes to bonding with other males, he's in his element. I'm not talking about homosexuality, repressed or otherwise, but about the universal human practice of male bonding, of men forming close friendships and alliances with other men. Every known human society has some form of male-bonding practices, usually including clubs, organisations or institutions (such as the London 'gentlemen's clubs' for which the English are famous), or at least special rituals, from which women are excluded.

It has been said that men's need for such bonding is as strong as their need for sex with women. In the average Englishman's case, it may be stronger. There is nothing wrong with the heterosexual English male's sex-drive, but he does seem to show a marked preference for the company of other men. This is not about the alleged closet homosexuality of English males: if anything, gay Englishmen tend to be more at ease in female company, and to enjoy it more. But it must be said that many of the English man's male-bonding rituals appear to be devoted to proving his masculinity and heterosexuality.

Foremost among these is the 'girl-watching' ritual – the English version of that time-honoured and probably universal male pastime of exchanging comments on the physical attributes of passing females. You can – if you are interested in such things – watch variations on this ritual in pretty much any pub, bar, café, night-club or street-corner on the planet. The English variant is, as you might by now expect, conducted in code. Very few of the set phrases used are intelligible without some interpretation. The code is not, however, difficult to decipher, and most of the stock phrases fall into one of two simple categories: approval (that female is attractive) and disapproval (that female is not attractive).

The most quintessentially and convolutedly English of these stock girl-watching remarks is my favourite: 'Don't fancy yours much!' This is a standard comment on any pair of females, one of whom the speaker considers to be less attractive than the other. As well as demonstrating that he can tell the difference (and has a healthy, red-blooded interest in attractive females), the speaker is 'laying claim' to the more desirable of the pair, by designating the less pretty one as 'yours'. Although technically reserved for commenting on a pair of women, 'Don't fancy yours much!' is often used to draw a male companion's attention to the unattractiveness of any passing female, whether or not she is accompanied by a more fanciable alternative. On one occasion, in a pub in Birmingham, I recorded the following exchange:

MALE 1 (*glancing up as a group of four women enters the pub*): 'Don't fancy yours much!'

MALE 2 (*turning to look at the women, then frowning in puzzlement*): 'Er, which?'

MALE 1 (*laughing*): 'Don't care, mate – take your pick: they're all yours!'

MALE 2 *laughs, but somewhat grudgingly, looking a bit put-out, as a point has been scored against him.*

Another somewhat cryptic English girl-watching phrase, this time of the 'approving' variety, is 'Not many of those to the pound!' This comment refers to the size of the observed female's breasts, implying that they are rather larger than average. The 'pound' means a pound in weight, not in sterling – so the phrase literally means that you would not get many of those breasts balanced like fruit on a grocer's weighing-scale against a pound weight. In fact it is an understatement, as large breasts would probably each weigh more than a pound, but let's not get too technical. In any case, it is a favourable judgement: large breasts are officially A Good Thing among English males; even those who secretly prefer small ones usually feel obliged to express approval. The 'Not many of those to the pound!' comment is often accompanied by a gesture suggesting the weighing of heavy objects in the hands: the hands are held out just in front of the chest – with palms upturned and fingers slightly curled in – then bounced up and down. Here is another overheard exchange, this time from a pub in London. It sounds like a comedy sketch, but I swear it is real:

MALE 1 (*commenting on a very well-endowed nearby female*): 'Cor! Not many of those to the pound, eh?'

MALE 2: 'Sssh! You can't say that any more, mate. 'Snot allowed any more.'

MALE 1: 'What? Don't give me that PC feminist crap! I can talk about a girl's tits if I like!'

MALE 2: 'Nah – it's not the feminists'll get you, it's the Weights and Measures lot. We can't use pounds any more, it's all metric now. You gotta say "kilos"!'

From his self-satisfied expression, I suspect that Male 2 rather fancies himself as a comedian, and had been waiting for an opportunity to use this gag, which he spoilt somewhat by laughing uproariously at his own wit, and labouring the point with: 'Heh heh – new regulation from Brussels, right? We gotta say, "Not many of those to the *kilo!*" Geddit? *Kilo!*'

'I would!' is a rather more obvious generic expression of approval, the message being that the speaker would be willing to have sex with the observed female. 'Definitely a ten-pinter!' is a derogatory remark, meaning that the speaker would have to consume ten pints of beer – that is, be very drunk – even to consider having sexual relations with the female in question. When you overhear a pair or group of English men saying 'six', 'four', 'two', 'seven' and so on, while surreptitiously scrutinising nearby or passing females, they may not be awarding the women 'marks out of ten', but referring to the number of pints they would have to drink in order to contemplate having sex with them. The fact that none of the women would be likely to give these self-appointed beauty-contest judges a second glance is immaterial. The girl-watching ritual is a display of masculine bravado, performed entirely for the benefit of male companions. By reciting the stock phrases, participants in this ritual affirm their status as macho, active heterosexuals. By tacit agreement, the assumption that they are in a position to pick and choose among the observed females is never questioned – and conspiring to promote this collective delusion reinforces the social bonds between the girl-watchers.

CLASS RULES

The Class-endogamy Rule

Like every other aspect of our lives, sex among the English is subject to class rules. For a start, there is an unofficial class-endogamy rule, whereby intermarriage between the social classes, although not actually forbidden, tends to be discouraged, and in practice does not occur very often. There are exceptions, of course, and such inter-class marriages are certainly more common than they used to be, but it is still very unusual for people from opposite ends of the social spectrum to marry.

Outside the pages of Barbara Cartland and P. G. Wodehouse, the sons of dukes and earls tend not to disoblige their families by insisting on marrying humble waitresses. Upper-class males may have sexual adventures or even infatuations with working-class females, but they generally end up marrying girls called Isabella, Henrietta and Cressida (with children's-book nicknames like Piggy and Tiggy) who grew up in large houses in Gloucestershire, with Labradors and ponies. The Henriettas and Cressidas, in turn, may have the odd rebellious youthful fling with a Jayden or a Darren, but usually 'come to their senses' (as their anxious mothers would put it), and marry someone 'from a similar background'.

Having said that, the two main factors affecting social mobility in England are still education and marriage. These two factors may often be connected, as universities are among the few places where young mate-seekers from different social classes are likely to meet 'as equals' (Prince William and Kate Middleton are an obvious example). Even here, the odds are against class-exogamous unions, as studies regularly show that when the English go to university, they have an uncanny knack of making friends almost exclusively with fellow students from identical social backgrounds.

But despite these herd instincts, people from different classes find themselves thrown together in seminars or tutorials, or through sports or other extra-curricular student activities, such as theatre or music. And there are even some students who make a deliberate, determined effort to avoid associating 'just with people from the same sort of families and schools as mine', as one intrepid upper-middle-class girl explained.

The 'Marrying-up' Rule

Working-class intellectual males are often attracted to precisely this type of slightly rebellious upper-middle-class female, and may end up marrying one. Although there are no doubt many exceptions, such marriages tend to be somewhat less successful than those in which the female partner is the one 'marrying up'. This is because an unwritten rule requires the partner who is 'marrying up' to adopt the tastes and manners of the class he or she is marrying into, or at least to make rather more compromises and adjustments than the higher-class partner, and upwardly mobile women tend to be more willing to do this than upwardly mobile men.

When working-class males 'marry up', there is a conflict between snobbery and sexism – between the marrying-up rule and traditional male-dominance rules whereby women are expected to do more adapting and adjusting. Bright working-class men who 'become middle class' by education, and particularly those who jump several classes by marrying upper-middle females they meet at university, can sometimes be a bit truculent and resentful about having to change their habits. They may, for example, persist in referring to their evening meal as 'tea', plant pampas grass and marigolds in the garden, refuse to squash peas onto the back of their fork, and deliberately embarrass their snobbish mother-in-law by using shibboleth words such as 'pardon', 'serviette' and 'toilet' at her Christmas party. Those upwardly mobile males who do adapt willingly to their new class tend to have problems with their own parents, whom they may find both resentful and embarrassing. You can't win.

Although again there are exceptions, women who 'marry up' are usually more compliant, and make more of an effort to fit in. If anything, they can sometimes be rather too eager to adopt the accent, vocabulary, tastes, habits and manners of their husband's class, and miss some of the all-important nuances in their anxious enthusiasm. They may wear the right clothes but wrongly combined, use the right words but in the wrong context, or grow the right flowers but in the wrong kind of pot – ending up with a sort of anagram of an upper-middle-class lifestyle. This fools nobody, embarrasses their in-laws, and alienates their parents. Trying too hard can be worse than not trying at all. And it involves committing a serious breach of the Importance of Not Being Earnest rule.

Partners do not have to come from opposite ends of the social spectrum for the marrying-up rule to cause tensions and conflicts. English people tend to despise the class immediately below theirs much more than the ones further down the scale. Upper-middles, for example, are often far more snooty and scathing about middle-middle tastes and habits than they are about those of the working classes. The boundary between middle-middle and upper-middle is full of booby-traps, and can be the hardest to cross.

The Working-class Potency Myth

Some upper-middle females are fascinated by working-class males at least partly because of a widely held belief that working-class men are more virile and better lovers than middle- or upper-class men. There is no empirical evidence to justify this belief. Working-class males may start having sex at a slightly earlier age than the higher echelons, but in general they do not have sex more often, nor is there any reason to believe that their partners enjoy it more. The notion that plebeian males are more sexually potent and uninhibited is a myth, perpetuated among the educated middle classes by people like D. H. Lawrence and John Osborne, and elsewhere by the soft-porn industry, where it seems to be an established fact that middle-class females all spend their time having fantasies about hunky working-class firemen, builders or plumbers. The working-class potency myth has been given a further boost by the rise of the 'Lad' and 'Lad culture' – which celebrates traditional, and stereotypically working-class, masculine values and interests (football, cars, tits, beer, etc.).

The persistence of this myth is, I think, mainly based on the mistaken assumption that the crass-and-boorish approach to flirtation, which is seen as more characteristic of lower-class males, is somehow indicative of greater sexual energy than the reticent-and-awkward manner, which is regarded as the preserve of the middle- and upper-class male. The truth is that *both* these approaches are symptoms of social dis-ease and sexual inhibition, and *neither* is a reliable indicator of virility or sexual competence. And in any case, the approach an Englishman adopts depends less on his social class than on the amount of alcohol he has consumed: all English males believe in the magical disinhibiting powers of the demon drink; the higher classes have particular faith in its capacity to make them as irresistibly crude and loutish as any proletarian sex-god.

AND SO TO BED . . .

But what about actual *sex*? Some of you may be feeling a bit cheated – in that I called this chapter 'Rules of Sex', and have so far said a lot about humour, flirtation, class-endogamy and so on but, apart from debunking the working-class potency myth, not a great deal about what the English are actually like in bed. And certainly nothing much about how our sexual performance differs from that of other nations.

There are two main reasons for this. First, being English, I find the whole thing a bit personal and embarrassing, so I've been procrastinating. (If you were here in my flat, I'd be prattling nervously about the weather and saying, 'I'll just go and put the kettle on . . .') Second, there is a bit of a, um, er, how shall I put this? A data problem. The participant-observation method is a wonderful thing, but the observation bit does not include direct observation of people's sex lives, and the participant element does not involve having sex with a full representative sample of natives, or with a cross-cultural sample of foreigners for comparison. Well, anthropologists have been known to become intimately involved with the people they study (my father tells me that such liaisons used to be jokingly called 'cultural penetration'), but this has always been rather frowned upon. I suppose it's allowed if you're studying your own native culture, as I am – and, yes, I have of course had English boyfriends, and a few foreign ones, but nothing like enough to constitute a scientifically representative sample. And in terms of direct experience, I'm not qualified to comment on the female half of the population at all.

But these are fairly lame excuses. A lot of social scientists write in great detail about sexual matters of which they have no direct personal experience. And although I have not had sex with a wide enough range of English people, my research has certainly involved enough *discussion* of the subject, with a respectably large and varied sample of both natives and foreigners, to gain at least some understanding of our sexual behaviour and its unwritten rules.

Sex-talk Rules

Discussing sexual matters with the English is not easy: although we are not particularly prudish, we find the subject embarrassing, and our methods of coping with or covering our embarrassment, such as knee-jerk humour and polite procrastination, mean that a great deal of my valuable research time is wasted on jokes, quips, witticisms, displacement weather-speak and tea-making. On top of this, the Importance of Not Being Earnest rule means that getting the

English to give straight, serious, non-ironic answers to one's questions about sex can be a struggle.

To make my task even more difficult, there is an unwritten rule whereby English males tend to assume that a female who talks about sex at all, however indirectly, must be at least signalling sexual availability, if not actively chatting them up. An American friend of mine got into some trouble with this rule: she couldn't understand why so many English men seemed to be 'making passes' at her, and taking offence when she rejected their precipitate advances, when she had 'given them no encouragement at all'. Anxious to help (and spotting an opportunity for an experiment), I hung around and eavesdropped on some of her conversations with men in our local pub, and found that she was saying things like 'but that was just after I discovered my first husband was gay, so I was feeling a bit confused about my sexuality . . .' within about ten minutes of being introduced to someone. I explained that this kind of intimate disclosure, although perhaps commonplace in the land of Oprah, would be interpreted by many English males as the next best thing to a written invitation. When she somewhat reluctantly curbed her natural candour, she found that the unwanted attentions ceased.

Great, I thought. Another successful rule-testing experiment – and with someone else acting as unwitting guinea-pig and breaking the rules for me. My favourite kind of field research. But although this test confirmed that I had correctly identified an unwritten rule, I could see that the rule itself was going to prove something of a handicap in my attempts to find out about English bedroom habits. I got round this problem in the usual ways – by fudging and cheating. I talked mainly to women, and to men I knew well enough to be sure that they would not misinterpret my questions. Women – even English women – can be quite open and honest with each other, in private, about the quirks and characteristics and attitudes of their male lovers, and indeed about their own, so I learnt a lot about both sexes just from them. And to be fair, I also gleaned quite a lot of useful information from discussions with male friends and informants, including one who somehow managed to combine an encyclopaedic knowledge of English females' sexual behaviour (thanks to a personal 'sample' of MORI-poll proportions) with an endearingly self-deprecating frankness about his own thoughts and habits.

The Rule-free Zone

So, after nearly twenty years of laborious, tactful information-gathering, what have I discovered about the private sex-life of the English? Actually, it's good news. Bed is the one place where we seem to shed almost all of our many and debilitating inhibitions; where we are, albeit temporarily, magically cured of our social dis-ease. Shut the curtains, dim the lights, take our clothes off, and you'll find we suddenly become quite human. We can, after all, engage emotionally with other humans. We can be passionate, open, warm, affectionate, excitable, impulsive – in a way you normally only see when we talk to our pets.

This is genuine disinhibition – not the rule-governed, so-called disinhibition of our Saturday-night or holiday-resort drunkenness, where we are merely acting out a prescribed social role, a sort of hammy caricature of what we think uninhibited behaviour ought to look like. Our sexual disinhibition is the real thing.

Of course, some of us are more free and abandoned between the sheets than others. In bed, we are ourselves, which means a wide range of different sexual styles – some a bit shy and tentative, others more confident; some talkative, others quiet; some clumsy, others expert; some creative or kinky, others more conventional; some perhaps a bit virtuoso-show-offy – depending on all sorts of factors, such as age, experience, personality, how we feel about a particular sexual partner, our mood, and so on. But the point is that these factors influencing our varied sexual styles are personal – nothing to do with the 'rules of Englishness' that govern our social behaviour.

Every step leading up to the sexual act is shaped by these Englishness rules: where we meet our partner, how we flirt, what we eat at dinner and how we eat it, how we talk, the jokes we make, what we drink and the effects of alcohol on our behaviour, the car we drive home in and how we drive it (or our conduct on the bus or in the taxi), the house we take our partner home to and how we feel and talk about it, the dog who greets us, the music we play, the nightcap we offer, how the bedroom is decorated, the curtains we close, the clothes we take off . . . Everything, right up to that point, whether we like it or not, is at least partly determined by one or another of the hidden rules of Englishness. We do not stop being English while we are engaged in the sexual act but, for that relatively brief time, our actions are not governed by any particular, distinctively English set of rules. We have the same basic instincts as other humans, and exhibit much the same range and variation in our personal sexual styles as humans of any other culture. Bed, at least while we are actually having sex, is a rule-free zone.

The Textbook-sex Imbalance

Having said that, one can make a few generalisations about English sex. For example, English males are, as a rule, less likely than their American counterparts to read those earnest self-help books and manuals about sexual techniques. English females, even if they don't read the books, get a lot of this kind of information from women's magazines. Until fairly recently, this has meant a slight imbalance in the sort of 'textbook' sexual expertise that one can acquire from such reading.

But the most 'laddish' English men's mags now feature illustrated articles on 'how to drive women wild' and 'three easy steps to multiple orgasm' and so on. Even the illiterate can watch late-night educational sex programmes, or pseudo-documentary soft-porn, on various television channels (programmes that are helpfully scheduled to start shortly after the pubs close), and most now have access to the vast amount of sexual self-help material available on the internet – so our men are rapidly catching up. Many younger males – and even some older ones – seem to have gathered, for instance, that performing a bit of token oral sex is *de rigueur*, just to prove you're not a total wham-bam Neanderthal. Some have even got past the stage of expecting to be awarded a medal for this.

Post-coital Englishness

Après sex or, if we have fallen asleep, the next morning, we revert to the usual state of awkward Englishness. We say:

'I'm terribly sorry, but I didn't quite catch your name . . . ?'

'Would you mind very much if I borrowed a towel?'

'I'll just go and put the kettle on . . .'

'No! Monty! Put it *down*! We *don't* eat the nice lady's bra! What *will* she think of us? Drop it! *Bad* dog!'

'Sorry it's a bit burnt: the toaster's a bit temperamental, I'm afraid – doesn't like Mondays or something . . .'

'Oh, no, it's very nice. Ooh, yes – tea! Lovely, thank you!' (This delivered with at least as much enthusiasm as the *cris de joie* of the night before.)

All right, I'm exaggerating a little – but not much: all these are genuine, verbatim morning-after quotes.

Le Vice Anglais and the Funny-bottoms Rule

In *The English*, Jeremy Paxman devotes the first four pages of his chapter on sexual matters to what the French call '*le vice Anglais*' – 'the English vice': flagellation (spanking, caning, and other assaults upon the bottom). At the end of his entertaining anecdotal survey of the topic, he admits, 'It would be silly to claim that "the English vice" is widespread among the English. It is not. Nor, despite its name, is it unique to the English.' Quite. And he might have added that even the name is hardly significant, as the French randomly designate as '*Anglais*' things they disapprove of or wish to poke fun at, often things that we in turn call 'French': their term for 'French leave' is '*filer à l'Anglaise*' – to run away like the English; a 'French letter' is a '*capote Anglaise*'.

But if this particular sexual kink is neither widespread among the English, nor unique to us, why give it such a lot of space and prominence? Paxman says that the 'central ambiguity' of this practice, 'that punishment is reward, and pain, pleasure – rings with English hypocrisy'. Well, maybe. But I think there is a simpler explanation for why he starts his sex chapter with this not-particularly-English vice, and that is the knee-jerk humour rule. When faced with any sort of discussion of sex, our humour reflex kicks in, and we make a joke of it. We also regard bottoms as intrinsically funny. So, if you've got to talk about sex, start with some funny stuff about bottoms.[114]

Page Three and the Un-erotic Bosoms Rule

Then, if possible, move on to bosoms, which we also find highly amusing. Paxman claims that 'English men are obsessed by breasts', citing the daily parade of page-three bosoms in the tabloid newspapers as proof of this fixation. I am not so sure. Breasts are a secondary sexual characteristic, and men in many parts of the world like to look at them – in magazines and so on, as well as in the flesh. I am not convinced that English men are any more obsessed with breasts than, say, American, Australian, Scandinavian, Japanese or German men. The daily breast-display on page three of the *Sun*, and in other tabloid papers, is, however, an interesting English phenomenon, and worth looking at a bit more closely.

In a national MORI survey, only 21 per cent of us expressed moral disapproval of the page-three breast parade. Of all the representations of sex in the media, topless page-three girls attracted the least condemnation, by a long way. Even among women, only 24 per cent had moral objections to page three, whereas nearly twice that number, 46 per cent, objected to soft-porn magazines in newsagents (such as *Playboy*, with similar images), and 54 per cent thought cinema pornography was immoral. Now, this does not, of course, mean that the other 76 per cent of women actively enjoy looking at page three, but it does suggest that many do not regard it as 'pornography' – perhaps seeing it as something more innocuous, even though the pictures are much the same as those in soft-porn magazines.

When I read these statistics, I was intrigued, and started asking my own questions, trying to find out why both men and women seemed to regard page three as somehow different from other

114. I hope it is clear that I mean no disrespect to Jeremy Paxman with all these quibbles. Quite the opposite: it is because his book is so good that it is worth quibbling with.

soft-porn images. In terms of numbers, although my 'sample' was much smaller, I got much the same results as the MORI poll – only about a fifth of my informants objected to page three. I was surprised to find that even some of my more feminist-minded informants could not work up much indignation about page three. Why was this?

'Because, well, page-three girls – I mean, they're just a bit of a joke,' said one woman. 'You can't really take it seriously.'

'Oh – I suppose we're just used to it,' explained another.

'Page three is more like those saucy seaside postcards,' said a particularly astute informant. 'It's just daft, with the silly captions full of awful puns. You can't really feel offended by it.'

A teenage girl was equally dismissive: 'Compared to what people download off the internet, or even what you see on the telly – well, page three is so *innocent*, it's sort of quaint and old-fashioned.'

I noticed that almost all of the people I asked about page three, even a few of those who expressed disapproval, tended to laugh or at least smile as they responded. They would roll their eyes or shake their heads, but in a resigned, tolerant way, much as people do when they are talking about the minor misdemeanours of a naughty child or pet. Page three is a tradition, an institution, somehow reassuringly familiar, like *The Archers* or rainy bank holidays. George Orwell described the English working class as 'devoted to bawdy jokes' and talked about the 'overpowering vulgarity' of rude comic postcards. The ludicrous puns, wordplay and *double-entendres* in the page-three captions are as much a part of this tradition as the naked breasts, reminding us that sex is a bit of a joke, not to be taken too seriously. It is hard to see the 'tits and puns' on page three as pornography, any more than the bosoms and puns in a jokey seaside postcard or a *Carry On* film are pornography. They are not even really sexy. Page three is somehow just too daft, too cartoonishly ridiculous, too *English* to be sexy.

'England may be a copulating country, but it is not an erotic country,' said George Mikes in 1977. This was an improvement on his original claim, in 1946, that 'Continental people have a sex-life; the English have hot-water bottles', but still not exactly flattering. He does have a point, though, which is borne out by my page-three findings: only the English could manage to make pictures of luscious, half-naked women into something quite as un-erotic as page three.

SEX RULES AND ENGLISHNESS

What does all this tell us about Englishness? The characteristics revealed here are mostly the 'usual suspects' – humour, social dis-ease, hypocrisy, fair play, class-consciousness, courtesy and so on. But what is becoming increasingly clear to me is that these defining characteristics of Englishness cannot be seen (*pace* Orwell, Priestley, Betjeman, Bryson, Paxman, Julian Barnes and all the other list-makers) just as a list of discrete, unconnected qualities or principles: they must be understood as a *system* of some sort.

Looking closely at the rules and behaviour patterns in this chapter, I see that most of them are products of a combination or interaction of at least two 'defining characteristics'. The knee-jerk humour rule is an example of the use of humour (a defining characteristic in its own right) to alleviate the symptoms of our social dis-ease (another defining characteristic).

Many of the flirting zones identified by the SAS Test also reveal interactions between defining characteristics. Our problems with singles' events and dating agencies – our need to pretend that we are gathering for some non-social purpose, and our squeamishness about the concept of 'dating' – seem to involve a combination of social dis-ease (again), hypocrisy and anti-earnestness (a subset of humour).

The EDM clubbers' 'no sex please, we're too cool' rule is mainly just about hypocrisy, but worth mentioning here as it seems to confirm something I have been suspecting for a while, which is that English hypocrisy really is a special *kind* of hypocrisy, involving collusion in a sort of unspoken agreement to delude ourselves, more than any deliberate deception of others.

The courtesy-flirting rule combines hypocrisy with another defining characteristic, courtesy. These two seem to go together a lot – 'polite egalitarianism' is another product of hypocrisy and courtesy, combined with class-consciousness.

The uncertainty principle is not a sign of repressed homosexuality, but an interaction of three defining characteristics of Englishness: social dis-ease + courtesy + fair play. The rules of banter are a product of social dis-ease + humour; the girl-watching rules involve both of these, with the addition of our special collective-delusion brand of hypocrisy. The marrying-up rule combines class-consciousness and hypocrisy; the sex-talk rules are social dis-ease symptoms treated with humour again, as is the funny-bottoms rule.

This is all rather crude at the moment – I'm sure the equations involved are more complex than these simple additions – but at least we're moving towards something that looks more like a diagram than a list. I haven't figured it all out yet, but I'm still hoping that by the end of the book I will have found some graphic way of illustrating the connections and interactions between the elements that make up our national character.

Finally, the 'punography' of page three, where the silly wordplay (which seems to be contagious, sorry) somehow cancels out the sexiness of the pictures, is another example of the English use of humour to neutralise potential embarrassment or offence – a 'social dis-ease + humour + courtesy' combo. Some cultures celebrate sex and the erotic; others (religious ones, mainly) neutralise sex by censorship; others (the US, parts of Scandinavia) neutralise it with po-faced, earnest political correctness. The English do it with humour.

RITES OF PASSAGE

'␣ve called this chapter Rites of Passage, rather than Religion, because religion as such is largely irrelevant to the lives of most English people nowadays, but the rituals to which Church of England vicars irreverently refer as 'hatchings, matchings and dispatchings', and other less momentous transitions, are still important. Most honest Anglican clerics will readily admit that the *rites de passage* of marriage, death, and to a lesser extent birth, are now their only point of contact with the majority of their parishioners. Some of us might attend a service at Christmas, and an even smaller number at Easter, but for most, church attendance is limited to weddings, funerals, and perhaps christenings.

THE DEFAULT-RELIGION RULE

The Elizabethan courtier John Lyly claimed that the English were God's 'chosen and peculiar people'. Well, if we are, this was certainly a rather peculiar choice on the Almighty's part, as we are probably the least religious people on Earth. In surveys, about 45 per cent of English people tick the box saying that they 'belong' to one or another of the Christian denominations[115] – usually the Church of England

---

115. I quoted a much higher percentage in the 2004 edition, but this figure is more up to date, and also based on more reliable survey methods. The national census survey (among other sins) phrases the religion question in a misleading way, asking people, 'What is your religion?', which presupposes that respondents have a religion, and giving them a list of world religions to choose from – whereas the British Social Attitudes survey, for example, asks, 'Do you regard yourself as belonging to any particular religion? If yes, which?' followed by denominations.

– but when asked, 'Are you religious?' only about 30 per cent say yes. Only 14 per cent of these 'Christians' say that they go to church on a regular basis, and when they say 'regular', only about eight per cent mean weekly. The vast majority of us attend church only for the aforementioned 'rites of passage', and for many of us, our only contact with religion is at the last of these rites – at funerals. Most of us (88 per cent at the last count) are not christened nowadays, and only about a third get married in church, but about 40 per cent of us have a Christian funeral of some sort, and most of us have probably attended one. This is not because death suddenly inspires the English to become religious, but because it has until recently been the automatic 'default' option: *not* having a Christian funeral required a determined effort, a clear notion of exactly what one wanted to do instead, and a lot of embarrassing fuss and bother. Now that other options have become more easily accessible, even the number of Christian funerals is declining. This lack of religious enthusiasm is not just a recent trend. In 1941, George Orwell wrote that 'the common people are without definite religious belief, and have been so for centuries. The Anglican Church never had a real hold on them, it was simply the preserve of the landed gentry, and the nonconformist sects only influenced minorities.' I suspect that churchgoing, for the English, has long been more of a social activity than a religious one.

In any case, the Church of England is the least religious church on Earth. It is notoriously woolly-minded, tolerant to a fault and amiably non-prescriptive. To put yourself down as 'C of E' (we prefer to use this abbreviation whenever possible, in speech as well as on forms, as the word 'church' sounds a bit religious, and 'England' might seem a bit patriotic) on a census or application form, as is customary, does not imply any religious observance or beliefs whatsoever – not even a belief in the existence of God. Alan Bennett once observed, in a speech to the Prayer Book Society, that in the Anglican Church 'whether or not one believes in God tends to be sidestepped. It's not quite in good taste. Someone said that the Church of England is so constituted that its members can really believe anything at all, but of course almost none of them do.'

I remember eavesdropping on a conversation in my doctor's waiting room. A schoolgirl of twelve or thirteen was filling in some medical form or other, with intermittent help from her mother. The daughter asked, 'Religion? What religion am I? We're not any religion, are we?'

'No, we're not,' replied her mother. 'Just put C of E.'

'What's C of E?' asked the daughter.

'Church of England.'

'Is that a religion?'

'Yes, sort of. Well, no, not really – it's just what you put.'

'C of E' is a default option. A bit like the 'neither agree nor disagree' box on questionnaires – a kind of apathetic, fence-sitting, middling sort of religion for the spiritually 'neutral'.

Ian Hislop, editor of the satirical magazine *Private Eye* and a self-confessed 'lukewarm' Anglican, illustrates this perfectly in his account of a sudden outbreak of religion at his C of E boarding school, caused by two former pupils who returned with a born-again, evangelical message, which somehow temporarily caught the imagination of the boys. 'It was very, very bizarre,' Hislop says. 'People were having prayer meetings in dormitories and the staff were terribly worried.' It might strike some people as a bit odd that the staff of a Church of England school – by definition a 'faith school' – would be so frightfully worried about pupils voluntarily saying prayers together, but as Hislop explains, 'You know, being sort of Church of England, people want a very quiet and moderate faith.' Hislop describes his own faith as 'so vague as to be sort of not really there at all' – which gives an idea of the degree of quietness and moderation instilled by his C of E education.

It is hard to find anyone who takes the Church of England seriously – even among its own ranks. In 1991, the then Archbishop of Canterbury, Dr George Carey, said, 'I see it as an elderly lady, who mutters away to herself in a corner, ignored most of the time.' And this typically Eeyorish comment was in an interview immediately following his appointment to the most exalted position in this church. If the Archbishop of Canterbury himself likens his church to an irrelevant senile old biddy, it is hardly surprising that the rest of us feel free to ignore it. Sure enough, in a sermon almost a decade later, he bemoaned the fact that 'A tacit atheism prevails.' Well, really – what did he expect?

More recently, in 2007, Dr Carey's successor as Archbishop of Canterbury, Dr Rowan Williams, described us as 'a country with a nominally Christian majority'. The key word here is 'nominally', and even the nominal Christians are no longer a majority.

THE BENIGN-INDIFFERENCE RULE

And the key word in Archbishop Carey's lament was 'tacit'. We are not a nation of explicit, unequivocal atheists. Nor are we agnostics. Both of these imply a degree of interest in whether or not there is a deity – enough either to reject or question the notion. Most English people are just not much bothered about it.

In opinion polls, about 55 to 60 per cent of the population answer 'yes' when asked if they believe in God,[116] but Dr Carey is right not to take this response at face value. When I asked people about it, I found that many of them answered 'yes' because they:

- are 'not particularly religious but sort of believe in Something'
- are vaguely willing to accept that there *might* be a God, so saying 'no' would be a bit too emphatic
- would quite like to think that there is a God, even though on the whole it seems rather unlikely
- don't really know but might as well give Him the benefit of the doubt
- haven't really thought about it much, to be honest, but, yeah, sure, whatever.

One woman told me, 'Well, I'd ticked "Christian" on the first page, in the sense that I suppose I'm sort of Christian as opposed to Muslim or Hindu or something, so then I thought I'd better tick God as well – otherwise I'd look a bit inconsistent.'

Others are clearly not so concerned about consistency, as surveys regularly show that up to 15 per cent of those identifying themselves as Christian freely admit that they do not believe in God. This may

116. Incidentally, only 56 per cent believe in opinion polls.

seem utterly bizarre, but Alan Bennett wasn't joking: in the C of E, belief in God is optional, and even raising the issue of belief would be in poor taste. Over half of those who tick 'Christian' do not believe in Christ[117].

My own research indicates that many of the unbelievers are ticking the 'Christian' box for the same reason as the woman quoted above: they mean 'Well, I suppose I'm sort of Christian as opposed to Muslim, Hindu, etc.' – which they see as more of a cultural than a religious identification. I have also interviewed many English people who tick 'Christian' on forms and surveys despite holding no religious beliefs whatsoever. The term, for them, represents a rather vague set of moral values and principles, only some of which, on further questioning, are even derived from the Bible, let alone the New Testament. Many of my informants quoted the Golden Rule ('Do unto others as you would have them do unto you'), which, although claimed by Christianity, is also espoused in some form by almost every other religion and ethical tradition, and found in many ancient texts from centuries before Christ. Other informants cited a range of non-Biblical moral precepts – almost all about tolerance and fairness – which have not to my knowledge been appropriated by Christianity, such as 'Live and let live' or 'Two wrongs don't make a right.' The participants in one of my discussion-groups were even convinced that 'From each according to his ability, to each according to his need' was one of Christ's teachings (I had to Google the quote for them to prove it came from Marx).

So, when you read about surveys showing that around 70 per cent of us think that our national identity is or should be based on 'Christian values', it's worth remembering that what many of the respondents mean by this has little or nothing to do with Christ, God, the Church or religion. Indeed, our current deputy prime minister, the Liberal Democrat leader Nick Clegg, is an avowed non-believer who nonetheless says that 'Christian values' are 'central' to his party's policies.

The clever researchers at MORI have done at least one survey asking their 'religion' questions in a way that is better suited to the

117. As the son of God, that is: they may believe that the historical person existed.

woolly beliefs and noncommittal attitudes of the English, offering the following options:

'*I am a practising member of an organised religion*': only 18 per cent of us tick this one, and that includes all the Muslims, Hindus, Sikhs and so on, who really *are* practising.

'*I am a non-practising member of an organised religion*': a bit like ticking the 'C of E' box, then; 25 per cent of us go for this undemanding option.

'*I am spiritually inclined but don't really 'belong' to an organised religion*': vague enough to appeal to 24 per cent of us – which presumably covers some of the 31 per cent who believe in astrology, the 38 per cent who believe in ghosts, the 42 per cent who believe in telepathy, the 40 per cent who believe in guardian angels, etc., etc.

'*I am agnostic (not sure if there's a God)*': requires too much thought, only 14 per cent.

'*I am atheist (convinced there is no God)*': ditto, and too decisive, only 12 per cent.

'*None of these*': well, they'd covered pretty much every possibility, just seven per cent.

'*Don't know*': with so many ambivalent, evasive options on offer, it would be churlish not to choose one, only one per cent.

So although only 12 per cent, at the last count, will go so far as to call themselves atheists, I think that the former Archbishop's notion of a prevailing 'tacit atheism' among the English is fairly accurate. If we were real atheists, he and his Church would have something to get their teeth into, someone to argue with. As it is, we just don't care enough.[118]

We are not only indifferent but, worse (from the Church's point of view), we are *politely* indifferent, *tolerantly* indifferent, *benignly* indifferent. We have no actual objection to God. If pushed, we even accept that He might exist – or that Something might exist, and we

---

118. The technical term for this is 'apatheism' (apathy + (a)theism), but this doesn't quite convey the peculiarly English type of indifference I'm trying to describe here.

might as well call it God, if only for the sake of peace and quiet. God is all very well, in His place, which is in a church. When we are in His house – at weddings and funerals – we make all the right polite noises, as one does in people's houses, although we find the earnestness of it all faintly ridiculous and a bit uncomfortable. Otherwise, He impinges very little on our lives or thoughts. Other people are very welcome to worship Him if they choose – it's a free country – but this is a private matter, and they should keep it to themselves and not bore or embarrass the rest of us by making an unnecessary *fuss* about it. (There is nothing the English hate more than a *fuss*.)

In many other countries – America, for example – politicians and other prominent public figures feel obliged to demonstrate their devoutness and invoke their deity at every opportunity. Here, they must do the exact opposite. Even to *mention* one's faith would be very bad form. The former prime minister Tony Blair was known to be a devout Christian, an affliction we tolerated in our usual grudgingly courteous fashion, but only because he had the good sense to keep extremely quiet about it – and was apparently under strict instructions from his spin-doctors never to use 'the G-word'. (His press spokesman once famously told reporters, 'We don't do God.') Despite this precaution, he was caricatured in *Private Eye* as a pompous and self-righteous country vicar, and his speeches and pronouncements were scrutinised for any sign of unseemly piety, the slightest hint of which was immediately pounced upon and ridiculed. (Here it is worth reminding ourselves again that satire is what the English have instead of revolutions and uprisings.) When it was alleged that Mr Blair and President Bush had actually *prayed* together during his visit to the White House, the media had a field day, and Blair is still denying that any such inappropriate act took place.

Our benign indifference remains benign only so long as the religious, of any persuasion, stay in their place and refrain from discomforting the non-practising, spiritually neutral majority with embarrassing or tedious displays of religious zeal. And any use of the G-word, unless obviously ironic or just a figure of speech (God forbid, God knows, Godforsaken, etc.) counts as an improper display.

Earnestness of any kind makes us squirm; religious earnestness makes us deeply suspicious and decidedly twitchy.

Another Blair example illustrates these unwritten rules: when some representatives of the Salvation Army came to visit Mr Blair, they asked to end the meeting with a prayer. Blair's aides were horrified at the suggestion, and when Blair insisted, one of them hissed, in disgust, 'For God's sake!' According to the rules of Englishness, this gritted-teeth protest was probably the only 'correct' use of the G-word in the entire meeting. It is hardly surprising that Blair waited until he was safely out of office before converting to Catholicism. He himself admitted, in 2007, that he was wary of talking about his Christian faith while still in office in case he was labelled a 'nutter'. We will tolerate a C of E prime minister, providing he is suitably discreet about his faith, as the Anglican Church barely counts as religion. Catholicism, however, is known to require actual religious beliefs – with no polite fudging or sidestepping – and a prime minister with such explicit and unambiguous convictions would be frightfully embarrassing. We knew perfectly well that Blair had been a 'closet' Catholic all along, of course, but openly declaring this is a different matter. There are plenty of openly gay politicians in our Parliament, but when it comes to religion, the unspoken rule is not entirely unlike the former 'Don't ask, don't tell' policy on homosexuality in the US military.

HATCHINGS, MATCHINGS AND DISPATCHINGS

So much for religion.[119] But what about those rites of passage that still often take place in churches, or involve vaguely religious ceremonies

---

119. Or at least, I thought I'd pretty much covered it, until an Anglican clergyman published a book (*The Faith of the English*) using *Watching the English* as his 'key text' and as the entire basis of an educational programme for church groups, with the aim of 'integrating' Christian faith and Englishness. I was surprised, to put it mildly, as all my observations on our tacit atheism, 'benign indifference' and so on in this chapter should have been enough to put anyone off such an attempt. But his book is intelligent and intriguing, and he deals with all my inconvenient observations – and my unflattering comments on his church – in typically English fashion, by politely ignoring them.

of some sort, if only by default or for the sake of convenience? The term '*rites de passage*' was coined in 1908 by the anthropologist Arnold van Gennep, who defined them as 'rites which accompany every change of place, state, social position and age'. Van Gennep had presumably noticed that while all animals are born, reach maturity, reproduce and die, only humans seem to feel the need to make an almighty song-and-dance over each of these life-cycle transitions – and quite a few calendrical ones as well[120] – surrounding them with elaborate rituals and investing every biological and seasonal change with deep social significance. Other animals also struggle for dominance and status within their herd or other social group, and form special bonds and alliances with selected peers. Again, humans make a big production number out of such matters, marking every rise in rank or affiliation to a sub-group with yet more rites and rituals and ceremonies. (Well, van Gennep didn't actually mention animals, and he certainly didn't make jokes about song-and-dance numbers, but he was French and rather earnest.)

There is nothing peculiarly English, then, about rites of passage. Every human society has these transitional rituals, and although the details and emphasis vary from one culture to another, van Gennep showed that these rites always have roughly the same basic structure, involving three stages or elements: separation (pre-liminal), marginality/transition (liminal) and re-incorporation (post-liminal).

Even in their details and emphasis, most English rites of passage are broadly similar to those of many other modern Western cultures: our babies are christened in white and have godparents; our brides also wear white and have bridesmaids and honeymoons; we wear black at funerals; we exchange gifts at Christmas – and so on. There is not much about the basic formula and sequence of events at, say, a typical English wedding or funeral that would seem particularly strange or unfamiliar to an American, Canadian, Australian or European visitor.

---

120. Victor Turner later redefined 'rites of passage' to exclude calendrical rites, focusing only on transitions in which an individual is socially transformed, but as van Gennep invented the term I feel he should get to decide what it means, and I'm using his rather broader definition.

Ambivalence Rules

So what, if anything, is distinctively English about English rites of passage? What, if anything, *might* seem odd or different to a visitor or immigrant from even a closely related modern Western culture? I started by taking the rather obvious step of asking them. 'It's not the customs or traditions,' said a perceptive American informant, who had herself participated in weddings (one as bride, one as mother-of) on both sides of the Atlantic. 'You're right, they're pretty much the same. It's more the attitude people have, something about their whole manner. It's hard to describe, but the English just don't seem to *participate* fully in a wedding the way we do – they always seem a bit, I don't know, a bit detached, kind of cynical but awkward at the same time – just not really *into* it, somehow.' Another trans-atlantic informant told me, 'I'd always thought the English were supposed to be good at ritual – you know, pomp and ceremony and all that. And you are: there's no one better when it comes to the really big public occasion – royal weddings, state funerals, that kind of thing; but when you go to ordinary private weddings and so on everyone just seems so . . . uncomfortable and stiff and stilted. Or they get completely drunk and stupid. There doesn't seem to be much in between.'

The problem is that rites of passage are by definition social occa-sions, involving a sustained period of obligatory interaction with other humans – and, worse, many are social occasions at which 'private' family matters (pair-bonding, bereavement, transition to adulthood) become 'public'. On top of all that, one is expected to express a bit of emotion. Not much, admittedly: the English do not go in for extravagant weeping and wailing at funerals, frenzied joy at weddings, or excessively gooey sentimentality at christenings; but even the minimal, token display of feeling that is customary at English rites of passage can be an ordeal for many of us.

(Most of us cannot even stomach 'the peace' – a ritual introduced into ordinary church services by well-meaning vicars, which merely requires us to shake hands with the person next to us and mumble, 'Peace be with you.'

'Everyone I've ever met *hates* "the peace",' said one informant. 'It sends shivers up my spine just thinking about it.')

Life-cycle transitional rites can be tense affairs in other countries as well, of course. The events marked by rites of passage often involve major transformations, which may be a source of considerable anxiety and fear. Even events regarded as positive transitions, occasions for celebration – such as christenings, coming-of-age or graduation ceremonies, engagement-parties and weddings – can be highly stressful. The passage from one social state to another is a difficult business, and it is no accident that such events, in most cultures, almost invariably involve the consumption of significant quantities of alcohol.

But the English do seem to find these transitional rites particularly challenging, and I think that our uneasiness reflects a curious ambivalence in our attitude towards ritual. We have an intense need for the rules and formalities of ritual, but at the same time we find these ceremonies acutely embarrassing and uncomfortable. As with dress, we are at our best when we are 'in uniform' – at those grand-scale royal and state rituals when every step is choreographed and every word scripted, leaving no room for uncertainty or inept social improvisation. The participants may not enjoy these occasions, but at least they know what to do and say. I pointed out in Dress Codes (page 385) that although the English do not *like* formality, and resent being dictated to by prim little rules and stuffy regulations, we lack the natural grace and social ease to cope with informality.

The rituals involved in private weddings, funerals and other 'passages' are just formal enough to make us feel stiff and resentful, but also informal enough to expose our social dis-ease. The formal pieties and platitudes are too affectedly earnest, too contrived and, in many cases, too embarrassingly *religious*, making us squirm and tug at our collars and shuffle our feet. But the informal bits where we are left to our own devices are even more awkward. Our difficulties at weddings and other transformational rites are essentially the same as those of a 'normal' English social encounter – those painfully inept introductions and greetings where nobody knows quite what to say or what they should do with their hands – only here our problems are magnified by the importance of the occasion. We feel we should try to say something suitably profound to a bride, proud parent, widow or graduate, without sounding pompous or sentimental, or resorting to worn-out clichés, and that we should arrange our features into a suitably pleased or downcast expression, again without overdoing either joy or grief. And we still don't know what to do with our hands, or whether or not to hug or kiss, resulting in the usual clumsy, tentative handshakes, stiffly self-conscious embraces and awkward bumping of cheeks (or, at weddings and christenings, bumping of hat-brims).

Hatching Rules

Only around a quarter of the English have their babies christened. This perhaps tells us more about English indifference to religion than about our attitude to children, but about a third of us do get married in church, and a similar number end up having a Christian funeral of some sort, so the relative unpopularity of christenings may reflect a certain cultural apathy towards children as well. It is not as though those who do not go in for christenings compensate with some other kind of momentous celebration to welcome the new arrival.[121] The birth of a child is a positive event, certainly, but the English do not make nearly as much of a big social fuss about it as most other cultures. The proud new father may buy a few rounds of drinks for his mates in the pub (a custom curiously known as 'wetting the baby's head', although the baby is not present, which is probably just as well), but then the English will happily seize upon almost any excuse for a celebratory drink or six. The child is not even the subject of conversation for very long: once the father has been subjected to a bit of good-natured ribbing, and a brief moaning ritual about the curtailment of freedom, sleepless nights, loss of libido and general noise and mess associated with babies, the topic is regarded as pretty much exhausted, and the head-wetters resume their normal pub-talk.

121. Secular baby-naming ceremonies are becoming more popular, but still only a few hundred of the 800,000 or so babies born each year are welcomed in this manner.

Grandparents, other close relatives and the mother's female friends may take more of a genuine interest in the infant, but this is largely a matter of informal private visits rather than any big social rites of passage. The American custom of a 'baby shower' for the new mother is sometimes adopted, but has not really caught on here to the same degree, and in any case usually takes place *before* the birth, with no actual baby involved. Christenings tend to be relatively small and quiet affairs[122]; and even at christenings, the baby is only the focus of attention for a very brief period – the English as a rule do not go in for too much excited goo-ing and coo-ing over infants. In some cases (enough for *Debrett's* to comment and frown upon the practice) christenings are merely an excuse for social-climbing parents to secure 'posh', rich or influential godparents for their child – known as 'trophy godparents'.

Please don't misunderstand me. I am *not* suggesting that individual English parents do not love and cherish their children. They clearly do, and they have the same natural parental instincts as any other humans. It is just that *as a culture* we do not seem to value children as highly as other cultures do. We love them as individuals, but we do not ritually welcome them into the social world with the same degree of enthusiasm. It is often said that the English care more about their animals than their children. This is an unfair exaggeration, but remember that our National Society for the Prevention of Cruelty to Children was not founded until some sixty years *after* the Royal Society for the Prevention of Cruelty to Animals, which gives some indication of the cultural order of priorities.

Kid-talk and the One-downmanship Rules

English parents are as proud of their children as parents in any other culture, but you would never know this from the way we talk about them. The modesty rules not only forbid boasting about one's offspring, but also specifically prescribe mock-denigration of them.

---

122. In terms of numbers of invited guests, at least. When christenings take place at a normal morning family service, numbers depend on how well attended the church is.

Even the proudest and most doting of English parents must roll their eyes, sigh heavily, and moan to each other about how noisy, tiresome, lazy, hopeless and impossible their children are. At a party, I heard one mother try to pay another a compliment: 'I hear your Peter's doing ten GCSEs – he must be terribly clever . . .' This was deflected with a snorting laugh and a disparaging complaint: 'Well, he'll have to be, as he certainly never seems to do any work – just plays those mindless computer games and listens to that Godawful music . . .' To which the first mother replied, 'Oh, don't tell me – Sam's bound to fail all his: the only thing he's any good at is skateboarding, and they don't have A levels in that, as I keep telling him, not that he takes a blind bit of notice of anything I say, of course . . .' The children in question might have been academic paragons, and both mothers perfectly aware of this – indeed, the lack of any real anxiety in their tones suggested that they were confidently expecting good results – but it would have been bad manners to say so.

The correct tone to adopt when talking about your children is a kind of detached, cynical, humorous resignation – as though you are *moderately* fond of them but nonetheless find them a bit of a bore and a nuisance. There are parents who break these unwritten rules, who show off and brag about their offspring's virtues and achievements, or gush sentimentally over them, but such behaviour is frowned upon as affected and pretentious, and such parents usually find themselves shunned and subtly excluded. Among family and close friends, English parents may express their real feelings about their children – whether bursting with love and pride or sick with worry – but among acquaintances at the school gates, or in other casual social chat, almost all of them assume the same air of mildly amused, critical detachment, and compete in bad-mouthing their hapless offspring.

But this typically English one-downmanship is not quite what it seems. The English, as I've said before, are no more naturally modest than any other nation, and although we obey the letter of the unwritten modesty laws, the spirit is another matter. Many of our derogatory comments about our children are in fact boasts in disguise, or at least highly disingenuous. Moaning about one's child's laziness and unwillingness to do homework indirectly conveys that he or she is bright enough to do well without trying. Complaining that one's 'impossible' children spend all their time on the telephone or out 'doing God knows what' with their friends is another way of saying how popular they are. A mother's eye-rolling mock-despair over her daughter's obsession with fashion and make-up reminds us that the girl is exceptionally pretty. We respond with a one-down expression of exasperation at our own child's tedious obsession with sport – really a covert boast about her athletic prowess.

If you are genuinely distressed about your children's habits or behaviour, it is still vitally important to adopt the correct *mock*-despairing tone. *Real* despair can only be expressed among very close friends (or anonymously on internet forums): at the school gates or at social gatherings, even if you are truly feeling desperate, you must pretend to be only pretending to feel desperate. Listening to these conversations, I would occasionally detect an edge of genuine hope-lessness creeping into a mother's tone as she described the transgres-sions of her 'hopeless' children. Her fellow moaners would start to look a little uncomfortable, avoiding eye contact with her and shifting uneasily about – their feet turning to point away from her, uncon-sciously signalling a desire to escape. Usually, the speaker would sense their discomfort, pull herself together and resume the proper tone of light-hearted, humorous, pretend distress. The unbearable lightness of being English.

The rules of the one-downmanship game also include a strict injunction against ever criticising the other person's child. You can denigrate your own as much as you like, but you must never say a disparaging word about your moaning-companions' offspring (or at least never to their face). Expressions of sympathy are allowed, in response to parents' complaints about their children's misdeeds or inadequacies, but must be carefully phrased to avoid causing offence. A deliberately vague 'Oh, I *know*' or a bit of empathetic tutting and rueful head-shaking are the only truly safe responses, and should be immediately followed by a one-down grumble about your own chil-dren's failings.

None of this is as calculated or deliberately hypocritical as it might sound. Most English parents obey the one-downmanship rules automatically, without thinking. They instinctively adopt the cynical, mock-despairing tones and appropriate facial expressions. They just somehow know, without consciously reminding themselves, that it isn't done to boast or get emotional. Even the subtle, indirect boasting – the showing-off disguised as deprecation – is not the result of careful thought. English parents do not say to themselves, 'Hmm, I'm not allowed to boast, so let me see, how can I bad-mouth my child while still somehow conveying that he/she is a genius?' This kind of indirectness just comes naturally to us. We are accustomed to not saying what we mean: irony, self-deprecation, understatement, obliqueness, ambiguity and polite pretence are all deeply ingrained, part of being English. This peculiar mindset is inculcated at an early age, and by the time our children go to primary school, they have usually already mastered the art of the indirect boast, and can do their own self-deprecatory trumpet-blowing.

English children's fear of undisguised boasting can be a handicap later on, in job interviews, when asking for promotions or pay rises and in other work situations where one is required to 'sell oneself' – or at least talk with some confidence about one's skills, abilities and achievements. Even the most privileged, well-educated and articulate English teenagers are so bad at this that one private school introduced a 'blow your own trumpet week', in which pupils were encouraged to acknowledge their strengths and successes, without fear of 'being seen as too confident'. Despite its jokey title, this was a fairly modest and understated exercise, in which pupils were asked, for example, to write some of their personal achievements on postcards and pin them to a tree. But this is England, so the newspapers were full of alarming headlines about 'boasting lessons', and quotes from the head teacher patiently denying that any unseemly boasting was involved.

The Self-deprecating Insult Rule

Speaking of privileged schoolchildren and the English art of indirectness, here is a quote I came across in a posh magazine from a mother whose daughter was in the same house as Kate Middleton (now the

Duchess of Cambridge, married to Prince William) at Marlborough, a very grand private boarding school: 'There was always something slightly galling about having your children at school with the Middletons. Every pristine item of clothing would have a beautifully sewn-in name tape, for instance. It was unthinkable that they would end up resorting to marker pens on labels like the rest of us. There were huge picnics at sports day, the smartest tennis racquets, that kind of thing. It made the rest of us all feel rather hopeless.'

To anyone who understands English class-indicators, this mother's apparently humble statement – all self-denigrating and full of admiration for the Middleton family's perfections – is not only an indirect boast, but also a subtle snobby put-down. Even if you are not English, if you've read the rest of this book, you should have no trouble deciphering the coded insults:

- You will know, as this mother clearly does, that caring about every item of clothing being 'pristine', with perfectly sewn-in name tapes, is a middle-middle or even lower-middle indicator. Even the word 'pristine' is a sneer: only the suburban bourgeoisie regard it as a term of approbation, and fuss about having everything 'pristine' or 'spotless'. Remember the lines from Betjeman's satirical poem, 'You kiddies have crumpled the serviettes/And I must have things daintily served'? (Or if you want a more modern example, think of the desperate social-climber Hyacinth Bucket, in the television comedy *Keeping Up Appearances*, and her constant fretting over such dainty details.)

- Upper class and secure-upper-middle mothers ('the rest of us', as this mother is careful to remind us, twice) would be carelessly indifferent about such trivia and perfectly happy to send their children back to Marlborough with crumpled clothes and their initials roughly scrawled in marker pen on their clothing labels. To say that the Middleton family would find this 'unthinkable' puts them firmly in their *petit-bourgeois* place.

- This mother's professed feeling of inferiority over the Middletons' big lavish picnics at school sports days, their expensive brand-new tennis racquets and 'that kind of thing', is utterly disingenuous. Worse than just insincere praise, this is yet another veiled insult: such ostentatious displays of wealth are clear *nouveau-riche* indicators.

- So, far from making this mother and 'the rest of us all' feel 'rather hopeless' by comparison, the Middletons' immaculate clothes, dainty name tapes, fancy picnics and high-priced sports equipment would in fact have made them all feel rather smugly superior.

- The repetition of 'the rest of us' (with the addition of 'all' the second time, just in case we missed the point) is a dead giveaway. What this mother is really saying is that among the truly upper/upper-middle Marlborough parents, the Middletons were not regarded as 'PLU' (People Like Us) but as jumped-up *nouveau* social-climbers. But this is England, so she says it in code: this quote is an exquisite example of English irony, in which every line is a snobbish put-down, cleverly disguised as a self-deprecating compliment.

The only thing that she and the other snooty Marlborough mothers may *genuinely* have found 'slightly galling' about the middle-class Middletons is that their daughter married the heir to the throne.

The Invisible-puberty Rule

The English, as a culture, tend to regard children as something of a tiresome encumbrance, and adolescents as a positive nuisance. Adolescents are seen as somehow both vulnerable and dangerous: objects of concern, but also potentially threatening; in need of protection, but also in need of restraint – and just generally *troublesome*. It is perhaps not surprising, then, that only minority faiths celebrate the onset of puberty in any significant way. The advent of this awkward, embarrassing, hormonally challenged phase of life is not widely regarded as a matter for celebration. The English prefer to bury their heads in the sand and try to pretend that it isn't happening. The C of E does offer a 'confirmation' ceremony at the appropriate age (traditionally between eleven and fourteen), but this is even less popular than christening, and there is no secular equivalent, so the vast majority of English children have no official rite of passage to mark their transition to adolescence.

Deprived of their rightful rites, English adolescents tend to invent their own unofficial initiation rituals – which usually involve getting into trouble for illegal drinking, experimenting with illicit recreational drugs, shoplifting, graffiti-spraying, joy-riding, etc. – or find other ways of drawing attention to their new sexual status: we have the highest rate of teenage pregnancy in Europe, for example.

But they are not formally 'welcomed' as fully fledged members of our society until *after* they have struggled through puberty, when the next official rite of passage, the eighteenth-birthday celebration, marks their transition to adulthood. For some, there is a mini rite of passage at seventeen, when they pass their driving test and get a driving licence, but eighteen is the age at which the English are officially entitled to vote, get married without parental consent, have homosexual sex, watch X-rated films and, most importantly for many, buy alcoholic drinks. Most will have been unofficially drinking, having whatever kind of sex they choose and watching 'adult' films (not to mention online pornography) for some years; many will have left school at sixteen and may be working full time; some may even be married or cohabiting, pregnant or with a baby of their own. But the eighteenth birthday is still regarded as an important landmark, and an excuse to have a big noisy party, or at least to get even more drunk than on an average Saturday night.

There may now, however, be a slight shift in the right direction. Although I doubt that my laments about 'invisible puberty' had anything to do with this, I am very pleased to report that a fairly new ritual, consisting of a big end-of-primary-school party/disco/prom, for eleven-year-olds moving on to secondary school, has become increasingly popular in English primary schools since this book was first published in 2004. Whatever one may think of the Hollywood-style extravagance and glitz involved in a small minority of these events, they are at least a step towards *some* kind of puberty rites for our ritual-deprived pubescents. Bar mitzvahs and bat mitzvahs are often very lavish affairs – and what some see as the excessive indulgence and glamour of these mini-proms seems to me no different from these ceremonies, or indeed from the highly elaborate and festive puberty rites held at or around the time of a girl's first menstruation in many other cultures, such as the four-day Navajo Kinaalda ceremony, or the eight-stage Apache Na'ii'ees or Sunrise Dance, to take just a couple of random examples. There is a reason that most cultures have these rituals: puberty is an important transition, and our pubescent youngsters are certainly aware of this, even if we choose to ignore it. They need to feel special and important and a bit 'grown-up' for a day, and we should be applauding any attempt to give them some kind of formal ceremony to mark and celebrate the beginning of their transition to adulthood. Those who disapprove of the primary schools' new final-year parties and proms are free to come up with something better – but of course they never do: they just grumble and carp in the usual Eeyorish manner.

The same applies, I think, to Sweet Sixteen parties, another ritual 'coming of age' celebration – already widespread in the US and with many equivalents in other countries, such as the *quinceañera* at fifteen in Latin America – that has recently become more popular in this country. Most of our Sweet Sixteens are fairly modest affairs, in no way resembling the 'My Super Sweet Sixteen UK' extravaganzas featured on the television show of that title, which are the preserve of a tiny minority of very rich, very spoiled brats. Again, perhaps it would be unwise to condemn all of the new coming-of-age parties on the basis of such an unrepresentative sample.

The Gap-year 'Ordeal'

Among the educated classes, the eighteenth-birthday rites are now often followed by the 'gap year', a passage between school and university involving a more prolonged 'liminal' period, in which it is customary for young people to spend some months travelling abroad, as their seventeenth- and eighteenth-century equivalents did in the Grand Tour, but now often incorporating some kind of charity work (helping Peruvian villagers to build a school, working in a Romanian orphanage, digging a well, saving a rainforest, etc.) and generally seeing the Real (i.e. poor) World and having meaningful, character-building Experiences. The gap-year trip is seen as a sort of initiation ordeal – a less arduous version of the custom in some tribal societies of sending adolescent males off into the jungle or wilderness for a time to endure a few pains and hardships and prove themselves worthy of official incorporation into adult society.

Among the English upper and upper-middle classes, this has often already been achieved by banishing one's offspring to character-building boarding schools for their entire adolescence. Until relatively recently, the upper class and aristocracy were determinedly anti-intellectual (a trait they shared, along with a penchant for sport and gambling, with the working classes), and rather looked down upon the middle classes' reverence for higher education. Their sons might go to university, but this was not regarded as essential – a spell in the army or at agricultural college or something would do just as well – and academic achievement was even less important for their daughters. The young Lady Diana Spencer never seemed particularly ashamed of her total lack of academic qualifications, joking cheerfully in public speeches about her dismal O-level results and how 'thick' she was. A middle-class girl would have been mortified. These attitudes are changing, particularly among the lower or less wealthy echelons of the upper class, whose offspring must now compete with the university-educated middle classes for the best jobs. Upper-class and even aristocratic or royal post-adolescents (including Diana's sons Princes William and Harry in 2000 and 2004) now find themselves bonding, team-building and comparing mosquito bites with middle-class teenagers on worthy gap-year adventures.

Gap-year initiates of all classes are expected to come back from their Experience transformed into mature, socially aware, reliable adults, ready to take on the enormous challenge and responsibility of living in a university hall of residence, doing their own laundry and occasionally having to open a tin of beans when they come back from the pub to find that the cafeteria is shut. First-year university students who have 'done a gap year' regard themselves as superior to those who have come 'straight from school' – more grown-up and worldly wise. They have a tendency to talk rather smugly about how much *older* they feel, compared to the immature, silly, un-gap-yeared freshers.

In some less privileged sections of English society, a spell in prison or in a young offenders' institution at around the same age is regarded as having a similar character-building, maturing effect – and graduates of this initiation-ordeal often exhibit much the same sense of smug superiority over their childish, uninitiated peers. In fact, if you look past the superficial ethnographic dazzle of accent and jargon, the similarities in the talk and manner of those who have 'been Inside' and those who have been gap-yeared are quite striking.

Student Rites

Freshers' Week Rules

For the privileged university-goers, the eighteenth-birthday rites, A-level exams and possibly gap-year 'ordeal' are followed by another important rite of passage known as Freshers' Week. This initiation ritual follows the classic pattern identified by van Gennep – preliminal separation, liminal transition/marginalisation and post-liminal incorporation. The initiates are first separated from their families, their familiar surroundings and their social status as school-children. Most arrive at university accompanied by one or both parents, in cars crammed with objects from their old life (clothes, books, CDs, duvet, favourite pillow, posters, photos, teddy-bear) and specially purchased objects for their new life (shiny new kettle, mug, bowl, plate, spoon, towel and so on).

Once they have helped to unload all this, parents become something of an embarrassing encumbrance, and are dismissed by the fresher with unceremonious haste and impatient reassurances: 'Yes, yes – I'll be *fine*. No, *don't* help me unpack, I can manage. Don't *fuss*, OK? Yes, I'll ring you tomorrow. Yes, all *right*. Bye now, bye . . .' The fresher may in fact be feeling anxious and even tearful at the prospect of parting, but knows without being told that it is not done – indeed, deeply uncool – to display these feelings in front of other freshers.

The fresher initiates barely have time to Blu-tac a few posters to their walls before the 'liminal' phase begins and they are hurled into a disorienting, noisy, exhausting succession of parties and fairs and events, staged by a bewildering variety of student clubs and societies – sporting, social, theatrical, artistic, political – all competing to sign them up for an impossible number of extra-curricular activities. These 'official' events are interspersed with pub-crawls, late-night pizzas and bleary-eyed, rambling coffee-sessions at three in the morning (as well as endless queuing to register for courses, obtain student identity cards and sign incomprehensible forms). This week-long 'liminal' phase is a period of cultural remission and inversion, in which the initiate's senses are disturbed by alcohol and sleepless-ness, social borders and categories are crossed and blurred, former identity is challenged and disrupted, and acceptance in the new social world is sought through pledges of affiliation to student clubs and societies. By the end of the week, the initiate has achieved a new social identity: he or she is incorporated as a student into the student 'tribe' – and finally allowed to rest a bit, calm down, start attending lectures and participating in normal student life.

Students like to describe Freshers' Week as 'mad' and 'anarchic' but, like most episodes of cultural remission, it is in fact a rule-governed, predictable, conventionalised deviation from convention. Certain normal social rules are suspended or inverted for the dura-tion of the festivities – talking to strangers, for example, is not only allowed but actively encouraged: one of the many guides to Freshers' Week produced by student unions reminds initiates that this is 'probably the only time in your life' that you will be free to approach and strike up conversation with complete strangers, and urges you to make the most of the opportunity. The subtext is equally clear: after Freshers' Week is over, the normal rules of Englishness apply, and talking to strangers without good cause is no longer acceptable. Freshers are encouraged to meet and make friends with as many fellow students as possible – a euphemism for ignoring class barriers – but also subtly reassured that friendships formed during the liminal period of Freshers' Week are not 'binding', that they will not be obliged to continue to associate with people from incompatible social backgrounds. 'You will meet countless new people (many of whom you will never see again after the first two weeks) and drink countless pints (many of which you will see again, the next morning)' are the instructions in one typical 'How to survive Freshers' Week' leaflet.

Getting drunk during Freshers' Week *is* more or less compulsory ('you *will* drink countless pints') and the English self-fulfilling belief in the magical disinhibiting powers of alcohol is essential – without it, the inversion of normal social rules about talking to strangers would be pointless, as most freshers would be too shy to approach anyone. Free social lubricant is provided at all of the parties and events during Freshers' Week, and initiates are expected to over-indulge and shed their inhibitions. In the prescribed manner, that is: there is a fairly limited range of acceptable drunken behaviours – 'mooning' (exposing one's bottom) is allowed, for example, but 'flashing' (exposing one's genitals) would be frowned upon; arguing and even fighting are approved, but queue-jumping is still strictly prohibited; telling bawdy jokes is fine, but racist ones are inappropriate. Among the English, drunken disinhibition is an orderly, well-regulated state – and Freshers' Week, despite the appearance of anarchy and debauchery, is actually a choreographed sequence of traditional, conventional rituals in which, every October, first-year students across the country shed exactly the same designated inhibitions in precisely the same time-honoured ways.

Exam and Graduation Rules

The next significant transitional rites for students are final exams, post-exam celebrations and graduation ceremonies: the passage from studenthood to proper adulthood. Studenthood can itself be seen as a rather prolonged 'liminal' stage – a sort of limbo state where one is neither an adolescent nor a full adult. University effectively post-pones true adulthood for an extra three years. As limbo states go, this is quite a pleasant one: students have almost all of the privileges of full adult members of society, but few of the responsibilities. English students moan and whine constantly to each other about their 'impossible' workload, and are always having what they call 'an essay crisis' (meaning they have to write an essay) – but the demands of most degree courses are not very onerous compared to those of an average full-time job.

The ordeal of final exams provides an excuse for even more therapeutic moaning rituals, with their own unwritten rules. The modesty rule is important: even if you are feeling reasonably calm and confident about an exam, it is not done to say so – you must pretend to be full of anxiety and self-doubt, convinced that you are going to fail, because it goes without saying (although you say it repeatedly) that you have not done anywhere near enough work. Only the most arrogant, pompous and socially insensitive students will ever admit to having done enough revision for their exams; such people are rare, and usually heartily disliked.

If you have clearly swotted like mad, you can admit this only in a self-deprecatory context: 'I've worked my butt off, but I'm still completely pants at genetics – I just know I'm going to screw up – and anyway there's bound to be a question on the one thing I haven't revised properly. Just Sod's Law, isn't it?' Any expression of confidence must be counterbalanced by an expression of insecurity: 'I think I'm OK on the sociology paper, but statistics is just totally doing my head in . . .'

An element of superstition, or fear of making a fool of oneself, may be an important factor before the exam, but the modest demeanour is maintained even *after* the desired result has been achieved. Those who do well must always appear surprised by their success, even if they secretly feel it was well deserved. Cries of 'Oh, my God! I don't believe it!' are the norm when such students receive their results, and while elation is expected, success should be attributed to good fortune ('I was lucky – all the right questions came up') rather than talent or hard work. An Oxford medical student who had got a First, and was being congratulated by friends and relatives at a celebratory lunch, kept ducking her head, shrugging and insisting that 'It's not really such a big deal in science subjects – you don't have to be clever or anything, it's all factual – you just memorise the stuff and give the right answers. It's just parrot-learning'.

At post-exam celebrations, it is also customary for all students to indulge in moaning rituals about their sense of 'anti-climax'. At every party, you will hear students complaining about how jaded they are. 'I know I'm supposed to be feeling all happy and celebrating,' they say, 'but actually it's a bit of an anti-climax'; 'Everyone's all euphoric, but I just feel like, yeah, OK, whatever . . .' Although every student seems to believe that he or she is the first to experience this, the anti-climax lament is so common that students who *do* feel euphoric and celebratory are in the minority.

The next opportunity not to get excited is the graduation ceremony. Students all claim to be bored and unimpressed by this occasion. None will admit to any sense of pride: it is just a tedious ritual, to be endured for the sake of doting parents. As at the start of the Freshers' Week rites, parents are again seen as something of an embarrassment. Many students go to some lengths to keep their parents and other relatives away from their friends and from any tutors or lecturers who might be present at the ceremony ('*No*, Dad! *Don't* ask him about my "career prospects". This isn't a bloody PTA meeting . . .'; 'Look, Mum, just don't do anything *soppy*, OK?'; 'Oh, for Christ's sake, Granny, don't *cry*! It's only a degree – I haven't won the fu– the flipping Nobel prize . . .'). Students with overly doting parents adopt bored, exasperated expressions, rolling their eyes and sighing heavily, particularly when anyone they know is within view or earshot.

School-leaver rites

The last few pages have focused disproportionately on educated-middle-class rites of passage – gap year, Freshers' Week, graduation. This is because there are no equivalent national, official rites for those who leave school at sixteen – or even for those who stop full-time education at eighteen. School leavers may celebrate in some way with their friends and/or family, but there is no formal ritual to mark their passage from school to vocational training, employment or unemployment. Yet one's first job (or dole cheque) is an important landmark, and arguably much more of a momentous change than simply going from school to university. Some schools have special speech days with prize-givings and so on, but no actual 'graduation' ceremony, and certainly nothing like an American high-school graduation, which is a big event, grander and more elaborate than most English university graduation ceremonies. GCSE and A-level exam results do not come out until late August, well after the school year has finished, so 'graduates' would in any case only be celebrating the end of their schooldays, rather than the academic success or achievement implied by the term 'graduation'. But it still seems a shame that the completion of secondary education, and the passage from school to adult working life, is not ritually marked in some more significant way.

Again I doubt that my whingeing had any influence, but I am happy to report that, although we still have few proper graduation ceremonies, this passage is at least now marked, in many schools, by a new, imported ritual: the 'high-school prom'. In the past decade, American-style proms – complete with hired stretch limos, girls in fancy ballgowns or cocktail dresses and sophisticated hairdos, boys in black tie or smart suits, many months of excited planning, etc. – have rapidly become hugely popular in English schools, over 85 per cent of which now hold them. These glamorous events have replaced the rather dull and half-hearted 'school discos' that some schools used to hold at the end of the summer term, but also sometimes at Christmas or at other times, such that they never held any particular significance for the graduating class, who were never given much, if any, special treatment or recognition. Indeed, it is still the case that one does not actually 'graduate' from an English school: one simply leaves, and one is called a 'school leaver', a depressing term with no connotations of achievement or accomplishment, especially when compared with the more impressive-sounding 'high-school graduate'. The new proms at least give our school leavers some sense of importance, and some kind of formal rite of passage to mark this socially significant transition.

English media pundits are of course now moaning about the cost of these new-fangled proms, expressing sardonic contempt for all the flashy, glitzy, ostentatious 'American' extravagance. They focus on the small minority of parents who spend ridiculous amounts of money on their daughters' designer outfits or horse-drawn carriages, rather than the majority who buy relatively cheap high-street frocks and club together to squeeze a dozen girls into a hired limo. Tabloid moralists express much virtuous indignation over all the ballgowns and make-up, which they deem too 'adult' for teenage schoolgirls – their diatribes invariably printed, with the usual hypocrisy, alongside large photographs of the most titillating examples they can find of scantily dressed prom-goers. They seem to miss the point that transition to adulthood is precisely what this rite of passage is all about, and dressing up in special 'grown-up' clothing is an integral part of the symbolic transformation. And although our proms have indeed been largely inspired by American films and television series, most other countries have some equivalent of the US high-school prom – and in many countries these celebrations are long-standing national or regional traditions. Graduation parties and balls are also, almost everywhere, more ceremonial and exciting events than the dreary, meaningless, ill-defined school discos that English teenagers had been enduring until very recently. We fail to mark their passage from childhood to adolescence with any puberty rites, we give them no graduation ceremony to mark the end of their schooldays, and now some would even begrudge them a bit of a festive ritual to celebrate their transition from school to the adult world.

In all the complaints about Americanisation, commentators have failed to notice that our proms do differ in at least one significant respect from the American variety: despite their supposedly slavish imitation of proms as portrayed in Hollywood films and American television series, our teenagers have generally not embraced the US custom of 'prom dates'. There are some exceptions, but most English school leavers attend their proms in groups – usually single-sex groups – not as couples. American prom photos all tend to feature couples, or rows of couples like animals waiting to board Noah's Ark, two by two. English prom photos, by contrast, are almost all of single-sex groups, ranging from trios to small herds. They may well end up pairing off during the course of the evening, but they do so in that typically English vague, ambivalent, non-dating manner. They might find themselves 'snogging', or even having furtive sex in some uncomfortable and undignified location at the after-party. Indeed, they may have been 'sexting' half-naked photos of themselves to each other, and having sex, for some time – but actually asking someone to be your 'date' for the prom would be too explicit, too cheesy, too embarrassingly intimate.

Matching Rites

At the beginning of this chapter, I pointed out that there is little about the format of an average English wedding that would seem odd or unfamiliar to a visitor from any other modern Western culture: we have the usual stag and hen nights (Americans call them bachelor and bachelorette parties); church or civil ceremony followed by reception; champagne; bride in white; wedding cake ditto; bridesmaids (optional); Best Man; speeches; special food; drink; dancing (optional); family tensions and feuds (more or less compulsory); etc. From an anthropologist's perspective, an English wedding also has much in common even with exotic tribal marriage rites that *would* seem odd to most modern Western eyes. Despite superficial differences, they all conform to van Gennep's basic rites-of-passage formula – separation, transition, incorporation – by which people are ceremoniously shunted from one sociocultural/life-cycle category to the next.

The English make rather less of a big social fuss about the 'engagement' than many other cultures – in some societies, the betrothal or engagement party can be as important an event as the wedding itself. (Perhaps to compensate, we make rather more of a fuss over the stag and hen nights, which are often considerably more protracted and festive than the wedding.)

Debrett's etiquette bible reminds us, somewhat pessimistically, that 'An important function of an engagement is to allow the two parental sides to get used to one another, and thus smooth out as early as possible any differences and difficulties.' This tells us a lot about the English attitude to weddings. We know that a wedding is supposed to be a joyous event, but in our usual Eeyorish fashion, we really see it as an ordeal, an occasion fraught with difficulties and dangers (or, as the ever-cheery *Debrett's* puts it, 'a minefield for the socially insecure and a logistical nightmare for the organisers' and, for good measure, 'a source of inter-family tension'). Something is bound to go drastically wrong, and someone is bound to be mortally offended – and because of our belief in the magical disinhibiting powers of alcohol, we know that the veneer of polite conviviality may crack, and the inevitable family tensions may erupt into unseemly tears and quarrels. Even if stiff upper lips are maintained on the day, there will be grumbles and recriminations in the aftermath, and in any case, even at best, we expect the whole ritual to be rather embarrassing.

The Money-talk Taboo

When the tensions are over money, which they often are – not least because weddings tend to be expensive affairs – the embarrassment factor is doubled. Unlike most other cultures, we persist in the notion that love and marriage have nothing to do with money – and that any mention of money would 'lower the tone' of the event. It is customary, for example, for the male partner to fork out about a month's salary on an engagement ring (in America it can be double that, or even more, as an engagement ring is seen as a more overt symbol of the male's status as a provider) but to ask or talk about how much the ring cost would be offensive. This does not stop everyone making their own private guesses, or asking about the stones and the setting as a roundabout way of estimating the price, but only the groom (and perhaps his bank manager) should know the exact cost, and only a very crass, vulgar groom would either boast or complain about it.

The cost of the wedding itself is traditionally borne by the bride's parents, but in these days of late marriages is now often met or at least shared by the couple themselves and/or grandparents or other relatives. But whoever has footed the lion's share of the bill, the groom will usually, in his speech, politely thank the bride's parents for 'this wonderful party' or some such euphemism. If the groom's parents, grandparents or uncle have contributed by paying for, say, the champagne or the honeymoon, they may be thanked for 'providing' or 'giving' these items – to use the words 'paying for' would imply that money was involved. We all know perfectly well that money is involved, but it would be bad manners to draw attention to the fact. The usual English hypocrisies. These polite euphemisms may conceal many petty financial squabbles, and in some cases much seething resentment over who paid for what or how unnecessarily extravagant the whole thing was. If you are hard-up, there is very little point in beggaring yourself to provide a lavishly expensive wedding for your daughter: other cultures might be impressed, but the English will only find it ostentatious, and wonder why you did not 'just do something simple and unpretentious'.

Humour Rules

Quite apart from the difficulties caused by money, or by the money-talk taboo, there is nowadays endless potential for tension in the composition of the two families involved in the ritual: it is highly likely that at least one set of parents will be divorced, and possibly remarried or cohabiting with new partners, perhaps with children from second or even third pair-bondings.

And even if nobody makes a drunken exhibition of themselves, and nobody is offended by the seating plan or the transport arrangements or the Best Man's speech, someone is bound to do or say something that will cause embarrassment. At the first English wedding I ever attended, I was that someone, although I was only about five years old. My parents had decided that my sisters and I should have some understanding of the important rite of passage we were about to witness. My father told us all about pair-bonding, described the wedding customs and practices of different cultures, and explained the intricacies of matrilateral cross-cousin marriage. My mother took it upon herself to explain the 'facts of life' – sex, where babies come from and so on. My sisters, aged about three and four, were perhaps a little too young to take much interest in this, but I was riveted. At the church the next day, I found the ceremony equally fascinating, and during a moment's silent pause (possibly after 'speak now, or forever hold your peace'), I turned to my mother and asked, in a loud, piercing whisper, 'Is he going to put the seed in now?'

I was not taken to any weddings for quite a few years after that, which seems a bit unfair, as I had clearly grasped the essential points, and only got the chronological order of things slightly mixed up. The next one I remember was in America, my father's second marriage. I was eight or nine – old enough this time for a lecture on bifurcate merging kinship terminology and virilocal versus uxorilocal post-marital residence patterns, with diagrams. This did not stop me suffering an attack of (mercifully quiet) giggles during the most solemn part of the ceremony. At the time, I felt rather ashamed of myself for being so childish (my father was always telling me to 'stop being childish'), but I now realise that my urge to laugh was a very English response. We find solemnity discomforting, and somehow faintly ridiculous; the most serious, formal, earnest bits of important ceremonies have an unfortunate tendency to make us want to laugh. This is an uneasy, nervous sort of laughter, a close relation of our knee-jerk humour reflex. Humour is our favourite coping mechanism, and laughter is our standard way of dealing with our social dis-ease.

We need this coping mechanism even more now that it has become customary at secular weddings for couples to exchange vows that they have written themselves. Curiously, the gist of these is usually much the same as the traditional church marriage vows, only less eloquently and succinctly expressed. But making earnest speeches, especially about personal feelings, is a supremely awkward undertaking for the English, and listening to these self-written vows makes us squirm with embarrassment, so the guests tend to spend this part of the ceremony trying to suppress giggles. Often, the couple themselves can't get through this embarrassing process without giggling either.

Once the uncomfortably earnest bits are over, English wedding receptions – and most other rites of passage – ring with laughter: virtually every conversational exchange is either overtly or subtly humorous. This is not, however, necessarily an indication that everyone is having a happy, jolly time. Some may well be feeling genuinely cheerful, but even they are also simply obeying the unwritten English humour rules – rules so deeply ingrained they have become an unthinking, involuntary impulse.

Dispatching Rites

Which is one of the reasons why we have a big problem with funerals. There are few rites of passage on Earth as stilted, uncomfortable and excruciatingly awkward as a typical English funeral.[123]

The Humour-vivisection Rule

At funerals we are deprived of our primary social coping mechanism, as our usual levels of humour and laughter are deemed inappropriate on such an officially sad occasion. At other times, we joke constantly about death, as we do about anything that frightens or disturbs us, but funerals are the one time when humour – or, at least, any humour beyond that which raises a wry, sad smile – would be disrespectful and out of place. Without it, we are left naked, unprotected, our social inadequacies exposed for all to see.

This is fascinating but painful to watch, like some cruel vivisectionist's animal-behaviour experiment: observing the English at funerals feels like watching turtles deprived of their shells. Denied the full use of our humour reflex, we seem horribly vulnerable, as though some vital social organ has been removed – which in effect it has. Humour is such an essential, hard-wired element of the English character that forbidding (or severely restricting) its use is the psychological equivalent of amputating our toes – we simply cannot function socially without humour. The English humour rules are 'rules' principally in the fourth sense of the term allowed by the *Oxford English Dictionary*: 'the normal or usual state of things'. Like having toes. Or breathing. At funerals we are left bereft and helpless. No irony! No mockery! No teasing! No banter! No jokey wordplay or *double-entendres*! How the hell are we supposed to communicate? Perhaps understandably, the vivisection rule is not always observed, as the English humour reflex often proves stronger than accepted

123. By which I mean an ordinary 'Christian' or 'traditional' funeral, the kind that the majority of us still have, and that most English readers will have attended at some point. I do realise that there are many other sorts, but there is not space here to cover all the funeral practices of minority faiths, which in any case could not be described as 'typically English' as only about seven per cent of the population belong to these faiths.

funeral etiquette. Although we may avoid the more obvious forms of humour, we find ways to sneak in at least a subtle bit of irony or understatement.

Earnestness-taboo Suspension and Tear Quotas

Not only are we not allowed to relieve tension, break ice and generally self-medicate our chronic social dis-ease by making a joke out of everything, but we are expected to be *solemn*. Not only is humour drastically restricted, but earnestness, normally tabooed, is actively prescribed. We are supposed to say solemn, earnest, heartfelt things to the bereaved relatives, or respond to these things in a solemn, earnest, heartfelt way if we are the bereaved.

But not *too* heartfelt. This is only a limited, qualified suspension of the normal taboo on earnestness and sentimentality. Even those family and friends who are genuinely sad are not allowed to indulge in any cathartic weeping and wailing. Tears are permitted; a bit of quiet, unobtrusive sobbing and sniffing is acceptable, but the sort of anguished bawling and howling that is considered normal, and indeed expected, at funerals in many other cultures, would in England be regarded as undignified and inappropriate.

Even the socially approved quiet tears and sniffles become embarrassing and make people uncomfortable if excessively prolonged, and England is possibly the only culture in the world in which *no tears at all* is entirely normal and acceptable. Most adult English males do not cry publicly at funerals; if their eyes do start to fill, they will usually brush the wetness away with a quick, angry gesture and 'pull themselves together'. Although female relatives and friends are more likely to shed a few tears, failure to do so is not taken as a sign of callousness or absence of grief, providing a suitably sombre expression is maintained, broken only by an occasional 'brave smile'.

In fact, many will regard such restraint as admirable. There may have been criticism of some members of the royal family for their 'uncaring' response to the death of Diana, Princess of Wales, but no one was surprised that her young sons shed only the most minimal, discreet tears at her funeral, having maintained their composure throughout the long walk behind her coffin and, indeed, throughout almost all of the funeral service. They were commended for their bravery and dignity; their smiles and murmured thanks as they accepted the condolences of the crowds during a 'walkabout' were widely praised, and somehow far more poignant than any amount of uninhibited noisy sobbing. The English do not measure grief in tears. Too many tears are regarded as somewhat self-indulgent, even a bit selfish and unfair. Grief-stricken relatives who do not cry, or cry only briefly, at a funeral are likely to be seen as showing great courtesy and consideration for others, putting on a brave face to reassure their guests, rather than demanding attention and comfort for themselves. To be more precise, and at the risk of getting into pea-counting mode again, my calculations indicate that the optimum 'tear quota' at an average English funeral is as follows:

- Adult males (close relatives or very close friends of the deceased): one or two brief 'eye-fillings' during the service, brusquely brushed away. Brave smiles.
- Adult males (other): none. But maintain sombre/sympathetic expression. Sad/concerned smiles.
- Adult females (close relatives or very close friends): one or two short weeps during the service, with optional sniffles; occasional eye-filling, apologetically dabbed with hanky, in response to condolences. Brave smiles.
- Adult females (other): none, or one eye-filling during service. Maintain sad/sympathetic expression. Sad/concerned smiles.
- Male children (close relatives/friends): unlimited if very young (under ten, say); older boys one weep during service. Brave smiles.
- Male children (other): same as for adult males (other).
- Female children (close relatives/friends): unlimited if very young; older girls roughly double the adult female tear quota. Brave smiles.
- Female children (other): none required, but brief eye-filling/ sniffing during service allowed.

I am, of course, talking here about a 'normal' funeral – exceptions to these unspoken rules and tear quotas will be seen at those desperately sad funerals where the deceased is a child, a young adult, or a mother or father of young children. But even on these occasions one does not often see any loud, unrestrained expression of grief – and if anyone does 'break down', their anguished sobbing will usually be punctuated with reflex 'sorries'.

Quite apart from any genuine grief we may be experiencing, the prohibition on humour, the suspension of the earnestness taboo and the tear quotas make English funerals a highly unpleasant business. We are supposed to switch off our humour reflex, express emotions we do not feel, and suppress most of those we do feel. On top of all this, the English regard death itself as rather embarrassing and unseemly, something we prefer not to think or talk about. Our instinctive response to death is a form of denial – we try to ignore it and pretend it is not happening, but this is rather hard to do at a funeral.

Not surprisingly, we tend to become tongue-tied, stiff and uncomfortable. There are no universally agreed-upon stock phrases or gestures (particularly among the higher social classes, who regard comforting clichés and platitudes as 'common') so we don't know what to say to each other or what to do with our hands, resulting in a lot of mumbled so-sorries, very-sads and what-can-I-says – and awkward embraces or wooden little arm-pats. Although many funerals are vaguely 'Christian', this does not indicate any religious beliefs at all, so references to God or the afterlife are inappropriate unless one is absolutely sure of someone's faith. If the deceased was over eighty (seventy-five at a pinch) we can mutter something about him or her having had a 'good innings' – and some gentle humour is permitted at the post-ceremony gathering – but otherwise we are often reduced to mutely rueful head-shaking and meaningful heavy sighs.

Clergymen and others delivering formal eulogies at funerals are lucky: they do have stock phrases they can use. Those used to describe the deceased person are a sort of ironic code. It is forbidden to speak ill of the dead, but everyone knows, for example, that 'always the life and soul of the party' is a euphemism for drunkenness; 'didn't suffer fools gladly' is a polite way of calling the deceased a mean-spirited, grumpy old sod; 'generous with her affections' means she was a promiscuous tart; 'a tireless raconteur' means a crashing bore who loved the sound of his/her own voice; and 'a confirmed bachelor' has always meant he was gay.

The 'Public Outpouring of Grief' Rule

Speaking of stock phrases: our reaction to the death and funeral of Diana, Princess of Wales was described by every newspaper, magazine, radio and television reporter as 'an unprecedented public outpouring of grief'. And I do mean every single one of them – it was almost spooky, the way they all used the exact same phrase. I have already pointed out that this allegedly un-English 'outpouring' consisted mainly of orderly, quiet and dignified queuing but, After Diana, the media became very attached to the phrase 'public outpouring of grief' and have trotted it out at every possible opportunity ever since. (In fact, contrary to popular opinion, there was no major cultural sea-change in expression of grief following the death of the Princess of Wales: my research on crying indicates that the English are, if anything, rather *less* inclined to be tearful now than we were before Diana died – and only 11 per cent of us have ever cried at the death of a public figure, so all those famous television images of people crying were of a highly unrepresentative minority. Most of us are made of sterner stuff, or emotionally constipated, depending on your point of view.)

The considerably more muted response to the Queen Mother's death (which, incidentally, also consisted largely of queuing) was inevitably described as 'a public outpouring of grief'. So was the even less impressive reaction to the death of the former Beatle George Harrison. Every time a child or teenager is murdered or dies in some other newsworthy manner, and a dozen or so friends and sympathisers lay flowers outside their house, school gates or local church, this is now a 'public outpouring of grief'. Pretty much anyone who dies in the public eye, unless they were for some reason widely detested, can nowadays expect nothing less than a 'public outpouring of grief'.

The death of a public figure who *is* widely detested, such as the former prime minister Margaret Thatcher, generally prompts a public outpouring of . . . jokes. Within seconds of the news breaking that Thatcher had died, the torrent of caustic humour began, starting in typical English fashion with a pun: 'Rust in Peace' – a reference to Thatcher's 'Iron Lady' nickname.

More elaborate jokes swiftly followed, including revellers drinking milk and handing out free glasses of milk on the streets, and a milk bottle placed in ironic tribute outside her house – references to an earlier epithet, 'Maggie Thatcher, Milk Snatcher', from 1971 when, as education minister, she abolished free milk for schoolchildren, an act seen as an early example of her callous lack of compassion for the less fortunate.

A media and internet debate ensued about whether or not Thatcher should be given the honour of a full 'state funeral', punctuated by jokes such as 'A state funeral for Thatcher? Surely she would want to go private?' This was, of course, a reference to her constant championing of private industry at the expense of the public sector, and her penchant for privatising formerly nationalised industries – also highlighted in jokes such as 'Maggie has only been in Hell for twenty minutes, and she's already privatised all the furnaces'. When the prolific joke-mongers were criticised for 'lack of compassion' towards the deceased, they responded with 'To those concerned about lack of compassion: don't worry, it's what she would have wanted.'

There were also many less humorous and more vitriolic comments, as well as demonstrations, burning of effigies and so on – and, of course, many reverent eulogies from Thatcher's equally numerous supporters. But these were all pretty much what one would expect at the death of a controversial leader in any country with free speech – although media reaction in the US to the death of Thatcher's equally controversial ally Ronald Reagan seemed to consist almost entirely of gushing tributes.

The media here, by contrast, generally seem to accept that the 'speak no ill of the dead' rule for friends and relations at private funerals does not apply to public discourse about a dead politician. They gave more or less equal coverage to the eulogisers and to the protesters and satirists. When one satirist's campaign managed within a week to propel the song 'Ding-Dong! The Witch Is Dead' to number two in that week's pop charts, the BBC came under intense pressure from Tory MPs not to play it on the official Radio 1 chart show. In typically English fashion, the BBC eventually compromised, playing a short clip that included all of the 'controversial' chorus, but not the entire song. Neither side was entirely happy with this decision, but both were able to claim a victory of sorts.

CALENDRICAL RITES AND OTHER TRANSITIONS

Calendrical rites include big celebrations such as Christmas and New Year's Eve, and others that occur at the same time every year, such as Easter, May Day, harvest festival, Hallowe'en and Guy Fawkes' Night, as well as Mothering Sunday, Valentine's Day and bank holidays. I'm including our annual summer holidays in this category, as they are seasonal and therefore essentially calendrical, even though they do not occur on fixed dates. (Some nit-pickers might argue that the summer holiday is not, strictly speaking, a 'rite', or at least not in the same sense as Christmas or harvest festival, but I think it qualifies, and will explain why later.) Also in this category would be the daily/weekly work-to-play transitional ritual of after-work drinks in the pub, but I've already covered this one in detail in Work to Rule (page 301).

Under 'other transitions', I'm including life-cycle rites of passage other than the major ones covered above – such as retirement celebrations, 'significant' birthdays (decade marks) and wedding anniversaries (silver, golden) – and rituals marking other social/place/status/lifestyle transitions, such as housewarmings and 'leaving dos'.

This all adds up to an awful lot of rites, many of which, like the major life-cycle transitions, are in most respects largely similar to their equivalents in other modern Western industrialised cultures. Gifts, parties, special meals, songs and decorations at Christmas; chocolate eggs at Easter; cards and flowers on Valentine's Day; alcohol at almost all festive occasions; food at most; etc. Rather than attempt to describe each rite in exhaustive detail, I will focus mainly on the broader unwritten social rules governing peculiarly English patterns of behaviour associated with these rites.

All human cultures have seasonal and transitional celebratory rites of some sort. Other animals just automatically register things such as the passing of the seasons, and adjust their behaviour accordingly: humans have to make a huge song-and-dance about every little calendrical punctuation mark. Fortunately for anthropologists, humans are also quite predictable, and tend to make pretty much the same *kind* of song-and-dance about such things – or, at least, the festivities of different cultures tend to have a lot of features in common. Singing and dancing, for example. Most also involve eating, and virtually all involve alcohol.

The Role of Alcohol

The role of alcohol in celebration is particularly important in understanding the English, and requires a little bit of explanation. In all cultures where alcohol is used at all, it is a central element of celebration. There are two main reasons for this. First, carnivals and festivals are more than just a bit of fun: in most cultures, these events involve a degree of 'cultural remission' or even 'festive inversion'. Behaviour that would normally be frowned upon or even explicitly forbidden (e.g. promiscuous flirting, raucous singing, cross-dressing, jumping in fountains, talking to strangers, etc.) may, for the duration of the festivities, be actively encouraged. These are liminal periods – marginal, borderline intervals, segregated from everyday existence, allowing us, briefly, to explore alternative ways of being. There is a natural affinity between alcohol and liminality, whereby the experience of intoxication mirrors the experience of ritually induced liminality. The chemical effects of alcohol echo the cultural chemistry of the festival.

But although humans seem to have a deep-seated need for these altered states of consciousness, for an escape from the restrictions of mundane existence, liminality is also rather scary. The fact that we restrict our collective pursuit of altered states and alternative realities to specific, limited contexts suggests that our desire for such liberation is by no means unequivocal – that it is balanced by an equally powerful need for the stability and security of everyday reality. We may be enthralled by the liminal experience of the carnival, but we are also afraid of it; we like to visit alternative worlds, but we wouldn't want to live there. Alcohol plays a double or 'balancing' role in the context of festive rituals: the altered states of consciousness induced by alcohol allow us to explore desired but potentially dangerous alternative realities, while the social meanings of drinking – the rules of convivial sociability invariably associated with the consumption of alcohol – provide a reassuring counterbalance. By drinking, we enable and enhance the experience of liminality that is central to festive rites, but the familiar, everyday, comforting, sociable rituals of sharing and pouring and round-buying, the social bonding that is synonymous with drinking, help us somehow to tame or even 'domesticate' the disturbing aspects of this liminal world.

So, there are the universals. But there are also some cross-cultural variations. Although alcohol and celebration are inextricably bound together in all societies where alcohol is used, the connection appears to be stronger in 'ambivalent' drinking cultures – those with a morally charged relationship with alcohol, where one needs a reason for drinking, such as England – than in 'integrated' drinking cultures, where drinking is a morally neutral element of normal life and requires no justification. The English (along with the US, Australia, most of Scandinavia, Iceland, etc.) feel that they have to have an *excuse* for drinking – and the most common and popular excuse is celebration. In 'integrated' drinking cultures (such as Latin/Mediterranean cultures) there is little or no disapprobation of alcohol, and therefore no need to find excuses for drinking. Festivity is strongly associated with alcohol in these integrated cultures, but is not invoked as a justification for every drinking occasion: a celebration most certainly requires alcohol, but every drink does not require a celebration.

The Celebration Excuse – and Magical Beliefs

As well as cross-cultural research with my SIRC colleagues on festive drinking, I did a study a few years ago specifically on English celebrations and attitudes to celebrating. This study involved the usual combination of observation-fieldwork, informal interviews and a national survey.

The main finding was that the English will seize upon almost any excuse for celebratory drinking. As well as the established calendrical festivals, a staggering 87 per cent of survey respondents mentioned bizarre or trivial events that had provided an excuse for a festive drinking session, including: 'my teddy-bear's birthday', 'my mate swallowing his tooth', 'when my neighbour's snake laid eggs after we'd thought it was a male', 'the first Friday of the week' and 'the fourteenth anniversary of the death of my pet hamster'.

In addition to the more outlandish excuses, over 60 per cent admitted that something as mundane and insignificant as 'a friend dropping in' had provided a good enough excuse for a bout of celebratory drinking. More than half the population celebrate 'Saturday night', just under half have celebratory drinks merely because 'It's Friday' and nearly 40 per cent of younger respondents felt that 'the end of the working day' was a valid excuse for drunken revelry.

Calling a drinking session a 'celebration' not only gets round our moral ambivalence about alcohol, providing a legitimate excuse for drinking, but also in itself gives us a sort of official licence to shed a few inhibitions. Celebrations are by definition 'liminal' episodes, in which certain normal social restraints can be temporarily suspended. A drink that has been labelled 'celebratory' therefore has even greater magical disinhibiting powers than a drink that is just a drink. 'Celebration' is a magic word: merely invoking the concept of celebration transforms an ordinary round of drinks into a 'party', with all the relaxation of social controls that this implies. Abracadabra! Instant liminality!

This kind of magic works in other cultures as well – and drinks themselves can be used to define and 'dictate' the nature of an occasion, without the need for words, magic or otherwise. Certain types of drink, for example, may be so strongly associated with particular forms of social interaction that serving them in itself acts as an effective indicator of expectations, or even as an instruction to behave in a specified way. In most Western cultures, for instance, champagne is synonymous with celebration, such that if it is ordered or served at an otherwise 'ordinary' occasion, someone will invariably ask, 'What are we celebrating?' Champagne prompts festive, cheerful light-heartedness, which is why it is generally regarded as inappropriate to serve it at funerals. In Austria, *sekt* is drunk on formal occasions, while *schnapps* is reserved for more intimate, convivial gatherings – the type of drink served defining both the nature of the event and the social relationship between the drinkers. The choice of drink dictates behaviour to the extent that the mere appearance of a bottle of *schnapps* can sometimes prompt a switch from the 'polite' form of address, *Sie*, to the intimate *du*. In England, although we do not have the same clear linguistic distinctions, beer is generally regarded as a more informal, casual drink than wine, and serving beer with a meal indicates expectations of informal, relaxed behaviour – even guests' body language will be more casual: slumping a bit rather than sitting up straight, adopting more open postures and using more expansive gestures.

In this respect, then, the English are not very different from other humans, but our belief in, and need for, the disinhibiting powers of both drinks and magic words is perhaps stronger than most other cultures', as our social inhibitions are more formidable. Our ambivalence and magical beliefs about alcohol are defining features of all English rites of passage, from the most important life-cycle transitions to the most trivial, trumped-up, teddy-bear's-birthday rituals.

Christmas and New Year's Eve Rules

The English year is punctuated by national calendrical holidays: some are mere commas, while others are more important semi-colons; the Christmas holiday and New Year's Eve are the final full stop. Most calendrical rites were originally religious events, often ancient pagan festivals appropriated by Christianity, but the Christian significance of many of these rites is largely ignored. Ironically, they might be said to have reverted to something more like their original pagan roots, which serves the Christians right for hijacking them in the first place, I suppose.

Christmas and New Year's Eve are by far the most important. Christmas Day (25 December) is firmly established as a 'family' ritual, while New Year's Eve is a much more raucous celebration with friends. But when English people talk about 'Christmas' (as in 'What are you doing for Christmas?' or 'I hate Christmas!'), they often mean the entire holiday period, from the 23/24 December right through to New Year's Day, including, typically and traditionally, at least some of the following:

- Christmas Eve (family; last-minute shopping; panics and squabbles; tree lights; drinking; too many nuts and chocolates; possibly church – early-evening carols or midnight service)
- Christmas Day (family; tree; present-giving rituals; marathon cooking and eating of huge Christmas lunch; the Queen's broadcast on television/radio – or pointedly *not* watching/listening to the Queen; fall asleep – perhaps while watching *Toy Story*, *ET* or similar; more food and drink; uncomfortable night)
- Boxing Day (hangover; family 'outing' of some sort, if only to local park; long country walk; visiting the other set of relatives; escape from family to pub)
- 27–30 December (slightly strange limbo period; some back at work, but often achieving very little; others shopping, going for walks, trying to keep children amused; more overeating and drinking; visiting friends/relatives; television; DVDs; pub)
- New Year's Eve (friends; big, boozy parties or pub-crawls; dressing up/fancy-dress; loud music; dancing; champagne, banging pans, etc. at midnight; fireworks; 'Auld Lang Syne'; New Year's resolutions; taxi-hunt/long cold walk home)
- New Year's Day (sleep late; hangover).

Many people's Christmases may not follow this pattern, but most will include a few of these ritual elements, and most English people will at least *recognise* this rough outline of an average, bog-standard Christmas.

Often, the term 'Christmas' comprises much more than this. When people say 'I hate Christmas' or moan about how 'Christmas' is becoming more and more of a nightmare or an ordeal, they are generally including all the 'preparations' for and 'run-up' to Christmas, which may start at least a month ahead, and which involve office/workplace Christmas parties, 'Christmas shopping', a 'Christmas panto' and quite possibly, for those with school-age children, a school 'nativity play' or Christmas concert – not to mention the annual ritual of writing and dispatching large quantities of Christmas cards. English people understand 'Christmas' to include any or all of these customs and activities, as well as the Christmas-week celebrations.

The school nativity play is, for many, the only event of any religious content that they will encounter during the Christmas period, although its religious significance tends to get lost in the social drama of the occasion – particularly the issue of whose children have been fortunate enough to secure the leading roles (Mary, Joseph) and the principal supporting ones (Three Kings, Innkeeper, Head Shepherd, Angel-of-the-Lord), and who must suffer the indignity of playing mere background shepherds, angels, sheep, cows, donkeys and so on. Or the school may have been gripped by a sudden fit of political correctness and attempted to replace the traditional nativity with something more 'multicultural'. This being England, the squabbles and skirmishes over casting and other issues are rarely conducted openly but are more a matter of indirect scheming, Machiavellian manipulation and indignant muttering.

The Christmas panto is a bizarre, quintessentially English custom. Almost every local theatre in the country puts on a pantomime at Christmas, in which a children's fairy-tale or folk tale – such as *Aladdin*, *Cinderella*, *Puss in Boots*, *Dick Whittington*, *Mother Goose*, etc. – is performed, always with men in drag (known as pantomime dames) playing the main female parts and a woman in men's clothes as 'principal boy'. Tradition requires a script full of salacious *double-entendres* for the grown-ups (at which many of the children laugh heartily), and much noisy audience-participation for the children, with cries of 'HE'S BEHIND YOU!' 'OH NO HE ISN'T!' 'OH YES HE IS!' – a ritual into which adult members of the audience often throw themselves with considerable gusto. No English politician could ever get away with Obama's 'YES WE CAN!' campaign chant: even in a sympathetic audience, many would be unable to resist shouting out the panto-response: 'OH NO WE CAN'T!'

The Christmas Moan-fest and the Bah-humbug Rule

'Christmas shopping' is the bit many English people are thinking of when they say that they hate Christmas, and usually means shopping for Christmas presents, food, cards, decorations and other trappings. As it is considered manly to profess to detest any sort of shopping, English men are particularly inclined to moan about how much they dislike Christmas. In a recent survey, 47 per cent of men admitted that they leave all their Christmas shopping until the last minute, on Christmas Eve, and 30 per cent confessed that they buy gifts from motorway service stations. (I say 'admitted' and 'confessed', but I suspect there may be an element of macho pride in such statements.) The Christmas-moan is now something of a national custom, and both sexes generally start moaning about Christmas in early November.

There is effectively an unwritten rule prescribing 'bah-humbug', anti-Christmas moaning rituals at this time of year, and it is unusual to encounter anyone over the age of eighteen who will admit to unequivocal enjoyment of Christmas. This does not stop those who dislike Christmas taking a certain pride in their distaste, as though they were the first people ever to notice 'how commercial the whole thing has become' or how 'it starts earlier every year – soon there'll be bloody Christmas decorations in August' or how it seems to get more and more expensive, or how impossibly crowded the streets and shops are.

Christmas-moaners recite the same platitudes every year, fondly imagining that these are original thoughts, and that they are a beleaguered, discerning minority, while the eccentric souls who actually *like* Christmas shopping and all the other rituals tend to keep quiet about their unorthodox tastes. They may even join in the annual moan-fest, just to be polite and sociable – much as people who enjoy rain will often courteously agree that the weather is beastly. The cynical 'bah, humbug!' position is the norm – particularly among men, many of whom find something almost suspiciously effeminate about an adult male who admits to liking Christmas – and everyone loves a good Christmas moan, so why spoil their fun? Those of us who actively enjoy Christmas tend to be almost apologetic about our perversity: 'Well, yes, but, um, to be honest, I actually like all the naff decorations and finding presents for people . . . I know it's deeply uncool . . .'

Not all Christmas-moaners are mindless, sheep-like followers of the 'bah-humbug' rule. Two groups of Christmas-haters who have good reason to complain, and for whom I do have sympathy, are parents struggling on low incomes, for whom the expense of buying presents that will please their children is a real problem, and working mothers for whom, even if they are not poor, the whole business can truly be more of a strain than a pleasure.

Christmas-present Rules

A gift, as any first-year anthropology student can tell you, is never free. In all cultures, gifts tend to come with some expectation of a return. This is not a bad thing: reciprocal exchanges of gifts are an important form of social bonding. Even gifts to small children, who cannot be expected to reciprocate in kind, are no exception to this universal rule: children receiving Christmas presents are supposed to reciprocate with gratitude and good behaviour. The fact that they often do no such thing is beside the point: a rule is not invalidated just because people break it. It is interesting to note that in the case of very young children, who cannot be expected to understand this rule, we do not give Christmas presents 'directly', but invent a magical being, Father Christmas, from whom the gifts are said to come. The traumatic discovery that Father Christmas does not exist is really the discovery of the laws of reciprocity, the fact that Christmas presents come with strings attached.

English squeamishness about money can be a problem in this context, particularly for the upper-middle and upper classes, who are especially sensitive about it. Talking about how much a Christmas present cost is regarded as terribly vulgar; actually telling someone the price of their present, or even that it was 'expensive', would be crass beyond belief. Although general, non-specific complaints about the cost of Christmas presents are allowed, harping on and on about the financial aspects of gift-exchange is uncouth and inconsiderate, as it makes recipients of gifts feel awkward.

Actual expenditure on Christmas presents seems to be inversely related to income, with poor, working-class families tending to give more lavish gifts, especially to children, often going heavily into debt in the process. The middle classes (particularly the 'interfering classes') tut-tut sanctimoniously over this, and congratulate themselves on their superior prudence, while tucking into their overpriced organic vegetables and admiring the tasteful Victorian ornaments on their tree.

New Year's Eve and the Orderly-disorder Rule

New Year's Eve, which more of us will admit to enjoying (although some of the bah-humbug brigade make the same complaints every year about the boring sameness of it all) is a more straightforward carnival – with all the usual, standard liminal stuff: cultural remission, legitimised deviance, festive inversions, altered states of consciousness, communitas, collective effervescence and so on – and it is more obviously a direct descendant of pagan mid-winter festivals, uncluttered by Christian meddling with the imagery or sanitisation of the rituals.

As with Freshers' Week, office Christmas parties and most other English carnival rites, the extent of actual debauchery and anarchy tends to be greatly overestimated, both by the puritanical killjoys who disapprove of such festivities and by those participants who like to see themselves as wild, fun-loving rebels. In reality, our New-Year's-Eve drunken debauchery is a fairly orderly sort of disorder, in which only certain specified taboos may be broken, only the usual designated inhibitions may be shed, and the standard rules of English drunken etiquette apply: mooning but not flashing; fighting but not queue-jumping; bawdy jokes but not racist ones; 'illicit' flirting and, in some circles, snogging, but not adulterous sex; promiscuity but not, if you are straight, homosexuality, nor heterosexual lapses if you are gay; vomiting and (if male) urinating in the street, but never defecating; forgetting your address or even your name, but never forgetting to buy your round, and so on.

Minor Calendricals – Commas and Semi-colons

And as New Year's Eve is understood to be the *most* debauched and disinhibited of our calendrical rites, the rest (Hallowe'en, Guy

Fawkes' Night, Easter, May Day, Valentine's, etc.) tend to be pretty tame – although they all have their origins in much more boisterous pagan festivals.

Our May Day, with staid, respectable, usually middle-aged morris dancers and the occasional innocent children's maypole, is a revival of the ancient pagan rites of Beltane. In some parts of the country, counter-culture/New Age revellers with dreadlocks, beads and multiple body-piercings celebrate May Day alongside the morris dancers and the Neighbourhood Watch/parish council types – an odd-looking juxtaposition, but generally amicable. Hallowe'en – fancy-dress and sweets – is a descendant of All Souls' Eve, a festival of communion with the dead, also of pagan origin and celebrated in various forms in many cultures around the world.

The practice of lighting bonfires and burning effigies in early November is another pagan one – common at 'fire festivals' welcoming the winter (the effigies represented the old year) – adapted in the seventeenth century to commemorate the defeat of Guy Fawkes's plot to blow up the Houses of Parliament. It is still also known as Bonfire Night and Fireworks Night,[124] and is now celebrated with firework-parties over a period of at least a fortnight, rather than just on the night of 5 November. Valentine's Day – cards, flowers, chocolate – is a sanitised Christian version of the ancient Roman festival of Lupercalia, originally held on 15 February, a much more raunchy celebration of the 'coming of spring' (in other words, the start of the mating season) designed to ensure the fertility of fields, flocks and people.

Many people think of Easter as one of the few genuinely Christian calendricals, but even its name is not Christian, being a variant of Eostre, the Saxon goddess of spring, and many of our Easter customs

---

124. We seem to have a habit of renaming festivals after the main symbols associated with them, rather than the events they are supposed to commemorate: Remembrance Day is more widely known as Poppy Day, for example, after the red paper poppies we wear to remember the war-dead. The charity Comic Relief had the good sense to pre-empt us by calling their national fund-raising day Red Nose Day, after the red plastic noses we are encouraged to buy and wear, rather than trying to call it Comic Relief Day.

– eggs and so on – are based on pagan fertility rites. Some otherwise non-practising Christians may go to a church service on Easter Sunday, and even some totally non-religious people 'give something up' for the traditional fasting period of Lent (it's a popular time to restart one's New Year's Resolution diet, which somehow lost its momentum by the third week in January).

As calendrical punctuation marks go, these are mostly just commas. Easter qualifies as a semi-colon, as it involves a day's holiday from work, and is used as a reference point – people talk about doing things 'by Easter' or 'after Easter', or something happening 'around Easter'. Valentine's Day also just about counts as a semi-colon, although we don't get a day off work, as it plays a significant part in our courtship and mating practices (significant enough to cause a big peak in the suicide rates, anyway).

In addition to these 'mainstream' national calendricals, every English ethnic and religious minority has its own annual punctuation marks: the Hindu Diwali and Janmashtami; the Sikh Diwali and Vaisakhi; Muslim Ramadan, Eid-ul-Fitr and Al-Hijrah; Jewish Hanukkah, Yom Kippur and Rosh Hashana, to name just the first few that immediately spring to mind. And every English subculture has its own calendricals – its own annual tribal gatherings and festivals. These include the upper-class 'Season', of which the Royal Ascot race-meeting, the Henley Regatta and the Wimbledon tennis championships (always abbreviated to just 'Ascot, Henley and Wimbledon') are the principal events. The racing fraternity have the Grand National, the Cheltenham Festival and the Derby in addition to Ascot; Goths have their annual convention at Whitby in Yorkshire; New Agers, other counter-culture groups and young music-lovers have their festival at Glastonbury; modern druids have the summer solstice at Stonehenge; the literati have Hay-on-Wye; opera-lovers have Glyndebourne and Garsington; dog-lovers have Crufts; bikers have the BMF Show at Peterborough; horsey folk have Badminton, Hickstead and the Horse of the Year Show; and so on. There are thousands of these subcultural calendricals, far too many to list, but each one, to its adherents, may be much more important than Christmas. And I have only mentioned the 'Christmases' – every subculture has its own minor calendricals as well, its own semi-colons and commas.

But even the minor punctuation marks are necessary: we need these special days, these little mini-festivals, to provide breaks from our routine and give structure to our year – just as regular mealtimes structure our days. That's 'we humans', of course, not just 'we English', but we English do seem to have a particular need for regular 'time out' from our rigid social controls.

Holidays . . .

Which brings me rather neatly to the concept of holidays,[125] and especially the summer holiday. I am including this under 'calendrical rites' (although nit-pickers might argue that technically it is neither) as it is an annually recurring event of possibly even greater cultural significance than Christmas, which in my book makes it calendrical, and a 'liminal' ritual conforming in important respects to the pattern identified by van Gennep as characteristic of rites of passage, which in my book makes it a 'rite'. (And this *is* my book, so I can call things calendrical rites if I choose.)

In terms of punctuation marks (I can labour metaphors too, if I wish), the summer holiday is an ellipsis (. . .), the three dots indicating passage of time, or something unspoken, or a significant pause or break in the narrative flow, often with a suggestion of mystery attached. I've always felt there was something decidedly liminal about those three dots. There is certainly something very liminal about the summer holiday: this two- or three-week break is a time outside regular, prosaic existence, a special time when the normal controls, routines and restraints are suspended, and we feel a sense of liberation from the workaday world. We are free from the exigencies of work, school or housekeeping routines – this is playtime, 'free' time, time that is 'ours'. On holiday, we say, 'your time is your own'.

Summer holidays are an alternative reality: if we can, we go to another country; we dress differently; we eat special, more indulgent

125. I'm using the term 'holidays' in the British sense, meaning what Americans would call 'vacations'.

food ('Go on, have another ice-cream, you're on holiday!') – and we behave differently. The English on their summer holiday are more relaxed, more sociable, more spontaneous, less hidebound and uptight. In a national study conducted by my SIRC colleagues, 'being more sociable' was one of the three most common responses when people were asked what they most associated with summer, the other two being 'pub gardens' and 'barbecues', which are both essentially also about sociability. We speak of holidays as a time to 'let our hair down', 'have fun', 'let off steam', 'unwind', 'go a bit mad'. We may even talk to strangers. The English don't get much more liminal than that.

English holidays – summer holidays in particular – are governed by the same laws of cultural remission as carnivals and festivals. Like 'celebration', 'holiday' is a magic word. As with festivals, however, cultural remission does not mean an unbridled, anarchic free-for-all, but rather a regulated sort of rowdiness, a selective spontaneity, in which specified inhibitions are shed in a prescribed, conventional manner.

The English on holiday do not suddenly stop being English. Even abroad, many English holidaymakers insist on eating the same food, drinking the same tea and beer and playing the same games that they enjoy at home. And many holiday resorts, particularly in Spain, pander to this insularity, providing fish-and-chip shops, tea-rooms, pubs, bingo, and other familiar comforts – essentially offering England in a warmer, sunnier setting, with maybe one Paella Night or a bit of flamenco and sangria for a little frisson of exotic excitement. Our defining qualities do not magically disappear either: even among the minority who take more adventurous holidays, behaviour is still dictated by the ingrained rules of humour, hypocrisy, modesty, class-consciousness, fair play, social dis-ease and so on.

But we do let our guard down a bit. The cultural remission of holiday law does not cure us of our social dis-ease, but the symptoms are to some extent 'in remission'. We do not miraculously become any more socially *skilled*, of course, but we do become more socially *inclined* – more open, less buttoned-up. This is not always a good thing, or even a pleasant sight, as the native inhabitants of some of our favoured foreign holiday resorts will testify. Some of us are quite frankly nicer when we are not shedding our inhibitions all over the place, along with our trousers, our bras, the contents of our stomachs and our dignity. As I keep pointing out, our famous polite reserve and our almost equally renowned loutish obnoxiousness are two sides of the same coin: for some of us, the magic word 'holiday' has an unfortunate tendency to flip that coin.

For good or ill, the liminal laws of carnival/holiday time apply to minor calendricals such as bank holidays as well – and even to ordinary weekends. (Some members of non-mainstream subculture tribes, for instance, may be able to adopt their 'alternative' dress, lifestyle and persona only during this weekend time-out. The more dedicated, or simply more fortunate, full-time members of these tribes refer to the part-timers rather dismissively as, for example, 'weekend Goths' or 'weekend bikers'.) Evenings and lunch-hours are also mini-remissions, and even coffee- and tea-breaks can be – what's even smaller? – nano-remissions, perhaps. Little oases of time-out; tiny, almost homeopathic doses of therapeutic liminality.

We talk about 'getting back to reality' or 'back to the real world' after a holiday, and part of the meaning and function of holidays is to define that 'real world' more sharply. Holidays and mini-remissions do not challenge or subvert the norms and laws that are sometimes suspended for their duration; quite the opposite: holidays highlight and reinforce these rules. By labelling holidays as 'different', 'special' and 'unreal', we remind ourselves of what is 'normal' and 'real'. By breaking the rules in a conscious, structured manner, we throw these important norms into sharp relief, and ensure our own obedience to them back in 'real' time. Every year, English holiday-makers, sighing at the prospect of 'getting back to reality', comfort each other with the wise words: 'But, of course, if it were like this all the time, we wouldn't appreciate it.' Quite true. But the reverse is also true: holidays help us to appreciate the structure and certainties – and even the restraints – of our 'normal' life and routines. The English can only take so much liminality. By the end of the summer holidays, we have had enough of indulgence and excess, and yearn for a bit of moderation.

Other Transitions – Intimate Rites and Irregular Verbs

Decade-marking birthdays and wedding anniversaries, house-warmings, retirement celebrations and workplace 'leaving dos' are usually smaller and more informal affairs than the big life-cycle transitions described earlier, although some may be no less important to the individuals concerned.

Retirement celebrations and 'leaving dos' that take place at work – where those involved may not be close friends of the person whose departure is being ritually marked – are the most likely to be characterised by the usual Englishnesses: social dis-ease symptoms, medicated with incessant humour and alcohol; polite egalitarianism masking class obsessions; modest, self-deprecating speeches full of indirect boasts and veiled put-downs; moaning rituals; jokey presentation of gifts; drunken 'disinhibition'; awkward handshakes, clumsy back-pats and uneasy embraces.

Truly private rites of passage – birthdays, anniversaries, house-warmings and retirements celebrated with family and one's very closest friends – are somewhat less predictable, apart from a few generic customs and conventions, such as cakes, balloons, singing, special food, drink and possibly toasts. These much more intimate rites are generally less socially challenging, and thus less awkward and stilted, than the bigger or more 'public' transitions. In private, among people we know very well, the English are quite capable of warmth, openness, intimacy and the full gamut of human emotions associated with friendship and family ties. Some of us are warmer and more open than others, but that is a matter of individual differences in personality, and has little or nothing to do with *national* character.

Even at these very private events, however, the most fundamental 'laws of Englishness' apply: we obey the humour rules, for example, particularly the anti-earnestness rule, much as we obey the law of gravity, so you are far more likely to hear jokey toasts than solemn, tearful or gushingly sentimental ones. We convey our feelings for the family member or close friend whose 'passage' is being celebrated through affectionate teasing and in-jokes, smiles, fond looks, little hugs, kisses or hand-squeezes and so on, rather than by explicitly declaring how much we love, cherish or admire them. I was at an English family party to celebrate a father's seventieth birthday, where all of these feelings had been expressed in typically minimal, understated ways, beautifully and touchingly, with much gentle humour and no speeches at all. Unfortunately, the father's American wife found all this English lightness unbearable, and took it upon herself to stand up and deliver an earnest, syrupy speech ('We've made this party for you because we all love you and we are all so proud of you and we want you to know that you're very special to us and . . .'). The English family suffered politely through all this, their extreme discomfort betrayed only by barely visible wincing, squirming, sidelong glances, discreet eye-rolls, suppressed snorts, stifled sighs and fidgety feet. When the painfully embarrassing ordeal was over, they clapped courteously – before quickly trying to restore the former light-hearted atmosphere with yet more joking. One of the family members muttered to me, 'I know she means well, but *ugh*!' Another imitated the American wife's accent and treacly tone: '"We made this party because we all love you." *No! Really?* Goes without saying, for Heaven's sake!' For the English, most emotional things 'go without saying'. Spelling them out, even at warm, 'uninhibited', intimate gatherings, is highly inappropriate.

Leaving aside these very basic, gravity-like laws, the behaviour of participants at intimate rites of passage will vary considerably, not just according to their age and class, as might be expected, but also their individual dispositions, personal quirks and histories, unique moods and motivations – the sort of stuff that is really the province of personality psychologists and psychiatrists, rather than us social scientists.

This is all true to some extent of the more formal, less private rites of passage as well – we are individuals on these occasions too, not mere automata acting entirely in accordance with the dictates of national character. But without wishing to deny each of us our individuality, I would maintain that our behaviour at these less intimate gatherings is broadly predictable, and conforms more consistently to the principal 'grammatical' rules of our culture.

Not that our rather less predictable behaviour at intimate celebrations is in any way 'ungrammatical'. Such events are a bit like irregular verbs: they have their own rules, which allow a greater degree of warmth, spontaneity and openness than we usually permit ourselves. We are not 'breaking the rules' at these intimate rites. In private, among people we know and trust, the rules of Englishness specifically allow us to behave much more like normal human beings, with normal human emotions. We just don't make earnest speeches about them.

CLASS RULES

But rather than end on that touching, encouraging note, I'm now going to talk about class. Again. Surely you didn't think we'd get through a whole chapter with just a couple of passing references to the class system?

You can probably do this bit yourself by now. C'mon, have a go: what are the main differences between a working-class funeral and a middle-class one? Or the indicators of a middle-middle versus an upper-middle wedding? Discuss with special reference to material-culture class indicators, sartorial class indicators and class-anxiety signals. Oh, all right, I'll do it – but don't expect anything very surprising: you can see, from what Jane Austen called 'the tell-tale compression of the pages', that we're nearly done here, and if we haven't got the hang of English class indicators and anxieties by now, we never will.

As you might expect, there is no such thing as a classless rite of passage among the English. Every detail of a wedding, Christmas, house-warming or funeral, from the vocabulary and dress of the participants to the number and positioning of peas on their forks, is determined, at least to some extent, by their social class.

Working-class Rites

As a general rule, working-class rites of passage are the most lavish (in terms of expenditure relative to income). A working-class wedding, for example, will nearly always be a big 'do', with a sit-down meal in a restaurant, pub 'function room' or hotel; a big fancy car or horse-drawn Cinderella-carriage to take the bride to the wedding venue; the full complement of matching bridesmaids in tight, revealing dresses; a huge, three-tiered cake; guests in glamorous, brand-new, Sunday-best outfits and matching accessories; a specialist wedding-photographer *and* a professional wedding-video firm; a big, noisy evening party with dancing and free-flowing booze; a honeymoon somewhere hot. No expense spared. 'Nothing but the best for our princess.' I have lost count of the number of working-class brides I've heard happily declaring that their own huge, elaborate, sequined-and-diamanté wedding dresses were much better and 'more princessy' than the simple, understated one worn by the Duchess of Cambridge for her marriage to Prince William.

Extravagant 'themed' weddings have become increasingly popular, and the costumes, props and décor more and more elaborate. Themes range from the relatively tame and vague Fairy Tale and Winter Wonderland to more specific and self-consciously 'wacky' themes such as Fifties Rock 'n' Roll, *Lord of the Rings*, Harry Potter, Zombie, Vampire, etc.

Working-class funerals (huge, elaborate wreaths; top-of-the-range coffin), Christmases (expensive gifts; copious quantities of food and drink), children's birthdays (the latest high-tech toys, high-priced football strip and top-brand-name trainers) and other rites operate on much the same principles. Even if one is struggling financially, it is important to *look* as though one has spent money and 'pushed the boat out'.

Lower-middle and Middle-middle Rites

Lower-middle and middle-middle rites of passage tend to be smaller and somewhat more prudent. To stick with the wedding example (although the same principles apply to other rites): lower- and middle-middle parents will be anxious to help the couple with a mortgage down-payment rather than irresponsibly 'blowing it all on a big wedding'. There is still great concern, however, that everything should be done 'properly' and 'tastefully' (these are the classes for whom wedding-etiquette books are written), and considerable stress and anxiety over relatives who might lower the tone or bring disgrace by getting drunk and 'making an exhibition of themselves'.

If the working-class ideal is the flamboyant, lavish 'celebrity' wedding, such as those of wealthy pop stars, footballers and glamour-models, the lower-middle and middle-middle aspirational benchmark is the royal wedding. For these classes, this generally means a fairly 'traditional' wedding with no wacky themes or gimmicks, although some of the more tame, generic and inoffensive themes, such as 'English Country Garden', are creeping up the social scale, and secular weddings in non-traditional locations are increasingly popular. The location must be suitably romantic and 'weddingy', though (no football clubs or amusement parks), and every detail must be dainty and effortfully elegant. These bourgeois or wannabe-bourgeois weddings are very contrived, carefully co-ordinated affairs. The 'serviettes' match the flowers, which 'tone with' the place-cards, which in turn 'pick up' the dominant colour of the mother-of-the-bride's pastel two-piece suit. But no one notices all this attention to detail until she draws their attention to it. The food is bland and safe, with hotel-style menus of the kind that call mash 'creamed potatoes'. The portions are not as generous as those at the working-class wedding, although they are more neatly presented, and 'garnished' with parsley and radishes carved into flower-shapes. The 'fine wines' run out too soon, calculations of glasses-per-head having been somewhat miserly, but the Best Man still manages to get drunk and break his promise to keep his speech 'clean'. The bride is mortified, her mother furious. Neither reprimands the offender, as they don't want to spoil the day with an unseemly row, but they hiss indignantly to each other and to some aunts, and treat the Best Man with frosty, tight-lipped disapproval for the rest of the afternoon.

Upper-middle Rites

Upper-middle rites of passage are usually less anxiously contrived and overdone – at least among those upper-middles who feel secure about their class status. Even among the anxious, an upper-middle wedding, funeral or Christmas aims for an air of effort*less* elegance, quite different from the middle-middles, who want you to *notice* how much hard work and thought has gone into it. Like 'natural-look' make-up, the upper-middle wedding's appearance of casual, unfussy stylishness can take a great deal of thought, effort and expense to achieve.

For class-anxious upper-middles, especially the urban, educated, 'chattering' class, concern is often focused not so much on doing things correctly as on doing them *distinctively*. Desperate to distinguish and distance themselves from the Philistine, uncultured middle-middles, they strive not only to avoid twee fussiness, but also to escape from the more banal aspects of 'traditional' weddings. They can't have the 'same old conventional Wedding March' or the 'same old boring hymns' as the mock-Tudor middle-middles or, God forbid, the inhabitants of semi-detached Pardonia. They choose obscure music for the bride's entrance, which no one recognises, so the guests are still chattering as the bride makes her way up the aisle – and little-known, difficult hymns that nobody can sing. The same principle often extends to the food, which is 'different' and imaginative but not necessarily easy or pleasant to eat, and the clothes, which may be the latest quirky, avant-garde fashions, but are not always easy to wear or to look at.

Unfortunately for these determinedly eccentric upper-middles, 'unusual' secular weddings have now become more popular among the working classes and lower-middle/middle-middle classes, so they are no longer charmingly distinctive and might even be compared with the vulgar 'themed' weddings favoured by the lower classes. The upper-middles are therefore reverting to more traditional locations, ceremonies and vows, which they can now reframe as charmingly 'retro'.

Upper-class Rites

Upper-class weddings tend to be fairly traditional, although not in the studied, textbook-traditional manner of many lower- and middle-middles. The upper classes are accustomed to big parties – charity balls, hunt balls, large private parties and the big events of the Season are a normal part of their social round – so they don't get as flustered about weddings and other rites of passage as the rest of us. An upper-class wedding is often a quite muted, simple affair. They do not all rush out to buy special new 'outfits' as they have plenty of suitable clothes already. The men all have their own morning suits and, as far as the women are concerned, Ascot may require something a bit special but 'One goes to so many weddings – can't be expected to keep ringing the changes every time,' as one very grand lady told me. Upper-class couples generally have no desire to make their weddings 'different' or distinctive, and very rarely write their own vows. Even at register-office weddings, where the traditional church vows are not permitted, they will choose the simplest of the 'standard' vows on offer.

The Sour-grapes Rule

If they cannot afford a big wedding (or funeral, Christmas, birthday, anniversary) the upper-middles and upper classes will often make a rather sour-grapey virtue of this, saying that they 'don't want a big, flashy production, just a simple family party with a few close friends', rather than running up credit-card debts, like the working classes, or dipping reluctantly into savings, like the lower- and middle-middles. The English modesty rule, with its associated distaste for ostentatious displays of wealth, serves the impecunious higher echelons well: anything they cannot afford can be dismissed as 'flashy' or 'vulgar'. (Big, glamorous weddings have long been regarded as decidedly 'naff', as Jane Austen pointedly reminds us by describing her upper-class heroine Emma Woodhouse's wedding as a small, quiet one in which 'the parties have no taste for finery or parade', and having the ghastly, pretentious, jumped-up Mrs Elton exhibit typically middle-class poor taste when she complains that the proceedings involved 'Very little white satin, very few lace veils; a most pitiful business!')

Lower- and middle-middles can use the same modesty principle to good effect by calling the extravagant celebrations they secretly envy 'wasteful' and 'silly', and talking disparagingly about people with 'more money than sense'. The 'respectable' upper-working class sometimes use this line as well: it emphasises their prudent respectability and makes them sound more middle class than the more common working-class approach, which is to express sniffy contempt for the 'stuck-up' 'showing off' of big, 'fancy' celebrations. '*She* had

to have a big posh do in a hotel,' said one of my informants, referring to a neighbour's silver wedding anniversary. 'This [their local
pub, where our conversation took place] wasn't good enough for
her. Stuck-up cow.'

The economic recession has resulted in a significant increase in
the use of these sour-grapes comments. The cloud of austerity has
a silver lining, in that lavish celebrations we cannot afford can now
be smugly dismissed not only as 'vulgar', 'wasteful' or 'stuck-up' (by
the higher, middle and working classes respectively), but also self-
righteously condemned, by all classes, as 'inappropriate when so
many people are struggling'.

RITES OF PASSAGE AND ENGLISHNESS

Poring over the rules in this chapter, trying to figure out what each one
tells us about Englishness and scribbling my verdicts in the margins, I
was struck by how often I found myself scribbling the word 'moderation'. This characteristic has featured significantly throughout the book,
but in a chapter focusing specifically on our 'high days and holidays',
our carnivals, festivals, parties and other celebrations, its predominance
is perhaps a little surprising. Or maybe not. We are talking about the
English, after all. By 'moderation', I don't only mean the English avoidance of extremes, excess and intensity, but also the need for a sense of
balance. Our need for moderation is closely related to our concern
with fair play. Our tendency to compromise, for example, is a product
of both fair play and moderation, as are a number of other English
habits, such as apathy, woolliness and conservatism.

Our benignly indifferent, fence-sitting, tolerant approach to religion is a product of moderation + fair play, with a dash of courtesy,
a dollop of humour, possibly a pinch or two of empiricism. (Oh
dear, I seem to have slipped from 'equation' to 'recipe' in mid-
sentence. This does not bode well for the final diagram.)

The other principal themes emerging from this chapter are pretty
much the usual suspects, but we can now see even more clearly how
many of the unwritten rules governing our behaviour involve a
combination of two or more defining characteristics. The

one-downmanship rules of kid-talk, for example, are clearly a product of modesty and hypocrisy (these two seem to go together a lot – in fact, we very rarely find modesty without an element of hypocrisy) with a generous slosh of humour. In the self-deprecating insult rule, we see a typical example of utterly hypocritical 'modesty', combined with acute class-consciousness and humour (in this case irony) used as a weapon.

The invisible-puberty rule is a more straightforward example of English social dis-ease. Pubescents and adolescents are essentially in an acute phase of this dis-ease (triggered or exacerbated by raging hormones). Our reluctance, as a society, to acknowledge the onset of puberty is a form of 'denial' – ostrichy behaviour that is in itself a reflection of our own social dis-ease. Social dis-ease can be 'medicated' to some extent with ritual, but our pubescents are denied any official rites of passage, and so invent their own. (The gap-year ordeal provides ritual medication, in the form of appropriate initiation rites, but rather late, and only for a privileged minority.) As noted earlier, however, we now finally have at least the beginnings of a ritual celebration of this transition, in the form of the increasingly popular end-of-primary-school 'prom'. I hope and expect that this new custom (and the slightly later Sweet Sixteen celebrations and secondary-school proms) will become more firmly established – but it is also worth noting that both Eeyorishness and hypocrisy were again evident in some reactions to these innovations.

The Freshers' Week rules involve a combination of social dis-ease – medicated with both ritual and alcohol – and that distinctively English brand of 'orderly disorder', a reflection of our need for moderation. The exam and graduation rules combine modesty with (as usual) an equal quantity of hypocrisy, plus a large dollop of Eeyorishness, seasoned with humour and a hint of moderation.

Our matching rites seem to trigger a rash of social dis-ease symptoms. The money-talk taboo is social dis-ease + modesty + hypocrisy, with class variations. At weddings, we find again that the symptoms of social dis-ease can be effectively alleviated with humour, and the painful 'natural experiment' of funerals shows us how bad the disease symptoms can get without this medication, as well as highlighting our penchant for moderation again. The tear quotas involve a combination of moderation, courtesy and fair play.

The celebration excuse and its associated magical beliefs are another example of social dis-ease medicated with alcohol and ritual. The Christmas moan-fest and bah-humbug rule combine Eeyorishness with courtesy and hypocrisy, while the Christmas-present rules blend courtesy and hypocrisy again. The New Year's Eve orderly-disorder rule is about moderation again, as well as the now very familiar attempts to control social dis-ease symptoms with alcohol and ritual – also evident in most of the minor calendricals. Holidays involve more of the same, and highlight our need to limit excess and indulgence – our need for moderation.

The class rules governing our rites of passage are about class-consciousness, of course, but also involve the usual close relation of this trait, hypocrisy – and in particular that special English blend of modesty and hypocrisy, which all the social classes seem to exhibit in equal degree.

Although we retain our squeamishness about earnestness at intimate, private transitional rites, they represent one of our very few genuine escapes from our debilitating social dis-ease. (The other main escape is sex, also a private matter.) Our fanatical obsession with privacy may be a symptom of our social dis-ease, but we also value privacy because it allows us some relief from this affliction. At home, among close family, friends and lovers, we can be warm and spontaneous and really quite remarkably human. This is the side of us that many visitors to this country never see, or only catch rare glimpses of. You have to be patient to witness it – like waiting for giant pandas to mate.

CONCLUSION:
DEFINING ENGLISHNESS

At the beginning, I set out to discover the 'defining characteristics of Englishness' by closely observing distinctive regularities in English behaviour, identifying the specific hidden rules governing these behaviour patterns, and then figuring out what these rules reveal about our national character. A sort of semi-scientific procedure, I suppose. Well, systematic, at least. But despite all the confident-sounding noises I was making in the Introduction, I had no idea whether or not it would work, as this approach to understanding a national character had not been tried before.

It seems to have worked. Or maybe that's a bit presumptuous. What I mean is that this approach has certainly given *me* a better understanding of the 'grammar' – or 'mindset' or 'ethos' or '*gemeingeist*' or 'cultural genome' or whatever you want to call it – of Englishness. Now, when I witness some apparently bizarre or ludicrous English behaviour (as I write this, we are in the middle of the Christmas-party season) I can say to myself, for example, 'Ah, yes: typical case of social dis-ease, medicated with alcohol and festive liminality, + humour + moderation'. (I don't usually say it out loud, because people would think I was bonkers.)

The point of this Englishness project, however, was not to allow me to feel quietly smug and omniscient. The idea was that other people might find it helpful too. Judging by all the letters I receive, the 2004 edition of this book has been helpful – or at least it has contributed towards the anthropological mission of 'making the strange familiar and the familiar strange'. But, as you know, I've been puzzling all this 'strangeness' out as we went along, chapter by chapter, so the book has been a bit like one of those maths tests where you have to 'show the workings-out' rather than just putting down the final answer. This means that if you think I've got the final answer to the 'What is Englishness?' question wrong, at least you can see exactly where I made my mistakes. It also means that, at this point, you know at least as much as I do about the defining characteristics of Englishness we've been trying to identify. I don't have anything up my sleeve to pull out for a grand finale. You could write this final chapter yourself if you felt like it.

THE LIST

But I promised, at the very least, a definitive list of our defining characteristics, and at best some sort of model or diagram or recipe showing how they fit together. So let's start with the List. During all the 'workings out', I seem to have developed a kind of shorthand way of referring to these characteristics, using a single term for each ('social dis-ease', 'moderation', 'Eeyorishness', etc.) without spelling out its entire meaning every time, and indeed often expanding, revising and refining my definitions of these terms in the light of new evidence, particularly when dissecting stereotypes such as English 'courtesy' and 'modesty', which turned out to be far more complex and full of contradictions than the colloquial use of these terms would suggest. Much as I love making up new words and playing with old ones, I do realise that there's a danger here of us ending up with enough home-made woolly jargon to knit ourselves a whole pointless new discipline (Englishness Studies or something equally inane), with its own impenetrable dialect. To avoid this, and to save you the trouble of going back to check exactly what I meant by 'empiricism' or 'fair play' or whatever, I'll try this time to give definitive definitions of each of the defining characteristics. There are ten of these: a central 'core' and then three 'clusters', which I have labelled reflexes, outlooks and values.

The Core: Social Dis-ease

The central 'core' of Englishness. Social dis-ease is a shorthand term for all our chronic social inhibitions and handicaps. The English social dis-ease is a congenital disorder, bordering on a sort of sub-clinical combination of autism and agoraphobia (the politically correct euphemism would be 'socially challenged'). It is our lack of ease, discomfort and incompetence in the field (minefield) of social interaction; our embarrassment, insularity, awkwardness, perverse obliqueness, emotional constipation and general inability to engage in a direct and straightforward fashion with other human beings. When we feel uncomfortable in social situations (that is, most of the time) we become either over-polite, buttoned up, defensive, passive-aggressive and awkwardly restrained or loud, loutish, crude, violent and generally obnoxious. Both our famous 'English reserve' and our infamous 'English hooliganism' are symptoms of this social dis-ease, as is our obsession with privacy. Some of us are more severely afflicted than others. The dis-ease is treatable. Temporary alleviation/remission can be achieved using the many ingenious props and facilitators with which we self-medicate, including games, sports, pubs, clubs, weather-speak, moaning, pets, hobbies, ritual, alcohol, magic words, the internet and, above all, humour. The sheer number and constant use of these medications indicates that we have the same natural need and desire for social contact and social bonding as any other culture – we just need more help to achieve it. We are *not* 'reserved' in the sense of misanthropic, unsociable or introverted: a truly reclusive culture would not generate so many highly effective social facilitators. We also enjoy periods of 'natural' remission from our dis-ease in private and among intimates, but it is never entirely curable. Most peculiarities of English behaviour are traceable, either directly or indirectly, to this unfortunate affliction. Key phrases include: 'An Englishman's home is his castle'; 'Nice day, isn't it?'; 'Oi – what you lookin' at?'; 'Mind your own business'; 'I don't like to pry, but . . .'; 'Don't make a fuss/scene'; 'Don't draw attention to yourself'; 'Keep yourself to yourself'; 'Come on, show us yer tits'; 'Great night out – got completely rat-arsed!'; 'Eng-er-land! Eng-er-land! Eng-er-land!'.

Reflexes

Our deeply ingrained impulses. Our automatic, unthinking ways of being/ways of doing things. Our knee-jerk responses. Our 'default modes'. Cultural equivalents of laws of gravity.

Humour

Probably the most important of our three basic reflexes. Humour is our most effective built-in antidote to our social dis-ease. When God (or Something) cursed us with the English Social Dis-ease, He/She/It softened the blow by also giving us the English Sense of Humour. The English do not have any sort of global monopoly on humour, but what is distinctive is the sheer pervasiveness and supreme importance of humour in English everyday life and culture. In other cultures, there is 'a time and a place' for humour; among the English it is a constant, a given – there is *always* an undercurrent of humour. Virtually all English conversations and social interactions involve at least some degree of banter, teasing, irony, wit, mockery, wordplay, satire, under-statement, humorous self-deprecation, sarcasm, pomposity-pricking or just silliness. Humour is not a special, separate kind of talk: it is our 'default mode'; it is like breathing; we cannot function without it. English humour is a reflex, a knee-jerk response, particularly when we are feeling uncomfortable or awkward – when in doubt, joke. The taboo on earnestness is deeply embedded in the English psyche. Our response to earnestness is a distinctively English and fundamentally 'empiricist' blend of armchair cynicism, ironic detachment, a squeamish distaste for sentimentality, a stubborn refusal to be duped or taken in by fine rhetoric, and a mischievous delight in pricking the balloons of pretension and self-importance. English humour is *not* to be confused with 'good humour' or cheerfulness. It is often quite the opposite: much of our humour is cynical, dark, hostile, or even downright cruel. English humour is also often passive-aggressive – a cowardly, calcu-lating, manipulative form of violence. It is said that the English have satire instead of violent revolutions and uprisings, which makes us sound fairly harmless, until you see just how vicious our satire can be. Our merciless mockery may not have actually brought down govern-ments, but it has certainly contributed significantly to the downfall of many political leaders. On a more positive note, humour is also our primary means of expressing affection, and achieving social bonding and intimacy. Key phrases include: 'Oh, come off it!' and the cynical 'Yeah, right!' (runners-up to 'Typical!' as our national catchphrase).

Others impossible to list – all conversation involves humour, and English humour is all in the *context*, e.g. understatement: 'Not bad' (meaning outstandingly brilliant); 'A bit of a nuisance' (meaning disastrous, traumatic, horrible); 'Not very friendly' (meaning abominably cruel); 'I may be some time' (meaning 'I'm going to die' – although, come to think of it, that one was possibly not intended to be funny).

Moderation

Another deep-seated, unconscious reflex or 'default mode'. I'm using the term 'moderation' as shorthand for a whole set of related qualities. Our avoidance of extremes, excess and intensity. Our fear of *fuss*. Our cautiousness and our preference for comfortable domesticity, familiarity, security and convenience. Our ambivalence, apathy, woolliness, middlingness, fence-sitting and conservatism – and to some extent our tolerance, which tends to be at least partly a matter of benign indifference. Our moderate industriousness and moderate hedonism (the 'work moderately, play moderately' principle most of us really live by, rather than the 'work hard, play hard' one we like to quote). Our penchant for order and our special brand of 'orderly disorder', with its choreographed shedding of designated inhibitions. Our tendency to compromise. Our sheer ordinariness. With some notable exceptions, even our alleged and much-vaunted eccentricities are mostly 'collective' and conformist. We do everything in moderation, except moderation, which we take to ludicrous extremes. Far from being wild and reckless, the English 'youth of today' are even more moderate, cautious and unadventurous than their parents' generation. (Only about 14 per cent do not suffer from this moderation-abuse – we must rely on these rare risk-seekers for future innovation and progress.) Key phrases include: 'Don't rock the boat'; 'Don't go overboard'; 'Don't overdo it'; 'Can't be bothered'; 'It'll do'; 'For the sake of peace and quiet'; 'Live and let live'; 'As long as they don't bother us'; 'All very well, in moderation'; 'Safe and sound'; 'Order! Order!'; 'A nice cup of tea'; 'If it were like this all the time, we wouldn't appreciate it'; 'Over-egging the pudding'; 'Too much of a good thing'; 'Happy medium'; 'What do we want? GRADUAL CHANGE! When do we want it? IN DUE COURSE!' (OK, that last one is my own jokey invention, not an actual chant, but you get the point.)

Hypocrisy

Another unthinking 'default mode'. One of the stereotypes I tried to 'get inside'. The English are rightly renowned for their hypocrisy. This is an omnipresent trait, insidiously infecting almost all of our behaviour – and even the 'ideals' we most prize, such as modesty, courtesy and fair play. But under the special microscope I used for this project, English hypocrisy emerged as somewhat less odious than it might appear to the naked eye. It depends on how you look at it. You could say that most of our politeness/modesty/fairness is hypocritical, but also that much of our hypocrisy is a form of politeness – concealment of real opinions and feelings to avoid causing offence or embarrassment (or just to avoid 'rocking the boat' – our hypocrisy is closely linked to our moderation). English hypocrisy often seems to be mainly a matter of unconscious, collective *self*-deception – collusion in an unspoken agreement to delude ourselves – rather than a deliberate, cynical, calculated attempt to deceive others. (Our 'polite egalitarianism' is perhaps the best example – an elaborate charade of courteous modesty and fairness, a severe case of what a psychotherapist would call 'denial' of our acute class-consciousness.) Hypocrisy comes easily to us not because we are by nature vile and perfidious (or no more so than any other culture) but because our social dis-ease makes us naturally cautious, oblique, indirect, passive-aggressive – disinclined to say what we mean or mean what we say, prone to polite pretence rather than honest assertiveness. (When we drop the hypocritical pretence, we tend to become incoherently aggressive, rather than calmly assertive.) Our hypocrisies also reveal our values. We are no more *naturally* modest, courteous or fair than any other culture, but we have more unwritten rules prescribing the *appearance* of these qualities, which are clearly very important to us. Key phrases: too numerous to list – English conversation is littered with polite euphemisms and other disguises, deceptions and denials – but, on average, at least every other 'please', 'thank-you', 'sorry', 'nice', 'lovely' (plus smiles, nods, etc.) is hypocritical.

Outlooks

Our world view. Our way of looking at, thinking about, structuring and understanding things. Our sociocultural 'cosmology'.

Empiricism

The most fundamental of this 'outlook' cluster. Empiricism is another shorthand term into which I am packing a large collection of English attitudes. Strictly speaking, empiricism is a philosophical doctrine holding that all knowledge is derived from sense-experience – and its close relation 'realism' should technically only be used to mean the tenet that matter exists independently of our perception of it. Englishness is deeply rooted in these philosophical principles, but I am also using these terms in a much broader, more informal sense, to include both the anti-theory, anti-abstraction, anti-dogma elements of our philosophical tradition (particularly our mistrust of obscurantist, airy-fairy 'Continental' theorising and rhetoric) and our stolid, stubborn preference for the factual, concrete and common-sense. 'Empiricism' is shorthand for our down-to-earthness; our matter-of-factness; our pragmatism; our cynical, no-nonsense groundedness; our gritty realism; our distaste for artifice and pretension (yes, I realise that last bit rather contradicts what I said about our hypocrisy, polite euphemisms, etc., but I never claimed that we were consistent). Key phrases include: 'Oh, come off it!'/'Yeah, right!' (overlap with 'Humour' – English humour is very empiricist); 'At the end of the day'; 'As a matter of fact'; 'In plain English'; 'I'll believe it when I see it'; 'Typical!' (overlap with 'Eeyorishness', also very empiricist); 'I refute it thus!' (No, we don't actually go around kicking stones and quoting Johnson, but his famous line encapsulates our mindset.)

Eeyorishness

More than just our incessant moaning. Quite apart from the sheer quantity of it, which is staggering, there is something qualitatively distinctive about English moaning. It is utterly ineffectual: we never complain to or confront the source of our discontent, but only whinge endlessly to each other, and proposing practical solutions is forbidden by the moaning rules. But it is socially therapeutic – highly effective as a facilitator of social interaction and bonding. Moaning is also highly enjoyable (there is nothing the English love so much as a good moan – it really is a pleasure to watch) and an opportunity for displays of wit. Almost all 'social' moaning is humorous *mock-moaning*. Real, tearful despair is not allowed, except among intimates. Even if you are feeling truly desperate, you must pretend to be only pretending to feel desperate (the unbearable lightness of being English). By 'Eeyorishness' I mean the mindset/outlook exemplified by our national catchphrase 'Typical!': our chronic pessimism, our assumption that it is in the nature of things to go wrong and be disappointing, but also our perverse satisfaction at seeing our gloomy predictions fulfilled – simultaneously peeved, stoically resigned and smugly omniscient. Our special brand of fatalism – a sort of curiously sunny pessimism. Key phrases include: '*Typical!*'; 'Huh! *Typical!*'; 'Bloody *typical!*' (and many other variations on this theme); 'What did you expect?'; 'I could have told you'; 'As per usual'; 'The country's going to the dogs'; 'There's always *some*thing'; 'Sod's Law!'; 'That'll never work'; 'Bound to rain: it's a bank holiday'; 'Mustn't grumble'; 'Better make the best of it'; 'Never mind'; 'Blessed are they who expect nothing, for they shall not be disappointed.'

Class-consciousness

All human societies have a social hierarchy and methods of indicating social status. What is distinctive about the English class system is (a) the fact that class is not judged at all on wealth, and very little on occupation, but purely on non-economic indicators such as speech, manner, taste and lifestyle choices; (b) the degree to which our class (and/or class-anxiety) determines our taste, behaviour and judgements; (c) the acute sensitivity of our on-board class-radar systems; and (d) our denial of all this and coy squeamishness about class: the hidden, indirect, unspoken, hypocritical/self-delusional nature of English class-consciousness (particularly among the middle classes)[126]. Our 'polite egalitarianism'. The vestigial prejudice against

126. For those still in denial, and who assume that class must be some personal obsession of mine: it is not. In discussions about Englishness, the issue of class/class-consciousness/preoccupation with class was raised by almost all of my English informants, and almost all of SIRC's English focus-group participants, and this characteristic came top of the list, by some distance, when we asked national survey respondents to identify the core features of our culture.

'trade'. The minutiae and sheer mind-boggling silliness of our class indicators and class anxieties. Our sense of humour about all this. Key phrases include: 'It is impossible for an Englishman to open his mouth without making some other Englishman hate him or despise him'; 'That sort of *background*'; 'Nice chap, but not really PLU'; 'Don't say "serviette", dear: *we* call it a napkin'; 'Mondeo Man'; 'S/he is a bit naff/common/*nouveau*/flashy/vulgar/unsmart/yobby/plebby/chavvy/ suburban-semi/mock-Tudor . . .'; 'Stuck-up posh tart (hooray/upper-class twit/old-school-tie/snob/public-school yah-yah/green-wellie . . .) thinks s/he's better than us'; 'What do you expect from a jumped-up grocer's daughter?'; 'That nice little man from the shop.'

Values

Our ideals. Our norms. Our fundamental guiding principles. The moral standards to which we subscribe and aspire, *even if we do not live up to them* – 'moral mythology' might be a better term.

Fair play

A national quasi-religious obsession. Much of English morality is essentially about fair play. Although we may often fail to live up to this ideal, breaches of the fair-play principle provoke more righteous indignation than any other sin. English 'fair play' is not a rigidly or unrealistically egalitarian concept – we accept that there will be winners and losers, but feel that everyone should be given a fair chance, providing they observe the rules (the unwritten social rules, I mean, not necessarily the official/legal ones, which may often be dismissed as 'unfair') and don't cheat or shirk their responsibilities. Fair play is an underlying theme in most aspects of our unwritten etiquette, not just the games and sports with which it is most famously associated: queuing is all about fair play; round-buying, table manners, 'orderly disorder', driving etiquette, flirting codes, business etiquette, polite egalitarianism, etc. are all influenced by this principle. Polite egalitarianism is hypocritical, concerned with the *appearance* of fairness, the concealment of embarrassing inequalities and inequities – but at least we care enough about these things to be embarrassed. Our penchant for compromise, our constant balancing and weighing up of 'on the one hand' and 'on the other hand' – often seen as woolliness, perhaps more kindly as tolerance – are a product of fair play + moderation. Our tendency to support the underdog – and to be wary of too much success – is also about fair play. Our acute sense of fairness is often mistaken for other things – including both socialism and conservatism, and even Christianity. What Julian Baggini calls English 'conservative communitarianism' is essentially moderation + fair play (plus the 'tribalism' that is a human universal, not peculiar to the English). Key phrases include: 'Well, to be fair . . .'; 'In all fairness . . .'; 'Given a fair chance'; 'Do your fair share'; 'Get your fair share'; 'Come on, it's only fair'; 'Fair's fair'; 'Fair enough'; 'Firm but fair'; 'Fair and square'; 'Wait your turn'; 'Take turns'; 'Be fair'; 'Fair cop'; 'Fair play to you/him/her!'; 'That's not cricket/not on/out of order!'; 'Level playing-field'; 'Don't be greedy'; 'Live and let live'; 'On the other hand'; 'There's always two sides'; 'On balance'; 'Let's just agree to disagree, shall we?'

Courtesy

A powerful ideal. Some of our politenesses are so deeply ingrained as to be almost involuntary, and thus fairly meaningless (the 'sorry' reflex, for example, is a knee-jerk response for most of us) but many require conscious or indeed acutely *self*-conscious effort. The English are often admired for our courtesy but condemned for our 'reserve', which is seen as arrogant, cold and unfriendly. Although our reserve is certainly a symptom of our social dis-ease, it is also, at least in part, a *form* of courtesy – the kind sociolinguists call 'negative politeness', which is concerned with other people's need not to be intruded or imposed upon (as opposed to 'positive politeness', which is concerned with their need for inclusion and social approval). We judge others by ourselves, and assume that everyone shares our obsessive need for privacy – so we mind our own business and politely ignore them. But our polite sorries, pleases and thank-yous are not heartfelt or sincere – there is nothing particularly warm or friendly about them. Politeness by definition involves a degree of artifice and hypocrisy, but English courtesy seems to be almost entirely a matter of form, of obedience to a set of rules rather than expression of genuine feelings. So when we do break our own courtesy rules, we tend if anything to be more obnoxious and unpleasant than other less 'polite' nations. We need all these rules to protect us from ourselves. Key phrases include: 'Sorry'; 'Please'; 'Thank you/Cheers/Ta/Thanks' (every culture has these words, but we use them more); 'I'm afraid that . . .'; 'I'm sorry, but . . .'; 'Would you mind . . . ?'; 'Could you possibly . . . ?'; 'I don't suppose . . .'; 'How do you do?'; 'Nice day, isn't it?'; 'Yes, isn't it?'; 'Excuse me, sorry, but you couldn't possibly pass the marmalade, could you?'; 'Excuse me, I'm terribly sorry but you seem to be standing on my foot'; 'With all due respect, the right honourable gentleman is being a bit economical with the truth'; 'Sorry, but I'm not going to apologise for that.'

Modesty

The English are no more naturally self-effacing than other nations – in fact, we are rather arrogant – but (as with courtesy) we have strict rules about the *appearance* of modesty, including prohibitions on boasting and any form of self-importance, and rules actively prescribing self-deprecation and self-mockery. We place a high value on modesty, we *aspire* to modesty. The modesty that we actually display is often false – or, to put it more charitably, ironic. Our famous self-deprecation is a form of irony – saying the opposite of what we intend people to understand, or using deliberate understatement. It's a kind of code: everyone knows that a self-deprecating statement probably means roughly the opposite of what is said, or involves a significant degree of understatement, and we are duly impressed, both by the speaker's achievements or abilities and by his/her reluctance to trumpet them. Problems arise when the English try to play this rather silly game with foreigners, who do not understand the ironic code and tend to take our self-deprecating or self-mocking remarks at face value. Modesty also requires that we try to play down or deny class/wealth/status differences – polite egalitarianism involves a combination of the three 'key values' (courtesy, modesty, fair play) with a generous helping of hypocrisy. English modesty is often *competitive* – 'one-downmanship' – although this game may involve a lot of indirect boasting, and self-deprecation can be used as a coded insult. English displays of modesty (whether competitive, hypocritical, insulting or genuine) are distinctive for the degree of *humour* involved. Our modesty rules often act as a counter-balance to our natural arrogance, just as our courtesy rules protect us from our own aggressive tendencies. Key phrases include: 'Don't boast'; 'Stop showing off'; 'Don't blow your own trumpet'; 'Don't be clever'; 'Don't be pushy'; 'I do a bit of sport' (meaning I've just won an Olympic medal); 'Well, I suppose I know a bit about that' (meaning I'm the acknowledged world expert on it); 'Oh, that's all a bit over my head, I'm afraid' (ditto); 'Not as hard as it looks/just lucky' (standard response to any praise for personal achievement); and, just in case you're starting to think we're quite sweet, 'Her house [or children, clothes, car, etc.] is always so pristine – makes me feel rather scruffy and hopeless' (coded insult, meaning she's a petit-bourgeois who cares about things being 'pristine' and actually makes the upper-middle/upper-class speaker feel smugly superior).

THE DIAGRAM

So. There are the defining characteristics of Englishness. They already seem to have arranged themselves into something a bit more structured than a list. We have a 'core' and we have identified three distinct categories – reflexes, outlooks and values – each with a 'cluster' of three characteristics. Diagrams are not really my strong point (for non-English readers: that is a *big* understatement) but it looks as though I might be able to keep my somewhat rash promise to represent all this visually in some way.[127]

It is impossible to show all of the individual interconnections and interactions between the characteristics. I spent several days trying, for example, to devise a visual illustration of the particularly close 'grammatical' links that I have described throughout the book between courtesy and hypocrisy, modesty and hypocrisy, humour and empiricism,

---

127. If I sound a bit reluctant and grudging about this, it is because I know that (a) people tend to expect rather a lot from diagrams, and may see them as an alternative to the effort of actually reading the book; and (b) it is much easier to spot flaws and failings in a simple diagram than in 500-odd pages of text, or even in the List above, with all its caveats and qualifications. A diagram is thus an easy target for cavillers and nit-pickers.

humour and Eeyorishness, fair play and moderation, and so on, but it always ended up looking like a tangled mass of spaghetti, only less appetising. And, in any case, I realised that these connections between defining characteristics are often only relevant or even apparent *in relation to* specific aspects or features or rules of English behaviour. The money-talk taboo, for example, is a product of social dis-ease + modesty + hypocrisy + class-consciousness (that is, the 'core' plus one from each 'cluster'). Our attitude to religion – a rather more complex matter – involves a combination of moderation + fair play + courtesy + humour + empiricism + Eeyorishness (a pick-and-mix from all the 'clusters', and all indirectly related to the 'core'). Our apparent anti-intellectualism is actually empiricism + modesty + humour (specifically anti-earnestness). And so on. You can have hours of fun – if, like me, you have nothing better to do – picking random aspects of English behaviour and 'mapping their cultural DNA' from the defining characteristics in the List. Some stereotypes can also be dissected in this manner: so-called 'English reserve', for example, is primarily a symptom of our social dis-ease (the chronically embarrassed/inhibited 'pole' of our 'bi-polar' social disorder) but also involves a combination of courtesy (specifically 'negative politeness') + modesty (with the usual link to hypocrisy) + moderation, with maybe a dash of grumpy Eeyorishness.

But in order to show all the connections and interactions between these characteristics in a diagram, I would have to include all the minutiae of our behaviour patterns, which would effectively mean including everything in the book – clearly an impossible task.

I think we'll just have to settle for something much simpler. Ditch the microscope, stand back and look at the big picture. This basic diagram of Englishness won't tell us anything we don't already know from the 'narrative' list above. It just shows what the defining characteristics are, how they can be classified, and that these characteristics are all linked both with each other and with the central 'core'. But the diagram does at least convey the notion that Englishness is a dynamic system rather than a static list. And it gets the whole thing on to one convenient page. For, um, easy reference or something. Englishness at-a-glance. And it looks rather nice and pleasingly symmetrical.

I'm afraid my little diagram of Englishness hasn't come out looking

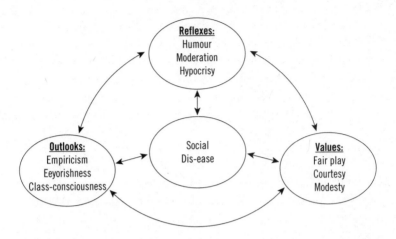

much like a 'genome', and it will no doubt be disappointing for those who were expecting something more complex and difficult and scientific-looking. But those genomes and so on were only metaphors, and much as I love to stretch, labour and generally abuse a metaphor, Englishness just would not be shoehorned into any existing scientific models, so I've had to make up my own rather crude and over-simplified structure. But it does look a bit sort of *molecular* – don't you think? – which is quite scientific enough for me. And anyway, the point was not to have a grandly impressive diagram, just something that would help us to understand and make sense of the peculiarities of ordinary English behaviour.

CAUSES

In our search for this understanding of Englishness, one question remains. If our unfortunate social dis-ease is indeed the central 'core' of Englishness, then we have to ask: what causes this dis-ease?

It is as though, throughout the book, I have been a sort of ethnological psychiatrist, examining a patient ('The English') who has 'presented with' a complex, apparently incoherent and unrelated set of odd behaviours, bizarre beliefs and strange, compulsive habits. After a long period of close observation and a lot of embarrassing questions,

I can see the recurring patterns and themes, and eventually arrive at a diagnosis: the condition I am calling the English Social Dis-ease. It is not a severely debilitating disorder: the patient self-medicates quite effectively in various ways, has developed a range of coping mechanisms, manages to lead a relatively normal life and regards his/her behaviour as perfectly reasonable (often claiming that it is the rest of the world that is odd and out of step). But others find the patient weird and often rather tiresomely anti-social, if sometimes quite charming. Although I cannot provide a cure, my diagnosis may in itself be of some help, at least in understanding the condition and its management.

But the aetiology of this dis-ease still remains something of a mystery. As with many psychological disorders, no one really knows what causes it. This is not for want of speculation on the subject. Although I believe this book is the first to identify the dis-ease properly – in the sense of giving a name to the odd collection of troubling symptoms that characterise the condition – I am certainly not the first to notice and comment on the symptoms themselves. Every attempt to describe our national character makes at least some mention of 'English reserve', and many also puzzle over its apparent opposite, English loutishness, hooliganism and other anti-social behaviours. My only contribution has been to suggest that these seemingly contradictory Jekyll-and-Hyde tendencies are part of the same syndrome (a bit like the manic and depressive elements of what is now called bi-polar disorder). This diagnosis may be helpful in understanding the English, but identifying and naming a disorder tells us nothing about its cause.

Several possible causes have been proposed by other writers. Many are inclined to blame the English climate. While our weather may indeed be a factor, I'm a bit sceptical about this explanation, as our climate is not really all that different from that of many other northern European countries – not to mention Scotland, Ireland and Wales – whose inhabitants do not exhibit the same sociopathic tendencies.[128]

128. Harry Mount attributes much of our social awkwardness to the English climate, but England has the same average hours of sunshine per year as Ireland, and almost identical average temperatures, rainfall, etc. We may have some traits in common with the Irish (as we do with many other cultures) but social dis-ease is clearly not one of them.

This does not rule out the weather as a cause (a lot of smokers do not get lung cancer), but it does suggest that other factors must be involved.

A number of writers point the finger at our history, but there seems to be little consensus on what parts of English history might be responsible for our current dis-ease. We had and lost an empire – well, so did the Romans, the Spanish, the French, the Russians, the Dutch, the Austrians, the Portuguese and a number of others, and they didn't all turn out like us. Some suggest that the tendencies I am concerned with are of relatively recent origin. G. J. Renier (author of *The English: Are They Human?*), for example, blamed public schools for the ludicrous excesses of English reserve; I have already discussed Harry Mount's attempts to attribute related social handicaps to gender-segregated state schools (when he's not blaming the weather); the anthropologist Geoffrey Gorer traced certain aspects of our national character, particularly our self-restraint and orderliness, to the establishment of our police force – and so on). Some even seem to believe that all of our loutish, yobbish, anti-social traits began, along with sex, in 1963, and that things were different and people knew how to behave back when they were a lad. Historians, however, provide evidence of both English 'reserve' and English loutishness dating back at least to the seventeenth century, and I have already mentioned reports of our medieval football violence. I am not a historian, so I may not be qualified to judge but as far as I can gather from reading the accounts of those who are, we would seem to have suffered from this social dis-ease for quite some time, perhaps in somewhat varying forms, and its onset or emergence cannot be attributed to any particular historical event or process.

So, if neither climate nor history can entirely account for our dis-ease, what about geography? The fact that we are 'an island race' has occasionally been put forward as an explanation for some aspects of our national character – such as our insularity. While there may well be some truth in this, I do not think that inhabiting an island can in itself account for much – there are, after all, plenty of other island peoples with very different national characters, although we may have some traits in common. But if we get a bit more specific, and take into account the size of our island and the density of its population, then the geographical argument starts to look a bit more promising. This is not just an island, but a relatively small, or at least very overcrowded island, and it is not too hard to see how such conditions might produce an inhibited, privacy-obsessed, socially wary, uneasy and sometimes obnoxiously anti-social people; a negative-politeness culture, whose courtesy is primarily concerned with the avoidance of intrusion and imposition; an acutely class-conscious culture, preoccupied with status and boundaries and demarcations; a society characterised by awkwardness, embarrassment, obliqueness, fear of intimacy/emotion/fuss – veering between buttoned-up overpoliteness and aggressive belligerence . . . Although we are in many ways very different, I have noted a number of important similarities between the English and the Japanese, and wondered whether the smallish-overcrowded-island factor might be significant.

But this crude geographical determinism is not really much more convincing than the climatic or historical arguments. If geography is so important in determining national character, why are the Danes so different from other Scandinavian nations? Why are the French and Germans so distinctively French and German, even when they live immediately either side of the arbitrary border between these two countries? Ditto Alpine French and Alpine Italians? I lived on that particular border for four years, and we would often cross into Italy purely to enjoy being in a very different culture for a bit, as the landscape was exactly the same. And what about Texans and Mexicans? Finns and Russians? And so on. No – geography may well play a part, but it clearly can't be the final answer.

Our social dis-ease, and indeed other key aspects of our national culture, did not come out of thin air, and so must presumably be due to our particular *combination* of climate, history and geography – which at least could be said to be unique. But as I have noted here and throughout the book, more detailed 'casual' explanations – attempts to attribute specific aspects of Englishness to our climate or geography, or to particular historical events or processes – simply do not stand up to close scrutiny or cross-cultural comparison. And one could even legitimately quibble that there is a 'chicken or egg' problem with the notion that our national character/culture is a 'product' of our unique climate/geography/history combination.

Although we may be at the mercy of our weather and some immutable aspects of geography, our environment is largely man-made, and our history entirely so.

I'm sorry, but I just don't think there is a simple 'casual' answer, and I'm not going to insult your intelligence with speculative 'Just So Stories' about 'How the English Got Their Social Handicaps'. To be honest, I can't really explain why the English are the way we are – and neither, if they are being honest, can anyone else. This does not invalidate my diagnosis of 'social dis-ease': I can pronounce the English to be a bit autistic or agoraphobic (or bi-polar for that matter), or just socially challenged, without knowing the causes of these disorders. Psychiatrists do this all the time, so I don't see why self-appointed national ethno-shrinks should not have the same privilege. And you can challenge my diagnosis or offer a second opinion if you disagree.

But before I stop (or get sectioned for metaphor-abuse), I should just issue a health warning: Englishness can be rather contagious. Some people are more susceptible than others, but if you hang around us long enough, you may find yourself greeting every misfortune, from a delayed train to an international disaster, with '*Typical!*', any hint of earnestness or pomposity with 'Oh, come off it!', and new people with embarrassed, stilted incompetence. You may find yourself believing that large quantities of alcohol will help you to shed these inhibitions, allowing you to greet people with 'Oi, what you lookin' at?' or 'C'mon, show us yer tits' instead. You may, however, be one of the many more fortunate visitors and immigrants whose strong cultural immune systems protect them from our dis-ease. If you still want to fit in, or just have a laugh at our expense, I suppose this book might help you to fake the symptoms.

The important point, which I hope is now clear, is that Englishness is not a matter of birth, race, colour or creed: it is a mindset, an ethos, a behavioural 'grammar' – a set of unwritten codes that might seem enigmatic, but that anyone can decipher and apply, now that we have the key.

EPILOGUE

I'm back at Paddington station. No brandy this time, as I don't have to do any more bumping or queue-jumping. Just a nice cup of tea and a biscuit – which strikes me as an appropriately moderate and understated way to mark the completion of my Englishness project.

Even though I am now 'off duty' – just waiting for the Oxford train, like a normal person – I realise that I have automatically chosen the best observation-position in the station café, with a particularly good view of the queue at the counter. Just habit, I suppose. The thing about participant-observation research is that it does rather tend to take over your whole life. Every routine train journey, every drink in the pub, every walk to the shops, every house you pass, every fleeting interaction with everyone you meet is a data-gathering or hypothesis-testing opportunity. You can't even watch television or listen to the radio without constantly making notes on bloody Englishness.

The book is done; I've left my notebook at home (I'm writing this on a napkin). But look: in that taxi earlier I couldn't help scribbling on the back of my hand something the driver said. I peer at the slightly smudged abbreviations. Something about 'all this rain and now they've issued drought warnings for next summer and isn't it just typical'. Oh, great, that must be my seven-hundred-thousandth recorded instance of English weather-moaning. Really useful information, Kate. Pathetic data-junkie. You've cracked the code; you've done your little bit towards resolving the English identity crisis. Now leave it alone. Stop all this obsessive queue-watching and pea-counting and recording random bits of weather-speak. Get a life.

Yes. Right. Absolutely. Enough is enough.

Ooh, but hang on a sec. What's that? A woman with a baby in a pushchair has approached the coffee-shop counter from the wrong end, and there's a queue of three people already waiting to be served. Is she trying to jump the queue, or just having a look at the dough-nuts and sandwiches before deciding whether to join the queue? It's not clear. But a jump-attempt here would be too blatant, surely? Not enough ambiguity in the situation. The three queuers are doing the paranoid pantomime – suspicious sideways looks, pointed throat-clearing, shuffling forward . . . Ah! Two of them have just exchanged raised eyebrows (but were they in the queue together, or are they strangers? Why wasn't I paying attention?). One of them sighs noisily – will the pushchair woman notice? Yes! She's got the message – she's moving towards the back of the queue, but looking mildly affronted. She'd never intended to jump the queue: she was just looking to see what sandwiches they had. The queuers look down or away, avoiding eye contact. Hah! She was innocent all along – I knew it! Now, I wonder if those two eyebrow-raisers are friends or strangers. This is very important – did that apparent queue-jump threat prompt eye contact between strangers or not? Let's see if they order together – damn, that's my train they've just announced! Huh! It *would* be on time for once, just when there's this fascinating queue-drama going on – *typical*! Maybe I could get the next one . . .

AFTERWORD TO THE REVISED EDITION

I missed my train, of course. It was worth it: the two eyebrow-raisers turned out to be strangers – they ordered separately and sat at different tables – so the queue-jump threat had indeed prompted very brief eye contact between strangers. I recorded this carefully on my napkin. And I have been compulsively observing queues, collecting examples of weather-speak, counting 'sorries' and so on ever since.

ACKNOWLEDGEMENTS

In a break with tradition, which for some reason always puts the author's family 'last but by no means least', I want to thank, first and very much foremost, my husband, Henry Marsh, and his children William, Sarah and Katharine. They've had to put up with many years of my stressing and obsessing over this book – and along with my mother, Liz, and sister, Anne, they read and commented on each chapter as it emerged. Anne also generously shared all her Ph.D. research data with me. My sister Ellie gave me wonderful holidays with her family in Lebanon and America, which I shamelessly used as opportunities for cross-cultural research. My father, Robin Fox, deserves most of the credit for any skills I may have as a participant-observer. They have all been unfailingly tolerant, helpful and encouraging. My co-director at the Social Issues Research Centre, Peter Marsh, gave me my first field-research job when I was seventeen, and has been my mentor and great friend ever since. I am also grateful to Desmond Morris for his help, advice and insights. *Watching the English* is based on nearly two decades of research, and it would be impossible to thank everyone who has contributed, but among those who have helped me in various ways, I would particularly like to thank Ranjit and Sara Banerji, Annalisa Barbieri, Don Barton, Krystina Belinska, Simon and Prisca Bradley, Angela Burdick, Brian Cathcart, Roger Chapman, Peter Collett, Karol Colonna-Czosnowski, Joe Connaire, Gina Cowen, James Cumes, Bianca Dahl, Paul Dornan, Alana Fawcett, Vernon and Anne Gibberd, William Glaser, Susan Greenfield, Janet Hodgson, Selwyn and Lisa Jones, Jean-Louis and Voikitza Juery, Kati Karnoven, Paull and Lorraine Khan, Eli Khater, Heidi Kingstone, Mathew Kneale, Sam Knowles, Slava and Masha

Kopiev, Meg Kozera, Hester Lacey, Jessaca Leinaweaver, Alistair Maag, Jeremy MacClancy, Laurence Marsh, Tania Mathias, Fiona McIlwham, Roger Miles, Daniel Miller, Paula Milne, Caroline Morrissey and Franz Andres Morrissey, Tony Muller, Simon Nye, Martin Parr, Grayson Perry, Marinella Simioli, Geoffrey Smith, Lindsey Smith, Steve Smith, Richard Stevens, Jamie Stevenson, Gudrun von Tevenar, Lionel Tiger, Patsy Toh, Simon Travis, Silvia Venturini, Jane Whitton and Roman Zoltowski. My thanks to everyone at Hodder & Stoughton, especially Rupert Lancaster, the world's kindest and most patient editor, and Kerry Hood, the nicest publicity-genius. Thanks also to Hazel Orme, the most quietly brilliant copy editor, and to Julian Alexander, the most hard-working and thoughtful agent.

REFERENCES

Appadurai, Arjun (1988): *The Social Life of Things*. Cambridge, Cambridge Uuniversity Press

Aslet, Clive (1997): *Anyone for England? A Search for British Identity*. London, Little, Brown

Austen, Jane (1815): *Emma*. London, The Folio Society, 1975

Austen, Jane (1813): *Pride and Prejudice*. London, The Folio Society, 1975

Baggini, Julian (2008): *Welcome to Everytown*. London, Granta

Barnes, Julian (1998): *England, England*. London, Jonathan Cape

Bennett, Alan (1978): *The Old Country*. London, Faber & Faber

Bond, R.W. (ed.) (1902) *The Complete Works of John Lyly*. Oxford, OUP

Bourdieu, P. (1986) 'The forms of capital'. In J. Richardson (Ed.) *Handbook of Theory and Research for the Sociology of Education*. New York, Greenwood

Boswell, James (1791): *The Life of Samuel Johnson*. London, Penguin, 2008

Breward, C, Conekin, B & Cox, C (eds.) (2002): *The Englishness of English Dress*. Oxford, Berg

Bryson, Bill (1995): *Notes from a Small Island*. London, Doubleday

Brown, P and Levinson, S.C. (2000): *Politeness: Some Universals in Language Usage*. Cambridge, Cambridge University Press

Collett, P and Furnham, A (eds) (1995): *Social Psychology at Work*. London, Routledge

Collyer, Peter (2002): *Rain Later, Good*. Bradford on Avon, Thomas Reed

Cooper, Jilly (1979): *Class: A View from Middle England*. London, Methuen

Crick, Bernard (ed.) (2001): *Citizens: Towards a Citizenship Culture*. Oxford, Blackwell Publishers

Crick, Bernard (ed) (1991): *National Identities: The Constitution of the United Kingdom*

Daudy, Philippe (1992): *Les Anglais: Portrait of a People*. London, Headline

De Muralt, B. L. (1725): *Lettres sur les Anglais*. Zurich

De Toqueville, Alexis (1958): *Journeys to England and Ireland*. London, Faber & Faber

Douglas, Mary (1966) *Purity and Danger: An Analysis of Concepts of Pollution and Taboo*. London, Routledge, 2002

Dunbar, Robin (1996): *Grooming, Gossip and the Evolution of Language*. London, Faber & Faber

Durkheim, Emile (1912) *The Elementary Forms of Religious Life*. Oxford, Oxford University Press, 2008

Easthope, Antony (1998): *Englishness and National Culture*. London, Routledge

Fox, Anne (2010) *Drink and Duty: Alcohol Use and the British Army* (unpublished Ph.D. thesis, Imperial College, University of London)

Fox, Kate (1999): *The Racing Tribe: Portrait of a British Subculture*. New Brunswick, Transaction

Fox, Robin (1991) *Encounter with Anthropology*. New Brunswick, Transaction

Fox, Robin (1980): *The Red Lamp of Incest*. New York, Penguin

Goffman, Erving (1961) *Asylums*. Anchor Books

Goodrum, Alison (2005) *The National Fabric: Fashion, Britishness, Globalization*. Oxford, Berg

Gorer, Geoffrey (1955): *Exploring English Character*. London, Cresset Press

Griffith, Phoebe *et al* (2011) *Charm Offensive: Cultivating Civility in 21st Century Britain*. London, The Young Foundation

Heath, D.B. (1991). 'Alcohol studies and anthropology'. In D. J. Pittman and H. R. White (eds.), *Society, Culture and Drinking Patterns Reexamined: Alcohol, Culture and Social Control Monograph Series*. New Brunswick, Rutgers Center for Alcohol Studies.

Hockey, John (2006) *Squaddies: Portrait of a Subculture*. Liverpool, Liverpool University Press

Hodkinson, Paul (2002): *Goth: Identity, Style and Subculture*. Oxford, Berg

Jacobs, Eric and Worcester, Robert (1990): *We British*. London, Weidenfeld and Nicholson

Jonson, Ben (1641) *Discoveries* ed. G. B. Harrison. New York: Barnes & Noble, 1966

Kron, R. (1901): *The Little Londoner: A Concise Account of the Life and Ways of the English*. Karlsruhe, J. Bielefelds Verlag, 1905

Kumar, Krishan (2003): *The Making of English National Identity*. Cambridge, CUP

Levi-Strauss, Claude (1955): *The Structural Study of Myth*. Structural Anthropology. Basic Books, 1963

Marsh, Peter *et al* (1978): *The Rules of Disorder*. London, Routledge

Marshall Thomas, Elizabeth (1960): *The Harmless People*. London, Secker & Warburg

McDonald-Walker, Suzanne (2000): *Bikers: Culture, Politics and Power*. Oxford, Berg

Mikes, George (1984): *How to be a Brit*. London, Penguin

Miller, Daniel (1998): *A Theory of Shopping*. Cambridge, Polity Press

Miller, Daniel (2009): *Stuff*. Cambridge, Polity Press

Miller, Geoffrey (2000): *The Mating Mind*. London, Heinemann

Mitford, Nancy (ed) (1956): *Noblesse Oblige*. London, Hamish Hamilton

Morgan, John (1999): *Debrett's New Guide to Etiquette & Modern Manners*. London, Headline

Mount, Harry (2012): *How England Made the English*. London, Penguin

Murdock, G. P. (1945) "The Common Denominator of Cultures," in Ralph Linton (ed.), *The Science of Man in the World Crisis*. New York, Columbia

Noon, M. & Delbridge, R. (1993): *News from behind my hand: Gossip in organizations*. Organization Studies, 14

Orwell, George (1970): *Collected Essays, Journalism and Letters* 2. London, Penguin

Paxman, Jeremy (1998): *The English: A Portrait of a People*. London, Michael Joseph

Pevsner, Nikolaus (1956): *The Englishness of English Art*. London, Architectural Press

Priestley, J. B. (1976): *English Humour*. London, William Heinemann

Quest-Ritson, Charles (2001): *The English Garden: A Social History*. London, Penguin

Renier, G.J. (1931): *The English: Are They Human?* London, Williams & Norgate

Richardson, Paul (2001): *Cornucopia: A Gastronomic Tour of Britain*. London, Abacus

Rooms, Nigel (2011): *The Faith of the English*. London, SPCK

Shaw, George Bernard (1916) *Pygmalion*. London, Penguin, 1998

Storry, Mike and Childs, Peter (eds) (1997): *British Cultural Identities*. London, Routledge

Scruton, Roger (2000): *England: An Elegy*. London, Chatto & Windus

Turner, Victor (1969): *The Ritual Process: Structure and Anti-Structure*. Chicago, AldineTransaction, 1995

Van Gennep, Arnold (1960) *Rites of Passage*, London, Routledge

Wilde, Oscar (1891): *The Picture of Dorian Gray*. London, Penguin Classics, 2003

Young, Michael (1958): *The Rise of the Meritocracy*. New Brunswick, Transaction 1994

Young, Michael (2001): 'Down with Meritocracy' The Guardian 29/6/2001

INDEX

ALSO FROM NICHOLAS BREALEY PUBLISHING

"A journalist who now lives in Switzerland, Bewes is a well-qualified guide to a country that, although familiar, requires expertise to understand... Bewes reveals how Switzerland is riddled with contradictions... Informative and entertaining."

—Harry Ritchie, *Mail on Sunday*

One country, four languages, 26 cantons and 7.8 million people (but only 78% of them Swiss): there's nowhere else in Europe like it. Switzerland may be almost 400km from the nearest drop of seawater, but it's an island at the centre of Europe. Welcome to the landlocked island.

Switzerland is the country that not only gave us triangular chocolate and holey cheese, but also the world's first Toilet Duck (1980) and Velcro (1955). It's a country famous for its punctual trains and strict neutrality - but what lies behind these stereotypes? What does Switzerland look like from the inside?

Swiss Watching is a revealing historical journey around Europe's most individual and misunderstood country. From seeking Heidi and finding the best chocolate to reliving a bloody past and exploring an uncertain future, *Swiss Watching* proves that there's more to Switzerland than banks and skis, francs and cheese. In the land of cultural contradictions, this is a picture of the real and normally unseen Switzerland, a place where the breathtaking scenery shaped a nation not just a tour itinerary, and where tradition is as important as innovation. It's also the story of its people, who have more power than their politicians, but can't speak to one another in the same language - and who own more guns per head than the people of Iraq. As for those national clichés, well, not all the cheese has holes, cuckoo clocks aren't Swiss and the trains don't always run exactly on time. And if you think Roger Federer is the only famous Swiss big cheese, think again!

ISBN 978-1-85788-587-3
eISBN 978-1-85788-991-8
Paperback $19.95
www.nicholasbrealey.com